LEARNING RESOURCES SERVICE

BRIDGWATER & TAUNTON COLLEGE

Taunton Campus
Wellington Road, Taunton TA1 5AX
01823 366 372
tauntonlrc@btc.ac.uk

Visit the *Early Childhood Studies* Companion Website at
www.pearsoned.co.uk/earlychildhoodstudies to find valuable student
learning material including:

- Video case studies with reflective activities
- Annotated web links
- PowerPoint slides of key figures and tables from the book
- Flashcards

We work with leading authors to develop the
strongest educational materials in childhood studies,
bringing cutting-edge thinking and best learning
practice to a global market.

Under a range of well-known imprints, including
Longman, we craft high quality print and electronic
publications which help readers to understand and
apply their content, whether studying or at work.

To find out more about the complete range of our
publishing please visit us on the World Wide Web at:
www.pearsoned.co.uk

Jane Johnston and
Lindy Nahmad-Williams

Early Childhood Studies

PEARSON

Longman

Harlow, England • London • New York • Boston • San Francisco • Toronto • Sydney • Singapore • Hong Kong
Tokyo • Seoul • Taipei • New Delhi • Cape Town • Madrid • Mexico City • Amsterdam • Munich • Paris • Milan

Pearson Education Limited
Edinburgh Gate
Harlow
Essex CM20 2JE
England

and Associated Companies throughout the world

Visit us on the World Wide Web at:
www.pearsoned.co.uk

First published 2009

ISBN: 978-1-4058-3532-9

British Library Cataloguing-in-Publication Data
A catalogue record for this book is available from the British Library

Library of Congress Cataloging-in-Publication Data

Johnston, Jane, 1954-
   Early childhood studies / Jane Johnston and Lindy Nahmad-Williams.
         p. cm.
   ISBN 978-1 4058-3532-9 (pbk.)
   1. Child develpment. 2. Childhood care. 3. Early childhood education. 4. Children--
Language. 5. Cognition in children. 6. Emotions in children. I. Nahmad-Williams,
Lindy. II. Title.
   HQ767.9.J64 2009
   305.231--dc22

                                        2008026679

10 9 8 7 6 5 4 3 2 1
12 11 10 09 08

Typeset in 9.5/12pt Giovanni Book by 30
Printed and bound by Graficas Estella, Navarro, Spain

The publisher's policy is to use paper manufactured from sustainable forests.

Brief contents

Guided tour   xii
About the authors and contributors   xiv
Acknowledgements   xvi
List of abbreviations   xviii

Introduction   1

Part 1 History and philosophy of early childhood studies   15

1   Theories and theorists   16
2   Developing your own philosophy   49

Part 2 Early years development   75

3   What is physical development?   76
4   Cognitive development   107
5   Language development   138
6   Emotional and moral development   171
7   Social development   204

Part 3 Early childhood   237

8   Families, homes and childhood   238
9   Early education   262
10 Special needs and inclusion: policy and practice   303

Part 4 Practitioners in early childhood   333

11 The early years professional   334
12 Reflective practice   362
13 Working together   391
14 Leadership and management of early years settings   422

Glossary   447
Index   451

Contents

Guided tour   xii
About the authors and contributors   xiv
Acknowledgements   xvi
List of abbreviations   xviii

Introduction   1
Aims of the book   1
Tools for Learning   2
Boxed features   9
Theorists in practice   10
How to use the book   11
References and further reading   12

Part 1 History and philosophy of early childhood studies   15

1 Theories and theorists   16
Jane Johnston

Introduction   16
Aims   17
A timeline of theorists   17
New and emerging theories   37
Summary   44
Key questions   45
References   45

2 Developing your own philosophy   49
Jane Johnston

Introduction   49
Aims   50
The nature of philosophy   50
Your personal philosophy   54
Developing individual philosophies   56
Examining our personal philosophy   57
The continuing development of philosophies   61
Integrated philosophies   65
Some underlying philosophies analysed   67
Summary   71
Key questions   71
References   72
Useful websites   73

Part 2 Early years development   75

3 What is physical development?   76
Linda Cooper

Introduction   76
Aims   77
Physical development   77
Early development: reflexes   79
Brain development   79
Grouping physical development: motor skills   80
Fine motor development   84
Coordination and balance   86
Factors affecting physical development   86
Social and emotional factors   89
Physical development in a nursery environment: indoor provision   91
Physical development and outdoor play   94
Physical development and the National Curriculum   96
Summary   103
Key questions   104
References   104
Useful websites   106

4 Cognitive development   107
Jane Johnston

Introduction   107
Aims   108
What is cognitive development?   108
The brain   108
Factor theories of cognitive development   113
Piaget's cognitive theory   114
Vygotsky's cognitive theory   116
Bruner's cognitive theory   117
Modern factor theories   118
Constructivist theories   123
Cognitive acceleration   125
Factors involved in cognitive development   128
Summary   134
Key questions   135
References   135

5 Language development   138
Lindy Nahmad-Williams

Introduction   138
Aims   139
Language   139
Non-verbal communication   139
Language acquisition theories   142
Sound – phonology   147
Grammar – morphology and syntax   154
Meaning – semantics   159
Pragmatics   161
Speaking and listening in the early years   162
Summary   167
Key questions   168
References   168

6 Emotional and moral development   171
Jane Johnston

Introduction   171
Aims   172
What are emotions?   174
What is emotional development?   174
Attachment   176
Confidence and self-esteem   186
How important is emotional development to other aspects of child development?   189
What is morality?   192
Summary   199
Key questions   201
References   201
Useful reading   203
Useful books for children   203

7 Social development   204
Jane Johnston and Angela House

Introduction   204
Aims   205
The relevance of sociology   205
What is social development?   206
Theories of social development   211
The influence of society   217
The influence of gender   219
The influence of the family   219
The influence of attitudes and behaviour   221
The influence of race and culture   226
The influence of social policy   229
The influence of the environment   231
Summary   232
Key questions   233
References   233
Useful websites   235

Part 3 Early childhood   237

8 Families, homes and childhood   238
Jane Johnston

Introduction   238
Aims   239
Families   239
Parenting   245
Homes   248
The development of children's rights   251
Childhood   253
Summary   258
Key questions   259
References   259
Useful websites   261

9 Early education   262
Lindy Nahmad-Williams

Introduction   262
Aims   263

Overview of key developments in education in the early years   263
Play   270
The role of adults   276
The learning environment   280
Planning and assessment   282
Personal, Social and Emotional Development   286
Communication, Language and Literacy   287
Knowledge and Understanding of the World   292
Transition from the Foundation Stage to Key Stage 1   297
Summary   298
Key questions   299
References   299

10 Special needs and inclusion: policy and practice   303
Carol Smith and Janice Reid

Introduction   303
Aims   304
A historical framework   304
Models of disability   306
An inclusive approach to education   310
Every Child Matters   314
Early years settings and recent legislation   316
Children with additional needs in early years settings   317
Multi-agency working   320
Conclusion   329
Summary   329
Key questions   330
References   330
Useful websites   332

Part 4 Practitioners in early childhood   333

11 The early years professional   334
Jane Johnston

Introduction   334
Aims   335
Different types of early years professionals   335
Standards for early years professionals   338
The early years professional and the Early Years Foundation Stage (EYFS)   343
The challenges facing early years professionals   355
Summary   358
Key questions   359
References   359
Useful reading   361
Useful websites   361

12 Reflective practice   362
Lindy Nahmad-Williams

Introduction   362
Aims   363
What is reflective practice?   364
Characteristics of reflective practice   368
Models to guide reflective practice   370
Developing individual reflective practice   372

Reflective practice and professional standards   378
Working with others to develop reflective practice   379
Supporting and evidencing reflective practice   385
Summary   387
Key questions   388
References   388

13 Working together   391
Jane Johnston

Introduction   391
Aims   392
Who should work together?   392
Working with children   395
Working with families, parents and carers   399
Working with the wider community   405
Working with other professionals   408
Working with professional associations   414
Summary   418
Key questions   419
References   419
Useful websites   421

14 Leadership and management of early years settings   422
Chris Johnston, Jane Johnston and Angela House

Introduction   422
Aims   423
The difference between management and leadership   423
Theories of leadership   423
Types of leadership and management   425
Situational leadership and management   430
Managing change   434
Managing communications   434
Managing the organisation   435
Managing the environment   436
Managing responsibility, policy and practice and supporting   437
the environment
Managing the team   438
Summary   443
Key questions   444
References   444
Useful reading   485

Glossary   448
Index   451

Guided Tour

Reflective Tasks

Philosophical thinking

Consider the model of philosophical thinking in Figure 2.2.

Level 1

Where do you think good education should be on this model? Provide some evidence from your own experience to say why you think this type of education is best.

Level 2

Reflect on your recent practice and consider which sector of the model best describes your practice. Provide some examples to illustrate your decision.

Level 3

Reflect on your setting. Where do you think your practice fits into the model. Provide some evidence to support this decision. Now identify where you would like to be on the model. How can you change your practice to better meet your philosophical ideal?

Your personal philosophy

'I have never let my schooling interfere with my education.'
Mark Twain (1835–1910)

Working collaboratively to support the development of children in the early years involves having a shared philosophy and vision for the future. A shared philosophy does not mean that everyone concerned should think alike, but that individual philosophies are coherent and shared, so that there is a common thread and vision for collaboration. My early teaching in the 1970s involved individual teachers with very different philosophical ideas and teaching practices, who happened to share a building and children! Children started school from playgroups and homecare and stayed in one vertically grouped class with one teacher for between 2 and 3 years depending on their birth dates. School admissions policies meant that children started school the term after their fifth birthday, and so those children born in September would have three years at Key Stage 1 (then Infants) and those born the following August would have two years at Key Stage 1. They then moved to Key Stage 2 (then Juniors) where they would have a different teacher each year. Each teacher would have different ideas about teaching and a different educational philosophy and practice, with one favouring child autonomy and decision-making and another a more didactic approach. Neither was there consistency of curriculum content and each teacher could make their own choices about the needs of the individual child and what areas of the curriculum to cover. From the perspective of the individual child moving through this educational experience, it must have been confusing at the very least. At worst, the individual child would feel alienated from the setting, with schooling being something that was done to them rather than something in which they were actively involved. While this is not a familiar situation in today's educational settings, collaborative philosophy is still an important issue.

When the setting involves one service (education, health or social care) then ensuring a collaborative philosophical approach is difficult enough, but when there are different

---

Reflective Tasks – many of these relate to the specific Tools for Learning skill being developed in a particular chapter. Each task has three levels: Level 1 is designed for students or those with limited professional experience; Level 2 assumes experience of working as an early years professional; Level 3 is designed for you if you are a lead professional or manager.

---

agencies, services and groups all trying hard to work together, it is possible that individual children can fall through gaps in the network. This leaves the child vulnerable or, worse, in danger, then we have failed that child.

The first step towards providing a clear, coherent and shared philosophy in practice is to be clear in your own personal philosophy. This chapter will help you to analyse your beliefs and compare them with the philosophies of your peers. It will then examine the philosophy which underpins practice and provision in the early years and give you opportunities to see where that philosophy comes from and compare it with your own developing philosophy.

Tools for Learning

Reflection and analysis

In this chapter we are focusing on reflection and analysis. Later in the book (in Part 3) we will look at deeper analysis and combining the analysis of primary and secondary data.

What is analysis?

Analysis means to take something apart or separate it in order to illuminate, reveal, uncover, understand, resolve, identify or clarify. It is a bit like playing pass the parcel, in that each layer reveals something new and tells you a bit more about what is in the middle of the parcel. When you analyse events, situations, experiences or reading, you begin to reveal what the main factors affecting them are, or understand why someone has acted in a particular way, or clarify the issues for further development/ action. Think also of a lottery scratch card, which involves scratching away a layer to reveal what is underneath. Analysis involves scratching beneath the surface of reading, ideas or observations to help us understand them. We may try to understand why something has happened or why an idea is held. Analysis also involves looking at alternative explanations or perspectives, such as looking at a situation from a parent, child or practitioner viewpoint.

Level 1

The first step towards developing analytical skills is to reflect on a situation or experience and answer analytical questions. Analytical questions ask how and why and so what, whereas descriptive questions ask when and where and what.

Look at the questions below and decide which ones are analytical and which ones are descriptive.

• Do you eat breakfast?
• Why is a healthy meal at the start of a day important for young children?
• Do you think that healthy school dinners are important for children?
• How can early years settings improve the healthy diet of children in their care?
• What are the main factors affecting the improvement of a healthy diet for young children?

Level 2

The next step towards developing analytical skills is to raise analytical questions after reflection. Remember that analytical questions ask how and why and so what and involve detailed answers.

Tools for Learning – are embedded within each chapter and encourage you to develop a range of key study skills essential for developing your own knowledge and expertise and improving professional practice.

---

years (Johnston and Gray, 1999) to discuss moral and ethical issues. The story of Darwin who was criticised for his ideas about evolution can lead to discussion about whether it is morally right to criticise people if their ideas are different from your own.

Practical Tasks

Stories to support moral development

Level 1

Find a story book that has a moral element to it. Plan how you can read/tell this story to children and follow it up with a discussion to focus on the moral issues. Try this out with a group of children and tape the discussion. Listen to the tape and analyse the children's responses to the story to try and ascertain their stage of moral development. How will you use this understanding of the children in your next work with children?

Level 2

Look at your planning for the next term and see what stories you are using that have a moral element to them. Incorporate into your planning how you can use each story to promote moral discussions. Tape or video the resulting discussions with children and use these to listen to the children's voices and analyse what they are saying about the moral issues. Identify the children's stages of moral development. What does this analysis tell you about your children? How can you use moral discussions in the future?

Level 3

As a staff, look at your long-term planning and ascertain what opportunities there are for moral discussions. Make a list of all the stories you use that have a moral element in them and aim to incorporate them into your planning. Try out your ideas with different age groups – you may try taking one story and using that in different ways with the different age groups in your setting. Video or tape the children's discussions and use the tapes to analyse the children's moral development. Reflect on the differences in moral reasoning in the different groups and consider what this analysis tells you about your setting's success in supporting the children's moral development. What do you need to do in the future to continue or improve your support for the children's moral development?

Puppets are also a useful resource (see Picture 6.5) to support both children's emotional and moral development, as well as their cognitive development (Keogh *et al.*, 2006). The first way in which this can be done is by children who find talking difficult talking through puppets explaining things they are not able to articulate to others. Another way, is during circle time, when the children can use the puppet to speak with the only responses allowed being through the puppet, thus helping the children to speak in turn and not shout out. A third way to use puppets is for the teacher to use one to help enact a moral story, with the children telling the puppet what they think about the moral dimension. Many children will feel happier telling the puppet, rather than an adult, even if it is on the hand of the adult!

Practical Tasks – provide an opportunity to undertake some more practical physical activities related to the content of the book. Again, the tasks can be tackled at three different levels, depending on your own personal experience and skill.

Case Studies – are included in most chapters and help relate theory and research to real practice.

Research Boxes – summarise specific current research related to the content of each chapter.

Critical Discussion Boxes – encourage you to critically evaluate and debate theories, case studies and tasks throughout the text.

Chapter Summaries and Key Questions – at the end of each chapter recap and reinforce the key points to take away from the chapter. They also provide a useful revision tool.

About the Authors and Contributors

Authors

Jane Johnston is a Reader in Education at Bishop Grosseteste University College Lincoln. She works extensively, both nationally and internationally, in early childhood studies and primary science education. Formerly, she worked in Nottinghamshire as a primary classroom practitioner, working with children from 5 to 11 years of age, and at the Nottingham Trent University as subject leader in primary science education. She led the development of Early Childhood Studies at Bishop Grosseteste University College, as Subject and Programme Leader for the BA (Hons) Early Childhood Studies. She has a particular interest in early years education, the development of scientific attitudes and the role of parents in scientific learning. Her many publications reflect this interest and she is the author of many books, articles and chapters on early years and science education. She is one of the first five science teachers to achieve Chartered Science Teacher (CSci Teach), which recognises high quality science teaching.

Lindy Nahmad-Williams is a Senior Lecturer in Primary Education and Early Childhood Studies at Bishop Grosseteste University College Lincoln. Lindy has over 16 years' teaching experience and has worked as a teacher in primary schools in Doncaster, Humberside and North Lincolnshire. She has an MEd in Early Years Education and also spent a year as a Registered Nursery OFSTED Inspector, working in private and voluntary settings. Lindy was seconded to North Lincolnshire LEA to assist with the introduction of the National Literacy Strategy, supporting teachers in schools and coordinating and presenting literacy courses and regional conferences. She was also on the research team of a TTA-funded project looking at the impact of taught discussion skills on students' teaching in schools. Lindy's interests span a number of areas, including language acquisition and development, early years education, teaching primary English and drama and the role of the teacher in different educational settings.

Contributors

Linda Cooper is a Senior Lecturer at Bishop Grosseteste University College Lincoln on the BA (Hons) Primary Education degree with QTS, where she specialises in early childhood physical development and PE. Formerly, she was a primary school teacher in West Sussex. Linda's interests are in dance and ICT. Pursuing her interest as an ICT coordinator, Linda spent time gaining her MSc in Information Systems where she was involved in studying and designing educational applications. In dance she has participated in many types of movement ranging from jazz and contemporary dance to the Alexander Technique. Her interest in movement has been continued throughout her teaching career.

Angela House has been at Bishop Grosseteste University College Lincoln for 5 years and has taught across a range of undergraduate courses including Initial Teacher Training, Early Childhood Studies and Foundation Degrees in Early Childhood Services, Children and

Youth Services and Educational Studies for Teaching Assistants. Having a background in applied social sciences and a Master's degree in education, Angela has enjoyed many years' experience working with children and their families in the UK, the Far and Middle East. Angela's main interests lie in the development and improvement of relationships between children, students and the teaching, learning environment.

Chris Johnston has worked in primary education in Nottinghamshire for 31 years, firstly as a teacher and for the last 16 years as a headteacher in two different schools. His success as a leader was highlighted at the school's last inspection in 2006, when the school was identified as outstanding in every category. In addition to his work in school, Chris is a Face-to-Face facilitator on the NPQH programme, is a consultant headteacher on the New Visions programme for the NCSL and is an accredited School Improvement Partner working for North Lincolnshire and Nottinghamshire.

Janice Reid has taught for 20 years in secondary, junior and primary schools. Her teaching roles have included head of drama, special educational needs coordinator, senior manager, nurture group coordinator and teacher governor. More recent professional development has focused on children with social, emotional and behavioural difficulties, with research papers on the Best Practice Research Scholarship website 2003 and in the *International Journal of Children's Spirituality*. She was a Farmington Institute Special Needs Award holder for 2001–2002 and Farmington mentor in 2003. Since 2004 Janice has worked for the Lincolnshire Birth to Five Service as an Early Years Advisory Teacher.

Carol Smith taught for many years in primary schools, from nursery to Year 6, in addition to working in a pre-school playgroup. She was a SENCO for 10 years, before becoming a Senior Lecturer in Education Studies at Bishop Grosseteste University College Lincoln. She is also an Associate Lecturer in Inclusion with the Open University. Her main areas of interest are inclusion, gifted and talented children and specific learning difficulties.

Acknowledgements

Authors' acknowledgements

The authors would like to acknowledge the contributions made to this book by all the early years professionals, students, academics and children with whom we have worked and who have influenced our practice. In particular we would like to thank the following who have made major contributions in the chapters: Linda Cooper, Angela House, Chris Johnston, Janice Reid and Carol Smith; as well as those who, although having made minor contributions, have significantly enhanced the text: Patricia Beckley, Sir Richard Bowlby, Pam Byrd, Ashley Compton, Helen Fielding, Christine Flint, Jane Harrison, Cyndy Hawkins, Helen Horner, Harriet Marland and Bia Sena.

Acknowledgements

We are grateful to the following for permission to reproduce copyright material:

Figure 1.1 from *Towards a Psychology of Being*, pub. Van Nostrand, reprinted with permission of John Wiley & Sons, Inc. (Maslow, A. H. 1968); Table 2.2 and extract from *About Integrated Services*, www.dfes.gov.uk, reproduced under the terms of the Click-Use Licence (DfES 2006); Figure 4.1 illustration after Leslie Laurien, reprinted by permission of Leslie Laurien; Figure 4.5 from Language in the Science Classroom, in *Learning in Science: The Implications of Children's Science* edited by R. Osborne and P. Freyberg, pub. Auckland, New Zealand: Heinemann, p. 31, ISBN-13: 978-0435572600, reprinted by permission of Beverley Bell (Bell, B. and Freyberg, P. 1985); Figure 5.1 from How Language Works, http://www.indiana.edu/~hlw/PhonUnits/vowels.html, reprinted by permission of Michael Gasser; Figure 5.2 from *Sound sense: the phonics element of the National Literacy Strategy. A report to the Department for Education and Skills*, http://www.standards.dfes. gov.uk/pdf/literacy/gbrooks_phonics.pdf, reprinted by permission of the author (Brooks, G. 2003); Table 7.2 adapted from Emotional Well-being and Social Mobility – A new urgency to the debate, in *Growing Strong. NCH Briefing*, reprinted by permission of NCH (NCH 2007); Figure 9.1 adapted from *Ideas, Evidence and Argument in Science (IDEAS) Project*, reprinted by permission of Jonathan Osborne (Osborne, J. et al. 2004); Figure 11.1 from *Prospectus Early Years Professional Status*, reprinted by permission of Children's Workforce Development Council (CWDC 2007); Figure 12.2 adapted from *Experiential Learning: Experience as the Source of Learning and Development*, Pearson Education, Inc. (Kolb, D. A. 1984).

We are grateful to the following for permission to reproduce the following texts:

Chapter 1 extract from *Children and their Primary School. A Report of the Central Advisory Council for Education (England) Vol. 1: Report*, Crown Copyright material is reproduced with the permission of the Controller of HMSO and the Queen's Printer for Scotland (DES 1967); Chapter 1 extract from *All Our Futures*, Crown Copyright material is reproduced with the permission of the Controller of HMSO and the Queen's Printer for Scotland (NACCCE 1999); Chapter 2 extract from *Early Years Foundation Stage. Direction of Travel*, Crown Copyright material is reproduced with the permission of the Controller of HMSO and the Queen's Printer for Scotland (DfES 2005); Chapter 8 extracts from *Focus on Families*, Crown Copyright material is reproduced with the permission of the Controller of HMSO and the Queen's Printer for Scotland (ONS 2005); Chapter 9 Critical Discussion Box, Letter to the Editor on Play, *Daily Telegraph*, 10 September 2007, courtesy of Baroness Greenfield; Chapter 10 extract from *Code of Practice on the Identification and Assessment of Children with Special Educational Needs*, Crown Copyright material is reproduced with the permission of the Controller of HMSO and the Queen's Printer for Scotland (DfES 2001); Chapter 12 extract from *Primary National Strategy – Reading: Developing Reflective Practice Through the Reading Quality Assurance Scheme*, Crown Copyright material is reproduced with the permission of the Controller of HMSO and the Queen's Printer for Scotland (DfES 2006); Chapter 13 extract from *Statutory Framework for the Early Years Foundation Stage: Setting the Standards for Learning, Development and Care for children from birth to five. Every Child Matters, Change for Children*, Crown Copyright material is reproduced with the permission of the Controller of HMSO and the Queen's Printer for Scotland (DfES 2007); Chapter 13 extracts from *Voluntary and Community Sector Review 2004: Working Together, Better Together*, reproduced under the terms of the Click-Use Licence (HM Treasury 2004); Chapter 13 Research Box, extract from *Moving Towards Integrated Working. Progress Report 2007*, reprinted by permission of Children's Workforce Development Council (CWDC 2007).

The publisher would like to thank the following for their kind permission to reproduce their photographs:

(Key: b-bottom; c-centre; l-left; r-right; t-top)

Alamy Images: Andre Jenny 34; Arclight 228t; Christina Kennedy 142; Jacky Chapman 345; Janine Wiedel Photolibrary 22, 271; Mary Evans Picture Library 20; Philip Wolmuth 346; Photolibrary Wales 69; The Print Collector 61; Vova Pomortzeff 228b; **Corbis:** Gideon Mendel 152; Jennie Woodcock, Reflections Photolibrary 96; **Education Photos:** John Walmsley 85, 163, 240t, 274, 288, 292, 308, 311, 399; **Getty Images:** AFP 27; Hulton Archive 25; Michael Wildsmith 81; **PunchStock:** Digital Vision 240b; **Report Digital:** Duncan Phillips 281; John Harris 344; Paul Box 379; Philip Wolmuth 249; **TopFoto:** RIA Novosti 28

In some instances we have been unable to trace the owners of copyright material, and we would appreciate any information that would enable us to do so.

Abbreviations

ADHD	attention deficit hyperactivity disorder
ASBO	antisocial behaviour order
ASD	autism spectrum disorder
BA (Hons)	Batchelor of Arts (Honours)
BERA	British Educational Research Association
BPS	British Psychological Society
BTec	Business 2 Technician Education Council
BTSS	Birth to Three Study
CACHE	Council for Awards in Children's Care and Education
CAF	Common Assessment Framework
CGfFS	*Curriculum Guidance for the Foundation Stage*
CP	cerebral palsy
CPD	continuing professional development
CSIE	Centre for Studies in Inclusive Education
CVC	consonant-vowel-consonant
CWDC	Children's Workforce Development Council
DATA	describe, analyse, theorise and act
DCSF	Department for Children, Schools and Families (from 2007)
DfES	Department for Education and Skills (to 2007)
DLOs	Desirable Learning Outcomes
DRC	Disability Rights Commission
EAL	English as an additional language
ECM	Every Child Matters
ECS	Early Childhood Studies
EEG	electroencephalogram
ELGs	Early Learning Goals
EPPE	Effective Provision of Pre-school Education
ESP	Early Support Programme
ESRC	Economic and Social Research Council
EYFS	Early Years Foundation Stage
EYP	early years professional
EYPS	Early Years Professional Status
FCCS	Families, Children and Child Care Study
FdA	foundation degree
FE	further education

HE	higher education
GCSE	General Certificate of Secondary Education
ICT	information and communication technology
IEP	individual education plan
IQ	intelligence quotient
LAD	language acquisition device
LASS	language acquisition support system
LCC	little 'c' creativity
LEA	local education authority
MLA	Museums, Libraries and Archives Council
NACCCE	National Advisory Committee on Creativity and Cultural Education
NAS	National Autistic Society
NBAS	Neonatal Behavioral Assessment Scale
NCB	National Children's Bureau
NCH	National Childrens Homes (The Children's Charity)
NCMA	Natinal Childminding Association of England and Wales
NCSL	National College for School Leadership
NPQICL	National Professional Qualification in Integrated Centre Leadership
NSPCC	National Society for the Prevention of Cruelty to Children
NVC	non-verbal communication
NVQ	National Vocational Qualification
OECD	Organization for Economic Co-operation and Development
OFSTED	Office for Standards in Education
OPM	Office for Public Management
ONS	Office for National Statistics
P4C	philosophy for children
PDD-NOS	pervasive developmental disorder – not otherwise specified
PEEP	Peers Early Education Partnership
PGCE	Post-Graduate Certificate of Education
PIES	physical, intellectual, emotional and social (development)
PILES	physical, intellectual, language, emotional and social (development)
PISA	Programme of International Student Assessment
PNS	Primary National Strategy
PPA	planning, preparation and assessment
PPD	personal and professional development
PSHE	personal, social and health education
QCA	Qualifications and Curriculum Authority
QTS	Qualified Teacher Status
REM	rapid eye movement
SAT	standard assessment task
SCAA	School Curriculum and Assessment Authority
SEN	special educational needs

SENCo	Special Educational Needs Coordinator
SENDA	Special Educational Needs and Disability Act (2001)
SIPs	School Improvement Partners
SMART	specific, measurable, analytical, relevant and time-related
TA	teaching assistant
TAC	Team around the child
TDA	Training and Development Agency
UN	United Nations
UNCRC	UN Convention on the Rights of the Child
UNESCO	UN Educational, Scientific and Cultural Organisation
UNICEF	UN Children's Fund
VAK	visual, audtiory, kinaesthetic
WHO	World Health Organization
YIP	Youth Inclusion Programme
ZPD	zone of proximal development

Introduction

This book is written to support early years professionals and students who are attempting to develop their knowledge, understanding and skills in an ever-complex multidisciplinary and integrated-agency context.

Early Childhood Studies encompasses a large range of aspects related to the childhood of young children between 0 and 8 years of age, including historical influences, psychology, sociology, education, legislation, management of early years settings and services, international perspectives and comparisons. As an academic discipline it is taught at secondary, further and higher education levels and combines disciplinary aspects from health, social, education, psychology and sociology in a complex balance. Professionals working in the early years often have expertise in one of these areas, but rarely in all, although the new integrated children's centres are designed to help different professionals who work together to help children and their families in a holistic way. The early years sector is a rapidly evolving and expanding one, which aims to equip and coordinate all those who work with children and their families. This development is in response to the Every Child Matters agenda (DfES, 2003), put in place after Victoria Climbié's tragic death when it was discovered that communication between different agencies responsible for supporting children and their families could have prevented the abuse and death of vulnerable children. Initiatives in early childhood include the establishment of the Children's Workforce Development Council (CWDC, 2007a), the introduction of initiatives to improve expertise in the workforce, such as the Early Years Professional Status (CWDC, 2007b) and the development of children's centres and schools to provide an integrated service to children and their families.

The target readers of the book reflect the changing nature of Early Childhood Studies and include:

- students on Early Childhood Studies HE courses (e.g. degrees in Early Childhood, Education Studies);
- students on Early Childhood Studies FE courses (e.g. BTech, Advanced Diplomas, etc. in Early Childhood);
- initial teacher education students on both primary and early years courses;
- early years professionals (teachers, classroom assistants, nursery managers, childcare managers, etc.);
- tutors in higher and further education.

Aims of the book

Within this book we attempt to support this holistic and integrated service by explicit development in a number of areas. First, we aim to develop knowledge and understanding in Early Childhood Studies and a critical understanding of its interdisciplinary nature, so that there is a balance of focus on the health, social care and education of children. This focus is one that has traditionally been compartmentalised, so that while families have considered the holistic well-being and development of their children, agencies and early years providers have often focused on one area almost exclusively. Secondly, we aim to build on basic understandings in all areas, extending knowledge and practice, so that professionals and student professionals can extend their expertise in areas where they are confident and competent and develop in those areas where they face particular challenges.

Throughout the book, the child is central to everything we do. Indeed the child is central to our own underpinning philosophy. In complex and ever-changing and developing areas of society it is easy to lose sight of the main reason for initiatives and developments. Our main aim is the same as that of the government, other children's agencies, parents and the whole of society: that is, supporting children in their development, so that they can become happy, safe, well-rounded individuals who are able to contribute to society and in turn support their children.

The key points of the book are the following:

- it contains easily accessible yet rigorous support for the development of understandings and skills in early childhood issues;
- it supports and extends effective practice in caring and educating children in the early years, being well grounded in research and good practice;
- it looks at Early Childhood Studies from a multidisciplinary perspective;
- it supports the beginner practitioner and extends the more experienced practitioner;
- it contains issues for reflection and practical tasks at three levels for student and existing professionals, thus appealing to the kinaesthetic practitioner/learner;
- it contains reference to recent research and practice, both nationally and internationally;
- it contains illustrations, tables, graphs and photographs as well as practical tasks, thus appealing to the more visual practitioner/learner;
- it provides additional reading suggestions and website addresses to support further understanding of issues.

Tools for Learning

The development of professional practice is dependent on more early years professionals gaining degree level expertise in Early Childhood Studies. This means that professionals should develop a range of study skills, which facilitate their professional practice and reflection on early childhood practice and provision. Within the book, these skills are termed the Tools for Learning and are embedded in reflective and practical tasks.

The order of the Tools for Learning in each chapter follows a developmental sequence (see Table 0.1), which should be helpful for students and professionals who are attempting to develop their expertise and practice. The first set of Tools for Learning, in Part 1 of the book, is connected to reading and reflection of reading. Chapter 1 is concerned with the selection and use of literature as follows:

- helping the reader to make appropriate choices in the type of literature: a combination of books, journals, policy documents and web-based sources, avoiding an over-reliance on one type of source;
- reading for understanding;
- making notes on their reading;
- using reading effectively in the development of persuasive arguments, rather than simply describing the reading.
- referencing using the Harvard system;
- using original sources rather than using books cited in other texts.

Table 0.1 The development of Tools for Learning within each chapter of the book

Chapter	Title	Tools for Learning
Part 1	History and philosophy of early childhood studies	
1	Theories and theorists	Selecting and using literature
2	Developing your own philosophy	Reflection and analysis
Part 2	Early years development	
3	Physical development	Observation as a research tool
4	Cognitive development	Interacting with children as a research tool
5	Language development	Narrative as a research tool
6	Emotional and moral development	Listening as a research tool
7	Social development	Interview as a research tool
Part 3	Early childhood	
8	Families, home and childhood	Deeper analysis
9	Early education	Combining primary and secondary analysis
10	Special needs	Synthesis of ideas
Part 4	Practitioners in early childhood	
11	The early years professional	Writing a literature review/ developing written arguments
12	Reflective practice	Writing models for different methodologies
13	Working together	Writing up a thesis
14	Leadership and management in early years settings	Presenting research

In order to select and use reading effectively, you need to be very clear what the reading is being used for. Usually, this means having clear questions that need to be answered. These may be SMART: Specific, Measurable, Analytical, Relevant and Time-related. Questions that are too broad and generic will be unanswerable, especially if you are focusing on a few texts. You need to be clear how you are going to measure success in finding evidence to answer the questions. You need to pose analytical questions (how, why, so what questions) as opposed to descriptive questions (what, when, who questions) and be clear how the evidence you collect will answer them (how relevant the evidence is to the questions). Finally, you need a clear timescale for collecting the reading necessary to answer the questions; it is very easy to spend a great proportion of the time you have in reading and collecting nice bits of information, as this is comforting and reassuring (see the Squirrel phase in Figure 0.1).

In Chapter 2 we focus on reflection and analysis. We start by looking at what analysis is: to take something apart or separate in order to illuminate, reveal, uncover, understand, resolve, identify or clarify. We look at how you can analyse events, situations, experiences or reading, revealing what the main factors affecting them are or understanding why someone has acted in a particular way or clarifying issues for further development/ action. Later in the book (in Part 3) we will look at deeper analysis and combining analysis of primary and secondary data.

Part 2 of the book focuses on the collection of primary data, with each chapter (3–7) looking at a different research tool. This is a scary phase of your research (see the lemming phase in Figure 0.1), as you cannot rely on the work or support of others. In this part, you need to consider the reliability, validity and ethics of the different data collection methods you use and how these methods fit into an overall methodology.

1. Sheep phase

In this phase of research you wander around grazing on interesting titbits but are not quite sure where you are going and why you are going there. You may find interesting bits of information, but they do not form a coherent whole and may not inspire you. The focus of your research appears as a distant speck on the horizon; one that you are wandering towards but not by any defined pathway. It can be a rather frustrating phase, although this frustration can be a motivating force to move towards a more defined focus.

2. Chick phase

In the chick phase, you need nurture and guidance. You rely on tutors for support but care needs to be taken that you do not become over-reliant and dependent on others. A healthy chick researcher will take advice, but become increasingly self-sufficient, thus moving from the comfort zone into new and more frightening territory. Less healthy chicks may need constant feeding, thus not achieving any independence, while cuckoo chicks expect that someone else will provide for all their needs at the expense of others. Yet other chicks (ducklings) may follow the lead without question and independent or original thought.

3. Squirrel phase

This is the phase where you know what you are doing and you read and collect information, which you squirrel away for future reference and use. It is a very comforting phase as you can collect a vast amount of information and feel very reassured by the reading which confirms your initial ideas. This comfort, however, can encourage you to stay in this phase for too long and keep hoarding information which may not see the light of day unless you move on.

4. Lemming phase

This is one of the most frightening phases and this fear provides the reason why some researchers try to avoid it. The lemming researcher needs to make a giant leap into the unknown; to take a big risk and voice new ideas, question assumptions and challenge perceptions. Researching involves taking risks but in this phase it is important to remember that you are not alone. There are other lemmings out there, who are just as frightened as you and will support you when you make the leap and may leap with you.

5. Sheepdog phase

The penultimate research phase is the sheepdog phase, in which you need to round up your research, collecting all the stray bits of information together and making a coherent whole of it. This is a very organised phase and can be very structured, which is of comfort to some researchers. However, a good sheepdog researcher will make decisions and act upon them and so will not just follow guidelines but reinterpret them to ensure the best possible outcome. So, the sheepdog researcher synthesises the data, draws conclusions, identifies implications and packages the research up in a final written form, making decisions for him or herself.

6. Songbird phase

This final phase is another frightening one, where you disseminate your research to a wider audience. You may present your research findings at appropriate conferences and write articles for further and wider dissemination or contribute to, or author, books.

Figure 0.1 Phases of Research (Based on Johnston, 2005)
With thanks to Ashley Compton and Lindy Nahmad-Williams for inspiration

Practical Tasks

Research terms

Table 0.2 has key research terms and their definitions. These are mixed up and you need to draw a line between the matching term and its definition. The answers for this can be found in Figure 0.3 at the end of the Introduction on p.12.

Table 0.2 Key concepts in educational research: task
(Definitions taken from Cohen, *et al.*, 2000: 44, 45, 74, 105, 117)

Term	Definition
Methodology	Issues which '*might be feasibly and fairly answered*' through research
Methods	'*The honesty, depth, richness and scope of the data achieved, the participants approached, the extent of triangulation and the disinterestedness or objectivity of the researcher*'
Research questions	Research approach which aims to '*help us to understand. In the broadest possible terms, not the products of scientific enquiry but the process itself*'
Reliability	'*The range of approaches used in educational research to gather data, which are to be used as a basis for inference and interpretation, for explanation and prediction*'
Analysis	'*Consistency and replicability over time, over instruments and over groups of respondents*'
Validity	Technique for understanding issues or factors by breaking them up into their constituent parts and reflecting upon them

There are many different methodologies or types of research and each one has its own individual characteristics. You need to understand different methodologies in order to make a decision about which type best describes your research. The types of research which best suit research in early childhood include the following:

- *Action research*, in which the professional attempts to improve or develop practice in a cyclical way, by planning the next step of action or development as a result of analysis of the previous action or development. This is significantly different from other research methodologies and it needs to be written up in a particular way (see Chapter 12 and Figure 12.1). You may be attempting to develop children's social skills, or developing role play in your setting and therefore research the effectiveness of your plans and practice in a plan–do–review research process.

- *Case study research*, which involves analysis of a number of specific instances to understand the bigger picture. You may be researching transition by looking at the different perspectives of parents, children and professionals (with each one being a case). Your cases may also be issues or factors affecting transition which emerge from the data, so that in research into transition this may be the role of the parents, the curriculum or other settings in the transition (see Chapter 14).

- *Correlational research*, which considers interrelationships among variables involved in the research. For example, you may research the relationship between the increase in children's emotional difficulties and early childcare away from the home (see Chapter 6), or the relationship between social class and childhood obesity.

- *Survey*, where opinions, factors, issues are identified. This may involve giving a questionnaire to parents to find out their attitudes towards a Steiner approach to learning, or talking to children to find out what games they like to play.

- *Historical research* does not depend on primary data but uses policy documents and research reports to analyse historical trends, or the effect of new developments. This may involve analysis of the changes in the early years curriculum, or special needs provision.

- *Ethnographic research* concerns analysis in the natural context, so that the study is unaffected by external factors. Children may be observed in their homes, while interacting with their parents or siblings, or professionals observed and informally interviewed within their own setting, during the course of their normal working day.

- *Ex post facto research* is retrospective research, which investigates possible cause-and-effect relationships. This is done by observing an existing condition or state of affairs and searching back in time for plausible causal factors. For example, an attempt may be made to trace the causes of a child's behavioural problems, or the causes of a child's health problems.

- *Accounts or narratives* are types of interpretive ethnography where situations are considered from the participants' perspectives. Professionals may narrate their life stories to help understanding of their career pathway, or critical incidents in your life may be analysed to illuminate your philosophical stance (see Chapter 2).

- *Illuminative research* is an attempt to explain or understand the data, looking for deep understandings. So analysis of an early years leader's concerns and the constraints in which they work, may help to explain or understand their actions.

You may find it helpful to articulate your ideas for your research (questions, methodology, methods and preliminary reading) in a research proposal. A format for this can be found in Figure 0.2. Planning your research in this way helps you to firm up your ideas, preparing yourself and giving yourself a greater chance of succeeding in your research, for, as Dwight Eisenhower (1890–1969) said, 'In preparing for, battle I have always found that plans are useless, but planning is indispensable.'

When writing a research proposal, the following headings can be a guide.

Focus of research. A brief statement about the focus of the research (perhaps with a title or an over-arching research question).

Research questions. We suggest three questions which will help you to explore the area or answer your over-arching research question.

Methodology. A brief statement about the type of research you are conducting. Identify research literature which is informing your choice of methodology and methods and annotate to identify how it supports your choices.

Methods. A list of methods to be used to collect evidence to answer your questions. Identify also how you can ensure your research methods are reliable and the data collected will be valid.

Ethical statement. Write a brief statement to explain how you have ensured your research adheres to ethical guidelines.

Literature. An alphabetical list of reading which will underpin your research and provide the basis for the literature review. For each piece of reading also supply a short annotation to explain the relevance to your research.

Figure 0.2 Structure of a Research Proposal

The research methods considered in Part 2, can be used in most of the methodologies described above. Research methods are considered in Chapters 3–7. Chapter 3 looks at developing the most important research skill for the early years professional as well as a skill that is essential to develop in young children: that is observation. Through the reflective tasks, we help to understand observation, expand observation skills and so understand processes, events and development. We look at different types of observations: focused, unfocused, participant and non-participant, and the use of observation schedules. In Chapter 4, we consider how we can collect data from children by interacting with them. Importantly, we consider the ethics of working with children and collecting data from them to support their development and our practice. We also introduce the idea of a planning ladder to help professionals to plan their interactions with children. Chapter 5 considers narrative as a research tool. In narrative, participants or informants tell a story. These stories are more than anecdotes, and can provide powerful insights into situations and support analysis and synthesis. Each chapter in this book contains such stories, sometimes in the form of case studies, exemplars of practice or research. Sometimes the story is told by different participants, triangulating data and getting a more vivid and comprehensive picture of the action, event or situation being described. A story told from a different perspective allows layers of data to be analysed and a more valid (truthful) picture begins to be revealed. Chapter 6 focuses on listening as a research tool. We can tell a great deal about a child by listening to them in a variety of situations. If children talk to us, ask us questions, this information can inform us about their worries, concerns, achievements and aspirations. Evidence collected from children can be a powerful way to find out about them and will help us to make decisions about how to continue to support them. On its own listening to children can provide evidence to assist our deep understanding; combined and triangulated with other evidence, from observation, narratives, discussions with parents and other professionals, the evidence is more valid and powerful. Chapter 6 also considers the ethos and environment that encourages children to talk and helps us to evaluate our own environment. We explore the type of adult interaction and the type of questions which encourage children to talk openly and honestly and so enable us to gain a better understanding of them and how we can support their development. In Chapter 7 we look at discussions and interviews as research tools. The chapter considers the different nature of formal interviews and more fluid and informal discussions and the different types of data that they can usefully provide, the limitations of that data and their role in verifying or triangulating evidence from other sources and other methods. We also consider the advantages and limitations of different data collection tools used in interviews and discussions (notebook, questions, video, audio-tape, etc.).

Part 3 of the book is focused on early childhood and the Tools for Learning in this part are the important skills of analysis and synthesis. In Chapter 8 the reflective tasks aim to develop your analytical skills. We start by looking at what analysis is and how it can help us to understand and identify the main factors, issues or components of ideas or actions. We look at analytical questions, so that you can begin to identify and use these, rather than descriptive questions, to help improve your understanding of children, childhood and your practice. Deeper analysis is supported through tasks that help mine data to different depths, understand different perspectives, identify patterns, chronology of events and illuminate meanings, all of which will help us in our professional practice with children. Chapter 9 is concerned with the combination of primary and secondary analysis. In this chapter the Tools for Learning involve the skill of combining analysis from both primary and secondary data. Analysis of secondary data is mainly found in a literature review, which reviews the literature in order to answer questions you have posed. Primary data are usually presented and analysed in sections of your work entitled 'Research findings' or 'Outcomes and analysis'. These sections, especially in action research, also contain analysis of secondary data and both are also combined in 'Discussion of findings'. Primary and secondary analysis should be combined and used to create strong arguments, using the data as evidence in support. In order to create arguments you need to understand what an argument is and the difference between an argument (an evidence-based belief) and an opinion (a non-evidence-based belief). You also need to know what makes for a good rather than a weak argument; one that provides reasons behind what you are claiming, evidence to support your argument, such as factual data, persuasive language and a counter-argument. We also look at how you can help yourself to develop strong arguments by asking yourself the sort of questions that promote argument.

In Chapter 10 we consider the skill of synthesis, which is a very important skill that enables you to take analyses from a wide range of primary and secondary evidence and put them together in order to draw conclusions, make sense of the whole and draw inferences, producing new ideas or models and identifying implications. Synthesising involves breadth and depth of understanding, making links between different analyses and engaging in a deep and critical discussion of the ideas, implication or models of thinking that have emerged from the analysis. Most importantly, it does not repeat the analysis but moves forward from it to greater clarity, sophistication of ideas and understanding.

Part 4 of the book is concerned with presenting ideas in written, pictorial or oral forms. This is an essential tool for those who are being assessed through their presentation of ideas in short written assignments, longer dissertations, oral and visual presentations. Chapter 11 focuses on what a literature review is and how to write one, developing persuasive written arguments. There is a mistaken view that a literature review should provide a general description of all the writing in a large area (for example, childhood, early education, childhood health), rather that a more specific analysis of literature to help answer posed questions and in narrower or more defined areas (for example, the effect of divorce on early emotional development, the effectiveness of a new phonics programme, or the increase in childhood obesity). The literature review of any study has two main functions:

1. to set the scene and provide an introduction to the research, through an critical examination of literature in the area;
2. to use the literature to provide a critical analysis to answer the research questions posed.

There are four steps to writing a literature review. The first one is to select appropriate literature, ensuring a balance between different types of texts, professional and academic; books, journals and websites; seminal and recent texts; policy documents and historical documents. The second step is to read and understand the literature and not skim-read to pick out juicy quotations to use in your writing. To understand a text fully, you may need to read and reread it and reflect upon it for a while before using it. Step three involves using the analysed ideas in the literature. The Tools for Learning sections in Chapters 8 and 9 will help you to understand analysis, and Chapter 11 will help you to articulate analysis of reading. In order to use the reading effectively, you need to develop a persuasive argument (Toulmin, 1958), that is, use ideas from literature to support your thinking or argue against and answer your research questions. Effective use of reading involves making these persuasive arguments (see also Chapter 9) by using reading to support your ideas, rather than citing reading, as this shows understanding of the issues through analysis of the ideas expressed in the text rather than description.

In Chapter 12 we focus on the different writing structures for different research methodologies. The different methodologies (the overarching type of research you are undertaking) were described earlier in this chapter. Different methodologies need to be written up in different ways. This is especially the case with action research and case study research. When deciding on your methodology, you need to consider what the research will look like in its final written form and keep this in mind throughout the data collection and analysis process. This will ensure that the relevant primary data are collected and written up in a form that is appropriate to the type of research. Figure 12.1 provides a basic structure of the written task. Each reader needs to provide their own structure for their written work, which best shows their understanding of both research and the subject being researched. The Tools for Learning in Chapter 13 are concerned with writing up a thesis, bearing in mind that it is *your* written thesis that is assessed and so it should show the depth and breadth of *your* understanding. Remember also that writing up the research takes far longer than most people envisage. Chapter 13 considers the sections and structure of your written work, some of the dilemmas you may face when writing up your research thesis and possible solutions to help you perfect your work. Within the chapter there is also a section to help you to focus on the criteria by which you will be assessed and some tasks specifically designed to help you reflect on your written work. The Tools for Learning theme for Chapter 14 is presenting research, both orally and visually. Oral presentation of ideas and findings helps to articulate understanding and ultimately will help with written communication. Oral communication is an essential element of degree level work and the individual who seeks out opportunities to speak out and articulate ideas is likely to enhance their personal and professional development. In this book there are plenty of opportunities for large and small group discussions in the reflective tasks and critical discussion boxes (see below). The skill of formally presenting ideas orally also needs to be developed, since presentations form a part of both assessments in higher education and in working life as an early childhood professional. The skill of oral presentation includes the ability to speak coherently, engage with the audience, referring to notes rather than reading from them, or using notes only as a prompt. An excellent visual and oral presentation would motivate and engage the audience and have clear sense of purpose. It is easy to spend considerable time making visual presentations visually striking and even engaging, but without a clear objective a presentation will fail in its purpose.

Boxed features

As well as the Tools for Learning boxes, there are other boxed features within the book. Each chapter has a number of Reflective Tasks and some also have Critical Discussion. Many of the Reflective Tasks relate specifically to the Tools for Learning skills being developed in the chapter and each has three levels. Level 1 is designed for the student or someone with little experience in either the skill being developed in the Tools for Learning or the subject matter of the chapter. Level 2 is designed for the working early years professional, or someone with some skill in the specific tool for learning being developed and/or in the subject matter of the chapter. Level 3 is designed for the lead professional, headteacher or manager, or someone who has already developed their skills and knowledge and wishes to extend them or support others in their personal and professional development and lead their setting in developments. Many chapters also have Case Studies and these are usually followed by a Reflective Task to help make sense of the Case Study. In this way the Case Studies are not simply illustrative, but lead to reflective and personal and professional development. Some chapters also have Practical Tasks, which encourage the reader to undertake some more practical physical activities related to the content of the chapter. These too are at three levels for the student, the professional and the lead professional. These are designed to support application of ideas in practice, thus supporting professional development and thinking. Each chapter is underpinned by extensive research and specific current research is summarised in each chapter in Research boxes.

The decision as to which level of task to undertake is one that each individual reader must take and the route through the book will, likewise, be individual. For example, an undergraduate student may wish to tackle the Level 1 tasks, which build on from their post-16 qualifications and are the sort of task undertaken on undergraduate degree programmes. However, there may be some areas of knowledge in which the reader has more expertise and so may choose to focus on Level 2 tasks, or move from Level 1 to Level 2 tasks. Some work-based undergraduate students (for example, foundation degree students, with extensive experience of working with young children) may wish to focus on Level 2 tasks and in areas where they have especial expertise they may choose to move on to some Level 3 tasks. Lead professionals, headteachers and managers will wish to focus on Level 3 tasks, which provide ideas for extending not only their own professional development, but also that of their team/staff through in-service training sessions and staff meetings. They may also wish to incorporate some of the Level 2 tasks to support the development of professionals in their setting.

We recognise that books of this nature contain many terms and acronyms or abbreviations not used in everyday life. Understanding these terms and what the acronyms stand for, as well as being able to use them, is increasingly important in professional life. The first time these key terms are used in the text they are coloured blue and the reader can then turn to the Glossary (p. 448) where the term will be defined. There is a list of Abbreviations on page xviii.

Theorists in practice

The book begins in Chapter 1 with an overview of historical practice and provision in the early years and the work of early pioneers, theorists and reformers who have influenced ideas and practice. Throughout the book we continue to reflect on these theorists, as well as introducing some new and more recent ideas. Table 1.1 identifies the main theorists you will meet in the book. Chapter 2 identifies the philosophical sayings of some theorists, in particular Steiner and McMillan; the latter's ideas about the importance of diet on children's health is picked up in Chapter 3. Maslow's hierarchy of needs is introduced in Chapter 1 (see Figure 1.1) and is used to support arguments about emotional development in Chapter 6, about social development in Chapter 7 and in looking at families in Chapter 8. It is also used to create new arguments and models in Chapter 14 (see Figure 14.3).

In Chapter 4 the ideas of Piaget, Vygotsky and Bruner are considered and two figures enlarge on Piaget cognitive theories (see Figure 4.4 and Table 4.1). Piaget's theories are further developed in relation to the following:

- language development in Chapter 5;
- moral development (see Table 6.5) in Chapter 6;
- social development in Chapter 7;
- education in Chapter 9;
- early years settings in Chapter 14.

Vygotsky's theories are further developed through discussion of language development in Chapters 5, 7, 9, 13 and 14. Other theorists whose ideas are recurrent themes throughout the book are:

- Bowlby, whose ideas about emotional development are fully developed in Chapter 6, but also form part of discussions in Chapters 7, 8 and 13;
- Bronfenbrenner, whose ecological systems theory is fully explored in Chapter 7 and through Figure 7.2, but is also considered in Chapters 6 and 13.

In addition the new work of Howard Gardner is introduced in Chapter 4.

As well as considering the ideas and theories of Piaget and Vygotsky in Chapter 5, the part played by Skinner and Bruner in understanding language development is discussed. We also introduce the work of Noam Chomsky, who provided an alternative viewpoint in the debate on language acquisition. Chapter 6 focuses on the work of four of our theorists, Sigmund Freud, Erik Erikson, John Bowlby and Laurence Kohlberg. Freud's psychoanalytical theory is explored and explained through the chapter and Table 6.3 and Erikson's psycho-social stages are illustrated in Table 6.4. Bowlby's theories on attachment are developed using the ideas of

Lorenz, and the new work of Mary Ainsworth and Sir Richard Bowlby (John Bowlby's son) are discussed. The debate on moral development focuses mainly on the theories of Piaget and Kohlberg (see especially Table 6.6), but the part played by Bandura's and Bronfenbrenner's work is also explored. Both Bandura and Bronfenbrenner feature strongly in Chapter 7, together with the behaviourist theories of Skinner and Lorenz. It is in this chapter that Bronfenbrenner's ecological systems theory is fully explained (see Figure 7.2) and links between emotional and social development explored using the work of Bowlby. The importance of Rousseau's work (1911) on thinking about social development is also discussed and Baumrind's work (1971) on parenting is introduced.

Diana Baumrind's ideas are more fully explored in the first chapter of Part 3, Early Childhood (see Figure 8.2). Chapter 8 begins with a quote from Rousseau about the family being the most ancient of societies and the recurrent ideas of Maslow and Bowlby are further discussed in this content.

Chapter 9 focuses on the work of Froebel, Bruner and Piaget, but also discusses the link between health and education using the ideas of Margaret McMillan, while Chapter 10 looks at the original focus of Montessori's ideas in supporting children with specific special needs.

In Part 4, Practitioners in Early Childhood, the practical applications of ideas are considered using the following examples:

- High/Scope, developed from the ideas of David Weikart (see Chapters 11, 12 and 13);
- Reggio Emelia, developed from the work of Loris Magaluzzi (see Chapters 12 and 13);
- Montessori education (see Chapter 13);
- Steiner education, developed from the philosophical work of Rudolph Steiner (see Chapter 13).

Chapter 12 also develops the ideas of Dewey and introduces new ideas in the form of Kolb's experiential learning cycle (1984; see Figure 12.2), while Chapter 13 develops the work of Bronfennbrenner, Vygotsky and Bowlby.

Finally, Chapter 14 develops the ideas of Bronfennbrenner, Rousseau, Vygotsky, Piaget and Maslow, discussing them in the context of leadership and management, and introducing new ways of applying their ideas, as well as introducing the ideas of Charles Handy (1992).

How to use the book

Like any book of this nature, it is not expected that you will read it from cover to cover, but rather use sections to support particular areas of study or personal and professional development. Neither is it designed to be 'dipped into' to find useful quotations to support your work, as this is an unscholarly approach that will not help your personal and professional development. Each chapter will stand alone, focusing on a specific area of Early Childhood Studies and should be read and reread; the relevant Reflective and Practical Tasks should be undertaken to support deep understanding. The Tools for Learning follow a sequence and these may be looked at in order or when the particular skill is being developed by the reader.

We hope that you will enjoy the book and find it useful in your personal and professional development.

Methodology

Research approach which aims to '*help us to understand. In the broadest possible terms, not the products of scientific enquiry but the process itself*'.

Methods

'*The range of approaches used in educational research to gather data, which are to be used as a basis for inference and interpretation, for explanation and prediction.*'

Research questions

Issues which '*might be feasibly and fairly answered*' through research.

Analysis

Technique for understanding issues or factors by breaking them up into their constituent parts and reflecting upon them.

Validity

'*The honesty, depth, richness and scope of the data achieved, the participants approached, the extent of triangulation and the disinterestedness or objectivity of the researcher.*'

Reliability

'*Consistency and replicability over time, over instruments and over groups of respondents.*'

Figure 0.3 Key Concepts in Educational Research Answers
(Definitions taken from Cohen, *et. al.*, 2000: 44, 45, 74, 105 and 117)

References and further reading

Ainsworth, M., Blehar, M., Waters, E. and Wall, S. (1978) *Patterns of Attachment*. Hillsdale, NJ: Erlbaum

Bandura, A. (1977) *Social Learning Theory*. Englewood Cliffs, NJ: Prentice-Hall

Baumrind, D. (1971) 'Current Patterns of Parental Authority', *Developmental Psychology*, Monograph 4.1, Part 2

Bowlby, J. (1958) 'The Nature of a Child's Tie to His Mother', *International Journal of Psychoanalysis* 39: 350–73

Bowlby, J. (1969) *Attachment and Loss*. New York: Basic Books

Bowlby, R. (2006) *The Need for Secondary Attachment Figures in Childcare*. www.telegraph.co.uk/opinion/main.jhtml?xml=/opinion/2006/10/21/nosplit/dt2101.xml#head5Childcare problems

Bronfenbrenner, U. (1995) 'The Bioecological Model from a Life Course Perspective: Reflections of a participant observer', in Moen, P., Elder Jnr, G.H. and Lüscher, K. (eds) *Examining Lives in Context*. Washington, DC: American Psychological Association: pp. 599–618

Bruner, J. (1983) *Child's Talk: Learning to Use Language*. New York: Norton

Chomsky, N (1972) *Language and Mind*. New York: Harcourt Brace Jovanovich

Cohen, L., Manion, L. and Morrison, K. (2000) *Research Methods in Education*, 5th edn. London: Routledge Falmer

CWDC (2007a) *About CWDC: What we Do* http://www.cwdcouncil.org.uk/aboutcwdc/whatwedo.htm

CWDC (2007b) *Prospectus: Early Years Professional Status*. Leeds: CWDC

Dewey, J. (1897) 'My pedagogic creed', *The School Journal*, LIV, 3: 77–80. Also available in the Informal Education Archives, http://www.infed.org/archives/e-texts/e-dew-pc.htm

Dewey, J. (1933) *How we Think*. Boston: D.C. Heath

DfES (2003) *Every Child Matters*. London: DfES

Erikson, E.H. (1950) *Childhood and Society*. New York: Norton

Freud, S. (1923) *The Ego and the Id*. London: Hogarth

Davenport, G.C. (1994) *An Introduction to Child Development*. London: Collins

Gardner, H. (2007a) 'Multiple Intelligences: Past, Present, Future.' *Proceedings of CONASTA 56 and ICASE 2007 World Conference on Science and Technology Education. Sustainable, Responsible, Global*. Perth: Science Teachers' Association of Western Australia, www.worldste2007.asn.au

Gardner, H. (2007b) *Five Minds for the Future*. Boston: Harvard Business School Press

Handy, C. (1992) *The Gods of Management*. London: Penguin

Johnston, J. (2005) 'Research Phases', *Newsletter of the Leicester Doctor of Education*, 13

Kolb, A. (1984) *Experiential Learning: Experience as the Source of Learning and Development*. Englewood Cliffs, NJ: Prentice-Hall

Maslow, A.H. (1968) *Towards a Psychology of Being*. New York: Van Nostrand

Piaget, J. (1929) *The Child's Conception of the World*. New York: Harcourt

Piaget, J. (1950) *The Psychology of Intelligence*. London: Routledge & Kegan Paul

Piaget, J. (1959) *The Language and Thought of the Child*. London: Routledge & Kegan Paul

Rinaldi, C. (2006) *In Dialogue with Reggio Emilia*. London: Routledge

Rousseau, J.J. (1911) *Emile*. London: J.M. Dent

Steiner, R. (1996) *The Education of the Child and Early Lectures on Education*. New York: Anthroposophic Press

Toulmin, S. (1958) *The Uses of Argument*. Cambridge: Cambridge University Press

Vygotsky, L. (1962) *Thought and Language*. Cambridge, MA: MIT Press

Vygotsky, L. and Cole, M. (eds) (1978) *Mind in Society, The Development of Higher Psychological Processes*. Cambridge, MA: Harvard University Press

Useful websites

Children's Workforce Development Council:
www.cwdcouncil.org.uk

Part 1

History and Philosophy of Early Childhood Studies

Chapter 1

Theories and Theorists

‘Our highest human endeavours must be to develop free human beings who are able of themselves to impart purpose and direction to their lives’
(Steiner, 1996)

Introduction

This chapter seeks to chart the emergence of influential theories on practice and policy in early childhood education and care, from the early eighteenth century onwards. Taking a chronological approach, it can be seen how the work of the earliest theorists and reformers impacts upon the work of the future generations of pioneers. Brief biographical details have been included to provide further insight into how experiences in their lives could have potentially influenced their work. In addition to providing factual details, the chapter also includes common themes and links between the theorists. Explicit connections are made between the work of the theorists and current early childhood practice and policy.

Aims

➜ To provide an overview of historical practice and provision in the early years through the work of early pioneers and reformers

➜ To provide key biographical details of the lives of these pioneers and reformers, in an attempt to understand the influences on them that have helped to formulate their beliefs

➜ To examine the key historical beliefs held by these pioneers and reformers and consider their influence on current practices and policy in early childhood education and care

➜ To consider recent, new and emerging theories and theorists emphasising the current issues in early childhood studies, both nationally and internationally

A timeline of theorists

We start our timeline see (Table 1.1) with **Jean Jacques Rousseau (1712–78)** who was a French 'philosopher, social and political theorist, musician, botanist, and one of the most eloquent writers of the Age of Enlightenment' (Microsoft, 1996a). Rousseau was born in Geneva on 18 June 1712 and raised by an aunt and uncle, as his mother died just after his birth. At 13, Rousseau was apprenticed to an engraver, but ran away after three years and became a companion and secretary to Madame Louise de Warens. It was here that Rousseau was influenced in his thinking. In 1742 he went to Paris and worked as a music teacher, music copyist and political secretary, becoming a close friend of the French philosopher Denis Diderot. Rousseau believed that childhood was distinctly different from adulthood. His ideas are based on the philosophy that humans are born free and good, but influenced by society, its conventions and through the process of socialisation, and that children have a different way of thinking to adults. Children were thought to develop inhibitions, vices and ideas during their childhood and to become increasingly constrained by the rules of society. Rousseau stressed that young children should be allowed to develop free of society's constraints and that early provision should provide a balance between societal freedom and happiness on one side and increasing independence and control on the other (Roopnarine and Johnson, 1987). Rousseau believed that education should *'accommodate itself to the child'* (Barnard, 1961: 33) rather than expecting the child to accommodate to the system, convincing educators that education should be child–centred, with expression rather than repression being central (Rousseau, 1911). Elements of Rousseau's principles have dominated early education for over 200 years and he has been called the 'Father of Education'. It is reasonably undisputed that his philosophy led to the understanding that practical development in the early years (experiential learning) was most effective and to the child-centred education in the UK in the 1960s and 1970s.

Our second reformer and thinker is **Johann Heinrich Pestalozzi (1746–1827),** a Swiss humanitarian and educational reformer, whose theories are thought to have been influential in the development of elementary education worldwide. Pesatalozzi was born in Zurich on 12 January 1746 and studied theology at the University of Zurich, intending to become a pastor. However, he was most concerned with the plight of the poor and in 1775 opened a school for the children of the poor on his estate near Zurich and another for orphans in 1798, both of which were not open for long because of financial difficulties. In 1799, Pestalozzi was more successful when he opened a school at Burgdorf, which

Table 1.1 Pioneers and reformers in early childhood

Rousseau, J.J.	(1712–1778)
Pestalozzi, J.H.	(1746–1827)
Oberlin, J.F.	(1740–1826)
Froebel, F.	(1782–1852)
Dewey, J.	(1859–1952)
Montessori, M.	(1870–1952)
McMillan, R.	(1859–1917)
McMillan, M.	(1860–1931)
Steiner, R.	(1861–1925)
Freud, S.	(1856–1939)
Piaget, J.	(1896–1980)
Vygotsky, L. S.	(1896–1934)
Erikson, E.	(1902–1994)
Skinner, B. F	(1904–1990)
Bowlby, J.	(1907–1990)
Maslow, A. H.	(1908–1970
Plowden, B.D.	(1910–2000)
Bruner, J.	(1915–)
Bronfenbrenner, U.	(1917–2005)
Magaluzzi, L.	(1920–1994)
Bandura, A.	(1925–)
Kohlberg, L.	(1927–1987)
Weikart, D.P.	(1931– 2003)

was moved to Yverdon in 1805 and was attended by pupils from all over Europe. This school was a testing ground for many of his ideas. Pestalozzi stressed the individuality of the child and believed that children learn through practice and observation 'through the natural employment of the senses' (Microsoft, 1996b). Like Rousseau, he stressed experiential learning and went on to identify that teachers should facilitate learning rather than impart knowledge to children. His beliefs have influenced not only elementary (primary) education throughout the Western world, but also teacher training in the UK, especially in the 1960s and 1970s.

Reflective Tasks

Experiential learning

Level 1

Consider Rousseau's and Pestalozzi's belief in experiential learning. What do you consider experiential learning to be? Identify which of the following would be part of experiential learning:

→

- finding out for yourself;
- being taught something;
- learning through your own experience;
- thinking through a problem;
- being supported by another person (adult or peer);
- learning through practical activities;
- discussing with others;
- learning from a book or the media.

Think about a positive learning experience you have had.

- What made it so positive?
- Was it experiential?

Level 2

Think of a successful learning experience you have provided for children.

- What were the features that made it successful?
- How could you have made the experience more experiential?
- Would this have made it even more successful? Why?

Level 3

Consider the future planning of your setting.

- Does it contain aspects of experiential learning?
- How can you work with your staff to develop the planning further to enhance children's experiential learning?
- Why might this be beneficial to the children?

Jean Frederic Oberlin (1740–1826) is a little known and probably under-rated reformer. He was a French educator who instituted a system of pre-school education which focused on language development and handicrafts, but had a varied and balanced curriculum, with some instruction, physical exercises to aid cooperative skills, handicrafts and no lesson plans or timetable. In 1767, together with three collaborators, Madeleine-Salome Oberlin, Sarah Banzet and Louise Scheppler, he set up a system of pre-school education and founded schools, which became known as the knitting schools, in poor villages in rural Alsace. At that time in rural areas, standard French was not commonly spoken and while this adversely affected his work it also characterised his system of learning. In the schools, groups of about 50 children sat around a leader while she knitted and chatted, teaching them names of objects, plants, animals, etc. in standard French. In this way, the children learnt from the leader who modelled speaking and listening and taught them about the world around them in an open and cheerful way. Oberlin also introduced a system for learning to read which was a form of early paired reading where children would listen to stories, look at illustrations and later read the text for themselves. His ideas and the practice in his schools formed a model for early education in France and he appears to be the first person to recognise the importance of a varied and balanced curriculum. His ideas were not adopted in France during his lifetime and his schools did not continue after his death in 1826, but today's provision for young children equally considers the importance of a varied curriculum and engages in group work to support developments such as literacy (DfEE, 1998).

Picture 1.1 Friedrich Froebel
Source: Mary Evans Picture Library/Alamy Images

Friedrich Froebel (1782–1852) (see Picture 1.1) was a German educator, who is widely recognised for his contribution to early childhood theories and practice. He was born in Oberweissbach in Germany on 21 April 1782 and was mainly self-educated, but undertook a University education in Jena, Göttingen and Berlin. He worked in forestry, surveying and architecture before becoming a teacher and was greatly influenced by Pestalozzi, with whom he worked from 1806 until 1810. In 1816 he founded a school called the Universal German Educational Institute. His ideas for the education of pre-school children, aged between 3 and 7, led to the first schools for pre-school children, which he called 'kindergarten' (children's garden). These kindergartens stressed the natural growth of children through action or play, as 'the purpose of education is to encourage and guide' (Froebel, 1826). Froebel's ideas were considered very radical for the time and largely rejected publicly; kindergartens were even banned in Prussia from 1851 to 1860. After his death in 1852, his ideas blossomed and kindergartens were established throughout western Europe and the USA and later throughout the world, so that he is now considered to have made an enormous contribution to education. As well as the importance of play, Froebel's legacy included the notion of practical experiences through the exploration of special materials, which Froebel called 'gifts'. These were a range of educational toys, such as shaped wooden bricks and balls, designed to develop a child physically and cognitively. Such educational toys are extremely common today, but this was a radically new idea in the early nineteenth century. Froebel also developed a series of educational activities, which he called 'occupations', and was very concerned about the education of young children through educational games in the family. Current practice involves the use of finger rhymes, nursery rhymes and educational songs, which are all used regularly with children from birth to aid social, cognitive and physical development.

Practical Tasks

Games, songs and rhymes

Level 1

Add to the list of rhymes and songs below:

Incy wincy spider

One, two, three, four, five, once I caught a fish alive

Round and round the garden, like a teddy bear

Here we go round the mulberry bush

We're going on a bear hunt

The wheels on the bus go round and round

Heads, shoulders, knees and toes

Each peach, pear, plum, I spy Tom Thumb

Identify which ones will develop a child physically, mathematically or linguistically.

Level 2

List all the games, songs and rhymes that will develop mathematical understandings and skills. Identify how you can use them to develop children mathematically.

Level 3

Make a new game for children, which will develop them mathematically or linguistically. This could be a magnetic fishing game, with basic key words written on the back of the fish, or a game of snap with numbers and objects on the backs of the cards (number 5 on one and five apples on another). Tip: Laminate the game to make it more durable. You can also add words, numbers, etc. after lamination, with a dry marker, and then you can make the game more or less difficult.

John Dewey (1859–1952) was an American philosopher, psychologist and educator who was interested in the reform of educational theory and practice. He studied at the University of Vermont and Johns Hopkins University. Throughout his career he lectured in education, acted as an educational consultant and studied the educational systems of China, Japan, Mexico, Turkey and the Soviet Union. Dewey opposed authoritarian methods of education, feeling that children should not be kept occupied or trained as that did not prepare for a democratic life. However, he did advocate guidance to support the child's development and preparation for this democratic life (Dewey, 1916). We can see this belief reflected in today's society as we are expected to support children in their decision-making and in developing aspects of citizenship through both the Early Years Foundation Stage (DfES, 2007) and Key Stage 1 (DfEE, 1999a). It is interesting to contemplate how Dewey's ideas about education, not just about keeping children occupied, fit with current initiatives for wrap-around care, the development of an early years foundation stage from birth to 5 years and the emotive debate about whether care at home or care in pre-school settings is best for development (FCCC, 2005).

We can see evidence in Dewey's ideas from other reformers and theorists. For example, Dewey followed Oberlin's belief in a varied curriculum and formulated educational principles, which emphasised learning through varied activities rather than a more formal curriculum. He also followed Rousseau's belief in child-centred childcare and began a shift from school-centred education towards more child-centred education, with his work and writings responsible for changes in **pedagogy** (the science of education) within the USA in the twentieth century. His ideas have been linked to progressive changes in education and he showed how philosophical ideas can work in practice.

Maria Montessori (1870–1952) was an Italian educator and physician who is best known for her method of teaching young children (see Picture 1.2), the Montessori method (Montessori, 1912). She was clearly a remarkable woman; the first female medical doctor in Italy who was only accepted at medical school by appealing to the Pope (Kramer, 1976), and an unmarried mother, whose experiences, background and observations led her to develop firmly held beliefs about early childhood. She believed that each

Picture 1.2 A Montessori nursery, showing children taking
part in practical activities to engage the senses
Source: Janine Wiedel Photography/Alamy Images

child was an individual with a unique personality and needed protection from adverse influences during childhood. These adverse influences included adult intervention, as she believed that adults hindered the child developing as an explorer, discoverer and manipulator of the environment. It was the role of adults to observe and support development. She was committed to a child-centred approach to childhood development, which involved child-sized furniture, a motivating environment and activities which supported, promoted and even accelerated all aspects of development.

The principles of the Montessori method (Montessori, 1912) are:

- early childhood should be child-centred but not child-led;
- there are five disciplines (practical, sensorial, language, mathematical, culture) and these are not sequenced and overtly separate;
- activities should satisfy the child's changing developmental needs and build upon each other;
- 'indirect preparation' should be built into the sequences (periods) of activities. There are seven periods during childhood;
- teachers should provide direction and structure;
- children determine their own rate of progression.

Children start in the first period by engaging with early practical activities and introductory sensorial, language and cultural activities. Today we can relate this to child development knowledge and early years education (Olaf, 2003) with children up to a year old focusing on listening, looking, learning, reaching out, crawling, pulling up and standing. In the Montessori method (Montessori, 1912), the early activities are developed in the second period by building on fundamental practical, sensorial (focusing on sight and sound), language and cultural skills. Olaf (2003) likens this to the young child from

1 to 3 years of age participating in family life, experiencing food, toys, puzzles, music and language. Montessori's third period develops more advanced practical skills, builds on the existing fundamental sensorial skills (focusing on smell, sound and taste), completing preparatory work in language, as well as fully entering culture work and starting mathematics. This relates to the period when children develop as part of a family and explore food, toys and games, blocks and puzzles as well as explore and care for their wider environment through interaction with the earth, plants, animals, people, language, music and art (Olaf, 2003).

Rachel McMillan (1859–1917) and her sister **Margaret (1860–1931)** were both born in New York but moved to Scotland during childhood. They were both committed to social welfare and reform of provision for young children. Rachel trained as a sanitary inspector and social worker, while Margaret trained as a governess. In 1908 Rachel opened a school clinic, followed in 1911 by an open-air nursery school in Deptford. Here, children aged between 2 and 5 would spend all day and be provided with meals. Margaret continued Rachel's work after her early death from cancer in 1917, opening the first nursery schools across the UK where caring was a central aspect. Indeed, the word 'nurture' was first coined by Margaret McMillan. Both Rachel and Margaret McMillan (1911) recognised the importance of a healthy body as well as a healthy mind in childhood. As Margaret wrote, without education and nurture in the first years 'all the rest of life is clouded and weakened' (McMillan, 1930). They identified that education is more effective when children are well fed and clothed and when it takes place in an environment that protects the child's health and welfare. They also established training colleges to prepare staff for work in nurseries; the Rachel McMillan Training College and nursery school remain in existence in Deptford today.

Margaret McMillan also placed a high value on the education of the imagination, identifying that creativity was an important aspect of early development, but could only progress if safety, health and welfare was adequately considered.

Tools for Learning

Selecting and using literature

In this chapter, the Tools for Learning, that is the tools we are developing to support your learning, are involved with choosing appropriate reading to support your understanding and using that reading effectively in oral and written arguments. The first step in this area is to make appropriate choices in the type of literature, using a few appropriate secondary sources of reading, which should also be a balance of books, journals, policy documents and web-based sources, avoiding over-reliance on one type. Appropriate reading involves choosing texts that help you to understand the issue you are researching and that can support the claims and counter-claims (arguments) you are making. Once chosen, reading should be for understanding rather than collecting lots of interesting titbits to quote, as this does not show understanding and tends merely to describe reading rather than use it effectively. Often to understand something thoroughly it needs to be read and reread while making notes from the reading, including a note of the full bibliographical reference. In this book we use the Harvard system of referencing, which involves putting the name(s) of author(s) and date in the text, and showing page numbers if you use a direct quotation. Full references should be made at the end of the piece of writing:

Name, initial. (date) *Title of Book*. Place of publication: Publisher

Name, initial. (date) 'Title of article', *Title of journal* Number. Volume. Pages

Name, initial. (date) 'Title of chapter', in name of editor, initial, in *Title of book*. Place of publication: Publisher, pages

At the end of this chapter, you will find references which illustrate how this works in practice.

When reading and referencing reading, you should always use original sources and they should always be read and referenced, rather than simply referencing texts that have been used within the book you are reading. This is necessary, not only for scholarly purposes and because it aids understanding of the original ideas and arguments, but also because you need to check that the details of the original author and the reference are correct.

The notes that you make on your reading can be used to support arguments you are making. Effective use of reading involves making persuasive arguments and using reading to support it, rather than simply citing reading, as this shows an understanding of the issues through analysis of the ideas expressed in the text rather than a description of them. This is discussed further in the Tools for Learning in Chapter 11. As the skill of using reading develops, then you need to use literature to create critical arguments.

Tools for Learning tasks

The beliefs of Maria Montessori and Margaret McMillan are well published, both in their own writings and in the writings of others.

Level 1

Find one book on either Maria Montessori or Margaret McMillan and read about their beliefs.

Level 2

Find one book written by either Maria Montessori or Margaret McMillan and one book written about them. Read both the books and compare the ideas expressed.

Level 3

Find one book which contains the beliefs of Maria Montessori or Margaret McMillan and another which critiques their beliefs. Read them both and compare the ideas expressed.

Reflective Tasks

The beliefs of Montessori and McMillan

Level 1

Consider how the beliefs of either Maria Montessori or Margaret McMillan are seen in today's early childhood practice. Make a list of practices today which could be attributed to their beliefs.

Level 2

Identify aspects of the practice of your class which can be attributed to the beliefs of either Maria Montessori or Margaret McMillan.

- How did these experiences relate to the beliefs of Montessori or McMillan?
- How did these experiences support or hinder early development?

Level 3

Identify aspects of the practice of your setting which can be attributed to the beliefs of either Maria Montessori or Margaret McMillan. From your experience, identify how these aspects of practice have supported child development in your context. How could you develop these aspects further?

Picture 1.3 Rudolf Steiner
Source: Hutton Archive/Getty Images

Rudolph Steiner (1861–1925) (see Picture 1.3) was a philosopher and scientist, born in part of Austria which is now in Croatia. He studied natural sciences at the University of Vienna and evolved the philosophical doctrine of anthroposophy, which focuses on disciplined inner activity and identifies the importance of the human being rather than God. In 1912, Steiner founded the Anthroposophical Society and in 1913 the Goetheanum, a school of spiritual science, to advance his educational methods. These methods are based on Steiner's philosophy, which advocates the importance of spiritual growth and holistic education. He believed that education involves supporting the unfolding of three human faculties:

- doing, associated with the hands;
- thinking, associated with the head;
- feeling, associated with the heart.

These followed the natural rhythm of life and engaged with the natural world. Like Montessori, Steiner cherished the unique individuality of every child. In Steiner's educational methods, nothing is rushed; there is nothing to fear since the natural rhythm is followed; nothing fails and children are allowed the satisfaction of experiencing and learning through play; there are no instructions, but rather self-direction with the teacher as a role model (Oldfield, 2001). Each session for young children will follow a rhythm of expansion and contraction. For example, the session may begin with a creative activity (painting, drawing, modelling, baking or cleaning), which allows expansion, followed by tidying up and circle-time (a contraction time). After washing hands and a snack and drink, children will have outdoor play time (expansion time) and finish the session with a story time or puppet show (contraction time). There is also a weekly rhythm, with each day of the week having specific identified activities and so there is no uncertainty or surprise for the child. Steiner also believed that children should not be forced into formal learning at an early age and that education involves developing purpose and direction (Steiner, 1996), in seven-year phases, with children not being felt ready to learn to read until they have completed the first phase at 7 years of age.

Tools for Learning

Selecting and using literature

Level 1

Find the chapter dealing with the natural rhythm and pace of early education in Oldfield (2001). Use the information in that chapter to reflect on the natural rhythm of your life.

Level 2

Find the chapter dealing with the natural rhythm and pace of early education in Oldfield (2001). Read this and compare it to the ideas expressed in Elkind (1989). Identify points of agreement in the ideas expressed.

Level 3

Find two different books which discuss Steiner's belief in the natural rhythm and pace of early education. Try to find alternative viewpoints in the literature and use these and your own experiences to critique his ideas.

Sigmund Freud (1856–1939) was an Austrian physician and the founder of the psychoanalytical perspective. Freud developed his theories from working with troubled adults, with a collection of nervous symptoms that appeared to have no foundation in the physical, and he believed that the way in which they manage their sexual and aggressive drives in the early years affected healthy personal development as adults. There are two main aspects to Freud's theories:

1. The development of personality, which Freud (1923) believed has three parts, the id, ego and super ego. The id dominates early life and behaviour and is a primitive, logical and totally demanding part of personality, focusing on things which give pleasure such as food and comfort. The ego is a more realistic awareness of self and the world, which develops with the child. The superego is a more developed part of personality which involves moral reasoning. These ideas are discussed further in Chapter 6.

2. Psychosexual development, which stresses the importance of early childhood relationships for healthy development, linking early sexual behaviour to parts of the body (oral, anal and genital) and the difficulty of balancing the basic needs in early childhood.

Freud's theories have received much criticism for three main reasons: because of the emphasis on sexual feelings in early development; because his theories failed to take into account cultural influences and could not be applied in other contexts; because he developed a theory of childhood by studying adults. However, his theories remain important because they were the first theories which recognised the importance of early experiences on future adult life and development, and also because they were developed and modified by other psychoanalysts, such as Anna Freud and Erik Erikson.

Picture 1.4 Jean Piaget
Source: AFP/Getty Images

Jean Piaget (1896–1980) (see Picture 1.4) was a Swiss developmental biologist who became interested in psychology and through studies of his own children identified four stages of cognitive development (Piaget, 1929; 1950):

- *pre-operational*, which is the earliest stage of cognition and is characterised by reflexive movements in response to stimuli and the development of early ideas as a result of experiences;

- *sensori-motor*, during which children develop their early ideas including mental imagery and thinking skills, although their thinking is very uncoordinated and irrational. It is also during this stage that language develops;

- *concrete operational*, which is a stage characterised by increasingly rational and coordinated thinking as long as the child is working concretely, that is, manipulating objects to aid understanding;

- *formal operational*, where thinking becomes more abstract and logical and children are able to solve mental problems.

Piaget's cognitive theories and those of other cognitive psychologists are discussed more fully in Chapter 4. His theories, and the work of other theorists, began an intense focus on cognition which has helped us to understand the way a child thinks. Piaget's work has been extensively criticised over the years by those who continued to work in the area, such as Lev Vygotsky (1962) and Robbie Case (Case and Okamoto, 1996). Some of his findings were found to be incorrect, especially with regard to the ages at which children develop cognitively; see for example, Berk's comparisons of developmental milestones (2003) with Piaget's stage theory. Piaget also posited theories about moral development (Piaget, 1965), which evolved in cognitive stages, illustrating the cognitive aspect of moral development and the belief that children were active participants in their moral development (see Chapter 6, for further detail). These ideas were also developed further by Kohlberg (1976).

Picture 1.5 Lev Vygotsky
Source: RIA Novosti/TopFoto

Lev Vygotsky (1896–1934) was a Russian teacher, psychologist and philosopher (see Picture 1.5). He initially studied law but became increasingly interested in how his pupils learned and as a result turned to research in developmental psychology in 1917, following the Russian Revolution. Developmental psychology became his lifelong passion and since the 1960s, when his writing was translated into English, his work has greatly influenced thinking in the UK and other Western countries. His ideas have had a great impact on educational developments in a number of areas:

- Vygotsky believed that the child's social and cultural environment affected cognitive development and that learning occured through the interaction of skilled adults (Vygotsky and Cole, 1978) and through social interaction with peers;

- he identified the zone of proximal development (ZPD), or the difference between tested levels of cognitive development and potential development that can be achieved through interaction with adults;

- he analysed children's play and concluded that it was important not just for emotional and physical development, but also for cognitive development;

- Vygotsky (1962) believed there was a strong interrelationship between language and thought and that speech was a tool developed in a social context which becomes a vehicle for thought;

- he also explored the transferability of higher order skills and of thinking processes from one context to another, concluding that some higher order thinking skills, such as classification and logical thought, were transferable.

Erik Erikson (1902–94) was particularly interested in the development of identity, an interest which arose out of his personal concerns about identity. He was born in Frankfurt, Germany, and his father was an unnamed Danish man, whom Erikson never met. His mother, who was Jewish, later married his paediatrician and Erikson appeared to suffer an identity crisis, changing his name (from Homburger to Erikson), citizenship (from German to American) and profession (from artist and teacher to psychoanalyst). He was greatly influenced by the work of Freud, having met psychoanalyst Anna Freud in Vienna, and developed Sigmund Freud's psychosexual theory into a psychosocial theory, which recognised the lifelong nature of emotional, moral and personality development. Erikson's first book (1950) became a classic in the field of psychosocial study. He identified the importance of a loving and emotionally stable home life, and the influence that culture and society had on a child's development. He also identified how conflict resolutions can be supported by carers. Despite the interest in Erikson's ideas, psychosocial theories are less popular today than behaviourist theories (for example, Skinner, 1953; Bandura, 1977; and see Chapter 7).

Burrhus Skinner (1904–90) developed a behaviourist theory of development, from the thinking of John Locke (1632–1704), and John Watson (1878–1958). Behaviourist theories work from the premise that the child is a tabula rasa or blank sheet, which social interaction writes upon or develops, in other words children develop through imitation, reinforcement and punishment. Skinner's theory of operant conditioning (1953) was developed after studying rats. Operant conditioning identifies that reward results in learned behaviour and provides an alternative to Pavlov's classical conditioning (1927), where a stimulus-response results in automatic behaviour. Skinner's theory has been successfully applied to human behaviour and forms the basis of many behaviour management theories in families and education, initially through the use of reward and punishment and more recently through positive reinforcement methods. The behaviourist theories have continued to be developed through the work of Bandura (1977).

Reflective Tasks

Reward or punishment

Level 1

Identify an example from your own experience which involved either reward or punishment.

- How did the experience affect your subsequent behaviour?
- Do you feel reward is more effective than punishment? Identify the reasoning behind your decision.

Level 2

Identify an example in your own practice where you use reward or punishment with children to influence behaviour.

- How successful is the strategy of using these?
- Do you use reward more than punishment? Identify why.

Level 3

Identify an example of both classical (Pavlov, 1927) and operant (Skinner, 1953) conditioning from your own experience or practice in your setting. Why do you think that operant conditioning is easier to identify in practice than classical conditioning?

John Bowlby (1907–90) studied medicine before moving into developmental psychology through psychiatry and psychoanalysis. While working voluntarily at a school for children with psychological problems, he became intrigued by the behaviour of two   children who showed signs of emotional problems; one, a teenager, being rather insular and remote, without a stable mother figure, and the other being an anxious, younger child who followed Bowlby around. As a result of these experiences, Bowlby began to consider the effects of early experiences on subsequent development and became convinced of the importance of the parental relationship in early life. Between 1958 and 1960 he published three papers on the theory of **attachment** in babies and young children (Bowlby, 1958; 1960a; 1960b). He identified the early bonding that occurs in babies and which is similar to Lorenz' imprinting in chicks (1952). There have been a number of criticisms of Bowlby's research, mainly because it focused primarily on children with emotional problems and the effects of parental deprivation (see Chapter 6 for further detail). There is also concern that Bowlby's research has been misrepresented to encourage post-war mothers to stay at home, thus reducing male unemployment, indicating a possible early political spin of the type more associated with modern society and politics.

Further research into attachment theories has been carried out by Ainsworth and her colleagues (1978), who measured the strength of attachment in young children and identified four different types:

- secure attachment;
- avoidance attachment;
- resistant attachment;
- disorientated attachment.

More recently, the Families, Children and Child Care Study (FCCC, 2005), a longitudinal study of 1,200 children, has been misreported in the media as finding that children are better cared for at home after Dr Penelope Leach spoke to the Childminders' Association on 3 October 2005. Although Dr Leach clearly corrected the misrepresentation in a press release, it is plain that the debate on care in the home versus pre-school care is one that is continually pertinent and challenges objectivity.

Reflective Tasks

Care at home

Level 1

Decide whether you feel that pre-school children are best cared for at home.

- How do you think your feelings are influenced by your own childhood experiences?
- How do you feel children benefit from pre-school care?

Level 2

- Are there aspects of a child's early development which can be more effectively supported at home rather than in a formal setting?
- Why do you think this?
- Can you support your views with evidence from your own experiences and practice?
- Do you think you are able to be objective in this debate?

Level 3

Identify those aspects of development which are best supported at home and those best supported in your setting. Identify the evidence from your own practice which has influenced your decisions.

- Could the evidence also support alternative viewpoints?
- What do the reflections mean for your own setting?

Abraham Maslow (1908–70) was born in Brooklyn, New York in 1908, the first of seven children born to uneducated Jewish immigrants from Russia. He studied law, but did not excel in his studies until he moved into the study of psychology at the University of Winsconsin. Here he worked with the animal psychologist Harry Harlow, who was researching attachment behaviour in rhesus monkeys, and later with Edward Thorndike (who was also a psychologist working in the area of animal behaviour), where he became interested in human sexuality. His work with monkeys and humans led him to consider social, physiological and emotional needs and he identified a hierarchy of basic needs which links the three areas (Maslow, 1968). In his hierarchy, each level needs to be fully met in order for development at the next level to take place (see Figure 1.1; Chapters 7, 3 and 6 for further consideration). Maslow believed that physiological needs are at the base of the hierarchy and if these physiological needs are not met, then children will not be able to move up the hierarchy and concern themselves with safety needs. Safety needs lead to emotional needs and then to esteem needs. Each level has to be met in order to achieve self-actualisation, the pinnacle of the hierarchy. If a need is fully met, then the motivation to achieve the need is removed, but if it is not fully met there is a desire for the need to be fulfilled. Significant problems in one area of development during childhood can result in lack of full development (Maslow, 1968). In this way Maslow extended the homeostatic principle to development: that is, the tendency for the internal environment of the body to remain constant and balanced despite external conditions. However, some needs are not felt to involve balance in the same way, so that as you move up the hierarchy you may become driven to succeed, not because of a lack of success but because you have experienced success and continue to desire it. Maslow studied a few people who were highly successful and determined that full self-actualisation involves the following (Boeree, 1998):

- truth;
- goodness;
- beauty;
- unity;
- aliveness;
- uniqueness;
- perfection and necessity;
- completion;

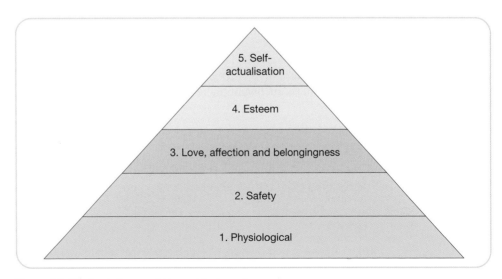

Figure 1.1 Maslow's theory of hierarchical needs.
Source: Maslow, 1968. Reprinted with permission of John Wiley & Sons, Inc.

- justice and order;
- simplicity;
- richness;
- effortlessness;
- playfulness;
- self-sufficiency;
- meaningfulness.

The importance of Maslow's ideas are in the link between the social, physiological and emotional areas of development and their combined importance on educational achievement, through self-actualisation.

Bridget Plowden (1910–2000) was the daughter of an admiral who married the British peer Lord Plowden. After years of voluntary work, she became a national figure in the UK after being asked in 1963 by the then education minister R.A. Butler to chair the Central Advisory Council on Education, whose report, often referred to as the Plowden Report, advocated a child-centred approach, whereby 'initial curiosity, often stimulated by the environment the teacher provides, leads to questions and to a consideration of what questions it is sensible to ask and how to find the answers' (DES, 1967: 242). The report had enormous influence on education in the 1960s and 1970s leading to a more child-centred approach to education which has subsequently influenced early education not only nationally (DfES, 2007) but also internationally. Through the report, Plowden identified her belief in:

- play;
- discovery learning;
- parental partnership in early education;
- the idea of 'learning readiness'.

These ideas were incorporated into early years education, although went out of fashion during the 1990s. For example, discovery learning became synonymous with children playing without purpose or learning objectives or support. In this view of discovery learning, children were thought to have no preconceived or existing conceptual ideas and they learned through unstructured, exploratory approaches. In the 1990s after the introduction of the national curriculum (DfEE, 1999a) and strategies for learning (DfEE, 1998; 1999b) there was a more structured approach to learning. We now realise that teaching and learning involves building on existing ideas, but also motivating young people. As W.B. Yeats once said: 'Education is not the filling of a pail, but the lighting of a fire'. In current early years settings, discovery is encouraged (DfES, 2007) and advocated through emphasis on creativity (see for example, DfES, 2003a; Wilson, 2005) and play (Lindon, 2001; Moyles, 2005). While learning in older children is often hampered through the lack of real discovery, some contexts are beginning to reintroduce more discovery play.

Tools for Learning

Selecting and using literature

Level 1

Find a current book which advocates play for effective development. Compare the ideas with those of the theorists and reformers who have advocated play (Froebel, Steiner, Vygotsky or Plowden).

Level 2

Read the part of the Plowden Report (DES, 1967) which describes discovery play and compare with Moyles' (2005) ideas.

Level 3

Read what Froebel (1826) and Plowden (DES, 1967) have to say about play and compare with the views of two modern writers.

Jerome Bruner (1915–) is an American who has played a major part in developing thinking in cognitive psychology. He identifies three modes of representation, or cognitive actions, which enable the mind to make meaning. The first is 'enactive representation', whereby cognition is expressed through physical actions; the second is 'iconic representation', whereby objects and events experienced through the senses are represented by mental images; and the third is 'symbolic representation', whereby thought is expressed through symbols, such as language. Bruner believed that cognitive development involves the ability to categorise the different representations and so build more complex mental images. During the 1970s, Bruner began to explore the role of language in cognition and the importance of cultural and language interaction on development, recognising the role of adults in scaffolding learning through skilled interaction. While this idea is not new (see, for example, Vygotsky earlier on in this chapter), Bruner's influence on early education in the latter part of the twentieth century is clear. His theory of constructivism (see Chapter 4) identifies that children develop cognitively through experience and interaction, actively constructing meaning as a result, and supported discovery learning as advocated by the Plowden Report (DES, 1967).

Urie Bronfenbrenner (1917–2005) was born in Russia in 1917 and went to live in the USA at the age of 6. He graduated in developmental psychology and continued his research in the area, putting forward theories and providing advice on the implications and applications of his theories. His ecological systems theory (Bronfenbrenner, 1995; Bronfenbrenner and Evans, 2000) views the child as developing within a complex social system, affected by relationships and the surrounding environments (see Figure 7.2). These environments extend beyond home, school and the local community, as follows:

- *Microsystem.* This is the closest system to the individual child and involves the child's immediate surroundings; their immediate family, their immediate carers and the community in which they live and play. The microsystem influences the child's behaviour, although not their innate characteristics (physical attributes, personality, abilities). Within this system, children who display positive characteristics are likely to have these positively reinforced. Adults who have positive relationships within this environment will also positively reinforce behaviours in children.

- *Mesosystem.* This system is once removed from the individual child and involves interactions between the child's microsystem: home, school, childcare, family, which affect the child's social and psychological development. For example, parental involvement in childcare and education affects long-term cognitive development and parents who interact with other parents in childcare or mother and toddler groups are likely to develop their parenting skills.

- *Exosystem.* This system is removed from the child, in that they are not directly involved with the interactions in the system and it does not directly influence children socially or psychologically. It involves both informal support for the child, such as the extended family (grandparents, aunts, uncles), friends, neighbours, workplace, church and community ties as well as more formal support, such as community and welfare services. Research has shown that families with few relationships in the exosystem are likely to have increased conflict and child abuse (Emery and Laumann-Billings, 1998).

- *Macrosystem.* This is the system furthest removed from the individual child and involves the cultural values, laws, customs and resources which affect the support children receive in the microsystem. For example, in societies where there is high-quality childcare and benefits for working parents, the children benefit in their everyday lives.

Loris Magaluzzi (1920–94) helped to found a system of pre-school education in Reggio Emilia, a small wealthy city in the Emilia Romagna region of northern Italy. The context for the Reggio Emilia system of pre-school education was that after the Second World War working parents in Italy wanted new schools for their children which would develop the thinking and social skills necessary for a new democratic society. In 1963, Reggio Emilia opened its first school and through the work of Magaluzzi disseminated its philosophy both nationally and internationally (see Picture 1.6). Magaluzzi believed that creativity is a characteristic way of thinking and responding to the world and wanted to change the culture of childhood, through debate on the rights and potentials of young children in our changing society. Fundamental to this debate is the Reggio Emilia image of the child, who is competent, active and critical, is able to develop relationships, construct meanings and decode symbols and codes (Rinaldi, 2006). The Reggio Emilia philosophy is based on partnership enquiry involving all concerned with the development of the young child and leading to effective home–school partnerships and relationship (Thornton and Brunton, 2005). As well as home–school liaison and the democratic rights of children, the principles of the Reggio Emilia early childhood approach include (Edwards *et al.*, 1993):

- the environment as a teacher;
- children's multiple symbolic languages;
- the teacher as a researcher;
- long-term projects.

Albert Bandura (1925–) is a Canadian psychologist who became very interested in behaviour theories and studied aggression in adolescence. In applying the behaviourist theory to his work on aggression, Bandura felt that the idea that it is the environment that causes behaviour was too simplistic and he suggested that behaviour in turn can cause the

Picture 1.6 Reggio Emilia
Source: Andre Jenny/Alamy Images

environment. This is known as reciprocal determinism. In his social learning theory (Bandura, 1986), personality results from an interaction between the environment, behaviour and psychological processes, and as such Bandura moved away from the strict behaviourist theories as described above (see Skinner) and recognised the role of cognition in behaviour. Through his observation of children and his famous research using the bobo doll, Bandura identified the role of imitation, modelling and self-regulation on behaviour (Bandura, 1977). In this study an inflatable doll, shown in a video, was seen by children to be hit aggressively; then, when allowed to play with the doll, the children imitated the aggressive behaviour they had witnessed, without rewards or punishments to reinforce behaviour. Bandura undertook a variety of different studies using the Bobo doll and established that the modelling process required the learner to:

- be attentive;
- retain the image: that is, to remember the behaviour;
- reproduce the behaviour;
- be motivated and wish to imitate the behaviour. This motivation could be because the behaviour has been reinforced through punishment or reward in the past, or because there are future incentives expected, or because the behaviour has been seen to be reinforced with others.

Another aspect of Bandura's social learning theory is the idea of self-regulation, or control of our own behaviour. Self-regulation occurs in three stages: self-observation, self-judgement and self-response (treating yourself if you succeed or punishing yourself if you do not). In this way, Bandura began to move into emotional aspects of learning, identifying certain unhealthy personality traits which can lead to self-punishment, aggression, depression and escapism. Bandura's ideas have led to the current belief in the importance of adults as good role models for behaviour and the concerns that famous role models should demonstrate exemplary behaviours. Many current educational practices apply both imitative and self-regulatory practices. For example, teachers will read books during quiet reading time, to encourage children to read. Some early years practices, such as Reggio Emilia and High/Scope are based on aspects of self-regulation, with children making decisions for themselves and evaluating the success of their work.

Lawrence Kohlberg (1927–87) was an American who started out as a developmental psychologist, studying under Piaget and then moving into the study of moral education, developing a cognitive theory of moral development. Like Piaget he used stories to investigate the way children develop moral reasoning. Kohlberg's theory of moral development (1976) identified three levels and six stages of moral reasoning (see Chapter 6):

- Level 1: Pre-conventional morality;
- Level 2: Conventional morality;
- Level 3: Post-conventional morality.

Kohlberg believed that moral development could be facilitated through discussion, argumentation and social interaction, enabling movement through the stages, although many adults are thought never to reach Kohlberg's final stage. The development of personal, social and health education (PSHE) and citizenship in the school curriculum can be argued to be based on Kohlberg's ideas for moral development through social interaction.

David Weikart (1931–2003) was an American psychologist who, in 1962, developed a coordinated set of ideas and practices in early childhood education based on Piaget's theories of development. This became known as the High/Scope Cognitively Orientated Curriculum, which is a curriculum underpinned by the belief that children are active learners who learn best from activities planned and executed by themselves (Hohmann and Weikart, 2002). The curriculum was designed for 3- and 4-year-old children in

Michigan, USA, to combat the negative effects of poverty. Weikart became head of the High/Scope Educational Foundation in the 1960s and 1970s. In the High/Scope curriculum children and practitioners work together to support child autonomy and independence, with children planning their activities before carrying them out and then reviewing them afterwards, in a child-centred reflective cycle of plan–do–review. The central principles of the High/Scope pre-school curriculum include the following (Hohmann and Weikart, 2002):

- children are active learners, creating their own meanings from their experiences;
- active learning is dependent on quality adult–child interactions;
- the learning environment needs to be well planned and well laid out to support development;
- daily routine is an essential element of active learning;
- assessment is a fundamental daily aspect of learning.

Many of these principles are not new and can be found in the theories of Froebel (active learning), Vygotsky (adult–child interaction), Steiner (daily routines), and reforms instigated by Plowden (active learning) and Reggio Emilia (learning environment). The difference is the complete package of ideas and the way in which they are put into practice.

The High/Scope Educational Foundation has also carried out considerable research into the effects of the programme on short- and long-term development, which seems to indicate that spending on early years is an investment. Through a longitudinal study High/Scope has shown that high-quality, cognitively-oriented nursery education, with adult-guided play and good home–school liaison, enables children to achieve better than their peers through school and function better in society as adults (Schwienhart *et al.*, 1993).

Reflective Tasks

Theorist, reformer, implementer or consolidator

Level 1

Consider the difference between a theorist, reformer, implementer or consolidator.

Level 2

Write a definition for a theorist, reformer, implementer and consolidator.

Level 3

Using your knowledge of the individuals, fill in Table 1.2:

1. by deciding who is a theorist/ philosopher, reformer, implementer or consolidator;
2. by considering whether they were concerned about the educational (intellectual), social, health (physical) or emotional welfare of the child.

See the Glossary for definitions.

Table 1.2 Theorist, reformer, implementer or consolidator? What was the contribution of these individuals to early childhood understanding and practice?

Name	Theorist/ Reformer/ Implementer/ Consolidator	Educational (intellectual)	Social	Health (physical)	Emotional

New and emerging theories

There are a number of new and emerging ideas which are influencing care and provision in the early years. This chapter will continue by looking at a few of these and then conclude with some recent research evidence which is informing current early years practitioners.

In recent years there has been a great deal written about creativity and it is emphasised in the early years curriculum (DfES, 2007) and many government initiatives (DfES, 2003a; QCA, 2003). One problem with the idea of creativity is that there is no one definition; different individuals or groups assign different meanings to it and it can often mean different things in different contexts (for example, in the arts, sciences, technologies).

Creativity is no longer considered to be exclusively the preserve of the arts (Prentice, 2000), but to incorporate aspects of problem-solving (de Bono, 1992), making connections (Duffy, 1998) and to be multifaceted (Beetlestone, 1998). Its inclusion in education (DfES, 2003a; QCA, 2003) is based on the belief that it is a potential in all children, which can be developed with support and encouragement (Craft, 2002; Wilson, 2005).

However, creative children require creative practitioners. These practitioners are ones who make connections between aspects of learning across the curriculum (DfES, 2003a), providing original and creative experiences in order to develop children in cross-curricular ways. They are knowledgeable, competent and independent, being able to make learning decisions, extending or adapting ideas, producing novel ideas for achieving objectives and as a result the children's learning will be enhanced. They would also balance the needs of the curriculum with those of the individual's creative development, balancing creativity and knowledge (Boden, 2001).

Research

The development of a model of creativity

Ashley Compton, Bishop Grosseteste University College Lincoln

As a former primary school teacher, now involved in initial teacher education, and as a parent of young children, I am very interested in the role of creativity in education. Creativity is often mentioned by government, by teachers, by parents and in the media. It seems to be something that we should promote but what exactly is it and how would we do that? To find some answers to these questions I began to read books, articles and government documents and I found that there were many different definitions for creativity. The definitions included 'big C' Creativity, representing major innovations in society, but also 'little c' creativity that involves the choices made by ordinary people. Some aspects, such as originality and problem-solving, are common to many definitions but none is universal. Although the government-commissioned report, All our Futures (1999), devised a formal definition of creativity: 'imaginative activity fashioned so as to produce outcomes that are both original and of value' (NACCCE, 1999: 30), some other government initiatives (QCA, 2003; Anderson *et al.*, 2005) have emphasised the importance of people establishing their own understanding of creativity. I decided that I needed to follow this advice and so examined a range of definitions for creativity from researchers, government agencies and practising teachers, considering the commonalities and differences, with the view of constructing a working definition for my future research. As well as looking at general definitions of creativity, I explored how the term has been used in curriculum documents. This led to me writing an article for a journal entitled, 'What does creativity mean in English education?' (Compton, 2007).

The preliminary reading I did led me to develop ideas of my own (theory building). I started with the definition that I felt best fitted my view of creativity in education, Beetlestone's three tiers of creativity (1998). This represents a continuum from self-expression in Tier 1 to big C creativity in Tier 3, incorporating many aspects of creativity that had been present in other people's definitions (Beetlestone, 1998: 95):

- *Tier 1* – everyone has the right and ability to express their thoughts and feelings, to create.
- *Tier 2* – making unusual connections, developing own style.
- *Tier 3* – making something new to society and, because of the technical expertise and vision involved, reaching a level of genius.

I felt that this definition would be useful within primary education since Tiers 1 and 2 could apply to both children and teachers, although Tier 3 would probably be out of reach of both. However, I felt that there were some important elements missing in this definition so I decided to augment Beetlestone's tiers (1998) with several elements drawn from other conceptualisations of creativity. Due to the influence of National Curriculum language I thought of them as levels of creativity rather than tiers. Each level builds on previous levels, and the pyramid is accessible to all, regardless of age. Perhaps also due to my background in teaching I felt that it was important that there was clear progression through the levels, without too much of a gap between them. There seemed to be too big a jump between the making of unusual connections at Tier 2 and the genius of Tier 3, so I subdivided Tier 3 to provide an entry level that acknowledged valuable novelty on a smaller scale. Thus, Level 3 allows children or adults to make something that is new to themselves or their peer group, rather than requiring that it be new to the whole world. The latter was reserved for Level 4.

Both Figures 1.2 and 1.3 attempt to display the continuum for an individual's creative development. The arrows in Figure 1.2 demonstrate the progression through the levels, but organising it in reading order resulted in the highest level of creativity being at the bottom of the page and implied that each stage supplanted the previous one. After some reflection I decided that Figure 1.3 was more effective than Figure 1.2 at demonstrating that the lower levels of creativity provide the foundation for the higher layers. The higher levels of creativity depend on and build upon the lower levels rather than replacing them. Highly creative people continue to question and notice while working at the top level, creating new and valuable things for society. A person may be at different stages of the creativity pyramid in different parts of life simultaneously. For example, one person might be winning the Nobel Prize for peace (Level 4); writing novels (Level 3); solving problems in computing (Level 2); and being interested in farming (Level 1). Everybody would have their own profile but this is not fixed. You might be very creative one day but then not at all the next. However, the premise of my pyramid is that all people and all ages can be creative at some level and in some part of their life. Most of us are unlikely to achieve Level 4 but we can certainly aspire to Level 3.

In addition to reading and reflection, I gathered views about creativity from other practitioners in order to design my creativity pyramid. I worked with a group of teachers undertaking a Master's degree in education and got them to record their definitions of creativity before and after an input. I analysed their responses to look at the specific words and categories of ideas they used. I then presented the emergent theory, my creativity pyramid, at a conference (Compton, 2006), which resulted in useful feedback allowing me to refine the pyramid further.

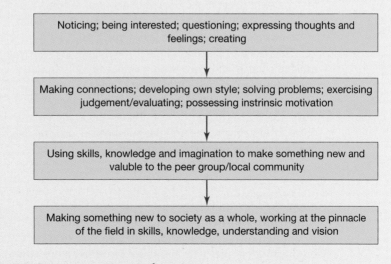

Figure 1.2 Compton's continuum of creativity
Source: Based on Beetlestone, 1998 (with considerable indebtedness)

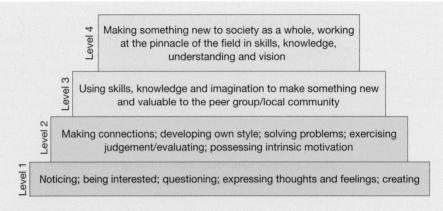

Figure 1.3 Compton's creativity pyramid
Source: Based on Beetlestone, 1998 (with considerable indebtedness)

Having designed the creativity pyramid I am now testing how it works (practitioner research). I started off by being interested in the cascade of creativity from tutors in higher education to our students, from our students as trainee teachers to their pupils. However, this is far too large a topic and I needed to narrow and focus. I meet regularly with a research support group where we talk through our ideas and ask challenging questions to help each other clarify our thoughts. Through these discussions with colleagues I came to realise that I was particularly interested in the role of creativity in assessment.

This led to several questions. Do we encourage creativity in assessment tasks and do we reward it when marking? Do students feel that they are being creative when doing assignments and do they feel this is recognised? Is creativity present at all grades or is it just at the top grades (A*, A or B) that students include it? Although these questions are aimed at university students, similar questions could be asked about planning for and assessing young children. Do the activities we design encourage creativity? Are they just at Level 1 of the pyramid or are we encouraging Levels 2 and 3? Do we encourage creativity just in the arts or across the whole curriculum?

In designing my research I have had to consider the methodology that is most appropriate for my question. I feel that qualitative methods are relevant because I am trying to understand a social phenomenon from several viewpoints. I wanted to use the creativity pyramid as a research tool but needed to test it. I decided to do this in three ways for triangulation. I used the creativity pyramid myself to look for evidence of creativity within documents (assignment briefs). I have also used it with a colleague in an interview to discuss whether the different levels of creativity are present in our assignments. Then I have used it with a group of students in an online forum to discuss whether they felt the different levels of creativity related to them. The initial findings indicate that the creativity pyramid is a useful tool that can be used in various ways and is understood by both tutors and students. I am now ready to write a proposal for my major research project that will use the creativity pyramid as a tool to examine the role of creativity within the assessment of initial teacher training students.

Learning theories are very popular and form the basis of much discussion in education, with practitioners attempting to adapt experiences for different sorts of learners. These theories often divide learners into three groups, those who favour visual methods, those favouring auditory methods and those favouring **kinaesthetic** methods (Dryden and Vos, 1999), although some (Johnston, 1996) identify four ways in which learners process information (see Chapter 4) and others multiple abilities or intelligences (Gardner, 1983). There does not appear to be any consensus on what learning theory is and a great concern that it is being advocated without firm research evidence of its worth (Coffield *et al.*, 2004). VAK theories (for visual, auditory, kinaesthetic) identify that although much early years provision is active, educational settings tend increasingly to favour the visual and auditory learners as children start school and move up the key stages. However, there is little common understanding of what is meant by kinaesthetic learning and how it differs in younger and older learners. Although popular, these theories do not appear to have a theoretical basis in research (Revell, 2005), with most research being practitioner-based and specific, with no conclusive evidence. Indeed, Gardner's theory of multiple intelligences (1983) has been adapted and used in many educational settings, although it was not intended to be used in this way (Revell, 2005). There is considerable popular support for these theories and evidence from practice to support them, but until the theories have a thorough research base and lead to real understanding of learning theories in practice we need to take great care in using and adapting them.

There are a number of cognitive theories which are having an impact in practice. Cognitive acceleration is another very popular theory but, like learning theories, it is not convincingly evidence-based and there is no common agreement about what it is. In some views it involves the process of supporting cognition by removing artificial obstacles to the development of gifted and talented children. For others, it involves advancing cognition through practices, such as meditation and Brain Gym (Dennison and Dennison, 1994). Brain Gym advocates drinking plenty of water and undertaking three minutes of exercise before mental activities to support left/right brain coordination and cognitive development. Many practitioners have incorporated aspects of Brain Gym into their practice with young children and some have found it successful, although others have found it of limited value. The link between drinking water and brain development is well known, as is the link between physical exercise and thinking. It may be that any activity which focuses children's energy and encourages them to think will support cognition and much more persuasive evidence is needed before we change practice significantly. Constructivist theories have developed from Piaget's and Vygotsky's cognitive theories and involve the child in constructing their own meaning, including alternative conceptions, from experiences and learning. These are acknowledged as occurring in many areas of learning (Littledyke and Huxford, 1998) and there is a huge body of research evidence in some areas (Johnston, 2005). Constructivist theories view learning as a continuous process, whereby children construct links with their prior knowledge generating new ideas, checking and restructuring old ideas or hypotheses, and is therefore very active. Such theories have been increasingly influencing changes in thinking in recent years, although changes in practice have been much less evident, possibly because of the difficulty in implementing real and sustained changes in practice. These ideas will be discussed more fully in Chapter 4.

Early years childcare settings are developing in a multidisciplinary way, with care focusing on the social development and health of children as well as education, with the introduction of SureStart, early excellence centres, extended school and wrap-around care. Settings are providing breakfast, after school-care, educational (nurseries, speech therapy) and social services (social workers, behaviour therapists), and health facilities (doctors, dentists, physiotherapy) on one site. These initiatives, together with the improved training for practitioners, have impacted on the early years sector. This focus on holistic care and development is incorporated into the government policy Every Child Matters (DfES, 2003b) and identifies five outcomes for every child:

- to be healthy;
- to stay safe;

- to enjoy and achieve;
- to make a positive contribution;
- to achieve economic well-being.

The principles embedded in the Children Act 2004 and Birth to Three Matters are generally welcomed, but hide a tension that exists between government philosophy and the practicalities of implementation, and there is no real evidence that the initiatives are having a positive, real or long-term, sustainable impact or that practitioners understand how to implement them. There is also a tension between families and early years providers, as parents are concerned that linking the different services may lead to breaches in confidentiality (NCB, 2005; Ward, 2005).

Tools for Learning

Selecting and using literature

Find some books on early years reformers and theorists and add names to Table 1.2.

Level 1

Using the information from the books, decide which of these reformers and theorists have influenced,

- early years social care;
- early years education;
- early years health care.

Level 2

Choose one reformer or theorist you have added to Table 1.2 and find out about them from three different books. Compare the information in the books and see if they are saying the same things about their beliefs.

Level 3

Choose one reformer or theorist you have added to Table 1.2 and find out about their lives from at least three different sources. You can use books, journals and web-based sources. Compare the sources of information and see if they are saying the same things about their beliefs.

Research

Childcare provision

The importance of play has been a recurring theme in early childhood theories; it has been discussed throughout this chapter and its importance will continue to be emphasised throughout this book. Play is strongly advocated in the Early Years Foundation Stage as 'a key way in which young children learn with enjoyment and challenge' (QCA, 2000: 25). During the 1990s early years policy and practice changed and play was de-emphasised (Johnston, 2002). Practice in the early years was influenced by those with little or no knowledge of how young children learn and who thought play 'a frivolous and low status activity' (Anning, 1994: 67), resulting in play being 'limited in frequency, duration and quality' (Bennett *et al.*, 1997). Considerable research underpins the belief that play advances learning (Bennett *et al.*, 1997; Moyles, *et al*, 2002; BERA, 2003) and this research is continuing to impact on early years settings.

Recent research has also focused on the type of care that has the most effect on development. Some of this research has been longitudinal, studying the long-term effects of childcare provision on development. For example:

- the EPPE (Effective Provision of Pre-school Education) project, a five-year study of the attainment and development of children aged between 3 and 7;
- the Families, Children and Child Care Study, a longitudinal study of 1,200 children, their families and their childcare (FCCC, 2005);
- the BTSS (Birth to Three Study), a longitudinal study of the PEEP (Peers Early Education Partnership) project, designed to benefit disadvantaged children in Oxford;
- research into the effects of the High/Scope pre-school programme (Schwienhart *et al.*, 1993), a longitudinal study of children from pre-school and into adulthood.

Research into childcare provision is considered difficult because early years practice is very complex, comprising a wide variety of practices underpinned by philosophies from a number of different contexts (Moyles, *et al.*, 2002). Research does appear to indicate that pre-school provision benefits children (Schwienhart *et al.*, 1993) and that formal settings that achieve the best outcome tend to view social and cognitive development as complementary (Siraj-Blatchford *et al.*, 2002; EPPE, 2002; 2003), although care must be exercised when drawing on research from other disciplines (BERA, 2003). Early intervention advantages children who are at risk of low educational achievement (Evangelou *et al.*, 2005) and the quality and duration of childcare affects the outcomes for young children (EPPE, 2003). Good outcomes are also linked to adult–child interactions that challenge children and extend thinking through open-ended questioning (Siraj-Blatchford *et al.*, 2002). Quality provision also appears to have a positive effect on parenting skills (Hohmann and Weikart, 2002; Evangelou *et al.*, 2005) and outcomes in later life (Evangelou *et al.*, 2005).

Tools for Learning

Selecting and using literature

Find some current research into one of the areas of early childhood:

- early years social care;
- early years education;
- early years health care.

Level 1

- What are the main findings of the research?
- How does the research impact on early years provision?

Level 2

- What do you feel about these findings?
- How will this research change your beliefs and practice?

Level 3

- How does this research impact on your setting?
- What changes will you make in your provision as a result of this research? Why?

Summary

→ Some of the earliest pioneers are from the eighteenth and nineteenth centuries. They include Jean Jacques Rousseau (1712–78), Johann Heinrich Pestalozzi (1746–1827), Jean Frederic Oberlin (1740–1826), Friedrich Froebel (1782–1852).

→ A common theme of these pioneers, particularly Rousseau, Pestalozzi and Froebel, stressed the individuality of the child and the importance of experiential learning. Oberlin believed in the importance of speaking and listening within a varied and balanced curriculum, noting the importance of the adult as role model. All influenced practice in early years education.

→ John Dewey (1859–1952) was particularly influential in educational philosophy. He believed in child-centred education and opposed authoritarian methods of education, feeling that children should make decisions and choices to prepare for a democratic life.

→ Philosophers whose beliefs have influenced education to such an extent that their names are used as a label to indicate that their philosophy permeates the school's approach include Maria Montessori (1870–1952) and Rudolph Steiner (1861–1925). Two of the principles of the Montessori method are that early childhood should be child-centred but not child-led, and that children determine their own rate of progression. Steiner's philosophy advocates the importance of spiritual growth and holistic education.

→ Other key influences in education are Loris Magaluzzi (1920–94) whose pre-schools in Reggio Emilia have international influence with the 'Reggio Emilia' philosophy; David Weikart (1931–2003) who is associated with the High/Scope approach; and Bridget Plowden (1910–2000) whose report had enormous influence on education in the 1960s and 1970s leading to a more child-centred approach to education which subsequently influenced early education not only nationally but also internationally. In the early 1990s many of Plowden's ideas went out of fashion.

→ Rachel McMillan (1859–1917) and her sister Margaret (1860–1931) were both committed to social welfare and reform of provision for young children. Margaret McMillan opened nursery schools with children's health and care as priorities. They opened the first 'open-air' nursery.

→ Influential developmental psychologists include John Bowlby (1907–90) with his theory on attachment; Urie Bronfenbrenner (1917–2005) whose ecological systems theory views the child as developing within a complex social system, affected by relationships and the surrounding environments; and Lawrence Kohlberg (1927–1987) who developed a theory of moral development.

→ Influential cognitive psychologists include Jean Piaget (1896–1980) who, through studies of his own children, identified four stages of cognitive development; Vygotsky (1896–1934) who identified the zone of proximal development (ZPD); and Jerome Bruner (1915–) with his theory of constructivism. All three of these psychologists have been highly influential in developing our understanding of how children learn.

→ Behaviourist theories have been developed by Burrhus Skinner (1904–90) with his theory of operant conditioning and Albert Bandura (1925–) with his social learning theory.

→ Other psychological theorists include: Freud (1856–1939) and his theories on the development of personality and psychosexual development; Erik Erikson (1902–94) and his psychosocial study on identity; and Abraham Maslow (1908–70) with his hierarchy of basic needs.

→ There are differences between a philosopher, reformer, implementer or consolidator.

→ The pioneers discussed were concerned with one or more of these aspects of development: educational (intellectual), social, health (physical) and emotional welfare of the child.

→ New and emerging theories and developments include issues around creative development; learning theories and questionable adaptations of Gardner's multiple intelligences; brain development; development of multidisciplinary settings, incorporating social care, health and education; and tensions between government policy and practice.

Key Questions

- Who are the influential early pioneers and reformers that have historically influenced practice and provision in the early years?
- What are the key events in their lives that have influenced them and helped to formulate their beliefs?
- What are the main features of each of the theories/beliefs held by the early pioneers and reformers?
- How have these beliefs influenced current practice and policy in early childhood education and care?
- Who and what are the recent, new and emerging theorists and theories emphasising the current issues in early childhood studies, both nationally and internationally?

References

Ainsworth, M., Blehar, M., Waters, E. and Wall, S. (1978) *Patterns of Attachment*. Hillsdale, NJ: Erlbaum

Anderson, F., Cockett, M. and McGuigan, P. (2005) *Journey – Handbook of Training Materials for Advanced Skills Teachers*. Leeds: CAPE UK. Available from http://www. creative-partnerships.com/resources/57650 (accessed 8.4.05)

Anning, A. (1994) Play and Legislated Curriculum. Back to Basics: An alternative view, in Moyles, J. (ed.) *The Excellence of Play*. Buckingham: Open University Press

Bandura, A. (1977) *Social Learning Theory*. Englewood Cliffs, NJ: Prentice-Hall

Bandura, A. (1986) *Social Foundations of Thought and Action: A social cognitive theory* Englewood Cliffs, NJ: Prentice-Hall

Barnard, H.C. (1961) *A History of English Education from 1760.* London: University of London

Beetlestone, F. (1998) *Creative Children, Imaginative Teaching.* Buckingham: Open University Press

Bennett, N., Wood, L. and Rodgers, S. (1997) *Teaching Through Play: Teachers' Thinking and Classroom Practice.* Buckingham: Open University Press

BERA Early Years Special Interest Group (2003) *Early Years Research: Pedagogy, Curriculum and Adult Roles, Training and Professionalism.* Southwell: BERA

Berk, L.E. (2003) *Child Development,* 6th edn. Boston: Allyn & Bacon

Boden, M.A. (2001) Creativity and Knowledge in Craft, in Jeffrey, B. and Leibling, M. (eds) *Creativity in Education.* London: Continuum

Boeree, C.G. (1998) 'Personality Theories. Abraham Maslow'. Available from www.ship.edu/~cgboeree/maslow.html

Bowlby, J. (1958) 'The Nature of a Child's Tie to His Mother', *International Journal of Psychoanalysis,* 39: 350–73

Bowlby, J. (1960a) 'Separation Anxiety', *International Journal of Child Psychoanalysis,* 4: 89–113

Bowlby, J. (1960b) 'Grief and Mourning in Infancy and Early Childhood', *The Psychoanalytic Study of the Child,* 15: 9–52

Bronfenbrenner, U. (1995) 'The Bioecological Model from a Life Course Perspective: Reflections of a participant observer', in Moen, P., Elder Jnr, G.H. and Lischer, K. (eds) *Examining Lives in Context.* Washington, DC: American Psychological Association, pp. 599–618

Bronfenbrenner, U. and Evans, G.W. (2000) 'Developmental Science in the 21st Century: Emerging theoretical models, research designs and empirical findings', *Social Development,* 9: 115–25

Case, R. and Okamoto, Y. (1996) (eds) 'The Role of Central Conceptual Structures in the Development of Children's thought', *Monographs of the Society of Research in Child Development,* 61(2), serial no. 246. Chicago: University of Chicago.

Coffield, F., Moseley, D., Hall, E. and Ecclestone, K. (2004) *Should We Be Using Learning Styles? What research has to say to practice.* London: Learning and Skills Development Agency

Compton, A. (2006) The Many faces of Creativity in English Education. Paper presented at BESA Conference, July 2006

Compton, A. (2007) 'What does creativity mean in Engish Education', *Education 3–13,* **35,** 2, 109–16

Craft, A. (2002) *Creativity and Early Years Education. A lifeworld foundation.* London: Continuum

De Bono, E. (1992) *Serious Creativity.* London: Harper Collins

Dennison, P. and Dennison, G. (1994) *Brain Gym.* Ventura, CA: The Educational Kinesiology Foundation

DES (1967) *Children and their Primary school. A report of the Central Advisory Council for Education (England) Vol. 1: Report.* London: HMSO

Dewey, J. (1916) *Democracy and Education: An introduction to the philosophy of education.* New York: Macmillan

DfEE (1998) *The National Literacy Strategy.* London: DFEE

DfEE (1999a) *The National Curriculum: Handbook for Teachers in England.* London: DfEE/QCA

DfEE (1999b) *The National Numeracy Strategy.* London: DFEE

DfES (2003a) *Excellence and Enjoyment. A strategy for primary schools.* London: DfES

DfES (2003b) *Every Child Matters.* London: DfES

DfES (2007) *The Early Years Foundation Stage; Setting the Standard for Learning, Development and Care for Children from Birth to Five.* London: DfES

Dryden, G. and Vos, J. (1999) *The Learning Revolution. To change the way the world learns.* Auckland New Zealand: The Learning Web

Duffy, B. (1998) *Supporting Creativity and Imagination in the Early Years.* Buckingham: Open University Press

Edwards, C., Gandini, L. and Forman, G. (eds) (1993) *The Hundred Languages of Children: The Reggio Emilia Approach to Early Childhood Education.* Norwood, NJ: Ablex

Elkind, D. (1989) *The Hurried Child: Growing up too fast.* London: Addison-Wesley

Emery, R.E. and Laumann-Billings, L. (1998) 'An Overview of the Nature, Causes and Consequences of Abusive Family Relationships: Toward differentiating maltreatment and violence', *American Psychologist*, 53: 121–35

EPPE (2002) 'Measuring the Impact of Pre-School on Children's Cognitive Progress over the Pre-School Period', *The EPPE (Effective Provision of Pre-school Education) Project Technical Paper 8a.* London: Institute of Education

EPPE (2003) 'Measuring the Impact of Pre-School on Children's Social/Behavioural Development over the Pre-School Period', *The EPPE (Effective Provision of Pre-school Education) Project Technical Paper 8b.* London: Institute of Education

Erikson, E.H. (1950) *Childhood and Society.* New York: Norton

Evangelou, M., Brooks, G., Smith, S. and Jennings, D. (2005) *Birth to School Study: A Longitudinal Evaluation of the Peers Early Education Partnership (PEEP) 1998–2005.* London: DfES

FCCC (2005) Families, Children and Child Care Study www.familieschildrenchildcare.org/fccc-home.html (accessed 11.11.05)

Freud, S. (1923) *The Ego and the Id.* London: Hogarth

Froebel, F. (1826) *On the Education of Man.* Keilhau, Leipzig: Wienbrach

Gardner, H. (1983) *Frames of Mind: The Theory of Multiple Intelligences.* London: Heinemann

Hohmann, M. and Weikart, D.P. (2002) *Educating Young Children*, 2nd edn. Ypsilanti, MI: High/Scope Press

Johnston, C. (1996) *Unlocking the Will to Learn.* Thousand Oaks CA: Corwin Press

Johnston, J. (2002) 'Teaching and Learning in the Early Years' in Johnston, J., Chater, M. and Bell, D. *Teaching the Primary Curriculum.* Buckingham: Open University Press

Johnston, J. (2005) *Early Explorations in Science*, 2nd edn. Buckingham: Open University Press

Kohlberg, L. (1976) 'Moral Stages and Moralization: The cognitive-developmental approach', in Lickona, T. (ed.) *Moral Development and Behaviour: Theory, Research and Social Issues.* New York: Holt, pp. 31–53

Kramer, R. (1976) *Maria Montessori. A biography.* London: Montessori International Publishing

Lindon, J. (2001) *Understanding Children's Play.* Cheltenham: Nelson Thornes

Littledyke, M. and Huxford, L. (1998) *Teaching the Primary Curriculum for Constructivist Learning.* London: David Fulton

Lorenz, K. (1952) *King Solomon's Ring.* New York: Crowell

Maslow, A.H. (1968) *Towards a Psychology of Being.* New York: Van Nostrand

McMillan, M. (1911) *The Child and the State.* Manchester: National Labour Press

McMillan, M. (1930) *The Nursery School.* London: Dent

Microsoft (1996a) 'Rousseau, Jean Jacques', *Microsoft® Encarta® 96*. © 1993–1995 Microsoft Corporation

Microsoft (1996b) 'Pestalozzi, Johann Heinrich (1746–1827)', *Microsoft® Encarta® 96*. 1993–1995 Microsoft Corporation

Montessori, M. (1912) *The Montessori Method.* London: Heinemann

Moyles, J.R. (ed.) (2005) *The Excellence of Play*, 2nd edn. Buckingham: Open University Press

Moyles, J., Adams, S., Musgrove, A. (2002) *Study of Pedagogical Effectiveness in Early Learning.* London: DfES

NACCCE (National Advisory Committee on Creativity and Cultural Education) (1999) 'All Our Futures'. Available from http://www.dcsf.gov.uk/naccce/index1.shtml (accessed 2.11.07)

NCB (National Children's Bureau) (2005) www.ncb.org.uk

Olaf, M. (2003) *The Joyful Child*, Arcata, CA: The Michael Olaf Company

Oldfield, L. (2001) *Free to Learn. Introducing Steiner Waldorf Early Childhood Education.* Stroud, Gloucestershire: Hawthorn Press

Pavlov, I.P. (1927) *Conditioned Reflexes.* Oxford: Oxford University Press

Piaget, J. (1929) *The Child's Conception of the World.* New York: Harcourt

Piaget, J. (1950) *The Psychology of Intelligence.* London: Routledge & Kegan Paul

Piaget, J. (1965) *The Moral Judgement of the Child.* New York: Free Press

Prentice, R. (2000) 'Creativity: A reaffirmation of its place in early childhood education', *The Curriculum Journal*, 11(2): 145–58

QCA (2003) *Creativity: Find it, Promote it!* London: QCA/DFEE. Available from http://www.ncaction.org.uk/creativity/index.htm (accessed 3.2.05)

Revell, P. (2005) 'Each to their own', *Education Guardian*, 21 May

Rinaldi, C. (2006) *In Dialogue with Reggio Emilia: listening, researching and learning.* London: Routledge

Roopnarine, J. and Johnson, R. (1987) *Approaches to Early Childhood Education.* Columbus, OH: Merrill

Rousseau, J.J. (1911) *Emile.* London: J.M. Dent

Schwienhart, L.J., Weikart, D.P. and Toderan, R. (1993) *High Quality Preschool Programs Found to Improve Adult Status.* Ypsilante, MI: High/Scope Foundation

Siraj-Blatchford, I., Sylva, K., Muttock, S., Gilden, R. and Bell, D. (2002) *Researching Effective Pedagogy in the Early Years.* London: DfES

Skinner, B.F. (1953) *Science and Human Behaviour.* London: Macmillan

Steiner, R. (1996) *The Education of the Child and Early Lectures on Education.* New York: Anthroposophic Press

Thornton, L. and Brunton, P. (2005) *Understanding the Reggio Approach.* London: David Fulton

Vygotsky, L. (1962) *Thought and Language.* Cambridge, MA: MIT Press

Vygotsky, L. and Cole, M. (eds) (1978) *Mind in Society, The Development of Higher Psychological Processes.* Cambridge, MA: Harvard University Press

Ward, H. (2005) 'Parents Reject Integrated Services', *Times Educational Supplement*, 7 October

Wilson, A. (2005) *Creativity in Primary Education.* London: Learning Matters

Chapter 2

Developing Your Own Philosophy

❛ I think, therefore I am ❜
Rene Descartes (1596–1650)

Introduction

This chapter will consider the nature of philosophy and will chart some of the most influential philosophers from ancient to modern times. We will explore the importance of a strong, well-founded philosophy underpinning the work of those in early childhood settings and the significance of the potential impact on children and their development. The chapter will lead you through the analysis and development of your own personal philosophy in the light of knowledge about key philosophers, the notion of integrated and shared philosophies within settings, and a consideration of the philosophies underpinning government initiatives.

Aims

→ To provide an overview of some of the most influential philosophers and philosophies which underpin practice and provision in the early years

→ To explore and analyse personal beliefs and consider what influences those beliefs

→ To support the development and articulation of a personal philosophy

→ To consider the notion of shared philosophies within integrated services

→ To consider the philosophies underpinning government initiatives

The nature of philosophy

Philosophy is concerned with the pursuit of wisdom and is a large and well-studied discipline in itself. Ancient and medieval philosophy was often concerned with deep thinking
and not with practical applications and it is no wonder that great, early scientists are
often known as philosophers, because often they did not practically investigate or experiment but instead thought deeply about issues. In ancient and medieval philosophy, these
deep issues included Aristotle's thinking on science, ethics, politics, and Socrates' thinking
on speculation and dispute, as well as Plato's ideas on society, education and justice. In
considering early childhood philosophies, Socrates' ideas about society are most relevant
and these are encapsulated in his book *Republic* (Plato, trans. Jowett, 1968). Plato argued
that society exists because individuals are not self-sufficient and rely on others to survive.
As a result, humans will group together into communities for the mutual support and
achievement of common goals and this is especially effective where the different members of society have different roles, responsibilities and functions, which together make a
coherent whole. Social classes within society were thought, by Plato, to be a result of this
need for society to comprise different individuals with different functions, led by
guardians (soldiers and rulers) responsible for the management of the society itself.
Guardians needed to be special members of society with an inclination towards philosophical thinking and they needed to be well educated. Since Plato had opened a school
in Athens, it is likely that this latter need was fulfilled by the education provided within
his school! Plato's philosophy on elementary education was that it was only for the elite,
who would become guardians of society. Education should also endeavour to achieve a
balance between physical, musical and intellectual development and therefore would not
be dissimilar to the key areas of development in the Early Years Foundation Stage (DfES,
2007). Plato also believed that strict control and censorship in education was essential as
fictional reading and dramatic pursuits would lead to self-deception and would dull children's judgements (a very different view from that held by Aristotle). Education for the
elite would also determine who was best equipped to be guardians of society and it was
the responsibility of society to design an educational system which would distinguish
between different children and to provide training appropriate to their abilities. This elementary education would involve the first 20 years of life, which is a very long early years!

Early modern philosophy is characterised by Locke, whose views on childhood are
examined later in this chapter. Locke and Hume were both very concerned with individual and collective morality. Locke's essay *Concerning Human Understanding* (see
Guttenplan *et al.*, 2003) explains the idea of a person as a moral agent who can be held
responsible for his or her actions only if he or she can remember the actions. Personal

identity comes when a child or adult can foresee the effects of actions and any rewards or punishments that may ensue. This way of thinking about personal identity has shaped discussions of the issue ever since. Hume, in his book *Treatise* (Hume and Selby-Bigge, 1888), identified his idea that our beliefs and actions are the products of custom or habit, and that human passions impact on action and human will by motivating actions. In this way, all human actions are a result of human feelings, without any interference from human reason. This is in contrast to modern beliefs about the development of **attitudes** which are that they are a complex interrelationship between the social (behaviour), the affective (feelings/emotions) and the cognitive (thinking/ideas), so for example, behaviour is affected by feeling and thinking (see Figure 2.1). Since attitudes involve the social, cognitive and emotional, they will also be looked at in other chapters within this book, but they are regarded as important in the early years (DfES, 2007), mainly because they influence all aspects of a child's holistic development. Attitudes are a crucial aspect of my own philosophy on early childhood and education. I believe that motivating attitudes, such as curiosity and enthusiasm, which are affective (concerned with feeling), and cognitive attitudes (concerned with thinking), influence our behaviour and relationships. In the same way, behavioural attitudes, such as flexibility, sensitivity and creativity, and social attitudes, such as cooperation, independence and social responsibility, will influence the way we feel and think and subsequent behaviours. For example, if we do not find sharing with others a pleasurable experience, then we will not be motivated to share in the future and this will affect our behaviour and social interactions, as we will choose to avoid sharing experiences.

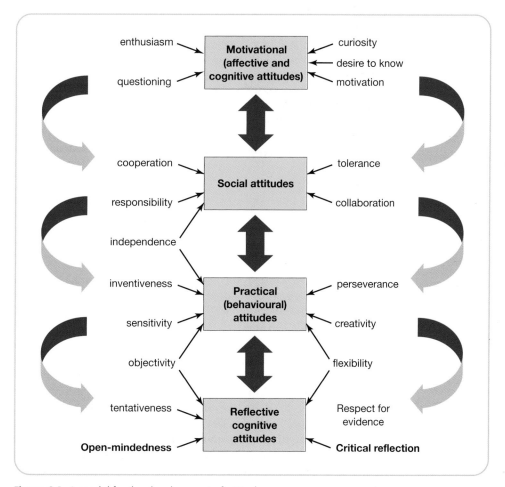

Figure 2.1 A model for the development of attitudes
Source: Adapted from Johnston, 2005a: 94

Reflective Tasks

Analysing attitudes

Divide the list of attitudes below into those which are affective, social/ behavioural and cognitive:

curious	enthusiastic	interested
tolerant	cooperative	grateful
responsible	proud	greedy
collaborative	aggressive	inventive
open-minded	tentative	respectful
flexible	independent	selfish
objective	sensitive	timid
conceited		

Level 1

Think about 'Goldilocks and the Three Bears' in the children's story. Using the list of attitudes above, consider which attitudes could be attributed to each of the characters. Provide evidence from the story to justify your ideas.

Level 2

Think about a child in your setting. Which attitudes (using the list above) could be attributed to the child? Provide evidence to support your ideas.

Level 3

Identify the attitudes you think are essential in early childhood and those you wish to develop within your setting. You can use the list above and add your own ideas. Consider how you can develop these attitudes within your setting.

Recent modern philosophy has influenced early childhood thinking, through the beliefs of Dewey (1916), considered briefly in Chapter 1. Dewey's pragmatic theories are applied to education and society in his book *Democracy and Education* (Dewey, 1916). Pragmatism is a philosophy that believes that practical action is more important than thought and that consequences, utility and practicality are vital components of meaning and truth. In an early childhood context, the emphasis is on behaviour rather than thinking and it is through the interactions children have with their environment that theories of early childhood become significant and it is only when these theories are shown to be successful in practice that they become 'true'. This does not mean that any theory that works for an individual or even a group of individuals is true, but rather that those theories that contribute to the common good in the long term are those that take precedence. If we apply this to an argument about the value of horoscopes, we could say that just because your horoscope occasionally seems to be accurate or may be accurate in parts, this does not mean that horoscopes in general are true and accurate reflections of our personality or future. In the same way, we can apply the idea to the argument in Chapter 1, about learning styles: just because learning style theory appears to have some significance for individual children and in some contexts, the evidence is not persuasive in the long term and so we need to treat the theory with caution, rather than consider it to be truthful and accurate.

Research

Philosophical thinking

Contemporary philosophy includes aspects of feminism and postmodernist theory. Postmodernist beliefs about education identify that it is more effective when children are engaged in discussions and argumentation, examining their own understanding, exploring abstract ideas and constructing their own understanding through challenge and discourse. This is opposed to the more traditional philosophy of learning which characterises the learner as passive and the teacher as an imparter of knowledge. Consider the model of philosophical thinking in Figure 2.2. This considers education in the context of two continua:

- *Traditionalist – Postmodernist*. Traditionalist education is concerned with authority, dissemination of knowledge and the training of skills, with the focus being on the teacher. Postmodernist education is concerned with the engagement of issues and the challenge of assumptions, with the focus being on the learner.

- *Positivist–Constructivist*. Positivist education is concerned with the pursuit of knowledge as truth, whereas in constructivist education the emphasis is on understanding rather than knowledge. Constructivism is concerned with the construction of understandings as a result of interaction and experience.

Highly structured practitioner-led education, where the practitioner imparts knowledge and trains children, is that within the traditionalist/positivist sector (see Figure 2.2). Structured explorations, where the practitioner sets up and structures activities, so that children can construct their own understandings and develop skills, are those within the traditionalist/constructivist sector. Play and discovery, where practitioners set up experiences and support, rather than guide children in their development, would fit within the constructivist/postmodernist sector. Challenges, discussion and argumentation would fit within the positivist/postmodernist sector.

TRADITIONALIST **Emphasis on authority, dissemination, imparting knowledge and training skills**	
Highly structured teacher-led instruction/demonstration	Teacher-led exploration
Structured teacher-led instruction/demonstration	Structured teacher-led exploration
POSITIVISM **Pursuit of knowledge as a truth**	**CONSTRUCTIVISM** **Constructing understandings** **from experience**
	Exploration
Debate/discussion/argumentation	Discovery
POSTMODERNIST **Emphasis on engaging with issues/ideas and challenging interpretations**	

Figure 2.2 Philosophical thinking in education
Source: Adapted from Johnston 2005b: 92; Longbottom, 1999

Reflective Tasks

Philosophical thinking

Consider the model of philosophical thinking in Figure 2.2.

Level 1

Where do you think good education should be on this model? Provide some evidence from your own experience to say why you think this type of education is best.

Level 2

Reflect on your recent practice and consider which sector of the model best describes your practice. Provide some examples to illustrate your decision.

Level 3

Reflect on your setting. Where do you think your practice fits into the model. Provide some evidence to support this decision. Now identify where you would like to be on the model. How can you change your practice to better meet your philosophical ideal?

Your personal philosophy

'I have never let my schooling interfere with my education.'
Mark Twain (1835–1910)

Working collaboratively to support the development of children in the early years involves having a shared philosophy and vision for the future. A shared philosophy does not mean that everyone concerned should think alike, but that individual philosophies are coherent and shared, so that there is a common thread and vision for collaboration. My early teaching in the 1970s involved individual teachers with very different philosophical ideas and teaching practices, who happened to share a building and children! Children started school from playgroups and homecare and stayed in one vertically grouped class with one teacher for between 2 and 3 years depending on their birth dates. School admissions policies meant that children started school the term after their fifth birthday, and so those children born in September would have three years at Key Stage 1 (then Infants) and those born the following August would have two years at Key Stage 1. They then moved to Key Stage 2 (then Juniors) where they would have a different teacher each year. Each teacher would have different ideas about teaching and a different educational philosophy and practice, with one favouring child autonomy and decision-making and another a more didactic approach. Neither was there consistency of curriculum content and each teacher could make their own choices about the needs of the children and what areas of the curriculum to cover. From the perspective of the individual child moving through this educational experience, it must have been confusing at the very least. At worst, the individual child would feel alienated from the setting, with schooling being something that was done to them rather than something in which they were actively involved. While this is not a familiar situation in today's educational settings, collaborative philosophy is still an important issue.

When the setting involves one service (education, health or social care) then ensuring a collaborative philosophical approach is difficult enough, but when there are different agencies, services and groups all trying hard to work together, it is possible that individual children can fall through gaps in the network. When this leaves the child vulnerable or, worse, in danger, then we have failed that child.

The first step towards providing a clear, coherent and shared philosophy in practice is to be clear in your own personal philosophy. This chapter will help you to analyse your beliefs and compare them with the philosophies of your peers. It will then examine the philosophy which underpins practice and provision in the early years and give you opportunities to see where that philosophy comes from and compare it with your own developing philosophy.

Tools for Learning

Reflection and analysis

In this chapter we are focusing on reflection and analysis. Later in the book (in Part 3) we will look at deeper analysis and combining the analysis of primary and secondary data.

What is analysis?

Analysis means to take something apart or separate it in order to illuminate, reveal, uncover, understand, resolve, identify or clarify. It is a bit like playing pass the parcel, in that each layer reveals something new and tells you a bit more about what is in the middle of the parcel. When you analyse events, situations, experiences or reading, you begin to reveal what the main factors affecting them are, or understand why someone has acted in a particular way, or clarify the issues for further development/action. Think also of a lottery scratch card, which involves scratching away a layer to reveal what is underneath. Analysis involves scratching beneath the surface of reading, ideas or observations to help us understand them. We may try to understand why something has happened or why an idea is held. Analysis also involves looking at alternative explanations or perspectives, such as looking at a situation from a parent, child or practitioner viewpoint.

Level 1

The first step towards developing analytical skills is to reflect on a situation or experience and answer analytical questions. Analytical questions ask how and why and so what, whereas descriptive questions ask when and where and what.

Look at the questions below and decide, which ones are analytical and which ones are descriptive.

- Do you eat breakfast?
- Why is a healthy meal at the start of a day important for young children?
- Do you think that healthy school dinners are important for children?
- How can early years settings improve the healthy diet of children in their care?
- What are the main factors affecting the improvement of a healthy diet for young children?

Level 2

The next step towards developing analytical skills is to raise analytical questions after reflection. Remember that analytical questions ask how and why and so what and involve detailed answers.

Read about Margaret McMillan's beliefs in Chapter 1 about the importance of a healthy body for a healthy mind. Considering your own experiences, raise some analytical questions that you can answer about meals provided in early years settings.

Level 3

Deeper analysis (which is covered more fully in Chapter 8) involves uncovering layers of analysis or looking at different perspectives. This might involve looking at the history of an incident (what came before and what after), patterns of behaviour, issues or factors affecting behaviour, or new ideas or thought resulting from reflection.

Read about Margaret McMillan's beliefs in Chapter 1 about the importance of a healthy body for a healthy mind. Consider what experiences influenced her beliefs. Consider, too, what we have done since to improve young children's diets and what more we need to do in the future.

Developing individual philosophies

'Happiness is having a large, loving, caring, close-knit family in another city.'
George Burns (1896–1996)

Our beliefs are the building blocks for our individual personal philosophy. These beliefs are influenced by the experiences we have, whether positive or negative. Our beliefs about good parenting will be based on our experiences as children, parents and practitioners (that is, observing parenting from an outside perspective). Our beliefs about health care will be based on our experiences in the health system, or the experiences of our family and friends. Our beliefs about education will be based on our own experiences as pupils. As a result, our beliefs are subjective and liable to be biased. This is because it is quite hard, if not impossible, to be objective when looking at anything we have been involved in. Since all of us have been through childhood, experienced parenting, health care, education and had to socialise with others, we all have beliefs about early years care. These experiences provide a template for our practice, so that poor experiences as a child can lead to poor parenting as an adult, or good experiences in building up self-esteem can lead to a confident adult, who in turn nurtures the self-esteem of children in their care. Sometimes we may reflect on these experiences and make a positive decision to do the opposite in our own practice, so that people who have had poor experiences at school during childhood may decide to home-educate their own children, or people who were the victims of physical abuse as children may use their abuser as a model of 'what not to do' as a parent. At times it is difficult to be objective about why you hold beliefs, or to see an alternative viewpoint. For example, if you are home educated, you may find it difficult to reflect on the experience objectively and consider the advantages or disadvantages of home education.

Some of my earliest memories are as a 3-year-old child, when I went to a nursery school. I can remember having a peg with a picture on it and the same picture being on my chair, bed and blanket. Every day we had a meal before our afternoon sleep and it was expected that we ate all our food up. I do not remember being a particularly fussy eater and am certainly not now, but I do remember being stubborn. On one occasion I flatly refused to eat boiled cabbage and was made to sit at the table with the plate in front of me, while other children prepared for their sleep. Eventually, an attempt to forcefeed me was made and I was promptly sick all over the floor! This incident led to my persistent dislike of boiled cabbage and also informed my beliefs about good practice as a parent and practitioner, so that while I would provide a balanced meal, with a helping of everything, children were not forced to eat but encouraged to try. My own children, who are now adults, are not fussy eaters, despite having fads during their childhood and so I am confirmed in my belief that this was the correct practice.

Reflective Tasks

Personal beliefs and influences

Level 1

Reflect on your own early life and identify one experience which has affected the way you think now. This could be a family, school, friendship, health, or other experience.

- Why was the experience important to you?
- How has the experience affected the way you feel?
- How do your beliefs relate to those of the theorists and reformers in Chapter 1?
- How will the experience and your subsequent belief change your practice in the future as a parent, carer, early years practitioner?

Level 2

Consider an early years setting you have experienced. Is there some aspect of practice or an incident of practice which has made you think about your own beliefs? This may be an experience which confirmed your beliefs or made you reconsider them. Raise some analytical questions about the experience to help you reflect upon it more deeply. Remember analytical questions look more deeply by asking how, why, or so what.

Level 3

Consider a recent policy or practice decision in your setting.

- Reflect on the influences that helped you reach a decision on the policy or practice.
- Examine your own objectivity in reaching that decision.
- Try to look at the decision from different viewpoints (practitioner, parent, child, etc.).
- On reflection, are you convinced that you made the correct decision? Why?

Examining our personal philosophy

'Health is worth more than learning.'
Thomas Jefferson (1743–1826) in a letter to his cousin John Garland Jefferson, 11 June 1790

Everyone reading this book will have a collection of experiences and beliefs about early years care and provision which have resulted from those experiences. In this part of the chapter we will try to explore the beliefs which form our personal philosophy, through a series of practical tasks.

Practical Tasks

What is Early Childhood Studies?

Using Table 2.1, write a list identifying all the things you think that Early Childhood Studies involves. *Do not* look at the contents page of this book or another book to help you, but identify the areas for yourself. Then compare your list with the contents page of this book and/or the contents page of another Early Childhood Studies textbook. Identify areas you have not identified or are not covered in the books. Why do you think this may be?

Divide your list into areas which deal with children's health, children's social care or children's education. Are there any other areas which do not fall into these categories? Can you find another category for other areas?

Look at your list and give yourself a score out of 10 for your understanding for each item, with 1 being low and 10 being high. Is there an area of Early Childhood Studies (health, social care, education or other) you feel most confident with? Why?

Highlight the items you feel less confident with (scored below 5) and rank them, with the lowest score at the top and the higher ones below.

Table 2.1 Identifying your Early Childhood Studies targets

Area	Competence	Action needed	Review

In this first set of practical tasks, you have undertaken your own personal needs analysis. First, you have identified the breadth of your understanding about Early Childhood Studies. If you look at the contents page of this book or another Early Childhood Studies book and there are items that are not on your list, then this may indicate that you are unaware of them or had forgotten them and so they are more likely to be aspects you need to focus on and learn more about. If you rank the items on your list which you feel less confident about, then you have prioritised your own learning and targets for your development. If the items on your list fall mostly in one area (health, social care or education), then you have identified which is your weakest area. It is likely that we are all stronger in one area than another, because of our background and experiences. My background as a primary school teacher and early years educator make education my strongest area. If you look at the contents page of this book and who is authoring each of the chapters, you should be able to identify each author's main area of strength.

Once you know your areas of strength and have identified the target areas for future development, you can select chapters of the book to support your development. You can also use your list while you use this book to reflect on your development and understanding throughout the book, reviewing your understanding in the different areas and adjusting your score. This will help you to identify the progress you are making in your own development.

Practical Tasks

What do you think?

In these tasks, you will begin to explore your personal philosophy on early childhood practice and provision. Remember that we are looking at all practice and provision for young children aged up to 8, so this includes prenatal, parental care, provision by childminders, nannies, playgroups, nurseries, social services and schools, and in all areas: social, health and education.

Produce a list or brainstorm identifying what you think is good early years provision and education. You may find answering these questions helpful to you in doing this:

- What do you think are the main areas of influence on a child's life? It may be easier for you if you break up childhood into different areas. You may wish to look at the section in Chapter 1 on Urie Bronfenbrenner and his ecological systems theory (Bronfenbrenner, 1995; Bronfenbrenner and Evans, 2000) for ideas. Alternatively, you may wish to consider stages in a child's life (prenatal, the first year of life, 1–3 years, 3–5 years, 5–8 years) and identify the main areas of influence during these stages. Another way of breaking up childhood is to consider the areas of development: physical, cognitive, social and emotional. You can, of course, break up childhood in other ways.

- Who do you think are the most influential people involved in a child's life?

- What care do you think is the best for children at different stages of development?

- What skills and attributes do you feel early years practitioners need to develop in order to support developing children?

This list or brainstorm can now be turned into a concept map. A concept map is a way of identifying more fully your ideas and the links between the different ideas. Concept maps (Novak and Gowan, 1984) look similar to 'brainstorming' spiders' webs but are more organised and indicate links between the ideas. In this way they not only identify what you think, as brainstorming does, but also why you think it, and they are analytical rather than descriptive. Your ideas are then linked using appropriate words or phrases to explain them (see the example in Figure 2.3). The following questions may help you to develop your own concept map:

- How do you think we should best care for children in the early years?
- Why do you think certain care is best for children at different stages of development?
- How (and why) do you think parents/family members/peers/practitioners/society should interact with young children?
- How (and why) do you think practitioners working with young children can best support their development?
- How should practice and provision be changed or developed in the future?

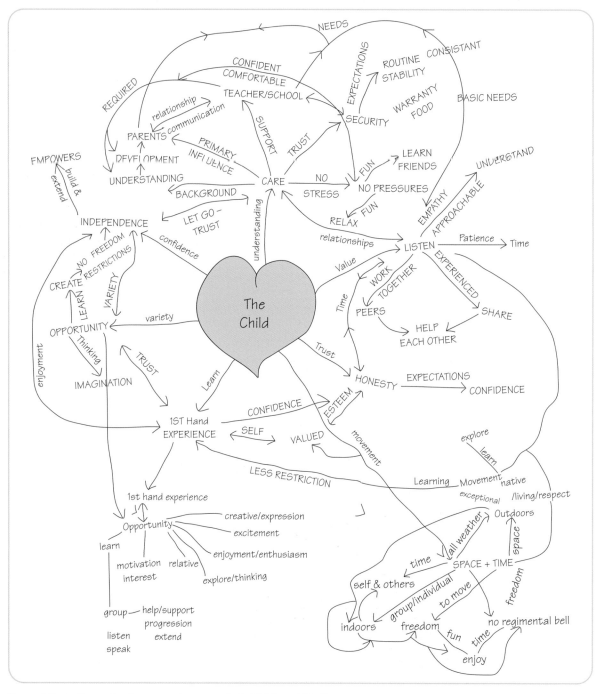

Figure 2.3 An Example of a concept map on Early Childhood Studies
Source: Courtesy of Christine Flint

The continuing development of philosophies

'Education is not the filling of a pail but the lighting of a fire.'
W.B. Yeats (1865–1939)

You have now begun to identify your personal philosophy on early childhood at this present time. This philosophy will be influenced by your past experiences and even by the recent reading and reflection you have undertaken, and by recent interaction with others who may have quite different ideas. It will also be affected by the current social context and interactions between children and adults (Alanen and Mayall, 2001). Childhood has no natural state and is not something that is defined by nature but rather constructed by society (Aries, 1972). Reflect upon philosophical changes in society's views of childhood, which have changed considerably over the centuries as public opinion, understanding and culture developed and with increased globalisation. In the fourth century, Britain and other countries were very insular and isolated. The view of childhood was influenced by the Church, who believed and instructed others in the belief that children were sinners and needed to obey and be disciplined by adults. In medieval society, children were considered to be miniature adults and as such could do all the work of an adult as soon as they could live without constant maternal care. If you look at pictures of medieval children, they have a tendency to be depicted as little adults. Childhood was therefore a very short period of time of total dependency. It was then followed by a lifetime of hard work, malnutrition and servitude. During the industrial revolution in the nineteenth century, children were seen as property and had a commercial use, working in factories, until the Factory Acts of 1833, 1843, 1864 and 1867 and the introduction of elementary education for all. Charles Dickens's novels, such as *Great Expectations*, published originally in weekly magazines (Dickens, 1861), along with social discussions, give some idea of what childhood was like for many children at this time (see Picture 2.1). Childhood in Victorian

Picture 2.1 Victorian children
Source: The Print Collector/Alamy Images

times (the latter part of the ninteenth century) can also be analysed through characteristic phrases, such as 'children should be seen, but not heard' and 'spare the rod and spoil the child'. In the twenty-first century these views are considered outdated as over the decades our views on discipline in childhood have changed; children are considered to have social rights (DfES, 2003a) and it is society's responsibility to ensure they are met. Children are disciplined through socialisation and education, rather than punishment, with antisocial behaviour orders (ASBOs) given to children but the responsibility for compliance given to parents.

After the nineteenth-century introduction of elementary education for all took effect, the twentieth century saw childhood as a time for learning, and schools became central in constructing a new image of childhood that separated children from the adult world. The cultural perspectives of Western cultures view childhood as a time when children are part of a family, dependent on the adults who care for them to assert their rights. These rights are limited by the child's vulnerability and dependency and childhood can be described as a structural and generational interplay (Alanen, 2001). In the twentieth century, the family was considered a private institution, although the beginning of the twenty-first century is characterised by government intervention in family life, with official views expressed on a range of formerly individual decisions, such as early childcare, vaccination, discipline, education, diet and exercise.

Reflective Tasks

Issues in early childhood

Choose one of the following: early childcare, vaccination, discipline, education, diet or exercise. Find and read some newspaper and magazine articles, and books about the issue.

Level 1

Answer the following questions.

- What are your beliefs about the issue you have chosen (early childcare, vaccination, discipline, education, diet or exercise)?
- How objective are your views?
- How do your views compare with those in the articles and books you have read?
- How is the writers' objectivity affected when considering the issue?
- Should the government intervene in childcare? Explain your beliefs.

Level 2

Raise some analytical questions about the issue you have chosen and read about in the articles and books. Remember that analytical questions will enable you to understand the issue more fully. Identify your beliefs about government intervention in childcare.

Level 3

Consider the historical changes in beliefs about the issue you have chosen. Try and explain how the social context and governmental influences have affected the changes you have identified.

Historical thinkers and philosophers have also reflected on childhood and there are three different views, which may be affected by the historical contexts of the time the philosophers were living. The view of Locke (1632–1704), known as empiricism, identifies that the child is an empty vessel to be filled, or a lump of clay to be moulded. Childhood is characterised by adults rigorously instructing children and moulding them into the form they would like. Rousseau (1712–78, see Chapter 1) was enlightened for his day. According to his philosophy of nativism, the child is vulnerable and generates in adults a desire to shelter them from the corrupt world, which is violent, oppressive, commercialised and exploitative. Adults do this by constructing a form of environment in which young children will be offered protection, continuity and security. In many ways, this view is compatible with many beliefs about childhood held in today's society. However, the reality is that while we may have shared beliefs in society today, they may not always be seen in practice. In the philosophy of Kant (1724–1804), known as interactionism, the focus is on the individual child who, irrespective of context, follows a standard sequence of biological stages that constitutes a path to full realisation, or a ladder-like progression to maturity. This idea was in many ways developed further by Piaget in his staged theory of cognition (see Chapters 1 and 5).

In the same way as philosophers' ideas change with the context and interaction with the ideas of others, so your philosophy will continue to develop as you continue to interact with others, read, reflect on reading, practice and provision, and develop your understanding.

Reflective Tasks

Reflecting on philosophies

Level 1

Read Chapter 1 and answer these questions:

- How are the ideas in your concept map similar or different from those of the philosophers discussed in the section A timeline of theorists?
- Whose ideas do you feel the most comfortable with and why?
- Whose ideas have made you think more about early childhood? Why?

Level 2

Choose one philosopher from Chapter 1, with whose ideas you feel comfortable. Identify the features of their philosophy you agree with and those you do not. Raise some analytical questions that you could ask about their philosophical ideas and try to answer them through reading Chapter 1 and books about the philosopher.

Level 3

Reflecting on your concept map, identify links with the ideas of the philosophers in Chapter 1. Choose one philosopher whose beliefs are close to your own. Find a book about the philosopher or an original piece of writing by them and identify features of the philosophy you agree with and those you do not. Make sure you also identify why you agree or not.

If we read about the lives of some of the philosophers and traditionalists identified in Chapter 1, we should be able to see how their life experiences have influenced their ideas and how their ideas have developed over time. For example, read an autobiography of Froebel (e.g. Froebel, *et al.*, 1892) and see how his life experiences led to his philosophical beliefs, such as the introduction of his gifts. As we can see from Chapter 1, Froebel's ideas were considered radical during his life but time and experience changed society's opinions towards his beliefs. In the child-centred, practical era of the 1960s and 1970s practical apparatus similar to Froebel's gifts was used extensively.

Research

Practical activities and cognitive development

We currently accept that practical activities support child development, although recent evidence on cognitive abilities compiled at Kings' College London by Philip Adey and Michael Shayer (Crace, 2006; Griffiths, 2006) indicates the need for children to play with practical resources, such as Plasticine, clay, sand, etc., in order to develop their cognitive understandings. The same research also informs us of current developments in Piaget's ideas about cognition and indicates that children in society today who are being taught to pass assessment tests, such as the standard assessment tasks (SATs) at 7 and 11 years of age, have less developed thinking skills than children in previous generations.

Piaget's ideas emerged from his studies of his own children, and if you read one of the numerous books about his life (e.g. Atkinson and Piaget, 1983) you can see how he developed his ideas. Read also one of the critiques of Piaget's work and you will be able to chart the rise and fall and rise again of his ideas and be able to analyse how social and academic views and subsequent research have affected the popularity or not of his philosophical beliefs.

If you read about the lives of Montessori (e.g. Kramer, 1976), Skinner (e.g. Skinner and Richelle, 1993), Freud (e.g. Gogerly and Freud, 2003) or McMillan (e.g. Steedman, 1990), you will be able to analyse how their ideas developed through personal and professional experiences, reflection and academic discourse. In fact, take any of the philosophers and traditionalists mentioned in Chapter 1 (see Table 1.1) and read about their life history and you should be able to see how their ideas were influenced and how they may have changed with time. Reading about these experiences may also make you think about your own beliefs and how they differ or are similar to those of the philosopher. You may be able to provide examples from your own experience which have helped you in this belief (see the first Reflective Task in this chapter on p. 54). In this way our personal philosophies are developing all the time and are never static. You can continue this development of your philosophy and understand the different ideas of others by engaging in discussion about philosophical statements.

Practical Tasks

Philosophical thinking

Level 1

Look at the philosophical statements (Figure 2.4) and consider your reaction to each statement. Identify why you agree or disagree with each statement. Share your ideas with a peer or a small group of peers. Look particularly at statements where you do not all agree and discuss why you hold different views.

Level 2

Look at the philosophical statements (Figure 2.4) and consider your reaction to each statement. Identify why you agree or disagree with each statement. Thinking about your setting or a setting in which you have had recent experience, compare your beliefs with those you have seen in practice in the setting. Share your ideas with a colleague/peer or a small group of colleagues/peers and see if they agree with your analysis.

Level 3

Use the statements in Figure 2.4 to help your setting decide what the individual philosophies of the staff are. In small groups or pairs, discuss each statement and decide which you agree/disagree with and why. Share your decisions with other staff. Using the statements you all agree with, look for evidence of this shared belief in practice in your setting.

- Children in the early years should be allowed to develop through experience and play.
- Early education should prepare children for school.
- Young children benefit more from early education rather than home care.
- Early education plays an important part in the social development of children.
- Health and nutrition are an important prerequisite for early learning and development.
- Children who attend nurseries, playgroups or pre-schools are adversely affected emotionally as children need a 'healthy', loving early home life before formal education.
- Early education has become too curriculum-focused and needs to reconsider the child.
- Parents are the first and consistent influence on children's lives and 'Parents and practitioners should work together in an atmosphere of mutual respect within which children can have security and confidence' (QCA 2000: 11).
- Children need routine and structure in order to support early development and learning.
- Young children need discipline rather than guidance.
- The role of the early years carer and educator is to support development and learning rather than teach.
- It is important for children to learn to read and write in nursery, pre-school, foundation stage.
- Adults are very important role models for young children.
- Without education and nurture in the first years 'all the rest of life is clouded and weakened' (McMillan 1930).
- Children will develop imagination and creativity without adult help and intervention.
- Moral development is best left to later years.
- 'Our highest human endeavours must be to develop free human beings who are able of themselves to impart purpose and direction to their lives' (Steiner, 1996).
- Children do not need to mix with other children in the first few years of life.

Figure 2.4 Philosophical statements

Integrated philosophies

'The greatest discovery of my generation is that a human being can alter his life by altering his attitudes of mind.'
William James (1842–1910)

The significance of shared and collaborative philosophies within a setting is becoming even more important as we move towards an integrated service for children. Integrated services involve a range of services that 'share a common location and a common philosophy, vision and agreed principles for working with children and families' (DfES, 2006).

Situated within the community, these integrated services aim to bring together health, social welfare and education services in a coherent way to support families and children, addressing the five outcomes identified in the Children Act 2004 (see DfES, 2003a; 2004a; 2004b), that children should:

- be healthy;
- stay safe;
- enjoy and achieve;
- make a positive contribution;
- achieve economic well-being.

Early years settings, such as nurseries, schools and community centres, are often well placed to offer an integrated service through use of multi-agency provision. The government (DfES, 2006) has identified two key developments integral to this type of provision: children's centres and extended schools, that is, care around educational provision, which takes into account the holistic needs of the family and the individual child. Provision for children in the integrated services is inclusive, available all year round and includes the 'wrap-around' care in extended schools. The multi-agency teams within the settings provide social, health and educational services for the whole family, such as employment and health advice for parents, antenatal care, and parenting classes for pregnant teenagers, single parents and socially deprived families, and not just support within the centre but also outreach services and informal and accredited courses for adults. A major aim is to involve and engage all carers, to advantage children and improve the quality of their childhood. The centres provide access to medical and dental treatment, physiotherapy, speech therapy, day care and education for children from birth through early childhood and often beyond.

The DfES (2006) has identified the benefits of and challenges facing the integrated services initiative and these are shown in Table 2.2. The first three of the challenges are concerned with the importance of collaborative philosophy, vision and practice, as in order to be successful, these settings need to work in a coordinated way and this is reliant on a shared philosophy and joint training of staff.

Table 2.2 The benefits of, and challenges facing, the integrated services

Benefits	Challenges
• Opportunity to address full range of issues around children's health and well-being in a non-stigmatising universal setting.	• Requires fresh thinking around the concept of the school or early years setting and their purpose in the community.
• Knock-on benefits for educational standards.	• How to bring a range of partners and the whole school community on board through 'collaborative leadership'.
• Greater co-working and cross-fertilisation of skills between agencies.	
• Opportunities for joint training.	• Developing a sense of joint purpose so that practitioners identify more with the new service than their role in their home agency.
• Shared base enhances communication between different services.	
• Members are still linked in to what is going on in their home agency.	• Managing any issues around pay and conditions for staff doing joint work at different levels of pay.
• Members likely to have access to training and personal development in their home agency.	

Source: Adapted from DfES, 2006

As discussed in Chapter 1, the integrated services are clearly an important development for young children, but it must not be assumed that the different partners involved in this multi-agency approach do share the same philosophy and vision and can work together in a coordinated way. It is most important that there is some shared common thread and vision in integrated, multi-agency, early childhood settings. In many ways, a coordinated philosophy is the first priority of the leader of an integrated setting, who may come from any of the partner backgrounds and who must value the different beliefs of individuals within the integrated services. Leadership issues are discussed further in Chapter 14 and how practitioners work together is discussed more fully in Chapter 13.

Some underlying philosophies analysed

'A fool's brain digests philosophy into folly, science into superstition, and art into pedantry. Hence University education.'
George Bernard Shaw (1856–1950)

In this section, we are looking at the underpinning philosophy of three important and recent early years initiatives, Every Child Matters (DfES, 2003a), the Foundation Stage curriculum (QCA, 2000) and the new Early Years Foundation Stage (DfES, 2007).

Every Child Matters (DfES, 2003a) was developed in order to close gaps that existed in provision for children and young people. These gaps had resulted in some high-profile, well-documented cases of child death and maltreatment and the rise in antisocial behaviour, teenage pregnancy, substance abuse and crime among children and young people. The underpinning philosophy is that every child matters and has a right to five outcomes:

- *health*, enjoying physical and mental well-being and living healthily;
- *safety*, being safe and protected from any form of harm or neglect;
- *enjoyment and achievement*, having access and benefiting from opportunities and developing important life skills;
- *contribution*, being involved in community and social life, so that they are able to make a positive contribution to society and take some responsibility for their own actions in society;
- *economic well-being*, being able to achieve their full potential and not be economically disadvantaged later in life because they have not had opportunities to fulfil their potential.

Consultation and the Children Act 2004 led to recognition (DfES, 2004a; DfES, 2004b) that in order to achieve this a radical reorganisation of children's services was needed so as to improve and integrate services in early years settings, schools and the health services, providing specialised support for families and children. The main change is a philosophical one, in that childcare and provision was to be come child-centred (DfES, 2004a) after a long period when the child was almost lost in the bureaucracy of the diverse and over-taxed services which were supposed to support and care for them. Practically, this means the integration and improvement of services including an increase in specialised help, the reconfiguration of services so that provision is all in one place, with professional, multidisciplinary teams working together and led by skilled and enterprising leaders (DfES, 2004a). The aim is that this will provide an informed service for children with shared responsibility for their safety and protection and which listens to children, young people and their families. As a result of the Children Act and the various documents which have followed consultation on Every Child Matters (DfES, 2003a; 2004a; 2004b), each local authority has carried out a comprehensive survey identifying local needs in order to support the principles of Every Child Matters and has produced action plans which provide an overview of actions in each area. While this is a first and essential step in delivering services, the local authorities were in danger of omitting the specifics of how the philosophy would be translated into action in practice by the various services, which are expected to work together in multi-agency settings. This lack of detail may prove to be a big obstacle, as it may provide gaps in the network of services which individual children may fall through. There do seem to be unproved assumptions that practitioners in Early Excellence Centres are coping with the complexity of new demands and policy shifts. There has also been limited research into 'joined-up' teams and the way they conceptualise and develop new services, and also limited practical support for new developments in terms of training, especially for 'community-led' initiatives such as SureStart. The main issues for the future of Every Child Matters (DfES, 2003a) appear to be concerned with partnership:

- the need for effective partnership within the services;
- the need for effective partnership/liaison/cooperation between the different agencies working in the field;
- the need for links with other authorities within the UK;
- the need for specifics as to how the different services will work together in order to translate the action plan into action in practice;
- the need for research on and development of practice and the link between the two.

Development in the Foundation Stage was first encompassed in curriculum guidance produced by SCAA (1996). This was fairly quickly replaced by new curriculum guidance in 2000 (QCA, 2000). The aims of the Foundation Stage were that the curriculum should provide the base and support for development for children aged between 3 and 5, in six key areas of development, which are fully explored in Chapter 9. The underpinning philosophy of the Foundation Stage can be split into four areas: practitioners, early experiences, parents and children.

The importance of early years practitioners is fundamental to the curriculum, as it is recognised that effective development relies on the understanding that practitioners have of early years development and the way they implement this understanding. Practitioners should understand how children develop, especially in the first few years of life, when development is extremely rapid (see Chapters 3 to 7, which look at children's physical, cognitive, language, emotional, moral and social development). They need to understand the practical applications of theories, such as Maslow's theory of hierarchical needs, Bronfenbrenner's ecological systems theory and Kohlberg's theory of moral development (see Chapter 1 and Figures 1.1). In this way, early years practitioners should consider all aspects of children's development, ensuring that all children feel included, secure and valued. Practitioners should also understand the effects of their interactions and interventions on children's development.

The experiences that children have within the early years curriculum is also an important aspect of the underpinning philosophy of the Foundation Stage curriculum. This curriculum should be relevant to the needs and experiences of the children, that is, it should develop from their interests and their world. There is no point in providing children with experiences that are so far outside their circumstances or interest that they become demotivated. These experiences should build on what children already know and can do, and respond to their interests by adapting the direction to accommodate the child (Rousseau, 1911). This does not mean that the experiences should be unplanned or unstructured, but that they should not only be directed by adults but initiated by the children. As a result, early years practitioners should be able skilfully to observe children, understand their needs and respond appropriately to children. Practitioners should also

Picture 2.2 A playful learning environment
Source: Photolibrary Wales/Alamy Images

understand the importance of the learning environment. This needs to be rich and stimulating, with experiences that motivate and inspire young children and support their future development (see Picture 2.2). Perhaps the most important aspect of the philosophy is that experiences should be play-based and practitioners should understand the importance of play, as 'well-planned play, both indoors and outdoors, is a key way in which young children learn with enjoyment and challenge' (QCA, 2000: 25).

Another important underpinning belief of the Foundation Stage curriculum is that 'parents are children's first and most enduring educators' (QCA, 2000: 9). Parents and practitioners are expected to formulate a partnership which effectively supports children's development. Parental influence is likely to be much greater than any influence exerted by a practitioner, since parents interact with children from the moment of conception, forming an important and enduring bond (see Bowlby's theory of attachment in Chapters 1 and 6). Children do need stability within their early years provision and it has been found (Field, 1991) that stable childcare arrangements, low turnover of staff and low adult–child ratios are key factors in emotional stability, contentment in early years and later achievements. However, practitioners are often transitory and within the early years, children will experience a large number of practitioner carers, from key workers to nursery nurses, class teachers, supply workers, etc., while parents are more likely to be enduring.

In addition to the importance of the curriculum accommodating the child and play, the final area that underpins the philosophy of the Foundation Stage curriculum is the principle that no child should be excluded or disadvantaged. Interestingly, the emphasis on the child as centrally important is not as strong as in the philosophy of the 1960s and 1970s as identified by the Plowden Report (DES, 1967).

Reflective Tasks

Principles of the foundation stage

Reflect on the principles which define the philosophy of the Foundation Stage curriculum (QCA, 2000).

Level 1

Which principle do you believe is the most important? Why do you think this?

Level 2

Reflect on your setting and consider which principle is the strongest in your setting's philosophy. Provide some evidence from your setting to support your argument that this is an important part of your collaborative philosophy.

Level 3

Compare the collaborative philosophy of your setting with the principles of the Foundation Stage curriculum. Identify differences between your philosophy and that of the Foundation Stage curriculum. Provide an argument to justify any differences in philosophy and practice.

The Early Years Foundation Stage (EYFS) (DfES, 2007) is a new development which aims to integrate the different initiatives for young children, such as:

- Birth to Three Matters (SureStart, 2003), which focuses on effective care of very young children by a variety of adults;
- the Foundation Stage curriculum (QCA, 2000), for children between 3 and 5 years of age;
- Every Child Matters (DfES, 2003a), which focuses on integrated care for children and young adults;
- a Childcare Bill and 10-year strategy for children, Choice for Parents, the Best Start for Children (DfES, 2004c), which attempts to give all children the best start in life and support parents in balancing life and work;
- The National Standards for Under 8s Daycare and Childminding (DfES, 2003b).

The main philosophical underpinning of the EYFS is not dissimilar to that embodied in Every Child Matters (DfES, 2003a, and see above) and the Foundation Stage of Learning (QCA, 2000, and see above), that is, the supply of flexible but coherent provision for children aged 0 to 5 years, which 'fosters and supports their development from birth, where they will interact with adults that are appropriately trained and experienced; in environments that are safe, caring and loving' (DfES, 2005: 2). This should allow children to progress through the first 5 years of their lives at a pace that is appropriate for them, taking into consideration individual needs, regardless of the different types of provision they are in. The aim is to provide consistent and high quality care for all children in maintained, voluntary and private sectors. The EYFS will have the same legal status as the current Foundation Stage for Learning (QCA, 2000), removing it from the National Curriculum and continuing to focus on the development within six areas of learning, building on research findings such as those identified in Chapter 1. Theoretically, the idea of combining the philosophical principles of the different strategies, consultations and documentation, as outlined above, appears sensible. Practically, this may be more difficult and produce confusion and incoherence, instead of the clarity and coherence it aims to achieve. As new initiatives and frameworks are introduced this may just add to the confusion.

Summary

→ Ancient yet influential philosophers, such as Aristotle and Socrates, were mainly concerned with deep thinking and not practical applications.

→ Early modern philosophy was concerned with moral development and personal identity, which is related to when a child or adult can foresee the effects of actions. This developed into the belief that all human actions are a result of human feelings without any interference from human reason.

→ Modern beliefs about the development of attitudes are that they are a complex interrelationship between the social (behaviour), the affective (feelings/emotions) and the cognitive (thinking/ideas).

→ Recent modern philosophy has influenced early childhood thinking, in particular through the beliefs of Dewey (1916).

→ Contemporary philosophy includes the postmodernist theory. Postmodernist beliefs about education identify that it is more effective when children are engaged in discussions and argumentation whereby they are constructing their own understanding through challenge and discourse.

→ Our beliefs are the building blocks for our individual personal philosophy and these beliefs are influenced by the experiences we have, whether positive or negative.

→ The development of a personal philosophy on early childhood will be influenced by past experiences, reading and reflection, interaction with others, and the current social context.

→ Childhood has no natural state and is not something that is defined by nature, but rather is constructed by society. This means that the notion of childhood has changed in different eras throughout history.

→ The importance of shared and collaborative philosophies within a setting are even more significant with the move towards an integrated service for children.

→ Three recent important government initiatives within early childhood are Every Child Matters (DfES, 2003a), the Foundation Stage curriculum (QCA, 2000) and the Early Years Foundation Stage (DfES, 2007). These can be examined through their underpinning philosophies.

→ The DfES (2006) has identified the benefits of and challenges facing the integrated services initiative, with the first three of the challenges concerned with the importance of collaborative philosophy, vision and practice.

→ The Early Years Foundation Stage (EYFS) replaced the Foundation Stage Curriculum (QCA, 2000) in 2008, integrating some of the different initiatives for young children, although much of the underlying philosophy remains the same.

Key Questions

● What are some of the most influential philosophies that have underpinned practice and provision in the early years?

● What life experiences have influenced your personal beliefs?

● What has contributed to the development of your personal philosophy?

● Can you articulate your developing personal philosophy with reference to various influences?

- What is meant by shared philosophies?
- How could shared philosophies be developed within integrated services?
- What philosophies are evident in recent government initiatives for the early years?

References

Alanen, L. (2001) 'Explorations in Generational Analysis', in Alanen, L. and Mayall, B. (eds) (2001) *Conceptualizing Child–Adult Relations.* London: Routledge Falmer

Alanen, L. and Mayall, B. (eds) (2001) *Conceptualizing Child–Adult Relations.* London: Routledge Falmer

Aries, P. (1972) *Centuries of Childhood.* Harmondsworth: Penguin

Atkinson, C. and Piaget, J. (1983) *Making sense of Piaget: the philosophical roots.* London: Routledge & Kegan Paul

Bronfenbrenner, U. (1995) The Bioecological Model from a Life Course Perspective: Reflections of a participant observer, in Moen, P., Elder Jnr, G.H. and Lüscher, K. (eds) *Examining Lives in Context.* Washington, DC: American Psychological Association, pp. 599–618

Bronfenbrenner, U. and Evans, G.W. (2000) 'Developmental Science in the 21st Century: Emerging theoretical models, research designs and empirical findings', *Social Development,* 9: 115–25

Crace, J. (2006) 'Children are less able than they use to be', *The Guardian,* 24 January

DES (1967) *Children and their Primary school. A report of the Central Advisory Council for Education (England) Vol. 1: Report.* London: HMSO

Dewey, J. (1916) *Democracy and education: An introduction to the philosophy of education.* New York: Macmillan

DfES (2003a) *Every Child Matters.* London: DfES

DfES (2003b) *National Standards for under 8s daycare and childminding.* London: DfES

DfES (2004a) *Every Child Matters: Change For Children.* London: DfES

DfES (2004b) *Every Child Matters: The Next Steps.* London: DfES

DfES (2004c) *Choice for Parents, the Best Start for Children: A Ten Year Strategy for Children.* London: DfES

DfES (2005) *Early Years Foundation Stage. Direction of Travel.* London: DfES

DfES (2006) 'About Integrated Services'. www.dfes.gov.uk (accessed February 2006)

DfES (2007) *Statutory Framework for the Early Years Foundation Stage: Setting the Standards for Learning, Development and Care for Children from Birth to Five.* London: DfES

Dickens, C. (1861) 'Great Expectations', in *All The Year Round. A Weekly Journal.* London: Chapman & Hall

Field, T. (1991) 'Quality Infant Daycare and Grade School Behaviour and Performance', *Child Development,* 62: 863–70

Froebel, F. W. A., Michaelis, E. and Moore, K. (1892) *Autobiography of Friedrich Froebel,* 4th edn. London: Swan Sonnenschein

Gogerly, L. and Freud, S. (2003) *Sigmund Freud: The Founder of Psychoanalysis.* London: Franklin Watts

Griffiths, S. (2006) 'Failing to teach them how to handle real life' *The Sunday Times,* 29 January

Guttenplan, S., Hornsby, J. and Janaway, C. (2003) *Reading Philosophy. Selected texts with a method for beginners.* Oxford: Blackwell

Hume, D. and Selby-Bigge, L.A. (1888) *Treatise of Human Nature.* Oxford: Clarendon Press

Johnston, J. (2005a) *Early Explorations in Science.* Buckingham: Open University Press

Johnston, J. (2005b) 'What is Creativity in Science Education', in Wilson, A. (Ed.) *Creativity in Primary Education.* Exeter: Learning Matters, pp. 88–101

Longbottom, J. (1999) Science Education for Democracy: Dilemmas, Decisions, Autonomy and Anarchy. Paper presented to the *European Science Education Research Association Second International Conference,* Kiel, Germany

Kramer, R. (1976) *Maria Montessori. A biography.* London: Montessori International

McMillan, M. (1911) *The Child and the State.* Manchester: National Labour Press

McMillan, M. (1930) *The Nursery School.* London: Dent

Novak, J. and Gowan, D.B. (1984) *Learning How to Learn.* Cambridge: Cambridge University Press

Plato, trans. Jowett, B. (1968) *Republic.* New York: Airmont Publishing

QCA (2000) *Curriculum Guidance for the Foundation Stage.* London: DFEE

Rousseau, J.J. (1911) *Emile.* London: J.M. Dent

SCAA (1996) *Nursery Education: Desirable Outcomes for Children's Learning on entering compulsory education.* London: DfEE

Skinner, B. F. and Richelle, M. (1993) *B.F. Skinner: A Reappraisal.* Hove: Lawrence Erlbaum Associates

Steedman, C. (1990) *Childhood, Culture and Class in Britain: Margaret McMillan, 1860–1930.* London: Virago Press

Steiner, R. (1996) *The Education of the Child and Early Lectures on Education.* New York: Anthroposophic Press

SureStart (2003) *Birth to Three Matters. A Framework to Support Children in their Earliest Years.* London: DfES

Useful websites

Every Child Matters: change for children: http://www.everychildmatters.gov.uk/

Birth to Three Matters: www.surestart.gov.uk/resources/childcareworkers/birthtothreematters/

Foundation Stage: www.surestart.gov.uk/improvingquality/ensuringquality/foundationstage/

Sure Start: www.surestart.gov.uk

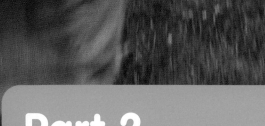

Part 2

Early Years Development

Chapter 3

What is Physical Development?

A bear, however hard he tries, grows tubby without exercise
A.A. Milne (1882–1956)

Introduction

This chapter seeks to investigate physical development in children from birth through to the age of 8. It will begin by exploring very early development and will examine some of the factors that can hinder the promotion of healthy development. It will then discuss how physical development can be promoted in pre-school settings. The chapter will conclude by analysing how physical skills are further progressed in school environments during physical education lessons.

Aims

→ To provide an overview of early physical development and the links with brain development

→ To outline the differences between gross motor skills, locomotor skills and fine motor skills

→ To consider the issues affecting physical development, such as hereditary factors, poverty, nutrition, obesity, and social and emotional development

→ To provide an understanding of the significance of the learning environment on physical development

→ To explore the potential of outdoor play

→ To provide an overview of physical education in school

Physical development

Physical development should not be confused with growth. Growth is the process by which cells divide to increase the size of the body. Physical development is the way in which children master control of their bodies (Beaver *et al.*, 1999; Tassoni *et al.*, 2002). This chapter studies physical development as opposed to growth. The way in which physical development occurs is a matter of much debate and the subject of extended academic discussion. Physical development relies on developments in the brain, which is stimulated by a combination of external experiences and the progression of an inborn maturational plan (Bee and Boyd, 2007). What cannot be denied, however, is the significance of this aspect of development. As educationalists have gained an increased understanding of how children learn and achieve, they have realised the absolutely central importance of encouraging physical skills in young children. For instance, the development of motor skills has implications for every other area of development. The ability to crawl opens up the world to a baby and gives a whole new range of features to explore (Slater and Lewis, 2002). Without this skill a child's world would be forever static and dependent on an adult changing and renewing the environment which the baby inhabits.

Tools for Learning

Observation as a research tool

Observation is an extremely useful research tool (or research method). It can help us to understand processes, events and development and it can support development, learning and professional practice. Observation is more than just looking. It involves:

● watching closely, for example as children are involved in a task;

● listening;

● discussing or questioning;

● analysing work/answers.

Observations can be focused, so that the observer is looking for something specific, or they can be unfocused, thus not excluding interesting but unexpected events and so supporting the generation of theory. The observer can be inside or outside the observations. For example, they may be the classroom teacher involved in the teaching or learning or an independent observer. All observations made need to be analysed and discussed with others for verification.

Using observation schedules

Observation schedules can aid observation and analysis, especially if you have specific foci for observation (see Figure 3.1).

Example schedule 1

Setting:	Observer's Name:	Date:
Time:	Focus: Behaviour Management	Context:
9.00 9.15	*Children are brought into the class by their parents who help them take off coats and settle on the carpet.* *Lead professional takes register and children sit quietly. D is chatting and professional waits until she has his attention before continuing.*	
Comments from the observation:		

Example schedule 2

Setting:	Observer's Name:	Date:
Time:	Focus: Behaviour Management	Context:

- **How do the children enter the setting at the beginning of the day?**
  Children are brought into the setting by their parents who help them take off coats and settle on the carpet
- **How does the lead professional deal with an inattentive child?**
  She waits quietly until she has the child's attention before continuing.

Comments from the observation:
It appears that the policy of the setting is one of quiet intervention.

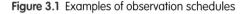

Figure 3.1 Examples of observation schedules

Early development: reflexes

When children are born they are equipped with a number of involuntary **reflexes** that determine movement. The reflexes are triggered in response to stimuli and the subsequent movements are not controlled by the child. Reflexes are present to help children survive and to aid them through their first weeks of life. For instance, babies are born with the inbuilt ability to 'root' and 'suck'. If a baby's mouth is stroked the infant will move its head and tongue towards the source of the movement. In addition, a baby will automatically suck on a finger, teat or breast placed in its mouth. These two reflexes help to ensure that a baby can obtain food after it is born (Bukato and Daehler, 2004). Other reflexes include those which help to protect the baby. The 'Moro' reflex is exhibited when the baby is startled and can often been seen in early infants if they are beginning to fall or if they hear a sudden noise like a banging door. In response, the baby will extend its arms, legs and fingers outwards, the back will be arched and the head will be drawn back (Papalia *et al.*, 2006). Other reflexes, like the 'grasping' reflex where a baby will make a strong fist around your finger, may be associated with later physical skills like reaching and holding. Similarly, the walking reflex reveals a baby making stepping motions when it is held upright with its feet just touching a surface (Bee and Boyd, 2007). All the reflexes mentioned above are called primitive reflexes and can be observed in babies from birth. These reflexes are tested soon after delivery as their absence can indicate abnormal development and possible potential neurological problems in the child's future life. Primitive reflexes disappear in the first months of life and are replaced by observable motor skills.

Goddard Blythe (2005) makes a very interesting connection between reflex development and early learning that reveals how vital physical development is even from the very start of life. She suggests that an incomplete transition from primitive reflexes to early motor development can result in problems in balance and coordination. For instance, retained rooting and sucking reflexes can interfere with the development of clear speech patterns and the coordination of the mouth muscles, while a prolonged grasping reflex can hinder the development of a good pencil grip. Her educational programme focusing on movement to correct immature reflexes appears to have great beneficial consequences for the academic progress of the children involved.

Brain development

The beginning of control of movement appears to depend on brain developments. The shift from reflex-like actions to voluntary movements occurs due to growth in the cerebral cortex (David *et al.*, 2003). This shift occurs when the brain has made enough connections or has been 'wired up' to allow further action to take place. It is not the purpose of this text to describe this very complex process minutely – that is the role of medical publications. However, a brief overview of brain development is given with its consequences for good physical development.

The brain is made up of neurons and glial cells. Neurons, or nerve cells, send and receive information. Glial cells support and protect the neurons (Papalia *et al.*, 2006: 139). The neuron is made up of dendrites and axons. The dendrite receives signals from other neurons. This information is transmitted along the axon which sends information across the synapse (the gap between neurons) to other neurons thus making a connection (Keenan, 2002: 79). Synaptogenesis (the formation of synapses) occurs in the cortex at a rapid rate in the first two years of life. Synaptogenesis happens in bursts and is followed by a 'pruning activity' when some connections are wiped out. How this synaptual pruning occurs is widely discussed. **Neurophysiologists** indicate that some synapses and their subsequent elimination are the result of an inbuilt pattern, whereas other elimination is the result of experiences. Each time an experience stimulates a neural pathway it leaves behind a chemical signal which is strengthened on every occasion it is reused by that same experience; the pathway gradually becomes immune to pruning (Bee and Boyd, 2007). Nash (1997) describes how babies deprived of a stimulating environment could suffer, by discussing the synaptual development of baby rats. Rats kept in toy-rich environments exhibited more complex behaviours than their deprived counterparts and their brains contained 25 per cent more synapses per neuron. She notes the timescale to brain development, stating that the most important year is the first. This increased understanding of how the brain develops has implications for how the child is stimulated during its very early life. Could lack of interaction or stimulation hinder synaptual development? This is simply too vast a question to answer in this publication. Theorists also point to the flexibility or the 'plasticity' of the young brain where children who suffer damage to certain regions of the cerebral cortex are often able to recover as neurons in other parts of the cortex take on this same function (Bukato and Daehler, 2004). Knowledge of how the brain develops does at least help stress the importance of not only loving a child but also providing high quality, interactive environments.

Advances in understanding the brain have been accompanied by commercial ventures. Shops are awash with products that claim to 'strengthen' a child's brain power. Lindon (2005: 127) urges that these products must be treated with caution and that they make overblown claims. Products like this prey on concerned parents and teachers who are trying to give a child 'the best start in life'. In addition, these 'toys' never replace high quality interaction and stimulation provided by a trusted adult. Lindon argues that the best possible way to achieve development comes from a loving relationship, stimulating interaction based around speaking and listening to a child and imaginative, varied play equipment.

As brain development allows a child to master various physical skills, this in turn allows a child to see the world in a different way. A child who can roll and reach can therefore investigate more objects than a child who remains still. A child who can pull itself up to stand has a very different viewpoint from one that lies on its back. Physical development, therefore, has wide-ranging implications for a child – advances in physical development allow for an increasingly independent life and make way for accompanying advances in a child's social and intellectual development.

Grouping physical development: motor skills

Motor skills acquisition is usually grouped into distinct areas: gross motor skills, locomotor skills and fine motor skills. (Fine motor skills are considered in the next section on page 84).

Gross motor skills involve large movements and use the bigger muscles in the body, such as whole limb movements which children use to walk, run, skip or hop, to name but a few movements that would fall into this category (see Picture 3.1). Gross motor skills develop according to a set sequence of activities which is easiest to remember as downwards and outwards. A baby, therefore, will gain control of its head first and control will progress through the body; development of extremities like fingers being the last features to be controlled. This is often referred to as:

- Cephalocaudal development – a growth pattern where development begins at the head and works its way downwards.
- Proximodistal development – a growth pattern that starts in the centre of the body and works it way outwards.

Picture 3.1 Using gross motor skills
Source: Michael Wildsmith/Getty Images

Locomotor skills are closely associated with gross motor skills but focus on movement from one place to another (Hughes, 2002). Hughes suggests that these start to emerge at about 8 months old when children begin to use crawling movements, although it is asserted that early movements like rolling could be considered to fall into this category as well (Bukato and Daehler, 2004).

As mentioned above, children acquire gross motor skills in a sequential manner; this development of skills is often termed as meeting 'milestones'. There are many textual sources that expand on and explain these milestones in order that a whole range of adults (e.g. parents, health professionals, educators) can assess children to ascertain if they fall into the 'norms' of development. Table 3.1 is a typical exemplar of how milestones are presented. While texts of this nature are extremely useful when assessing physical development it must be remembered that the acquisition of skills will not be the same for every child; children follow their own, unique pattern of development. Young children of the same age will reveal themselves to be at quite different stages of development, but all may be categorised as being 'normal', healthy children.

Table 3.2 The development of gross and fine motor skills

Age	Gross motor skills	Fine motor skills
2 months 3 months	holds head up rolls over kicks vigorously	control of eye movement; smiles engages in finger play
5–8 months	sits without support if held standing, legs and feet bear weight	passes toy from hand to hand grasps a toy
9 months	beginning to crawl pulls to standing	bangs objects together beginning to point with index finger can grasp small object with finger and thumb (beginnings of a pincer grip)

Table 3.2 *Continued*

Age	Gross motor skills	Fine motor skills
12 months	'cruises' around furniture shuffles on bottom, crawls proficiently may walk may stand alone	holds own cup picks up fine objects with a pincer grasp points at objects of interest
18 months	walks confidently pushes and pulls large toys carries toys while moving	holds crayon, will scribble with gusto using to and fro motion makes dots on page might show preference for using one hand
2 years	throws ball overhand beginning to kick a ball runs squats to play and rises without difficulty	turns pages of a book can unwrap objects eats with spoon picks up and returns objects to resting place with ease holds pencil using thumb and two fingers
3 years	walks upstairs using alternating feet; jumps climbs on small apparatus (small slides, climbing frames) kicks with ease sits with crossed legs rides a tricycle with confidence and uses the pedals	builds a tower of nine cubes cuts paper with scissors threads beads uses lines to form boundaries of objects when drawing pictures draws 'kisses' (cross) with pencil held in preferred hand near its point

Source: Adapted from Sherian, 1997; Keenan, 2002; Slater and Lewis, 2002; Bukato and Daehler, 2004

Research

Definitions of observation

This research (Johnston, 2007) involved 43 students in the first year of undergraduate studies on a BA(Hons) Early Childhood Studies course and took place during a teaching session. It attempted to find out what student practitioners understand the skill of observation to be, and involved each student writing an individual definition of observation.

Twenty-seven students mentioned watching or looking in their definitions of observation, such as '*looking at the things someone does and watching what has happened or is happening*'. Of those, six identified looking in depth, four mentioned looking to learn from or find out and two that looking involved deduction, hypothesis and explanation. Gathering words and actions was mentioned by one student and absorbing information by another. Observation as a skill was identified by five students and other skills such as analysis (nine), recording (eight) and questioning (one) were also mentioned:

- *The ability to analyse surroundings and take in every detail, resulting in the ability to describe whatever it may be later.*

- *This is when you watch/look at somebody and something and record what you have seen or just take in mentally what has been observed.*

However, mention of these skills appeared to consider the skill of the observer rather than the observed.

→

Interestingly 18 students mentioned people or children in their definition:

- *An observation is when someone observes children or adults as an individual or in groups. An observation is carried out in order to find out information, which will be important. Observations are usually recorded.*

- *This is a way in which we can watch people in their environment and analyse their abilities.*

Further, it appears that they have been influenced by their immediate studies, which have involved observations of children in settings (schools, nurseries and playgroups). Other characteristics of observation were listening (three) and using all the senses (one):

- *To watch and to learn from something that can be seen. Observation can use all five senses (touch, taste, smell, hear, see) and can include practical or theory activities.*

Only two students considered observations in the environment and no student considered observation as a scientific skill.

The importance of contextual factors in understanding observation is evidenced by the number of students whose initial perceptions of observation involved watching or looking at children and adults. These students had previously undertaken specific modules of work in observing children, settings and interactions. Despite the context of this research being a session looking at skills in children, they all utilised their prior knowledge and understanding in defining observation. The interactions enabled the students to achieve a better understanding of the complex nature of observation and how it leads to other process skills, particularly classification, explanation and interpretation. This understanding was further supported by the interaction, indicating the importance of professional dialogue in the construction of pedagogical skills.

Case Study

Playing on the climbing frame

Adam, Robert, Flora and Sarah are each 20 months old. The children and their parents have known each other from birth and frequently meet in order that the children can play. The children, on this occasion, were playing in the garden on a small, plastic climbing frame that had a slide emerging from it. The frame was specifically designed for children of this age and was about 1m in height. The children had to climb on to a low platform before using the slide to descend from the apparatus. All the children investigated the equipment according to their own level of ability and depending on their gross motor skills. Flora could climb on to the frame with ease and would then sit down in order to descend to the ground. Adam had an adventurous approach to the task; after climbing on the equipment he would then experiment with running down the slide. Adam's mum ensured that he was able to challenge himself in the way he wished but was there to see that he did not harm himself. Robert found it difficult to organise his limbs on the frame – and sought the help of his mother. Once on the frame he was able to slide down to the ground but preferred to keep hold of his mother's hand. Sarah had only just started to walk very confidently (Sarah had spent a long time competently shuffling on her bottom and found this a very good way to get around) and was still fairly unsure when balancing. She could attempt to ascend the climbing frame and had to be given much support in order to investigate the equipment. Sarah's mother gave her as much help as she could in order that her daughter should feel included in the activity and enjoy the experience.

Critical Discussion

Case study of climbing frame

The children discussed in the Case Study have wide-ranging gross motor skills but all would, just about, lie within the norms of development. At a young age differences between children can appear quite marked but this does not always mean that children who may lag behind in a certain area should be labelled as unable. Sarah could be classed as 'late' in walking but one must be wary of diagnosing or suggesting a medical condition related to this. In addition, 'lateness' in walking does not indicate delayed progress in other developmental areas, e.g. cognitive achievement.

Level 1

Consider how you could challenge Adam to further progress in his next stage of physical development.

Level 2

Consider how you could challenge Adam to further progress in his next stage of physical development. How could you also plan to help Sarah in her own learning journey when looking after both these children at the same time?

Level 3

Do you think Adam's mother was right to let her child run down the slide? Consider how you would plan challenging physical activities that let children take risks but that also keep them safe.

Fine motor development

This emphasises the development of manipulative skills and use of smaller muscles. Typically, this would involve actions such as picking up small objects, bead threading, drawing, manipulating eating utensils, cutting with scissors, undoing buttons or pulling a zip (see Picture 3.2). Fine motor skills develop at a slightly later stage than gross motor skills (Bee and Boyd, 2007). Certainly a child's first attempt at cutting and drawing tasks involves much concentration and can look awkward and cumbersome. Good fine motor skills develop only with much patience and practice.

The acquisition of fine motor development also depends on growth, particularly bone development. The hand, wrist, ankle and foot have fewer bones at birth than at adulthood. A fully grown wrist exhibits nine bones. These bones are visible in girls at 51 months of age and in boys at 66 months of age (Bee and Boyd, 2007). This is significant as girls, at an early age, may have more developed fine motor skills than boys. This can have consequences for the experiences of children in school. The observation of boys carrying out early writing shows that they can appear stilted and small amounts of writing can take some time to produce; this can be frustrating for them. Girls on the other hand often find it easier and more satisfying to write and particularly appear able to acquire a cursive style. 'Joined-up' handwriting is usually taught in Year 2 of Key Stage 1. The ability to join up letters makes up part of a child's score in the Standard Assessment Tests (SATs). This feature might, therefore, be harder for boys to attain. Certainly this demonstrates the importance of how having a good understanding of physical development can aid a practitioner involved with a Key Stage 1/Foundation Stage class.

Picture 3.2 Using fine motor skills
Source: John Walmsley/Education Photos

Practical Tasks

Fine motor skills

Early on in training it is easy to make generalised statements of early years children, such as, 'they can't "do" anything' or 'they know so little' and even, 'everything I plan takes them about 30 seconds to complete'. It is interesting to observe how these attitudes change as students spend an increasing amount of time in educational settings working alongside this age group. As their awareness of child development broadens, students often acquire a much greater appreciation of outcomes from the children. Trainee practitioners begin to understand how to look at the first drawings of children and see how much knowledge that child has about the world to be able to produce the work. They also observe the concentration the child has had to apply to produce the outcome. Study Picture 3.3 (overleaf).

Level 1

- How would you assess this child's fine motor development?

Level 2

- Assess this child's fine motor development.
- What else does this picture reveal about her general level of development and her conceptual understanding?
- If she were a child in your care how would you use the assessment information to support her future development?

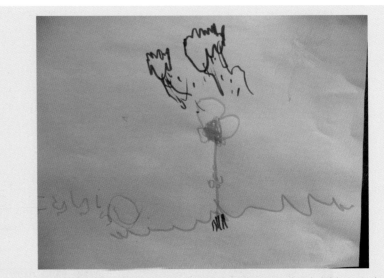

Picture 3.3 A picture of a growing flower completed by a pre-school child named Isabelle ('Issie'), aged 3 years 9 months

Level 3

- Use this task with your staff and assess this child's fine motor development and general conceptual development. Use the assessment framework from the Early Years Foundation Stage (DfES, 2007) to help you. Decide how your setting might encourage the child to talk about the drawing.
- How does your setting encourage children to progress fine motor skills?

Coordination and balance

As children reach middle childhood they concentrate on refining their motor skills. Once major milestones like walking and running have been mastered, a period of consolidation occurs when they become increasingly coordinated, balanced and agile. Children will now have no problems in executing moves like kicking a ball but they might have to persevere when it comes to dribbling it or scoring a goal – this requires a combination of coordinated skills. Children will experiment with balancing on increasingly narrower objects. They will learn to use their eye–hand coordination to hit a ball with a bat. To acquire and improve in these skills, children need plenty of opportunity to practise them.

Factors affecting physical development

The rate at which young children develop is determined by a mixture and interaction of hereditary and environmental factors.

Hereditary factors

Our genetic makeup is a result of a mixing of our parents' genes – this is termed a '**genotype**' (Davenport, 2001). This make-up can predispose a child to certain characteristics and its physical disposition. It is likely that children will grow to a height similar to that of their parents. A person's eye and hair colour is genetically influenced. Genetic inheritance can also result in children inheriting conditions that hinder their physical development (e.g. asthma). In the Second World War era Sheldon (1940) proposed a widely accepted classification of physical type:

- *Endomorphs* have a rounded, soft body with short arms and legs.
- *Mesomorphs* have hard, firm, upright bodies, with highly developed muscles.
- *Ectomorphs* have thin, underdeveloped bodies with little muscle and fat.

Humans are genetically predisposed to fit in one of these groups. It used to be widely assumed that hereditary components were largely responsible for many physical and character traits and that there was very little a person could do to change this. Today, a more sophisticated approach is recognised and while we cannot 'reinvent ourselves' environmental factors are now considered very influential on our eventual level of physical skills and the final definition of a person's character.

Maturation

Maturation is the name given for the *rate* at which we develop physically. Maturation is genetically influenced. Papalia *et al.*, (2006: 13) refers to maturation as the 'unfolding of a natural sequence of physical and behavioural changes, including the readiness to master new abilities'.

Certain behaviours in children cannot be achieved because they are not maturationally ready – for instance, you cannot toilet train an 8-month-old because the body has not matured sufficiently. All people pass through the same stages in maturation in a certain order. For instance, walking occurs before running. Children do not, however, mature at the same rate due to their maturation level and their genetic make-up (Davenport, 2001: 4). The influence of maturation in physical development is a matter of some debate. Papalia *et al.*, (2006) argue that seeing all motor development as a result of brain development is simplistic and seek to explain rather that it should be viewed as a process of continual development between the brain (maturation) and environmental factors such as the child's motivation to achieve a physical milestone and the opportunities it has to explore and practise skills. Bertram and Pascal (2006) note that to understand development theorists must look beyond biological explanations and realise that learning is significantly influenced by individual social and cultural experiences.

Poverty

Poverty has a negative effect on a child's holistic outlook and this includes physical development. It is difficult to think of the UK as a country that still experiences significant levels of poverty. However, Bertram and Pascal (2006) note that in comparison with other developed countries, England continues to experience high levels of poverty. They go on to assert that poverty is the single most damaging influence on a child's life and is associated with a range of negative factors connected to child development. Poverty, for example, might result in conditions like poor, damp housing which in turn acts a trigger for children genetically disposed to certain conditions (Beaver *et al.*, 1999: 130). A child placed in inadequate housing might develop asthma. Poverty might also result in a mother experiencing poor levels of nutrition during pregnancy which places a child at a disadvantage even before it is born. Smoking and drinking too much alcohol and caffeine are found to be more prevalent among poorer sections of society and this can potentially influence the health of a child (David *et al.*, 2003). Ennal's report (2004) for the National Children's Bureau on child poverty makes for depressing reading. This reveals that the UK has the fourth largest economy in the world and yet one of the highest levels of child poverty of all industrialised countries. Children born into poverty have a lower birth weight, higher infant mortality and poorer health. Higher stress levels, less access to transport facilities, less stimulating environments and less help with bringing up the children reduce the young's capacity to learn both physically and academically. Moreover, poor families are more likely to have a disabled child or one with social and emotional needs.

Nutrition

Poor nutrition is also linked to poverty and is one of its consequences. However, diet has been a topical issue in schools for the past few years and will therefore be discussed separately.

Good nutrition aids growth. Nutrition has also been linked to global development in children. Malnutrition can have disastrous consequences for a young child. Gallahue and Ozmun (2006) note that if severe malnutrition occurs during the first four years of life a child not only never recovers the growth norms for its age range but also fails to catch up in its mental and physical development because of harmful effects on the brain. Bukato and Daehler (2004) discuss how nutritional depravation can influence development at many different levels. These authors state that possible consequences include more frequent and severe illness, delayed growth, slower motor skill development as well as lower intellectual development. While the UK does not see diseases associated with severe malnutrition (e.g. Kwashiorkor), the effect of diet on the global development of a child remains a concern. It is argued that poor nutrition can lead to poor cognitive development and hindered progress at school. David et al. (2003) discuss findings about the inadequacy of the fruit intake of young children and emphasises the effect on cognitive development, particularly in boys.

Obesity concerns

In the past few years there has been a growing awareness and recognition of rising levels of obesity in children. The causes for this seem to be wide-ranging. It would appear that children are participating in less exercise out of school hours. With an increase in concern about the safety of children they are less likely to play outside where parents cannot monitor them. This trend has been accompanied by a shift in the type of 'play' activities in which a child might engage. Physically passive pastimes like watching television or playing computer games are now the likely choice of many young people. Children have also experienced changing eating habits. Consuming processed food with high sugar, fat and salt content encourages already physically inactive children to put on weight. Obesity statistics show that its prevalence in children aged 2–10 years rose from 9.9 per cent to 14.3 per cent between 1995 and 2004. Without preventive action it is estimated that one in five children will be obese by the year 2010 (DoH, 2006).

The problems caused by a poor diet have been recognised by central government and they have sought to deal with it through a variety of responses. With Every Child Matters (DfES, 2003b) naming one of its five main outcomes as 'being healthy', this has firmly pushed food choices to the fore. The *Healthy Living Blueprint for Schools* (DfES, 2004) sets out its vision for how children should be taught about nutritional choices, in particular, promoting the availability of fresh water in schools and encouraging children to access this via water bottles and water coolers. It stated that all 4–6-year-olds should be eligible for a free piece of fruit per day. It encouraged the provision of a healthy diet through school meals provided at lunchtimes and at breakfast clubs. Schools can now 'prove' their commitment to becoming 'healthy' by being awarded the National Healthy Schools Standard once they have provided evidence of the provision of certain criteria, which include promoting healthy eating. Half of all schools were targeted to achieve this by 2006 with the rest working towards this status by 2009 (DoH, 2005).

OFSTED (2006) evaluated the effectiveness of the responses to these initiatives. It found that primary schools are more successfully educating their children to make informed decisions about their food choices and that efforts have been made, through the promotion of healthy school dinners, to influence the diet of children. The best schools have a 'whole school food policy' that has been formulated via consultation with the whole school community, including pupils and parents. So far, it would appear that primary schools are achieving more success than secondary schools when educating their children about nutrition.

Reflective Tasks

Healthy eating

Healthy Eating in School (OFSTED, 2006) advocates promoting healthy eating to young children through a planned approach using a whole range of curriculum subjects.

Level 1

- What are the key features of a healthy diet that children need to consider?

Level 2

- Think of some ways in which you could teach children to make healthy choices through different key areas of the Early Years Foundation Stage (Knowledge and Understanding of the World, Personal, Social and Emotional Development, etc.) and National Curriculum subjects, e.g. history, geography, art, PSHE.

Level 3

- How can does your setting encourage children to learn about healthy foods through structured play?

Social and emotional factors

The Birth to Three Matters (DfES, 2003a) documentation and the subsequent Early Years Foundation Stage Framework (DfES, 2007) both stress the importance of good emotional health promoted by strong attachments to trusted and caring adults – the feeling of 'being special' to particular adults is paramount in the development of the whole child. For a child to develop physically as well as socially and intellectually there is the overriding need for emotional security and the development of 'resilience'. Indeed, such is the importance of emotional stability it would appear that some children can be provided with an adequately nutritional diet but can fail to grow; this is commonly called *non-organic failure to thrive syndrome*. The causes of this syndrome are somewhat obscure but are sometimes thought to be due to poor emotional attachments, poor bonding experiences and low **self-esteem**. David *et al.* (2003) suggest that failure to thrive could even be indicative of abuse. Such an assertion, although a possibility, needs to be considered with caution and contemplation of a whole series of contributing factors.

Delayed physical development

Macfadyen and Osbourne (2000: 143) assert that children with average physical abilities are accepted and have more status than those who underachieve. They note that children with better motor skills are likely to have positive peer relations. Gallahue and Ozmun (2006: 285) state that both boys and girls place great value on competence in physical activities, and this is an essential factor in their global self-esteem. It is certainly easy to recall anecdotal evidence of children giving a high value to their peers who were good at 'football' or always chosen for team games. Adults certainly do not forget the pain and humiliation of being the last to be chosen due to some misguided individual allowing children to pick teams for sports activities. Those children with noticeably lower physical skills entering new schools may lack confidence or have more difficulty making friends. Furthermore, David *et al.* (2003) suggest that delayed physical development has even wider implications. Physical development not only determines movement but can have ramifications for the 'wiring' of the brain. Babies who can explore feel safe in locations as they are able to make 'mental maps' of the places they go – those children who cannot do this do not make these connections. Children who cannot move easily may not be able to access sensory and stimulating materials available to others in a nursery situation. In addition, those who cannot move independently may develop perceptual difficulties as a consequence and this may influence their educational progress.

Case Study

Hyper-mobility

Reaching, or not, reaching milestones in physical development can influence the manner in which people respond to and communicate with children. Three-year-old Grace had recently been diagnosed with hyper-mobility in her joints. This resulted in increased movement, particularly in her ankles, wrists and hips. Grace had been 'slow' to walk, but when she did achieve this milestone she walked short distances with 'gusto' but found longer distance much more difficult. She was then slow to run and at 3 she was achieving a fast 'canter', not a fully flexed running movement. Grace demonstrated rather confusing physical development. She could walk and also ride a bike with great ease. She could not, however, skip (although she could gallop and jump) or hop and often fell over for 'no apparent reason'. These symptoms prompted Grace's mother to seek medical help and she was diagnosed with over mobile joints. Grace's mother tried to encourage her daughter as much as possible but found that Grace tired easily and sometimes relied on a pushchair or had to be carried more frequently. During routine trips out, she noticed the variety of comments her daughter received. If in a pushchair, Grace was often completely overlooked by adults or perceived as younger than her peer group. When Grace started to ride her bike she received comments like 'Gosh! she's a clever girl'. Grace found that using a toy pushchair with a toy in it helped her when walking. When she did this people would often pass comment such as 'hasn't Grace grown' or 'she'll be ready for school soon'.

Reflective Tasks

Providing an inclusive environment

Level 1

Consider why it is important to provide an inclusive environment.

Locate relevant information on inclusion in the Early Years Foundation Stage documentation (DfES, 2007) and read what they have to say about inclusion.

- What sorts of observations would you undertake to find out about inclusion in a setting?

Level 2

Observe the children in your care and note those who have less developed physical skills than others. Ask a colleague to observe you interacting with these children and focus on these questions:

- How do you communicate with children of the same age but with different physical skills?
- Do your interactions change or do you treat all children equally?

Level 3

As a setting, discuss how you would plan for a child who had severely impaired physical development.

- How could you try to ensure that their experience in your setting was on a par with others in the group?

Physical development in a nursery environment: indoor provision

Physical development is often associated with the outdoor environment in an educational setting. It is, however, important to provide indoor opportunities for the development of both fine and gross motor skills.

Gross motor development

Gross motor development can be catered for in an indoor space by careful planning and a little creativity. Most important is the availability of unoccupied space where children can move freely. Greenland (2006: 163) discusses the relevance of providing such space as this helps develop senses connected to movement. The 'proprioceptive' sense relates to the position of our body parts in relation to one another and the 'vestibular' sense promotes movement and its relationship to the ground. These senses are developed through the use of floor play where children spend time in contact with the ground, belly crawling, crawling, pushing, pulling, spinning and falling. This need might be catered for by decreasing the amount of table-top activities available. Greenland discusses how nurseries have placed some of their activities on the floor so that children are in contact with it while they pursue tasks. Roopnarine and Johnson (2005) state that indoor settings must be designed for movement and that climbing, running, standing and jumping are as as equally important as sitting – a lack of opportunity to move results in behavioural problems as children seek to express themselves. Wetton (1997) discusses the regrettable amount of physical play planned for in the home. Children, particularly boys, need to be able to practise their motor skills in an unstructured manner during periods of free play – they need the opportunity to participate in 'rough and tumble' activities in a safe environment. Physical play of this nature can often be confused with 'bad behaviour' in young children and can be accompanied with comments like 'don't be rough', or 'sit still'. Children of this age find it easy to switch from high spirited ventures to calmer occupations and both states should be catered for. A nursery environment that is characterised by children sitting around tables quietly involved in activities may, at first, appear very orderly but might not be offering the most suitable learning activities.

Dance activities also promote gross motor skills and coordination. Early dance is an excellent way for children to be able to express themselves and show their understanding of stories to illustrate their imaginative creations; allowing children to express themselves through dance also enables them to access other areas of the Early Years Foundation Stage curriculum (DfES, 2007). Dance movement promotes the proprioceptive and the vestibular senses. Dance is also a good way for children to experience the joy of just moving their bodies and of thinking only about the present, not the past or what they are doing next. In busy, stimulating environments it is good to get children just thinking about movement for movement's sake. This sentiment echoes some of the principles of the Alexander Technique, a movement scheme that was developed by F.M. Alexander 1869–1955. He focused on body alignment, poise, balance, coordination and the connection of the body and the mind. The Alexander Technique has also been promoted in schools to help children with their posture while sitting and to prevent them from collapsing over the desk when working, or from holding a pencil incorrectly (Merry, 2000). Sharing dances with appreciative adults has beneficial effects on a child's self-esteem and shows that their expression of thought is appreciated and valued. Including props such as scarves and ribbons which a child can wave or flick, can have the added bonus of encouraging a child's eye and hand coordination – a vital ingredient that is required for early letter formation (Tassoni, 2002).

Fine motor skills

There are numerous activities that can be planned for the development of fine motor skills. Ideas can be taken from the diverse breadth of play opportunities, and might include such activities as painting, sewing, threading beads, picking out small objects from treasure baskets, picking up and gluing sequins to collages, manipulating play dough into shapes, bursting spare bubble wrap, dressing dolls and teddies in clothes and fastening their buttons, and early mark-making.

Case Study

Bead-threading

Jack was participating in a bead-threading activity. Jack and student teacher, Kerry, were making necklaces for the bears in the role play corner. Both Jack and Kerry sat together and made their own necklaces. Discussion ensued as to how to tie a knot at the end of their thread so the beads might not fall off; Jack had a go at tying a knot and then was aided by Kerry. Jack and Kerry discussed the variety and shape of beads on offer; they also talked about the colours of the beads they threaded. Some beads had fairly big holes by which they could be attached; smaller beads were more difficult to thread and it took some perseverance on Jack's part in order to succeed.

Towards the end of the activity Kerry counted her beads on her necklace, and then they both counted Jack's creation. Kerry had also threaded her beads in a sequence of repeated colours – they spent time talking about the pattern she had made. When the necklaces were finished they took them to the bears in the role play corner and tied them on. Jack talked about where the bears might be going in order to show off their necklaces. He then proceeded to dress up the teddies in clothes, getting them ready for their trip.

Reflective Tasks

Fine motor skills

Consider the Case Study above.

Level 1

This activity develops Jack's fine motor skills and hand–eye coordination.

- What other skills were also being enhanced here?
- How could the activity be further extended?
- Why did Kerry sit and make her own bead necklace?

Level 2

- What activities do you use with the children in your care to develop fine motor skills and hand–eye coordination?
- What other skills do these activities develop?
- How else can you develop fine motor skills?

Level 3

As a staff, decide all the different ways you can develop fine motor skills and hand–eye coordination in your setting.

- How can observation help you identify the skills the children currently have?
- Is there a development in the skills through your setting?
- How could you further support the development of fine motor skills?

Case Study

Baking

Amy and her play worker were baking. Amy thoroughly enjoyed baking and particularly looked forward to the activity. The first job for Amy was to place cake cups in the cake tray – separating the cake cups was tricky. Amy helped to spoon the sugar and butter into a mixing bowl taking care to try not to spill the sugar. She was then allowed to crack the egg and break it in the bowl – this was one of the best bits of the whole task! Amy helped to mix up the ingredients with a wooden spoon – she commented that this made her arm ache. Next, she helped to measure out two spoonfuls of water and finally she carefully added the flour. The mixture was given a final stir, and then Amy helped to spoon the cake mixture into the waiting cake cups. When the cakes had cooked and cooled Amy helped to ice them by spreading icing over the tops. Finally, using currants and other dried fruits, Amy had to make faces on the cakes.

Reflective Tasks

Developing fine and gross motor skills

Consider the Case Study above.

Level 1

Identify all the fine and gross motor skills this activity used. What other cross-curricular skills were being developed here?

Level 2

Identify all the fine and gross motor skills this activity used. What other cross-curricular skills were being developed here? Make a studied observation and assessment of the fine and gross motor skills of a child in your care. Think and plan how this child's development could be further progressed in this area.

Level 3

As a staff, observe how children use the equipment in your setting over a week. Think how you could further develop these activities to promote fine and gross motor skills. Are there any other resources or activities that you could use to develop fine and gross motor skills?

Physical development and outdoor play

It is of paramount importance that children have a chance to access quality play in an outdoor space. Experiences of childhood have changed, and are still changing, from previous expectations of growing up. In the past children had much more opportunity to play outside and in this way they had a chance to strengthen their muscles, gain stamina and challenge themselves by taking calculated risks like climbing trees, crawling through scratchy bushes, leaping over obstacles and racing on bikes with friends. This type of outdoor play provided the opportunity to build confidence both physically and mentally. As already stated in the section on obesity, children are not spending so much time outdoors. Some children do not have gardens but even if an outdoor space is available it might not be suitable for a 3-year-old. As Edgington and Titchmarsh (2002: 9) state, gardens are changing their purpose and might not be child-oriented. Gardens, although very attractive, might have an adult purpose rather than being a large open space that children can run in. The increasingly common gravelled areas of specially designed gardens might look enormously tempting to young children offering numerous opportunities for them to dig, touch, bury things, etc. This activity, however, might be met with comments like 'don't touch the gravel, don't touch the garden ornaments, don't touch the pot plants'.

Furthermore, green spaces have been commandeered in favour of the different parts to a garden that render them unsuitable for riding a scooter around, or pitching a play house on. Gardens are becoming ascetically pleasing spaces to be in and are seen as another 'room' in the house; they may not, however, provide exciting spaces from the child's viewpoint. As a result, it is crucial that nurseries and Foundation Stage settings understand the importance of providing outdoor spaces.

Outdoor provision and physical development

Provision needs to be made for children to develop control of different parts of their bodies and this can be achieved by carefully organising the outdoor space (Edgington and Titchmarsh, 2002: 19).

Outdoor spaces equipped with play apparatus like climbing frames, ropes, slides and swings encourage the use of large muscles and gross motor skills. In the past few years there has been an emphasis on providing equipment in schools and nurseries akin to apparatus that might be found in a play park; this is often referred to as fixed equipment. The installation of fixed equipment can look very attractive to prospective parents and children looking around an educational establishment and provides the 'wow' factor. This kind of apparatus plays an important role in providing physical opportunities to children in ways that are probably not possible indoors. It also offers challenge to children as a place where they can take risks and stretch themselves. Fixed apparatus, however, does possess potential disadvantages. It can be extremely costly and take up a lot of space – nurseries and schools have to question the value of letting one piece of equipment dominate a small outdoor area (Edgington and Titchmarsh, 2002). Safety aspects also need to be considered; the provision of an appropriate floor material like bark deep enough to meet specific safety legislation needs to be purchased. Bilton (2002: 39) argues that this kind of equipment offers only limited play choices for children and that it provides no opportunity for change. She also suggests that fixed apparatus encourages 'competitive' rather than cooperative play options. She advocates that the best kind of equipment of this size should be able to have attachments made to it so that the children can maximise the possible play opportunities. Physical challenge of this nature can be provided by alternative, less costly, flexible solutions like planks, boxes, tyres, ropes and A-frames (Bilton, 2002). If fixed equipment is purchased, Drake (2005: 78) advocates utilising it with an imaginative approach. For instance, she discusses reading stories and then incorporating the equipment for the children to re-enact an event. In this manner the climbing fame might be used as an imaginary mountain, or balancing on the rope bridge over an imaginary stream.

Large apparatus should not be the only type of outdoor equipment that offers physical challenge to children. The availability of bikes and wheeled toys provides the chance to improve coordination and balance; these toys should be given their own distinct space where they can be used to their full potential but avoid interrupting other types of play (see Picture 3.4). There should also be smaller equipment like hoops, soft balls and beanbags that can be thrown between children or at suitable targets in order to develop the skills necessary for proficient throwing and catching. In addition, there should be free space where children can simply run around and raise their heartbeat (Edgington and Titchmarsh, 2002: 13).

Decisions need to be made about the availability and access to the outdoor space. Lindon (2005: 134) discusses the effects of limiting time spent in this area to one distinct period in the day. When 'playtime' does then occur, children tend to choose outside options over all other available indoor activities resulting in short bursts of extremely energetic play. Conversely, unlimited access to outdoor space at all times has the effect of children playing calmly and being less boisterous. Lindon observes that the free flow of children between outdoor and indoor activities results in more equal use of all the equipment on offer in the nursery.

Picture 3.4 Developing gross motor skills on the tricycle
Source: Jennie Woodcock/Reflections Photolibrary/Corbis

The outdoor classroom

It is important to be aware that outdoor space should not be seen as an area that is used for physical activity alone. The outdoor space connected to a nursery or school can be used to explore all areas of the curriculum. In addition, physical development cannot be viewed and discussed in isolation. Activities principally designed to encourage other curriculum areas may incidentally promote physical skills as well.

Physical development and the National Curriculum

As children leave nursery settings to enter infant school, physical development and its stimulation is largely taught in specific PE lessons, the content of which is determined by the National Curriculum (DfEE, 1999) and early learning goals in the Early Years Foundation Stage (DfES, 2007). Over the past 10 years raising standards in literacy and numeracy has dominated the world of education. Emphasis on the importance of physical development has been muted. Success in schools and early education has been increasingly measured in terms of early academic achievement. Lindon (2005: 132) tracks the profile of physical development arguing that the task of early years settings in the UK has come to be defined as academically preparing children for school, or more specifically, not to fail in school. Standard Attainment Tests (SATs) administered in Year 2 (or at 7 years of age) to assess performance in literacy and numeracy further increase the importance of these subjects. Physical development in children has been somewhat taken for granted and, until recently, has been forced to take a back seat while literacy and numeracy remained at centre stage. Schools have passed through some 'drought' years where the importance and benefits of physical education have not been lauded.

Very gradually, concerns about the fitness and health of the younger generation have caused the physical aspects of education to receive renewed and long-awaited recognition. Government green papers, like *Every Child Matters* (DfES, 2003b), which has proposed 'staying healthy' as one of its five central tenets, have helped physical development be acknowledged as just as important as any other curriculum area. Moreover, it is now being argued that encouragement of physical skills has a knock-on benefit for those sought-after academic developments. Edgington and Titchmarsh (2002: 8) state that developed physical strength gives a sense of physical well-being. They then proceed to argue that outdoor exercise encourages control over the limbs which, in turn, not only helps areas like kicking balls but also using pencils and scissors accurately. In addition, Bilton (2002) asserts that children need the experience of large muscle movement as these muscles develop before smaller ones, so children need to be able to experience swinging from a bar or digging in the garden to strengthen arm muscles as this will enable smaller muscles to be used when drawing or writing. Finally, Bruce (2004: 104) asserts that the development of learning is 'hindered' and even 'damaged' if young children are placed in classrooms that require numerous paper and pencil exercises and long periods of sitting still. For young children, sitting still may be the hardest action for them to achieve. Pupils need sufficient time, space and planned opportunities during which they can explore and develop their physical skills. Motor skills, it would seem, are the primary tools for learning (Goddard Blythe, 2005). Ultimately, a good education promotes 'whole child' development in which physical development shares an equal partnership with all other aspects of the curriculum.

The following sections discuss the progression of physical skills within the context of dance, gymnastics and games activities.

The emergence of dance

The outcomes that most relate to dance in the Early Years Foundation Stage framework (DfES, 2007) are that children should:

- move with confidence, imagination and in safety;
- move with control and coordination;
- show awareness of space, of themselves and of others.

By the end of Key Stage 1, the National Curriculum (DfEE, 1999) requires children in dance to:

- use movement imaginatively, responding to stimuli, including music and performing basic skills;
- change the rhythm, speed, level and direction of their movements;
- create and perform dances using simple movement patterns including those from different times and cultures;
- express and communicate ideas and feelings.

Dance lessons in schools can be a joyous and uplifting experience which should re-energise and stimulate children. There are many benefits to be gained from children participating in dance lessons in schools as opposed to the early forms of dance discussed in the section on nursery education. For infant children dance provides a vital non-verbal form of expression. For pupils who find literacy difficult or for young children who are learning to write, dance can free them from the struggle to record their thoughts symbolically in favour of communicating meaning with their bodies. Success in dance can have a direct, positive influence on self-esteem and self-confidence. Those children who excel creatively will be stimulated and motivated by this part of the curriculum; this confidence might then, in turn, help in areas in which they are not so strong. This area of the curriculum also aids social development. Formulating a dance in groups or pairs requires communication, discussion, planning, organisation, compromise and decision-making.

Finally, as well as improving general fitness, dance helps children to coordinate and control their bodies and posture in an increasingly refined and masterful manner. Here physical development is progressed from the nursery experience as the children are required to produce more exact and controlled movement patterns.

The above explanation gives a small indication of how important dance is in the curriculum. Unfortunately the experience of dance in the primary school can be variable. Dance can be viewed as a 'difficult' subject to deliver and some teachers lack enthusiasm for this area. Dance can be associated with specialist techniques which teachers feel unable to replicate in schools adequately. Practitioners can lack confidence and creative 'ideas' when planning lessons. In addition, as Wetton (1997: 118) argues, dance requires creativity, imagination and ascetic responses to stimuli. She points out that it is difficult to 'conjure' this up at an appointed time prescribed by the school's timetable – a cold Monday morning 9.00 am slot in the hall may not be the best time to inspire and motivate both teachers and children. The problems of teaching dance have been recognised by both educationalists and publishers and as a result there is a plethora of information and ready-made 'dance programmes' that can be implemented in schools. This book does not serve the purpose of a 'dance manual' but the next few paragraphs do attempt to explain features that should be considered when approaching dance lessons in school in relation to physical development.

Thematic approaches

The best dance lessons revolve around a well-chosen and correctly pitched theme; the theme provides useful 'hooks' on which to base the movement ideas. Themes chosen for younger children should be within their own context and experience so that they can understand them and can work from this starting point. Taking traditional stories like 'The Three Little Pigs' can provide a ready-made structure for a dance lesson. A practitioner who knows their class, their likes and dislikes, can use this information to pick a theme that will stimulate the imagination of their children. A theme that reflects the work or 'topic' being carried out in class can also give satisfying results and allows children to interpret their topic in a creative way. Published materials that give ideas on dance lessons can be adapted to meet the needs of a particular class. The least satisfying lessons can result from following a selection of ready-made lessons that are delivered in a manner that is out of context to the children and the school and does not take account of the needs and progression of the class.

Once a theme for a series of lessons has been settled upon it is useful to introduce this through the use of visual materials. Imagination needs to be triggered in dance just as it would in any other curriculum area. This might be achieved through the use of story, music or showing the children some pictures of the theme and discussing it. This might even be tackled via film clips or viewing dances made by others. The important issue here is that children are supplied with materials that trigger ideas, discussion and enthusiasm.

Planning

A dance lesson should be well planned; too often lessons fall down at this stage. Plans can lack enough content to keep children learning and progressing. For beginning practitioners, sectioning a lesson into 5–10 minute components can produce a more structured and compelling plan which teachers feel confident in delivering. The plan should consider four distinct parts to the lesson: warm up, skills development, dance climax and cool down. The plan should adequately consider assessment in relation to the progression of physical skills. For dance lessons to be of worth at the end of a year a teacher has to be able to express how a child has improved and progressed in their physical capability and in the control of their bodies.

The warm up

This is a vital part of the lesson which physically and mentally prepares a child for what is to come. The warm up should reflect the overall theme of the lesson. The warm up should not exist as something that is separate to the rest of the lesson but as a time when the children are introduced to the theme for study while they are warming their bodies up. A dance warm up should allow the children to focus on all parts of their body in different ways and should improve their body awareness. This is a time to think only about what their bodies can do and enjoy experimenting with movement. One of the keys to encouraging this depends on a teacher's awareness of language. Asking the children to crawl, shake, slither, slide, jump, hop, knock, shimmy, roll, stride, skip, stretch, bounce, rock, shuffle, creep, tap, scuttle, swish, soar, tumble, glide, crash, bang, stamp, march, point, wiggle, nod, shadow, crouch, jog, gallop, leap, drift, dart, shudder or swoop will help young pupils to move all their body parts.

Skills development

This critical part of the lesson is about allowing children to develop an expressive movement vocabulary; this can often be overlooked and undervalued. A common mistake made is to spend too little time on this area, then for a teacher to play some music which they wish children to interpret. Disappointment usually follows as the children just do not have enough ideas to work on in order to produce something of worth. When children are writing a story practitioners give much input into story structure, character development and vocabulary choices before expecting children to produce a story of worth. In dance, educators need to provide the same sort of input before expecting the children to perform simple sequences of movement. This is the part of the lesson where movement interpretation is introduced and improved upon. Young children need time to experiment with and work on different methods of controlling their bodies. For instance, if a class were working on a theme of 'winter' they might spend time producing movements that could consist of curling and rolling to represent a snowball, twisting or spinning to represent winds, swaying, drifting to represent breeze, a leaping, stretched movement to represent crashing thunder. During this time there should be an opportunity to reflect on their ideas and view others in order that movement is improved and executed with refined skill.

Dance climax

This is the part of the lesson where children take their movement ideas and put them together into sequences of movement. Young children do not have to create 'group dances' as this can be too complex. However, connecting individual moves and performing them to their peers should be an enjoyable and satisfying climax to the lesson. The opportunity to show their classmates and teacher their movement sequences is essential as it gives status to their work. At this point children also learn the skills of evaluation and constructive criticism so that movement can be further improved.

Cool down

It is important to allow time for a proper cool down. This part of the lesson is where children know that the session is ending and they are to return to the classroom. A cool down will prepare the body physically and mentally for the next period of learning.

Case Study

A dance lesson

Read the following exemplar of a dance lesson with a class of 6–7-year-olds.

Class 1 were undertaking a dance class studying traditional dances from the British Isles. This session was the first in a series of six lessons looking at dance of this kind. The first activity of the lesson involved the children counting to eight while walking, running, jogging and skipping to the counts. Extra time was dedicated to skipping and encouragement was given to the children to draw up their knees. The class then started to listen to some traditional folk music and clapping to the beat. Next, they participated in a variety of movements that encouraged the children to move in time to the music. Initially, the children had to click their fingers for eight beats, march for eight beats, pat their thighs for eight beats and then skip for eight beats. The class then had to repeat this exercise but make sure they clapped on count eight of each type of movement.

The lesson then progressed to study some generic movements related to traditional dancing. The children learnt how to perform a cross-hand swing (a pair of children cross their arms and hold hands, they then swing around in a clockwise direction for eight beats), a promenade (a pair of children join together with crossed hands and turn to face the front of the room, they walk forwards for eight), a do-si-do (partners face each other and travel around the opposite person passing right shoulders, maintaining a back-to-back stance and returning to face each other again) and a star (travel around in a clockwise direction with your right hand in the air with one or more people, repeat in an anticlockwise direction using your left hand).

The children were then asked to work in pairs and put the movements they had learnt all together in eight-bar phrases. The children were asked to choose three of the movements learnt in class and join them to another eight-bar phrase that they had made up by themselves. The children were given 10 minutes to do this. After five minutes the teacher played music to let them practise their sequences. The class were then split in half and the children were asked to perform to each other. The audience were each asked to watch one particular pair of children dancing and then identify one movement they enjoyed about the dancing and one feature that could be improved.

At the end of the class the children participated in gentle stretches, curling and uncurling exercises. The children finished by lying on the floor. They were asked to identify the best part of the lesson and how they could further improve their dances during the next session.

Reflective Tasks

A dance lesson

Level 1

- How does the lesson in the Case Study above encourage dance skills and physical development?
- How has the physical requirement progressed from early childhood?
- Consider what might be effective about this dance lesson.
- Consider how it might be improved.

Level 2

- How would you evaluate this lesson?
- How would you assess individual children's development against the assessment criteria for Physical Development?
- How would you progress the development in the next lesson?
- How will the pupils' motor skills be further developed?

Level 3

Consider the use of traditional dances to develop physical skills.

- Why is traditional dance such an effective form of movement to use with young children?
- How might traditional dance be related to elements of play?
- How could you incorporate traditional dance into your setting?
- How would you evaluate its effectiveness?

The emergence of gymnastics activities

It might be easy to question why gymnastics appears in the National Curriculum when very few people see their careers as gymnasts or carry out gymnastics in their adult life. This form of exercise, however, can have noticeable benefits for young children. The principle benefit of gymnastics is to promote body control and flexibility, to encourage muscle tone and to increase stamina. Wetton (1996) argues that gymnastics encourages children to acquire various physical qualities which will enable them to meet the challenges of the environment in which they live. Manners and Carroll (1995), in their discussion of gymnastics, suggest that up until the age of 6 the more exercise the body gets, the thicker the layer of cartilage in the joints which, in turn, protects against injury. Gymnastics also correlates with dance in that it increases body awareness in children; it, too, can also promote social interaction through the planning and performing of sequences of movement.

The outcomes that most relate to gymnastics in the Early Years Foundation Stage document (DfES, 2007) are that children should:

- move with confidence, imagination and in safety;
- move with control and coordination;
- travel around, under, over and through balancing and climbing equipment;
- show awareness of space, of themselves and of others;
- use a range of large and small equipment.

By the end of Key Stage 1, the National Curriculum (DfEE, 1999) requires children in gymnastics to:

- perform basic skills in travelling, being still, finding space and using it safely, both on the floor and using apparatus;
- develop the range of their skills and actions;
- choose and link skills and actions in short movement phrases;
- create and perform short, linked sequences that show clear beginnings, middles and ends and have contrasts in direction, level and speed.

Planning for gymnastics

Good gymnastics lessons are well planned and prepared. As with dance, a gymnastics lesson has a warm-up section, skills development section (floor work), an apparatus section, an opportunity to perform skills and a cool-down period. Gymnastic lessons need to follow well-chosen themes, which might include rolling, jumping, flight, turning, balancing, running, travelling, weight transference, bouncing, rocking, curling or stretching to name but a few. The emphasis in a good lesson will be on encouraging children to be imaginative in the way they use their bodies and enabling them to demonstrate their skills progression by increasing the complexity of the movements. Most importantly, children should be required to refine and improve the execution of moves. Improvement of physical skills is achieved only by letting children perform their moves to their peers and teacher and receiving good quality, well-timed verbal intervention. Infant lessons that are effective also provide challenging, open-ended tasks that *'all'* children can respond to at their own level of physical skill (Manners and Carroll, 1995).

Apparatus

Gymnastic skills that are initiated on the floor should be extended and developed through the use of apparatus. Apparatus increases the number of possible options children can utilise in order to develop challenging movement sequences. As such, apparatus should always be viewed as an extension of floor movement, not something that is investigated as a separate learning opportunity. Apparatus should normally follow floor work in any one lesson, but due to the practicalities of the school timetable, and the time-consuming aspect of getting out equipment, it is often used in a dedicated 'apparatus' lesson. It is therefore important that medium-term planning shows how floor work tackled earlier in the term is to be developed on the apparatus. Practitioners are often apprehensive about using apparatus with young children due to health and safety reasons. As long as these types of lessons are carefully planned, the equipment is the right height for small children and in good condition, potential for accidents is minimised. Children need to be able to take risks, challenge themselves and explore their physical capabilities in order to extend and flex muscle. Apparatus provides the extension of the 'rough and tumble' nursery play and allows young people to take controlled risks – it is a vital part of the curriculum.

The emergence of games activities

Structured games lessons in schools provide a further opportunity to build strength and stamina as well as allowing children to control their bodies and develop muscle tone. Games also encourage a child's moral and social development by requiring them to participate eventually in team games and to understand how to conduct themselves as a good 'sports person'.

The Early Years Foundation Stage (DfES, 2007) statements that are most relevant to this aspect of physical education are:

- move with control and coordination;
- show awareness of space, of themselves and of others;
- use a range of large and small equipment;
- recognise the changes that happen to their body when they are active.

At the end of Key Stage 1, the National Curriculum (DfEE, 1999) requires children to be able to:

- travel with, send and receive a ball and other equipment in different ways;

- develop these skills for simple net, striking/fielding and invasion type games;
- play simple, competitive net, striking/fielding and invasion type games that they and other have made, using simple tactics for attacking and defending.

Effective games teaching

Wetton (1996) comments on the apprehension of practitioners when delivering games lessons; she notes that they often 'fear' this area of the curriculum as they might teach in a way that is deemed 'old fashioned' or that a technique might be incorrectly explained. This leads some professionals to avoid PE situations in which they might not feel confident. Wetton argues that while subject knowledge is indeed important, it is subordinate to the need to ensure that children gain sufficient access to games education. With children spending more time inside it is vital that they are provided with physical education experiences that preferably take place outdoors in the fresh air. Macfadyen and Osbourne (2000) also note feelings of inadequacy but suggest effective practice consists predominantly of setting up situations where all pupils are provided with the opportunity to 'have a go' and then to assess how well they are achieving a skill. As in other areas of the curriculum, the practitioner should be adept at choosing the correct place for analysis and intervention in order to facilitate in the progression of physical skills.

Early years games activities should focus on those that encourage the refinement of motor skills in sending objects in a variety of ways as well as retrieving them. Macfadyen and Osbourne (2000) encourage the lesson emphasis to be on self-improvement and problem-solving rather than on pupils winning or being 'better' than a classmate. They suggest that motor skills might be performed in predictable, unchanging situations that focus on the exploration of equipment as well as the acquisition of skills, e.g. rolling a ball towards a target. Challenge is provided by decreasing target size or increasing distance. In these lessons emphasis is placed upon individualised learning situations rather than group work. Formative assessment and planning to meet the needs of the children is of paramount importance. Hopper et al. (2000: 11) proposes that many infant children experience failure and frustration in games activities as practitioners begin teaching too far along the journey of a skill. For instance, practice in catching becomes a lesson on dropping and retrieving. It is easy for adults to forget how difficult it was to learn to dribble a football or catch a small ball. As children progress through Key Stage 1 exploration of equipment and skills development is still a focus although some paired work might be additionally anticipated. It is only as children reach the end of this Key Stage that small team games can be implemented (Hopper et al., 2000: 17). Young children do not have the physical strength or the conceptual understanding to participate in games that are exact replicas of adult versions. Fun, well-pitched games should be applied that centre on participation rather than on their outcome.

Summary

- → Physical development is the way in which children master control of their bodies.
- → Physical development is significant to learning as it enables children to be involved in active exploration.
- → Babies are born with involuntary reflexes and develop control over their movements with the development of the brain.
- → Gross motor skills develop according to a set sequence of activities which is easiest to remember as downwards and outwards.

➔ Locomotor skills are closely associated with gross motor skills but focus on movement from one place to another.

➔ The acquisition of fine motor development depends on growth, particularly bone development. The hand, wrist, ankle and foot have fewer bones at birth than in adulthood. Therefore fine motor development develops slightly later than gross motor development.

➔ Our genetic make-up can predispose us to certain characteristics and physical disposition, including some inherited conditions that hinder physical development.

➔ Social and cultural experiences also affect physical development, in addition to brain development.

➔ Poverty can have a detrimental effect on physical development and this includes poverty in the UK, not only in underdeveloped countries.

➔ Poor nutrition can affect physical development through both under-nourishment and through an inappropriate diet leading to obesity.

➔ There are possible links between poor physical development and extreme emotional insecurity.

➔ The learning environment indoors can promote fine motor, locomotor and gross motor skills if carefully planned and monitored.

➔ The outdoor environment should offer physical challenge to children and be equipped with resources that maximise play opportunities through being flexible in their use.

➔ Physical education is gaining more emphasis in schools due to recent concerns about children's health and the increase in obesity.

➔ PE lessons should have a clear structure, including warm-up activities, skills development, an opportunity to put the skills into practice and a cool down.

➔ Dance, gymnastics and games all need to be planned for appropriately according to the needs and stages of physical development of the children.

Key Questions

- How is early physical development affected by the development of the brain?
- What are gross motor skills, locomotor skills and fine motor skills?
- What are the factors that can adversely affect physical development? Are any of these preventable?
- How can the indoor learning environment be planned to promote all aspects of physical development?
- How can the outdoor environment be resourced to maximise children's play and maximise opportunities for the development of physical skills?
- What should a good PE lesson include?

References

Beaver, M., Brewster, J., Jones, P., Keene, A., Tallack, J. and Neaum, S. (1999) *Babies and Young Children. Book 1. Early Years Development.* Cheltenham: Stanley Thornes.

Bee, H. and Boyd, D. (2007) *The Developing Child.* New York: Pearson Education

Bertram, T. and Pascal, C. (2006) Introducing Child Development, in Bruce, T. (ed.) *Early Childhood: A Guide for Students.* London: Sage

Bilton, H. (2002) *Outdoor Play in the Early Years: Management and Innovation.* London: David Fulton.

Bruce, T. (2004) *Developing Learning in Early Childhood.* London: Sage

Bukato, D., and Daehler, M. (2004) *Child Development. A Thematic Approach.* New York: Houghton Mifflin

Davenport, G.C. (2001) *An Introduction to Child Development,* 2nd edn. London: Collins

David, T., Goouch, K., Powell, S. and Abbot, L. (2003) *Birth to Three Matters: A Review of the Literature.* Available from http://www.dfes.gov.uk/research/data/uploadfiles/RR444.pdf (accessed April 2007)

DfEE, (1999) *The National Curriculum. Handbook for primary teachers in England.* London: QCA

DfES (2003a) *Birth to Three Matters. A Framework to Support Children in their Earliest Years.* London: DfES

DfES (2003b) *Every Child Matters.* London: DfES

DfES (2004) *Healthy Living Blueprint for Schools.* Available from: http://publications.teachernet.gov.uk/eOrderingDownload/0781-2004.pdf (accessed March 2007)

DfES (2007) *Statutory Framework for the Early Years Foundation Stage: Setting the Standards for Learning, Development and Care for children from birth to five. Every Child Matters, Change for Children.* London: DfES

DoH (Department of Health) (2005) *National Healthy Schools Status. A Guide for Schools.* Available from: http://www.wiredforhealth.gov.uk/PDF/NHSS_A_Guide_for_Schools_10_05.pdf (accessed March 2007)

DoH (Department of Health) (2006) *Choosing Health: Obesity Bulletin Issue 1.* Available from: http://www.teachernet.gov.uk/_doc/9763/Department%20of%20Health%20-%20Obesity.pdf (accessed March 2007)

Drake, J. (2005) *Planning Children's Play and Learning in the Foundation Stage.* London: David Fulton

Edgington, M. and Titchmarsh, A. (2002) *The Great Outdoors: Developing Children's Learning Through Outdoor Provision.* London: Early Education

Ennals, P. (2004) *Child Poverty and Education.* Report for the National Children's Bureau Available from: http://pegasus.xssl.net/~admin315/assets/files/reports/Education_and_Child_Poverty.pdf (accessed May 2007)

Gallahue, D. and Ozmun, J. (2006) *Understanding Motor Development. Infants, Children, Adolescents, Adults, 6th edn.* New York: McGraw-Hill

Greenland, P. (2006). Physical Development, in Bruce, T. (ed.) *Early Childhood: A Guide for Students.* London: Sage

Goddard Blythe, S. (2005) *Releasing Intelligence Through Movement.* Available from: http://www.inpp.org.uk/intmovement.htm# (accessed May 2007)

Hopper, B., Grey, J. and Maude, T. (2000) *Teaching Physical Education in the Primary School.* London: Routledge Falmer

Hughes, L. (2002) *Paving Pathways. Child and Adolescent Development.* London: Wadsworth Thomson Learning

Johnston, J. (2007) 'How can we support the development of the skill of observation in young children?' Paper presented to the Australasian Science Education Association (ASERA) Conference, Freemantle, Western Australia, July 2007

Keenan, T. (2002) *An Introduction to Child Development.* London: Sage

Lindon, J. (2005) *Understanding Child Development. Linking Theory and Practice.* Abingdon: Hodder Arnold

Macfadyen, T. and Osbourne, M. (2000) Teaching Games, in Bailey, R. and Macfadyen, T. (eds) *Teaching Physical Education 5–11.* London: Continuum

Manners, H. and Carroll, M. (1995) *A Framework for Physical Education in the Early Years.* London: Falmer

Merry, S. (2000) *Education 2000. The Alexander Techniques for Children.* Available from: http://www.ed2k.org.uk/Ed2kindex.htm (accessed May 2007)

Nash, M. (1997) Fertile Minds. *Child Growth and Development,* 01/02, 24–8

OFSTED (2006) *Healthy Eating in Schools.* Available from: http://www.ofsted.gov.uk/publications/2625 (accessed January 2008)

Papalia, D., Olds, S. and Feldman, R. (2006) *A Child's World. Infancy through to Adolescence.* New York: McGraw-Hill

Roopnarine, J. and Johnson, J. (2005) *Approaches to Early Childhood Education.* Upper Saddle River, NJ: Pearson

Sheldon, W.H. (1940) *The Varieties of Human Physique. A Constitutional Psychology.* New York: Harper & Brothers.

Sheridan, M. (1997) *From Birth to Five Years: Children's Developmental Progress,* 4th edn. London: Routledge

Slater, A. and Lewis, M. (2002) *Introduction to infant development.* Oxford: Oxford University Press

Tassoni, P. (2002) *Planning for the Foundation Stage.* Oxford: Heinneman Child Care

Tassoni, P., Beith, K., Eldrige, A. and Gough, A. (2002) *Diploma in Childcare and Education.* Oxford: Heinneman Child Care

Wetton , P. (1996) *Physical Education in the Nursery and Infant School.* London: Routledge

Wetton, P. (1997) *Physical Education in the Early Years.* London: Routledge

Useful websites

Statutory Framework for the Early Years Foundation Stage; Setting the Standards for Learning, Development and Care for children from birth to five. Every Child Matters, Change for Children: www.standards.dfes.gov.uk/eyfs/resources/downloads/statutory-framework.pdf

Chapter 4

Cognitive Development

'A mind that is stretched by a new experience can never go back to its old dimensions'

Oliver Wendell Holmes (1809–1894)

Introduction

After a brief introduction to cognitive development and the brain, this chapter takes a chronological view of our understanding of cognition, starting with early philosophers and looking at current ideas. The chapter will begin by looking at the brain and the mind and, in particular, a child's mind, and will consider differences between a child's and, an adult's mind and mental processing. It will continue by looking at different cognitive theories and factors affecting cognitive development. Throughout it will provide examples of cognitive development in practice in children up to 8 years of age. By the end of the chapter, you should be in a better position to answer the question posed at the beginning of the first section 'What is cognitive development?'

Aims

→ To provide an overview of the function of the brain, including the development of the brain.

→ To consider the two main theories of cognitive development: factor theories and cognitive theories

→ To provide an overview of the constructivist theory of teaching and learning

→ To consider the nature of the learning environment in the light of these theories

→ To explore ideas related to cognitive acceleration

→ To consider the significance of the process of memory in cognitive development

→ To consider the roles of consciousness, metacognition, culture, language and age in supporting cognitive processes

What is cognitive development?

At one time, the terms intelligence and intellectual development were used to refer to cognition and cognitive development. These terms are rather limiting, as they refer to a small aspect of the thinking process and also have been thought to be socially divisive. As a result, we tend to use the more encompassing and inclusive terms of cognition and cognitive development. Cognitive development is the development of cognition or conceptual knowledge and understanding. It involves the development of concepts or 'pictures in the mind', products of reasoning, which help us to make sense of the world. There are many aspects of cognition, which will be discussed through this chapter:

- memory – the ability to remember;
- abstraction – the ability to form a general concept;
- logic – the ability to reason;
- problem-solving – the ability to solve mental problems;
- intelligence – a measure of thinking ability, as measured by intelligence quotients;
- reasoning – providing evidence or justification for a belief;
- thinking – using or exercising the mind;
- knowledge – an assured belief of something that is known;
- understanding – to comprehend something or *'grasp with the mind'* (*Chambers*, 1972: 1487);
- metacognition – to be aware and understand your own thought processes.

The brain

There are three main types of brain; the lizard brain, the bird brain and the mammal brain. The lizard brain is very primitive and has simple primitive functions, reacting to dangers and stimulus. The bird brain is slightly more developed with the ability to recognise and with a rudimental intelligence as seen in birds who solve simple problems, such as how to get seeds, etc. The mammal brain is more developed and enables more complex problem-solving and creativity. Within the mammal brain there are differences from mammal to mammal and there are also differences between different human brains. There are differences between male and female brains, with men having 4 per cent more brain cells than women and about 100 grams more of brain tissue, and women having more dendritic cellular connections (that is, nerve connections) between brain cells and a larger deep limbic system and corpus collosum. The corpus collosum connects the left and right hemispheres of the brain (see Figure 4.1) and allows the two main parts of the brain to communicate with each other. This enables coordinated physical movement to occur and the transfer of learning from one hemisphere to the other. There have been many suggestions as to the results of male/female brain differences, from superior intelligence, different thinking mechanisms and greater intuition, but little is conclusively proved. Most people have a dominant side of the brain. For men, language is most often just in the dominant hemisphere, while a larger number of women are able to use both sides for language, probably because of the increased corpus collosum. Left-brain thinking is:

- linear;
- sequential;
- symbolic;
- logical;
- verbal;

and involves the processing of reality. Right-brain thinking is:

- holistic;
- random;
- concrete;
- intuitive;
- non-verbal;

and involves fantasy processing.

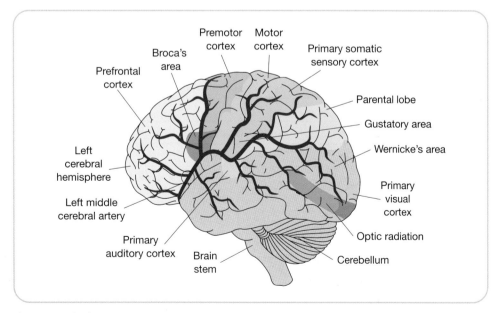

Figure 4.1 The brain
Source: Illustration after Leslie Laurien

Tools for Learning

Interacting with children as a research tool

In this chapter we are considering how we can collect data from children by interacting with them. Children can be very powerful sources of data to help us develop our practice and support their cognitive development. However, we need to consider the ethics of working with children in this way. The following points will help you when you plan to collect data from and with children:

- Consider the child at the centre of the research and do nothing to harm their development. Remember that unethical research that harms a child physically or psychologically can be regarded as child abuse.
- You should not do anything with children if you consider that another approach would be more beneficial to their development.

NOW YOU CAN BEGIN
Have you checked everything?
How would this knowledge improve your work with children?
How would you ensure the validity of your data and analysis?
How will you maintain confidentiality?
How ethical is your research idea?
How could you collect data on this area of cognition? What techniques will you use (observation, questioning, interaction, test, task)?
What has already been found out in this area?
What do you know about this aspect of cognition?
Why do you want to research this area?
What do you want to find out about children's cognition?
START HERE

Figure 4.2 Planning for the study of children's cognition

- When studying children you need to have their consent and their parents'/carers' consent and the consent of the setting.

- The identity of all children/ parents/schools studied should not be disclosed.

- Children and their parents/carers/professionals have a right to see any data collected and analysis of that data.

The reflective and practical tasks in this chapter involve interaction with children as a means to collect data on cognitive development. When you plan to collect data with and from children, you may wish to use the planning ladder in Figure 4.2. Start at the bottom of the ladder and answer each of the questions in full. Once you have done this you will be ready to collect the data and will have ensured, as best as you can, that the children are not adversely affected by the research.

Practical Tasks

Which hemisphere dominates?

There are a number of different tests you can do to see if you are more left- or right-brained. See Figure 4.3 to test yourself.

1. I always wear a watch.
2. I keep a diary/filofax.
3. I believe there is a right and wrong way to do everything.
4. I hate following directions.
5. The expression 'Life is just a bowl of cherries' makes no sense to me.
6. I find that sticking to a schedule is boring.
7. I'd rather draw someone a map than tell them how to get somewhere.
8. If I lost something, I'd try to remember where I saw it last.
9. If I don't know which way to turn, I let my emotions guide me.
10. I'm pretty good at maths.
11. If I had to assemble something, I'd read the directions first.
12. I'm always late getting places.
13. Some people think I'm intuitive.
14. Setting goals for myself helps keep me working.
15. When somebody asks me a question, I turn my head to the left.
16. If I have a tough decision to make, I write down the pros and the cons.
17. I'd make a good police detective.
18. I am musically inclined.
19. If I have a problem, I try to work it out by relating it to one I've had in the past.
20. When I talk, I gesture a lot.
21. If someone asks me a question, I turn my head to the right.
22. I believe there are two sides to every story.
23. I can tell if someone is guilty just by looking at them.
24. I keep a 'to do' list.
25. I feel comfortable expressing myself with words.
26. Before I take a stand on an issue, I get all the facts.
27. I've considered becoming a poet, a politician, an architect, or a dancer.
28. I lose track of time easily.
29. If I forgot someone's name, I'd go through the alphabet until I remembered it.
30. I like to draw.
31. When I'm confused, I usually go with my instincts.
32. I have considered becoming a lawyer, journalist, or doctor.

Left brain – 1, 2, 3, 5, 8, 10, 11, 14, 15, 16, 17, 19, 24, 26, 29, 32

Right brain – 4, 6, 7, 9, 12, 13, 18, 20, 21, 22, 23, 25, 27, 28, 30, 31

Figure 4.3 Which hemisphere dominates?

Reflective Tasks

Which hemisphere dominates?

Level 1

After finding out which is your more dominant hemisphere, look at the lists on page 109 that identify the characteristics of the different hemispheres of the brain. Reflect on yourself and if you agree with the description of yourself.

- Are you logical and verbal and organised (left-hemisphere dominance) or are you holistic, random, intuitive and non-verbal (right-hemisphere dominance)?
- See how other people you know answer and reflect on any differences between males and females.
- How might this knowledge affect your understanding of the way you learn?

Level 2

Having found out which is your more dominant hemisphere, focus on the children in your care. Consider which children are logical and verbal and organised (left-hemisphere dominance) and which holistic, random, intuitive and non-verbal (right-hemisphere dominance).

- See if there is a difference between the boys and girls.
- How does this knowledge of your children affect the way you will interact with them?

Level 3

Having found out which is your more dominant hemisphere, find out about your colleagues in your setting.

- Are you and your colleagues mainly left- or right-hemisphere dominant?
- How might this affect the way you work with children?
- Are the children in your setting left-hemisphere dominant (logical and verbal and organised) or right hemisphere-dominant (holistic, random, intuitive and non-verbal)?
- Is there a difference between the children and the staff?
- How does this knowledge of your staff and children affect the way you will interact with them in the future?

The brain also controls some hormones and these can create differences in spatial ability and coordination, with some of these differences being seen in males and females. Research by Money and Ehrhardt (1972), studying girls who have high levels of male hormones, has shown that they are likely to be more masculine (tomboyish) and less likely to play with other girls of the same age. Knowing that there are such differences which can affect developing children leads us to consider whether we can control these biological differences and whether we can excuse our behaviour or simply explain it. Other brain differences occur when the brain is damaged in some way, through injury (maybe as a result of birth damage), illness (such as maternal rubella in pregnancy), chemical damage (such as pre-natal alcohol abuse) or congenital problems (such as Down's syndrome or Fragile X syndrome). There can be some positive brain differences occurring as a result of playing music to the developing foetus, talking to the bump, swimming and some food cravings (as the body craves what it lacks and needs).

The brain begins to develop from 8 weeks after conception, before which time there is no brain. The first things to develop, when the foetus is 5–8 weeks old, are neurons (which send and receive messages). At 13 weeks, glial cells (which manage the neurons) develop and at 8–9 months dendrites form. Synapses develop after birth. These occur where neurons meet, enabling communication via neurotransmitters and electric charges and sending chemical such as serotonin around the body. At birth the medulla and mid-brain are fully developed, although the cerebellum and cortex continue to develop over the next 5 years. Newborn babies have some inbuilt reactions, such as sucking, gripping and startle responses, which are designed to safeguard them and which are similar to the inbuilt reactions of apes in the wild. These are not really cognitive functions as they involve no thought or deliberation. Within 1 month babies begin to develop cognitive functions. They can smile and meet a gaze, smell (especially their mother), hear (especially high pitched noises), taste (sweet, sour, salt, bitter) and feel (heat, pain, etc.). By the time they are 6 months old the brain can govern perception, body movement, thinking and language, and primitive reflexes disappear. At 2 years glial cells stop forming, although the brain continues to develop through similar 'bursts and prunings' and is greatly influenced by experience. So, for example, language which develops at 3 years will be advanced by the child's experience.

There have been many different ideas about the mind throughout history. Plato (see Plato, trans. Jowett, 1968) and Descartes (1596–1650), famous for the phrase 'I think, therefore I am', both believed the mind was a spiritual entity with innate ideas, while Locke (see Guttenplan *et al.*, 2003) believed that the mind was a tabula rasa or blank sheet that could be written on through experience or the moulding/teaching of others. Modern neural physiologists, such as Professor Susan Greenwood (2001), believe that the mind is a biological entity, whilst psychologists might advocate something in between. There are also beliefs (Wood, 1998) that the child's mind is significantly different from the adult's, not just because of the physiological differences in their brain as described above. Children's perceptions appear to be different from an adult's; for example, they see colours differently. We also know that children are often unable to think abstractly, rationalise, reason or apply logic. So, does this mean that their minds are different?

Factor theories of cognitive development

There are a number of different theories of cognitive development, which fall into two main categories: factor theories and cognitive theories. These will be discussed in chronological order, starting with the earliest theories. The first theories are factor theories of intelligence (intelligence being the term used prior to cognition). Factor theories regard cognitive development to be a result of different factors. Spearman (1927) claimed that general intelligence (the g factor) was responsible for success in a large number of seemingly unrelated skills such as mathematical, musical or spelling ability, because they all involved the same general intelligence. In addition to this general ability there was specific ability (the s factor) which was responsible for success in some skills. Thurstone and Thurstone (1941) identified seven primary mental abilities:

S or spatial ability

P or perceptual speed

N or numerical ability

V or verbal reasoning

M or memory

W or word fluency

I or inductive reasoning.

There are more modern factor theories, such as Gardner's theory of multiple intelligence which is discussed below.

Piaget's cognitive theory

The next set of theories are cognitive theories, which involve processing information and are concerned with the steps or processes of problem-solving. The most famous of these staged theories of cognitive development is Piaget's (1950). Piaget (see Chapter 1) was a developmental biologist who studied many children, including his own, and whose ideas are still extremely influential in education today. In Piaget's theory (see Figure 4.4), cognitive development involves the building up of mental structures called schemas (mental representations) and operations (combinations of schemas). All development occurs in the same order; that is, the child moves through the stages in order (invariant functioning). However, each individual has different experiences and so their cognition will vary (variant functioning).

Piaget is not without his critics. This is because of his small sample, the assertive nature of his theories and rigidity of stages and the ages assigned to them (Bruner *et al.*, 1956). Children's development is often considered to be more gradual and complex (see below). However, Piaget's theories have dominated education for many years and have formed the basis for much further research and developed understanding of the way in which children learn.

Table 4.1 shows Piaget's stages in summary. His first stage is the sensori-motor stage, which involves the very youngest children after birth. These children are primarily concerned with their own needs and act instinctively, through simple reflex responses that help them to survive. They suck and swallow, moving their heads as a result of a stimulus, such as stroking their cheek, to find food. They are able to grasp firmly when their fingers touch something, which enables them to cling on (a primitive reflex action that enabled our early ancestors to cling to their mothers' backs as they moved quickly through trees; as can be seen in apes and monkeys). My son, who was born by Caesarean section, was delivered by grasping the surgeon's fingers! Within a few weeks developing children are able to demonstrate some more coordinated movements, focus their eyes and recognise

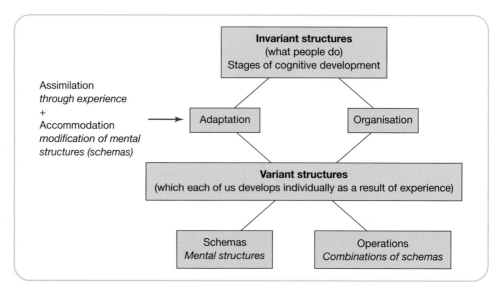

Figure 4.4 Piaget's model of cognition
Source: Adapted from Davenport, 1994: 132

the human face. They are still very dominated by the here and now and react to their needs, communicating their hunger, pain, etc., through crying. They soon learn that their cries are recognised and responded to. However, they are initially unable to distinguish between themselves and the rest of the world and cannot recognise the existence of an object once it has been removed or hidden from their view, although soon they realise that objects not in sight do exist and they can learn to follow an object with their eyes. They look at the human face with concentration and learn to recognise the face of their mother (as well as her smell, learnt while in the womb) and father. They can concentrate for long periods of time, just looking at faces, and begin to smile at about 6 weeks of age, which supports the development of attachment bonds and supports survival by motivating adults to care for them (Bowlby, 1958). As children develop their movements become less erratic and more coordinated and their gross and fine motor skills develop (see Chapter 3). Through practical experience of observing, using all their senses and early toys, they learn about the world around them and solve simple problems, such as how shaking a rattle makes a noise, how different toys have different textures, shapes and colours. In this way they begin to develop their simple ideas about their world into increasingly more complex ones.

Table 4.1 Piaget's stages of cognitive development and scientific understanding

Stage	Age	Description
Sensori-motor	0–2	Much behaviour is reflexive, for example, babies turn towards sounds and touch. Their first ideas developing about the world are action schemas. They assimilate information through their senses and via experiences. In this way they learn about scientific phenomena by extending and modifying schemas (accommodation), building up mental pictures of the world.
Pre-operational	2–7	Children's thought processes are developing but are not necessarily ordered and logical. They are very egocentric, believe that everything has a consciousness (animism) and all moving objects are alive. They also believe that their opinions are correct (moral realism).
Symbolic	2–4	Children recognise symbols which have meaning (e.g. words, signs, etc.). Language becomes important in mental imagery and understanding about the world.
Intuitive	4–7	The child's perceptions dominate their thinking, which shows a lack of reversibility. Changes in objects mean that there are changes in quantity/number. They are unable to think about several features of an object at once (conservation) and will be unable to sort using a number of criteria at the same time or handle variables in scientific investigation.
Concrete operational	7–11	Children's thinking gradually becomes more coordinated, rational and adult-like. At this stage, egocentric thought declines as does animism. Children can think logically if they can manipulate the object that they are thinking about. Appearance of objects influences thought, so a large object will be thought of as heavy and will make a loud sound. Children are unlikely to change their ideas unless persuasive evidence is present.
Formal operational	11–16	Children begin to rely more on ideas than the need to manipulate objects. Their thinking becomes more abstract. They are able to solve mental problems and to build up mental models of the world. Formal operations involve propositions, hypotheses, logical relationships and contradictions. They are able to see and manipulate variables involved in investigations.

Source: Adapted from Johnston, 2005: 62–3

The second of Piaget's stages is the pre-operational stage, which is divided into two sub-stages: the symbolic stage and the intuitive stage. The symbolic sub-stage is characterised by the development of increasingly complex communication in the form of language; important in cognition through mental imagery. Language continues to develop in the second sub-stage within the pre-operational stage: the intuitive sub-stage. This sub-stage is characterised by increasing mental imagery, dominated by the child's perceptions, and they are often unwilling to change their initial ideas. It was when researching this stage that Piaget identified children's inability to conserve, so that perceived changes in objects meant that the objects were different. Children at this stage cannot identify that:

- a number of objects which are rearranged remain the same number;
- the mass of an object remains the same even when the shape changes (as with balls of dough rolled into sausage shapes);
- the volume of liquid remains the same, even when poured into different shaped/sized containers.

The third of Piaget's stages of cognitive development is the concrete operational stage, during which children's thinking gradually develops, becoming more coordinated, rational and adultlike. Children are less dominated by their perceptions, although they do need to manipulate objects to support their understanding of them. In this way they can understand the conservation of number, mass or volume if they can manipulate the objects while they are thinking. They also begin to listen to the ideas of others and realise that their ideas are not the only ones, although their own intuitive ideas still take precedence and they are unlikely to change their ideas unless really persuaded to do so. So at this stage meaning actively and practically develops through a gradual process involving observation, experience, play, social interaction and social discourse (talking). Children construct links with their prior knowledge to generate new ideas, check and restructure old ideas and move away from simplistic ideas towards more sophisticated ones.

The formal operational stage is Piaget's last cognitive stage and is characterised by children using their minds rather than their hands. In this stage, children begin to be able to group, separate, order and combine in their minds. They can solve mental problems and think in abstract ways. This is a stage that Piaget felt that children would move through from about 11 years of age. However, there is evidence that some children can conserve at 5 or 6 years of age (Bruner *et al.*, 1956) and can think logically at earlier ages (Johnston, 2005), while some adults do not reach this stage and are never able to achieve logical, abstract thought.

Vygotsky's cognitive theory

Vygotsky (see Chapter 1) developed his cognitive theory (1962) building on from Piaget's. He identified the importance of language in cognitive development, so that as children's language develops it becomes more complex (see Chapter 5) and they are able to talk about their ideas, thus helping their understanding to develop. However, Vygotsky recognised (1962) that language and thought are different functions which develop separately but support each other. Vygotsky and Cole (1978) also identified the importance of sensitive interaction by expert adults to support children's cognitive development. Vygotsky identified that there was an area just beyond current understanding (the zone of proximal development), which sensitive interaction, in ways suited to the child's age, culture and social needs, can help to reach. Skilled adult interaction or scaffolding can help the learner move beyond their initial ideas and develop their conceptual understanding, a theme taken up by Bruner (1977), who argued that education should be constructed to support cognition through a spiral curriculum, which revisits ideas and phenomena and motivates the children. Peer support can also help to scaffold children's learning, as children learn through cooperative interaction that the ideas of others may be different.

Practical Tasks

Cognitive learning activities

Level 1

Plan a cognitive learning activity with a small group of children and try to incorporate some peer and adult interaction. Carry out and evaluate the activity and identify how successful it was in developing the children's cognition.

- How important was the peer interaction in the success of the activity?
- How did your interaction support the children's learning?
- How could you improve your interaction to further develop the children's learning and your practice?

Level 2

Plan a cognitive learning activity for your class of children that incorporates both peer and adult interaction. Carry out and evaluate the activity and identify how successful it was in developing the children's cognition.

- How important was the peer interaction in the success of the activity?
- How did your interaction support the children's learning?
- How could you improve your interaction to further develop the children's learning and your practice?
- How did the children feel about the activity? Did they learn best from the peer or adult interaction?

Level 3

Ask staff and children in your setting to identify what recent learning experiences they have liked/found most successful. Analyse their ideas and identify those that were individual activity, those that involved peer interaction and those that involved more adult interaction. Try to identify what type of adult interaction was involved in the activities:

- Organisational: involved the adult in organising the children;
- Motivational: involved the adult in motivating the children to learn for themselves;
- Instructional: involved the adult in didactic teaching of the children;
- Interactional: involved the adult in interacting with the children during the activity and learning with them;
- Other: not one of the above.

Identify what type of interaction you and your staff feel most comfortable with and why.

Bruner's cognitive theory

Bruner's cognitive theory involves cognitive growth and is influenced by and builds upon Vygotsky's theories. Bruner (1960) considers environmental and experiential factors in the development of cognition and suggests that cognitive ability develops depending on how the mind is used. His modes of representation are based on categorisation, as follows (Bruner, 1966, see Chapter 1):

- 'enactive representation', cognition expressed through physical actions (action-based);
- 'iconic representation', objects and events experienced through the senses are represented by mental images (image-based);
- 'symbolic representation', thought is expressed through symbols, such as language (language-based).

Bruner believed that whenever we observe something, interact with something, learn something and make decisions, we are mentally sorting and arranging our ideas to form a hierarchical arrangement of related categories, echoing Bloom's taxonomy (Bloom, 1956). For Bruner, these modes of representation are interrelated and only loosely sequential, although the third one, symbolic representation, is the most mysterious and ultimate mode.

Bruner (1960) identified a number of important factors affecting children's cognitive development and which successful cognitive support or teaching needs to consider:

- structure in learning;
- readiness for learning;
- the spiral curriculum;
- intuitive and analytical thinking;
- motivation.

More recently, Bruner (1991) has argued that the mind structures its sense of reality through cultural mediation (or interaction with ideas, others and situations in the cultural context) and he specifically focuses on the idea of narrative (personal explanation or storytelling) as one of these cultural products that supports cognitive development.

Modern factor theories

Sternberg's triarchic theory (1985) is a type of factor theory which identifies three types of intelligence. The first is contextual intelligence or the ability to manage daily life, and people with common sense, business sense or who are streetwise fit into this category. The second is experimental intelligence or creativity and the ability to cope with new situations. People who are risk-takers and thrive on stress may fit into this category. The third type is componential intelligence or the ability to analyse and think critically, and people who score well in IQ tests will fit into this category.

Another factor theory is Gardner's theory of multiple intelligence. Gardner (1983) believes that there are a number of different intelligences:

- *Bodily-kinaesthetic*, or using the body to solve problems and express ideas and feelings. Children who rate highly in this intelligence are likely to be ones who like making things, dancing and physical activities. They are likely to do well as actors, athletes and dancers or as mechanics.
- *Interpersonal*, or the ability to gauge moods, feelings and needs. Children who fit into this category tend to be good listeners and supportive friends and they are likely to make good salespeople, teachers, counsellors or to work in caring professions.
- *Intrapersonal*, or the ability to use knowledge about themselves. Children who have a well-developed intrapersonal intelligence will also have a well-developed sense of self and use this knowledge to manage their own learning. They are prepared to solve problems in ways that they determine, rather than follow the lead of others. Adults

who have highly developed intrapersonal skills will be reflective, meditate, attend counselling sessions, keep a diary, etc.

- *Linguistic*, or the ability to use words, oral or written. Children who are good linguists, will be good orally, perhaps telling stories or chatting away to others during activities. They are thought to make good storytellers, politicians, comedians and writers.

- *Logical-mathematical*, or the ability to understand and use numbers and reason well. Children who have good logical-mathematical intelligence are likely to be good with numbers, think logically, solve problems and would make good mathematicians, scientists, computer programmers and accountants.

- *Musical*, children who are musical are likely to hum while they work, tap their fingers and feet to imaginary beats, and adults who are musical will find themselves as musicians, composers, music critics and music lovers.

- *Naturalist*, or the ability to organise and classify both the animal and plant kingdoms as well as showing understanding of natural phenomena. Children who have a high naturalist intelligence will enjoy outdoor education, animals, plants and environmental experiences. Adults who fit into this category would be biologists, environmentalists, animal lovers, etc.

- *Spatial*, or the ability to perceive the visual-spatial world accurately. Children who are good in this category will be able to orient themselves and produce good painting, models and solve problems. Adults who excel in this category would be hunters, sailors, engineers, inventors, surgeons as well as decorators, sculptors, painters, etc.

Critical Discussion

Multiple intelligences

Howard Gardner has spoken about the myths and realities of multiple intelligences (Gardner, 2007a). Since his original work on multiple intelligences was published (Gardner, 1983), it has been associated with the following claims:

- that it provides evidence for a VAK (visual, auditory and kinaesthetic) approach;
- that intelligence is a teaching style;
- that multiple intelligences describe a single construct and relate to single disciplines;
- that there is an 'official' multiple intelligence approach;
- that talents are 'God-given', independent of external factors and cannot be developed.

Gardner (2007a) argues that these are myths which weaken multiple intelligence as a theory and we should:

- by all means broaden the concept of multiple intelligences but avoid proscription when attempting description;
- consider the contextual influences on intelligences;
- consider what environments promote intelligences. Gardner considers that Reggio Emilia is such an environment (see Chapter 1);
- consider scientific evidence from genetics and neuroscience, as they can help to inform our understanding and practice.

Consider your understanding of multiple intelligences, how you have used, or seen others use, the theory and Gardner's claims and arguments. What are the implications of these arguments for your future practice? How does the 'new look' multiple intelligences relate to the personalised learning agenda (see DfES, 2006; Johnston et al., 2007).

Research

Gardner's five minds

Howard Gardner (2007b) has identified five different minds, which he considers will be increasingly important in our future.

The disciplined mind

The disciplined mind is one that is developed through education and supports individuals in becoming 'expert' in one discipline. Historically, being expert in one area/discipline was sufficient, but the complexities of our current and future societies means that we need to become interdisciplinary or multidisciplinary, gain expertise in new disciplines and gain mastery over changing disciplines. However, this must not lead to a watering down of expertise, but rather the opposite.

The synthesising mind

The ability to synthesise – to survey a wide range of sources or experiences, make decisions about importance, combine information in a meaningful way and communicate that in an understandable way – is an intellectual skill of increasing importance in modern society. This is especially important as sources of information are rapidly increasing. Teachers, politicians, leaders and communicators need to be able to synthesise huge amounts of information. A synthesising mind will have an area of expertise (a discipline), know the trusted sources of information within the discipline, be able to keep an overview of the area being considered (the big picture) and consider the details. A synthesising mind can be both a searchlight, having a broad overview, seeing and making use of the links between disciplines/areas and monitoring changes in the area, and also be a laser beam, having in-depth knowledge within the area.

The creating mind

The creating mind develops new ideas, practices and procedures, solves complex problems and is innovative or engages in big C creativity (Csikszentmihalyi, 1997). Like the disciplined mind, the creating mind does not rest once something has been created, but is constantly motivated to risk failure and continue to develop and create. Gardner (2007b) recognises the importance of both the disciplined and synthesising minds on the creating mind, as new and innovative developments in disciplines are unlikely to occur without the ability to synthesise.

The respectful mind

The respectful mind welcomes social contact, displays initial trust, gives individuals the benefit of the doubt, tries to form links, is tolerant and avoids making judgements. For a respectful mind, difference does not equal wrong. This type of mind is increasingly important in a complex multicultural society, with the opening up of borders between countries and increasing pluralisation.

The ethical mind

The ethical mind considers more sophisticated moral issues in an abstract way. Decisions, behaviour and beliefs of those around you can influence the development of an ethical mind and provide role models for the development of such a mind. An ethical mind will not cut corners, will speak out if injustices are seen, even if that is at the cost of respect for individuals. This illustrates a tension between the respectful mind and the ethical mind, which can, mistakenly, be regarded as synonymous, rather than linked in a looser correlation.

There is no hierarchy within the minds, although Gardner (2007b) does believe that there is a rhythm. A disciplined mind is needed to be able to synthesise and be creative, and creativity involves some degree of synthesis, although a very disciplined mind is less likely to be creative and a highly synthesising mind may not lead to creativity.

Johnston (1996) identified cognition as multidimensional. Her theory is that there are four interactive learning schemas, which combine together in different ways in individual learners.

The first is *Sequential Processing*, or the ability to be ordered and organised, having the desire for clear instructions and time to complete work. Early years professionals who are sequential processors are highly organised, will keep their setting tidy, plan activities in detail and will prize these attributes in the children they care for. Children who are sequential processors will organise their time well, find planning for their day easy, as in High/Scope settings (Hohmann and Weikart, 2002), and will fit into mainstream settings well, for as Johnston (1996) has identified many teachers and education professionals are highly sequential.

The second interactive learning schema is *Precise Processing*, or the ability to be precise and detailed, desiring information and enjoying acquiring knowledge. Adults who are precise processors will have a good general knowledge, enjoy and be good at quizzes, read factual books, watch factual television programmes and do well at examinations that ask them to remember and recall factual information. Since these attributes are ones that are favoured in our education system, children who are precise processors are likely to do well in academic terms, be knowledgeable and precise and pay attention to detail.

The third schema is *Technical Processing*, or the ability to be practical, technical or scientific and liking hands-on projects and first-hand experience. Adults who are technical processors are those who like gadgets and technical tools. I have seen teachers in schools who have a wide range of technical gadgets from electric pencil sharpeners to multimedia and use them without any qualms or anxiety. They are likely always to have a practical technical project running, involving making things and solving technical problems. Children who are good technical processors will enjoy technical and scientific activities. They will enjoy taking things apart to see how they work and will prefer making things or drawing diagrams, rather than writing or sitting and listening.

The final interactive schema is *Confluent Processing*, or the ability to be creative or artistic, having confidence and liking to use imagination and take risks. Early years professionals who are confluent processors will be creative risk-takers who may find following government directives difficult, especially if they have another way that they can see would work better. They are likely to modify national strategies to meet the needs of the children in their care and provide motivating cross-curricular activities that develop the children in a variety of ways. Children are likely to be the quirky, challenging children who love drama, music or art, who are independent thinkers and can make life challenging for those who care for them. In my own work with young children, I have always enjoyed those children who will banter with me and have creative solutions to problems and who challenge me if they can see a different and better way to do something. I found it more challenging when my own son was one of these children and who 'marched to the beat of his own drum' rather than mine or the setting he was in. At various times he was regarded as 'difficult', 'naughty', 'problematic'. In nursery he once put sand in the pram of a visiting baby, because he wanted the baby to be able to play with the sand too; when he started school he ate the sleeve of his coat, up to the elbow, as he was bored during long story times at the end of the day; he would constantly hum and sing (he later went on to take a degree in music), and he once opened the door of his classroom and, jumping in, exclaimed to all the children sitting on the carpet listening attentively, 'I'm back! Have you missed me?'

Johnston (1996) believes that our education and care system favours those children who are sequential and precise, and indeed that most professionals are sequential and precise processors. For children who are more technical or confluent, this makes formal settings difficult; they will find it much harder to fit in and this is likely to have an adverse affect on their development. Perhaps we need to remember that, as Rousseau (1911) believed, the setting should accommodate itself to the child and not expect that the child should change to fit into the setting. Certainly it is our responsibility as professionals to help children to accommodate in ways they need to so that they can fit into society and develop socially and emotionally as well as cognitively. In order to do this we need to accommodate them and differentiate our practice to meet their needs.

Practical Tasks

Factor theory test

Level 1

Use the internet to find a factor theory test (or see Johnston, 1996 or Gardner, 1983). Complete the test and see what type of learner you are. Think how you can modify your planning for and practice with children to accommodate their different learning preferences. Make a five-bullet point list of things you need to consider when you are working with children to ensure you are meeting all children's needs.

Level 2

Use the internet to find a factor theory test (or see Johnston, 1996 or Gardner, 1983). Complete the test for yourself and your children and see what type of learners you are.

- What do the results of this test tell you about your own practice?
- How can you modify your practice and accommodate all the learners in your setting?
- Try out some of your ideas and see what the effect is. Try asking the children what they think of the changes/modifications. Try asking other professionals as well.

Level 3

Use the internet to find a factor theory test (or see Johnston, 1996 or Gardner, 1983). As a staff complete the test for yourselves and your children and see what type of learners you are. Look at the activities you provide in your setting and see if they favour one type of learner more than others. Decide as a staff how you can change your practice to accommodate different types of learners. Try out your ideas and evaluate the effects by asking professionals, parents and children what they think of the changes.

Constructivist theories

Constructivist theories have emerged from Piaget's cognitive theory (1950), developed further by Vygotsky (1962; Vygotsky and Cole *et al.*,1978) and Bruner (1960; 1966). These theories involve the child in constructing their own meaning from experiences and learning. We expect that as children get older they will develop their ideas in a linear way, rather like climbing up a set of stairs. This is often what we do see with children's understandings developing as they get older and with more experience of the world around them. However, Strauss (1981) noticed that cognitive development was not always linear but that some concepts appeared to develop in a U-shaped curve.

Research

U-shaped development

The U-shaped curve devised by Strauss (1981) can be seen in Figure 4.5, which shows the responses children made to the question 'Is it an animal?' when shown images of a person, a cow, a spider, a worm and a whale (Bell and Freyberg, 1985: 31). Analysis of the responses indicate that the linear development shown for pictures of people can be understood if we consider that 5-year-old children, who will be in the pre-operational stage of development according to Piaget (1950), are very egocentric and will not see themselves as an animal but as they develop they will understand more of the animal kingdom and their place in it. The high response to the question 'Is a cow an animal?' can be explained as the result of the early child's experiences with farmyard animal books, toys and other experiences which firmly place a cow as an animal at an early stage. The U-shaped curve seems less easy to explain, but if we consider the world of the average 5-year-old, which is fairly simplistic, we can see how they may easily classify whales, worms and spiders as animals. As children develop they learn that the animal kingdom is more complex. Whales are mammals and not fish, worms and spiders are not insects but belong in separate groupings in the animal kingdom. They are developing their understanding but as they struggle to understand the complexity of the whole they give an apparently incorrect response to the question 'Is it an animal?' This U-shaped development is very common and can be seen in all aspects of children's cognition (Littledyke and Huxford, 1998).

Sometimes children develop alternative conceptions as a result of their experiences. These have been extensively studied in science education (Driver, 1985), but are acknowledged as occurring in many other areas of learning (Littledyke and Huxford, 1998) and seen in work with young children (Johnston, 2002; 2005). Cognition is not just about adding to and extending existing concepts; it may necessitate radical reorganisation of existing thinking. Re-modification of these misconceptions and new learning occurs when individual children are allowed to construct their own meaning through experience with the physical environment and through social interaction. This is an active and continuous process whereby children construct links with their prior knowledge, generating new ideas, checking and restructuring old ideas or hypotheses. In this way learning is thought of as an active rather than a passive pursuit and children are responsible for controlling their own learning. This is the basis of the constructivist view of teaching and learning (see Figure 4.6). In the early years our role as professionals is to find out what ideas children hold and then to plan experiences which will develop, modify or challenge their existing ideas so that they move towards a more sophisticated and scientifically acceptable view of the world.

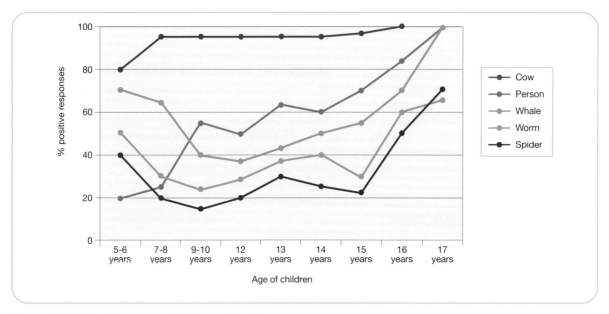

Figure 4.5 Children's responses to 'Is it an animal?'
Source: Bell and Freyberg, 1985: 31

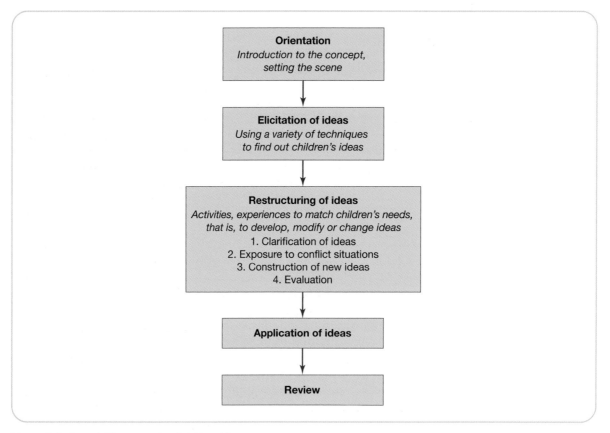

Figure 4.6 A model for a constructivist teaching sequence
Source: Adapted from Scott, 1987: 9

Cognitive acceleration

Cognitive acceleration is the process of supporting the construction of children's ideas. This may involve the removal of factors that adversely affect cognitive development, such as rigid curricular requirements that treat children as a group and plan activities suitable for the average child rather than for the individual. It may mean that gifted children can move faster and further through the early years curriculum and that children who have any kind of difficulties because of ill health, special needs or developmental delay can move at a slower rate (see Chapter 10). For example, there are many children who are born prematurely and who spend weeks or months in neonatal care before they are able to go home. These children are likely to experience developmental delay, at the very least until the time they were expected to be born. However, the expectation is that they will attend formal care groups and compulsory education depending on their age (related to their actual birth date) and not their developmental stage. Some cognitive acceleration occurs in subject areas and these are particularly appropriate for children who are gifted and talented. There are some arguments against cognitive acceleration which focuses on some areas of development or subjects, mainly because the rest of the child's development is unlikely to progress at such a rate and this may cause social and emotional problems later in life.

Research

Cognitive acceleration

Research into cognitive acceleration carried out at King's College London (see Shayer and Adey, 2002) has led to curriculum materials being developed in mathematics, science, technology and the arts which aim to support cognitive development and accelerate children's thinking skills. The resources are based on Piaget's cognitive theories and stimulate the development of thinking abilities through the three pillars of cognitive acceleration: cognitive conflict, social construction and metacognition.

Cognitive conflict is the conflict children feel when their ideas are different from the ideas held by others and do not fit the evidence of their experiences. For example, young children will often believe that heavy things will sink when put into the water trough. They can be challenged by objects that are heavy but float and even more challenged when they can take something that floats, such as a lemon and make it sink by removing the peel and pith (this happens because the inside of the lemon is more dense than water, but the pith is less dense and so will float).

Social construction is when children work cooperatively with others and together construct knowledge by exploring and testing out their different ideas. In an example, children were playing in the role play area, which was set up as a building site. They were building a large structure with cardboard boxes and discussing how to make the tallest tower using the boxes. One child thought that they needed to make the tower tall and thin, while another said that it needed to have the big boxes at the bottom and the small ones at the top and a third child thought that the big boxes should be at the top and the small ones at the bottom. They tried out all their ideas and found that the best structure was pyramidal in shape, with the big boxes at the bottom and the smaller ones at the top. This social construction helped each child to see the ideas held by other children and they were able to work together to come to a better understanding of structures. There are a number of forms that this social construction can take, such as formal discussions and debates, discussion of pictures, concept cartoons (Naylor and Keogh, 2000) and puppets who have alternative ideas to the children and challenge their thinking.

When children understand their own thinking processes (*metacognition*), they can work individually or socially to support their own development. In one example from Philip Adey's work on developing thinking skills with 7- and 8-year-olds (Adey *et al.*, 2003), children were encouraged to explore a collection of seeds and non-seeds (e.g., small beads). They began with a concrete preparation activity in groups, such as discussing stories involving seeds, for example, Eric Carle's, *The Tiny Seed* (1987) or Raymond Briggs's, *Jim and the Beanstalk* (1970), or discussing when they had seen or planted seeds at home or in their settings. They were then asked to work together in a group to sort the collection of seeds and non-seeds, providing an opportunity for cognitive conflict and social construction (see Picture 4.1). After this the teacher asked them to reflect on their criteria for sorting the collection and to provide explanations for their decisions, enabling them to begin to understand their own ideas and reasons for holding them (metacognition). They were then asked to think about how they could show that the seeds are seeds and the others not, and finally they shared their ideas for testing and shared what they had learnt about seeds through the process (metacognition).

Picture 4.1 Children sorting seeds

Children's cognition can also be accelerated by brain stimulation such as forms of transcendental meditation (Dixon, 2002) and Brain Gym (Dennison and Dennison, 1994). Brain Gym (which advocates drinking plenty of water) and PACE (a three-minute exercise to support left/right brain coordination and cognitive development) is proving very popular in many settings to improve children's concentration and thinking skills and there is a great deal of anecdotal evidence to support its use. However, there is little real research evidence to indicate whether it is the full programme that has the effect, or a part of it, or the enthusiasm of the practitioners using it that makes it work. There is a persuasive argument that children respond well to Brain Gym because long activities are being broken up into smaller ones, motivating them and keeping their attention. There is another argument that any change to the normal routine can have an effect on concentration by keeping children's attention, and another that any form of physical activity supports thinking.

Case Study

Classification skills

This case study involved an observation of a class of Year 1 children, whose first language was not English, who were sitting in a circle playing and sorting toys. The collection involved the concept of forces, as some toys used electricity, were held together by or moved because of magnetism, were spinners or wind-up toys, etc. The learning objectives also involved developing classification skills. The collection of toys was shared among the class, so that each child had one toy. They were encouraged to play with it for a few minutes and then show the child sitting next to them how it worked. A few children shared this with the whole class and then all were encouraged to sort the toys according to their properties, putting them into sorting hoops. The children were challenged to sort the toys according to their own categories. One child said that we should put all the spinning toys in one hoop, whilst another child suggested a collection of magnetic toys. Other categories suggested were electrical and wind-up toys and so there were four categories for sorting. When the hoops were put on the floor, each child had to decide whether their toy should be placed in the spinning, magnetic, wind-up or electrical hoops. Ferdinand, having a magnetic gyroscope which spins on a metal frame with two metal rails, identified that his toy was both a spinner and magnetic and he did not know which hoop to put it in. I asked him what he thought we should do and he decided that we could place the gyroscope between the spinning and magnetic hoops, so that it touched both. I then asked the other children if there was another way to do this and Louisa said that we could separate the two parts of the gyroscope and put the spinning part in the spinning hoop and the metal frame in the magnetic hoop (although it was not itself magnetic, this was a good idea). A third child, Bernardo suggested an alternative solution, by overlapping the hoops so that there was another section for magnetic spinning toys.

Reflective questions

1   What do you think the skill of classification is and how does it develop?
2   Is this the type of thinking you would expect from young children?

Critical Discussion

Thinking skills

The observation recorded in the Case Study above identified the level of thinking skills which 5-year-old children could engage in, given a flexible pedagogical approach. Not only did the children show good problem-solving ability for their age, their solutions were very different from an adult solution, which would be influenced by their education and experience, seeing past the simplistic logic of the child and using Venn diagrams. Children's thinking skills are very different from adults' and adult practitioners need to consider this when planning activities and making judgements of achievement.

There were some key pedagogical factors in this activity which enabled thinking skills to be used successfully. First, the activity was structured, but with the flexibility to enable the children to make decisions and solve problems. A highly structured activity would probably not have allowed for alternative solutions. Secondly, it was practical, with the end product being the sorted collection, thus not disadvantaging the children because of their language skills. Thirdly, it was important to provide a challenge and thinking time to enable the children to solve problems. Too little time and the children would not have the opportunity to develop and use their skills; too much time and the children would become bored or frustrated. In the same way, group or whole class activities such as this need to be of short duration and at a pace that challenges the more able child and supports the less able and does not bore or frustrate.

Factors involved in cognitive development

As children develop cognitively their ideas become more abstract and sophisticated and they are able to apply them more widely, linking related phenomena together in first familiar and then unfamiliar situations. Professionals can support this development by giving them time and encouraging them to reflect on their ideas, testing them out through interaction with other children and communicating all their ideas to others.

There are a number of factors that can affect a child's cognitive development and these are discussed in the following sections.

Memory

Memory is highly prized in society and in education. If you have a good memory then you are more likely to succeed academically. Memory is a process by which we receive, encode, reorganise and retrieve information. It is an active process in which the brain alters and organises information rather than just recording it. We receive an enormous amount of information in the course of one day; far more than we can remember. What we remember depends on physical factors, such as the development of the brain and functioning of the brain; psychological factors, such as emotions and motivation; and behavioural factors, such as strategies to develop and improve memory. The process of memory involves three stages:

1. *Encoding*. Information is converted into codes so that it can be represented mentally. We use visual codes when we remember a face, picture or a scene; auditory codes, when we remember spoken language or a piece of music; and semantic codes when we remember meanings (the meaning of a story or a song rather than the whole story or song). We also encode memories of physical skills such as riding a bike, driving, swimming, etc.

2. *Storage*. Information is stored in our brains for either a short time (short-term memory) or a longer time (long-term memory). Short-term memory involves memorising small bits of information for a short period of time. This may include retaining unrehearsed information, such looking at a set of objects or a screen for a short time and remembering a few aspects of them for about 20 to 30 seconds. It may also include memorising rehearsed information for a longer period of time, such as remembering a telephone number while you dial the number. Our short-term memories can hold only a few items at any one time (seven, plus or minus two), although

if we group some information together we can hold more (e.g. grouping telephone numbers into groups of three or four digits). Once the capacity of the short-term memory is exceeded, newer information displaces the older. Some information can be transferred from short-term to long term-memory by rehearsal. Long-term memory involves the more or less permanent storage of information and a change in the nervous system, with a memory trace or engram. Our long-term memories have unlimited capacities and can hold information for indefinite periods of time. Forgetting information is thought to be a matter of of retrieval problems rather than storage problems (Atkinson and Shiffrin, 1968).

3. *Retrieval*. This involves recovering stored information from long-term memory. Some information (name, address, telephone number) can be retrieved instantaneously. Larger amounts of information, or information only partly understood, can be difficult to retrieve. We retrieve information from our memories by recognition, recall and reconstruction. Recognition is the simplest form of retrieval and can be seen in young children (see Picture 4.2). It involves recognising the similarities between information. If we look at a set of 10 objects or pictures and then mix them up with some unfamiliar ones, we can pick out some of the original set. This is recognition. Recall is more complex as it involves generating a mental image of information. If we look at a set of objects or pictures, it would involve recalling them later (as in some television quiz games). Reconstruction involves reorganising information, making sense of it. We may retell a story in our own words, perhaps emphasising different things from the original story (Brainerd and Reyna, 1993).

There are two main types of memories, procedural memories (remembering how to do something, such as ride a bike, swim, write a cheque) and declarative memories (remembering knowledge). Declarative memories are the most important for cognitive development. They can be subdivided into two groups: episodic memories, or the memory of personal events such as your first day at school or what you did at the weekend, and semantic memories, or knowledge about the world, that is facts, concepts, etc.

Picture 4.2 Children playing Kim's game

not set into a context. It is semantic memory that is traditionally tested in educational tests and examinations.

Young children show evidence of memory as soon as they are born. A baby recognises its mother's heartbeat or sounds familiar to it from the womb. Young children recognise faces and familiar toys, and during pre-school age develop this recognition to near adult levels (Berk, 2003). It does appear that it is a fairly automatic process requiring little long-term memory.

Young children during their first year can often recall when memories are strongly cued. Ashmead and Perlmutter (1980) found that a 7-month-old child would look at the door when he heard his father's voice greeting him on the telephone, recalling that his voice usually could be heard greeting him as he came home from work. At pre-school age, children show evidence of rehearsal to support short-term memory by repeating names of toys as they play with them (Berk, 2003). They also show evidence of organisation (grouping related items together) to aid memory. For example, they will sort objects into categories (spatial organisation), although they are not able to make meaningful categories (semantic organisation). As they get older they develop their memory strategies, so that rehearsal has a bigger impact on their memories after about 6 years of age. Berk (2003) believes that children will utilise rehearsal strategies more consistently from around 7 years of age and organisation strategies from around 8 years of age, but they are not consistent or always effective. Once rehearsal and organisation are firmly established, children are able to combine the strategies, repeating names and stating categories. This develops until they find combination strategies that work for them. For example, by organising items first, then rehearsing category names and then individual names they can remember quite complex information (e.g. sorting information for an exam).

By the age of 5, children begin to reconstruct events. They can tell you the main events in a story, often forgetting things that appear unimportant. They may reorder events, condense information or add information that fits into the meaning they have of the story. As they develop they produce more inferences and interpretations from memorised information and the original information decays. This makes the information more coherent to the child, although it does mean that memories can be inaccurate. Brainerd and Reyna (1993) identified that sometimes reconstruction involves a gist of the information (fuzzy trace) and that this gist of the information is retained for longer than a verbatim memory. With age, children rely less on the verbatim reconstruction (e.g. methods for doing something, recipes, etc.) and more on the gist of the original, which they elaborate and develop.

Elaboration is the strategy of creating relationships between pieces of information in different categories. This develops in older children, once they have constructed and organised information. Children are able to elaborate from about 10 years of age. For example, in order to remember the words fish and pipe they may picture a fish smoking a pipe. Once this strategy is established it can be very successful in supporting memory. It is much more common during adolescence. There are other strategies to developing semantic memory and supporting cognitive development, including:

- rote: remembering information in the hope that it becomes automatic (alphabet, tables);
- rehearsal: repeating information to support memory and perhaps elaborating on it;
- organisation: grouping related items together/classifying/sorting/the development of schema;
- making notes: bullet pointing main pieces of information;
- mnemonic devices: using an initial letter strategy to support memory, such as a rhyme or sentence, or a rhyme to remember facts;
- motivation: you are more likely to remember something if you have a motivation to do so and intrinsic motivation is more powerful than extrinsic motivation;

- association; we are more likely to remember complex information if we associate it with something. Some people can remember long lists of objects by associating them with events in a story. Others remember to do a particular thing if they associate it with an everyday event, such as cleaning their teeth, or brushing their hair;

- rhythm; we remember advertising jingles because of the rhythm involved. How many advertising jingles can you remember?

Practical Tasks

Mnemonics

Can you work out the meaning or finish the following mnemonics?

1 Never Eat Shredded Wheat

2 Thirty days has September ...

3 Every Good Boy Deserves Favour

4 My Very Easy Method ...

Level 1

- Are any of these mnemonics suitable for children in the early years?
- Can you think of any other mnemonics that are helpful to children in the early years?
- Look at the other strategies to support memory (see the list of bullet points above) and identify which ones would be useful with children from 0 to 3 years of age, 3 to 5 years of age, and 5 to 8 years of age.

Level 2

- Which of the strategies above do you currently use with children in your setting?
- Which of the strategies would be suitable for use with your children?
- Use one or more of the strategies with your children and evaluate how useful they are in supporting children's semantic memory and cognitive development.

Level 3

As a staff, consider how you can incorporate different strategies (see the list of bullet points above) into your work with children. Try out these strategies over a period of time and evaluate their usefulness in supporting children's semantic memory and cognitive development.

Consciousness and metacognition

If we are not conscious of having knowledge, can that be said to be knowledge? Is it only conscious thought which is involved in cognition? In its widest sense cognition includes both the conscious and the unconscious mind; peripheral, as well as focal awareness (White, 2002). Skills and attitudes can also be conscious or unconscious. For example, we might be naturally (unconsciously) generous, but also make a conscious effort to be more generous in our everyday life. In some ways consciousness is associated with metacognition or the awareness and understanding of aspects of thought. As children develop, their cognitive processes expand as they become aware of their cognitive capacities. For example, they know that attention and effort are necessary and that learning is not a passive act. 'Attention is fundamental to human thinking' (Berk, 2003: 279) and develops along with other aspects of child development. Very young children are easily distracted and find it difficult to focus on one thing if other, more exciting and novel things attract their attention. As they develop, they are able to be increasingly selective in focusing on the relevant aspects to help them achieve a goal. Selective attention appears to develop rapidly between the ages of 6 and 9 (Berk, 2003) and is dependent on cognitive inhibition (the ability to control both internal and external distracting stimuli) and the development of attention and planning strategies. Miller (2000) has identified that children use attention strategies on many different tasks and that they tend to develop these strategies in four phases:

1. *production deficiency*: pre-school children are not able to utilise any strategies;

2. *control deficiency*: from school age, children apply strategies inconsistently;

3. *utilization deficiency*: as children develop, they are more able to apply strategies consistently, but the effect on their performance is limited;

4. *effective strategy use*: children are able to use a strategy consistently and their performance improves.

Some children suffer from Attention Deficit Hyperactivity Disorder (ADHD) and find it difficult to focus on one task for any length of time. Boys are 3–9 times more likely to be diagnosed with ADHD than girls (Berk, 2003), although it may be that ADHD behaviour in girls is not as obvious rather than that they do not suffer from it (Gaub and Carlson, 1997). ADHD is thought to have a genetic tendency, but is associated with environmental factors including social/family difficulties and prenatal drug and alcohol exposure.

Children also learn to use a variety of other strategies to support their own cognitive development and set themselves targets to develop their thinking skills. Moreover, as they develop children learn more strategies for processing information. They learn about the importance of effective memory and develop rehearsing and categorising techniques that improve their cognition. As children develop independence (and this in turn is affected by the amount and types of independent tasks they are encouraged to do), they also learn that it is easier and more effective to focus on one task rather than trying to multitask, and that memorising a list of unrelated words is more difficult than a list of related ones. Children are, however, still very inexpert at cognitive self-regulation, or monitoring their own cognitive progress, as this develops at a much later stage as they move towards adulthood.

Mental modelling is another metacognitive strategy for representing data, ideas, objects, events or processes. Children develop intuitive models about the world around them. These are not always correct and further experiences can develop these models or cause them to be restructured. For example, children who think that heavy things sink and light things float have developed a mental model about the world which can be challenged by further experiences, such as water play involving a variety of different objects (different in size and mass). During this water play they can be challenged to make something that normally floats sink, such as a lemon, referred to earlier, or some aluminium foil. They can also be challenged to make something that normally sinks float, such as a ball of plasticine which can be made into a boat shape, or marbles which can float in the plasticine boats (Johnston, 2005). Teaching can also affect the restructuring of these models, resulting in a synthetic model which may be a combination of the original intuitive model and the new ideas presented in the teaching and which may still be incorrect.

Culture, language and age

Culture and language appears to support some children in cognitive processing and not others. For example, Asian children appear to be better at manipulating multi-digit numbers than American children (Fuson and Kwon, 1992) because of a variety of factors, including language, teaching, use of additional resources such as an abacus, and earlier introduction to multi-digit numbers. The information processing view of cognition is that it is a complex neural process, not unlike the workings of a computer. The ability to process information increases with age, as children's neural networks develop and they are able to store and memorise information more effectively.

Reflective Tasks

Interdependency of cognitive development

Level 1

Consider how cognitive development affects, and is affected by, other aspects of development. Write your thoughts down in Table 4.2.

Level 2

Consider how language development is affecting the cognitive development of children in your setting. How could you develop their cognition through language? Try out some of your ideas and monitor the effects on the children's cognition.

Level 3

Analyse the current practice in your setting and consider how you develop cognition through and alongside other areas of development. What changes could you suggest to staff to change practice and further develop the children cognitively? Try out some of your ideas and evaluate the effects on the children's cognition.

Table 4.2 How does cognitive development affect, and become affected by, other aspects of development?

Area of development	Effect of cognitive development
Physical	
Social	
Emotional	
Moral	

Practical Tasks

Observing cognitive development

Level 1

Observe a child to ascertain their cognitive development:

- Consider how the child is developing in this area.
- Consider what is affecting the child's cognitive development.
- Analyse what experiences the child needs to develop, modify or change their ideas and support their cognitive development.

Ideas

You could observe a child playing with a moving toy and consider what their play tells you about their understanding, or observe a child exploring capacity in the water trough, or listen to a child describing or explaining something to a peer.

Level 2

Plan a change in your setting to support one aspect of cognitive development. Evaluate the effect of this change on children's cognitive development.

Ideas

You could set up an interest or tinkering table to encourage children to explore the world around them, or try some Brain Gym exercises with your children, or challenge children during their play and explorations to solve simple problems.

Level 3

Having analysed current practice (see Reflective Tasks above), discuss your ideas for change with staff in your setting. Modify your ideas as a result of this discussion and implement the changes in partnership with colleagues. Evaluate the effects of the changes with the staff.

Ideas

You could introduce the idea of Brain Gym exercises to your staff, or set up role play areas to promote understandings, or promote home/setting challenges to encourage thinking skills.

Summary

→ The brain has both a left and a right hemisphere and it is usual for one to be more dominant than the other.

→ The brain starts to develop when the foetus is approximately 5–8 weeks old. When a baby is born much of the brain is fully developed, although the cerebellum and cortex continue to develop over 5 years.

→ There are many different theories about the mind and how it works, with distinctions between physiologists' views and psychologists' views.

→ There are two main theories of cognitive development: factor theories and cognitive theories.

→ Cognitive theorists include Piaget, Vysgotsky and Bruner.

→ Factor theorists include Sternberg with the triarchic theory and Gardner with the theory of multiple intelligences.

→ Johnston (1996) identified cognition as multidimensional with four interactive learning schemas.

→ Theories of cognitive development have implications for the type of learning environment provided for children.

→ Constructivist theories involve children in constructing their own meaning from experiences and learning.

→ Cognitive acceleration is the process of supporting the construction of children's ideas.

→ There are a number of factors that can affect a child's cognitive development, including memory and metacognition.

→ Memory is an active process in which the brain alters and organises information rather than just records it.

→ Although there are two main types of memories, declarative memories are the most important for cognitive development.

→ There are a number of different strategies to develop semantic memory and support cognitive development.

→ Metacognition is the awareness and understanding of aspects of thought and children's cognitive processes expand as they become aware of their cognitive capacities.

→ Culture, language and age have an effect on certain aspects of cognitive processing.

Key Questions

- How does the brain function and what is the difference between the right and left hemispheres?
- What are the main factor theories?
- What are the main cognitive theories?
- What is the constructivist theory of teaching and learning and how does it relate to cognitive development theories?
- How would a constructivist approach impact upon the learning environment?
- What are some of the ideas related to cognitive acceleration?
- What are the three stages in the memory process?
- What is the significance of the process of memory in cognitive development?
- How do the roles of consciousness, metacognition, culture, language and age impact upon the cognitive process?

References

Adey, P., Nagy, F., Robertson, A., Serret, N. and Wadsworth, P. (2003) *Let's Think Through Science: A programme for developing thinking in Year 3.* Windsor: NFER-Nelson

Ashmead, D.H. and Perlmutter, M. (1980) Infant Memories in Everyday Life, in Perlmutter, M. (ed.) *New Direction for Child Development*, Vol. 10. San Francisco: Jossey-Bass, pp. 1–16

Atkinson, R.C. and Shiffrin, R.M. (1968) Human Memory: A proposal system and its control processes, in Spence, K.W. and Spence, J.T. (eds) *Advances in the Psychology of Learning and Motivation*, Vol. 2. New York: Academic Press, pp. 90–195

Bell, B. and Freyberg, P. (1985) *Language in the Science Classroom*, in Osborne, R. and Freyberg, P. (Eds) *Learning in Science*. Auckland, New Zealand: Heinemann

Berk, L. E. (2003) *Child Development, 6th edn.* Boston, MA: Allyn & Bacon

Bloom, B.S., Krathwohl, D.R., Engelhart, M.D., Furst, E.J. and Hill, W.H. (1956) *Taxonomy of Educational Objectives: Cognitive Domain.* London: Longman

Bowlby, J. (1958) 'The Nature of a Child's Tie to His Mother' *International Journal of Psychoanalysis*, 39: 350–73

Brainerd, C.J. and Reyna, V.F. (1993) 'Memory Interdependence and Memory Interference in Cognitive Development', *Psychological Review*, 100: 42–67

Briggs, R. (1970) *Jim and the Beanstalk.* London: Penguin (Picture Puffin).

Bruner, J.S. (1960) *The Process of Education.* Cambridge, MA: Harvard University Press

Bruner, J.S. (1966) *Toward a Theory of Instruction.* Cambridge, MA: Belknap Press

Bruner, J.S. (1977) *The Process of Education,* 2nd edn Cambridge, MA: Harvard University Press

Bruner, J.S. (1991) 'The Narrative Construction of Reality', *Critical Inquiry*, 18, 1: 1–21

Bruner, J.S., Goodnow, J.J. and Austin, G. A. (1956) *A Study of Thinking.* New York: Wiley

Carle, E. (1987) *The Tiny Seed.* London: Hodder & Stoughton

Chambers Twentieth Century Dictionary, Ed. A.M. Macdonald (1972). Edinburgh: W. & R. Chambers

Csikszentmihalyi, M. (1997) *Creativity.* New York, HarperPerennial

Davenport, G.C. (1994) *An Introduction to Child Development.* London: Collins

de Bóo, M. (ed) (2004) *Early Years Handbook. Support for Practitioners in the Foundation Stage* Sheffield: The Curriculum Partnership/ Geography Association

Dennison, P. and Dennison, G. (1994) *Brain Gym.* Ventura CA: Educational Kinesiology Foundation

DfES (2006) *Personalised Learning.* www.standards.dfes.gov.uk/personalisedlearning/

Dixon, C.A. (2002) 'Consciousness and Cognitive Development: A six-month longditudinal study of four-year-olds practising the children's TM technique. Dissertation extract. Available from www.mum.edu/library/abstracts/dixon.html

Driver, R. (1985) *The Pupil as a Scientist.* Buckingham: Open University Press

Fuson, K.C. and Kwon, Y. (1992) 'Korean Children's Understanding of Mutlidigit Addition and Subtraction', *Child Development*, 63: 491–506

Gardner, H. (1983) *Frames of Mind: The Theory of Multiple Intelligence,* 2nd edn. London: Heinemann

Gardner, H. (2007a) 'Multiple Intelligences: Past, Present, Future'. *Proceedings of CONASTA 56 and ICASE 2007 World Conference on Science and Technology Education. Sustainable, Responsible, Global.* Perth: Science Teachers' Association of Western Australia. www.worldste2007.asn.au

Gardner, H. (2007b) *Five Minds for the Future.* Boston: Harvard Business School Press

Gaub, M. and Carlson, C.L. (1997) 'Gender Differences in ADHD: A meta-analysis and critical review', *Journal of the American Academy of Child and Adolescent* Psychiatry, 36: 1036–45

Greenwood, S.A. (2001) *The Private Life of the Brain.* London: Penguin

Guttenplan, S., Hornsby, J. and Janaway, C. (2003) *Reading Philosophy. Selected texts with a method for beginners.* Oxford: Blackwell

Hohmann, M. and Weikart, D.P. (2002) *Educating Young Children, 2nd edn.* Ypsilanti, MI: High/Scope Press

Johnston, C. (1996) *Unlocking the Will to Learn.* Thousand Oaks, CA: Corwin Press

Johnston, J. (2002) Supplement on Making Sense of the World in *Early Years Educator*, June

Johnston, J. (2005) *Early Explorations in Science*, 2nd edn. Buckingham: Open University Press

Johnston, J., Halocha, J. and Chater, M. (2007) *Developing Teaching Skills in the Primary School*. Maidenhead: Open University Press

Littledyke, M. and Huxford, L. (1998) *Teaching the Primary Curriculum for Constructivist Learning*. London: David Falmer

Miller P. H. (2000) 'How Best to Utilize a Deficiency', *Child Development*, 71: 1013–17

Money, J. and Ehrhardt, A.A. (1972) *Man and Woman, Boy and Girl*. Baltimore: Johns Hopkins University Press

Naylor, S. and Keogh, B. (2000) *Concept Cartoon in Science Education*. Crewe: Millgate House Publishing

Piaget, J. (1950) *The Psychology of Intelligence*. London: Routledge & Kegan Paul

Plato, trans. Jowett, B. (1968) *Republic*. New York: Airmont Publishing

Rousseau, J.J. (1911) *Emile* London: J.M. Dent

Scott, P. (1987) *A Constructivist View of Teaching and Learning Science*. Leeds: Leeds University

Shayer, M. and Adey, P. (eds) (2002) *Learning Intelligence. Cognitive Acceleration Across the Curriculum from 5 to 15 Years*. Buckingham: Open University Press.

Spearman, C. (1927) *Abilities of Man*. Basingstoke: Macmillan

Sternberg, R.J. (1985) *Beyond IQ: A Triarchic Theory of Human Intelligence*. Cambridge: Cambridge University Press

Strauss, S. (1981) *U-shaped Behavioural Growth*. London: Academic Press

Thurstone, L.L. and Thurstone, T.G. (1941) 'Factorial Studies of Intelligence', *Psychometric Monographs*, No.2

Vygotsky, L. (1962) *Thought and Language*. Cambridge, MA: MIT Press

Vygotsky, L. and Cole, M. (eds) (1978) *Mind in Society, The Development of Higher Psychological Processes*. Cambridge, MA: Harvard University Press

White, J. (2002) *The Child's Mind*. London: Routledge Falmer

Wood, D. (1998) *How Children Think and Learn: The Social Contexts of Cognitive Development*, 2nd edn. Oxford: Blackwell

Chapter 5

Language Development

The limits of my language mean the limits of my world.
Ludwig Wittgenstein (1889–1951)

Introduction

Language acquisition is one of the most fascinating areas of study and has been the subject of much debate between many linguists, psycholinguists and cognitive psychologists. There are various theories on how we learn to speak which will be examined in this chapter, but if we think about the fact that a 5- or 6-year-old child has virtually commanded adult grammar, we can see why this uniquely human skill has generated so much study and controversy. Crystal (1995: 427) states that language acquisition is 'the most complex skill anyone ever learns'. It is difficult to disagree with him. This chapter will outline influential language acquisition theories; the components of language: sound, grammar and meaning; pragmatics; and speaking and listening in the early years.

Language

Linguistics is the scientific study of language, but what do we mean by 'language'? In everyday use, the word 'language' has broader meaning than 'speech'. If we consider some of the usages (such as body language, sign language, bad language, the language of flowers) we can see that the term is used quite loosely. In linguistic terms, however, language is an organised system of symbols that we use to communicate. Animals can and do communicate with one another and with humans. For example, my cat tells me when he is hungry by standing at his bowl and miaowing loudly and persistently. Even a less basic instinct such as wanting to be stroked is communicated to me by the pat of his paw on my arm. This is communication, but it is not language. Human language can be distinguished by three main features: it is symbolic; it is grammatical; and it has no single system, as different groups of humans use different languages (Tomasello, 2003). The number of languages in use over the world is vast, with different calculations suggesting approximately somewhere between 5,000 and 6,000. This means that children learn to use the linguistic conventions of the community in which they live: their first language.

Non-verbal communication

In the previous paragraph reference was made to sign language, which is based on a symbolic code, and body language, which is not. Yet gesture, stance and facial expression are embedded in our communication and although this is not governed by symbols, it would be a failure to acknowledge the deep significance of our non-verbal signals if it were not included in this chapter on language development. Graddol *et al.* (1994) argue that if linguists focus only on verbal communication they will neglect the importance of non-verbal communication in enabling us to understand and exchange meanings. They highlight six features of non-verbal communication (NVC), also known as kinesics: gesture, proxemics, body contact, posture and body orientation, facial expression, gaze.

● *Gesture* can be either symbolic or non-specific. Symbolic includes signals with a recognised message, such as a wave, thumbs up or a shake of the head. Symbolic gesture may not be interpreted in the same way in different cultures and what may be a perfectly innocent gesture in one culture may well cause offence in another! Non-specific gesture is more vague and is best described as 'talking' with our hands. Some people do this more than others. It is interesting to watch politicians on television use certain gestures to emphasise key points.

- *Proxemics* refers to our personal space, that is, how close we are to the person we are speaking to. The closer we are to the person we are speaking to the more intimate we are. Sometimes we feel people are 'invading' our space because their notion of a comfortable distance is different from ours.

- *Body contact* can be formal, such as a handshake, or less formal, such as squeezing a person's arm when thanking them. Some people find physical contact uncomfortable, whereas others have a more 'touchy-feely' approach. This varies across cultures, illustrated by the way some cultures greet each other with a kiss on both cheeks. In Britain, this may happen, but often only within certain social groups and rarely between two men, unlike Arab countries.

- *Posture and body orientation* relate to how we hold ourselves and sit or stand. If one person is standing and the other is sitting, the person standing is seen to be in a dominant position. If we slouch back in a chair it appears more informal than if we are sitting upright. Some people might turn slightly away from someone if they do not want to include that person in the conversation.

- *Facial expression* is fairly self-explanatory, but emotion cannot be signalled by one specific facial movement as it is far more complex. For example, a smile (upward movement of the mouth) cannot signify happiness or friendliness if the eyes are signifying sadness, anger or threat. The face uses many muscles to show expression to signify an emotional state and this is intensified by other aspects of NVC, such as posture. Some facial and emotional expressions are culturally informed (see Chapter 6).

- *Gaze* is basically looking at another person. When one person looks at another and the look is returned resulting in mutual gaze, it is termed eye-contact. We are quite sensitive to eye-contact and expect to be looked at when we are speaking. If you have ever been in a position when you are speaking to people and their gaze is diverted to somewhere else, you may well have felt that they are no longer listening and have become interested in another person's conversation or something they have seen. This can be quite off-putting for the speaker. Speakers, however, often glance away when they are speaking because they are also thinking as they speak. Again there are also cultural differences, with some Afro-Caribbean children looking away in deference to dominant adults.

All of these aspects of NVC contribute to our communication with others and may often send out more powerful messages than the words we use. There have been many estimates of how much of our communication is non-verbal, from 65 to 95 per cent, but what is clear is that it is an essential part of our interaction with others.

Practical Tasks

Non-verbal communication

Level 1

List as many different types of symbolic gestures as you can think of.

- Do any have more than one meaning?
- Could this lead to confusion or is the meaning apparent by the context?
- How many have you seen children using?

Level 2

Observe an adult speaking to a child/children. Note down the NVC exhibited by both the adult and the child/children.

- What does this indicate about their involvement, interest, emotional state (relaxed, happy, intimidated, uncomfortable, bored)?
- Could you be misreading any signals?

Level 3

- Observe more than one adult speaking to a child/children. Note down the NVC exhibited by both the adults and the child/children.
- Is any one type of NVC more prevalent than another?
- Are the different types of NVC used by both adults and children or does NVC differ between adults and adults, children and children and between adults and children?
- If so, why might this be?

Forming relationships is vital to child development. The key way in which we form relationships is through communication and much of that is non-verbal. Touching, looking, smiling and holding are ever-present in a loving relationship between a baby and the caring adult and help to secure a strong bond. David *et al.* (2003: 70) highlight the importance of a 'warm and loving relationship' to enable the child to become a *skilful communicator,* one of the four components that was part of the Birth to Three Matters Framework (SureStart, 2003). Babies have very clear NVC signals long before they begin to grasp speech. Lindon (2005) outlines some of the common gestures babies make, such as an outstretched hand to request an object, and body movements to indicate refusal, such as turning the head away. Just looking at a baby's face can tell us about how he/she is feeling, such as contented, happy, curious or distressed. Looking at photographs can be illuminating, such as those supplied by Murray and Andrews (2000) to show the ways babies communicate and the importance of a sensitive adult to respond to this. Listening to children is not only verbal. We 'listen' with more than our hearing. We can feel if someone tenses and we can see if someone looks upset and respond appropriately. The Director of the Coram Family Listening to Young Children Project, Lancaster (2003: 7), maintains that 'babies' voices are there for us to hear from birth'; it is the role of the adult to be sensitive to that voice, to understand it and to respond.

Research

Baby signing

Baby signing (see Picture 5.1) is fairly new concept, beginning in America in the late 1980s, but having wider recognition following research by Goodwin *et al.* (2000). They noted that research in language development tended to focus almost exclusively on the development of verbal language, and they were interested in babies' use of gesture (reaching, pointing) and 3–5-year-olds' use of mime in play. Their research involved working with babies from 11 months old using a recognised set of sign language symbols for parents to use and teach their babies. The results indicated that signing also appeared to facilitate verbal development, although, as they acknowledge, this could be due to the signing encouraging additional verbal prompts and reactions from the adults. There are now various courses running in the UK for parents and babies to learn this sign language. Grove *et al.* (2004) are somewhat sceptical, criticising the cost of the courses and emphasising the value of babies' natural gestures and the potentially rich communication occurring between parents and child in response to these. Whatever personal view is held about baby signing, what is positive is the recognition of the vital role of non-verbal communication and the importance of viewing language development in its widest sense.

Picture 5.1 Baby signing
Source: Christina Kennedy/Alamy Images

Language acquisition theories

Having emphasised the importance of non-verbal communication in language, this chapter will now turn to that which is unique to humans and the subject of much debate: speech. Spoken language is our primary means of communication, leading to our secondary means of communication, which is reading and writing. Without oracy there would be no literacy. Being proficient in our first language is therefore paramount to our success as a social being within a literate society.

The study of linguistics is highly complex, but one part of this science is how we acquire our first language. There are a number of theories, but we shall look at an overview of those most discussed to highlight the key areas of debate. Perhaps the two most talked about are the opposing nature versus nurture views, or as they are more commonly known within language development: nativist and empiricist. The two theorists most associated with these two differing views on language acquisition, brought to the fore in the 1950s and 1960s, are Noam Chomsky and B.F. Skinner.

B.F. Skinner (1904–90)

Skinner's behaviourist theory has already been discussed in Chapter 1, and it is this theory which he applied to language acquisition. This nurture/empiricist view of development focuses on language as a learned behaviour by emphasising the child's imitation of the language of others and the role of adult reinforcement. Skinner viewed a baby's babbling as the beginnings of speech and that the positive response of adults to this babbling promotes further attempts to use verbal language. As the babbling is reinforced, it gradually becomes recognisable words. Mukherji and O'Dea (2000) cite the many natural behaviours adults exhibit with babies and toddlers, such as responding positively to attempts at communication; being proactive, such as waving and repeating 'bye bye' or 'ta ta'; and naming objects and events. These certainly would reinforce language and encourage repetition.

'Motherese' is a term used to describe the unique voice adults use when talking to babies which is used all over the world, but not in all cultures. It is generally slower, with shorter sentences, higher-pitched and more exaggerated in intonation than the speech of adult-to-adult. There is little evidence to suggest that this improves children's capacity to learn language and has been criticised by Chomsky, although the musicality of motherese has been shown to be preferred by babies in research by Trevarthen (1999). Lindon (2005) notes that the name 'motherese' suggests that it is only mothers that use this modified language with babies, which is clearly not the case, and refers instead to 'infant-directed speech'.

The behaviourist theory led to some people experimenting with teaching primates language, usually with American sign language due to the physiological differences in the mouths and throats of humans and apes, with varying and disputable degrees of success. Two high profile cases were the Gardners with Washoe in the 1960s and Patterson with Koko in the 1970s; although the primates were able to form some of the signs, there is debate about their understanding, and therefore whether this could be viewed as learning language. Research into developing language in primates is continuing at Central Washington University's Chimpanzee and Human Communication Institute, with descendants of Washoe, so clearly this is still a theory held strongly by some. Pinker (1995) questions this link with our apparent closest relative, the chimpanzee. He cites the fact that chimpanzees in the various studies have needed extensive, explicit teaching to learn a few words, in sharp contrast with children who learn thousand of words in complex structures without any apparent direct teaching. He reasons that chimpanzees and humans evolved from one common ancestor, but they then split and it is the human species that developed the capacity for language, not chimpanzees. Pinker clearly believes humans have an innate ability for language, a theory introduced by Chomsky.

Noam Chomsky (1928–)

Chomsky challenged Skinner's behavioural theory on language acquisition, taking a nature/nativist approach. He strongly questioned the notion that children learned language through repetition, particularly noting the fact that children regularly use grammatically incorrect words such as 'he runned away', which are unlikely to have been used by adults. Our natural speech patterns are littered with hesitancies and repeated words, not model sentences to be easily copied. He used the term 'poverty of the stimulus' to define this. He also believed that language is unique to the user and is not repetition of previously heard utterances (Chomsky, 1972). This led to his assertion that we have an innate ability to learn language, known as the Language Acquisition Device (LAD). In effect, this theory states that we are physiologically programmed to learn the language that we hear as a baby. Therefore, a baby hearing French will learn to speak French and a baby hearing English will learn to speak English, because this is the language they are exposed to, but they both have the same LAD. This is also known as universal grammar, which is both innate and unique to humans and separate from general cognitive principles. It enables children to process the sounds they hear and make a response which, over time, refines into proficient language use. Chomsky's explanation of young children's incorrect use of grammar, such as 'runned', was due to a child abstracting a rule and overgeneralising. Chomsky's view certainly became popular, as Skinner's reinforcement paradigm did seem somewhat simplistic to explain such a complex phenomenon.

There are other theories and critics of Chomsky's theory, which will be discussed after the Practical Tasks below. One of the main criticisms is Chomsky's apparent lack of acknowledgement of the role of the adult or the human need for social interaction. Lyons (1977: 145) makes the important point that Chomsky did not 'entirely abandon' the behaviourist account of language acquisition, but felt it needed to be supplemented with a more substantial theoretical framework. He did not value infant-directed speech, but he did value the external world and the world of social activity.

Practical Tasks

Applying the theories

Level 1

Tape yourself having a conversation with another adult. Listen to the tape and note down your vocal tags (terms, 'you know', 'right', etc.), repetitions of words or the beginnings of words, hesitations, rewording of phrases/sentences, substitute words ('thingy', 'whatsit'), unfinished sentences and interruptions Consider Skinner's behaviourist theory in the light of this.

- What elements of your speech would support a child learning language and what elements would be a hindrance?

Level 2

Observe a child and adult talking. Consider Skinner's behaviourist theory and note down ways in which the adult is reinforcing/supporting the child's talk. Listen closely to the adult.

- Are there any elements of the talk (see Level 1) that are not a perfect model of language?
- How does this fit with the behaviourist theory?

Level 3

Observe a child and adult talking (see Levels 1 and 2). Consider both Skinner's behaviourist theory and Chomsky's nativist theory. Argue both for and against each theory based on your observations.

Additional theories

There are critics of Chomsky's theory, particularly as it is difficult to test and provide evidence. Trask and Mayblin (2000: 129) state that critics of nativism feel that it is not a hypothesis as it lacks any meaningful scientific investigation. Tomasello (2003) challenges Chomsky's assertion that children's grammatical errors support his theory, stating that children *learn* the rules of grammar through learning words and then learning how to put them together as a cognitive process. This is referred to as the 'usage-based' theory, in which language is learned through regular use, with this familiarity leading to mastery and sophistication. Gasser (2006) also challenges the notion that language is too highly complex for it to be learned without a language acquisition device. He asserts that there is regularity in language and that humans have powerful statistical learning mechanisms that make language accessible. He also believes that although language is not overtly 'taught', adults put in place unconscious strategies to support a child in language development. The infant-directed speech discussed earlier would be an example of this in the early stages of language development. Tomasello and Gasser are more sympathetic to the empiricist theory, viewing language as learned, but within our complex cognitive framework.

Bruner (1983) took the socio-interactionist view, which does not dismiss Chomsky's theory of the LAD, but puts more emphasis on the social and cultural setting in which the language is learned. He introduced the term Language Acquisition Support System (LASS), to accompany the LAD, in which the adults provide a supportive framework to promote language development. The intrinsic human need to interact is the basis for this, and Bruner's theory of adults 'scaffolding' children's learning is central to this idea. Feral children, sad cases where children have been abandoned and have had to survive in extreme deprivation, are examples of children growing up without human interaction. High profile cases, such as Genie, who was found at the age of 13 having been strapped onto a potty chair all day and locked in a room throughout her life, and Victor, known as 'the wild boy of Aveyron' who lived in the wild until discovered at the age of 12, both had no language on discovery. Despite attempts to teach them language, there was little success. Genie did manage to learn words and some two-word sentences, but never learnt grammar and therefore could not put the words together in coherent sentences. The reasons why feral children struggle to learn language could be several, but lack of human interaction in their formative years could be one. Lenneberg (1921–75) said that there is a critical period after which language acquisition is impossible. He believed that after puberty it was no longer possible to learn language; in a sense, the LAD could no longer be activated. More recent studies on feral children have suggested that this critical period could be shorter, with children over 6 still unable to learn to speak. Pinker (1995) also cites the critical period for normal language development as being up to 6 years of age. Studies on feral children are fraught with difficulties as there are so many other variables and each case is so different that it is impossible to draw any firm conclusions, but it does provide a different dimension to further discussion.

Vygotsky (1896–1934) and Piaget (1896–1980) both saw language acquisition as part of the cognitive process, within the general structures of thinking. This is often known as the cognitive approach (Whitehead, 1990). However, this is where the similarity ends. Piaget (1929; 1950) believed that cognitive development came first and then language helped to put symbols to those thoughts. As the child develops schemas, words are used to describe and then refine those schemas. For example, a child understands that the four-legged, furry being is different from a human and learns the word for that animal is 'cat'. The child then calls another four-legged, furry being 'cat' and is told it is a dog. The role of language is to refine the schema, but the schema was in existence in the child's mind before the word. Pinker (1995) dismisses Piaget's theory as just labelling thoughts and Lambirth (2005: 76) states that: 'concepts are formed, organised and structured through the use of language'. Vygotsky (1978) had very different ideas about language and thought. He believed that there was a more distinct relationship between language and thought and stated that thought comes into existence through language. He saw speech as a way in which children make sense of the world alongside the physical exploration of first-hand experience (Vygotsky, 1978). He also believed that thought and speech were separate at birth, going through a variety of processes, but by about the age of 2 these processes combined with the creation of verbal thinking.

Piaget and Vygotsky also had different views about language development. Piaget (1959) classified the function of children's speech into two areas: egocentric and socialised. Egocentric speech is repetition and monologue which serves to accompany an action, with no social function, which Piaget claimed disappears as the child matures. Vygotsky (1978) did not believe egocentric speech to be 'primitive and infantile' as Piaget had put it (Piaget, 1959:17), but an important tool for cognitive development. According to Vygotsky (1978), as children mature egocentric speech does not disappear, it becomes inner speech. Vygotsky, like Bruner (1983), also noted the influence of the adult or competent speaker in scaffolding and developing children's speech, which is related to the zone of proximal development discussed in earlier chapters. Goodwin (2001) highlights the value of talking out loud to consolidate learning, making the point that the process of articulation is important to our understanding. This suggests that egocentric speech is not always internalised, but continues to some extent throughout our lives. If we think about activities such as learning to drive, 'mirror, signal, manoeuvre' is a phrase spoken by many. Basil Fawlty gave his car a good talking to before finally thrashing it with the branch of a tree. As Homer Simpson would say: 'It's funny 'cos it's true'. We use language to clarify our thoughts, aid our memory, deepen our understanding and as an outlet for our emotions to help us to come to terms with how we are feeling.

Reflective Tasks

Language and thought

Level 1

Consider times when you have talked out loud to yourself. In what types of situations does this occur? Why do you think you spoke the words rather than internalised them and how did it help you?

Level 2

Explain to a friend/colleague the differences between Piaget's and Vygotsky's views on language and thought. Did this process help you to clarify your own knowledge? If so, why might that be?

Level 3

Explain to a friend/colleague Bruner's, Vygotsky's and Piaget's views. Provide your own examples to illustrate the theories.

- Did this process help you to clarify both your knowledge and understanding and its application to your own practice.
- If so, why might that be?
- Has this process prompted you to ask further questions about the theories? If so, note these down and try to find the answers.
- What have you learnt from this exercise?

To conclude this part of the chapter on theories of language acquisition and development, it is clear that the debate will continue, but what is apparent is children's need for social interaction and the important role of the adult in scaffolding their development. These hold true whether due to biological or social factors. Many researchers adopt a balanced view which accepts humans' **innate** ability for language, but which also accepts the role of the adult as facilitator. The remarkable capacity of children to master language is now going to be examined in more detail as we focus on the three components that constitute spoken language: sound, grammar and meaning.

Sound – phonology

Phonology is concerned with the organisation and patterning of sounds in a language. It includes important indicators of meaning, such as intonation and use of emphasis. The pitch, loudness and duration of speech sounds are called prosody (Graddol *et al.*, 1994) and enable us to clarify meaning which goes beyond the actual words that we are using. In other words, the *way* we say something. If someone asked you what you thought of this book, your reply could be, 'It's really interesting', but we would have to hear you say it to know if you were genuinely interested or thoroughly bored and using sarcasm (we hope it would be the former!). Crystal (1995) also refers to the importance of pauses in prosody, and anybody who is good at telling jokes knows how to use the pause to good effect in order to elicit the biggest laugh. The stress placed on certain words can also emphasise meaning:

1 *I* bought the wine (it was me, nobody else – perhaps *you* need to pay for something).

2 I *bought* the wine (I didn't steal it).

3 I bought the *wine* (someone else bought the other stuff).

If you try saying 'yes' or 'no' in as many different ways as possible, you can begin to see how important prosody is to the spoken word.

Paralinguistics is another way in which we use sound to convey meaning. This can include the type of voice we use (e.g. a whisper), or the types of noises we often use when listening to someone, such as 'ah' and 'mmm'. You may well have been on the telephone and questioned whether or not the person you are speaking to is still there if there is an absence of these types of sounds. Paralinguistics is often used with babies when the parent/carer sensitively imitates the baby's cooing and babbling sounds as a form of interaction.

Phonology describes and charts the varieties of speech sounds and pronunciation. Within the UK there are a variety of accents which use different sounds, such as the emphasised rolled 'r' of the Scots and the flat vowel sounds of the North of England. We can often tell which foreign language is being spoken by the sounds and rhythm, even though we might not understand the words, for example the difference between the sounds of Italian and the sounds of German. Before examining phonology in more detail it might be useful to define the many similar words used within this discipline:

- **Phonetics** is the way we form, transmit and hear sounds. Whitehead (1990) refers to this as applied linguistics. It is a technical study of the physical vocal system.

- Phonology is the sound system of a particular language and therefore does not apply to all sounds the vocal system can make. For example, the English language does not produce a guttural sound common in Middle Eastern languages and Manderin does not use the 'r' sound as it is used in England. This is why some sounds common in English are difficult for some people speaking English as a second language whose first language does not contain those sounds.

- A **phoneme** is a sound. It may not be represented in the same way in writing. For example, 'fish' and 'phonetics' have the same phoneme at the start (they both begin with the same sound), but are spelt differently.
- **Phonics** is the teaching and learning of letter/sound correspondence for reading and writing.

We are going to be concentrating on phonology in this chapter.

Articulation

In addition to our vocal chords (see Figure 5.1), we use a variety of mouthparts to make different sounds when speaking. These are:

- lips (upper and lower);
- tongue (tip, middle and back);
- alveolar ridge (the ridge just behind the top teeth);
- hard palate;
- soft palate;
- teeth (upper and lower).

Although there are only 26 letters in the English alphabet, there are actually about 44 phonemes in the English language of which 20 or more are vowel sounds (Crystal, 1995). We tend to refer to vowel sounds as 'open' sounds because no part of the mouth is closed and the different mouthparts do not come into contact with one another. Regional accents do affect the way that some sounds are made, particularly, but not exclusively, vowel sounds. The next task will encourage you to think about how the mouthparts are used to make some of the consonant sounds in English, outlined in the Practical Tasks overleaf.

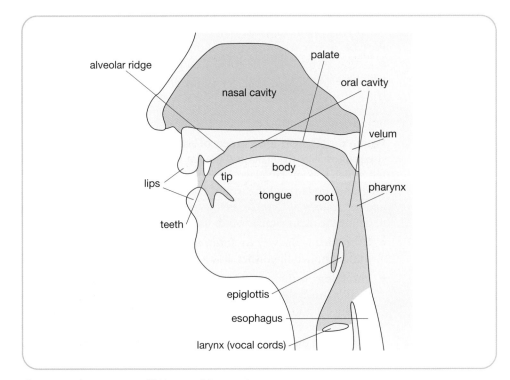

Figure 5.1 The anatomical location of the vocal tract
Source: http://www.indiana.edu/~hlw/PhonUnits/vowels.html

Practical Tasks

The way we produce sounds

'b' as in bat; 'c' as in cat, 'd' as in dog, 'f' as in fish, 'g' as in goat, 'j' as in jig, 'l' as in leg, 'm' as in milk, 'n' as in name, 'p' as in pig, 'r' as in red, 's' as in said, 't' as in top, 'v' as in vet, 'w' as in wet, 'y' as in yes, 'z' as in zoo, 'th' as in think, 'th' as in the. (Taken from Graddol *et al.*, 1994: 31).

Level 1

Say each of the above sounds and try to work out which mouthparts you are using to articulate them. Use a mirror to help you.

Level 2

Complete the Level 1 task and note down any that use the same mouthparts but sound different. Why do you think this is?

Level 3

Complete the tasks for Levels 1 and 2. A baby's babbling consists of repetitions of consonants such as: 'bbbb', 'mmmm' 'dddd' 'sssss' 'wwww' 'ttttt', but rarely of 'th' 'ffff' 'vvvv' 'lllll' and 'rrrr'. Explain why you think this is.

An outline of the way we produce these sounds can be found in Table 5.1. Only look at this list when you have tried for yourself first.

Source: Graddol *et al.*, 1994

Table 5.1 The way we produce sounds

Sound	Mouth parts used
b as in bat	Upper and lower lips
c as in cat	Back of tongue and soft palate
d as in dog	Tip of tongue and alveolar ridge
f as in fish	Top teeth and lower lip
g as in goat	Back of tongue and soft palate
j as in jig	Middle of tongue against the alveolar ridge and hard palate, sides of tongue against side top teeth
l as in leg	Tip of tongue and alveolar ridge
m as in milk	Upper and lower lips
n as in name	Tongue tip and alveolar ridge, sides of tongue against side top teeth
p as in pig	Upper and lower lips
r as in red	Tip of tongue rolled back nearly touching the alveolar ridge, sides of tongue against side top teeth, middle of tongue lowered. In a rolled 'r', the tip of tongue 'trills' against the alveolar ridge
s as in said	Tongue tip and middle making light contact with the alveolar ridge, sides of tongue touching sides of top teeth. Air escapes through a groove in the tongue
t as in top	Tip of tongue and alveolar ridge
v as in vet	Top teeth and lower lip

Table 5.1 *Continued*

Sound	Mouth parts used
w as in wet	Upper and lower lips rounded, back of tongue held high
y as in yes	Tongue high in the mouth with the sides touching the top side teeth
z as in zoo	Tongue tip and middle making light contact with the alveolar ridge, sides of tongue touching sides of top teeth. Air escapes through a groove in the tongue
th as in think	Tip of tongue between top and bottom teeth
th as in the	Tip of tongue between top and bottom teeth

One of the key differences in making these sounds is that some are voiced and some are unvoiced. This means that some have vocal-chord vibrations (we use our voice to say it) and others do not. For example, you probably noted that 'p' and 'b' were made in the same way, using upper and lower lips, but they sound slightly different. This is because 'b' is a voiced sound and 'p' is unvoiced. Graddol *et al.* (1994) include this useful exercise, which is your next practical task, to help illustrate the point.

Practical Tasks

Voiced and unvoiced sounds

Articulate the final sound of each of these words below:

1. rum – 'mmmmm'
2. buzz – 'zzzzzzz'
3. love – 'vvvv'
4. run – 'nnnnnn'
5. bus – 'ssssssss'
6. buff – 'ffffffff'

And the initial sounds of:

7. 'this' – 'ththth' and
8. 'thistle' – 'ththth'.

Say the word and then the sound. Prolong the sound for a few seconds. Now try singing each sound by producing a pitched note. You should find that only some of the sounds can be sung like this. The others cannot be sung unless they are turned into one of the sounds that can. Those that can be sung are voiced sounds and those that cannot are unvoiced.

Level 1

Do the task above. Using two columns, note which of the sounds above can be sung in one column and the ones that cannot in the other. Map a line from each sound in the second column to the sound it turns into in the first column when you try to sing it.

Level 2

Do the task above. Take all the sounds from the previous task and sort them into voiced and unvoiced.

Level 3

Do the task above and the Level 2 task. Explain what impact this knowledge would have on your pronunciation of sounds if you were teaching phonics to help a child learn to read or helping a child with articulation difficulties.

Source: Graddol *et al*., 1994

Articulation and phonics

When teaching children the different phonemes, it is important that we articulate them as accurately as possible. Our accent might affect the way we pronounce some sounds and if we have an accent that is different from the accent of the children we work with this is something to bear in mind. As a teacher, I was once told by a parent to stop teaching her child to speak with a Yorkshire accent because he was pronouncing the 'u' as in bus with a flat vowel sound. We had been looking at 'u' in the middle of consonant-vowel-consonant (CVC) words and the child was using my northern pronunciation! There is no correct or incorrect accent and this should not become an issue if we are aware of the differences and acknowledge them. The way we pronounce consonants depends on the mouthparts we use to form them. The 'plosives' are formed by holding and then exploding the air to make the sound in p/, b/, t/, d/, k/, g. It is difficult to say these sounds without adding a vowel 'uh' after them. It is important to make this as minimal as possible, but it is impossible not to make a small vowel sound. All other consonant sounds can be articulated without the 'uh' vowel following them. The 'fricatives' are sounds that are made by forcing the air through a passage, as in s/, f/, v/, h,/ z. These can all be held on to make the sound without adding the 'uh' vowel sound, so it should be: 'sssss', 'vvvvv', not 'suh', 'vuh'. It is the same for 'nasal' consonants: 'nnnnn', 'mmmm', not 'nuh', 'muh'. It is useful to call these continuous sounds because we can hold them on continuously and do not need to add a vowel sound to them. When teaching phonics, it is important to keep the sound as pure as possible.

There has been much debate about the teaching of phonics in recent years and the Rose Report (DfES, 2006a) highlighted the need for systematic phonics teaching in the early years of school to provide children with the best start to early reading and writing (see Picture 5.2). Two different types of phonics are regularly mentioned: synthetic and analytic, with synthetic phonics being the preferred method cited by the government. This chapter is concerned with language development rather than reading and writing development, but brief definitions of **synthetic** and **analytic phonics** have been included in Figure 5.2.

Babbling

Having knowledge of how sounds are produced can help us to understand phonological processes in a child's language development. In the first two or three months the sounds babies make are mostly associated with cooing. From about 4- to 5 months onwards children begin to make speech-like sounds, which are the initial stage of babbling, called 'marginal babbling' (O'Grady, 2005). These early stages also include the child experimenting with 'fun' noises, such as blowing bubbles and blowing raspberries (Whitehead, 1990). This stage is sometimes referred to as 'vocal play' (Crystal, 1995), with the baby

The following definitions of 'synthetic' and 'analytic' phonics have been taken from Greg Brooks' report Sound Sense: *The Phonics Element of the National Literacy Strategy – A Report to the Department for Education and Skills*, University of Sheffield (2003).

Synthetic phonics – refers to an approach to the teaching of reading in which phonemes (sounds) associated with particular graphemes (letters) are pronounced in isolation and blended together (synthesised). For example, children are taught to take a single-syllable word such as *cat* apart into its three letters, pronounce a phoneme for each letter in turn /k, æ, t/, and blend the phonemes together to form a word. Synthetic phonics for writing reverses the sequence: children are taught to say the word they wish to write, segment it into its phonemes and say them in turn, for example /d, ɒ, g/, and write a grapheme for each phoneme in turn to produce the written word, *dog*.

Analytic phonics – refers to an approach to the teaching of reading in which the phonemes associated with particular graphemes are not pronounced in isolation. Children identify (analyse) the common phoneme in a set of words in which each word contains the phoneme under study. For example, teacher and pupils discuss how the following words are alike: *pat, park, push* and *pen*. Analytic phonics for writing similarly relies on inferential learning: realising that the initial phoneme in /pɪg/ is the same as that in /pæt, paːk, pʊʃ/ and /pen/, children deduce that they must write that phoneme with grapheme <p>.

Figure 5.2 Definition of synthetic and analytic phonics
Source: http://www.standards.dfes.gov.uk/pdf/literacy/gbrooks_phonics.pdf

Picture 5.2 A phonics lesson
Source: Gideon Mendel/Corbis

experimenting with wide pitch glides and noises made with the lips. By 6 months the vocal play has totally developed into babbling. This tends to consist of repeated syllables, such as 'dadada', increasing in consistency up until 10–12 months of age, often overlapping slightly with the child's first words. At about 9 months, the babbling is consistent with the phonology of the child's first language, so there is a notable difference between the babbling of a baby exposed to English from that of a baby exposed to another phonology, such as Urdu (Mukherji and O'Dea, 2000). Babies spend a lot of time watching and listening. They see the lips moving as an adult talks to them and hear the pattern and rhythm of their voices. There is also evidence that babies can hear when they are still in the womb. DeCasper and Spence (1986) report on their study involving the mother reading the same story for six weeks prior to the birth. They show evidence that the baby recognised the story, perhaps due to the rhythm, two days after birth. Kisilvsky *et al.* (2003) report on their study which showed evidence of the foetus recognising the mother's voice over that of a stranger, by recording the change in its heartbeat when the mother spoke. Babbling is present in both hearing and deaf babies, which raises questions about whether or not it is a stage of language development, as it is not a direct response to the sounds heard by the baby. Deaf babies' babbling does eventually cease at about 9 months (Herman, 2002), which also coincides with the stage at which the babbling takes on the phonology of the language the baby is hearing. We could conclude from this that babbling becomes the first stage of speech development at approximately 9 months, or when the phonology becomes distinct.

First words

Children develop at different rates, but at about 12 months babies produce their first words. Often the repeated sounds in babbling, such as 'dada', are thought to be a reference to 'daddy', but are in fact just the child playing with sounds. The first word may not be recognisable to the adult, but it is the child's attempts to communicate using a specific word (Mukherji and O'Dea, 2000). The learning of first words is often quite slow, and these are usually nouns, naming people (mummy), animals (dog) or familiar objects (cup). Often the adult will support these early words by repeating them or asking questions to prompt the use of them, such as 'who is this?' or showing a picture and asking 'what is that?' The adult will also extend the word into a sentence, such as 'yes, this is your cup', which is perhaps an example of Gasser's unconscious support strategies (2006), mentioned earlier in the chapter. The word a child uses could have a variety of meanings, for example, 'cup' could mean: 'I want my cup', 'I'm thirsty', 'My cup is on the floor', 'Where is my cup?' 'That cup is like mine', to name a few. When my niece was a baby and she used the word 'hot' it could mean a number of things, such as 'too cold', 'too sour', 'too sweet', 'I'm full' and, occasionally, 'too hot'! She was basically telling us that something was wrong with the food and it was our job to find out what. This is known as the 'holophrase', which is when one word is used to represent a whole sentence. The relationship between the adult and the child and the sensitivity of the adult to the child's language should make this holophrase part of a meaningful interaction.

The articulation of sounds is still at an early stage of development and the child will make many substitutions and deletions (O'Grady, 2005). These are some of the common examples:

- deleting the end consonant: boat = bow, dog = doh;
- deleting the second sound of an initial consonant cluster: blanket = banket, try = tie, sleep = seep;
- deleting the 's' when followed by another consonant: stop = top, small = mall;
- deleting syllables: elephant = effant, giraffe = jaff;
- confusing voiced and unvoiced consonants at the beginnings and endings of words: cup = gup, bed = bet, push = bush;
- common substitutions, as can be seen in Table 5.2.

These are all common pronunciation problems and are quite usual between the ages of 2 and 5. As the child becomes more fluent, the pronunciation becomes more accurate. Children will also understand far more words than they can speak in the initial stages. Understanding words is called 'receptive' language and using spoken words is called 'expressive' language. Receptive language is usually far more advanced than expressive

Table 5.2 Common linguistic substitutions

Actual word	Child's pronunciation	Sustitution
lake	yake	Uses a 'y' for 'l'
look	wook	Uses a 'w' for 'l'
red	wed	Uses 'w' for 'r'
sheep	seep	Uses 's' for 'sh'
this	dis or vis	Uses 'd' or 'v/f' for 'th'

language, which is apparent when the adult asks the child to do something, such as point to a particular animal in a picture or to go and get something familiar. Children respond because they understand even though their expressive language is not as advanced. This is why having conversations with young children is so important.

Nursery rhymes and tongue-twisters are excellent ways to develop children's articulation. Some of the well-known rhymes have alliteration (repetition of the initial sound) which helps children to become more aware of the sounds in their language and helps them to practise their pronunciation. This is known as phonological awareness. Try some of these tongue-twisters:

Betty bought a bit of butter × 5

Red lorry, yellow lorry × 5

Red leather, yellow leather × 5

Peggy Babcock, Peggy Babcock × 5

There are some more in Figure 5.3. Try saying them slowly for clarity first and then gradually increase your speed. Ensure you articulate each word properly, even at speed.

Practical Tasks

Nursery rhymes

Level 1

List as many nursery rhymes as you can.

- What are the repeated sounds in each rhyme?
- Which do you think would be easiest for children to say and why?

Level 2

List as many nursery rhymes as you can. Try a few with children in your setting. Looking at the list of common deletions and substitutions, select the rhymes that would be most useful in helping to develop each of the articulation problems.

Level 3

Select three of the common substitution/deletion examples. Create your own rhymes and tongue-twisters which would help children to develop their articulation in the three areas of difficulty identified. Identify a child that you work with who has articulation difficulties and create a rhyme and tongue-twister that would help him or her.

A box of biscuits, a batch of mixed biscuits

A big black bug bit a big black bear,
made the big black bear bleed blood.

A flea and a fly flew up in a flue.
Said the flea, 'Let us fly!'
Said the fly, 'Let us flee!'
So they flew through a flaw in the flue.

Swan swam over the sea,
Swim, swan, swim!
Swan swam back again
Well swum, swan!

Peter Piper picked a peck of pickled pepper
A peck of pickled pepper Peter Piper picked
If Peter Piper picked a peck of pickled pepper
Where's the peck of pickled pepper Peter Piper picked?

Sister Suzie's sewing shirts for soldiers
Such skill at sewing shirts my fine young sister Suzie shows
Some soldiers send epistles say they'd sooner sleep on thistles
Than the saucy soft short shirts for soldiers sister Suzie sews

Des does a dastardly deed

Round the rugged rocks the ragged rascal ran

Brad's big black bath brush broke.

She sifted thistles through her thistle-sifter.

Quick kiss. Quicker kiss.

Please pay promptly.

If Stu chews shoes, should Stu choose the shoes he chews?

I wish to wash my Irish wristwatch.

The sixth sick sheik's sixth sheep's sick.

Thin sticks, thick bricks.

Figure 5.3 Some more tongue-twisters

Once a child has learnt about 50 words, learning is accelerated. By the age of 6, children have a vocabulary of about 14,000 words (O'Grady, 2005). It is at about 15–18 months onwards when children begin to put words together, which is the early stage of grammar. This chapter will now look more closely the development of the grammatical constructs which underpin the English language.

Grammar – morphology and syntax

The word 'grammar' is used by linguists in a variety of ways (Graddol *et al.*, 1994), but essentially it is the way words are put together to produce meaning, so as soon as children use more than one word they are beginning to show an understanding of grammar. Crystal (1995: 190) puts it more simply: 'It's all to do with making sense.' Some people feel quite worried by the word 'grammar', but there is a distinction between 'knowing grammar' and 'knowing *about* grammar' (Crystal, 1995: 191); in this instance we will be concentrating on the former. We have specified two aspects of grammar: morphology and syntax. **Morphology** is the study of word structure and this aspect of grammar is involved when children learn the way words change, such as adding an 's' to make a word a plural or 'ed' to put it in the past tense. **Syntax** is the study of sentence structure and it is this aspect of grammar when children learn to order words within a sentence to communicate meaning fully. The learning of grammar is a continual process, but there are identifiable stages.

Roger Brown (1973), a pioneer in children's language development, outlined five main stages of language acquisition:

1. *15–30 months*. Two-word sentences, which could have different grammatical attributes such as a verb and a noun, 'push truck'; a reference to location, 'in here'; negation, 'allgone milk'; or saying who possesses something, 'mummy shoe'. Like the holophrase, these two-word sentences could each have a variety of meanings. These are sometimes referred to as telegraphic sentences because they only use the key words.

2. *28–36 months*. Use of morphemic structure, such as 'ing' and plurals: 'falling down', 'my biscuits'.

3. *36–42 months*. More three word sentences and beginning to ask questions: 'Where is mummy?' 'Is she coming?'

4. *40–46 months*. Longer simple sentences and more consistent use of correct morphemic endings: 'Mummy walked to the shops.'

5. *42–52+ months*. Use of contractions, 'She's coming' and use of compound and complex sentences with more than one subject, 'Mummy has gone to the shops and daddy is making tea.' 'Mummy has gone to the shops because we need some milk.'

There are many different charts outlining speech development in various detail, such as those in Sheridan (1997) and Bee (2004), but the main stages are all very similar. During these stages, children are also very creative with their use of language, applying some of the grammatical rules to invent new verbs, particularly between the ages of 2 and 3. O'Grady (2005: 29) gives these examples: 'How do you know where to scissor it?' (cut it open), 'Did you needle this?' (sew this) and 'I'm talling' (growing taller). These created words are a good sign that children are understanding their language and that they are enjoying using it. They are playing with the tools of language and finding out about it in the same way that they might play with objects and find out about them with their eyes and hands.

Some of the common errors that children make are related to morphology. It is understandable due to the inconsistency of the English language, although children do learn irregular nouns and verbs surprisingly quickly. Common examples are:

- Adding 'ed' to irregular verbs: runned (ran), goed (went), sleeped (slept), 'getted' (got), singed (sang), see'd (saw), sinked (sank), broked (broken).
- Occasionally adding 'ed' to the past participle of irregular verb: gotted (got), ranned (ran), although this is less common.
- Adding 's' to irregular nouns that do not form plurals with an 's': sheeps, mouses.

Others are related to the use of pronouns, using 'me' instead of 'I'. So the pronoun is used correctly in the sentence 'will you cuddle me', but is used incorrectly in the sentence, 'me want a cuddle'. Some children rarely make grammatical errors, but even those who make a lot will eventually learn the correct form. Some adults also have problems with the occasional irregular verb. Common mistakes include the use of 'sat' and 'stood'. I have heard television presenters, who are supposed to be using standard English, say 'I am stood' rather than 'I am standing' or 'I am sat' rather than 'I am sitting', so the English language is not easy to get right all of the time! Different dialects also put words together in a non-standard way, using their own syntax systems. Non-standard use of the pronoun, for example, 'give I the apple' instead of 'give me the apple' used in some dialects, such as in parts of the South-West, is not due to lack of knowledge and experience, but is part of the dialect. The way the significant adults in a child's life speak will, of course, have a direct influence on the child's speech. It is therefore important to distinguish between the syntax of a dialect and grammatical errors due to a child's stage of speech development.

Jean Berko (1958) constructed an experiment to try to find out more about children's learning of morphology. She used nonsense words rather than real words to ensure that the children were applying rules of morphology rather than using existing knowledge of words. She was particularly interested in pluralisations and putting words into the past tense. She invented a little character called a 'wug' and showed a picture of one wug saying 'this is a wug' and then showed a picture of two, saying 'now there is another one, now there are two …', providing the child with the opportunity to pluralise. Seventy-five per cent of the 4–5-year-olds were able to pluralise and 97 per cent of 6–7-year-olds. As the study progressed she used more irregular words. She found that children modelled their answers on the most common, regular word endings, which is perhaps why they use 'ed' on irregular verbs. What is significant is that children are able to apply grammatical rules and the more experienced language users they are, the more they are able to deal with irregularity.

Speech and language problems

Children develop articulation and syntax at different rates, but it is useful to be aware of the developmental stages to identify potential problems. For example, if a child is not putting together two word sentences by the age of $2-2\frac{1}{2}$ years of age, then it suggests possible language delay. Communication disorders can be defined as either articulation/speech disorders or language disorders. Articulation disorders can be difficulty with specific sounds, two of the most common being unable to articulate 'r' and substituting it with 'w', or being unable to articulate 's' and 'z' and substituting them with 'th'. Sometimes these can be corrected with speech therapy (Retuccia, 2002), but often they are not corrected and will continue throughout the child's life into adulthood without causing any problem. A more potentially upsetting speech disorder is that of stammering or stuttering. This is a fluency disorder which commonly appears between the ages of 2 and 4 and often disappears just as quickly. If a child stammers for over a period of three years then it is likely to be a more persistent problem. Speech therapy can help a child to control the stammer, but it may reappear during times of stress (Craig and Tran, 2005).

Language disorders are related to communicating thoughts and putting them into a sequential, logical order so that they can be understood. It also relates to understanding language, so it can affect both receptive and expressive language. Sometimes a child might have a hearing problem which will affect their language development. Children on the autistic spectrum or those with dyslexia or dyspraxia may also have language difficulties. There are also children who choose not to speak, known as selective mutisim. I worked with a child who did not speak in infant school for the full three years. He did not say one word, not even to friends in the playground. His mother brought tapes of him talking at home, but for some reason he would not talk in school. We were not able to help this child during his time with us, but it is important to be aware of communication disorders and to seek specialist help where necessary.

Tools for Learning

Narrative as a research tool

Narrative can be a useful research tool. It involves research participants or informants telling their story. Stories can be on any theme, such as critical incidents that influence your ideas/behaviour/development, as for example described in Chapter 2; your first day at school; an emotional experience (see Chapter 6); parenting (see Chapter 8).

If the same story is told by different participants, then there is a form of triangulation occurring, with the story being told from different perspectives. For example, a child, teacher and parent may provide their stories about teaching/learning to read, or a child with a speech impediment and a speech therapist may tell their stories about overcoming difficulties and what strategies worked best from their perspective.

Reflective Tasks

Stammering

Read the following narrative extract from an 8-year-old who has a stammer:

> I feel embarrassed sometimes when I have to speak in front of the class. I worry about not being able to speak in front of them. I have been picked on and I used to hate going into lunch. I wanted to be on my own. I don't like reading in front of people. Sometimes people try to help by saying 'slow down' or 'take a deep breath' which I hate because it is not that easy. If it was, I wouldn't have a stutter. I don't like it when people fill in what they think I am going to say. I like to put my hand up rather than be picked on to speak. I don't want to be treated any differently though.

Level 1

- Have you ever felt similar emotions when being asked to speak in front of people?
- What makes you feel anxious?
- What would help you?

Level 2

Find out more about stammering. There are several useful websites on speech therapy which provide factual information, case studies and ways to help. The British Stammering Association (www.stammering.org) could be a good starting point. What strategies could help this child?

Level 3

Do the task for Level 2.

- Is this child's story typical of others who stammer or do people feel differently?
- This child clearly does not like doing some things which are everyday events in schools and yet does not want to be treated differently. How would you approach this if this child was in your class/setting?

Meaning – semantics

Semantics is concerned with the study of meaning and is therefore extremely complex. It includes the study of vocabulary (lexis) because the contexts in which words are used can totally determine their meaning. Consider the sentence: 'The rabbit is ready to eat.' What do you think it means? It could mean: 'I've cleaned Fluffy's hutch out and she's hungry so I'll go and get her food', or it could mean: 'I've set the table and brought the rabbit out of the oven, so let's tuck in.' It all depends on the context.

Word usage affects meaning and therefore our language is never static but continually changing. Additions to the *Oxford English Dictionary* reflect our developing language. The English language has many influences, including Latin, Greek, French, German and Scandinavian. We now also have American, Canadian and Australian influences, particularly with the numerous imported television programmes and high street chains. 'Regular' used to mean 'often', but is now also used to represent a size – 'do you want regular or large fries with that?' Speaking of fries, our love of food from around the world has increased our vocabulary to include words to describe food from places such as Italy, India, China, Thailand, Mexico and Africa. Technology has demanded the introduction of new words to name the new inventions and processes, such as 'mobile phone' and 'texting'. Young, social groupings also like to have their own language to distinguish them from the older generation, such as 'wicked' meaning 'bad and evil' to my mother but meaning 'brilliant' to my niece. The language of business and the media infiltrates everyday language with words and phrases, so that now we all 'think outside the box' and try to avoid 'fudging the issue'. The sheer size of our vocabulary is fantastic.

In addition to the number of words, the way we use words also varies considerably. Consider the following idioms which are all related to parts of the body:

- I jumped out of my skin.
- He made my blood boil.
- It was a slip of the tongue.
- He was brainwashed.
- She's really got her teeth into it now.

If you take them literally they are absolute nonsense and yet we all know what they mean. Children, however, do take things literally until they have more experience. I remember, in my first year of teaching, saying to two boys who had been less than focused during the lesson, 'you two had better pull your socks up', to which they both bent down and actually pulled their socks up. I meant 'start working harder', but I used an idiom instead which was clearly not familiar to the two 5-year-old boys. Children on the autistic spectrum tend to take a literal approach to language and therefore use of idioms and metaphors could be very confusing.

Communication is highly complex. We can often communicate more by what we do not say than what we do say. If a man has had an argument with his wife and then asks her if she is all right, she might say, 'yes – fine', but her tone of voice and body language are clearly saying the opposite, with the husband in no doubt about how she really feels. The complexities of communication, including the inferences we can make from 'reading between the lines', will be explored in the next tasks.

Reflective Tasks

The complexities of communication

Read the narrative extract below about an 18-year-old's first day at work in a nursery:

It was murder trying to get up this morning! I was nearly late because I missed the first bus – I don't know why I was bothered though. I felt like a spare part when I got there. Mind you – you want to make a good impression on your first day; I won't be so bothered tomorrow. The other girls, Kate and Shelley, are lovely – really friendly. Gail seems a bit of a cow though. She had a go at me for filing my nails, said 'it wasn't appropriate'. I was only filing them because one broke! She wouldn't have thought it 'appropriate' if I'd scratched a baby with my broken nail, would she? Oh, the babies! They're gorgeous! I love babies. I could eat them up on hot buttered toast!! There's this little lad, Nathan, who kept crying. The others didn't bother with him – said he's always like that. I kept going to him and talking to him and showing him things. He really seemed to calm down. All he wants is a bit of attention. The toddlers are quite sweet too. I hated the pre-school room though. They're at you all the time. There's this one girl, Faith, she's a monster! She never does as she's told and she talks constantly. Julie was trying to read a story and she was running round the room! She's a real pain in the neck. Julie is so patient with her but I don't reckon that'll work. She needs a firm hand, that one. One good shout and that will be her sorted, I reckon. I don't know how Julie kept her cool. I could feel myself getting worked up and I didn't have to deal with her!

You don't get many breaks. I was planning on going into town in my lunch break, but there's no time. I'd only just eaten my crisps and it was time to go back. We have different break times too, so it's a bit boring. I took my chocolate back with me, but Gail said it 'wasn't a good role model to eat unhealthy food in front of the children'. What's that about?! Absolute rubbish. No one is telling me what I can and can't eat. As if seeing me doing something is going make the children do it.

I love talking to the parents. Some like to stay and talk at the end of the day. They want to know what their child has been doing. Well so would I. I really like telling them. Shelley stops and talks but Gail and Kate seem to be too busy rushing about tidying up. I don't know whether Gail approved. She kept looking at me but I don't care. I'd want to know what my child had been doing. I mean, they've been away from you all day. You've missed that bit of them growing up.

I was cream-crackered at the end of the day! I was going to go out for a drink but all I wanted was to sit and veg out in front of the telly. I'm pleased I got the first day over. The first day is always hard. I can't wait to see Nathan and the other babies tomorrow. I'd better make sure I get up in time. It'll be better when I get used to it and know what to do.

Level 1

Identify any idioms or phrases used that should not be taken literally.

- Why do you think these were used?
- What did the speaker think about her first day?
- Why have you drawn these conclusions?
- Comment on her relationship with Gail.

Level 2

- What did the speaker think about her first day?
- List the types of emotions she might have experienced.
- In which areas does she appear to need more experience?
- In which areas does she appear confident?
- Why have you drawn these conclusions?
- Comment on her relationship with Gail.

Level 3

- If you were the manager of the nursery and overheard this, how would you feel about this person's attitude to her work?
- What did she say that informed your opinion?
- What support strategies do you think she needs? Why?
- Are there any aspects of training that would help her?
- What are her apparent strengths?
- What does her relationship with Gail suggest to you?

Pragmatics

Pragmatics is basically the art of conversation. Graddol *et al.* (1994: 16) refer to it as the study of language 'in its communicative context' and Crystal (1995: 457) as the 'factors influencing a person's choice of language'. What it is concerned with is the way we are able to interact with different people in different situations, for example being able to banter with friends during a night out in the pub and being equally adept at discussing a serious work-based issue in a meeting with colleagues. Whitehead (1990) refers to the ways we speak in different situations as using different 'registers'. It is also a part of the English National Curriculum within Speaking and Listening, referred to in Language Variation (DfEE, 1999). Children learn pragmatics with experience and exposure to different situations. We have probably all heard a child say something deemed somewhat inappropriate, yet entirely innocent, due to their lack of experience. I remember a child asking our delightful elderly teaching assistant why she had got a moustache. Inappropriate, but no malice intended. As children learn social rules and experience different language contexts, their pragmatic skills should develop.

Lindon (2005) highlights the concern that has been raised about children's limited language skills on entry to school. The National Literacy Trust (http://www.literacytrust.org.uk) published several articles on its website on children's lack of basic language skills and the perceived increase in speech difficulties. Television and poor parenting were cited as two possible reasons. Certainly there are arguments for and against television, but although it may help to develop some language skills, it is essentially a passive activity and therefore is less likely to develop the skills of conversation. Bernstein (1971) and Tough (1977) identified differences in language and social class, with a clear distinction between language use, being more restricted in the working classes and more elaborate in the middle classes. Other influential studies (Tizard and Hughes, 1984; Wells, 1987) have indicated that language in the home is rich and varied, regardless of social class. They suggest that children's language can be restricted by the school context, which is why it is essential that early years settings and schools value children's linguistic experiences in the home and have clear strategies to promote and continue this language development in the school.

Research

Opportunities for conversation

Research by UNICEF (2007) into the well-being of children in 21 countries drew upon previous research by the Programme of International Student Assessment or PISA (Adams and Wu, 2002; OECD, 2004), which looked at family resources and structure in 43 countries. Two questions were asked which indicate how the art of conversation is faring in different countries:

- In general, how often do your parents eat the main meal with you around a table?
- In general, how often do your parents spend time just talking to you?

The UK was one of the lowest ranked countries for sharing a meal with their family, even though almost two-thirds of children still regularly eat the main meal of the day with their families. Family meals are often where good conversations occur and a similar number of UK children (70 per cent) reported talking regularly to their parents (being in the top half of the reported countries). Young people find it easier to talk to their mothers than their fathers and this figures rises with age.

Speaking and listening in the early years

There are two aspects to developing speaking and listening skills in the early years setting: one is providing specific activities and tasks for children to complete; the other is raising the status of talk through dialogic teaching. Alexander (2004) believes that talk in the classroom goes beyond that which the National Curriculum (DfEE, 1999) calls 'speaking and listening' to a more intrinsic, pedagogical approach which promotes the right kind of talk and encourages thinking and learning. This is the basis of dialogic teaching. The importance of adult–child conversation is emphasised, which should be reciprocal, supportive and purposeful. Adult questioning should encourage child questioning, rather than questions to test recall (see Picture 5.3). If we take the story of 'Goldilocks and the Three Bears', a question to test recall might be: 'Whose chair did Goldilocks break?' A question to promote further thinking and questioning might be: 'Why do you think Goldilocks was out in the woods on her own?' The first question requires recall but does not develop any further thinking; if you know the story, you know the answer. The second question is open to interpretation and several answers could be offered and extended. Siraj-Blatchford *et al.* (2002) refers to a similar approach in early years settings, known as sustained shared thinking, also referred to in Chapter 9. It is important for the classroom ethos to be one that values talk, provides time for talk and promotes learning through talk. Some primary schools are now teaching philosophy, which is based on developing thinking skills through pupil-led, teacher-facilitated discussion. Lipman (see Lipman *et al.*, 1980) was one of the pioneers of philosophy for children (P4C), believing that a subject-led curriculum resulted in children learning facts, but not how to think. P4C is concerned with reasoning and creative imagination, exploring themes found in stories that are meaningful to children and that stimulate discussion and debate. Valuing purposeful talk should permeate the whole curriculum and not just be promoted within 'communication, language and literacy' and 'speaking and listening' activities.

Picture 5.3 An adult questioning children
Source: John Walmsley/Education Photos

Practical Tasks

Using stories

Level 1

Take a traditional tale you know well. Make two columns on a piece of paper and think of questions to test recall in one column and questions to probe further thinking in the other column. Consider things such as how a character might feel, what they could do next, etc.

Level 2

Take a traditional tale you know well. Consider ways to involve children in considering different aspects of the story (the hidden parts), such as (in 'Goldilocks and the Three Bears') what the bears did when they went into the woods, what her family were doing while Goldilocks was away, or what the three bears did after Goldilocks ran away.

Level 3

Do the Level 2 task and then work with a group of children on developing these 'new' stories to extend the original. Allow the children to discuss and think of their own ideas, so that you act as a facilitator not the leader. Evaluate the experience by reflecting on the children's talk and the level to which you were involved. Is there anything you would have done differently? Write up the experience as narrative, but make sure you are also analytical.

Specific activities, such as circle time (Mosley, 1996), can promote children's speaking and listening skills in a very structured way. Each child takes it in turn to speak round the circle and can pass if they do not wish to say anything. Figure 5.4 has some examples of circle-time activities to promote speaking and listening. Circle-time is also used in some schools as a behaviour management tool, to discuss sensitive issues such as bullying, but any circle-time leader must be aware of potential difficulties, such as a child making a personal disclosure. One of the advantages of circle time is the focus on promoting listening skills. Listening is a largely untaught skill and is difficult to assess. We often half listen, homing in on things which interest us and then 'drifting off' when they do not. Active listening involves other skills such as concentrating and remembering, and Figure 5.5 has some examples of activities to promote this with young children.

Circle time
- Self-discipline
- Self-esteem
- Social skills
- Sharing/sense of belonging
- Relationship building
- Responsibility
- Empathy

Golden rule
- No-one may say anything negative about another person by name.
- Look at the person who is speaking.
- Listen to the person who is speaking.

Circle games
- 'Cross the circle if …' (e.g. you watched television last night; you like chocolate; you are hungry). The children get up and swap places with someone else if they agree with the statement.
- 'I am thinking of…' Select a category, e.g. fruit or animals. Go around the circle, clapping to a rhythm, in turn, saying, 'I am thinking of pears'; next person: 'I am thinking of apples', etc.
- Finish the statement. Provide the opening of a statement for each child to continue, e.g. 'I feel happy when …', 'I feel sad when …', 'I feel angry when …', 'The most exciting thing that happened to me was …', 'if I had one wish I would wish for …', etc.
- Telling a story. This can be done round the circle one word at a time, one sentence at a time, or using an object that you pass round randomly to indicate the storyteller.
- Nursery rhyme. Recite a nursery rhyme round the circle one word at a time or one syllable at a time.
- Animals. Give each pupil an animal name using no more than four animals altogether, so that several pupils share each animal's name. When you call out an animal's name, all the pupils with that name have to swap places.
- Alternative animals. Stork on one leg, chicken on two legs, monkey on two legs and one hand, cat on two legs and two hands.
- Pass the squeeze. You squeeze the hand of the child next to you as many times as you wish. The child then passes that squeeze on. It goes round the circle until it comes back to you. You will then be able to tell if the squeeze has been passed round successfully.
- Partners 1. Have a circle of chairs with two children to a chair. You need an odd number to play this, as one chair needs only one child. One child stands behind the chair and the other sits on it. The child on his/her own stands behind the chair. This child has to get one of the other sitting down children onto his/her chair by winking at them. If the child behind the child winked at sees, he/she must stop his/her partner by touching (not dragging) his/her shoulders.
- Partners 2. Do the same exercise as above, only this time, instead of winking, the child calls out a name.
- Can I come in? Give every child a logi-block shape. Each pupil asks 'Can I come into your zoo?' You (having decided previously the requirement, e.g. all yellow shapes, or all small shapes) answer, 'Yes, you can come into my zoo today', or 'No, not today'. The children have to guess the requirement.
- What can it be? The children sit in a circle and the teacher picks up any object – a book for example, and begins to use the book as another object. The children have to guess what the object is, and the book is then passed on to the next person.

- Pass the mask. In a circle, one child makes a mask of their face – it can be gruesome or funny. Then the next child goes up to their partner's face, takes the 'mask' and passes it to the next child who puts it up to their face and imitates it, before wiping it off and making one of their own, which they, in turn, pass to the next child, etc. Variation – the mask can be thrown across the circle to someone else.
- Something kind. Each child takes it in turns to finish the statement 'I was kind when…'.
- Spider's web. Number the children in the circle alternately 1, 2, 1, 2, 1, 2…. One child stands in the centre as a spider; the rest of the children are flies. When the teacher shouts a number, those children run across the circle to swap places. If the spider catches them, they become spiders too and stay in the middle.
- Blindfold a child and sit him/her in the middle of the circle. When the teacher taps another child on the shoulder, he/she says 'Good morning/afternoon John [or whatever the blindfolded child is called]', and the blindfolded child has to guess the speaker. When he/she guesses correctly, that child becomes blindfolded.
- My turn/your turn. Ask children to think of their favourite cereal/television programme/game etc. One child starts by saying 'My turn, cornflakes, your turn,…' and says another child's name. The named child then continues 'My turn, porridge, your turn, …', until all children have had a turn.
- Eye contact. One child stands up and locks eyes with someone sitting. That child then stands up and does the same with another child, while the first child sits in his or her place, etc.
- Magic sweets. 'I have a bag of magic sweets. Would you like one?' The sweets are handed round, with each child pretending they are different sweets.
- One clap means 'sit'.
  Two claps mean 'walk' on the spot'.
  Three claps mean 'walk in one direction round the circle'.
  The teacher or child stands in the centre and claps the instructions.
- Go round the circle and each child claps the syllables of his/her name.
- Copy the rhythm. The teacher claps a rhythm and the children copy. Add a chant to the rhythm:

clap	clap	clap
I	like	tea

clap	clap	clap	clap	clap	clap
I	–	like	–	tea	–

Working together
- Partners. One person talks for 1 minute about him/herslf. The other has to tell the rest of the group what his/her partner has said.
- Kind comments. Children form pairs, and each in turn makes a positive comment about his/her partner, starting with the name of the child.
- Mirrors. Two children face each other. One is the mirror, the other is the reflection. Teacher sets the scene and the children have to work together, e.g. putting make-up on, washing, cleaning teeth, etc.
- Rhythm. One person taps a rhythm on the back of another and it is passed round the class (like Chinese whispers).

Figure 5.4 Circle time features and games

Oracy in schools has been viewed with varying degrees of importance over the past 30 years. In 1975, the Bullock Report (DfES, 1975) highlighted the significance of oral language in the development of literacy skills. In 1992, the work of the National Oracy Project was published (Norman, 1992), aiming to enhance the role of speech in teaching and learning, which had been deemed as less significant since the introduction of the National Curriculum. The National Literacy Strategy (DfES, 1998), focused on reading and writing; however, the third aspect of English, speaking and listening was left out. With oracy being such an important element in the successful learning of literacy skills, this omission is

Listening games

- Copying a simple clapping rhythm.
- Follow my leader, only saying the actions rather than doing them (e.g. the leader *saying* put your hands in the air rather than doing it).
- Simon says.
- Go on a listening walk and list all the sounds you can hear.
- Hide a timer that buzzes somewhere in the room. The child/group has to find it when it buzzes.
- Have two or three musical instruments. Play one of them behind a screen and ask the children to identify which one.
- Tape some familiar sounds and then ask the children to identify them.
- Ask one child to turn away from the rest of the children. Select another child to say 'Hello, do you know who I am?' The child has to try to identify who is speaking.
- Pass a bell or bunch of keys around the circle without allowing it/them to make a noise.
- Ask the children to pretend to be asleep and to wake up when they hear a pre-agreed sound.
- Use musical instruments as signals, e.g. bells mean run around, the drum means stop, the tambourine means jump up and down, etc.
- Use 10 solid identical plastic containers with lids – fill two with paper clips, two with nails, etc. Ask the children to find the pairs.
- Have a tape with animal noises or everyday sounds and corresponding pictures. Match the sound to the picture.
- Choose a specific word or name of a character. Tell a story and ask the children to put up their hand every time they hear the word/name.
- Do/don't. Have a selection of objects and give the child an instruction using 'do' and 'don't', e.g. do bring the doll, don't bring the teddy.

Concentration and memory games

- Play 'Grandma went to market'. Go round the circle and add a new item each time, e.g. 'Grandma went to market and bought some bacon', the next child repeats that and adds another item '… some bacon and some bread'. It can be simplified by fewer children and also by having a visual clue by providing a shopping bag with objects in for children to pull out. Choosing items in alphabetical order is another variation, e.g. first person has to think of something beginning with 'a', second person with 'b', etc.
- Kim's game. Have a tray with objects and let the children look at it. Put the tray behind a screen and remove something. The children have to say what is missing.
- Build a simple tower with different coloured bricks. Ask the children to look carefully at it before knocking it down. Ask the children to help you build it again so that the colours/shapes are in the same order.
- Give a list of instructions. Start simply with one or two, e.g. put your hand on your head and stick out your tongue. Gradually use longer strings of instructions, e.g. put your hand on your head, stick out your tongue, turn around and sit down.
- On my way to school I saw … Show several pictures of things you saw on your way to school. You can then either ask the children to tell you in the correct order, or add some extra pictures and ask the children to remove the things you didn't see and put the other pictures into the correct order.
- In a circle, ask the children to pull an object out of the bag and hold it up for the rest of the children to see. Pass the bag round the circle. At the end, ask the children who held up a particular object, e.g. who held up the teddy? It could be more than one child if two or more pulled the same object out of the bag.
- With the children in pairs, ask them to look carefully at each other for one minute. They then turn their backs to their partners and change one (or more when experienced) aspect of their appearance, e.g. tuck hair behind ears, roll up sleeves, then on command ask the children to face their partner and say what has changed.
- Give the children some shapes and then give instructions, e.g. put the shapes in a line, put the square at the beginning of the line, put the circle next to the square, etc. Increase the number of instructions you give in one go as the children become more experienced.

(See Bailey and Broadbent, 2001, which has some useful listening, concentration and memory games. It also has a soft toy leopard called Lola, which is used with the games.)

Figure 5.5 Activities to promote active listening

quite unforgivable. In 2000, language and literacy became *communication*, language and literacy in the *Curriculum Guidance for the Foundation Stage* (QCA/DfEE, 2000) and in 2003, at last, speaking, listening and learning materials (DfES, 2003) were introduced as a supplement to the National Literacy Strategy. The renewed literacy strategy has actually included speaking and listening within the first four of its 12 strands. It is apparent that the importance of oracy is again being recognised. It is our role to ensure it remains a high priority.

Summary

→ Non-verbal communication (NVC), also known as kinesics, has six main aspects: gesture, proxemics, body contact, posture and body orientation, facial expression, gaze.

→ Our non-verbal communication is far more significant than many people realise.

→ Forming relationships is important to children's language development.

→ There are a number of language acquisition theories and there is considerable debate about how we acquire language.

→ Two of the most significant are the opposing nature versus nurture views, or as they are more commonly known within language development: nativist and empiricist.

→ The two theorists most associated with these two differing views on language acquisition, brought to the fore in the 1950s and 1960s, are Noam Chomsky and B. F. Skinner.

→ Although Chomsky's theory is the most popular, there are critics of this theory and there is no consensus of opinion about how we acquire language.

→ Phonology is concerned with the organisation and patterning of sounds in a language. It includes important indicators of meaning, such as intonation and use of emphasis.

→ Phonology is the sound system of a particular language and therefore does not apply to all sounds the vocal system can make.

→ From about 4–5 months onwards children begin to make speech-like sounds, which are the initial stage of babbling. At about 9 months, the babbling is consistent with the phonology of the child's first language.

→ Children develop at different rates, but at about 12 months babies produce their first words.

→ Children will understand far more words than they can speak in the initial stages.

→ Understanding words is called 'receptive' language and using spoken words is called 'expressive' language.

→ Once a child has learnt about 50 words, learning is accelerated. By the age of 6, children have a vocabulary of about 14,000 words.

→ As children become more proficient they are able apply grammatical rules, although these can result in misapplying rules to irregular words, such as 'runned' instead of 'ran'. The more experienced language users they are, the more they are able to deal with irregularity.

→ Communication disorders can be defined as either articulation/speech disorders or language disorders.

→ Word usage affects meaning and therefore our language is never static, but continually changing.

→ Pragmatics is the art of conversation and children learn that there are different contexts for language, both informal and formal.

→ As children learn social rules and experience different language contexts, their pragmatic skills should develop.

→ There are two aspects to developing speaking and listening skills in the early years setting: one is providing specific activities and tasks for children to complete; the other is raising the status of talk through dialogic teaching.

→ Valuing purposeful talk should permeate the whole curriculum and not just be promoted within 'communication, language and literacy' and 'speaking and listening' activities.

Key Questions

- What is non-verbal communication and what are the different ways in which we communicate without speech?
- Outline of some of the key language acquisition theories. What are the criticisms of each?
- What are the different aspects of phonology?
- How do we articulate different sounds within our phonology?
- What are the broad stages of language acquisition?
- What are some of the difficulties that children might encounter as their speech and language is developing?
- How can teachers develop speaking and listening in the primary school?

References

Adams, R. and Wu, M. (eds) (2002) *PISA 2000 Technical Report.* Paris, OECD

Alexander, R. (2004) *Towards Dialogic Teaching.* Cambridge: Dialogos

Bailey, R. and Broadbent, L. (2001) *Helping Young Children to Listen.* Birmingham: Lawrence Educational

Bee, H. (2004) *The Developing Child, International Edition,* 10th edn. Boston Allyn & Bacon

Berko, J. (1958) 'The Child's Learning of English Morphology', *Word,* 14: 150–77

Bernstein, B. (1971) *Class, Codes and Control, Vols 1 and 2.* London: Routledge & Kegan Paul

Brown, R. (1973) *A First Language: The Early Stages.* London: Allen & Unwin

Bruner, J. (1983) *Child's Talk: Learning to Use Language.* New York: Norton

Chomsky, N. (1972) *Language and Mind.* New York: Harcourt Brace Jovanovich.

Craig, A. and Tran, Y. (2005) 'What is the Relationship between Stuttering and Anxiety?' Available from: www.stammering.org (The British Stammering Association).

Crystal, D. (1995) *The Cambridge Encyclopedia of the English Language.* Cambridge: Cambridge University Press.

David, T., Goouch, K., Powell, S. and Abbott, L. (2003) *Birth to Three Matters: A Review of the Literature.* Nottingham: DfES

DeCasper, H. and Spence, M. (1986) 'Maternal Speech Influences Newborns' Perceptions of Speech Sounds', *Infant Behaviour and Development,* 9: 133–50

DfEE (1999) *The National Curriculum: Handbook For Teachers In England.* London: DfEE/QCA

DfES (1975) *A Language for Life* (The Bullock Report). London: HMSO

DfES (1998) *The National Literacy Strategy: Framework for Teaching.* London: DfES

DfES (2003) *Speaking. Listening and Learning: A Framework for Key Stage 1 and 2.* London: DfES

DfES (2006a) *Independent Review of the Teaching of Early Reading, Final Report. The Rose Report.* London: DfES

DfES (2006b) *The Early Years Foundation Stage. Every Child Matters. Change for Children.* London: DfES

Gasser, M. (2006) *Research Overview of Language Acquisition and Evolution.* Available from: www.cs.indiana.edu/~gasser/

Goodwin, P. (2001) *The Articulate Classroom: Talking and Learning in the Primary Classroom.* London: David Fulton

Goodwin, S., Acredolo, L. and Brown, C. (2000) 'Impact of Symbolic Gesturing on Early Language Development', *Journal of Non-Verbal Behaviour,* 24: 81–103

Graddol, D., Cheshire, J. and Swann, J. (1994) *Describing Language.* Buckingham: Open University Press

Grove, N., Herman, R., Morgan, G. and Woll, B. (2004) 'Baby Signing: the View from the Sceptics', *Royal College of Speech and Language Therapists Bulletin.* Available from: www.nationalliteracytrust.co.uk

Herman, R. (2002) *Characteristic Developmental Patterns of Language and Communication in Hearing and Deaf Babies 0–2 Years.* London: Department of Language and Communication, City University

Kisilevsky, B., Hains, S., Lee, K., Xie, X., Huang, H., Ye, H., Khang, K. and Wang, Z. (2003) 'Effects of Experience on Fetal Voice Recognition', *Psychological Science,* 14, 3: 220–24

Lambirth, A. (2005) *Primary English – Reflective Reader.* Exeter: Learning Matters

Lancaster, Y.P. (2003) *Promoting Listening to Young Children – The Reader. Coram Family Listening to Young Children Project.* Maidenhead: Open University Press

Lindon, J. (2005) *Understanding Child Development.* London: Hodder Arnold

Lipman, M., Sharp, A.M. and Oscanyan, F. (1980) *Philosophy in the Classroom,* 2nd edn. Philadelphia: Temple University Press.

Lyons, J. (1977) *Chomsky* (revised edn). Glasgow: Fontana/Collins

Mosely, J. (1996) *Quality Circle Time.* Cambridge: LDA

Mukherji, P. and O'Dea, T. (2000) *Understanding Children's Language and Literacy.* Cheltenham: Stanley Thornes

Murray, L. and Andrews, E. (2000) *The Social Baby.* London: Richmond Press

Norman, K. (1992) (ed.) *Thinking Voices: The work of the National Oracy Project.* London: NCC/Hodder & Stoughton

OECD (2004) *Learning for Tomorrow's World: First Results from PISA 2003.* Paris, OECD

O'Grady, W. (2005) *How Children Use Language.* Cambridge: Cambridge University Press

Piaget, J. (1929) *The Child's Conception of the World.* New York: Harcourt

Piaget, J. (1950) *The Psychology of Intelligence.* London: Routledge & Kegan Paul

Piaget, J. (1959) *The Language and Thought of the Child.* London: Routledge & Kegan Paul

Pinker, S. (1995) Language Acquisition, in Gleitman, L.R., Liberman, M. and Osherson, D.N. (Eds) *An Invitation to Cognitive Science,* 2nd edn, Vol. 1. Cambridge, MA: MIT Press

QCA/DfEE (2000) *Curriculum Guidance for the Foundation Stage.* London: QCA

Retuccia, C. (2002) 'Phonologic Strategy for /r/ Remediation', *ADVANCE for Speech-Language Pathologists and Audiologists,* 12, 39: 12

Sheridan, M. (1997) *From Birth To Five Years: Children's Developmental Progress,* 4th edn. London: Routledge

Siraj-Blatchford, I., Sylva, K., Muttock, S., Gilden, R. and Bell, D. (2002) *Researching Effective Pedagogy in the Early Years.* Nottingham: DFES

SureStart (2003) *Birth to Three Matters.* London: DfES

Tizard, B. and Hughes, M. (1984) *Young Children Learning.* London: Fontana Press

Tomasello, M. (2003) *Constructing a Language – A Usage-Based Theory of Language Acquisition.* Cambridge: MA: Harvard University Press

Tough, J. (1977) *The Development of Meaning: A Study of Children's Use of Language.* London: Allen and Unwin

Trask, R. and Mayblin, B. (2000) *Introducing Linguistics.* Cambridge: Icon Books.

Trevarthen, C. (1999) *Adventures with the IMP: The Psychology of Musical Narrative in Mother's Songs and Chats with Infants.* Available from: http://marcs.uws.edu.au/links/amps/index.htm

UNICEF (2007) 'The state of the world's children'. Available from: http://www.unicef.org/sowc07/report/report.php

Vygotsky, L. (1978) *Thought and Language.* Cambridge MA: MIT Press

Wells, G. (1987) *The Meaning Makers.* London: Hodder & Stoughton

Whitehead, M. (1990) *Language and Literacy in the Early Years.* London: Paul Chapman Publishing

Chapter 6

Emotional and Moral Development

'There can be no knowledge without emotion. We may be aware of a truth, yet until we have felt its force, it is not ours. To the cognition of the brain must be added the experience of the soul'

Arnold Bennett (1867–1931)

Introduction

This chapter will explore the significant influences on emotional and moral development. In recent times, there has been a particular emphasis on children's physical health and safety with perhaps far less focus on children's emotional needs. It is much easier to recognise when a child has hurt themselves physically, with clear procedures to follow, than when a child is hurt emotionally. This chapter seeks to highlight the central place emotional and moral development has on the development of the whole child and will outline the key factors to be taken into consideration.

Aims

→ To consider what constitutes emotional development

→ To provide a critical overview of attachment theories

→ To explore self-concept and self-esteem and consider influences which can impact on them

→ To consider the importance of emotional development on other aspects of development

→ To provide an overview of the theories of moral development

→ To explore ways of supporting moral development

Tools for Learning

Listening as a research tool

In this chapter, we are looking at listening as a research tool. We can tell a great deal about a child by listening to them. We want to encourage children to talk to us, to ask questions and to be curious about the world around them. We also want to find out how they feel, what worries them, what they enjoy doing and why and how we can support them in stressful situations. In order to assess children's ideas and feelings and provide experiences to support their development, we need to access them. This is best done by listening to them in a relaxing, questioning environment which encourages children to express themselves and to ask questions but not to feel stupid in doing so. While the children are playing, exploring, investigating, discussing we can listen to them. If they feel free to talk about their ideas and emotions while they are working their discussions can be very revealing. Taping conversations can be very enlightening and tell us a lot about the children's thinking and sometimes reveal some hidden ideas and concerns which have been overlooked in a busy classroom. We can also listen to the way in which children answer our questions. When asking questions of children, we are more successful at finding out about them if we are non-threatening and personalise questions. For example, it is better to ask 'What do you think will happen next?' rather than 'What will happen next?' The first question appears to value the child's opinion. The second question can appear to require a specific, 'correct' answer.

As well as personalising questions it is better to ask open-ended questions as these are usually more successful than specific questions in eliciting children's ideas and feelings. Open-ended questions are ones which do not have a predetermined or limited choice answer, for example we may ask 'What can you tell me about this?' rather than 'What is this?'

Practical Tasks

Gauging emotion by listening

List as many different emotions as you can. Sort the emotions into those that are negative emotions, those that are positive and those that are neutral.

Level 1

Try taping a conversation between you and some peers and listen to it to see if you can gauge their emotions by listening to them.

Level 2

Set up an interactive activity for a small group of children and tape their discussions. Listen to the tape and see if you can gauge their emotions by listening to them. What does this knowledge of the children tell you about them?

Level 3

Listen to children in different contexts, such as outside play, story-time, literacy hour or interactive activities. You could try videoing or taping them and use the tapes for deeper analysis. What does their discussion tell you about your setting? How could you improve your provision to make the setting a happy and secure environment for all children?

Reflective Tasks

Gauging emotions

Level 1

- How can you tell if a baby is happy or sad from their cry?
- How can a child's tone of voice tell you how they are feeling?
- How do you think you can access a child's emotions by listening to them?

Level 2

- How can you gauge the emotions of the children in your care?
- Do the children express their emotions equally through expression, body language and vocal language?

Level 3

- How can you tell if the children in your setting are happy and settled in your care?

What are emotions?

Emotions are an expression of feelings which show a readiness for action. This may mean that the individual continues with an action already started, or modifies it or even changes it. The main reasons for the action are environmental factors (Saarni *et al.*, 1998) and social stimuli. The resulting emotions are the result of an interrelationship between our biochemistry and environmental and social events, so that, biologically, parts of the brain respond to emotional arousal. Damage to the brain can result in emotional difficulties and personality changes.

In the newly-born child, simple emotional needs are expressed through crying. As children develop, different emotions are expressed through different cries and mothers can not only tell their baby's cries from other babies', they can also tell what the cry means. They can tell if the baby is tired, uncomfortable, hungry, bored or happy. As children develop, they begin to use facial expressions to convey emotions. Facial expressions are a clear way to observe emotions even in children with visual and aural impairments. As children develop language (see Chapter 5), emotions are also expressed through linguistic emphases and body language. Many of these ways of expressing emotion are unconscious rather than conscious and it is very difficult even for the best actor to hide emotions from a keen observer.

What is emotional development?

Early emotional development occurs in response to children's needs and wants (see Table 6.1). They cry, babble, laugh, showing distress, anger, frustration, fear and pleasure. They show emotional responses to changes and to stability in their environment. Babies appear to be born with some basic emotions, common to all primates, such as attraction to a pleasurable stimulation and withdrawal from an unpleasant stimulation. Other emotions develop gradually. Berk (2003) has identified four emotions (happiness, anger, sadness and fear), which have been fairly extensively researched, although there are many other emotions that a child can express (see the tasks above).

Table 6.1 Emotional development

Age	Emotional development
Birth–6 months	The child at this age: • shows signs of almost all emotions from birth; • begins to smile socially; • begins to laugh as an expression of happiness; • shows facial expressions of happiness with familiar carers; • expresses emotions in a well-organised way, related to events.
7–12 months	At this age: • anger and fear increase, especially in situations with strangers; • the child will avoid unfamiliar or uncomfortable situations; • the child needs a secure base, provided by those who care for them; • the child can become distressed or withdrawn in unstable situations.

Table 6.1 *Continued*

Age	Emotional development
1–2 years	The child at this age: • is aware of themselves; • will be guided in their emotions by their carers and close adults; • is very dependent on adults.
3–6 years	As the child develops: • they show more self-conscious emotions and these are clearly linked to self-esteem; • they use their developing language to express emotions; • they can develop active strategies for regulating emotions; • they begin to conform in social contexts, even when this is against their emotions.
7–11 years	In the older child: • self-conscious emotions become integrated with inner standards of behaviour; • internal strategies for emotional self-regulation are evident and these can be adjusted to situations; • the need to conform and show awareness of emotional rules is evident.

The right side of the brain is where intuitive skills develop and these are needed in order for the child to develop relationships, emotions and empathic understanding. In the first three years, this side of the brain develops rapidly and is more dominant than the left side of the brain. After 3 years of age, the left side of the brain becomes dominant, and language and memory develop (see Chapter 4). High levels of stress in the first three years of development are thought to have an adverse effect on brain and emotional development, resulting in aggressive and anti-social behaviour in childhood and later life (Bowlby, 2006).

Young babies smile soon after birth. They usually do this when fully fed, during REM (rapid eye movement) sleep, in response to gentle touching, rocking and their mother's voice. At about 6–10 weeks they will smile when they recognise a familiar face. This is a social smile and it helps them to form an attachment with their carer, so that in the first 2–3 months they tend to reserve smiles for familiar faces. From about 3 or 4 months, babies begin to laugh; again as a result of a social stimulation, such as playful events. As they approach the end of their first year, children show more than one kind of smile, a reserved one for strangers and a full one for familiar faces, and in their second year a smile 'becomes a deliberate social signal' (Berk, 2003: 399).

Distress is shown from an early age to indicate unpleasant experiences, such as hunger, pain, etc. During their first year the expressions of anger and sadness become more complex and frequent. Anger is particularly intense when children associate an unpleasant experience with a carer with whom they have learned to associate warmth and pleasant experiences. For example, a child who is reprimanded by a carer who is normally loving and kind may react by crying and may appear quite distressed. A child who is denied a sweet by an adult who may provide all other nutritional needs may respond in an extreme way by throwing a tantrum and screaming. This helps us to understand infant tantrums, but not necessarily find them easy to handle.

Sadness occurs early in response to separation from objects and carers. The effect can be that the child avoids separation and strengthens attachments to objects and people. Both sadness and fear (which develops from 6 to 12 months) are common expressions of anxiety in the presence of strangers. This response can vary from mild wariness through to sadness and to different levels of anxiety to fear. Fear, like other emotions, can be conditioned (see Pavlov, 1927). For example, if children are scratched by a cat, they may express fear or dislike each time they see a cat.

Attachment

Babies quickly form attachments with their carers. This attachment begins in the womb, when the developing foetus recognises its mother. Early bonding is thought to have a biological origin and be a primitive response to need, as the developing baby needs support from an adult as it develops; in fact, human babies need the most care and support not only in the early years but also through adolescence (see also Chapter 4). When a baby is born, the maternal bonding occurs quickly. If something occurs to prevent that bonding the effects can be quite severe for both mother and child. Both my children were born by Caesarian section: my daughter an emergency with general anesthetic, whom I did not consciously meet until she was about 5 hours old; my son an elected section with an epidural anaesthetic. As my son was being delivered and I was told I had a baby boy, I felt very detached from him and had no feelings about my new baby at all and I was unsure if I wanted him or even loved him. This is not uncommon with mothers who have Caesarian sections, as they may feel detached from the process of childbirth and so detached from the resulting baby. After a few minutes, once he had been assessed, the nurses put him in my arms and the bonding was immediate and very intense (so deep, that as I write this, I feel very emotional). There are many reasons why mothers fail to bond with their babies, including bad experiences during childbirth, hormonal reasons including post-natal depression, and children who have physical needs. Of course babies bond with other close carers, fathers, grandparents, secondary carers, and these bonds can be close and intense too, but the maternal bond is important as it is the first bond the child has, beginning pre-birth.

Bowlby (1969) studied the effects of maternal deprivation on attachment and future emotional development and concluded that it was essential for future mental health. His theory is that:

- children have a biological need for an attachment with a maternal figure;
- the attachment is monotropic (with one person);
- the attachment forms from around 7 months when children begin to be able to crawl and move away from their carer;
- children are biologically adapted to form an attachment between 7 months and 3 years;
- maternal deprivation has short- and long-term consequences for health.

This attachment was thought to be similar to Lorenz' imprinting in chicks (1952) (see Chapters 1 and 7). Studies of monkeys and apes have strengthened the view that there is a biological factor influencing attachment. There have been a number of criticisms of Bowlby's research. Perhaps the most important criticism is that Bowlby failed to consider the effect of privation, that is the effect of never having an attachment, on emotional development. He also did not take into account the effect of discord and stress in family relationships on emotional development. Finally, he did not consider attachments other than maternal attachments (paternal, peers, siblings, etc.) and multiple attachments.

Research

The strength of attachment

The strength of attachment has been measured (Ainsworth *et al.*, 1978) using a technique called Strange Situation, whereby eight episodes are used to note a child's attachment behaviours (see Table 6.2). This research has helped us to understand attachment and the effects on a child's behaviour and development. Through the research, different types of attachment were recognised:

1. *Secure attachment*. The parent is used as a base and the child shows preference for the parent over a stranger, seeking them out when they return after a period of absence. This type of attachment was evident in 65 per cent of the US children observed.

2. *Avoidance attachment*. The child is unresponsive to the parent when present and is not distressed when they leave. They are slow to greet the parent when they return. This type of attachment was evident in 20 per cent of US children observed in the study.

3. *Resistant attachment*. The child seeks closeness to the parent and does not explore on their own. The child shows anger and resistant behaviours when the parent returns and is not easily comforted. This type of attachment was observed in between 10 and 15 per cent of the US children studied.

4. *Disorganized, disorientated attachment*. Children show confused, contradictory behaviours when reunited with the parent, looking away. They may also show dazed facial expressions. This type of attachment was seen in between 5 and 10 per cent of the US children in the study.

Table 6.2 Episodes in the Strange Situation

Episode	Events	Attachment behaviours observed
1	Experimenter introduces parent and baby to playroom and then leaves	
2	Parent is seated while baby plays with toys	Parent as a secure base
3	Stranger enters, is seated, and talks to parent	Reaction to unfamiliar adult
4	Parent leaves room. Stranger responds to baby and offers comfort if upset	Separation anxiety
5	Parent returns, greets baby, and offers comfort if necessary. Stranger leaves room	Reaction to reunion
6	Parent leaves room	Separation anxiety
7	Stranger enters room and offers comfort	Ability to be soothed by stranger
8	Parent returns, greets baby, offers comfort if necessary, and tries to re-interest baby in toys	Reaction to reunion

Source: Adapted from Berk, 2003: 420

Factors that affect attachment in the developing child are varied and include some of the factors that affect the bonding of a new-born baby. It is important that children have the opportunity for attachment. They need to have consistent carers, so they know and become familiar with them. Within the family, they need to have familiar carers (mother, father and other family members), so a child who is taken into care or institutionalised during the first year is vulnerable to attachment problems. Children who are in day care not only need to have a secure family base, but also to have consistency in their carers during the day (Field, 1991). Recent initiatives to integrate services, improve the workforce and improve provision for children (Surestart, 2003; DfES, 2003, 2006; CWDC, 2006) may have an adverse effect on attachments in day care and early education, as skilled staff are engaged in development which takes them away from some of the face-to-face interactions with children. As Siraj-Blatchford *et al.* (2002) have indicated, good outcomes for children are linked to effective adult–child interaction. The quality of care is very important for attachment. The child needs to have carers who engage with them emotionally; indeed caring, by its very nature, has an emotional element. In this way attachment is also dependent on the mental health of the carers, so that depressed carers can fail to make these essential attachments and adversely affect later emotional development. Attachment can also be affected by the child's individual circumstances, such as prematurity, illness, special needs or temperament and other biological factors as well as environmental factors. Family circumstances, such as poverty, working parents, single parents or marital friction, will also make a difference to the quality of attachment (see Part 3, Early Childhood).

Secure attachment in the early years is thought to have an important effect on later development, with children with secure attachments in early childhood showing more positive attitudes, such as enthusiasm, flexibility and persistence, and using more imaginative play (Matas *et al.*, 1978; Eliker *et al.*, 1992). Sir Richard Bowlby, President of the Centre for Child Mental Health, has expressed his concern about children in day care and emotional development, in a joint letter to the *Daily Telegraph* (2006) together with other leading experts in childhood. They identify the need for consistent, continuous care in children's long-term emotional development. There is a need for good secondary attachments (that is, attachments other than the child's parents, such as siblings, grandparents, nannies or childminders) to be formed in childcare, as these help children to develop as stress-free individuals (Bowlby, 2006). There is evidence (Bowlby, 2006) that children under 3 years of age who have strong primary or secondary attachments will not be adversely affected by a few hours of separation a day, provided they are left with carers with whom they have a strong secondary attachment bond and who are consistent, sensitive and responsive. Children over 3 years of age are more likely to benefit socially and cognitively from high-quality care (Schwienhart *et al.*, 1993; Bowlby, 2006) and if they have strong secondary attachment bonds it will also support their emotional development. However, the very nature of day care in SureStart nurseries, with relatively high ratios of children to adults and a high turnover of staff, means that children who receive extended care are less likely to develop strong and effective attachments than children cared for at home or with childminders.

Research

Examining the causes of stress in babies and toddlers in group daycare: Sir Richard Bowlby

Throughout human evolution, mothers have been helped to care for their young by members of the extended family. Some of these will have known the baby since birth and become secondary attachment figures, and their motivation to provide care would have come from shared attachment bonds. Then, the carer and baby would have had ready access to mother for feeding on demand and co-sleeping at night, and would usually have been within sight or earshot of her. Of course we don't have absolute scientific proof that this description is correct, but there's a very high probability that it is.

Scientific probability

Most of science is based on the *probability* of a theory being correct, and if a theory is still current after many years of critical investigation, there's a high probability that it *is* correct. Attachment theory has been attacked, praised and tested from many angles. It was first outlined in 1958 and nearly 50 years later it has emerged as the world's largest subject of academic research into child development – in October 2006 there were more than 500,000 sites listed on Google referencing 'attachment-theory'.

I grew up with attachment theory and since 1994 I've been studying it and gathering information from conferences and discussions with practitioners and academics. I'm not a scientist, but my father John Bowlby was, and attachment theory has been so thoroughly tested by scientists that there is now a very high probability of its being correct. My views are based mostly on scientific research findings and partly on circumstantial evidence.

Primary and secondary

The term primary attachment figure refers to the person with whom a child develops a lifelong emotional bond, and whom they most want to be with when they are frightened or hurt – usually but not necessarily their birth mother. The term secondary attachment figure refers to the few special people in children's lives with whom they have developed a close subsidiary or secondary attachment bond such as siblings, grandparents, nannies or childminders and especially fathers. Having three or more of these secondary attachment relationships usually increases children's resilience to stress and acts as a protective factor.

Secure and insecure attachment

Secure attachment is when children have a predictable and safe affectionate bond with their attachment figure (either the primary or a secondary). Securely attached infants aged between about 6 and 30 months are not usually affected by a few hours of separation from their primary attachment figure if they're being looked after by a person with whom they have developed a secure *secondary* attachment bond. When these carers are consistent, sensitive and responsive they can benefit toddlers' social and cognitive development and provide support to families. Children older than 36 months will usually benefit socially and cognitively from age appropriate amounts of high quality pre-school nursery education.

Insecure attachment is when children have a less predictable bond with an attachment figure (either primary or secondary), and by itself insecure attachment is very difficult to identify unless the Strange Situation Procedure is employed. Insecure attachment is found in approximately 40% of toddlers in the UK and USA and is acknowledged as a risk factor that often contributes to the mental health problems of children and adults. Insecurely attached toddlers are less emotionally robust and more vulnerable to separation distress than securely attached toddlers.

Risk factors

Risk factors that contribute to emotional disturbance in children vary in their severity. Serious risk factors include having a parent who was raised in care or accommodated, having parents who are chronically neglectful or have a drug or alcohol problem, or who are abusive or violent. Childhood risk factors that are not *as* serious include parental depression, young unsupported parenthood and lack of parenting skills. The effects of these are exaggerated by poverty. Children with one or even two of the less serious risk factors may not appear to be too upset by them, but having three or more in combination is likely to result in significant emotional or behavioural problems. Another example of a risk factor is when children become *primarily* attached to a carer, who then leaves the family and the child's primary attachment bond is broken. The chances of becoming *primarily* attached to a *carer* are more likely:

when the baby starts being cared for before they're 6 months old;

when the carer spends more time with the baby than the primary attachment figure does;

when the carer is living in the baby's family home;

when the carer comforts the baby at night;

when the carer is unclear about relationship boundaries.

Attachment based childcare

One childcare model which can minimise the risk factors for babies and toddlers is attachment based childcare where, for instance, a family group allows a carer to provide age appropriate care for each child. The sort of features that distinguish attachment based childcare are:

that babies and toddlers between the ages of 6 and 30 months have access to a trusted secondary attachment figure whenever their primary attachment figure is not available to them;

that carers look after no more than three children well spaced in age: one aged 6 to 18 months, one between 18 and 36 months, and one over 36 months;

that carers have sufficient energy, and are trained and supported to meet the physical and emotional demands of the babies, toddlers and young children in their care;

that babies' and toddlers' secondary attachment needs are met, maintained and monitored;

that carers' emotional attachment to the children they care for is sensitively supported and monitored;

that parents are supported in maintaining their child's primary attachment bond to them.

Before starting in childcare, babies must already have formed a *primary* attachment bond to the person who's raising them long term (usually but not necessarily the birth mother) during the first 6 to 9 months of life. Even the most sensitive non-parental childcare is usually more stressful to babies and toddlers between 6 and 30 months, than home care with their primary attachment figure. However, having age appropriate amounts of childcare with a secondary attachment figure does not seem to constitute a significant long-term risk factor for either secure or insecure children.
Note: In particular circumstances some toddlers can benefit from daycare with a sensitive secondary attachment figure.

Resistance

Attachment theory focuses on the quality of the loving bond between parents and children, and although the theory is widely accepted as being scientifically valid, there still remains a resistance to it in some quarters. I think this is partly due to the emotional nature of the childhood memories that may be awakened by studying it, and partly due to its implications for modern-day family life. One area that worries parents and researchers is that some babies are being looked after by unfamiliar carers and lack continuity in personalised care-giving.

Brain development

Babies and toddlers younger than about 30 months have the right hemisphere of their brain developing more rapidly and exerting more control over them than the left side of their brain. The right side is where intuitive skills develop which are needed for relationships, emotions, and the empathic understanding of another person's feelings. These unconscious skills are learned by babies and toddlers whilst experiencing them over and over again, and it's the quality of the relationships and the feelings they experience day after day that can have a significant influence on their developing brain. These formative early experiences cannot be consciously recalled by the child later on, because they occur during the pre-verbal phase of brain development.

By about 36 months, toddlers' brains have undergone a very significant change. The growth spurt of the right side of the brain has slowed down and the sensitive period for developing social and emotional intelligence has made way for a growth spurt on the left side instead. The left side of the brain then becomes dominant, and promotes the development of complex speech and the ability to remember past events and anticipate future ones.

Stress and cortisol

Although cortisol is the stress hormone, normal levels are needed by the body for healthy functioning, and cortisol will rise and fall throughout the day depending on many different physiological and psychological factors. However, babies and toddlers have extremely fragile brains that are developing very rapidly, and some researchers are growing very concerned about babies and toddlers who have elevated levels of cortisol all day. Researchers worry that because babies' brains develop in response to the neurochemicals in their body, their brains may become adapted to high levels of cortisol, and this may be affecting children's ability to control their emotions and behaviour.

Group daycare

Researchers have found that many babies and toddlers have elevated levels of cortisol whilst experiencing certain forms of group daycare. The causes may include physiological stress from loud noises, minor accidents, conflicts and aggressive play, or from psychological stress if they lack continuity of personalised care-giving. Group daycare does not naturally lend itself to babies and toddlers developing an enduring secondary attachment bond to one carer. This may be because babies and toddlers have more than one carer providing their needs each day, and some carers may not have the time or inclination to form an attachment to a child, and some carers may be young and not intending to stay in post very long. Sometimes babies or toddlers do form attachments but policy may require babies to move to new groupings, or for carers to be moved to other duties. If this happens too frequently the pain of loss can make babies reluctant to form a secondary attachment bond to another carer. The combination of both physiological and psychological stress may account for the elevated levels of cortisol associated with some centre based group daycare.

Note: The occasional loss of a secondary attachment figure need not be too distressing to a toddler if sensitively handled, but regular swapping of carers to prevent any attachment bond developing can be a risk factor.

Separation anxiety

Babies and toddlers between the age of 6 and 30 months who do not receive sensory evidence (sight, sound, touch, smell or taste) that any of their known and trusted attachment figures are present, will have an instinctive feeling that the situation is becoming dangerous. This will induce some level of fear and raise their cortisol levels. At this age their emergency response to fear is flight towards an attachment figure, and the longer there is no sensory input from a trusted attachment figure, the greater the level of danger sensed, especially if the surroundings are not very familiar.

When left by their primary attachment figure, most babies and toddlers who have not had the opportunity to develop a secondary attachment to one carer will initially protest by crying and searching for their attachment figure. When this does not result in reunion, the instinctive reaction of some babies and younger toddlers is to become a bit subdued or withdrawn (although others appear to manage better). This compliant behaviour is usually seen as the toddler settling in and accepting their new surroundings, but their level of cortisol is often elevated which indicates that they're stressed, and if they then sense danger some may 'freeze' or 'still'. This situation is more common in group settings which lack continuity in personalised care-giving.

Note: This reminds me of toddlers in the 1950s when they were left in hospital without an attachment figure.

Securely attached

When securely attached babies and toddlers are eventually reunited with their primary attachment figure, and receive enough time and sensitive attention, they are usually able to be sufficiently comforted that their cortisol level returns to normal before bedtime, and in the morning the cycle can start again. Without additional risk factors, securely attached babies and toddlers appear to tolerate this cycle of daily separation and repair without noticeable long-term effects. Nevertheless, childcare in the absence of an attachment figure is likely to be a risk factor which usually goes undetected, increasing children's vulnerability to the impact of any additional risk factors they may experience later on.

Insecurely attached

Some babies and toddlers who are insecurely attached to their primary attachment figure and experience long periods without access to an attachment figure may have continuously elevated levels of cortisol. When they are reunited with their primary attachment figures, the insecurity in the relationships may prevent some of these babies and toddlers from being adequately comforted, and their cortisol level may not be returned to normal before bedtime. By morning the cortisol level may still be elevated and the cycle continues.

Two risk factors

Toddlers have a risk factor if they are insecurely attached to their primary attachment figure; some securely attached toddlers in group daycare without an attachment figure present may have a risk factor. If toddlers are both insecurely attached *and* have no access to an attachment figure they may be experiencing two risk factors that are difficult to detect *individually*, but which acting together produce small but noticeable increases in aggressive and disruptive behaviour.

Three risk factors

A third risk factor to children is insensitively handled parental separation. If it's well handled it can usually be tolerated by securely attached children if they have no other risk factors. But if insecure attachment is added to regular care without an attachment figure, and then there is family breakdown as well, the three risk factors acting together will usually overwhelm children, and can result in the sort of behavioural and emotional problems we are increasingly seeing today. It's worth noting that these attachment risk factors impact children's ability to make stable relationships.

Conclusions

My final conclusions are as follows. Many toddlers receive a risk factor at home from insecure attachment, and another risk factor from any sort of childcare where there is not a 'good enough' secondary attachment figure. These two risk factors are becoming normalised within society and are hidden contributors to children's future social and emotional problems. A combination of three or more risk factors has a high probability of producing increased levels of behavioural problems and emotional instability.

By reorganising childcare to provide secondary attachment bonds for babies and toddlers we can remove one increasingly common risk factor. Childminders can be professionally supported and encouraged to make links; parents could be allowed to use their childcare allowance to pay a grandmother or other relative to care for their child, or parents could choose to use the allowance to look after the child themselves.

In a society which encourages both parents to work outside the home while their children are under 3, it is attachment focused childcare arrangements that have a crucial role to play in facilitating the healthy emotional development of children.

It is in our power to provide this if we care enough about our children's well-being. It can be done!

References

Mother Nature, Sarah Blaffer Hardy, 1999.

Fifty Years of Attachment Theory, R. Bowlby, 2004.

The Nature of the Child's Tie to His Mother, *I. J. of Psycho-Analysis*, J. Bowlby, 1958.

Attachment and Loss, vol. I Attachment, J. Bowlby, 1969.

Attachment and Loss, vol. II Separation, J. Bowlby, 1973.

Separation and the Very Young, James and Joyce Robertson, 1989.

'Transition to Child Care: Associations With Infant-Mother Attachment, Infant Negative Emotion, and Cortisol Elevations.' Ahnert, Gunnar, Lamb, Barthel. *Child Development*, 2004.

'Early Child Care and Children's Development in the Primary Grades: Follow-Up Results from the NICHD Study of Early Child Care', NICHD Early Child Care Research Network, *American Educational Research Journal*, 2005.

Affect Regulation and the Origin of the Self, A.N. Schore, 1994.

'Adolescent Mental Health Problems on the Increase.' Maughan *et al. J. of Child Psychology and Psychiatry*, 2004.

Maternal and Perinatal Risk Factors for Later Delinquency, Farrington and West, 1993. *Observational Study of Daycare at the Soho Family Centre*, Barnard (in preparation 2006).

Additional reading

Raising Babies: should under 3s go to nursery, Steve Biddulph, 2006.
Why Love Matters: how affection shapes a baby's brain. Sue Gerhardt, 2004.

Source: Reprinted with permission of Sir Richard Bowlby. For a 'fuller elaborated picture', please see: Bowlby, R. (2007). 'Babies and toddlers in non-parental daycare can avoid stress and anxiety if they develop a lasting secondary attachment bond with one carer who is consistently accessible to them', *Attachment and Human Development*, 9(4).

I have been concerned about the lack of focus on emotional development in care and education of children for some time. We have focused our attention on the physical safety of children, because of high profile child abuse cases, so that the delicate balance in holistic care has shifted to the detriment of emotional development. As Bowlby (2006) has pointed out, children in nurseries may be safer physically, but not emotionally and we are uncertain of the long-term effects of emotional deprivation. This trend is not seen in other countries, which set a high store on the emotional responses to children. In Brazil, for example, society expects children throughout early years and primary education to be emotionally developed and parents are more likely to complain if their child is not hugged, kissed and cared for after a minor accident, rather than complain about the accident itself. What message do we send to children if we do not care for them when they are distressed because we have to keep our emotional distance from them? Emotional development can be affected if a number of the risk factors that affect attachment are present, such as:

- attachment failure;
- illness;
- maternal depression;
- poverty;
- loss of a carer with whom a strong attachment has been made;
- lack of skills of the carer;
- neglect;
- violence or abuse;
- time spent with different carers (more time should be spent with primary rather than secondary carers)

Even when the primary attachment is strong and great care is taken to ensure that secondary care is skilled and caring, the child may experience emotional difficulties. I have experienced this for myself when my son was $2\frac{1}{2}$ years old and was cared for two days a week by a childminder who was a neighbour and friend. After a long summer break, my family moved home a few miles away from the childminder. Two days later my son was due to start at playgroup for two mornings a week (in retrospect he was too immature for this to be really successful), but unfortunately the childminder's husband died suddenly and alternative childcare needed to be found quickly. All these factors were stressful enough for me, but they were equally and more devastatingly difficult for my son. A few months and a number of different carers later, he first asked to go home (he had enjoyed his holiday in the new house!) and exhibited some characteristics of a distressed child:

not wishing to be left, reverting to bedwetting, etc. As a result, alternative arrangements had to be made to ensure his emotional well-being. This type of stress can be rectified if the child has a secure home environment, with strong primary attachments. If, however, the family is impoverished, or bereaved or disrupted by illness, divorce or any other factor, the child is more likely to have emotional difficulties and be aggressive, antisocial or disruptive of other children and the family, class, etc.

Reflective Tasks

Early childcare

Level 1

Discuss with your peers, your own early childcare.

- Can you identify any of the stress factors (listed above) in your own early life and care?
- In retrospect, how could your own emotional development have been supported further in early childhood?

Observe and talk to an individual child to ascertain how they are settling in a care or educational setting.

- How might the setting further support the child's emotional development?

Level 2

Observe the children in your care and ascertain if they suffer from any of the stress factors identified above. Take care not to judge based on a snapshot of the child in your setting.

- How might you support the children's emotional development?

Put some of your ideas in practice and observe and listen to the children to ascertain how effective your support is.

Level 3

Observe and listen to children and adults interacting in your setting.

- Is your setting a loud or calm environment?
- Are the children passive or aggressive, interactive, social or solitary?
- Are there lots of conflicts or minor accidents?
- Are your professionals young and inexperienced or older and experienced?
- Have they been in post for a considerable time?
- Do professionals stay with your setting for a long time or do they move on to other settings?
- Do you keep groups of children together during their time with you?
- How can you make your setting a more stress-free environment for the children?

Try out some of your ideas and evaluate the success by observing and listening to the children.

Confidence and self-esteem

Children develop confidence in themselves and their abilities because of their interactions with the world. A result of these interactions is that children develop their personalities. Freud's work on personality and temperament (1923) led him to believe that there were two instincts which influence our personality and emotional development: the 'libido' (a positive force for survival, good, love and kindness) and the 'death wish' (a negative force for aggression, evil, hate and anger). In Freud's psychoanalytical theory (1923), personality consists of three related elements:

1. *The id*. This is a primitive, logical and totally demanding part of personality, focusing on things which give pleasure such as food and comfort and dominates early life and behaviour.

2. *The ego*. As children develop, they gain a more realistic awareness of themselves and the world. This awareness is called the ego. The id still has a big effect on their personality, but they become aware of the need for logic and rationality. They have to ask for things they need. They increasingly recognise the need to solve problems (to satisfy the id) by planning, negotiation, etc.

3. *The superego*. Moral reasoning, as a result of the child's recognition of themselves and others (id and ego), is called their superego. The superego results in a conscience and morality and recognises the moral dimensions of need (e.g. we should not steal to meet our needs).

See also Table 6.3.

Table 6.3 Freud's psychoanalytical theory (1923)

Stage and age	Erogenous zone	Main characteristics	Tasks to achieve
Oral 0–1	Mouth	Main source of pleasure is the mouth, lips, tongue. Biting, licking, swallowing. Main concern is with immediate gratification of urges so id dominates	Satisfactory feeding (weaning)
Anal 1–2	Anus	Controlling and not controlling bowels and bladder. The ego starts to control id.	Potty and toilet training
Phallic 2–6	Phallus	Some pleasure is gained from playing with genitals. This pleasure is associated with opposite-sex parent leading to Oedipus and Electra Complexes. Id demands, ego tries to satisfy id and superego tries to impose moral choices	Successful solutions to Oedipal and Electral Complexes
Latency 6–11	None	Oedipus and Electra identification with same-sex parent and loss of interest in opposite sex. Id, ego and superego continue to compete	None
Genital 11 onwards	Genitals	Increasing concern with adult ways of experiencing sexual pleasure	Good relationships with members of both sexes

Self-esteem is the evaluative aspect of self-concept: what we think of ourselves, or how we judge ourselves. Children develop the idea of themselves as an individual from birth in a staged process interlinked with their emotional development. From a few months old, children show awareness of themselves and show recognition of the effects of their own actions. Secure children can explore themselves in their surroundings, safe in the knowledge that they are protected and well looked after. In their second year, children become more aware of themselves. They begin to recognise themselves in pictures and refer to themselves as 'me'. If emotionally secure they will begin to develop a more positive view of themselves. They begin to develop understanding of their objects, family and those belonging to other children 'my mummy', 'mine'. As language develops, children are better able to express their emotions about themselves and describe themselves and their feelings about events and their achievements. They also develop the ability to 'make-believe', think about things and have private thoughts and imaginings. This occurs from their third year and is linked with the development of cognition, moral development and imagination. In this way they develop a concept about themselves, their attributes, attitudes and values. This development of self can be seen in children's drawings, which focus first on themselves and those close to them, initially drawing faces and then stick figures with large faces, and then their whole family. These drawings can be analysed by trained psychologists, who can begin to see emotional rifts in the family and aspects of concern in the child's emotional development.

The development of self-concept and self-esteem is dependent on children's physiological needs being developed, as defined by Maslow's hierarchical needs (1968) (see Chapter 1, Figure 1.1). A child who has a high self-esteem will be happy with the type of person they are, aware of their competencies, clear about their behaviour and how it will be viewed by others. Self-esteem includes a number of categories of self-worth. The first is academic competence and children will have a good self-esteem if they perform well academically. This does not have to be only achievement in the strict academic areas of English, mathematics and science, but also artistic, musical or technological ability and achievement in other subjects. A second category of self-worth is social competence and this involves the children's relationships with both their peers and their family. Children who have good, close family relationships and a close circle of friends will have more social confidence and a more positively developed sense of self. A third category of self-worth involves physical and athletic competence. Children who are good at sports, play for teams and are picked by their peers for team games will have a strong sense of self-worth and self-esteem. Children who find all kinds of physical activity and competitive sports difficult and are always the last to be picked by their peers to join teams will have less sense of self-worth and a lower self-esteem. The last category involves physical appearance. All adults have at least one part of their body which they would like to change and it is worrying that more young children also seem to have this concern about their bodies. Indeed, in more developed, Western countries, the number of children who are having plastic surgery for non-essential physical differences is worrying. Unfortunately, children are most unforgiving when it comes to another child with a physical difference, such as a large nose, lips or ears, just as they can be with children with different hair or skin colour. If the children are emotionally secure in other aspects of their lives, then they will put up with some comments on their appearance, but if not, then it can cause some real emotional difficulties, as seen in children who suffer from eating disorders and self-mutilation.

Gender identity, or the perception that an individual has of themselves in masculine or feminine terms, can have an influence on self-esteem. Gender identity is developed through a process of gender typing, a complex process involving genetic, cognitive and social factors. Gender typing also helps to develop gender-linked beliefs and gender roles, and is affected by gender stereotypes (common beliefs in society about males and females). Gender identity is developed from birth as a result of biological factors, such as hormone levels, and research (Money and Ehrhardt, 1972) has shown that girls who have high levels of male hormones are likely to be more masculine (tomboyish) and less likely to play with other girls of the same age. Families and society may both describe girls and boys differently and their behaviour towards them may be different, and this too can affect their self-esteem. Williams and Best (1990) found that it is a commonly held view in 30 different countries around the world that boys have more instrumental traits (reflecting competence, assertiveness and competitiveness) and girls have more expressive traits (reflecting care, sensitivity and consideration of others).

Culture can also affect self-esteem. This may be related to the way different cultures view children or treat boys and girls differently. For example, in some cultures (in countries such as China, the UK and Pakistan) the differences between the genders are very marked, with girls and boys having clear identity differences and being treated differently from a very young age. In some cases these differences are connected to religion (e.g. Islam). In other cultures, such as Finland and Sweden, equality is very important. Initially, this was politically and economically driven, because of the need for women to work, because of the expanding economy and/or because of a diminished male workforce (the effect of war). Sweden has developed the notion of gender equality to an extent that younger generations of Swedish children regard themselves as having a mixture of instrumental and expressive traits (Intons-Peterson, 1988) and girls feel more comfortable with their gender than in other countries. Cultural differences can also affect self-esteem if the child considers that their culture is at odds with the mainstream culture of the society in which they live. Cultural deprivation and difference can cause a child to have a lesser sense of self-worth. Some minority children achieve a greater sense of self-esteem by joining together into groups or gangs and while this can raise self-esteem in the shorter term and in the immediate locality it causes division and can lower self-esteem in the wider society and longer term.

Parenting styles (see Chapter 8) can also affect the child's self-esteem. Children who come from families with more **democratic** or authoritative styles (Baumrind, 1971) are more likely to have a higher self-esteem than those who come from more **authoritarian** families. The reason for this is because children from more democratic families are likely to be involved in family decision-making about a range of things, such as holidays, schooling, moving house, etc. This is likely to give the children a greater sense of self-worth as they will feel their opinion is of value and makes a difference to their lives and the lives of others. These children are more likely to engage in discussion in schools and other social contexts and feel confident about expressing their opinions. If the children are academic achievers as well, they will also feel more confident about speaking out in schools and less concerned about the social pressures and comments of their peers, who may feel that it is 'uncool' to speak out and express yourself publicly.

Practical Tasks

What effect does self-esteem have on other aspects of early childhood development?

Level 1

Consider the part self-esteem plays on the following areas of development:

- physical;
- cognitive;
- language;
- social;
- moral.

Choose one of the areas of development above and plan an activity for children that will have learning outcomes in the area and support the development of self-esteem. If you can, try out the activity and evaluate its effect on the children's self-esteem by observing them and listening to them.

Level 2

Consider your current planning for children in your setting and reflect on how activities planned to develop the children socially, physically, morally, cognitively and linguistically are affecting the children's self-esteem. You can gather this information by observing the children and listening to them.

Modify your planning (or produce new planning) to develop the children in one or more key areas and also support the development of their self-esteem. Try out your activity and evaluate its effectiveness by observing and listening to the children.

Level 3

Consider the planning for your setting for the next term and the opportunities within the plans to develop self-esteem in the children. Modify the activities planned to incorporate as many of the key areas as possible (physical, language, cognitive, social and moral development) and also to develop the children's self-esteem.

Put your modified plans into action and evaluate the effect on the children's self-esteem. You can do this by observing and listening to the children. Reflect on your findings with your staff and group the effects into positive, negative and none (that is, those that have a positive or negative or no effect on the development of self-esteem).

Consider how you can further develop your planning and practice to support the development of the children's self-esteem.

How important is emotional development to other aspects of child development?

The **functionalist** view of emotions is that they serve a function to prompt action to change, modify or develop the world around us and achieve personal goals. Your emotional reaction to an event determines your desire to repeat the experience and emotional development is thought, by functionalists, to be central to all aspects of development. Emotional development is thought to be extremely important in order for self-actualisation, achievement and other aspects of development. Children whose emotional development has been impaired in some way, through maternal depression, insecure attachment, poor parenting, family/home difficulties or disruption (such as, divorce, bereavement, poverty, illness, etc.), or biological deficiencies (such as, chemical or hormonal imbalances) are likely to experience emotional difficulties throughout childhood and in later life. Chronic depression, which affects 8–10 per cent of women, can disrupt a parent's ability to engage with their child and this can lead to irritable, depressed children who are unable to develop relationships later in life and who are more likely to have social problems at school and parenting problems in later life. Where maternal depression is associated with other family problems (see p. 184), the emotional difficulties are likely to be greater. Emotional development is thought (Matas *et al.*, 1978; Eliker *et al.*, 1992) to affect social development, by supporting positive social attitudes such as, enthusiasm, flexibility and persistence, and the development of creative development, by supporting imagination and imaginative play (see Figure 6.1).

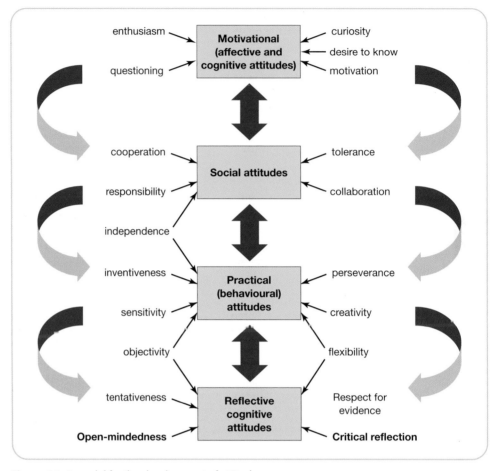

Figure 6.1 A model for the development of attitudes
Source: Adapted from Johnston, 2005: 94

Cognitive development will also be affected by emotions and emotional development. Motivation to learn, enthusiasm, perseverance, flexibility and tolerance of ideas will be affected by emotions (Johnston, 2005). The development in complexity and intensiveness in emotions during early childhood is thought to be the result of cognition (Alessandri *et al.*, 1990). As children develop, they begin to understand the effect of their own actions on people and events, and as their cognitive capacities develop, they are also able to determine situations and people's emotions. For example, they begin to develop awareness of situations which may be threatening and those which can be explored further. They can explain emotions in others, by giving explanations for sadness, happiness, fear. They can predict what emotions others will express in different situations. They can remember the feelings associated with certain situations and avoid or seek them out. As they develop, they realise that they can hold more than one emotion at the same time, have mixed feelings, and can argue for and against actions, considering the emotional advantages of actions. They also learn to hide some emotions for social reasons. In this way emotional development is closely related to Piaget's stages of cognitive development (1950; see Chapter 4, Figure 4.4), Kohlberg's stages of moral development (1976; see below), Freud's psychoanalytical theory (1923; see above and Table 6.3) and Erikson's psycho-social stages (1950; see Table 6.4).

Table 6.4 Erikson's psycho-social stages (1950)

	Stage	Approximate age
1	Trust v Mistrust	0–8 months
2	Autonomy v Doubt, Shame	8–18 months
3	Initiative v Guilt	18 months–6 years
4	Industry v Inferiority	6–11 years
5	Identity v Identity Diffusion	11 years onwards

There are social and cultural variations with regard to emotions, which identifies that there may be a learnt aspect to emotions and strengthens the evidence of a cognitive element in emotional development. Intercultural studies (Munn, 1966) have shown differences in expression in different cultures. For example, we show surprise by raising our eyebrows, while in Chinese society the tongue is stuck out when they are surprised. Clapping hands is a sign that we are happy, but in Chinese society it expresses worry or disappointment. Other studies have shown cultural differences regarding attachment. German children have been shown to display avoidance attachment, but this can be explained by the encouragement of independence in young children in German society (Grossmann *et al.*, 1985). On the other hand, Japanese children show great distress when left by a parent, but since in Japanese culture children are rarely left this is unsurprising. In societies where parents share tasks and fathers work from home, for example, the Aka hunters in central Africa (Hewlitt, 1992), children have closer relationships with their fathers than in societies where the father works away and is more distant. Cultural variations are also found with regard to stranger anxiety and these are thought to be due to differences in child-rearing techniques. Efe hunters in Africa (Tronick *et al.*, 1992) show little stranger anxiety because as babies they are passed from one adult to another, whereas in Israel kibbutz children show great stranger anxiety, possibly because of their isolated community's fear of terrorism (Saarni *et al.*, 1998).

In Chapter 9, the story *The Snow Lambs* (Glori, 1995) is used within a cross-curricular theme to support development across subjects and key areas, including emotional development (see Figure 9.2). The story itself has a distinct emotional element and can be used to explore feelings, with children being asked to identify with the main characters and recognise the emotions they will experience during the story. The children can also be asked to identify experiences they have had that have made them feel the same as the characters. The storytelling and follow-up play can use the resources in the sheep play area (see Picture 6.1); a stuffed lamb, a sheep's fleece (washed and brushed), a stuffed dog. This can support emotional development as children are motivated by the play and can learn about their own emotions through the play (see also Picture 6.1).

Music can support children emotionally and it is no coincidence that music is also used therapeutically to support children who have suffered trauma or who are emotionally disturbed because of childhood crises (illness, divorce, bereavement, abuse, etc.). Children can listen to music, play with musical instruments, explore how music makes them feel and make their own musical instruments out of junk material. These instruments can be ones that make a sound by being banged, blown, plucked or shaken. Children can begin to make their own music and even note this down in their own way, using symbols of their choice. They can also use the instruments made or other instruments to create a sound track for a favourite story book, focusing on how the music can create the mood for the story. In this way the children are developing:

Picture 6.1 Playing sheep and emotional development

- their fine motor skills, as they play instruments and make their own instruments (physical development);
- their understanding of how the instrument makes a sound (cognitive development);
- their ability to work with other children, sharing instruments and resources and making music with others (social development);
- their creativity by making their own music and using their own symbols to record their music (creative development);
- their understanding of their own feelings during different parts of the activity and the way music can create mood (emotional development).

Parachute play (see Picture 6.2) is often used to support children physically and socially as it both involves gross motor development and encourages children to take turns and work cooperatively with their peers. It can also support emotional development by making children feel good about themselves and motivated to work with other children as they play and have fun.

What is morality?

Morality, defined as 'the doctrine of actions as right or wrong' (*Chambers*, 1972), is society's process of enforcing rules of right and wrong on its members. It is important for any social group (family, class, school, gang, club) and for society as a whole that there is some common morality. This is because all social groups can only function if individual members share common goals and have common rules and regulations. However, not all groups have to have the same set of rules; in fact, different societies may have different moral codes and beliefs about right and wrong.

Picture 6.2 Parachute play

Moral development is 'the process by which children adopt and internalise the rules and expectations of society and develop a sense of right or wrong' (Dwyer and Scampion, 1995: 254) and is an important part of socialisation.

Behaviourist theories of moral development

Behaviourists believe that children develop morals through imitation, reinforcement and punishment. These are behaviourist theories, of which there are three main types (see also Chapters 1 and 7). The first is classical conditioning, which is a learned stimulus response and results in automatic behaviour. Pavlov (1927) showed this response with his dog, by ringing a bell just before he fed the dog. The dog learned to associate the bell with food and would salivate as soon as it heard the bell. So, for example, children may learn to use social responses such as 'please', 'thank you' and 'excuse me' automatically. However, they are more likely to learn these social responses as a result of being rewarded for using them or punished for not using them (operant conditioning) and by imitating the behaviour of others who do use them (social learning). Operant conditioning occurs where behaviour is learned as a result of reward and/or punishment and was identified by Skinner (1953), who experimented on rats to develop his theory (see Chapters 1 and 7). Operant conditioning provides extrinsic motivation for children to adhere to social and moral conventions, by rewarding behaviour that is socially acceptable and punishing behaviour that is not acceptable. I was once asked by my son (aged 3): ' Can I have a drink?' My response was to say 'Excuse me, what did you ask for?' and his response was to ask again, although adding to his request: 'Can I have a drink and a biscuit?' I told him that he had forgotten something in his request and he responded by asking for a drink, a biscuit and a sweet! Clearly this was my fault for being unclear about the social cue that I wanted, but he quickly learnt that he was more likely to get a drink and a biscuit (although not necessarily a sweet) if he used the word please. Unfortunately, many young children do not use social niceties as a matter of course because they have not learned that these are necessary in order to have their wishes fulfilled, probably because in their early lives it was not necessary.

In early years settings, children are more likely to learn by reward than punishment, although they are punished if they:

- have to wait for something they want to play with because they have snatched it from another child;
- are excluded from an activity because they have disrupted the play of others;
- are made to apologise to a peer they have hurt.

Through punishments such as this and rewards such as being praised, being allowed to do a favourite activity, or acknowledgement of their efforts, children learn that if they listen to others and not shout out, they will be rewarded by being listened too. They learn to take their turn and not snatch toys, and to play with and alongside other children. They learn that if they play nicely and are good friends they will have more friends and feel better about themselves. In recent years there has been considerable focus on positive behaviour management, so that negative behaviours are ignored where possible, and the focus is on rewarding and celebrating positive behaviours, other than empty and meaningless praise, which the child does not value. Care has to be taken to ensure that the focus does not get distorted and becomes reward for not doing something negative, such as not pinching or not speaking out of turn. We can avoid this distortion if the targets for behaviour and adhering to moral and social codes are individual and specific. In this way a young child who starts in a nursery with little or no experience of socialising, and who finds it difficult to be part of a large group and to cooperate and share, will not have the same expectations as a child who has been in the nursery for a while and has been used to socialising and sharing within a large family. Professionals need to ensure that they do not see differentiation in social and moral targets as 'double standards'. In my experience, children find this easier than the adults who care for them. Johnston *et al.* (2007) identify some positive ways to focus on behaviour, such as:

- concentrating on the behaviour or the social or moral rule and not the person;
- avoiding rhetorical questions, sarcasm and humiliation;
- allowing children to make decisions for themselves (perhaps from a limited choice);
- avoiding non-productive confrontations and arguments.

Negative reactions to behaviour will often create further difficulties. Webster-Stratton (1999) believes that teachers' negative reactions to what is perceived as poor behaviour will usually escalate the problem, not provide the good role models children need to develop morally.

Children also learn by observing and imitating others, particularly the behaviour of those who are role models. This is the main characteristic of Bandura's social learning theory (1977; see especially Chapter 1). This theory identifies that children learn behaviours by observation and imitation. In this way carers and professionals who are good role models will help children to learn social and moral conventions, while poor role models will not help children to learn the socially and morally acceptable behaviours we want.

Cognitive theories of moral development

As well as learning through extrinsic ways about moral codes and conventions, children need to develop intrinsic motivations for behaving in socially and morally acceptable ways. They need to behave in certain ways because they want to rather than because they are made to. In order for this to happen they need to think about what they are doing and understand the effects of certain behaviours on others. This is the basis of cognitive theories of moral development (see also Chapter 4).

Cognitive psychologists believe that morality is developed as children's cognitive skills develop. Freud's psychoanalytical theory and theory of moral development (1923) concludes that children develop morally through identification with parents of both sexes and is deeply interconnected with his psychoanalytical theory (see p. 186). In this theory, the child is quite passive in the process of moral development. Young children will not recognise the need to work with others to achieve their desires (id), while as they mature and gain experiences they learn that they need to take others into consideration (ego). It is only as they develop with age and experience that they learn that they may also consider the effect of their actions on the wider community and society (superego). Piaget also developed a cognitive theory of moral development (1965). He believed that children were active participants in their moral development and their ability to use and understand rules developed in cognitive stages related to their cognitive development (see Chapter 4 and Table 6.5). Children in the sensori-motor stage of development will have no moral codes, while those in the pre-operational stage will begin to obey rules by imitating their role models, but there will be no real understanding of what they are doing and why. They are also egocentric in their adherence to rules and we can see this when we observe young children playing games: they will bend or change the rules to suit themselves. At the concrete operational stage children will accept rules and obey them, but real understanding and application in different circumstances will come as they move to the formal operational stage.

Piaget found out about children's moral development and developed his staged theory after listening to children's responses to moral stories and by asking them to make a moral judgement. In one story one little girl stole a loaf of bread from a shop because she was poor and starving, while another stole a small cake from a shop because she wanted it. Piaget found that pre-operational children could not take into account intentions and felt that the crime of stealing a large loaf was worse than stealing a small cake. Children in the concrete and formal operational stages of development were more able to take other things into account when making decisions and could see the social and moral aspects of the stories.

Kohlberg (1976) also had a cognitive theory on moral development and like Piaget he used stories to investigate the way children develop moral reasoning. Kohlberg identified three levels and six stages of moral reasoning. In the first stage of the first level (pre-conventional morality) children are concerned with the outcomes, rather than the motives, of some behaviour, so they will work towards reward and avoid punishment. In the second stage of pre-conventional morality, the children will still be very egocentric and concerned with their own pleasure and reward, but they will also begin to be concerned about others who are close to them, especially their close family. The second level, called conventional morality, is where children begin to consider others, but the motive for this is still selfish. In the first stage at this level (stage 3), children will try to win approval

Table 6.5 Piaget's cognitive theory of moral development (1965)

Stage	Age	Use of rules
Sensori-motor	0–3	None
Pre-operational	4–7	Imitation and egocentric application
Concrete operational	7–11	Accept and obey

from others and so will behave in ways that they know will please them. They know that the behaviour will please, but they do not understand why. At the second stage at this level (stage 4), children will slavishly follow conventions and obey rules and expect punishment for non-adherence. They are, however, beginning to understand some aspects of why we have rules. It is at this stage that children begin to feel guilt when they do something that they know is wrong. The final level is post-conventional morality, which again has two stages. Stage 5 is characterised by an increasing awareness of the interests of others, so in a setting they will consider the feelings and needs of their peers, even if they are not friends with them. However, most children are unlikely to reach this stage in the early years (up to 8 years of age). The final stage (stage 6) is characterised by deep moral principles and understanding of religious, political, social and ethical issues and few adults reach this stage, let alone children. Kohlberg (1976) identified that the stage of moral development can be ascertained by the way an individual reasons about the dilemma facing them, rather than by the decision they come to which determines their moral maturity. So those who favour individual rights over society's laws are thought to be at a lower stage of moral development than an individual who considers the wider implications of actions.

Like Piaget (1965), Kohlberg (1976) found out about the stage of moral development by listening to the responses to moral stories and moral discussions. These discussions are also important for children in helping them to develop understanding of moral issues and see things from the perspective of others. I use moral stories in much of my teaching with young children and they provide them with opportunities to think (develop cognitively), understand the views of others (develop socially) and feel their ideas are valued (develop emotionally). They also provide me with opportunities to ascertain their development. In one school, a class of 8-year-old children had been discussing the miracles of Jesus in a religious education lesson and were asked to identify what miracle they would ask of Jesus if they were to meet him today. Most children identified that they would like something to happen to them; become a professional footballer, be rich and famous, etc. These children were working at stage 1 of Kohlberg's pre-conventional level and were mainly concerned with themselves. Some children wanted something to happen to their family or friends, such as make a grandparent who was ill better, or get a job for a father who had just been made redundant. These children appeared to be working at stage 2 of Kohlberg's pre-conventional level and were considering others and not just themselves. A few children thought about global or national events and wanted to eliminate poverty or stop wars for the greater good and not just their own. These children were beginning to show characteristics of post-conventional morality (Kohlberg, 1976; see also Table 6.6).

Table 6.6 Kohlberg's cognitive theory of moral development (1976)

Level	Stages	Moral characteristics
1 Pre-conventional morality	1	Children are concerned with the outcomes of some behaviour. They do not take motives into account and avoid punishment
	2	Children judge in terms of their own pleasure and that of those close to them
2 Conventional morality	3	Children try to win approval from others
	4	Children insist rules should be obeyed or punishment will follow. Guilt begins at this stage
3 Post-conventional morality	5	There is increasing awareness of the interests of others in the community. Their needs may be more important than individual needs
	6	There are deep moral principles (religious, political, social). Few reach this stage

Supporting moral development

Moral development can be supported in a number of ways. Most importantly, children need an environment in which they can take responsibility for their own development and make decisions for themselves. They also need good role models to imitate and develop their own ideas of responsibility from, and learn to from their role models and experiences that they are responsible for their own actions. Young children will often deny responsibility for an action because they did not intend the result. They may not realise that another child will be upset or hurt if they behave in a certain way or that something will break or go wrong if they do something. However, they have to learn to take responsibility for the action, apologise and attempt to right any wrongs. Many young children deny responsibility if they did not mean something to happen and will say 'It's not my fault, I didn't mean to.' Unfortunately, this kind of response is all too apparent in societies and adults as well as children, and it is hardly surprising that children are not developing a sense of responsibility for their actions. Children need to develop social attitudes, such as cooperation, tolerance, and responsibility and leadership (see Johnston, 2005 and Figure 6.1), but we should remember that they do not exist naturally and we need to support their development. The curriculum for children in the Foundation Stage for Learning (DfES, 2006), that is, for children aged 0–5 years of age, and for children in Key Stages 1 and 2 (DfEE, 1999), for children aged 5–11 years, identifies the need to *promote children's 'spiritual, moral, social and cultural development, and prepare all pupils for the opportunities, responsibilities and experiences of life'* (DfEE, 1999: 11). The curriculum divides values into four cluster areas (DfEE, 1999: 195–7):

- valuing the self (self-esteem, health);
- valuing others (property, toleration, respect);
- valuing society (participation);
- valuing the environment (sustainability, biodiversity and repair of damage); and it is the responsibility of settings to provide an environment where development is moral and child-centred, thus showing their care for the holistic development of the child.

This environment would be one that values children as individuals (Rousseau, 1911) and has clear rules and boundaries for the children, so that they can make their own decisions but within a structure that supports them and helps them to realise the consequences of their decisions and actions. In this way, a setting that provides a routine and security (see Steiner, 1996; Webster-Stratton, 1999), together with explicit reminders through discussion of the rules, will enable children to feel secure in the knowledge of what is acceptable and what is not. The relationship between professionals, children and their families is vital for this to occur effectively (see Bronfenbrenner, 1995, and Chapters 1 and 7). This learning partnership, discussed more fully in Chapter 13, helps to provide the safe and secure learning environment in which children can develop morally.

Professionals also utilise strategies for supporting behaviours in their setting. These include the use of quiet and pausing to gain attention, eye contact and focusing children on positives rather than negatives. Many children's stories have a moral element and this can be used to support moral development. Reading the story can be followed by a discussion on the moral dilemmas faced by the characters and how the children would respond in a similar situation. Stories like 'The Three Little Pigs' and 'Goldilocks and the Three Bears' can lead to discussions on how the characters felt at different stages in the story and whether they were right to act as they did. For example, should Goldilocks have entered the bears' house and eaten their food? Was she responsible for breaking their chairs? Was it surprising that the bears reacted as they did? How would you react if a stranger entered you house and ate your porridge? Like Piaget (1965) and Kohlberg (1976) I have used stories, both fictional and historical, to encourage children in the early years (Johnston and Gray, 1999) to discuss moral and ethical issues. The story of Darwin who was criticised for his ideas about evolution can lead to discussion about whether it is morally right to criticise people if their ideas are different from your own.

Practical Tasks

Stories to support moral development

Level 1

Find a story book that has a moral element to it. Plan how you can read/tell this story to children and follow it up with a discussion to focus on the moral issues. Try this out with a group of children and tape the discussion. Listen to the tape and analyse the children's responses to the story to try and ascertain their stage of moral development. How will you use this understanding of the children in your next work with children?

Level 2

Look at your planning for the next term and see what stories you are using that have a moral element to them. Incorporate into your planning how you can use each story to promote moral discussions. Tape or video the resulting discussions with children and use these to listen to the children's voices and analyse what they are saying about the moral issues. Identify the children's stages of moral development. What does this analysis tell you about your children? How can you use moral discussions in the future?

Level 3

As a staff, look at your long-term planning and ascertain what opportunities there are for moral discussions. Make a list of all the stories you use that have a moral element in them and aim to incorporate them into your planning. Try out your ideas with different age groups – you may try taking one story and using that in different ways with the different age groups in your setting. Video or tape the children's discussions and use the tapes to analyse the children's moral development. Reflect on the differences in moral reasoning in the different groups and consider what this analysis tells you about your setting's success in supporting the children's moral development. What do you need to do in the future to continue or improve your support for the children's moral development?

Puppets are also a useful resource (see Picture 6.3) to support both children's emotional and moral development, as well as their cognitive development (Keogh *et al.*, 2006). The first way in which this can be done is by children who find talking difficult talking through puppets explaining things they are not able to articulate to others. Another way, is during circle time, when the children can use the puppet to speak with the only responses allowed being through the puppet, thus helping the children to speak in turn and not shout out. A third way to use puppets is for the teacher to use one to help enact a moral story, with the children telling the puppet what they think about the moral dimension. Many children will feel happier telling the puppet, rather than an adult, even if it is on the hand of the adult!

Picture 6.3 Puppets to support emotional and moral development

The most important consideration in supporting a child's development is that it is multi-faceted. Emotional development is a vital part of a child's holistic development and if the balance between the different aspects are not considered and planned for the child will suffer. In recent years, the focus on physical development (physical safety of the child) and cognitive development has been at the expense of emotional development. This balance now needs to be restored.

Summary

→ Emotions are an expression of feelings which show a readiness for action and are a result of an interrelationship between our biochemistry and environmental and social events.

→ Early emotional development occurs in response to children's needs and wants.

→ High levels of stress in the first three years of development are thought to have an adverse effect on brain and emotional development.

→ Babies quickly form attachments with their carers.

→ When a baby is born, the maternal bonding occurs quickly. If something occurs to prevent that bonding the effects can be quite severe for both mother and child.

→ Bowlby (1969) studied the effects of maternal deprivation on attachment and future emotional development and concluded that attachment was essential for future mental health.

→ There have been a number of criticisms of Bowlby's research. Perhaps the most important is that Bowlby failed to consider the effect of privation, that is, the effect of never having an attachment, on emotional development.

→ There is a need for good secondary attachments to be formed in childcare, as these help children to develop as stress-free individuals (Bowlby, 2006).

→ There is concern about the nature of day care in some nurseries and the potential detrimental impact on secondary attachments, owing to relatively high ratios of children to adults and high turnovers of staff.

→ Recent research by Sir Richard Bowlby (2006) examined the causes of stress in babies and toddlers in group day care and concluded that a combination of three or more risk factors has a high probability of producing increased levels of behavioural problems and emotional instability.

→ Children develop confidence in themselves and their abilities because of their interactions with the world. A result of these interactions is that children develop their personalities.

→ In Freud's psychoanalytical theory (1923), personality consists of three related elements, the id, the ego and the superego.

→ The development of self-concept and self-esteem is dependent on children's physiological needs being developed, as defined by Maslow's theory of hierarchical needs (1968).

→ Self-esteem includes a number of categories of self-worth, including academic competence, social competence, physical and athletic competence, and physical appearance.

→ Gender identity or the perception that an individual has of themselves in masculine or feminine terms can have an influence on self-esteem.

→ Other influences on self-esteem include culture and parenting styles.

→ Emotional development is thought to be extremely important for self-actualisation, achievement and other aspects of development.

→ Cognitive development will also be affected by emotional development. Motivation to learn, enthusiasm, perseverance, flexibility and tolerance of ideas will be affected by emotions.

→ Emotional development is closely related to Piaget's stages of cognitive development (1950), Kohlberg's stages of moral development (1976), Freud's psychoanalytical theory (1923) and Erikson's psycho-social stages (1950).

→ Music can support children emotionally and it is often used therapeutically to support children who have suffered trauma or who are emotionally disturbed because of childhood crises (illness, divorce, bereavement, abuse, etc.).

→ Moral development is 'the process by which children adopt and internalise the rules and expectations of society and develop a sense of right or wrong' (Dwyer and Scampion, 1995: 254) and is an important part of socialisation.

→ Behaviourists believe that children develop morals through imitation, reinforcement and punishment.

→ Cognitive psychologists believe that morality is developed as children's cognitive skills develop. Piaget developed a cognitive theory of moral development (1965). He believed that children were active participants in their moral development and their ability to use and understand rules developed in cognitive stages related to their cognitive development.

→ Freud's psychoanalytical theory and theory of moral development (1923) identifies that children develop morally through identification with parents of both sexes and is deeply interconnected with his psychoanalytical theory.

→ Kohlberg (1976) identified three levels and six stages of moral reasoning, from the first stage of the first level, where children are concerned with the outcomes rather than the motives, to the final stage (stage 6), which is characterised by deep moral principles and understanding of religious, political, social and ethical issues. Few adults are thought to reach this stage, let alone children.

→ Moral development can be supported in a number of ways. Most importantly, children need an environment in which they can take responsibility for their own development and make decisions for themselves.

Key Questions

- What constitutes emotional development?
- What are the key aspects of attachment theories and why are some criticised?
- What can influence the development of self-concept and self-esteem?
- How does emotional development impact on other areas of development?
- What are the main theories of moral development?
- How can adults support children's moral development within their settings?

References

Ainsworth, M., Blehar, M., Waters, E. and Wall, S. (1978) *Patterns of Attachment.* Hillsdale, NJ: Erlbaum

Alessandri, S.M., Sullivan, M.W. and Lewis, M. (1990) 'Violation of Expectancy and Frustration in Early Infancy', *Developmental Psychology*, 26: 738–44

Bandura, A. (1977) *Social Learning Theory.* Englewood Cliffs, NJ: Prentice-Hall

Baumrind, D. (1971) 'Current Patterns of Parental Authority', *Developmental Psychology*, Monograph 4.1 Part 2

Berk, L.E. (2003) *Child Development*, 6th edn. Boston: Allyn & Bacon

Bowlby, J. (1969) *Attachment and Loss.* New York: Basic Books

Bowlby, R. (2006) *The Need for Secondary Attachment Figures in Childcare.* www.telegraph.co.uk/opinion/main.jhtml?xml=/opinion/2006/10/21/nosplit/dt2101.x ml#head5Childcare problems

Bronfenbrenner, U. (1995) The Bioecological Model from a Life Course Perspective: Reflections of a participant observer, in Moen P., Elder Jnr, G. H. and Lüscher, K. (eds) *Examining Lives in Context.* Washington, DC: American Psychological Association, 599–618

Chambers Twentieth Century Dictionary, ed. A.M. Macdonald (1972). Edinburgh: W. & R. Chambers

CWDC (2006) *Early Years Professional National Standards.* London: CWDC

Daily Telegraph (2006) Letter to the Editor, Saturday 21 October

Davenport, G.C. (1994) *An Introduction to Child Development.* London: Collins

DfEE (1999) *The National Curriculum: Handbook for Teachers in England.* London: DfEE/QCA

DfES (2003) *Every Child Matters.* London: DfES

DfES (2006) *Early Years Foundation Stage.* London: DfES

Dwyer, D. and Scampion, J. (1995) *A Level Psychology.* London: Macmillan

Eliker, J., Englund, M. and Sroufe, L. (1992) Predicting Peer Competence and Peer Relationships in Childhood from Early Parent-Child Relationships, in Parke, R. D. and Ladd, G.W. (eds) *Family-Peer Relationships: Modes of Linkage.* Hillsdale, NJ: Erlbaum: pp. 77–106

Erikson, E.H. (1950) *Childhood and Society.* New York: Norton

Field, T. (1991) 'Quality Infant Daycare and Grade School Behaviour and Performance', *Child Development*, 62: 863–70

Freud, S. (1923) *The Ego and the Id.* London: Hogarth

Glori, D. (1995) *The Snow Lambs.* London: Scholastic

Grossmann, K., Grossmann, K.E., Spangler, G., Suess, G. and Unzner, L. (1985) Maternal Sensitivity and Newborns' Orientation Responses as Related to Quality of Attachment in Northern Germany, in Brotherton, I. and Waters, E. (eds) Growing Points of

Attachment Theory and Research. *Monographs of the Society for Research in Child Development*, 50: 1–2

Hewlitt, B. S. (1992) Husband–Wife Reciprocity and the Father–Infant Relationship among Aka Pygmies, in Hewlett, B.S. (ed.) *Father–Child Relations: Cultural and Biological Contexts*. New York: Aldine De Gruyter, pp. 153–76

Intons-Peterson, M.J. (1988) *Gender Concepts of Swedish and American Youth*. Hillsdale, NJ: Erlbaum

Johnston, J. (2005) *Early Explorations in Science*, 2nd edn. Buckingham: Open University Press

Johnston, J. and Gray, A. (1999) *Enriching Early Scientific Learning*. Buckingham: Open University Press

Johnston, J., Halocha, J. and Chater, M. (2007) *Developing Teaching Skills in the Primary School*. Buckingham: Open University Press

Keogh, B., Naylor, S., Downing, B., Maloney, J. and Simon, S. (2006) 'Puppets Bringing Stories to Life in Science', *Primary Science Review* 92: 26–8

Kohlberg, L. (1976) Moral Stages and Moralization: The cognitive-developmental approach, in Lickona, T. (ed.) *Moral Development and Behaviour: Theory, Research and Social Issues*. New York: Holt, pp. 31–53

Lorenz, K. (1952) *King Solomon's Ring*. New York: Crowell

Maslow, A.H. (1968) *Towards a Psychology of Being*. New York: Van Nostrand

Matas, L., Arend, R. and Sroufe, L.A. (1978) 'Continuity of Adaption in the Second Year: The relationship between quality of attachment and later competence', *Child Development*, 49: 547–56

Money, J. and Ehrhardt, A.A. (1972) *Man and Woman, Boy and Girl*. Baltimore: Johns Hopkins University Press

Munn, N. (1966) *Psychology*, 5th edn. London: Harrap

Pavlov, I.P. (1927) *Conditioned Reflexes*. Oxford: Oxford University Press

Piaget, J. (1950) *The Psychology of Intelligence*. London: Routledge & Kegan Paul

Piaget, J. (1965) *The Moral Judgement of the Child*. New York: Free Press

Rousseau, J.J. (1911) *Emile*. London: J.M. Dent

Saarni, C., Mumme, D.L. and Campos, J.J. (1998) Emotional Development: Action, Communication and Understanding, In Eisenberg, N. (ed.) *Handbook of Child Psychology: Vol 3 Social, Emotional and Personality Development*, 5th edn. New York: Wiley, pp. 237–309

Schwienhart, L.J, Weikart, D.P. and Toderan, R. (1993) *High Quality Preschool Programs Found to Improve Adult Status*. Ypsilante, MI: High/Scope Foundation

Siraj-Blatchford, I., Sylva, K., Muttock, S., Gilden, R. and Bell, D. (2002) *Researching Effective Pedagogy in the Early Years*. London: DfES

Skinner, B.F. (1953) *Science and Human Behaviour*. London: Macmillan

Steiner, R. (1996) *The Education of the Child and Early Lectures on Education*. New York: Anthroposophic Press

SureStart, (2003) *Birth to Three Matters. A Framework to Support Children in their Earliest Years*. London: DfES

Tronick, E.Z. Morelli, G. and Ivey, P. (1992) 'The Efe Forager Infant and Toddler's Pattern of Social Relationships: Multiple and Simultaneous', *Developmental Psychology*, 28: 568–77

Webster-Stratton, C. (1999) *How to Promote Children's Social and Emotional Competence*. London: Paul Chapman.

Williams, J.E. and Best, D.L. (1990) *Measuring Sex Stereotypes: A multi-nation study*. Newbury Park, CA: Sage

Useful reading

Cooper, P. (ed.) (1999) *Understanding and Supporting Children with emotional and Behavioural Difficulties.* London: Jessica Kingsley

Pearson, M. (1998) *Emotional Healing and self-Esteem.* Melbourne: ACER

Pearson, M. and Nolan, P. (1995) *Emotional release for Children. Repairing the past – preparing the future.* Melbourne: ACER

Useful books for children

Amos, J. and Spenceley, A. (1997) *Being Helpful.* London: Cherrytree Books

Amos, J. and Spenceley, A. (1997) *Sharing.* London: Cherrytree Books

Amos, J. and Spenceley, A. (1997) *Being Kind.* London: Cherrytree Books

Amos, J. and Spenceley, A. (1997) *Making Friends.* London: Cherrytree Books

Amos, J. and Spenceley, A. (1999) *Owning Up.* London: Cherrytree Books

Bryant-Mole, K. (1998) *I'm Shy.* London: Hodder Children's Books

Bryant-Mole, K. (1998) *I'm Happy.* London: Hodder Children's Books

Green, J. (1999) *I Feel Bullied.* London: Hodder Children's Books

Green, J. (2002) *Why Should I Recycle?* London: Hodder Children's Books

Llewellyn, C. (1998) *Nice or Nasty? Learning about drugs and your health.* London: Hodder Children's Books

Llewellyn, C. (2001) *Why Should I Eat Well?* London: Hodder Children's Books

Moses, B. (1993) *I Feel Sad.* London: Hodder Children's Books

Moses, B. (1993) *I Feel Frightened.* London: Hodder Children's Books

Moses, B. (1993) *I Feel Angry.* London: Hodder Children's Books

Moses, B. (1993) *I'm Worried.* London: Hodder Children's Books

Moses, B. (1993) *I Feel Jealous.* London: Hodder Children's Books

Moses, B. (1997) *I Don't Care! Learning about respect.* London: Hodder Children's Books

Chapter 7

Social Development

'There can be no keener revelation of a society's soul than the way in which it treats its children'
Nelson Mandela (b. 1918–)

Introduction

This chapter focuses on the social development of children from birth to 8 years of age. It examines the influence that society and culture have on young children's social development as well as how theories of social development permeate and affect our understanding of children. There will be opportunities to reflect upon key issues and to analyse the impact of social contexts upon children's holistic development.

Aims

→ To provide an understanding of the main aspects of social development

→ To provide an overview of the key theories of social development

→ To explore what constitutes a society

→ To consider some of the influences on social development, including gender, the family, culture and race

→ To consider some of the behaviour problems children may experience

→ To consider some of the external influences on social development, such as social policy and the environment

The relevance of sociology

The Penguin Dictionary of Sociology (Abercrombie *et al.*, 1984: 199) states that the term sociology derives from two roots: the Latin·*socius* (meaning companion) and the Greek *ology* (meaning the study of), and literally means 'the study of the processes of companionship'. In a more technical sense sociology is 'the analysis of the structure of social relationships as constituted by social interaction'.

Sociology is concerned with the observation and analysis of relationships occurring in society. It attempts to measure patterns of social behaviours carried out by individuals and seeks to explain these through the social conditions (environment or nurture) in which they live and develop. The most significant and influential of these environments is the family. Sociological research has, in the past, been influential in supporting the cultural and idealised stereotypical view of family life within Western societies. For example, Bowlby's (1951) study of attachment (see Chapters 1 and 6) advocated a childhood cared for by primary carers and thus stereotypical family life. More recently, sociological research has increasingly become the bedrock on which governments develop their social policies for benefits and childcare provision. By collecting national figures on the divorce rates and the number of dependent children within the UK, sociologists influence policy by using an analysis of their results to forecast what support and intervention may be required in the future.

Research

The make-up of society

Data collected by the Office for National Statistics (2007) is showing a shift in the make-up of society. In 2007, there were just over 4 million children aged 5 and under, with 660,080 babies, 680,725 children aged 1 year, 699,913 aged 2 years, 712,460 3-year-olds, 733,291 4-year-olds and 721,433 children aged under 5 years. While the differences in numbers are not significant, they do show a steady decline in births. If this decline is taken together with a large increase in the numbers of adults approaching, or having reached, retirement age, we can predict a society comprising older people being cared for by fewer younger people. The implications for our future society include the impact on the economy, health and education services, and social integration.

The study of society, through sociology, originated shortly after the French Revolution of 1789. The Revolution not only shook Western societies to their roots but also appears to have forced the pace of social reform. Through the Revolution ordinary people, especially women, began to make demands for their democratic rights. These were to be *heard and considered*; women wanted the right to be educated (Fitzgerald, 2006). Some 27 years previously, Jean-Jacques Rousseau had first published his influential work *Emile, ou l'education* (1911, see also Chapter 1). The eighteenth century was the century of the European Enlightenment, a period of lively uncertainty, daring social criticism, and unprecedented faith in reason. Rousseau took issue with much of the critical thrust of his age's philosophical reasoning and championed the rights of the child in society.

What is social development?

Social development is concerned with learning to live with others in a social learning environment: in society. Child development is divided up in different ways depending on whether you are a psychologist, educationalist or child developmentalist. Psychologists talk about cognitive, conative and affective development (thinking, doing and feeling). Educationalists talk about the key areas of the Early Years Foundation Stage: personal, social and emotional, communication, language and literacy, problem solving, reasoning and numeracy, knowledge and understanding of the world, physical and creative development. Those concerned with child development talk about PIES (physical, intellectual, emotional and social development) or PILES, by including language, which is actually part of intellectual (or, to be more politically correct, cognitive) development. In all cases the development is the same, but just divided into different categories. In this chapter we are concerned with all the social aspects of development (social knowledge, behaviour, skills and attitudes). It is, however, difficult to compartmentalise development neatly as there are considerable overlaps. For example (see Figure 7.1):

- drawing involves both a cognitive and a physical response;
- attachment involves an emotional and a social response (see also Chapter 6);
- moral reasoning involves cognitive, emotional and social responses (see also Chapter 6);
- play involves a response in all areas: cognitive, emotional, social and physical.

Reflective Tasks

The interrelationship of development

Level 1

Consider where to place the following into the Venn diagram in Figure 7.1:

- walking;
- feeding yourself;
- making friends;
- riding a tricycle;
- language;
- crying;
- asking questions;

- self-confidence;
- cutting;
- recognising shapes.

Make sure you can argue why you made the choice you did for each one.

Level 2

List all the activities a child in your setting will do in one day. Try to place each one into the Venn diagram in Figure 7.1. Consider whether there is a balance of activities in the different areas. Should the different areas be balanced? Make sure you identify why you have answered in a particular way.

Level 3

With your colleagues, list different types of activities your children engage in over a period of a term. Try to place each one into the Venn diagram in Figure 7.1. Identify all those which have a social element to them and consider whether they represent the full range of social activities needed for effective social development (see below for more detail on social development). If there are any social activities not undertaken in your setting, identify how you can incorporate them.

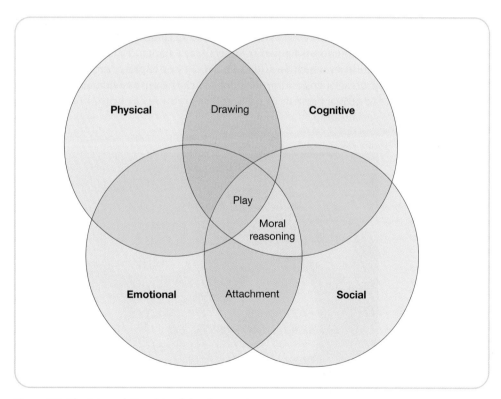

Figure 7.1 The inter-relationship of development

Children begin to develop socially as soon as they are born and interact with others. At first the newborn baby attracts attention by crying, informing its parents or carers that it needs feeding, changing, attention. The baby also listens to the sounds of those around it and responds to sounds and other stimuli and those who make them. Babies particularly respond to their family in a positive way and to strangers in a more negative way (see Chapter 6). As young children move in other social circles outside the family, they respond to their peers, develop language to help them to communicate with others (see Chapter 5) and begin to be more independent. All this is part of social development and it occurs through the process of socialisation. *The Penguin Dictionary of Sociology* (Abercrombie *et al.*, 1984: 201) states that the term socialisation describes the 'process whereby people learn to conform to social norms'. The process of social development can be considered as the internalisation of social norms or social rules which become internal to the individual. These social rules may be an essential element of social interaction.

Early social development, through the process of socialisation, can be observed by attending to the behaviour of, and interactions between, infants and their carers and also within the environment. Babies can attract attention by moving, making noises or by crying, in an effort to make their needs known because they are hungry or lonely and desire company. They can be seen listening and responding to sounds and movement in the environment, through different gurgling or babbling noises and facial expressions, in different ways depending on whether they are responding, playing or interacting with family members, with strangers or peers.

Infants and young children spend much of their time playing, and play is a significant factor in social development (see Picture 7.1). Through play we can both observe and be observed practising the actions and situations most relevant and common in our society. Play is recognised (e.g. Lindon, 2005; Moyles, 2005) as an important part of all aspects of learning (see Chapters 9 and 4) and of development (e.g. Jenkinson, 2001; Johnston, 2005) in a creative and cross-curricular way (de Bóo, 2004)

The emergence of language plays a large part in early social development by copying others and recognising sounds, and developing independence through making our needs and intentions known to others (see Chapter 5). The development of language is a social action in which an individual must participate. At the minimum, it is a two-way social process of communication, in which there is a sender and a receiver. Language is not just an abstract system of rules and conventions to learn, but an active part of the process of socialisation.

Picture 7.1 Children playing together

The reactions and responses of others in meeting the needs of young children help them to develop a sense of self-identity, an understanding of who they are and where they fit within the social structure. This understanding grows steadily as the child matures and is linked with other areas of development, especially cognition (see Chapter 4). Social development is influenced by the conditions or environment in which children find themselves growing up and is deeply dependent on how children are interacted with and nurtured: 'the process of caring for and teaching a child as the child grows' (Wikipedea, 2006). Through continual interaction with their environment children begin to understand what is acceptable behaviour, how to get along with people, where there is danger and pleasure and how to react in different situations. Much of this is learned within the first few years of a child's life and within the family.

It cannot be denied that from the moment infants are born they create an impression on their surroundings. Babies are born with innate qualities or reflexes which are pre-programmed; these are known as primitive reflexes, including swallowing and sucking reflexes, rooting reflexes and the grasping reflex. They are designed to gain from their environment both the attention and care necessary to survive. Newborn babies also have rudimentary social skills such as turning their head to light and sound. They are fascinated by human faces and gaze attentively at their carer's face when being fed or cuddled. Babies also often imitate facial expressions. They will blink in response to sound or movement and can be startled by sudden noises; babies will respond to the sound of their mother's voice and can distinguish the smell of their mother's breasts from those of other women who are breastfeeding (Meggitt and Sunderland, 2004: 5–11). The behaviours which occur in primarily social situations are both auditory and visual and are designed to operate with adults and to give the infant an initial orientation to social situations (Smith *et al.*, 1998: 70).

This is, however, only one facet of social development. In order for any of these reflexes or actions to be recognised or to be acknowledged there has to be a response and therefore for every action there is a reaction. The action of the infant, whether it be crying due to discomfort or hunger, results in a response from the carer. This could be being changed or being fed. As a result of being cuddled when feeding, the baby may gaze at the carer and this in turn will build the bond of mutual satisfaction between carer and infant (see Chapter 6). These are behaviours which, according to Smith *et al.* (1998), require a social response and adults tending to the needs of the infant will respond in a social way, by smiling and talking back or picking up and comforting or playing with the child. This is how infants learn social behaviours, through these first interactions, and they learn what is expected and what is accepted within the society in which they live.

Tools for Learning

Interview as a research tool

Discussions and interviews are a useful way to collect evidence. You can interview a range of adults, such as parents and professionals, and ascertain their views on a range of issues, tapping into their expertise and ideas. You can instigate discussions with adults and children and listen to their responses and interactions (see also Chapter 6, which looks at listening as a research tool). Discussions and interviews can also help to verify and illuminate data collected in other ways. Discussions and interviews may:

- be fluid in nature to allow for unexpected lines of discussion and subsequent unexpected data;
- have a structure to ensure that the questions needed are answered;

- be an open forum involving some active participation/negotiation. This can lead to a more positive attitude towards the researcher;
- be captured on video or audio tapes or in a notebook.

Interviews tend to be more formally structured, with rigid questions, while discussions may be more informal and fluid in nature. The advantages of an interview is that the structure provides a safeguard to keep the interview focused, although it may be that the interviewee does not feel comfortable about disclosing some information in a more formal structure, especially where notes or tapes of the interview are being made. Discussions have the advantage of making the participant(s) feel at ease and they can follow prompts or questions which help to focus them. I have found that discussions often provide real insights into situations, actions and contexts, which a more formal interview will not, and participants are more likely to 'open up' if you do not have a notebook or tape. However, the disadvantage is that you need to record the responses quickly after the event to ensure you capture them. You may also need to verify the evidence at a later date to ensure you have captured it correctly.

Reflective Tasks

Social and biological factors

Level 1

Discuss with your peers and decide between you what the social and biological aspects of child development are. Now consider how society affects child development. Make a list of your differences.

Level 2

Discuss with your colleagues which aspects of the development of the children In your care are determined by social and which by biological factors.

- How does the social context within your setting affect the children's development?
- How can you support the children's social development?

Level 3

Initiate a nature versus nurture debate with the staff in your setting. Decide whether you agree with the statement 'Most of a child's early development is the result of nurture'.

The building of strong social and emotional foundations is an important function of development for children to reach their full potential. This is not only supported by Bowlby's attachment theory (1951) as discussed in Chapter 6, but also illustrated in the application of Maslow's hierarchy of needs (1968; see Figure 1.1). When the lower level physiological or immediate survival needs, such as food and drink, are satisfied, there is a necessity to feel safe and secure and protected (see Chapter 1). According to Maslow (1968), when these lower needs are fulfilled a person can psychologically move on up the hierarchy to satisfy the needs for love and belongingness. This is where one can feel part of the larger social group, feel accepted and develop friendship with other beings. Upon the satisfaction of the need one can again rise through the hierarchy, finally achieving self-fulfilment in which one realises one's own potential (Dryden *et al.*, 2005: 3).

Theories of social development

Rousseau (1712–78) was interested in children. He emphasised the role of nature or internal forces on development, stressing that children were very different from adults; he saw them as 'noble savages' with a natural sense of right and wrong (see Rousseau, 1911). Rousseau's developmental account of childhood and the two central concepts of maturation and stages of development laid the foundations for later researchers. However, the earlier English philosopher and physician John Locke (1632–1704) had emphasised the crucial role of nurture or external forces as routes for development (see Guttenplan *et al.*, 2003). He proposed that children were a 'blank slate' at birth and it was the experiences and interaction with people and the environment which affected their development. He saw the parents as the tutors or first teachers of children, capable of moulding the child in any way they liked. While the roots of modern theories stretch back to Rousseau and Locke, we will continue by looking at some of the most influential of the theories in the twentieth century. Although early experiments were usually carried out under laboratory conditions and with animals, some require a leap of faith when attributing the findings to the characteristics of early human social growth; nevertheless they do have a significant role to play in understanding the effects of the environment and parental/society's views on social development.

Behaviourism

Social behaviour occurs whenever two or more organisms interact. There are a number of basic social behaviour:

- attachment (identified first by Bowlby (1951; 1969) and described more fully in Chapter 6);
- imprinting (see Lorenz, 1952);
- conditioning (see Pavlov, 1927; Skinner, 1953);
- social organisation;
- cooperation and competition.

Many social animals appear to be drawn to each other or to show attachment. This results in the animals grouping together. This type of behaviour may be due to outside factors, such as insects swarming around a lamp because they are positively phototropic, or birds migrating because of climatic changes. Some behaviours are a result of social interaction, such as certain birds taking the lead in migrations, wolves hunting together or apes caring for the young of others in the community. Some attachment is also emotional (Bowlby, 1969) and aids survival, especially when the animal has a long dependent infancy. Imprinting is a form of attachment seen in some animals which does not have an emotional component. An animal is imprinted (attached) to the first thing it sees after birth (usually the mother) and will follow it. This behaviour explains the way young animals follow their parent. However, as Konrad Lorenz (1952) showed, ducklings would be imprinted to the first thing they saw (Lorenz) and this attachment to him was irreversible.

Classical conditioning as identified by Pavlov (1927) is where an animal learns a behaviour resulting from a stimulus. In Pavlov's experiment he conditioned a dog to salivate when hearing a bell by always ringing the bell before feeding. Therefore the stimulus was the bell and the response the salivation. Watson and Raynor (1920) taught an 11-month-old child called Albert to be afraid of a soft white rabbit by showing it to him accompanied by a loud noise which frightened him. B.F. Skinner (see Chapter 1) argued that we should only be interested in what we could observe with our own eyes, i.e. the behaviour of the child, and not concern ourselves with the internal workings like feelings, motives and intentions, which are not easily seen. He was most concerned with how the external environment controls behaviour. He also believed that by understanding behaviour we could predict what people would do in a given situation, or arrange circumstances to control and interpret behaviour. He studied any response changes as a result of what he called 'reinforcement' (Skinner, 1953). He thought that behaviour could be modified by reinforcement, called 'operant conditioning'. Positive rewards like praise, approval and affection or concrete rewards like toys, money and sweets increased the likelihood of behaviour being repeated and the lack of rewards or reinforcements would lead to the behaviour lessening and eventually disappearing. He thus believed that children could be 'shaped' to behave in socially acceptable ways. In other words, reward results in learned behaviour.

Reflective Tasks

Reward or punishment

Level 1

Ask a group of your peers to identify an example from their own experience which involved either reward or punishment. Question them to find out:

- how the experience affected their subsequent behaviour;
- if they feel reward is more affective than punishment.

Ask them to identify the reasoning behind each decision.

Level 2

Ask a group of children in your care:

- if they can remember being rewarded or punished;
- whether the experience changed their behaviour.

Identify whether memories of rewards or punishments are more prevalent. What does this knowledge tell you about the children and their social development? Does this knowledge change your interactions with them? If so, how?

Level 3

Discuss with colleagues in your setting what rewards and punishments you use with children in your care, to control social behaviour. Ask each other which rewards and/or punishments are the most effective.

Ask the children which practices they find effective and see if they match those you have identified.

What does this knowledge tell you about the children and your practices? Does this knowledge change your practice? If so, how?

Some animals (hens, wolves, lions) show evidence of social organisation, in which some individuals are dominant and some submissive. Schjelderup-Ebbe (1935) observed this behaviour in hens and identified that hens quickly established themselves into a 'pecking order' hierarchy, so that the dominant hen pecked all the rest and the most submissive hen was pecked by everyone. The pecking order is learned behaviour, with the largest animal learning that it can win any fight and the weakest that it cannot. The introduction of a new member into the society changes the hierarchy and a period of re-establishment occurs, during which each member of the society learns its place in the 'pecking order'. This type of behaviour can be seen in any group of children, as Golding's novel *Lord of the Flies* (1954) shows.

Some animals (including humans) behave differently when they are in a social situation from when they are alone. This social facilitation (occurring in ants, rats, apes) can be cooperation or competition. Ants will compete with each other to show that they can dig the most or find the most food. Rats will compete for food although they have also been seen to be cooperative in some experiments (Daniel, 1942) in order to get food. Cooperative behaviour is seen more often in more complex animal societies. Apes can cooperate to a high degree and this is facilitated in humans by language and gestures. When children begin to socialise within the family, they quickly learn that they need to cooperate in order to achieve their desires. Some young children, especially those in large families with a large number of siblings or young relatives, learn to compete for things they want, although there is a persuasive argument that some aspects of competition are biological rather that developed through experience. Hull (1943) developed the drive reduction theory which attempts to explain cooperation. He identified that human behaviour acts to satisfy primary physiological needs and these behaviours can then be learned and reinforced. For example, children prefer adults who have given them food, security, gifts and will behave in ways to please these adults and elicit further rewards.

Social learning theories

Social learning theories attempt to explain behaviour in terms of social learning rather than psychoanalytical theories as discussed in Chapter 6 (Freud, 1923; Erikson, 1950). The emotional and biological factors affecting social behaviour are accepted in the social learning theory, although a child's personality is seen as the result of social interaction. One type of social learning is thought to occur through modelling. There are particular role models in children's lives who they are likely to identify with and imitate. These include parents, siblings, peers and teachers. Children will model aspects of behaviour of their role models. The theory emphasises the importance of social forces on behaviour.

Research

Bandura's Bobo doll experiment

Albert Bandura (1977) was a social theorist who based his ideas on extensive laboratory research known as the 'Bobo doll' experiment (see also Chapter 1). He conducted studies of three groups of nursery children to see how they would respond to a short film. In the film the children would see a plastic doll (Bobo doll) being hit with a mallet, kicked, etc. One group of children saw an ending where this behaviour was rewarded, one group saw an ending where it was punished and one group saw no response at all to the behaviour. The children were then allowed to play with the doll. The resulting behaviour showed that those children who saw aggression being rewarded or ignored were more likely to be aggressive to the doll. The theory is an offshoot of behaviourism and concludes that children are more likely to imitate models who are warm and powerful and who possess objects or characteristics valued by the children; by acting in the same way the children hope to obtain the characteristics valued.

Therefore observation and imitating result in learned behaviour (Oates, 1994: 24). We can use Bandura's theory when considering how children develop stereotypical gender behaviours and also to consider how identification with characters in books, on television and in films influences behaviour. Modelling alone is not felt by many psychologists to explain children's behaviour. Piaget's theories of cognitive development (1950) argue that children actively construct their knowledge as they explore the world in which they live. As a result their behaviour will be influenced by their understandings and the experiences which influence their construction. Paiget's theories are discussed more fully in Chapter 4.

Vygotsky believed that cultural and environmental influences contributed to differences in behaviour. He developed his sociocultural theory (see Vygotsky, 1987; Wertsch and Tulviste, 1992) to explain how social interaction leads children to beliefs and behaviours characteristic of that society or culture. The types of social interactions which develop these behaviours include cooperative dialogues, where adults and more expert peers communicate, and the ideas, beliefs and behaviours of society. These ideas become internalised by the child, who will then use language to help them master behaviours and actions shown to them by the more knowledgeable members of the society. In this way, development (both cognitive and behavioural) is a socially mediated process, in which language is key to making sense of the world. As a result, children's thinking and behaviour dramatically develop alongside their language.

Systems theories

The ecological systems theory was put forward by Bronfenbrenner (1995; Bronfenbrenner and Evans, 2000) and views the child as developing within a complex social system, affected by relationships and the surrounding environments. He proposed a four-nested system of potential influences in development, most commonly illustrated as a set of circles (see Figure 7.2 and Chapter 1). At the heart sits the *microsystem* (meaning small) and the child sits in the centre of this system and indeed all the systems. A young child has several microsystems influencing their individual development, the most influential being the family (this includes the home environment, parents and siblings) and another the setting or school environment (including professionals and peers). The microsystem is based on an individual's actual experiences which sit within the next level or circle, the (meaning middle) *mesosystem*, a system of connections, a two-way traffic system, which links individual experiences within the microsystem. For example, a breakdown in family relationships ending in divorce may affect another microsystem, school, resulting in poor academic performance, withdrawal or disruptive behaviour. The mesosystem is like a circuit breaker in an electrical system, as when an overloaded switch in the kitchen results in a blown fuse, the action of one resulting in a reaction in another. The third circle of influence, termed the *exosystem* (external; without direct influence), shows us that what happens outside the direct experience of the child will influence what happens within the microsystem. For example, the type of employment and earnings generated by the parents may affect the quality of care and potential life chances of the child. Finally the *macrosystem* (the larger or wider society) is the all-encompassing circle, where society's rules and regulation, the legislation and conditions affecting individuals and family life and within the society are held. These have a direct bearing on all other systems and on how individuals act and react within society.

The dynamic systems theory (Fischer and Biddell, 1998; Thelen and Smith, 1998) involves the child's mind, body, physical world and social world in an integrated system that guides behaviour. This is a dynamic interaction, in which changes to one part (physical or social) disrupt the system and the child reorganises their behaviour so that the system works effectively, but in a more complex and effective way.

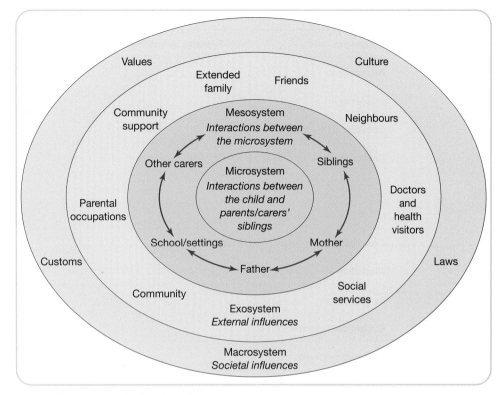

Figure 7.2 The ecological systems theory
Source: Bronfenbrenner, 1995, The Bioecological Model from a Life Course Perspective, in Moen, P. *et al*. (eds) *Examining Lives in Context*, American Psychological Association, Washington, DC, Copyright 1995. Reprinted with permission.

Practical Tasks

The ecological systems theory

Read the section above before you try these tasks.

Level 1

Add examples from your own experience into Table 7.1. Try to add something in every section.

Level 2

Add examples in each section of Table 7.1 from your experience with children in your care. Decide how you can support each child in their social development.

Level 3

Add examples in each section of Table 7.1 from children in your setting. How can you support these children in their social development?

Table 7.1 Add your own examples of different types of behaviour in children

Behaviour	Example in children
Attachment	
Imprinting	
Social organisation	
Competition	
Cooperation	
Conditioning – classical	
Conditioning – operant	
Modelling	
Sociocultural	
Ecological systems	
Dynamic systems	

Constructivist theories

Jean Piaget (1896–1980) is credited with constructing the first full child development theory. Piaget was interested in epistemology (the study of the nature of knowledge and its origins), or how we come to know something and whether this knowledge is innate or acquired. He argued that from birth we actively seek and interpret environmental information (Piaget, 1929). Children are born with the ability to adapt to and learn from the environment with basic patterns of actions which he termed sensori-motor schemes. These action patterns are the foundations of knowledge on which we build or construct knowledge into more sophisticated structures (see Chapter 4; Piaget, 1950). Piaget's theories relate to social development through his work on the progression of play as we come to realise the importance of the environment and social development. Play is also the most easily observed behaviour to witness. Very young children will play alone amusing themselves with toys and everyday objects. As they mature children will begin to notice other children and watch and copy their actions during play situations. With continued growth and the emergence of language children now begin to communicate and share with others in play, initially by playing alongside each other rather than together (parallel play). In the early years of school, children move to collaborative play, where they together enact scenes from everyday life and often incorporate exaggerated rules and conditions before the start of games or play situations (see Chapter 9). Therefore it may be assumed that family circumstances or social situations play a large part in affecting children's development, through the ability of the family/teacher/carer to produce the required environment. It was, however, the internalisation of personal experience that formed the basis of the Piagetian theory of development.

Social constructivism was developed by Lev Vygotsky (1896–1934), who worked until his early death at the Moscow Institute of Psychology (see Chapter 1). Although he had read the work of Piaget, his own work had a more political slant in which he meant to build a better socialist society. Vygotsky and Cole (1978) emphasised the role of the social environment in children's development. Like Piaget, Vygotsky saw children as active organisers of their own knowledge. He believed that the emergence of language at around the age of 2 years, and the characteristics and interactions with the people with whom the child grew up influenced their social development (Vygotsky, 1962). He called this the 'cultural line', which means that by continually practising and observing social interactions young children came to understand and accept them as being norms of society. Central to his ideas were the characteristics of the people involved with the child and especially the interaction between the child and another person. He firmly believed that early speech and close relationships aided children's social and cognitive development. Although Piaget's and Vygotsky's theories have similarities, they differ in this approach of the cultural line. Piaget believed in the solitary learner while Vygotsky believed that human beings could only be understood in the context of their social and historical environment.

The influence of society

From a social scientist perspective 'a society would be a grouping of people who share the same culture, and culture includes everything that one learns as a member of a human society' (Yeo and Lovell, 2001: 4).

Reflective Tasks

Considering and setting the social context

Level 1

- How would you describe society?
- Discuss with a group of your peers and come up with your collaborative definition of society. How does this differ from your own definition or the individual definitions?
- How do you think society affects children's social development?

Level 2

- Ask a group of professionals how they describe society. How do their views differ?
- How do you think their views have been shaped by their experiences?
- During the discussions, did they come to a collaborative or shared definition? If so how did this happen?
- Ask individual professionals how they think society influences an aspect of development (physical, emotional, social, cognitive). How are their responses different?

Level 3

- Within your setting, discuss with your colleagues what they consider society to be. Analyse their responses and identify how the discussion has influenced their ideas.
- Consider what influence society has on the children in your care.
- How does society affect the children's development?
- How can you help the children's social development?

When a group of early childhood students were asked the question 'what is society?', they responded 'it's about rules and regulations, it's about our values and our culture, and it's about people living together and getting along with each other'. You may have come up with something similar to the students and extended their ideas by identifying that society is a group of individual persons, large or small, living, working and socialising together. Did you consider that a family could be viewed as a society? The function of a society is to protect, to provide comfort and emotional stability, to provide common goals and shared objectives, which are mutually beneficial to the people living within the society and for the progress and sustenance of the society. In this way a family can be said to be a society.

French philosopher and sociologist Emile Durkheim (1858–1917) identified an important factor of influence as being the 'social structure' of a society. He perceived that the way in which people within society acted and behaved was characterised by their social practices, for example family life, marriage, education and work. These structures were what held people together, woven into the tapestry of life within the society, the bonding or glue which held fast the beliefs and morals of the people. However, he also strongly believed that where you were placed within the social structure, the social positions held by people, through family position, wealth, education and employment, would not be equal and that individual desires would be held in check only by the collective need for social order.

> Tell me the marriage patterns, the morals dominating family life, and I will tell you the principal characteristics of its organisation.
> (Durkheim, trans. Simpson, 1960)

In this view, children are moulded by society from birth and actions which are carried out by groups or individuals within a society can be observed as organised patterns of living which influence thinking and behaviour. Members of society have a shared or common understanding of what should happen. They share a value system which influences behaviour. For example, the social phenomenon of marriage, mentioned in the quote above, organises the way in which people of a certain age (in the culture of the UK) can live together, legally, and begin to develop a family structure which is acceptable to the society as a whole.

Marriage has been generally accepted as a normal pattern of development in the lives of individuals who wish to live together and rear a family. The laws of the country and social policy of the government supports and protects this behaviour and anything that falls outside this pattern may be viewed with suspicion and or be subject to criticism. It has certainly been an accepted idea that marriage was viewed as being the preferred state in which couples should bring up children. Certainly the continuity and stability of relationships between the parents and the child are thought by society and politicians to be the best for social development through socialisation. However, changes in the law have made it possible for a wider range of people who are living together to have equal rights within the definition of marriage and child-rearing practices. Durkheim (trans. Simpson, 1960) suggested that socialisation and education internalises these ideas in individuals. There are then social constraints, guides and moral obligations to obey social rules; or as Durkhiem suggests 'a collective conscience' to conform. This is a functionalist approach, in which 'society' is a unity of integrated working parts and each part of the whole has a role to play in maintaining the continued existence of the whole society.

Society thus influences social development through interaction with others and education about the social world in which we live. So it would appear that influences on social aspects of child development may include the family background, circumstances into which children are born and brought up, opportunities for education and the potential to achieve economic well-being through education and employment. Underpinning these issues would be the tenet 'for the collective good of the people' to live in and with social order, which would be supported by laws and policy, such as the welfare state, ensuring the 'well-being' of its citizens.

The influence of gender

Within his writing, Rousseau (1762) emphasised that the distinction between the male and female role and differences between the sexes defined social order and in turn the different roles for boys and girls in childhood and men and women in adulthood. Although it could be clearly seen that men and women had different body shapes and functions, for example, the rounded hips and full bosom of women were clearly for child-bearing and rearing, while men had a different body shape, size and stature, Rousseau puzzled over the extent to which these sex differences affected other aspects of nature and society (Rousseau, 1762) and he concluded that the relationship and natural differences between men and women must influence moral behaviour, with boys strong and girls weak. The role of women was clearly defined biologically and therefore morally. The view that women were naturally homemakers, providing nurture for their children and supporting the family by being attentive to their needs, set the female domain clearly within the home as creator of the 'natural environment' for bringing up children and pleasing the male, as opposed to being outside in the social, male-dominated realm of work and providing for the family. This view clearly affected Rousseau's view of childhood for girls and for boys.

The debate about the different roles in society for males and females has continued for over two centuries, even when at various times in history girls and women have worked alongside boys and men in agriculture, shops, factories and businesses, for example, during the French Revolution and the two world wars. It was during these times that the need for early childcare provision was established. Much of the care was informal and children were left with elderly relatives or neighbours, although day-care nurseries were established to look after the factory workers' children. In the period after the Second World War many day nurseries were closed down as the care was found to be lacking and a period of regulation was initiated for childminders and nurseries, 'due mainly to moral panic about the dangers of accidental harm to children while they were in the care of people other than their mothers' (Baldock *et al.*, 2005: 17). This argument is a recurring theme, even today when discussing the role of women, mothers and childcare. We will return to this later when we examine the early work of Bowlby (1951, see also Chapter 1) which added fuel to this argument.

The influence of the family

Families are discussed more fully in Chapter 8. Here we discuss the influence of the family on a child's social development. A family is the first influence on social development. Bowlby's research on attachment (1969; see above and Chapter 6) has been used to try to explain social phenomena or 'problems', such as teenage delinquency, as individual characteristics of the child, rather than a problem in society. Bowlby convincingly found a correlation between what we would now call antisocial behaviour and the early patterns of the child/parent relationship. On reflection, we might feel that such research laid the blame for antisocial behaviour squarely at the feet of the individual family, child and parent.

Children can be affected by the breakdown of the family. Divorce, the breakdown of cohabiting unions and/or the creation of new partnerships and blended families can all affect the child and their social development. Some children do not live in families at all; for example, in 2001, 139,000 children were living in other households in the UK, including living with adults or other relatives who are not their parents. An additional 52,000 children under 16 lived in communal establishments such as children's homes (Office for National Statistics, 2005). In 2001, 10 per cent of all families with dependent children in the UK were stepfamilies; 0.7 million stepfamilies had dependent children living in households in the UK. Although there is a tendency for children to stay with their mother following the break-up of a partnership, the loss of one primary attachment and the reconstitution of the family does appear to have an effect on social development. For a start, these stepfamilies are generally larger than non-stepfamilies; 27 per cent of stepfamilies had three or more dependent children compared with 18 per cent of non-stepfamilies (Office for National Statistics, 2005).

Parenting can also affect a child's social development. Schaffer (1999) suggested that there were three types of parental attributes:

- *universal attributes*: those common to all human parents which can be regarded as part of the heritage of our species;
- *cultural-specific attributes*: those that are specific to particular societies and thus distinguishing one grouping of parents from another;
- *individual attributes*: those which differentiate one parent from another within cultural groups and can therefore be considered as an expression of the individual's personality.

Baumrind (1971) suggested that parenting styles were responsible for producing certain characteristics within children and that children with authoritative parents were found to be the most competent, tending to be self-reliant, keen to achieve, socially responsible, self-controlled and cooperative. Children with permissive parents on the other hand, tended to be aimless, lacking in self-assertiveness and generally uninterested in achievement. Those with authoritarian parents were surly, defiant, dependent and, especially in boys, socially incompetent. Those children with rejecting-neglecting parents tended to be the least mature of all in both cognitive and social development. See Figure 8.2 in Chapter 8 for more information on parenting styles. Although initially Baumrind (1971) assumed that the parenting styles alone can produce these effects she does, in her later writing, acknowledge that children's personalities and also their sex play a part in their social development. It may be significant to consider that children's personality types may affect and influence the way parents respond to some behaviours, so that parents may not naturally adopt these styles and may be forced into them as an example of the 'action–reaction–response' facet of social development.

There are a number of other aspects of the family that can influence an individual child's social development:

- **Family size**: The number of children in the family and their position in the family can make a difference to their social development. An only child will not have to compete with other children for attention and may find it difficult to relate to peers, although they may be more able to socialise with adults. The youngest child in a large family may be less socially mature and independent than the average child of the same age, because they are treated as the 'baby' of the family. The eldest child in a large family may have to take more responsibility for caring for the younger members and may be more responsible and independent and nurturing as a result. The age gap between siblings can also make a difference to a child's social development in similar ways. Children living in extended family groups (living with or near each other) will have a wide social network from birth, but children living in nuclear families a distance from other relatives and family friends are likely to be less socially aware and active, although reduced family size does seem to increase the quality of interaction between members, so this may reduce any other adverse effect.

- **Ethnicity (race/culture)**: Different cultures have different styles of parenting and different types of families. It is difficult to stereotype different ethnic groups, but some may be more controlling, with a strict belief in discipline, respect for elders, etc. However, it is difficult to research these differences without bringing your own cultural beliefs and expectations with you.

- **Socio-economic**: Poverty has a profound effect on child development in all areas. It causes stress and conflict and living in poorer areas is often associated with gangs, violence and crime, with effects on children's physical development, mental health, intelligence and school achievement. It is no coincidence that raising children out of poverty is an important underpinning philosophy of the Every Child Matters agenda (DfES, 2003).
- **Divorce**: Divorce is usually associated with conflict in the family and a drop in income. Longitudinal research (Hope *et al.*, 1999) has indicated that divorce is associated with maternal stress, depression, anxiety and 'minimal parenting'. Fathers are likely to be permissive, conflicting with maternal style, making conflict greater for the child. Age, temperament, gender and social support all make a difference to how a child manages divorce.
- **Remarriage**: The blended or reconstituted family also brings problems for the child and his/her development. Switching to new rules and parenting types can be stressful. Boys will often welcome a new stepfather who is warm and approachable, while older children and girls may experience difficulties. Children from broken homes and who experience remarriage and the difficulties resulting from blended families are more likely to experience problems in their social and married lives.
- **Bereavement**: Children, too, can suffer extreme stress and mental anguish when they are bereaved and this can make them withdrawn and affect their social development as well as their emotional development.
- **Illness**: Children who have to take on the role of carers for sick parents are likely to miss out on important aspects of their own development. However, they do appear to become very self-reliant and organised at an earlier age.
- **Working parents**: Girls may benefit from having a working role model for a mother. However, it is likely that working mothers are more authoritative, and this will give the children more independence and support their social development.
- **Early child care**: The type of childcare (childminders, day nurseries, nannies, relations, playgroups, school and after school clubs), numbers of carers, type of parenting style and conflict between home style and carer's style will all affect a child and their social and emotional development (Field, 1991). As Bowlby (2006) has identified, we should not assume that greater day-care provision for children outside the home will automatically result in social improvement (see Chapter 6). It appears that we need to move slowly with new initiatives and assess their impact on children in a holistic way. This, however, does not suit politicians who want to make big changes and cannot wait to see what their long-term effects are.

The influence of attitudes and behaviour

Attitudes or adopted positions or expressions of ideas can be observed behaviours and can affect development in general, and in the early years specifically (QCA, 2000). A model for the development of attitudes adapted from Johnston (2005: 94) can be seen in Figure 2.1. One attitude group comprise social attitudes, which include cooperation, collaboration, responsibility, independence and tolerance. These attitudes are necessary for children to live and work effectively with others in family, educational and social groups. Early years settings are organised in social ways with children having to share and play independently, collaboratively and cooperatively. Play can be useful in supporting social development (Bruner *et al.*, 1976), although first play is often individual or parallel play and cooperative play occurs only later. Indeed, although children can play together at an early age (Lindon, 2001) cooperative play is not felt to be encouraged in most educational settings

(Moyles, 1989; Moyles *et al.*, 2002). In this way, social development can be affected by the opportunities provided for social play in settings and also by adult interaction (Bennett *et al.*, 1997). Cooperation is not something that comes naturally and needs to be structured, supported and planned for. Grouping children according to friendship, gender, ability or any other criteria can help them to learn to cooperate with different types of people. It is more natural for young children to be competitive (Dean, 2001) rather than cooperative and they are often reluctant to share with others. Children need to be tolerant towards other children, recognising the needs of and respecting the views of others. When children learn to compete rather than cooperate, this can affect the delicate social balance within a family or setting and affect children's subsequent social development. For example, competition can make some children so anxious not to fail that they will refuse to compete or even cooperate. Children also need to develop a sense of responsibility for their behaviour and to become increasingly independent and responsible individuals. Young children need support from adults (see Vygotsky, 1987) to reach this stage in their social development as it presupposes a maturity and experience they lack.

The attitudes children develop in their early lives interrelate to form a set of attitudes which affect the way they view others and situations, and also their behaviour. Attitudes towards gender will affect the way children see roles in society and whether girls and boys can do the same tasks as each other or adults. Political attitudes will affect social policy (see below) and subsequent provision and social development. Attitudes towards race, culture (see below), social class, religion and disabilities will affect the way children interact with children who look or think differently from them. One of the main social attitudes affecting attitudes towards others is tolerance. Children are naturally egocentric, but need to learn that their ideas and views do not take precedence over others. They need to learn to tolerate and accept others' views and to reflect on their own ideas and behaviours and learn from their social interactions.

Reflective Tasks

Social attitudes

Level 1

Can you think of examples from your own life of:

- how your attitudes differ from those of your parents?
- how your attitudes conflicted with those in your school or friends' families?

Level 2

Reflect on the children in your care and consider what attitudes they have developed from their families that conflict with attitudes you hold. How can you support the children in developing their social attitudes so that they can interact more effectively with others in your setting?

Level 3

As a staff, decide what social attitudes you think are important and how you will support their development.

Practical Tasks

Social attitudes

Level 1

Interview a professional (e.g. teacher, nursery manager, early years professional) to find out what social attitudes they think are necessary for children's effective social development and what potential conflicts exist between the attitudes of home and the setting.

Level 2

Interview a parent and a professional (e.g. social worker, educational psychologist) to see how they would support the development of social attitudes.

Level 3

Interview parents and different professionals (e.g. social workers, educational psychologists, behavioural therapists) to find out what social attitudes they think are important and how they would support their development.

Consider if there is a potential conflict between the views of your setting, the families who use the setting and the professionals who support children's development. How can you work effectively together to reduce conflict and support children's social development?

Children's social behaviour can be assessed in a number of ways and this assessment can provide useful information to help support children in their social development. The Neonatal Behavioral Assessment Scale (NBAS) looks at a newborn baby's reflexes, response to stimuli (social or physical) and other reactions. It has been given to many children around the world and has shown cultural differences in newborn behaviour. For example, newborn Asian and American Indian babies are less irritable than white American babies, possibly because in these cultures swaddling, close physical contact and nursing at first signs of discomfort are encouraged (Berk, 2003). Some cultures encourage babies to be carried about all day on the mother's back or hip and these babies receive more sensory stimulation and are more alert and content than less active babies. The cultural differences seen in newborn babies indicate the problems of having a scale which assesses such behaviour! Regular health and development checks are available by midwives at birth and by health visitors at local health clinics or doctors' surgeries. They normally occur at birth, 6 weeks and then at regular intervals throughout a child's early childhood. They record the milestones of a child, including physical, language and social development. Health visitors can assess behaviour and provide information to support parenting and child development. Occasionally, children may be observed and assessed by child psychologists, behaviourists, social services, etc. They may assess the child's behaviour and make suggestions for parents, teachers and others to modify behaviour and support the child's development.

Tests can be administered to look at some aspects of behaviour, although there are no holistic tests of behaviour. Problem-solving tests have been used to test behaviour under certain conditions in adults. For instance, the 'brook test' (Munn, 1966) looked at how men behaved when faced with a raging brook to cross with a large amount of equipment.

Also, many 'reality' television programmes look at behaviour in extreme circumstances and a number of job interviews now include a behavioural test, role play or an observation of some task. School reports identify the child's behaviour in school and comment on it. School assessments of behaviour should be in line with good practice in assessment and focus on evidence and not be emotive or judgemental

There are a large number of behavioural disorders that a child may exhibit, ranging from mild or occasional to extreme or habitual. Most children will have some behavioural problems during their childhood and most are resolved quickly through social interaction. Some may require outside support and intervention.

- **Eating**: Food can have an effect on behaviour in a number of ways. Poorly nourished children are likely to be listless, inactive and inattentive. Obese children are more likely to have health, mental and behavioural problems (Berk, 2003). Certain food substances (high sugar content, caffeine, orange juice) can cause hyperactivity and even be the partial cause of social aberrations. Most children use food at some point in time as a social weapon. They may become temporarily or more permanently faddy about food. They may use meal times as an opportunity for attention (negative or positive). In extreme cases, they may develop eating disorders (anorexia nervosa or bulimia nervosa).

- **Sexual**: Young children are exposed to sexual behaviour in all aspects of their lives and they are often ill-prepared for it. Boys are thought (Berk, 2003) to receive less support for their pubescence changes than girls and the support girls receive is often too late for their physical needs. There are different cultural responses to sexual education and pubescent changes, with some cultures having ceremonies or rites of passage (the Jewish bat or bar mitzvah, scarring on the face of some African tribes, Australian Tiwi aborigines' initiation camps and ceremonies). Some sexual disorders may be socially learned or be the result of problems with self-esteem. Some sexual problems are socially and culturally ingrained, such as the circumcision of women in some societies.

- **Habit**: Habit disorders can be common in all ages. Young children may develop a habit, such as sucking their thumbs, pulling their hair, biting their nails, rubbing their nose, licking their lips. More obsessive disorders include repetitive behaviours such as getting dressed in a certain way, chewing food for a certain time or number of chews, washing themselves repeatedly. If these behaviours become obsessive, then this will affect a child socially and in extreme cases children can become socially excluded (e.g. agoraphobic).

- **Social**: Social disorders include temper tantrums, stealing, lying, truancy, cruelty, bullying, etc. Many psychologists and sociologists have identified the role played by the home and society on antisocial behaviour. The Plowden Report (1967) is one of many research reports which have identified the effects of social deprivation on behaviour and education. There have been many projects (SureStart, Education Action Zones) which have attempted to counter the effects of social deprivation on the development of children's behaviour.

- **Psychological**: Psychological disorders include autism, Asperger's syndrome and problems with self-esteem. These problems can be mild or severe and may need special help from experts and individual educational plans (IEPs).

- **Psychotic**: Psychotic disorders may result in bizarre behaviours. Children who have psychotic disorders (schizophrenia, delusions, hallucinations) may have to be treated medically and educationally apart from other children. They may spend some time in mainstream education and some time in a psychiatric unit. This combined approach to their behaviour attempts to enable them to integrate in society.

- **Educational**: Educational disorders may include problems with concentration and attention deficit, which may affect a child's behaviour and development. Children may need additional support to enable them to function in mainstream education.

There are a number of different ways in which behaviour can be shaped or changed:

- *Systematic desensitisation* is a method of making some painful or unpleasant experience more acceptable. A child who will not go to school may have had some unpleasant experience or feeling which is now associated with going to school. Initially it is essential to find out what the child likes about school (school work, friends, teachers, etc.) and what they do not like (playtime, lunchtime, etc.). Once you ascertain what the child will and will not do, they can be encouraged by rewards, praise, etc. to go into the playground for short periods of time or stay for part of the lunch period.

- *Implosion therapy* is a type of therapy which involves confrontation with the cause of anxiety or dislike. Eventually, with exposure, the panic and behaviour resulting from confrontation will abate. This is possibly not a very good type of therapy to use with children as it could cause greater problems.

- *Aversion therapy* involves punishment for undesirable behaviour, so that children associate it with unpleasant emotions. It therefore replaces a pleasant response with an unpleasant response (see Skinner's operant conditioning, 1953). For example, children who persistently bed-wet may be treated with aversion therapy, by being given a sheet which sounds a buzzer and wakes them when they begin to urinate. They soon learn not to urinate in the bed. This type of therapy is used only in extreme cases, such as severe bed-wetting and some instances of drug abuse, where other methods have not worked.

- *Behaviour shaping* involves the changing of behaviour until it resembles behaviour we want. We do this by responding to behaviour with either pleasure or disgust, reinforcing and encouraging positive behaviour and discouraging poor behaviour or any behaviour we do not like. Behaviour shaping is another form of operant conditioning (Skinner, 1953).

- *Behaviour modification* is similar to behaviour shaping, but does not involve the causes of the behaviour, merely the behaviour itself. It involves defining exactly the problem behaviour and the desired behaviour and sets small target steps to achieve the latter. It may also involve ignoring undesirable behaviour and praising behaviour that is more acceptable. Bandura (1977) used behaviour modification in his modelling therapy. Changes in behaviour in school children commonly result from this type of behavioural therapy.

- *Psychoanalytical therapy* has many different forms. Typically, it involves reclining on a couch and being encouraged to say anything which comes into mind, or engage in free association, or respond to prompts or questions. During the discourse, problems may be identified; they can be analysed by the therapist and can then be dealt with. Taking children back to relive past experiences can be a form of regressive psychoanalytical therapy, although it is felt that sometimes memories may be incorrect or reconstructed in alternative ways.

- *Play therapy* is more suitable for behavioural therapy with children than psychoanalytical therapy, and was developed by Anna Freud, who followed her father Sigmund Freud in looking at psychotherapy. Children are thought to express problems through play and further play activities can help the child understand the problems and modify behaviour and attitudes.

Research

Citizenship and crime

The Howard League for Penal Reform collected evidence from over 3,000 children across the country, as part of a wider nine-year educational programme on Citizenship and Crime. The key findings of the survey (The Howard League for Penal Reform, 2007) are,

- ninety-five per cent of children surveyed had been victims of crime on at least one occasion;
- property had been stolen from 49 per cent of children while at school and 18 per cent between school and home;
- fifty-seven per cent of the children surveyed had experienced their property being deliberately damaged;
- bullying or assaults were common, with 46 per cent being called racist names, and 56 per cent threatened on at least one occasion. Nearly three-quarters of children in the survey had been assaulted;
- children commonly reported problems to family and friends and less commonly (in one-third of cases) to police or teachers;
- children feared crime, felt vulnerable and scared and wanted safe places to play. Their perception was that adults saw them as perpetrators rather than victims of crime;
- children felt that improved recreation facilities and places for children to meet and play would prevent crime;
- children had clear ideas of justice and fairness;
- most incidents of crime were low-level incidents occuring in schools and play-grounds.

The Howard League for Penal Reform (2007) recommends that improvement in children's lives will not occur through a top-down approach, but rather through an integrated approach involving local education authorities, police, victim support, the local community safety and youth offending teams, key community groups and others. Children need to learn about crime and victimisation, the criminal justice system and about conflict resolution and mediation in order to change and challenge attitudes to offending and antisocial behaviour. Restorative justice approaches will support schools by providing them with techniques to help resolve conflicts. Most importantly, the report recommends that children should be listened to and included in discussions and policy-making.

The influence of race and culture

Race is a result of biological evolution which has occurred over 2 million years from the first human primate out of Africa to the modern *Homo sapiens*. Culture is a result of social evolution, which has occurred over the last 12,000 years and has been more rapid than biological evolution (Bronowski, 1973). Cultural evolution has involved the develop-ment of complex social structures (nomad life to self-sufficient agricultural to collaborative bartering, etc.) and with the complexity comes collective traditions, norms, values, morals and beliefs which enable humans to live together in complex social systems (see above), which can be described as the pinnacle of Maslow's hierarchical needs (1968). Culture is then everything we learn about how to be included within and become members of our society; it's about expected behaviours, the social norms and the laws guiding us, it's about our values and attitudes, our language and literature, our religious beliefs and traditions. It is worth considering at this point cultures other than our own in order to understand and acknowledge 'that our behaviour is largely the result of our socialisation, how we are brought up in a particular society with its particular culture' (Yeo and Lovell, 2001: 4–5).

Race and culture can affect a child's view of society and their social development as they see themselves as outside or inside the dominant culture of the society in which they live. Ethnic minority children, whose family culture is very different from the society they live in and the setting they are placed in, may view themselves as the outsiders. Children who are from lower social classes than their carers in nurseries, playgroups and school may consider themselves the 'have-nots', the socially deprived. Children from economically deprived countries may consider themselves to be socially deprived because they are living in relative poverty and their families may seek to emigrate to richer countries. This does not always bring with it a richer social life. I have worked in a number of countries which have extreme poverty for a number of reasons; for example, the Former Yugoslavian Republic of Macedonia and Bosnia as a result of war and conflict (see Picture 7.2) and western Russia as a result of political changes (this area of Russia has been part of Finland, Sweden and Russia in the past 100 years, see Picture 7.3). In these countries we can apply Maslow's hierarchical needs (1968) to social and cultural development of a society. At the base of the hierarchy is physiological needs for all members of the society, which at times of stress and conflict may be difficult to achieve. Safety comes a close second, if not a joint first, with physiological needs as if you are in fear of your life and cannot access medical help this become a priority for you. Education, which we take for granted in the UK, is much less important and indeed children in the former Yugoslavia may have missed out on education for 8 to 10 years during the conflict during the 1990s. This must have had a profound effect on their emotional and social development as well as their cognitive development. Financial security is less important and can only be achieved if the society is safe and has fulfilled its other needs. Issues like culture and the environment are the pinnacle of the hierarchy and can only be achieved if the society is safe, well educated and financially secure.

There are some cultural differences that influence parenting, with some societies advocating that fathers care for their children or that care is shared between mothers and fathers. Other societies have extended families (Asian or African) or the number of children is limited (China) and this will have an effect on the children's social development. Some societies have different attitudes towards gender and treat girls and boys differently (see p. 219) and others have different expectations of their children. For example, Japanese parents have high expectations of their children's academic achievement.

Settings in the UK tend to have a white middle-class, urban culture and when families do not fit this stereotype the relationship between the family and the setting is troubled and the child is stuck in the middle. Not only do middle-class families share the cultural values with the setting, but middle-class parents have a greater capacity for intervention in the life of the setting. This actually can make the professional feel unsettled and so rather than advance the relationship, it can harm it. Working-class parents relate to the setting in a subservient way and professionals are more likely to feel the relationship is good. This view is not shared by the parents who are less happy with the relationship. In this way, the setting may actually be an obstacle in the child's development, rather than supportive of it. Our education and care systems for young children are politically, socially and culturally driven. The systems can alienate children if they are forced to adapt to a culturally different system and values and this can lead to academic failure. If the curriculum and context is not well matched to the children's age and abilities this can lead to a cycle of persistent failure. There are differences in the academic success of children due to cultural

Picture 7.2 Some different European social contexts: a town in the Former Yugoslavian Republic of Macedonia
Source: Arclight/Alamy Images

Picture 7.3 Some different European social contexts: a village in Western Russia
Source: Vova Pomortzeff/Alamy Images

differences because of social class, ethnic culture and even regional cultures. These differences between school and home cultures can lead to cultural discontinuity and shock. This can help to explain school failure among some groups of children. Settings can discriminate because they treat children equally rather than differentiate to accommodate cultural differences.

There are different types of professionals who can help or hinder the cultural and social development of the children in their care. The *monocultural* professional sees cultural diversity as an obstacle in their work with children, as it has potentially discrimination effects. They look upon cultural diversity in the setting as a deficit (concerning themselves with that which is missing in cultures that deviate from the norm) and they believe that cultural homogeneity in the classroom is important, given that it is the vehicle of national culture in official mass schooling. They proclaim their own cultural identity as a fixed and indisputable historical fact, are focused on the culture of the setting and believe that it is their role to educate for modernisation. They recognise cultural differences, without wanting to know them (in order to avoid preferences for any sociocultural group).

The *multicultural* teacher attempts to understand the cultural differences that exist in the community. The benign multicultural professional sees the obvious cultural differences that exist, while the critical multicultural professional deals with different ways of life and opportunities of life in a proactive way. *Intercultural* teachers attempt to bridge the cultural divide, seeing cultural diversity as a way of enriching the teaching/ learning process, promoting different knowledge and cultures. They take into consideration cultural diversity in the setting in order to produce a confrontation of cultures and remake their personal map of cultural identity so as to overcome cultural ethnocentrism. They will argue in favour of decentring the setting so the school becomes part of the local community and try to understand cultural differences through the development of pedagogical devices on the basis of the notion of culture as a social practice.

The influence of social policy

In 1942 Sir William Beveridge, a member of the then Liberal Party, presented a report to the British government in which he stated that, at the end of the Second World War, a post-war country should be driven to 'abolish want' and 'banish poverty'. He identified five main goals for the government; these were to eradicate ignorance (lack of education), disease (lack of health care provision), squalor (lack of good housing), want (lack of income) and idleness (lack of employment). This indeed was the beginning of our social welfare system and the legislation to underpin such a system was brought into being in 1945 by the Labour Government, including the establishment of the National Health Service in 1948 with free medical services for all and a national system of benefits to provide social security, so that the population would be protected from 'the cradle to the grave' (World War 2 People's War Team, 2003).

Earlier, the 1944 Education Act, known as 'the Butler Act' was introduced to the government by R.A. Butler (see Chapter 9). This laid the foundation for a post-war system in which free education for all children to the age of 15 years was introduced. This Act replaced all previous education legislation and reflected the vital importance of education to the nation and the individual. The Act also echoed political tendencies, the social and economic needs of the nation which recognised that individuals' needs are not merely academic and neither are those of the community. It was recognised that education was not only communicating academic information, but also fostering the spiritual, mental, physical and vocational well-being of the community. The focus must be on the education of the individual member for the common good of the community.

Elsewhere, people like Margaret and Rachel McMillan (see McMillan, 1911 and Chapter 1) had begun to publicise and raise awareness of social conditions as a possible weakness for our society, especially in areas of deprivation. They were concerned that through a lack of nourishment young children were not developing and learning and set about opening the kitchen schools, where young children were fed and their mothers had the opportunity of learning, informally, how to cook nourishing meals. Although immediately concerned with the welfare of the children, the McMillan sisters were among the first to realise the potential health and education benefits of adequate sustenance to children and indirectly for society.

It is apparent that in the twenty-first century these principles are still supporting ideas which will benefit society and effect social change. With the publication of the green paper, *Every Child Matters; Change for Children* (DfES, 2004), five areas are identified as necessary to build strong foundations for family and child welfare which will support continuing social development in the UK. These are:

- *being healthy*: to enjoy good physical and mental health and live a healthy lifestyle;
- *staying safe*: by being protected from harm and neglect;
- *enjoying and achieving*: by getting the most out of life and developing the skills for adulthood;
- *making a positive contribution*: through being involved with the community and society and not engaging in anti-social or offending behaviour;
- *economic well-being*: by not being prevented by economic disadvantage from achieving full potential.

It is interesting to note the resemblance these outcomes have to the Beveridge report. In particular, the last of these statements, 'economic well-being', indicates the political stance which would appear to play a significant part in social development. It may in fact lie at the heart of social development. In order for people to survive, the need to provide sustenance for mind and body has been vital and a contributor to social development. This idea seemed to be confirmed when John Bowlby wrote a report, in the early 1950s, of his research on separation of children from their parents, later published by the World Health Organization (WHO).

> *Just as children are absolutely dependent on their parents for sustenance, so in all but the most primitive communities, are parents, especially their mothers, dependent on a greater society for economic provision. If a community values its children so must it cherish their parents.*
> (Bowlby, 1951: 84)

Bowlby had began to develop his ideas on early attachment and the importance of safe, secure relationships in the early years for children, so that they would grow and develop into stable, well-adjusted adults. Based on a Freudian view that later patterns are fixed by 5 years of age (Gross, 2001: 459), the idea of a critical period in which young children form an attachment to their main carer (usually the mother, in Bowlby's theory) is still relevant today, and has been instrumental in developing our thoughts and provision for early years childcare practice (see Chapter 6).

Reflective Tasks

The effect of recent government initiatives

Level 1

Discuss with a group of your peers what recent government initiatives may have an effect on children's social development. Identify what effect you think the initiative will have.

Level 2

Discuss with your colleagues how recent government initiatives will affect the social make-up of your setting and the social development of the children in your care. How can you implement any new initiatives to support social development further?

Level 3

Discuss with staff, parents and governors of your setting the implications of recent government initiatives on the social make-up of your setting and the social development of the children in your care. How can you work together to implement any new initiatives to support social development further?

The influence of the environment

Urie Bronfenbrenner emphasised the importance of studying 'development-in-context', that is, the environment in which an individual is situated and is experiencing. Bronfenbrenner (1995) felt that it is necessary to understand our experiences before we can restructure and adapt to our surroundings. 'Ecological transitions' are how children begin to develop their understanding of society and how to react and behave within it (Smith *et al.*,1998: 11). As Lindon (2005: 45) reminds us, an ecological approach, such as Bronfenbrenner's, shows us that children do not develop in isolation and although he concentrated on the experiences of individual children within the context of their family he clearly illustrated, in his model (see Figure 7.2), the layers of society in which children had no direct participation, but which affect early socialisation (Schaffer, 1999). In this way social development is dependent on complex interrelationships between other social systems and society, with changes in one having a 'knock-on' effect on others. Thus it is very difficult to make social policy, practice or individual life changes without it affecting the child in ways that cannot be fully understood.

Research

Factors affecting social mobility

Research conducted in 2007 on behalf of National Children's Homes by Julia Margo and Sonia Sodha, from the Institute of Public Policy Research, has indicated the factors affecting social mobility (see Table 7.2).

Table 7.2 Factors that determine social mobility, ranked in order of importance to the general public

Rank	Responses to a general question about social mobility	The respondent's response in light of their own life experience
1	Family income	Education
2	Education	Stability of family structure
3	Emotional well-being	Emotional well-being
4	Where you live	IQ
5	Physical health	Physical health
6	Stability of family structure	Family income
7	IQ	Where you live
8	Social class	Social class
9	Physical attractiveness	Physical attractiveness
10	Experience of discrimination	Experience of discrimination

Source: Adapted from NCH, 2007

The findings indicate the importance of emotional well-being (emotional health) to social mobility and that this is becoming more significant.

Emotional wellbeing became four and a half times more important as a factor that determined social mobility for those born in 1970 compared to those born in 1958. Every indicator suggests that it will be even more important for children born now.

(NCH, 2007: 1)

IQ, physical health, family income, where a person lives and social class are considered to be less important than emotional well-being. The NCH considered the links between children's personal interactions, the increase in drug and alcohol misuse, mental health problems and antisocial behaviour and conclude that they are having an adverse effect on children's emotional well-being.

Summary

→ Sociology is concerned with the observation and analysis of relationships occurring in society. The most significant and influential of these is the family.

→ Sociologists influence government policy by using an analysis of their results to forecast what support and intervention may be required in the future.

→ Social development is concerned with learning to live with others in a social learning environment: that is, society.

→ Social aspects of development include social knowledge, behaviour, skills and attitudes. It is, however, difficult to compartmentalise development neatly as there are considerable overlaps.

→ The process of social development can be considered as the internalisation of social norms or social rules which become internal to the individual.

→ Play is very important to social development. Through play we can both observe and be observed practising the actions and situations most relevant and common in our society.

→ Through continual interaction with their environment, children begin to understand what acceptable behaviour is, how to get along with people, where there is danger and pleasure and how to react in different situations.

→ The roots of modern theories stretch back to Rousseau and Locke, although some of the most influential theories were formed in the twentieth century.

→ These theories include: behaviourism, social learning theories, systems theories and constructivist theories.

→ Society and social development are inextricably linked. From a social scientist perspective 'a society would be a grouping of people who share the same culture, and culture includes everything that one learns as a member of a human society' (Yeo and Lovell, 2001: 4).

→ Within a society there are many influences on social development.

→ Some of the most significant of these are gender, the family, culture and race.

→ Attitudes and behaviour have a distinct impact on social development. The attitudes children develop in their early lives interrelate to form a set of attitudes which affect the way they view others and situations and also their behaviour.

→ There are a large number of behavioural disorders that a child may exhibit, ranging from mild or occasional to extreme or habitual.

→ Most children will have some behavioural problems during their childhood and most are resolved quickly through social interaction. There are some that may require outside support and intervention.

→ Social policy and political views have a direct influence society.

→ Our education and care systems for young children are politically, socially and culturally driven.

→ The layers of society in which children have no direct participation affect early socialisation.

Key Questions

- What is meant by social development?
- What are the key theories of social development and how do they differ?
- What constitutes a society?
- In what different ways does the family influence social development?
- How does gender, culture and race influence social development?
- What are some of the behaviour problems children may experience?
- What types of support for these behaviour problems may be provided if necessary?
- What impact does social policy and the environment have on social development?

References

Abercrombie, N., Hill, S. and Turner, B.S. (1984) *The Penguin Dictionary of Sociology*, Harmondsworth: Penguin

Baldock, P., Fitzgerald, D. and Kay, J. (2005) *Understanding Early Years Policy*, London: Paul Chapman

Bandura, A. (1977) *Social Learning Theory*. Englewood Cliffs, NJ: Prentice-Hall

Baumrind, D. (1971) 'Current Patterns of Parental Authority', *Developmental Psychology*, Monograph 4.1, Part 2

Bennett, N., Wood, L. and Rogers, S. (1997) *Teaching Through Play: Teachers' thinking and classroom practice*. Buckingham: Open University Press

Berk, L.E. (2003) *Child Development*, 6th edn. Boston: Allyn & Bacon

Bowlby, J. (1951). *Maternal Care and Mental Health*. World Health Organisation Monograph (Serial No. 2)

Bowlby, J. (1969) *Attachment and Loss, Volume 1. Attachment*. New York: Basic Books

Bowlby, R. (2006) *The Need for Secondary Attachment Figures in Childcare* www.telegraph.co.uk/opinion/main.jhtml?xml=/opinion/2006/10/21/nosplit/dt2101.xml#head5Childcareproblems

Bronfenbrenner, U. (1995) The Bioecological Model from a Life Course Perspective: Reflections of a participant observer, in Moen, P., Elder Jnr, G.H. & Lüscher, K. (eds) *Examining Lives in Context*. Washington, DC: American Psychological Association, pp. 599–618

Bronfenbrenner, U. and Evans, G.W. (2000) 'Developmental Science in the 21st Century: Emerging theoretical models, research designs and empirical findings', *Social Development*, 9: 115–25

Bronowski, J (1973) *The Ascent of Man*. London: Sir Joseph Causton & Sons

Bruner, J.S., Jolly, A. and Sylva, K. (1976) *Play: Its role in development and education*. Harmondsworth: Penguin

Daniel, W.J. (1942) 'Cooperative Problem Solving in Rats', *Journal of Comparative Psychology*, 34: 361–8

Dean, J. (2001) *Organising Learning in the Primary Classroom*, 3rd edn. London: Routledge Falmer

De Bóo, M. (ed.) (2004) *The Early Years Handbook. Support for practitioners in the foundation stage*. Sheffield: Geography Association

DfES (2003) *Every Child Matters*. London: DfES

DfES (2004) *Every Child Matters: Change For Children*. London: DfES

Dryden, L., Forbes, R., Mukherji, P. and Pound, L. (2005) *Essential Early Years*. London: Hodder Arnold

Durkheim, E., trans. Simpson, G. (1960) *The Divisions of Labour in Society* (1893). New York: The Free Press

Erikson, E.H. (1950) *Childhood and Society*. New York: Norton

Field, T. (1991) 'Quality Infant Daycare and Grade School Behaviour and Performance', *Child Development*, 62: 863–70

Fischer, K.W. and Biddell, T.R. (1998) Dynamic Development of Psychological Structures in Action and Thought, in Lerner, R.M. (ed.) *Handbook of Child Psychology. Vol. 1 Theoretical models of human development*. New York: Wiley, pp. 467–561

Fitzgerald, T. (2006) *Sociology OnLine, Concepts in Sociology*. http://www.sociologyonline.co.uk/soc_essays/Origins.shtml (accessed February 2006)

Freud, S. (1923) *The Ego and the Id*. London: Hogarth

Golding, W.G. (1954) *Lord of the Flies*. London: Faber & Faber

Gross, R. (2001) *Psychology, The Science of Mind and Behaviour*, 4th edn. London: Hodder & Stoughton

Guttenplan, S., Hornsby, J. and Janaway, C. (2003) *Reading Philosophy. Selected texts with a method for beginners*. Oxford: Blackwell

Hope, S., Power, C. and Rodgers, B. (1999) 'Does Financial Hardship Account for Elevated Psychological Distress in Lone Mothers?', *Social Science and Medicine*, 29: 381–9

Howard League for Penal Reform (2007) *Children as victims: Child-sized crimes in a child-sized world*. London: The Howard League for Penal Reform

Hull, C.L. (1943) *Principles of Behavior*. New Haven: Yale University Press

Jenkinson, S. (2001) *The Genius of Play. Celebrating the Spirit of Childhood*. Stroud: Hawthorn Press

Johnston, J. (2005) *Early Explorations in Science*, 2nd edn. Buckingham: Open University Press

Lindon, J. (2001) *Understanding Children's Play*. Cheltenham: Nelson Thornes

Lindon, J. (2005). *Understanding Child Development, Linking Theory and Practice*, London: Hodder Arnold

Lorenz, K. (1952) *King Solomon's Ring*. New York: Crowell

Maslow, A.H. (1968) *Towards a Psychology of Being*. New York: Van Nostrand

McMillan, M. (1911) *The Child and the State*. Manchester: National Labour Press

Meggitt, C. and Sunderland, G. (2004) *Child Development, An illustrated guide, Birth to 8 years*. Oxford: Heinemann

Moyles, J.R. (1989) *Just Playing? The role and status of play in early childhood education*. Buckingham: Open University Press

Moyles, J.R. (ed.) (2005) *The Excellence of Play*, 2nd edn Buckingham: Open University Press

Moyles, J., Adams, S. and Musgrove, A. (2002) *Study of Pedagogical Effectiveness in Early Learning*. London: DfES

Munn, N. (1966) *Psychology. The Fundamentals of Human Adjustment*, 5th edn. London: Harrap

NCH (2007) 'Emotional Well-being and Social Mobility – A new urgency to the debate', *Growing Strong. NCH Briefing*. London: NCH

Oates, J. (ed.), (1994) *The Foundations of Child Development*. Oxford: Blackwell

Office for National Statistics (2005) www.statistics.gov.uk/focuson/families (accessed June 2006)

Office for National Statistics (2007) www.statistics.gov.uk/ (accessed September 2007)

Pavlov, I.P. (1927) *Conditioned Reflexes*. Oxford: Oxford University Press

Piaget, J. (1929) *The Child's Conception of the World*. New York: Harcourt

Piaget, J. (1950) *The Psychology of Intelligence*. London: Routledge & Kegan Paul

Plowden, B.H. (1967) *Children and their Primary Schools*. London: HMSO

QCA (2000) *Curriculum Guidance for the Foundation Stage*. London: DFEE

Rousseau, J.J. (1762) *The Social Contract or Principles of Political Right,* translated by G.D.H. Cole, Public Domain, rendered into HTML and text by Jon Roland of the Constitution Society: http://www.constitution.org/jjr/socon.htm; http://www.lucidcafe.com/library/96jun/rousseau.html (accessed June 2006)

Rousseau, J.J. (1911) *Emile.* London: J.M. Dent

Schaffer, H.R. (1999) *Social Development.* Oxford: Blackwell Publishers

Schjelderup-Ebbe, T. (1935) Social Behaviour of Birds, in Murchison, C. (ed.) *Handbook of Social Psychology.* Worcester, MA: Clark University Press

Skinner, B.F. (1953) *Science and Human Behaviour.* London: Macmillan

Smith, P.K., Cowie, H. and Blades, M. (1998) *Understanding Children's Development,* 3rd edn. Oxford: Blackwell Publishers

Thelen, E. and Smith, L.B. (1998) Dynamic Systems Theories' Lerner, in R.M. (ed.) *Handbook of Child Psychology, Vol. 1 Theoretical models of human development.* New York: Wiley, pp. 563–634

Vygotsky, L. (1962) *Thought and Language.* Cambridge, MA: MIT Press

Vygotsky, L. and Cole, M. (eds) (1978) *Mind in Society, The Development of Higher Psychological Processes.* Cambridge, MA: Harvard University Press

Vygotsky, L.S. (1987) *The Collected Works of L.S. Vygotsky. Vol. 1. Problems of General Psychology.* New York: Plenum

Watson J.B. and Raynor, R. (1920) 'Conditioned Emotional Reactions', *Journal of Experimental Psychology,* 3: 1–14

Wertsch, J.V. and Tulviste, P. (1992) 'L.S. Vygotsky and Contemporary Developmental Psychology', *Developmental Psychology,* 28: 548–57

Wikipedia (2006) The Free Encyclopedia: http://en.wikipedia.org/wiki/Nurture (accessed June 2006)

World War 2 People's War Team (2003) http://www.bbc.co.uk/dna/ww2/A1143578 (accessed June 2006)

Yeo, A. and Lovell, T. (2001). *Sociology for Childhood Studies.* London: Hodder & Stoughton

Useful websites

The Howard League for Penal Reform: www.howardleague.org

Part 3

Early Childhood

Chapter 8

Families, Home and Childhood

"The most ancient of all societies, and the only one that is natural, is the family"
Jean-Jacques Rousseau (1762)

Introduction

This chapter will consider the role of the family and parenting in child development. As society changes, so does the family, with the notion of two married parents bringing up their children with the support of the extended family no longer the recognised norm. Family units vary considerably and we will explore the different types of family, their roles in child rearing and the impact of parenting on the child. The nature of childhood and the influence of family and home will be discussed both from a historical perspective and within the current debates about the changing nature of childhood within our modern society.

Aims

→ To provide an overview of the different types of family units within our society

→ To develop an awareness of some of the different parenting styles and the potential impact on child development

→ To consider some of the different types of homes and environments in which children live and how these are central to a child's culture

→ To provide an overview of the development of children's rights

→ To consider some of the negative influences on childhood and how these can adversely affect the child

→ To consider some of the more recent views on the nature of childhood

Families

Sociologists and anthropologists define the family as a group biologically connected through kin connections (Maybin and Woodhead, 2003). This is, however, a historical, white and Western definition and does not reflect the situation in other societies and in the twenty-first century. In current social contexts the family is considered to be a household, or all those who live in one house (as parents, children, servants); parents and their children; the children alone or common descendants. The Office for National Statistics (2005) uses this definition of a family: 'a married/cohabiting couple with or without child(ren), or a lone-parent with child(ren)'. Other definitions used by the Office for National Statistics are:

- **household**: a person living alone, or a group of people living at the same address who have the address as their only or main residence and either share one main meal a day or share the living accommodation (or both);
- **dependent children**: aged under 16, or aged 16–18 in full-time education and never married;
- **multi-family households**: families sharing a household with at least one other family.

The main function of a family is to reproduce and survive in future generations. The family cares for the developing child, providing food, warmth and shelter, and nursing the child when sick. The family also socialises children and supports them in learning the norms and values of the culture in which they live. This reduces conflict and maintains order within the family unit and within society. The family also provides emotional support, by comforting children and supporting them in their emotional development, helping them to become independent in society (see Chapter 6). They help a child to develop self-esteem and a sense of purpose and commitment to the family unit and to society.

There can be many different types of family. The one that springs to most minds and is cited by politicians as the 'norm' or 'ideal' (Owens, 1997), is the nuclear family; the mother, father and children (see Picture 8.1). However, there are many variations from this norm and for children and carers involved each situation appears 'normal'. We are often informed by the media and government that the married, nuclear family is best for the child, but it is clear that it is social and emotional stability (see Chapters 6 and 7) or a loving, caring and stable family that is important (see Picture 8.2). There have been many changes in the traditional family structure of a married couple and their children. Statistics taken from the Office for National Statistics (2005) suggest that social trends show mar-

Picture 8.1 A 'typical' nuclear family
Source: John Walmsley/Education Photos

Picture 8.2 A less traditional family unit with same-sex partners
Source: Digital Vision/PunchStock

riages in UK are still popular. They also show an increase in the diversity of family type, with marriages increasing at the beginning of the twenty-first century, after a 30-year decline, to half their 1970 peak of almost 340,000. Statistics also show that in 2004 66 per cent of dependent children in the UK lived in a married couple family, although there was a continued rise in the proportion of births outside marriages: 42.8 per cent in 2005, compared with 42.2 per cent in 2004; in 1995, 1 in 3 births were outside marriage.

Research

Family structure

Comprehensive research from the Office for National Statistics (Smallwood and Wilson, 2007) has looked at many different aspects of families, such as family structure and formation (see Figure 8.1), education, unpaid care, living arrangements and health and geography, with much of the data coming from the 2001 Census. The data show that in 2006:

- fourty-three per cent of UK families had no children;
- fourteen per cent had only non-dependent children;
- cohabiting couples were more likely to have no children (57 per cent) than married couples (50 per cent);
- thirty-nine per cent of cohabiting couples and 38 per cent of married couples had dependent children;
- seventy-three per cent of lone mothers had dependent children, against 50 per cent of lone fathers.

Family types are very similar for England, Scotland and Wales.

Families: *Focus on Families* (Smallwood and Wilson, 2007) looks at family types and explores similarities and differences between them. It also draws on demographic information to look at the many dimensions of families in the UK today and shows that married-couple families are still the majority. The total number of families reached 17 million in 2004, and around 7 in 10 were headed by a married couple, but the number of families headed by a married couple fell by half a million between 1996 and 2004, to just over 12 million. At the same time both lone-mother and cohabiting couple families increased, to 2.3 million and 2.2 million respectively.

Cohabiting-couple families are much younger than married-couple families. In 2001 half of cohabiting couple families in the UK were headed by a person aged under 35, compared with just over a tenth of married couples. A couple's age is taken from one of the adults. The difference in age between cohabiting and married-couple families is mostly explained by whether they have children living with them. Cohabiting couples with no children tended to be younger than married couples, reflecting the increase in the number of people choosing to cohabit instead of, or before, getting married.

Lone-parent families were younger than married-couple families, and lone-mother families were younger than lone-father families. One in three lone-mothers was aged under 35, whereas fewer than one in 10 lone-fathers were under 35. In a lone-parent family young children are more likely to live with their mother than their father. In 2001 families with dependent children were more likely to be headed by a younger person than families with non-dependent children or families with no children living with them. (Labour Force Survey, spring 1996 and 2004; Office for National Statistics, 2005).

Dependent children: Children in lone-parent families were more likely to live with their mother than their father. In 2004 nearly nine out of 10 lone parents were lone mothers.

Figure 8.1 Statistics taken from the National Statistics Office
Source: Adapted from ONS, 2005

The nuclear family can be subsumed within an extended family group. Extended families come in two main types: those where children, parents, grandparents or other relatives (aunts, uncles, cousins, etc.) live under one roof and those where the extended family lives close by (in the same street or town). The advantages of the extended family are that there is support for the child, and the parents, and parenting skills are learned from effective role models and care is shared. When families are separated by long distances, especially coupled with an increasingly fragmented society where parents are driven by economics to work long hours and spend less time with their family, the development of parenting skills and support are weakened. Increasingly common in Western society is the single-parent family, with that parent usually (but not exclusively) the mother. The Office for National Statistics (2005) have identified that 1 in 4 dependent children live in a single-parent family. This is an increase from 1 in 14 in 1972. Sometimes this occurs because of the break-up of the nuclear family, or because of unplanned or teenage pregnancies, where the father does not remain with the mother. Occasionally the single parent is the father, although younger children are more likely to stay with their mothers (Pryor, 2004). The UK has a high proportion of single parent families and these can be either well supported within extended family units or reliant on government agencies and sporadic family support.

The blended or reconstituted family is another common feature of modern Western societies. This occurs when adults and children from different family groups combine to make a new family (or stepfamily). Blended families are more likely to be economically stable, but the reconstitution of families does result in 'changes in family dynamics' (Pryor, 2004: 117) with social and emotional repercussions, as discussed in earlier chapters. In 2001, 10 per cent of all families with dependent children in the UK were stepfamilies; 0.7 million stepfamilies had dependent children living in households in the UK. Although there is a tendency for children to stay with their mother following the break-up of a partnership, the loss of one primary attachment and the reconstitution of the family does appear to have an effect on social development. For a start, these stepfamilies are generally larger than non-stepfamilies; 27 per cent of stepfamilies had three or more dependent children compared with 18 per cent of non-stepfamilies (Office for National Statistics, 2005). All family members need to adjust to the new group and renegotiate social rules and responsibilities and this can be difficult for young children.

Other reconstituted families are adoptive or foster families, where children may have to enter an established family. Many adopted children do not consider the family to be a biological construct but a social one, while some adopted children do not feel part of their adoptive family, although whether this is for biological or social reasons is unclear. Adoption was legalised in the UK through the 1926 Adoption Act. At that time, the adopted child had no contact with their biological parents. For older children being adopted, this was probably not only an enormous upheaval but must have caused some developmental delay or problems. By the 1970s adoption was becoming less common, due to shifts in social thinking, and the 1976 Adoption Act allowed children to locate their biological parents. Foster children may still have contact with their biological parents and this can also create difficulties as they may have to come to terms with two very different social situations and manage the emotional relationships with both the foster and biological parents. If the children are young, this can make the transition to the adoptive or foster family easier, although I have had experience of children who have lived in a very secure and loving foster/adoptive family, from 18 months of age, but who still exhibit severe manifestations from early abuse or neglect. In some societies, informal fostering of children is common, with grandparents or other relatives caring for children (Burr and Montgomery, 2003a). In the UK, children have been placed in single-parent foster families for many years, especially where the child is older or has a disability. However, a change in the law in 2007 has made it easier for homosexual families to care for adoptive or foster children. This is a very controversial issue, especially for Church adoption groups. Homosexual couples have also formed families as a result of artificial insemination or surrogacy and this too has received criticism from some quarters.

Children can be affected by the breakdown of the family. Divorce, the breakdown of cohabiting unions and/or the creation of new partnerships and blended families can all affect the child and their social development. Some children do not live in families at all; for example, in 2001 139,000 children were living in other households in the UK, including living with adults or other relatives who are not their parents, and an additional 52,000 children under 16 lived in communal establishments such as children's homes (Office for National Statistics, 2005).

Tools for Learning

Deeper analysis

The reflective tasks for this chapter are aimed at supporting your analytical skills. Analysis in concerned with 'resolving or separating of a thing into its elements or component parts' (*Chambers*, 1972: 43). It involves understanding, clarification and illumination. When analysing an observation, a situation, or data of any kind, we attempt to understand what is happening, why individuals react in certain ways and in certain situations. We look underneath the obvious and reveal why something happens and resolve problems and clarify purposes and intentions. Through analysis we may identify what are the main factors/issues components of ideas or actions. We may scratch beneath the surface of reading, ideas or observations. We may try to understand why something has happened or why an idea is held. We may try to provide alternative explanation. We may try to look at a situation from other perspectives or points of view.

One way to ensure you are being analytical rather than descriptive is to make sure that you are asking yourself (and answering) analytical questions. Analytical questions ask how and why and so what, whereas descriptive questions ask when and where and what.

As you develop your analytical skills, you should look more deeply at events, situations, evidence and begin to identify different layers of analysis. This may mean looking at a situation from a number of different perspectives, perhaps getting evidence from different parties. You can think of this deeper analysis as a bit like mining to different depths, so you encounter different types of soil or rocks, and evidence of life in different centuries. You may also liken it to unwrapping a parcel (like in the game pass-the-parcel) to expose different layers and begin to reveal what is underneath. Another analogy is sorting a collection of objects in different ways, so that you get a better understanding of the collection as a whole and of the individual objects. Layers of analysis may reveal a chronology or history, as for example in looking at the history of childhood (Cunningham, 2006). Layers may involve a number of questions about families, such as:

- How do families support social development?
- How is the social development of children affected by the emotional ties within the family?
- Why do some children struggle to develop socially within the family unit?

Together these build up a holistic and informative picture of how a family influences the social development of the child.

Deep analysis also involves looking at data collected to identify patterns which will help you not only to understand but to support. For example, you may identify patterns in parenting behaviour and the effects on the child and this may help you to support the family in caring for the child. The analysis may reveal issues or factors that affect parenting.

Reflective Tasks

Family structure

Level 1

Consider your own family structure (type of family, number of siblings, position in the family, etc.) and identify what effect this structure had on your social development. You will need to challenge your own objectivity, as it is likely that you will find it difficult to be truly objective when looking at your own life or your own family. Try looking at your family from another perspective, or discussing your views with someone from a different family structure.

Level 2

Consider the different family structures of children in your care.

- How do the different structures affect the children's social development within the setting?
- Do you find it easier to understand and accommodate some types of family structures?
- Why might this be?
- How can you support children who come from families that you find difficult to understand?

Level 3

Consider the different family structures of children in your care.

- Does your setting advantage (accommodate) one type of family structure over others?
- Why might this be?
- What factors affect your ability to accommodate different family structures and support the children's social development?

Research

Social and cognitive skills

Research undertaken on behalf of the Department for Children, Schools and Families (DCSF) by the Centre for the Economics of Education has looked at the impact of early cognitive and non-cognitive skills on later outcomes (Carneiro *et al.*, 2007). The research has identified the importance of these skills for schooling attainment, labour market outcomes and social behaviours at various ages. The key findings indicate that both cognitive and non-cognitive skills are strongly dependent on family background and other characteristics of the home learning environment. This is due to both genetic and environmental reasons. By the time children are 7 years of age, there are gaps in social and cognitive abilities related to socio-economic status (identified by the father's social class), so that children from both professional and non-manual family backgrounds exhibit significantly greater cognitive and social skills than children from manual backgrounds. Social skills appear to be unaffected by the number of years a parent has spent in education (although this does have an effect on cognitive skills). Other aspects of the home learning environment (amount of reading by parents and the interest shown in the children's education) are found to affect the development of social skills.

There were other factors that affected the development of social skills (Carneiro *et al.*, 2007):

- family problems, such as alcoholism, mental health issues and divorce;
- birth order;
- slow early development;
- poor health and/or disability at birth and/or during early childhood.

Parenting

Salter (1998) identifies parenting as a shared activity involving two adults who care, nurture, guide, educate and interact with the developing child. Mothering, on the other hand, is considered (Salter, 1998: viii) to be 'essentially a spiritual activity, a woman's intimate connection with her child – one that only a mother can have', and begins after conception. If mothering is a biological construct, then adoptive parents and fathers cannot provide this function. However, we know that children do form close and primary attachments with adults other than their biological mother (see Chapter 6) and so parenting seems to be a better term to use for this chapter. Parenting has been identified (Whiting and Pope-Edwards, 1988) as having four functions:

- survival, by protecting and nurturing the child;
- attachment, by offering emotional support and love (see Chapter 6);
- basic health, by supporting children in personal hygiene and offering medical support;
- social behaviour, by supporting social development.

In many ways these functions can be related to Maslow's hierarchical needs (1968; see Figure 1.1), in that children will not develop fully unless their physiological, safety and affective needs are developed. Families too cannot function fully, fulfil their true potential, or be harmonious unless they provide the physiological, safety and affective needs of children. Differences in parenting may be due to culture (Berk, 2003; Montgomery, 2003), so that each family will still fulfil the functions, but in different ways depending on the cultural context. Society considers that natural parents are competent at fulfilling these functions, unless something goes wrong within the family. This is not the same with adoptive and foster parents, who are subject to rigorous and continual scrutiny to ensure they are effective parents (Burr and Montgomery, 2003a).

Schaffer (1999) suggested that there were three types of parental attributes:

- *universal attributes*: those common to all human parents which can be regarded as part of the heritage of our species;
- *cultural-specific attributes*: those that are specific to particular societies and thus distinguish one grouping of parents from another;
- *individual attributes*: those which differentiate one parent from another within cultural groups and can therefore be considered as an expression of the individual's personality.

Research

Parenting styles

In the late 1960s and early 1970s Diana Baumrind (1971) extensively researched and categorised the parenting styles that she observed in the child-rearing practices of mothers and fathers of over 130 pre-school children. She identified four areas of parental behaviour – control, nurturance, clarity of communication and maturity demands – and she found that parenting could be best described as a combination of these, as can be seen in Figure 8.2.

Authoritarian parenting. Parents are in power and control and direct their children. They expect unquestioning obedience and may use scare tactics to control, and force and punishment if the child does not obey. They can appear cold and mocking. They do not consult their children and rarely give praise or show pleasure in the children's achievements.

Permissive parenting. Parents allow themselves to be used as a resource by the children. They exercise limited control but are noticeably loving and affectionate. They may be inconsistent about discipline and generally consult with the children over family decisions and rules. These parents are usually less active in taking responsibility for the children's behaviour. These parents can appear over-indulgent or inattentive to their child.

Authoritative parenting. Parents show high levels of warmth and achievement demands. They have firm control over the children but in a way which encourages verbal give and take and mutual respect. Good levels of communication are evident and children are always clear about what is expected and why. Parents are more likely to reason with the children and show more warmth than in other groups. These parents are high in acceptance and involvement, responsive, attentive and sensitive to the child's needs.

Rejecting–neglecting parenting. Parents show an essentially disengaged style and appear emotionally detached. Child rearing barely exceeds the minimum effort to feed and clothe the child. Parents are neither responsive to nor demanding of their child. They do not monitor or support their child's activities and provide little structure for understanding the world or the social rules required to live in it. At its extreme parents can be guilty of neglect. They may actively reject their child-rearing responsibilities and have a combination of low acceptance and low involvement with little control and general indifference to issues of autonomy (decision-making).

Figure 8.2 Baumrind's taxonomy of parenting
Source: Based on Baumrind, 1971

Reflective Tasks

Parenting styles

Level 1

Look at the parenting styles in Figure 8.2 and assign each of the following behaviours of children in a supermarket to different parenting styles,

- the child who is screaming '*I want*' and running around;
- the child who is screaming '*I want*' and has a temper tantrum and receives a smack from his/her parent;
- the child who has his/her own shopping list and is involved in collecting items;

- the child who has his/her own trolley and list and helps their parent get the shopping;
- the child who shouts '*I want*' and gets food off the shelf and is allowed to eat the food on the way round, before paying for it;
- the child who shouts '*I want*' and the parent talks to them and discusses why his/her behaviour is unacceptable and disciplines the child if it continues.

Level 2

Look at the children in your care and try and find examples of children who are the recipients of the different parenting styles in Figure 8.2. Provide an example of behaviour to justify each decision.

Level 3

As a staff, decide which parenting style (see Figure 8.2) is more akin to the style of behaviour management in your setting. How can you support the social development of children who have experienced different styles and who may be alienated by the styles used in your setting?

Parenting is affected by the different type of family structure (see p. 241) as well as different types of care and support for the child and family. If outside agencies, such as social services or the National Council for One-Parent Families, support the family, or the parents attend parenting classes at local SureStart centres, then it is likely parenting will be positively affected. If children are cared for in settings (such as nurseries or crèches) for long periods of the day, or by childminders and nannies, there may be a conflict of parenting, with children having different rules and social conventions to consider within the different types of care. Children cared for in institutions, such as children's homes, or even those in extended care in settings may also receive some diverse and inconsistent parenting, becoming detached and emotionally and socially unstable. As Pryor (2004: 126) has identified, 'as family structures become more diverse, so too do parenting arrangements and practices', but parenting still 'remains pivotal to the well-being of children and is the conduit through which most other factors impinge upon them'.

The size of the family group will also affect parenting. Children in large families, especially the older children, are more likely to have to gain early parenting skills and help care for younger family members. Younger members of large families may be quite independent, having had to look after themselves. They may also be gregarious, being used to the social mix of large numbers of others. On the other hand, they may seek solitude or try to blend into the background, which is difficult to achieve when they move into larger settings and are in an even bigger group. An only child may have considerable adult attention and come to rely on this type of interaction and be quite demanding. They may also find it difficult when they begin to attend playgroup, nursery or school, as they will not have the individual attention that their early years have led them to expect. The only girl in a family may be treated differently from male siblings and the youngest may be treated differently from the eldest. Middle children may just feel left out! I was a middle child, with a sister nearly three years older and a brother two years younger. My parents treated each child in as similar a way as possible and every opportunity given to one was given to another. However, each of us (my siblings and me) have different perceptions of how our parents treated us.

Reflective Tasks

Different family structures

Level 1

Try imagining yourself in a different type of family or a different position within your family. How do you think your perceptions of your family, parents and siblings would be different?

Level 2

Try imaging what it must be like for a child from a small/large family to adjust in your setting. Ask the children to describe their family and to imagine what it is like to be part of a different family. Do you think this knowledge of different families will help you and the children to interact more effectively?

Level 3

As a staff discuss your own family structures and parenting experiences. Identify children in your setting who come from different family structures and experience different parenting styles from your own experiences. Try to imagine what it is like for those children and their parents, when in your setting. Do you think this knowledge of different families will help you, the parents and the children to adjust to life in your setting?

Homes

There are different types of homes for family units and this will have an effect on the childhood (see Picture 8.3). Children can live in flats, bungalows, terraced houses, semi-detached or detached houses. They can live in caravans or boats, or in communes or community hostels and children's homes. They can remain in the same home for a long period of time, or they can move frequently (change home or location). This does raise the question, whether a house is a home. Clearly, the experience of my son, described in Chapter 6, indicates that the actual house does have some effect on the child's emotional stability, but more important must be the individuals who live together and make up the family. As Maybin and Woodhead (2003) have identified, there are many different types of homes and experiences, including for some children 'homes' wherever they can sleep, with groups of other 'street children' who make up their 'family' unit. In the UK, there are few checks on homes, unless a family is in need of support. Indeed, not only are there more checks on adoptive and foster families and homes, but cat and dog charities make more checks on prospective families before allowing animals to be housed within a family!

There are also different types of environment that the family may live in (rural, urban, suburban, multicultural, working class, etc.). If the home is in a monocultural environment, then most of the families in the local area will share cultural norms. A family living in this monoculture, but which does not share the culture, will possibly feel isolated and may be alienated from the local community. Children living in multicultural communities may find it easier to understand and respect other cultures. However, as the children develop and begin to attend formal care and education settings, they may find it difficult to adjust, especially if their culture is not one that is understood or respected by the setting. Cultural differences can be regional, with subcultural groups existing in the inner cities north and south of the UK, and can involve differences in social class as well as

Picture 8.3 Traveller site
Source: Philip Wolmuth/Report Digital

ethnic differences. Indeed, there are many cultural factors which can affect the developing child, their family and their childhood. If the home and setting attended by the child have cultural differences, then this can lead to cultural discontinuity. This can occur because different cultures have different facial expressions, habits, mannerisms, etc. (see Berk, 2003; Curtis and O'Hagan, 2003) which can conflict with those encountered within the setting. For example, I once worked with an American who brought his family to the UK for a few years, and his 7-year old son started school, for the first time, on arrival. On his first day at school, he was reprimanded by a school dinner lady for cutting up his food and then transferring his fork into his right hand to eat. This naturally caused problems for the child, who was quite quickly alienated from the school.

In many ways this lack of understanding of different cultures is explained by the lack of research into cultural differences (Curtis and O'Hagan, 2003) because of the sensitivity of analysis of previous studies (see Eysenck, 1971, whose research indicated that black African-Americans were of lower intelligence than white Americans or black Africans). As a result, settings discriminate because they treat children equally rather than differentiate to accommodate cultural differences. A monocultural setting sees cultural diversity as an obstacle due to its potential discrimination effects and looks upon cultural diversity in the setting as a deficit (that is, they are concerned with that which is missing in cultures that deviate from the norm). They believe that cultural homogeneity in the setting is important, as the cultural identity of the setting and the community is a fixed and indisputable historical fact. The multicultural setting attempts to understand the cultural differences that exist in the community. They may be benignly multicultural in that they see the obvious cultural differences that exist, but take no action, or critically multicultural in that they deal with different ways of life and opportunities of life in a proactive way. An intercultural setting attempts to bridge the cultural divide, seeing cultural diversity as a way of enriching the setting. They promote differences, taking advantage of different knowledge and cultures and taking into consideration cultural diversity in order to produce a confrontation of cultures, thus attempting to overcome cultural ethnocentrism. In this way, the intercultural ethos supports the setting in becoming part of the local community, making the transition from home to the formal setting less traumatic for the child.

Reflective Tasks

Culture and potential conflict

Level 1

Consider the effect of home experience on physical, cognitive, emotional social, moral, or language development.

- How might these areas of development be affected?
- Can you think of an experience in your own life where the culture of home and school conflicted?
- How did this affect you?
- How did you resolve/reconcile/deal with this conflict?

Use this example and some background reading to provide an argument as to how children's development is affected by cultural conflict.

Level 2

- Does the culture of your setting affect the physical, cognitive, emotional social, moral, or language development of any children in your care?
- Do children find it easy to move from home to your setting?
- How could you support or assist the children to overcome the effects of any cultural conflict?

Use this example and background reading to provide an argument as to how we can support children who experience cultural conflict between home and the setting.

Level 3

Consider your setting in the local community.

- Is your setting at the centre of the community?
- Is your setting monocultural, multicultural or intercultural?
- How can you develop your setting to support the children's transition from home to the setting?
- How might outside agencies provide support?

Use analysis of your setting and reading to provide a persuasive argument as to why you need to develop/modify/change the culture of your setting.

The importance of good home–setting liaison or partnership is well recognised (Bastiani and Wolfendale, 1996; QCA, 2000; DfES, 2003a, 2003b; Abbott and Langston, 2004; Sage and Wilkie, 2004) and will be discussed further in Chapter 13. It is, however, important to stress that all who care and work with children have a duty of care that involves easing the various transitions they make throughout their lives. This includes making the cultural transition from home to a formal setting easier. Of course, some children need to make these transitions earlier, if they are cared for by day nurseries, childminders or nannies, and effective liaison and partnership is also important here (Riddall-Leech, 2002).

The development of children's rights

Childhood is not only affected by family, home and settings, it is also influenced by historical events, political policy, law and public opinion (Aries, 1972; Lawrence, 2004). Cunningham's excellent tour of the history of childhood (2006) identifies how childhood was different in different eras, from the short, physically hard childhood in the Middle Ages, when childhood was interrupted by work, illness or death, to the more complex social childhood of modern times (see also Chapter 2). Childhood is also determined by the different perspectives of those involved, as Montgomery (2003) identified in her discussions with children and parents from different cultures, places and contexts. She identifies three Western constructions of childhood:

- the *Puritan* discourse, where childhood is considered a time of evil and wildness, during which the child needs to be disciplined and punished to break their will and prevent sinning. This is characterised by the thinking of Thomas Hobbes (1588–1679);
- the *Tabula Rasa* discourse, where childhood is a time of development. This is characterised by Locke (1632–1704), who thought that children were blank slates to be filled and that childhood was the time when adults influenced the developing child;
- The Romantic discourse, where childhood is seen as a period of innocence, as also identified in the New Testament and characterised by Rousseau (1712–78) and his writing (Rousseau, 1911).

Montgomery (2003) also identifies a fourth theme of *Globalisation*, which is characterized by the writing of Giddens (1997), who believes that childhood is increasingly dependent on the world society.

Throughout the different stages of history, childhood has also been characterised by children's rights, although this has only been legalised in the last few centuries. Perhaps one of the most important historical actions was the Factories Act of 1833, which began the legal protection of children from exploitation, and established half-time school, allowing children to both work and attend school. However, it was not until 1948 that the United Nations Declaration of Human Rights identified that everyone had rights, regardless of their wealth, skin colour, sex or age. Burr and Montgomery (2003b) identify some arguments against applying human rights to children, such as their immaturity, lack of knowledge and experience, inability to communicate and lack of power. Kay (2001) believes that children's rights are not taken seriously. As a result, children often remain exploited by adults who are expected to care for them.

The Children Act 1989 developed children's rights from the UN Declaration and the United Nations Convention on the Rights of the Child (UNCRC). It identifies that children's welfare is 'paramount' and should be actively considered and consulted in all decisions about their own welfare. This has changed childhood considerably, as the child's wishes and feelings are now taken into consideration in all matters. Children's rights are thought (Burr and Montgomery, 2003b) to be the four Ps of provision, prevention, protection and participation. *Provision rights* support the first level of Maslow's hierarchy (1968), so that all children are entitled to have their physiological needs met, although they go further and entitle the child to education and care that supports their holistic development. *Prevention rights* are concerned with the systems in society that ensure safety and prevent abuse. *Protection rights* protect the developing child from any exploitation by adults, society and cultures. *Participation rights* allow the child to be part of the decision-making process, encouraging them to develop opinions and make decisions, and so are the beginning of citizenship. It is interesting that at various times in the development of the National Curriculum (DfEE, 1999), the curriculum has either encouraged or dissuaded teachers from supporting children in their development as citizens and in making moral and ethical decisions (see Johnston, 2002; 2005).

The UNCRC has made a considerable impact on childhood worldwide and the Children Act 1989 a big impact on childhood in the UK. Children's rights have been further developed through the Children Act 2004 and the Every Child Matters initiative (DfES, 2003b) which identifies five outcomes for every child from birth to 19 years of age. Every child has the right to be healthy, safe, to enjoy and achieve, to make a positive contribution and achieve economic well-being, and all local authorities are obliged to produce action plans to ensure that they achieve the Every Child Matters agenda. In this way childhood today is a very different experience from childhood in the past and there is considerable support available for families and children, such as:

- Parentlineplus;
- Save the Children;
- Relate;
- Parents' Advice Centre;
- Twins and Multiple Births Association;
- National Council for One-Parent Families;
- NCH;
- National Childbirth Trust;
- NSPCC.

Reflective Tasks

Support agencies

Level 1

Choose two or three of the support agencies listed above (see also the list of useful websites at the end of the chapter). Analyse the support they have to offer children and their families. Analyse how the agencies support the children's entitlement to the four Ps: provision, prevention, protection and participation (Burr and Montgomery, 2003a).

Level 2

Research the support offered by the above agencies. Analyse how these agencies can support your work with young children. Identify children in your care whom the agencies can support in enabling them access to the four Ps: provision, prevention, protection and participation (Burr and Montgomery, 2003a).

Level 3

Identify all the families in your setting who need help to enable them to care for their children and provide them with their entitlement under the Every Child Matters agenda (DfES, 2003b). Research the support offered by the above agencies and identify what help they can provide. How can you utilise the agencies in your future work to benefit the children in your care?

Childhood

Childhood is determined by the family, home, community and the legal and political context in which the child lives. Modern childhood is longer than in previous centuries (Cunningham, 2003; 2006), probably because of the complex society in which we now live. In the past 50 years we have seen the school-leaving age rise from 14 to 16, with discussions and plans to raise it to 18. I find it confusing that you can be adult enough to leave school, buy cigarettes, have sexual intercourse and marry (with parental consent) at 16; learn to drive a car at 17; and officially come of age, drink alcohol, vote and marry (without parental consent) at 18. It is even more confusing when many young people still celebrate 21 as the start of adulthood, over 30 years after adulthood was determined as 18 years of age!

Childhood is also determined by the lifestyle choices of the adults who care for the child. Children who live in single-sex families, are brought up by grandparents, live communally with others, are home educated or live a religious life, will have different childhoods from the 'norm' in society. The variations of experience in childhood are all generally successful in supporting child development and 'transforming helpless, self-centred infants into more or less self-supporting, responsible members of their communities' (Hoghughi and Long, 2004: 68). However, childhood is not without its problems and is not necessarily a happy experience for all children. Sibling rivalry can create problems that continue into adulthood and old age. It may also influence parenting skills, with parents attempting to provide a childhood unlike their own. My own childhood was characterised by my being a middle child, with a dominant elder sibling, and four house and location moves before I was 11, with resultant changes in friends. This made me determined to provide a different childhood for my children and I was determined not to move locations (even though I did move house, with resulting problems as described above and in Chapter 6) and to avoid warring between my children. I am sure that my children will, in turn, pick on aspects of their childhood that they would like to change for their own children; perhaps even those things I was determined to maintain for them.

Special physical, emotional, behavioural and social needs can also affect the quality of childhood (see Chapter 10), creating challenges for the whole family. Children who have special needs may have their childhood characterised by stays in hospital, medication or separation from their family, and may even have their childhood cut short. If another family member is unwell or has a special needs, this will also affect childhood, as all children may be involved in caring and having to make adjustments to their family life. Bereavement, especially the loss of a close family member, will also affect childhood. One of my earliest memories is being cared for by my maternal aunt while my parents attended my fraternal grandmother's funeral. This was just after her own father's and my maternal grandfather's death, and I remember it because the grief felt by my parents and aunt was evident on their faces and not something I had ever experienced before. Miscarriage, sudden infant death or death of a sibling can have a devastating affect on the whole family and even very young children will be touched by the effects. For some children, the death of a much-loved sibling can lead them to attempt to emulate their deceased brother or sister and this can have repercussions throughout childhood and later in life. These problems are exacerbated in modern society where child health is measurably of a higher standard (Lawrence, 2004) and child mortality is less common than in previous generations, when childhood was often cut short by death and disease (Cunningham, 2006).

Domestic violence and abuse will also affect childhood. Our present society has made great progress in preventing child abuse of any kind, through legislation and provision of resources, in the knowledge that 'every child matters' (DfES, 2003b), although it is impossible to prevent all children witnessing or being part of abuse of some kind. I have worked with children who have experienced situations that I, fortunately, have not. We need a whole new set of understandings, attitudes and skills when working with children who are experiencing difficult childhood situations, such as:

- when a child is trying to focus on their education, having been awake most of the night, listening to parents rowing and witnessing mother being beaten or thrown out of the house;
- when a child has to attend a new setting because they are living in a hostel for abused families;
- when a child is aggressive or abusive, because that is the only response they have ever experienced;
- when a child arrives one morning with the imprint of a hand or shoe on their body;
- when a parent is released from a long stay in prison and returns to the inevitable changes in their family life.

We need extra patience and tolerance for behaviours that are less than desirable. We need to understand that children lead different lives from us and not to make judgements based on our naivety and inexperience. We need to support these children in different ways and make the childhood within our settings as 'normal' and stable as possible.

Reflective Tasks

Crises in childhood

Level 1

Read about the different crises that children may experience in childhood. Use the reading and your personal experiences to create an argument as to how you could assist a child to overcome jealousy, fears, effects of loss and grief, or the separation and divorce of their parents.

Level 2

Focus on a child in your setting who has particular difficulties due to jealousy, fears, effects of loss and grief, or the separation and divorce of their parents. Read to help you to understand the child's responses and use that reading to inform a decision as to how you can support the child to overcome the difficulties they face.

Consider also how, as a practitioner, you can promote relationships between the setting and home to support the child further.

Level 3

As a staff look at the common crises that children in your setting face. Read to help you to understand the crises from the child's perspective and decide:

- how you can support the children;
- how you can improve liaison between the home and the setting;
- how you can, and when you should, involve support agencies to provide further support for the children and the family.

Research

A caveat: Sweeping generalisations

Childhood can also be adversely disrupted by the break-up of the family through divorce, separation or bereavement, and findings from a study, commissioned by the Conservative Party and reported in the *Sunday Times* (Oakeshott, 2006), blamed unmarried and single parents for the social crisis in childhood. The claim is that anti-social behaviour, drug and alcohol addiction, educational failure and welfare dependency are the result of family break-up and poor parenting. It is unclear what evidence supports these claims and it does seem a little assertive to blame all society's problems on families and poor childhood.

Critical Discussion

Modern childhood

We know that childhood today is different from the childhood of yesterday and many of these differences benefit the child. Childhood is longer, children are healthier, receive more educational opportunities and have more rights. However, not all changes in childhood are thought to be good.

In September 2006, a letter written to the *Daily Telegraph* by over a hundred child experts, academics, writers etc. led by Baroness Greenfield, Director of the Royal Institution, expressed concern at 'the escalating incidence of childhood depression and children's behavioural and developmental conditions'. The concern is that childhood has become characterised by junk food, sedentary technological play and a paucity of quality interaction with adult role models. Most importantly, the letter identified the importance of giving children time as 'in a fast-moving, hyper-competitive culture, today's children are expected to cope with an ever earlier start to formal schoolwork and an overly academic test-driven primary curriculum' (*Daily Telegraph*, 2006: 23). This letter was supported by a second about six weeks later (Bowlby, 2006), with Sir Richard Bowlby, President of the Centre for Child Mental Health as a lead signatory, which expressed concern that the focus on extended group day care has a detrimental effect on social and emotional development (see also Chapter 6). Both letters called for the long-overdue debate on childhood.

Palmer (2006) begins her book on what she calls 'toxic childhood' by describing a young child who is dressed beyond her years, with an unsuitable slogan on her t-shirt. We see this scenario all too often, with small girls wearing clothes that send explicit sexual messages to the world and shoes that damage growing feet; with boys mimicking celebrity role models who do not set a good example for the developing child. Childhood for the modern child is likely to include learning difficulties, such as dyslexia, and syndromes, such as ADHD (Attention Deficit Hyperactivity Disorder), processed foods with additives (Palmer, 2006), less time to be children and play (Elkind, 2001) and childhood stress and emotional problems (Gerhardt, 2004; Bowlby, 2006).

In modern childhood children appear to be pressurised to grow up too fast. Often their parents cannot afford to stop at home and care for them, even if they want to. Nurseries provide physical care for children, but cannot replace the primary attachments of parents, or even provide the same quality of secondary attachments

(Bowlby, 2006). Good quality pre-school provision can provide positive effects (EPPE, 2002; 2003), especially for children who are disadvantaged, although there is equal evidence that good quality home care provides positive effects too (FCCC, 2005). Certainly an institutionalised childhood is not one that anyone would benefit from unless it was tempered by quality home interaction. Unfortunately, a toxic childhood (Palmer, 2006) has few such quality interactions, as parents are often stressed by modern life, self-absorbed by their own concerns, anxieties and feelings (Elkind, 2001) and do not spend quality time with their children. Childhood is spent passively, playing with electronic games or watching television, with the resulting health problems, from obesity to attention disorders and poor brain development (Gerhardt, 2004), caused by excess sugar and processed food.

The introduction of early formal education (DfEE, 1999; QCA, 2000) has disrupted childhood by institutionalising children at too early an age, over-testing them, and has not always encouraged them to learn through play. Further, school dinners have deteriorated and packed lunches are so nutritionally poor that even celebrity chefs have entered the debate on how we feed our children. Busy working parents are getting home from work, picking up their children from day care and feeding them with processed food while they watch television, so that some children do not know how to socialise over a meal and do not know how to use cutlery. The sedentary lifestyle also has an effect on bedtimes, as the sugar-laden children are buzzing at bedtime and have had no opportunities to run off the energy they have consumed. They then have insufficient sleep to enable them to focus on learning the next day and the cycle continues.

Another type of toxic childhood is the one where parents structure the childhood for their children to such an extent that children are rushed from school to homework clubs and then to other clubs and societies, to music, athletics and swimming classes, horse riding, football matches, etc, but never spend quality time interacting with their parents. On one level, a childhood where children are given opportunities to learn skills, make music and exercise, is great, but only within a childhood that is not pressurising the child to 'perform' better than anyone else and only if the parents make time to 'be with' their children and enjoy their company. I am particularly critical of homework for children in the early years, or even in the full primary years, as I feel that learning is more effective in school, during the day and with qualified teachers, and if this time is not sufficient then the curriculum needs to be changed and not childhood. I would rather children went for a walk with their parents, read a book for pleasure with their parents, or cooked and ate a family meal with their parents.

What are your thoughts on the arguments about toxic childhood? Do you think that childhood today is a poorer experience for our children?

As I have been writing this chapter, I received the following in an email, which I think sums up much of what we mean about changing childhoods:

According to today's regulators and bureaucrats, those of us who were kids in the 60s, 70s and early 80s probably shouldn't have survived, because our baby cots were covered with brightly coloured lead-based paint which was promptly chewed and licked.

We had no childproof lids on medicine bottles, or latches on doors or cabinets and it was fine to play with pans.

When we rode our bikes, we wore no helmets, just flip-flops and fluorescent 'spokydokies' on our wheels.

As children, we would ride in cars with no seat belts or airbags – riding in the passenger seat was a treat.

We drank water from the garden hose and not from a bottle and it tasted the same.

We ate chips, bread and butter pudding and drank fizzy juice with sugar in it, but we were never overweight because we were always outside playing.

We shared one drink with four friends, from one bottle or can and no one actually died from this.

We would spend hours building go-carts out of scraps and then went top speed down the hill, only to find out we forgot the brakes.

After running into stinging nettles a few times, we learned to solve the problem.

We would leave home in the morning and could play all day, as long as we were back before it got dark. No one was able to reach us and no one minded.

We did not have Playstations or X-Boxes, no video games at all. No 99 channels on TV, no videotape movies, no surround sound, no mobile phones, no personal computers, no DVDs, no Internet chatrooms and no TVs for those of us a wee bit older

We had friends – we went outside and found them.

We played elastics and rounders, and sometimes that ball really hurt!

We fell out of trees, got cut, and broke bones but there were no law suits.

We had full on fist fights but no prosecution followed from other parents.

We played knock-the-door-run-away and were actually afraid of the owners catching us.

We walked to friends' homes.

We also, believe it or not, WALKED to school; we didn't rely on mummy or daddy to drive us to school, which was just round the corner.

We made up games with sticks and tennis balls.

We rode bikes in packs of seven and wore our coats by only the hood.

The idea of a parent bailing us out if we broke a law was unheard of ... they actually sided with the law.

This generation has produced some of the best risk-takers and problem solvers and inventors, ever. The past 50 years have been an explosion of innovation and new ideas. We had freedom, failure, success and responsibility, and we learned how to deal with it all.

Reflective Tasks

Different childhoods

Level 1

Discuss with some of your peers the different childhoods you experienced. Compare and contrast your childhoods.

- In retrospect, what aspects of your childhood would you like to have changed? Why?
- How could you have changed your childhood?
- How could settings/society/the government have helped you?

Level 2

Compare and contrast the different childhoods of children in your care.

- What do you consider to be the biggest challenge for childhood today?

- How can you support children and help to provide an improved childhood for the children?

Level 3

As a staff identify the different childhoods experienced by children in your setting.

- What challenges face childhood today?
- How can your setting respond to the challenges facing childhood today?
- How can you support families in creating suitable childhoods for their children?

Summary

→ Sociologists and anthropologists define the family as a group biologically connected through kin connections.

→ In current social contexts the family is considered to be a household, or all those who live in one house.

→ The main function of a family is to reproduce and survive in future generations, but the family also cares for and looks after their developing child, socialises their child, provides emotional support, helps a child to develop self-esteem, and to develop a sense of purpose and commitment to the family unit and to society.

→ There are many different types of family, including biological and non-biological.

→ The break-up of a family unit can have an impact on child development.

→ Differences in parenting may be cultural (Berk, 2003; Montgomery, 2003), so that each family will still fulfil the functions, but in different ways depending on the cultural context.

→ Both the structure and the size of the family group will affect parenting.

→ There are different parenting styles and some parents seek support from outside agencies to learn alternative parenting styles to manage their children's behaviour effectively.

→ There are different types of homes for family units and the type of home, number of times children move home and nature of the environment will all have an effect on childhood.

→ Cultural differences can be regional and they can involve differences in social class as well as ethnic differences. There are many cultural factors which can affect developing children, their families and their childhood.

→ If the home and setting attended by the child have cultural differences, then this can lead to cultural discontinuity.

→ An intercultural setting attempts to bridge the cultural divide, seeing cultural diversity as a way of enriching the setting. In this way, the intercultural ethos supports the setting in becoming part of the local community, making the transition from home to the formal setting less traumatic for the child.

→ Childhood is not only affected by family, home and settings, it is also influenced by historical events, political policy, law and public opinion.

→ Children's rights have developed considerably, particularly since the Children Act in 1989.

→ Children's rights, among other things, protect the developing child from any exploitation by adults, society and cultures, allow the child to be part of the decision-making process and encourages them to develop opinions and make decisions. This is a world away from the old adage *children should be seen and not heard*.

→ Childhood is determined by the family, home, community, legal and political context in which the child lives and it is also determined by the lifestyle choices of the adults who care for the child.

→ There are a number of factors which affect childhood, including special physical, emotional or learning needs, illness, bereavement, and negative external influences such as abuse and neglect.

→ There are differing views about the nature of childhood in a modern society, both positive and negative.

Key Questions

- What are the different types of family units within our society?
- How might different parenting styles have a potential impact on child development?
- What are some of the different types of homes and environments in which children live and how are these central to a child's culture?
- How have children's rights developed over the past 30 years?
- What are some of the negative influences on childhood and how might these affect the child?
- What are some of the more recent views on the nature of childhood, and do you agree with them?

References

Abbott, L. and Langston, A. (eds) (2004) *Birth to Three Matters. Supporting the framework of effective practice.* Buckingham: Open University Press

Aries, P. (1972) *Centuries of Childhood.* Harmondsworth: Penguin

Bastiani, J. and Wolfendale, S. (1996) *Home–School Work in Britain: Review, Reflection and Development.* London: David Fulton

Baumrind, D. (1971) 'Current Patterns of Parental Authority', *Developmental Psychology*, Monograph 4.1, Part 2

Berk, L.E. (2003) *Child Development*, 6th edn. Boston: Allyn & Bacon

Bowlby, R. (2006) *The Need for Secondary Attachment Figures in Childcare* www.telegraph.co.uk/opinion/main.jhtml?xml=/opinion/2006/10/21/nosplit/dt2101.xml#head5Childcareproblems

Burr, R. and Montgomery, H. (2003a) Family, Kinship and Beyond, in Maybin, J. and Woodhead, M. (eds) *Childhood in Context* Chichester: John Wiley & Sons/Open University Press

Burr, R. and Montgomery, H. (2003b) Children's Rights, in Woodhead, M. and Montgomery, H. (eds) *Understanding Childhood: an interdisciplinary approach.* Chichester: John Wiley/Open University Press

Carneiro, P., Crawford, C. and Goodman, A. (2007) *The Impact of Early Cognitive and Non-Cognitive Skills on Later Outcomes.* London: Centre for the Economics of Education

Chambers Twentieth Century Dictionary, ed. A.M. Macdonald (1972). Edingburgh: W. & R. Chambers

Cunningham, H. (2003) Children's Changing Lives from 1800 to 2000, in Maybin, J. and Woodhead, M. (eds) *Childhood in Context*. Chichester: John Wiley/Open University

Cunningham, H. (2006) *The Invention of Childhood*. London: BBC

Curtis, A. and O'Hagan, M. (2003) *Care and Education in Early Childhood. A Student's Guide to Theory and Practice*. London: Routledge Falmer

Daily Telegraph (2006) Letters to the Editor – Modern Life Leads to More Depression among Children, Tuesday 12 September: 23

DfEE (1999) *The National Curriculum: Handbook for Teachers in England*. London: DfEE/QCA

DfES (2003a) *Excellence and Enjoyment. A strategy for primary schools*. London: DfES

DfES, (2003b) *Every Child Matters*. London: DfES

Elkind, D. (2001) *The Hurried Child. Growing Up Too Fast Too Soon*, 3rd edn. Cambridge, MA: Da Capio Press

EPPE (2002) 'Measuring the Impact of Pre-School on Children's Cognitive Progress over the Pre-School Period', *The EPPE (Effective Provision of Pre-school Education) Project Technical Paper 8a*. London: Institute of Education

EPPE (2003) 'Measuring the Impact of Pre-School on Children's Social/Behavioural Development over the Pre-School Period', *The EPPE (Effective Provision of Pre-school Education) Project Technical Paper 8b*. London: Institute of Education

Eysenck, H.J. (1971) *Race, Intelligence and Education*. London: Maurice Temple Smith

FCCC (2005) Families, Children and Child Care Study www.familieschildrenchildcare.org/fccc-home.html (accessed 11.11.05)

Gerhardt, S. (2004) *Why Love Matters: How affection shapes a baby's brain*. London: Routledge

Giddens, A. (1997) *Sociology*. Cambridge: Polity Press

Hoghughi M. and Long, N. (eds) (2004) *Handbook of Parenting: Theory and research for practice*. London: Sage

Johnston, J. (2002) The Changing Face of Teaching and Learning, in Johnston, J., Chater, M. and Bell, D. (eds) *Teaching the Primary Curriculum*. Buckingham: Open University Press

Johnston, J. (2005) *Early Explorations in Science*, 2nd edn. Maidenhead: Open University Press

Kay, J. (2001) *Good Practice in Childcare*. London: Continuum

Lawrence, A. (2004) *Principles of Child Protection: Management and Practice*. Maidenhead: Open University Press

Maslow, A.H. (1968) *Towards a Psychology of Being*. New York: Van Nostrand

Maybin, J. and Woodhead, M. (2003) Socializing Children, in Maybin, J. and Woodhead, M. (eds) *Childhood in Context*. Chichester: John Wiley / Open University

Montgomery, H. (2003) Childhood in Time and Place, in Woodhead, M. and Montgomery, H. *Understanding Childhood: An interdisciplinary approach*. Chichester: John Wiley/ Open University

Oakeshott, I. (2006) 'Unwed Parents Causing Social Crisis, say Tories', *The Sunday Times* 10 December: 11

Office for National Statistics (2005) '*Focus on Families*'. www.statistics.gov.uk/ focuson/families (accessed June 2006).

Owens, P. (1997) *Early Childhood Education and Care*. Stoke-on-Trent: Trentham Books

Palmer, S. (2006) *Toxic Childhood. How the modern world is damaging our children and what we can do about it*. London: Orion

Pryor, J. (2004) Parenting in Reconstituted and Surrogate Families, in Hoghughi, M. and Long, N. (eds) *Handbook of Parenting: Theory and research for practice*. London: Sage

QCA (2000) *Curriculum Guidance for the Foundation Stage.* London:DFEE

Riddall-Leech, S. (2002) *Childminding.* Oxford: Heinemann

Rousseau, J. J. (1911) *Emile.* London: J.M. Dent

Sage, R. and Wilkie, M. (2004) *Supporting Learning in Primary Schools,* 2nd edn. Exeter: Learning Matters

Salter, J. (1998) *Mothering with Soul: Raising children as special work.* Stroud: Hawthorne Press

Schaffer, H.R. (1999) *Social Development.* Oxford: Blackwell Publishers

Smallwood, S. and Wilson, B. (eds) (2007) *Focus on Families 2007 Edition.* London: Office for National Statistics/Palgrave Macmillan

Whiting, B. and Pope-Edwards, C. (1988) *Children of Different Worlds: The Formation of Social Behaviour.* Cambridge, MA: Harvard University Press

Useful websites

Birth to Three Matters: www.surestart.gov.uk/resources/childcareworkers/birthtothreematters/

Childline: www.childline.org.uk

DCFS (Department for Children, Schools and Families) Research: www.dcsf.gov.uk/research

Every Child Matters: change for children: www.everychildmatters.gov.uk

National Childbirth Trust (NCT): www.nct.org.uk

National Council for One Parent Families: www.oneparentfamilies.org.uk

NCH – The Children's Charity: www.nch.org.uk

NSPCC: www.nspcc.org.uk

Parentlineplus: www.parentlineplus.org.uk

Parents' Advice Centre: www.pachelp.org

Relate: www.relate.org.uk

Save the Children: www.savethechildren.org.uk

SureStart: www.surestart.gov.uk

Twins and Multiple Births Association: www.tamba.org.uk

United Nations Children's Fund: www.unicef.org

Chapter 9

Early Education

Education is not the filling of a pail but the lighting of a fire
W.B. Yeats (1865–1939)

Introduction

This chapter will examine the policy, practice and provision for early years education. Recent government initiatives and policies will be discussed and reviewed to see whether or not they fully cater for the needs of young children and their learning. The chapter will, first, outline a brief history of early years education; secondly, consider the essential features of high quality practice, and, finally, focus on the learning areas within the Foundation Stage and transition to Key Stage 1.

It is only in recent years that education in the early years has become a feature in the government's agenda for policy and practice in education. When the National Curriculum was introduced in 1988, Key Stage 1 began in Year 1; reception children were not included. Local education authorities varied in their support for the early years, and guidance on appropriate educational experiences espoused by early years experts often ran contrary to more formal expectations within the school. OFSTED inspections focused on achievements from Year 1 onwards and only inspected the early years within a school setting. Early years practitioners were working in a 'no-man's land' in terms of recognition by local and central government. Thankfully this has changed and this chapter will now chart the history of these changes, starting from the early twentieth century.

→ To provide a historical overview of the key developments in policy and practice in early years education

→ To consider the value of play in learning and to review the vocabulary of play

→ To consider the role of adults in children's learning

→ To explore the potential of the learning environment

→ To provide an understanding of the planning and assessment cycle

→ To provide a brief overview of each of the six areas of learning

Overview of key developments in education in the early years

In 1900, over 50 per cent of 2-, 3-and 4-year-olds were in nursery schools (Devereau and Miller, 2003). The problem was that these very young children had to fit into a system designed for older children and which did not take account of the needs of the under-5s. In 1905, Katherine Bathurst, a school inspector, called for a revised system which outlined the need for national nursery schools with separate facilities and more appropriate teaching methods. The Consultative Committee Report (1905) stated that there should be: 'no mental pressure, no formal lessons and no undue physical discipline'. It also recommended that there should be no more than 30 children in the class. The 1918 Education Act allowed all local education authorities to establish nursery schools, but they did not use their new powers extensively to put this into action (Bertram and Pascal, 2001).

Tools for Learning

Combining primary and secondary analysis

In this chapter the Tools for Learning involve the skill of combining analysis from both primary and secondary data. Secondary data collection and analysis is the focus of Part 1 of the book. Secondary data is collected from reading policies, research reports, books and journals (as covered in the Tools for Learning in Chapter 1). Analysis of secondary data (see Chapter 2) is mainly found in a literature review, which reviews the literature to help answer questions you have posed. Primary data collection is the focus of Part 2 and considers observation, interaction, narrative, listening and interview. Primary data is usually presented and analysed in sections of your work entitled 'Research findings' or 'Outcomes and analysis'. These sections, especially in action research, also contain analysis of secondary data and both are also combined in 'Discussion of findings' (see also Chapter 10).

Primary and secondary analysis should be combined and used to create strong arguments. In this way you do not simply describe what you have seen or read, but use the data as evidence to support an argument or point you are making. For example, you may have read that play supports development and you may have seen that it does in practice, and so you put both your primary and secondary evidence together. This can be seen in each chapter of this book when we share our own experiences and research and combine them with the literature in the area.

An argument consists of (Toulmin, 1958):

- *claims*: assertions about what exists or what values people hold;
- *data*: statements that are used as evidence to support assertion;
- *warrants*: statements that explain the relationship of the data to the claim;
- *qualifiers*: specified conditions under which claims hold true;
- *backings*: underlying assumptions which are often not made explicit;
- *rebuttals*: statements which contradict either the data, warrant, backing or qualifier of an argument;
- *counter-claims*: opposing assertions.

If you only make claims without data, warrants, qualifiers and backings, then you are merely stating an opinion, which is unlikely to persuade a reader to support you. An argument will persuade a reader through the use of the evidence, the balanced discussion of counter-claims and persuasive language. (See Figure 9.1.)

Good arguments involve reasons behind what you are claiming and evidence to support your argument, such as factual data. The language will be persuasive and there is likely to be a counter-argument. There are five levels of argument and the level of work that you are engaged in demands more at the higher levels (Level 5) than lower levels.

Level 1: arguments that are a simple claim versus a counter-claim or a claim versus a claim.
Level 2: arguments that consist of claims with either data, warrants or backings, but which do not contain any rebuttals.
Level 3: arguments that consist of a series of claims or counter-claims with either data, warrants or backings, with the occasional weak rebuttals.
Level 4: arguments that consist of a claim with a clearly identifiable rebuttal. They may have several claims and counter-claims.
Level 5: an extended argument with claims, supported by data and warrants with more than one rebuttal.

You can help yourself to develop strong arguments by asking yourself questions that help to promote argument:

- Why do you think that?
- What is your reasons for that?
- Can you think of another argument for your view?
- Can you think of an argument against your view?
- How do you know?
- What is your evidence?
- Is there another argument for what you believe?

The Hadow Report in 1931 recommended nursery schooling, particularly in deprived areas. This report took evidence from Susan Isaacs, who was a philosopher, psychologist and teacher in the 1920s and 1930s (Isaacs, 1954), emphasising the need to help children to be independent and to socialise with other children. The Second World War (1939–1945) saw a great many nurseries hastily opened to meet the needs of childcare, with mothers going out to work to help the war effort. These nurseries tended to be of

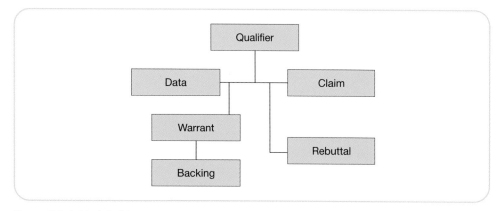

Figure 9.1 A Model of Argument
Source: Adapted from Osborne, Erduran and Simon (2004)

poor quality and lacking in suitably qualified staff (Devereau and Miller, 2003). After the war, many were closed and mothers were encouraged to stay at home to look after their children, particularly following the recommendations from the Ministry of Health in 1945 and the interpretation of Bowlby's research (Bowlby, 1958; see Chapter 1). The next key influence was the Plowden Report (DES, 1967) which advocated the need for high quality early years provision, but not for children under the age of 3 and only part-time. Again, the influence of Bowlby is evident.

Following two decades of relatively little change, the next major influence was the1988 Education Reform Act, and with this came the introduction of the National Curriculum. This did not have a direct impact on the early years, but some argue that the pressure on Key Stage 1 teachers to ensure children performed well in the SATs impacted on the early years curriculum by formalising learning earlier (Cox and Sanders, 1994; Pollard *et al.*, 1994; Anning, 1995; Lally, 1995; Nahmad-Williams, 1998). Children starting school aged 4 were often introduced to a more formal curriculum, with less emphasis on play, than was appropriate for children of that age.

The 1990s saw the catalyst for change in early years provision. A highly influential report, *Starting with Quality*, commissioned by the DfES (1990) into the quality of education offered to 3- and 4-year-olds, was the start of the shake-up in early years educational provision. This became known as the Rumbold Report. The report suggested that the process of education and its content were inseparable, that the context, the people involved and their values and beliefs had a direct impact on children's learning. The report stated that the implementation of education should consider:

- basic provision and organisation;
- approaches to learning;
- curriculum integration;
- role of adults;
- partnership with parents.

The report also noted the variation in provision at a local level and called for central government to give a clear lead and to set a national framework in which local development could take place.

It took six years, but in 1996, *Desirable Outcomes for Children's Learning on Entering Compulsory Education* was published by the School Curriculum and Assessment Authority (SCAA, 1996). This document set out six areas of learning (Desirable Learning Outcomes or DLOs) and the goals that should have been achieved by children of compulsory school age (the term after their fifth birthday). The goals were called Early Learning Goals (ELGs). The learning areas were:

- Personal and Emotional Development;
- Language and Literacy;
- Mathematical Development;
- Knowledge and Understanding of the World;
- Creative Development;
- Physical Development.

The document was clearly influenced by the Rumbold Report and emphasised the importance of partnership with parents. This was the first 'curriculum' document focusing specifically on the early years and it raised the profile of education for the under-5s and the vital role it has to play in a child's development.

With the DLOs came the nursery voucher scheme. The vouchers were available to all parents for three terms, commencing the term after the child's fourth birthday, and paid for five sessions of nursery provision per week. They could be redeemed at any institution providing nursery education which in turn had to be inspected by OFSTED and follow the guidelines of the DLOs. The voucher scheme was supposed to provide parents with choice and access to quality. In fact it was extremely controversial and there were suggestions that schools were altering their admissions policies to allow children to start school earlier without appropriate provision for 4-year-olds (Hofkins, 1996). In 1997, the scheme was abolished. The government provided funding for an expansion of nursery provision for all 4-year-olds and, after time, for all 3-year-olds too.

In 2000, the CGfFS – *Curriculum Guidance for the Foundation Stage* (QCA/DfEE, 2000) – was published and this document took the place of the DLOs. There were the same six areas of learning, although Personal and Social Development became Personal, Social and *Emotional* Development, and Language and Literacy became *Communication*, Language and Literacy. Because the Foundation Stage included the term after a child's third birthday to the end of the reception year, the ELGs remained but were accompanied by 'Stepping Stones' which provided guidance for younger children. The documentation was also far more detailed than the DLOs and focused on aspects of teaching and learning in each area, providing specific examples of practice. The new Early Years Foundation Stage (DfES, 2007), statutory from September 2008, includes the six areas areas of learning but without the stepping stones, although there are stages in each area based on age ranges.

Reflective Tasks

Tracking the changes

There have been a number of changes in the documentation and requirements of the Foundation Stage curriculum since its introduction in 1996. *Desirable Outcomes for Children's Learning on Entering Compulsory Education* (SCAA, 1996) became *Curriculum Guidance for the Foundation Stage* (QCA/DfEE, 2000) and *The Early Years Foundation Stage; Setting the standard for learning, development and care for children from birth to five* (DfES, 2007).

The names of some of the key areas of development have changed over the years since the introduction of the early years curriculum. In the Foundation Stage curriculum documentation (QCA/DfEE, 2000) words were added to the names of the key areas of Language, Literacy and *Communication* and Personal, Social and *Emotional* Development (additions in italics). In the Early Years Foundation Stage (DfES, 2007) Mathematical Development has become *Problem-solving, Reasoning and Numeracy*.

Level 1

Look at the three different documents, *Desirable Outcomes for Children's Learning on Entering Compulsory Education* (SCAA, 1996); *Curriculum Guidance for the Foundation Stage* (QCA/DfEE, 2000) and *The Early Years Foundation Stage; Setting the standard for learning, development and care for children from birth to five* (DfES, 2007). Map out the changes to the requirements in the areas of Language, Literacy and Communication; Personal, Social and Emotional Development and Problem, Solving, Reasoning and Numeracy.

- Why do you think any changes were made? Use theories and ideas from the previous chapters to support your views.

Level 2

- What aspects do you think come under 'emotional development' that differ from 'personal and social development'?

- What aspects do you think come under 'communication' that differ from language and literacy'?

- How does 'problem-solving, reasoning and numeracy' differ from 'mathematical development'?

- What differences do the changes/additions make to you in your work with children? Use theories and ideas from the previous chapters to support your views.

Level 3

As a staff, analyse the Early Years Foundation Stage document (DfES, 2007) and consider how you think any changes in wording will impact upon practice in your setting. Justify your views with examples from your practice and reading/research.

In 2002, the Foundation Stage was established as part of the National Curriculum. At last, this crucial period in a child's development was recognised as a stage in its own right, something that had been called for since the beginning of the last century. It is important, however, to emphasise that there is not a Foundation Stage curriculum; the document is practice *guidance*. It is therefore important for practitioners to provide high-quality experiences based on play and experiential learning initiated by children, rather than a prescribed curriculum.

In 2003, *Birth to Three Matters* (SureStart, 2003) was published as a framework to provide guidelines for practitioners and carers working with children up to 3 years of age. It was not intended to be curriculum guidance in any sense, but did highlight key areas of development and the ways in which the adult can provide and build on experiences which are natural and relevant to the child. The literature review underpinning the framework (David *et al.*, 2003) drew upon a wide range of knowledge, including social work, health and medicine, developmental psychology and sociology. One of the most useful features of this review is the plethora of evidence provided which can be used by practitioners to justify and support their practice. Adams *et al.* (2004: 24), note that practitioners would benefit from a 'clearly argued rationale for the Foundation Stage' in addition to the 'how to do it' document. I would suggest that a similar review of the literature for the Foundation Stage would certainly highlight the theoretical underpinnings and make them explicit to all involved with the education of young children.

The four key aspects of development identified in *Birth to Three Matters* were given the following titles:

- The Strong Child;
- The Skilful Communicator;
- The Competent Learner;
- The Healthy Child.

The aspects were then divided into four components, looking at each aspect in more detail. Although these divisions are in place, it is acknowledged that there is considerable overlap and that development cannot be compartmentalised. This relates to Bruce's principles (1987) and those highlighted in the Early Years Foundation Stage (DfES, 2007) emphasising the importance of a holistic approach to children's development. The significant changes introduced with the new Early Years Foundation Stage (DfES, 2007) is that it incorporates birth to 5, which should focus on continuity and progression through the child's first 5 years of life.

There still appears to be the notion that the reception year is a preparation for Year 1 (Adams *et al.*, 2004) which is in direct contrast to the rhetoric identifying this as a distinct stage within the Foundation Stage. Perhaps we should keep Bruce's revised first principle (2005) in mind, which emphasises that we should provide children with appropriate experiences for their needs as children rather than preparation for adulthood. To narrow this down even further, we could say that the best way to prepare children for the next stage is to give them what they need at their current stage. If we get this right, concerns about progression should not be an issue.

Practical Tasks

Using literacy sources

Level 1

Find a book which has a more detailed account of key events in the history of early childhood education. Make a timeline showing dates, key publications and significant changes. Include more detail when outlining changes after 1996. Compare the historical changes in the documents with your own experiences as a child and the experiences of older family members and colleagues.

Level 2

Look at *Starting with Quality: Report of the Committee of Inquiry into the Educational Experiences Offered to 3 and 4 year olds* (DfES, 1990), known as the Rumbold Report, the *Curriculum Guidance for the Foundation Stage* (QCA/DfEE, 2000) and *The Early Years Foundation Stage* (DfES, 2007). Note down where you can see the Rumbold Report's influence and any significant differences. Provide evidence from your own experiences in education to analyse and compare with your findings from reading.

Level 3

Find a range of responses to the introduction of *Desirable Outcomes for Children's Learning on Entering Compulsory Education* (SCAA, 1996), *Curriculum Guidance for the Foundation Stage* (QCA/DfEE, 2000) and *The Early Years Foundation Stage* (DfES, 2007).

- What are their key arguments for/against?
- What might be influencing their views?
- Has your reading altered your views or influenced your thinking in any way?
- Analyse your own experiences as a child and/or teacher and compare with your findings from reading.

Reflective Tasks

Using the chapters in this book

Level 1

Consider Chapter 4 on Cognitive development and Chapter 5 on Language development. Note how one area of development can affect the other and any similarities in the theories. Analyse your own experiences and provide evidence for and against the argument that language development involves cognition.

Level 2

Consider Chapter 5 on Language development, Chapter 6 on Emotional and moral development and Chapter 7 on Social development. Note how the areas interrelate and the potential impact upon the development of each area. How do the areas interrelate in practice from your observations of children?

Level 3

Consider each chapter in Part 2. As a staff, identify the interrelationship between the areas and the significance of this in terms of a multi-agency approach. Using examples from your own experiences and setting, provide evidence of the impact/significance (or not) of a multi-agency approach.

Schools are also responding to *Every Child Matters* (DfES, 2004) by outlining the way they will address the five outcomes which are listed in Chapter 1. As this document encompasses all children, from birth to 19, there has to be a more coherent approach for it to be successful in its aims. It has a clear objective to make sure children have the best possible start in life by ensuring health, family support, childcare and education services work together using a multi-agency approach. This represents another cycle of change under the remit of the newly formed Children's Services in each local authority. In addition, a new early years professional role will be established for those leading children's centres. This is to ensure that the lead person is trained in child development from birth to 5, rather than the qualified teacher, whose training at present is from 3-year-olds upwards. All children's centres require a qualified teacher to oversee the education side of the provision. One such teacher commented to me on the fact that she did not know anything about children under 3 and felt this was an area she needed to develop. This new early years professional role should go some way towards eradicating the problem. It will be interesting to see how this will impact on early years education.

The focus so far has been on the educational experiences of children up to 5 years of age, but it is also important to note that appropriate early years provision should be reflected in Key Stage 1 (for children aged 5–7). Some schools are using the areas of learning throughout the Foundation Stage and Key Stage 1 to ensure children's experiences do not become too formal and subject-led. The notion of whole school planning, in which Key Stage 1 and Key Stage 2 teachers plan compatible themes and topics to run concurrently, suggests coherence and continuuity. However, if it is a top-down approach with the focus on Key Stage 2 and preparation for this stage, the early years experiences may well not be appropriate. In 1991, when I was teaching a reception class, some of the topics suggested, particularly history-based topics, were wholly inappropriate for younger children and it took some pursuasive argument to ensure my Key Stage 2 colleagues could see that their suggestions lacked relevance for the children in my class! The significance of education in the early years has been raised in recent years and, with it, a broader recognition of the need for a recognised early years curriculum.

The first part of this chapter has provided a historical overview from the 1900s to the present day. Reference has been made to high quality provision and practice, but what are the key features of high quality provision and practice in early years education? We will now turn our attention to four important components:

- play;
- the role of adults;
- the learning environment;
- planning and assessment.

Play

Practical Tasks

Play

For each level, make a list of all the games you enjoyed playing as a child (it might take some time to remember!). Then consider the following questions:

Level 1

- Where did you play?
- Who did you play with?
- Was the play influenced by anything, e.g. television programmes, stories, films?
- Did you engage with a particular toy, e.g. My Little Pony, Barbie, Action Man, Transformers, etc.
- Did you collect anything?

Level 2

- Can you categorise your own play into imaginary play (e.g. role play, playing with toys, etc.) and play with rules (board games, playground games such as 'tig', etc.).
- What sort of play did you enjoy the most?
- Why do you think that was?
- What impact does this knowledge have on the type of play you offer in your work with children?

Level 3

As a staff, consider whether you play as an adult. If so, what do you play and how does it make you feel? If not, why do you think this is?

- In your setting, how you are distinguishing play from other activities?
- Try to categorise the play in your setting into different types.
- How can you develop play in your setting?

We often refer to play and the importance of a play-based curriculum for the early years, but how do we define play? The CGfFS states: 'Well-planned play, both indoors and outdoors, is a key way in which children learn with enjoyment and challenge' (QCA DfEE, 2000: 25). In order for practitioners to provide 'well-planned play' they must have a clear understanding of what play is and how to provide for it. There are many books wholly devoted to the subject of play in early childhood, yet there still seems to be confusion about play in educational settings. In contrast, play in the home seems much easier to define, perhaps because the compound 'well-planned' is not usually associated with it. Bruce (2004a) argues that adult-dominated tasks cannot be described as play, yet as Moyles (1989: 17) suggests, parents 'have a right' to expect play to be different in school from that in the home. This is an interesting point. I am not sure play at school should always be different from play in the home, but as the emphasis at school is on *learning* through play, this needs to be identified. So what is the role of the teacher/practitioner? If play is too directed it is deemed not to be play, yet there is a clear directive and need for play to be planned as part of the educational curriculum. This creates a dichotomy for teachers/practitioners and highlights the need for a clear rationale for play in school.

The value of play is undisputed, and from the theories discussed in Chapter 1 (Froebel, 1826; Piaget, 1950; Bruner *et al.*, 1976; Vygotsky and Cole, 1978) it is apparent that children learn through play. In fact, we all learn through play, both as children and adults. How many of us 'played' on the computer to learn about the different functions and practise their use? Even role play is practised by adults, from people who enjoy amateur acting or historical re-enactments to pretending we are a celebrity chef when cooking, or rehearsing the way we will tackle somebody about a potentially confrontational issue. We learn new skills, explore feelings and deepen our understanding when playing and therefore it is an important tool for learning. Perhaps at the heart of any rationale for play in school should be a good understanding of the value of play, underpinned by theory, to justify its inclusion in an educational setting (see Picture 9.1).

The vocabulary of play can be helpful in terms of defining the type of play, but can also be confusing because of the differing interpretations of the meanings of the words. Some are fairly straightforward:

Picture 9.1 Play in an educational setting
Source: Janine Wiedel Photolibrary/Alamy Images

- **Solitary play** – playing alone.
- **Parallel play** – playing alongside one another, perhaps with the same resources, but each involved in individual play with no explicit communication or collaboration. Bruce (2004a) prefers to call this companionship play to highlight the intrinsic value of being in another's company.
- **Cooperative/collaborative play** – playing together in pairs or as a group, communicating with each other and responding to one another within the play activity.
- **Play with rules** – games with established rules that each participant must follow. Some negotiation in the interpretation of the rules.

Some other terms could be referred to as jargon: technical terms which need explanation:

- **Symbolic play** – Piaget's theory of children's play between the ages of 2 and 6, with children's ideas about the world visible through their play (Piaget, 1976).
- **Epistemic play** – related to the acquisition of knowledge and skills through problem-solving. Asking the question: 'What does this object do?'
- **Ludic play** – fantasy play and practice play. Asking the question: 'What can I do with this object?'

The last two definitions were established by Corrine Hutt and John Hutt (Hutt *et al.*, 1988). It could be considered that over-reliance on epistemic play would provide children with skills but not the ability to transfer those skills to other contexts. Over-reliance on ludic play would help children to express themselves and think creatively, but would not develop knowledge and skills sufficiently. Macintyre (2001: 6) distinguishes two types of play in a similar way, but refers to them as 'play as learning' and 'play as practice'.

Continuing with our examination of terms:

- **Socio-dramatic play:** children acting out social exchanges which they may have experienced or may be imagining, based on issues of personal significance.
- **Exploratory play:** children playing with materials, using their senses to learn more about them and begin to develop concepts about the world in which they live.
- **Imaginative play:** children creating their own imaginary worlds or scenarios, sometimes without resources, other times using resources to represent other things.

Others terms are open to different interpretations and can therefore cause confusion. If we are to have a common language in which to talk about play, it is important that we have a shared understanding. During an in-service course, practitioners were asked to define the following terms: free play, structured play and outdoor play. The differing results indicate the importance of having a shared understanding of the vocabulary:

- **Free play:**

1. Totally child-initiated, with the child selecting the resources.
2. Resources selected by the teacher/practitioner, but with the child able to choose from the selection and to move freely between activities.
3. Resources selected by the teacher/practitioner, with the children in groups, moving to new activities when told.
4. Free to play after finishing work set by the teacher.

It could be argued that the first two points are free play because children are in control of the play and have time to immerse themselves in their play. The second two lack that freedom. If children know that they have only a limited time before being moved on, or are forced to play with other children they have not chosen themselves, this will restrict their involvement and purpose. If children can play only when they have finished the adult-directed activity, some will never get the chance to play and others will rush the directed activity knowing that the time for play is restricted. Bruce (2004a) refers to 'free-flow' play, and has formulated principles for it. Two key factors are time for full involvement, and space, both indoors and outdoors, to move freely. It is important that children are aware of rules, for example, resources which are available and those which are not, but this should not restrict the quality of the involvement in the play.

- **Structured play:**

1. Resources selected by the teacher/practitioner, but with children able to choose from the selection and to move freely between the activities.

2. Resources selected by the teacher/practitioner with a specific task to complete, e.g. an instruction to make a hedgehog with the playdough, but without the teacher working alongside for much of the time.

3. Teacher-led activity, with the teacher working alongside the children to achieve a specific outcome determined by the teacher.

Moyles (1989) argues that the term 'structured play' has not been helpful to teachers/practitioners in that it creates the notion that structured play means with teacher involvement, and unstructured play means with no teacher involvement. The fact remains that the teacher/practitioner is always involved in the provision of time, space, and variety and scope of resources, and in that sense there will always be an element of structure. It is how much involvement the adult has during the play that is important. The final point above, with the teacher/practitioner directing the activity to achieve an imposed outcome, raises the question: can this be defined as play? Perhaps the idea of 'shared control', based on the High/Scope philosophy, is helpful here. If the teacher dominates, the element of play is bound to be affected. The teacher has to take account of the child's interests and allow the child to take the play into another direction. The relationship between teacher and child is paramount, with a positive play culture established in the setting.

- **Outdoor play** (See Picture 9.2)

1. A carefully planned outdoor environment that covers the six areas of learning on a larger scale – in essence, an outdoor classroom. Children are able to access the indoors and outdoors freely.

2. An outdoor environment that has more emphasis on physical play (climbing frame, wheeled toys, small apparatus, etc.), but does address some of the other areas of learning. Children tend to go out in groups.

3. An outdoor environment that promotes physical play with planned physical activities. Children go out in groups or as a class.

4. A large playground that is accessed at the same time by a number of different classes for 'playtime' during assigned breaks through the day.

Clearly there are variations within the above points, but these illustrate the breadth of experiences offered to children. High quality outdoor play is an essential part of a child's development and it is encouraging to note that it has been more carefully considered in recent years. The CGfFS (QCA/DfEE, 2000) highlights the importance of planning play outdoors, which has raised its profile in OFSTED inspections. Bilton (1998) suggests the indoors and outdoors should be viewed as one combined environment, with both areas equally available to the children, a view also taken by Bruce (2004a) in her principles for free-flow play. In many settings, however, this ideal (as outlined in the first point above) is not possible due to staffing, position and size of the area. Settings such as playgroups in church halls, with a car park but no outdoor area for children to access, clearly face a challenge. The key issue is that practitioners recognise the value of outdoor play and plan

Picture 9.2 Outdoor play
Source: John Walmsley/Education Photos

for it within the limits of their provision, with aspirations and an action plan for improvements in order to strive constantly towards the ideal.

In addition to variations in levels of provision, health and safety issues have had a negative impact on the freedom we give to children in the outdoors. As outlined in Chapter 1, Magaret McMillan (1860–1931) realised the importance of the outdoors for health and also for education. Her garden was not the same as the large tarmac playgrounds so commonly seen in schools today; the outdoors was viewed as a place to learn, not a place to take a break from learning. Early years settings have tried to emulate this, but we are often perhaps a little overprotective. A rain shower can cause mayhem with the rush to get inside as though it were acid, not rainwater! Yet children love splashing in puddles and learn so much about their environment through seeing and experiencing the changes. The Scandinavian saying 'there is no such thing as bad weather, only bad clothing' should be a motto in all settings. There is also the concern that children may sustain physical injury which can inhibit the resources and activities provided. Of course it is important to consider all aspects of safety, but it should be risk assessment to *enable* (Alliance for Childhood, 2004), with rules that promote freedom and allow children to take risks within a safe environment.

Critical Discussion

The debate on the nature of childhood

The following letter was published in *The Daily Telegraph* on 10 September 2007. It was signed by a group of academics (including one of the authors of this book), children's authors and charity leaders including Baroness Greenfield, the Director of the Royal Institution, the authors Philip Pullman and Michael Morpurgo, Dr Penelope Leach, the childcare expert and Sue Palmer, author of *Toxic Childhood* (Palmer, 2006). It was published 12 months after a similar letter to the *Telegraph* which led to the paper's 'Hold on to childhood' campaign and provoked a national debate on young people, with contributions from the Archbishop of Canterbury and all major political parties.

Read the letter and decide where you stand in this critical debate. Develop persuasive arguments to support your ideas.

Since last September, when a group of professionals, academics and writers wrote to the *Daily Telegraph* expressing concern about the marked deterioration in children's mental health, research evidence supporting this case has continued to mount. Compelling examples have included UNICEF's alarming finding that Britain's children are amongst the unhappiest in the developed world, and the NCH's report of an explosion in children's clinically diagnosable mental health problems.

We believe that a key factor in this disturbing trend is the marked decline over the last fifteen years in children's play.

Play – particularly outdoor, unstructured, loosely supervised play – appears to be vital to children's all-round health and well-being. It develops their physical coordination and control; provides opportunities for the first-hand experiences that underpin their understanding of and engagement with the world; facilitates social development (making and keeping friends, dealing with problems, working collaboratively); and cultivates creativity, imagination and emotional resilience. This includes the growth of self-reliance, independence and personal strategies for dealing with and integrating challenging or traumatic experiences.

Many features of modern life seem to have eroded children's play. They include: increases in traffic that make even residential areas unsafe for children; the ready availability of sedentary, sometimes addictive screen-based entertainment; the aggressive marketing of over-elaborate, commercialised toys (which seem to inhibit rather than stimulate creative play); parental anxiety about 'stranger danger', meaning that children are increasingly kept indoors; a test-driven school and pre-school 'curriculum' in which formal learning has substantially taken the place of free, unstructured play; and a more pervasive cultural anxiety which, when uncontained by the policy-making process, routinely contaminates the space needed for authentic play to flourish.

A year on from the original letter to the *Telegraph*, therefore, original signatories are joined by other concerned colleagues in calling for a wide-ranging and informed public dialogue about the intrinsic nature and value of play in children's healthy development, and how we might ensure its place at the heart of twenty-first-century childhood.

Research conducted by Moyles *et al.* (2002) found that although play was at the root of practitioners' philosophy and practice, few could provide a theoretical basis, and this lack of understanding was evident in the observations that were made. From the research, it would appear that a shared understanding and common language about play is vital if we are to justify explicitly what we know instinctively about the importance of play in an educational context. The specific words we use to classify and describe play may vary from setting to setting; however, within each individual setting a common language is important, as is the ability to speak from an informed position and communicate this clearly to parents and carers.

Reflective Tasks

Definitions and classifications of play

Level 1

Find some different definitions to describe types of play. Consider the personal play experiences that you outlined in the first play task (p. 270) and see if you can classify those experiences under the definitions you have found.

Level 2

Using a number of different sources, look at the different ways play can be classified. Look at the similarities and differences in the definitions and group together those that you feel are similar. Use your own headings to classify your groupings. Consider your personal play experiences and play you have observed in your own work with children and list them under the appropriate headings you have devised.

Level 3

As a staff and using a number of different sources, consider the classification of play into different categories.

- Why do you think these categories have been chosen? How do they relate to the areas of child development?
- Consider play experiences in your setting. How do you or would you categorise the play?
- Which set of classifications do you feel is the most useful for your setting and why?

The role of adults

The importance of the role of adults in early years settings should not be underestimated. It is a highly specialised, multifaceted role which perhaps does not get the recognition it deserves. Well-qualified staff with a good understanding of how young children learn can ensure that children's early educational experiences are positive and developmental. Research (Siraj-Blatchford *et al.*, 2002) into effective pedagogy in the early years concluded that the most highly qualified staff were the most effective in promoting children's learning. The National Commission on Education (1993) highlighted concerns about the lack of training for teachers in reception classrooms. A small-scale research study found that over half of the reception teachers interviewed were not specifically trained to teach early years children (Nahmad-Williams, 1998). Clearly there are implications for the staffing of early years settings to ensure teachers have the appropriate knowledge in early years practice. The recognition of the importance of the early years, resulting in more government funding, has ensured wider availability of appropriate training. This is a far cry from the 'mum's army' approach advocated in the 1990s by the government, suggesting that the only qualification needed to teach young children was to be a mother. Unsurprisingly, this outraged early years practitioners and the idea was abandoned!

I have outlined the importance of practitioners sharing a common language and being able to speak from an informed position to communicate to parents, but now we need to consider the role of practitioners in their daily interactions with children. The most effective practitioners ensure there is balance between child-initiated and adult-led activities

(Siraj-Blatchford *et al.*, 2002). What is also significant is the practitioner's ability to extend children's learning through high-quality interactions, defined by Siraj-Blatchford *et al.* (2002) as sustained shared thinking. The potential of sustained shared thinking, in which children are involved in in-depth one to one or small group discussions with their peers and adults to further their understanding, is emphasised as a key way in which practitioners can promote learning. Vygotsky's zone of proximal development (Vygotsky and Cole, 1978) highlights the potential for learning through sensitive and appropriate interactions, moving children's learning beyond that which could be achieved alone.

The role of the adult can take many forms:

- *The adult playing alongside children as a friend*: listening, responding, collaborating and sharing.
- *The adult as a model*: taking on a role and modelling the behaviour, such as a doctor or concerned patient in a role play area set up as a hospital.
- *The adult as a facilitator*: providing time, space and resources and adapting these according to the needs of the children, ensuring a balance between child-initiated and adult-initiated activities.
- *The adult as a mediator*: supporting children talking through conflicts and rationalising their behaviour.
- *The adult as initiator*: planning and initiating appropriate focused group work to meet specific learning objectives.
- *The adult as an observer*: planning time to observe children during child-initiated activities to learn more about them as individuals and to assess their development.
- *The adult as a reflective practitioner*: constantly evaluating the provision and making changes as necessary.
- *The adult as a listener and responder*: actively listening and encouraging children to vocalise their views and feelings in a meaningful discussion, rather than a question and answer scenario.
- *The adult as a guide*: encouraging exploration and problem-solving through sensitive intervention and open-ended questioning.

Case Study

Various scenarios

Scenario 1

Helena, Adele and Katie, are playing in the home corner. Helena is issuing instructions to the other girls regarding roles and what they should wear. Both Katie and Adele are ignoring her. Adele is happy in a 'baby' role, squatting down and making 'baby' noises. Katie is trying to encourage the others to help her create a caravan. She has already positioned two chairs as driver and passenger seat and is talking to the others about going on holiday. Helena and Adele are ignoring her, with Adele in her 'baby' role, and Helena issuing orders, unconcerned that no one is listening.

Scenario 2

Paul, Ryan and Rashid are playing with the large wooden bricks. They are building towers and smashing them down rather noisily. There are a number of other activities going on in the classroom, including reading and writing.

Scenario 3

You have set up the water tray with filling and pouring equipment to encourage an understanding of capacity and the language 'full' and 'empty' – this is written into your plan. Jason, Aine and Paul are engrossed in a 'rescue' game, using the containers as boats which they are sinking and then setting up a rescue mission.

Scenario 4

You have a reading corner, which is where children go to sit quietly and read or listen to story tapes. It is also used by you to sit and talk to the whole class on the carpet. You hear a noise coming from the area, and see that the quiet reading corner is being used as a classroom. One child is 'in role' as the teacher, and a small group of children are 'in role' as the rest of the class. The 'teacher' is taking register and using the flip chart to 'teach' the class initial letter sounds.

Reflective Tasks

Role of the adult

Consider the various scenarios in the Case Study above.

Level 1

Apply one of the following roles of the adult to each scenario:

- adult as mediator;
- adult as observer;
- adult as reflective practitioner;
- adult as guide.

Explain why you made these choices.

Level 2

How would you define the role of the adult in each scenario? Could the adult have more than one role in each scenario?

Level 3

Decide if, when and how an adult should intervene in each of the scenarios and give your reasons. How would you define the role of the adult in each scenario? Consider how each scenario might affect future planning.

In considering the importance of the role of the adult as practitioner, we must acknowledge the roles of the most significant and influential adults in a child's life: the parents/carers. As practitioners we should value the child's first educators and strive to establish good partnerships with them. This has not always been the case. Tizard *et al.* (1981) conducted research between 1976 and 1979 into parental involvement in nursery schools. They state that before the 1960s parents were not encouraged to be involved in their children's schooling: 'notices stipulating NO PARENTS BEYOND THIS POINT were not uncommon in state schools in the sixties' (Tizard *et al.*, 1981:5). In the late 1950s and early 1960s, my mother was told not to attempt to teach her children anything before they started school in case she did it incorrectly and caused more problems for the teachers! Thankfully this has changed and partnership with parents is a key aspect of the EYFS (DfES, 2007). Current initiatives such as BookStart, which encourages parents to share books with their babies, and SureStart, which supports families in learning how to communicate and play with their children, indicate a more holistic approach, embracing the value and influence of a child's home life. Communicating with parents/carers is therefore another key role of the early years practitioner and will provide further insight into each child's experiences before and beyond the classroom.

Research

Key findings from research

Early years education has seen enormous developments in recent years and alongside the developments have been research into the effectiveness of educational approaches, new initiatives and changes in policy and practice. Some of the research has informed practice, but much follows changes and so evaluates unproved assumptions that new approaches are effective. Changes made on such assumptions include the introduction of the national literacy (DfEE, 1998) and numeracy strategies (DfEE, 1999b), advice about how to teach phonics (PNS, 2007) and the integration of children's services in children's centres.

We provide a brief description below of some of the key findings from different research projects.

Aubrey *et al.* (2000) in a survey of early years research found that there had been a dip in research from the mid 1980s to 1990s and much of the research has traditionally been funded by the Economic and Social Research Council (ESRC), Nuffield or Rowntree Foundations or encouraged by the Teacher Development Agency. They also found that much research evidence on early childhood development comes from psychology rather than education. They concluded that we had much to learn from international practice and research and that the best research needed to be careful not to be ethnocentric (assume a dominant theory as a measure for judgement). The BERA Early Years Special Interest Group (2003) conducted a survey of children aged between 3 and 6. They found that existing research had either not asked some questions or there were gaps in research; because of the changing contexts of early years education, past research cannot necessarily answer the questions of current practice and care must be exercised when drawing on research from other disciplines.

Siraj-Blatchford *et al.* (2002) researched effective pedagogy in the early years and their key findings were that:

- good outcomes for children are linked to adult–child interactions that involve 'sustained shared thinking' and open-ended questioning to extend children's thinking;
- the most effective settings provide both teacher-initiated group work and freely chosen yet potentially instructive play activities;
- the settings that view cognitive and social development as complementary achieve the best outcomes.

Moyles *et al.* (2002) also researched pedagogical effectiveness in the early years and found that:

- early years pedagogy is an extremely complex phenomenon comprising a wide variety of practices underpinned by philosophies from a number of different contexts;

- effective pedagogical practices are dependent on headteachers/managers developing a strong ethos which values practitioners;
- play is the root of practitioners' thinking and philosophy, but does not have a firm theoretical base and is not always evident in practice;
- practitioners understand and value parental roles and contributions.

Schwienhart *et al.* (1993) undertook a longitudinal research study, which focused on the High/Scope approach. They concluded that spending on early years is an investment and that high-quality, cognitively-oriented nursery education, with adult-guided play and good home–school liaison, enables children to achieve better than their peers through school and function better in society as adults.

The learning environment

'Have nothing in your house that you do not know to be useful, or believe to be beautiful.'
William Morris (1834–96)

We are all affected by the environment in which we live and work. At work, if it is too hot or too cold our concentration and ability to complete our tasks is affected. If there are many distractions or if we have insufficient space we feel frustrated. Tiny details can have a negative impact on our work: poor lighting, an uncomfortable chair or a blunt pencil can affect our whole attitude to the task in hand. Even paint colours in hospitals are carefully chosen because of their calming effects. Young children spend many of their waking hours in early years settings and it is their right to spend that time in a clean, well-lit, comfortable, attractive and well-cared-for environment. I remember visiting a nursery in a deprived inner city district of Sheffield. The nursery staff had to clean the outside area of debris thrown out of the overlooking flats every day before the children arrived. The inside was a haven. Table lamps, settees, attractive soft furnishings and high-quality resources served to provide a safe, warm and caring environment: a place where children wanted to be and where they knew they would be cared for. If we show respect for the environment this in turn reflects the respect we have for the children.

In addition to the aesthetic and practical considerations, the environment can help to promote learning and this is particularly relevant in an early years setting. The Reggio Emilia approach to education places an important emphasis on the environment; in fact, the environment is seen as an integral part of the education process, as Bishop (2001: 73) states: 'The intention has always been that the internal and external spaces of Reggio pre-schools should have educational significance and symbolic meaning for those who use them.' The architecture of early years settings in the UK varies depending on whether they are purpose-built with open spaces and large, low windows, or Victorian buildings with high ceilings and windows. We do not always have a choice about the building, but we can have control over the way the space is organised.

The Early Years Curriculum is provided through the careful planning and resourcing of the indoor and outdoor environment: they are of equal importance. It is essential to view them as one learning environment (see Picture 9.3). The children should be confident and able to pursue their own interests by moving between the areas, both indoors and outdoors. The child's interaction with the environment is central to early learning (Bruce, 1987). The High/Scope approach (Hohmann and Weikart, 2002) highlights the importance of clearly organised space which promotes children's autonomy. Usually the space is divided into different areas. These could be influenced by the areas of learning in the EYFS (DfES, 2007) or National Curriculum subjects (DfES, 1999a), or could be related to different types of play. Depending on the space available, some possible examples are:

Picture 9.3 The learning environment
Source: Duncan Phillips/Report Digital

- home corner and role play
- creative
- small construction
- large construction and blocks
- sand (dry, damp, wet)
- water
- books
- writing
- malleable and tactile
- small world
- music and sound making
- mathematics
- science/explorations
- woodwork/DT
- ICT.

The outdoor environment can be similarly divided, with the activities on a larger, messier scale. There could be additional areas such as wheeled toys/vehicles, climbing apparatus, small apparatus, sensory garden and wildlife area.

When organising the learning environment it is essential to ensure that all areas of provision are inviting and stimulating; clearly defined for both adults and children; carefully planned for every day; monitored and evaluated; maintained and replenished; safe; and clean and tidy.

Within these areas, it is important that resources are organised, and clearly labelled and accessible to both adults and children to encourage independent selection and return. A wide selection of resources should be available at child level to encourage children to make independent choices to support their own learning

Featherstone and Bayley (2001) highlight other considerations, such as light, colour, different floor coverings, textures and senses, furniture, storage and displays. Another aspect is the flexibility of the organisation of furniture so that areas can be enlarged or reduced to suit the activity. Individual settings may prefer to organise the learning environment in slightly different ways or describe the areas using different headings, but the important aspect of the provision is not what it is called, but that it exists in a developmentally appropriate form. This leads on to the next section of the chapter in which we consider both planning and assessment in the early years.

Planning and assessment

The planning and assessment cycle is an important part of any phase of education. A well-planned, appropriate curriculum which builds on the children's previous experiences to develop their learning is at the heart of the process. What is perhaps more challenging for early years practitioners is the lack of knowledge they have about the children before entering the setting, unlike teachers of older children who have records of achievement from the previous class. Another challenge is the uniqueness of the early years curriculum, which is not knowledge-based but experience-based. In addition, there is also the important balance between child-initiated and adult-led activities (Siraj-Blatchford *et al.*, 2002). Planning for adult-led activities is fairly straightforward, but how do you plan for child-initiated learning? Drake (2001: 7) stresses the need to develop a 'fertile environment' which should be thoroughly planned to maximise the potential for learning. The need for children to have time for play is well documented (Lindon, 2001; Bruce, 2004a; Moyles 2005;) and is also highlighted in the CGfFS 'Children need time to become engrossed, work in-depth and complete activities' (QCA/DfEE, 2000: 11). Planning for the Foundation Stage and Key Stage 1 must therefore include planning the appropriate space, time and resources, as outlined in the previous section, to promote the empowerment of children, leading to autonomy and independence.

Planning the curriculum is usually separated into long-, medium- and short-term planning. Long-term plans provide an overview of the curriculum to ensure it is broad and balanced, thoroughly covering all areas of learning. This can be over a year or longer, depending on the policy of the school/setting. Medium-term plans usually focus on half a term to a term and 'chunk' the curriculum outlined in the long-term plans, often into topics or themes. The focus is on progression through the different areas of learning or subjects, ensuring that there is continuity. Short-term plans can be over a week, a day or can be individual lesson plans. These break down the medium-term plans into individual sessions and provide details of timings, the activities, groupings, differentiation, deployment of adults and assessment opportunities. Fisher (1998) identifies long/medium-term plans as planning for the curriculum and short-term plans as planning for the child. This is quite a useful definition, but it could be argued that the child should be at the heart of all planning and therefore planning will vary from setting to setting in order to suits the needs of their children. When the CGfFS (QCA/DfEE, 2000) was introduced there was no planning guidance and many practitioners found it difficult to find appropriate planning formats to work with. In 2001, QCA published additional guidance called *Planning for Learning in the Foundation Stage*. This did not stipulate one way of planning for all, but contained examples of planning from a variety of contexts and settings. The document did not include medium-term plans, only referring to long and short term. The majority of schools, however, plan in three cycles: long, medium and short. The EYFS (DfES, 2007) does not include any specific planning guidance but does provide suggestions for all statements within the six areas of learning. The National Curriculum has never included planning guidance, but has left this to individual schools to decide.

For settings with younger children, there are often two types of short-term plans: an overview of the play experiences for child-initiated activities, focusing mainly on provision of resources, and adult-focused plans with clear learning objectives and differentiation. Again, this will vary from setting to setting. This is a significant difference between planning in the Foundation Stage and planning the curriculum for older children in Key Stage 1. Some of the other considerations are outlined below:

- *Planning and working as a team*: all those who work with the children should participate in the planning process. The lead teacher will have overall responsibility for monitoring the planning and it should clearly identify each adult's role during the sessions.

- *The unplanned curriculum*: the planning should allow flexibility to respond to children's interests and unexpected opportunities for stimulating learning experiences, such as the first snow of the year.

- *Assessment opportunities*: specific opportunities need to be identified and an adult needs to take responsibility for observation and/or recording.

- *Theme/topic*: this is a common and effective way of integrating different areas of learning. It is also a way of beginning from children's interests and experiences. Many topics can provide useful links between home and the setting, allowing children and their parents to contribute and become involved.

It is difficult to separate planning and assessment as the two are inextricably linked, so we will now consider the role of assessment in the overall process.

> Assessment gives insight into children's interests, achievements and possible difficulties in their learning from which next steps in learning and teaching can be planned. It also helps ensure early identification of special educational need and particular abilities.
> (QCA/DfEE, 2000: 24)

Assessment allows us to gather information about a wide range of pupil characteristics in order to make decisions about the curriculum they need; help children's confidence and motivation; set targets; accumulate records of progress; inform others who have to make decisions about pupils; and help us to evaluate the curriculum and the setting to provide information on our effectiveness as teachers. In addition, we are also to be accountable to a wide range of people and have to meet legislative requirements. These last two must not overshadow the needs of the child; we must remember that we assess in order to enable us to support all individuals so that they can reach their full potential, and external pressures should not have a negative impact by creating a climate of pressure to push children on before they are ready. Assessment should be used to serve the curriculum rather than be its master. In other words, we should not 'teach to the test', but use our assessments of the children to ensure we are providing an appropriate curriculum matched to their needs.

There are two main types of assessment: formative and summative. **Formative assessment** informs the planning of the curriculum. It is often based on informal observations of children but can also involve planned observations of individuals or groups and is also used to record significant achievements during day-to-day experiences. It is ongoing, and effective practitioners are constantly assessing children during a range of activities in different contexts. **Summative assessment** is simply a summary of a child's attainments and often involves a numerical score or grade. The information is used to report to parents or could support the identification of special needs. A set of scores for a class or group can be used for target-setting or other decision-making, such as whole curriculum planning; whole school evaluation; value added information; and local and national accountability. Thankfully, in the early years summative assessment does not involve tests as it does in the later years.

The principles of assessment include using existing skills, knowledge and understanding as a starting point by valuing children's past experiences and existing achievements. Practitioners can use baseline assessments (initial assessments on entry to a setting) to provide appropriate starting points and to monitor progress. Building good relationships with parents and carers will allow the assessment process to be a partnership, enabling the achievements in the home to contribute to the child's profile in the setting (Siraj-Blatchford, 1998). Assessment in the early years should also be holistic, which means assessing across different areas of learning within one activity or observation. In other words, an activity might be planned to develop mathematical understanding, but children do not compartmentalise their learning and neither should we! So if a child demonstrates excellent communication skills within this activity, it should be recorded. Manageable recording systems should be developed so that significant progress can be noted at any time and added to a child's profile.

Strategies for assessment include:

- *observation*: incidental, planned, participant and non-participant;
- *talking and listening to children*: discussions, conversations and questioning;
- *assessing products*: drawings, early writing, paintings and models.

Observations should be built into the planning so that time is established to ensure all children are observed and assessed over an identified period of time.

Case Study

Playing in the water tray

Two children are playing in the water tray. They are filling bowls with plastic fruit. A teacher from another class joins them.

Child A:	We're making fruit salad!
Teacher:	Oh lovely, can I have some please?
Child B:	Yes – you'll need a spoon (*gives teacher a spoon*)
Teacher:	This is delicious – what is this? (*pointing to the water in with the fruit in the bowl*)
Child A:	Fruit
Teacher:	No, I mean the liquid at the bottom of the fruit (*pointing again to the water*)
Child B:	Um … juice … orange juice! Let's squeeze some oranges to make the juice!
Child A:	Yes … we need the oranges.

Both children grab the bowls excitedly, take out all the plastic oranges and begin to 'squeeze' out the juice into the bowls.

Child B:	We did this when we made smoothies.
Teacher:	Oh have you been making smoothies?
Child A:	Yeh – we made smoothies
Teacher:	I've never made a smoothie – what did you do?
Child B:	We had to squeeze out the juice like this (*demonstrates with the plastic fruit*)
Teacher:	Did you like them?
Child B:	Yes!

Child A has got a plastic orange stuck in the bottom of a sundae glass and is trying to remove it.

Teacher:	Oh dear, is it stuck? How can you get it out?

Child B (*grabbing the glass*) I can do it (*tries to grasp it with his fingers, but it doesn't move*)
Teacher: Can you try another way?
Child B tries a spoon but it doesn't work.
Teacher: What happens if you fill it with water?
Child B pours water into the sundae glass and the orange bobs up.
Child B (*laughing*) Look … did you see it? It bounced. Look!
The teacher leaves as the two children continue to pour water into the glass to watch the orange bounce.

Reflective Tasks

Identifying learning through play

Level 1

- In the Case Study above, identify the two children's previous experiences.
- Can you identify any learning taking place during this interaction?

Level 2

- How does the teacher's interaction impact upon the learning in this activity?
- Plan an adult-focused activity to build on this learning.

Level 3

Consider the learning taking place.

- What are the implications for practice and provision in your setting?
- How will you have to change your plans?

The Foundation Stage Profile

In the Foundation Stage summative assessment is completed through use of the Foundation Stage Profile (QCA, 2003). Prior to its introduction in 2002, statutory base-line assessments were used to assess children in their first term in the reception year. The education authorities could select from a number of different schemes, of which there were over 50. This meant that results could not be analysed and compared within a national context as there was no parity in the schemes used. This led to the adoption of one assessment profile to be used by all schools and completed by the end of the reception year. The implementation of the profile has had a mixed reaction, with differing viewpoints about its usefulness and application. As with all summative assessments, the judgements provide an indication of a child's achievements and attainment, but should not be used in isolation and should be accompanied by a portfolio of evidence. Effective record-keeping is therefore an important aspect of assessment.

Key Stage 1 – SATs

In Key Stage 1, children in Year 2 have to complete statutory assessments, known as SATs, in English and maths. These used to take the form of tests, but after the years of controversy after their introduction within the National Curriculum changes have occurred. Many educators and parents questioned the appropriateness of testing young children, and in 2005 new arrangements were introduced focusing on teacher assessments rather than the tests. The tests have not been abolished; the guidance is to use them to support teacher assessment with teacher discretion applied in deciding on how many and which tests to use. This has gone some way towards appeasing the negative views on testing, but the fact that the tests still exist falls short of the total abolition demanded by many.

Having considered the key features of high-quality practice, we will now look more closely at the six areas of learning within the Foundation Stage. The purpose is to raise issues rather than examine each area in detail. We will take the areas in the order they appear in the EYFS.

Personal, social and emotional development

Personal, Social and Emotional Development permeates the whole curriculum. There are six aspects within this key area of learning: dispositions and attitudes; self-confidence and self-esteem; making relationships; behaviour and self-control; self-care; and sense of community. Pascal (2003) outlines three core elements of early learning: emotional well-being; social competence and self-identity; and attitudes and dispositions. These core elements are attributed to learning in the broadest sense and emphasise the fundamental impact this area of learning has on all the others. Although there is no evidence to suggest that the areas of learning are in any way hierarchical, it is pertinent that this is the first area of learning.

It is significant that the word 'emotional' was added to the learning area in the CGfFS (QCA/DfEE, 2000) when it was not included in the Desirable Outcomes (SCAA, 1996). The importance of emotional intelligence (Goleman, 1996) and emotional literacy have been emphasised in recent years and focus on developing our ability to understand and handle our own emotions in addition to understanding and responding appropriately to others' emotions. Important factors to take into account are: significant others, self-esteem, independence, interpersonal skills and moral development. The values we demonstrate within our settings and the way we communicate these will have an influence on the children in our care. Personal and social skills are learned in daily interactions with others. Our sense of self is directly related to the relationships we form with others. This area of learning cannot be measured in the same way as literacy and numeracy; we do not hear about it when it is successful, only when there are issues such as inappropriate behaviour or poor social skills. In relation to dealing with challenging behaviour, Cooper *et al.* (2001) highlight the advantages of a holistic approach, also advocated by the Steer Report (Steer, 2005). This holistic approach is a key feature of the Foundation Stage, underpinned by this key area of learning. Personal, Social and Emotional Development is only specified in the Foundation Stage; from Key Stage 1 onwards there is a framework for personal, social and health education, and citizenship, but this is non-statutory guidance at Key Stages 1 and 2. This is somewhat puzzling and could be construed as undermining the importance of this area in comparison with the statutory subjects outlined in the National Curriculum.

Reflective Tasks

Rules

Level 1

Think back to your own childhood and consider the rules in your house.

● Who enforced these rules and in what way?

- Can you remember any phrases that your parents regularly used to remind you how to behave?
- How did you respond?
- Have these values influenced your behaviour today, either by your following them or deliberately doing the opposite?

Level 2

Consider your observations of the children you work with.

- Were you aware of any rules?
- How did the you and other adults communicate values to the children?
- How was 'appropriate' behaviour encouraged?
- Did you agree with all you observed? If not, why not? Does this indicate a different set of values?

Level 3

Consider how you promote positive values in your setting.

- Do you have rules and if so, why?
- Do you all agree with the rules?
- Take one aspect of learning within Personal, Social and Emotional Development and think of a variety of practical activities which would promote this area of development.

Communication, Language and Literacy

Since the introduction of the SATs at the end of Key Stage 1 and the literacy hour in primary schools (DfES, 1998), teachers can become preoccupied with literacy – the teaching of reading and writing – and put less emphasis on the development of speaking and listening skills. The Literacy Framework was revised in 2007, with the inclusion of speaking and listening which was mysteriously absent from the 1998 version. It is encouraging that in the Foundation Stage, both communication and language are emphasised and 'literacy' is the final, rather then the first, word in the title of this area of learning. Oral skills are the foundations for learning and the development of these skills are paramount to creating successful readers and writers (Tough, 1977; Wells, 1986; Norman, 1990).

Communication, Language and Literacy is separated into six aspects: language for communication; language for thinking; linking sounds and letters; reading; writing; and handwriting.

- *Language for communication* involves the development of pragmatic skills, which is about interacting with others, participating in conversations and responding and taking turns. This includes phonology, syntax and semantics, which have been explored in more detail in Chapter 5.
- *Language for thinking* could be referred to as 'talking to learn' (McDonagh and McDonagh, 1999). This involves cognitive development: 'using talk to organise, sequence and clarify thinking, ideas, feelings and events' (QCA/DfEE, 2000: 58). It also recognises the significance of imagination and using language to express our creativity.
- *Linking sounds and letters* is the development of phonological awareness through nursery rhymes and language play, leading on to a more structured teaching of phonics for reading and writing. The Rose Report (DfES, 2006) highlights the importance of high-quality phonics teaching. The website provides further information on this topic.

● *Reading* includes wide experiences of a range of books, both fiction and non-fiction, to foster a love of reading; knowledge about print and developing a sight vocabulary; using different strategies to read, including applying phonics skills; and using books as a model to promote writing development. (See Picture 9.4.)

Picture 9.4 Sharing books
Source: John Walmsley/Education Photos

- *Writing* includes role play or emergent writing when the child makes marks during play to represent meaning (shopping list, waitress writing down orders); structuring writing; applying phonic skills; and different types of writing.
- *Handwriting* is about the physical act of forming letters, including hand/eye coordination; the development of fine motor skills; pencil hold; letter formation and the development of handwriting style.

In the UK we focus on literacy skills earlier than many other European countries (Dryden *et al.,* 2005). Four of the aspects outlined above relate to literacy; it is essential to place due emphasis on oracy skills and not to feel pressurised by the external pressures of testing to overlook this crucial area of development. Phonics is often taught through use of worksheets and writing-based activities, yet phonological awareness is all about hearing and making the sounds of words. The oral work in phonics is essential to develop both reading and writing. Talking before writing is very important and encourages children to clarify and expand their ideas before committing them to paper. Oracy, or speaking and listening, should therefore be at the centre of our approach to teaching and learning.

At Key Stage 1, the National Curriculum area of English is subdivided into three areas: speaking and listening, reading and writing. Since the publication of the Rose Report (DfES, 2006), early reading has come under much scrutiny. The teaching of phonics has been hotly debated, with the conclusions from the report indicting that a systematic synthetic approach is the most successful. The debate will continue, but what is important is that schools acknowledge some of the other key messages from the report, including providing children with rich reading experiences and the importance of the development of oral language.

Reflective Tasks

Learning to read

Level 1

- Can you remember learning to read?
- Can you remember any books you read at primary school?
- What do you do now as an adult if you come across a word you have never seen before?
- What are the strategies you put in place?

Access and read the explanation of the 'Simple View of Reading' on the standards website by going http://www.standards.dcsf.gov.uk/primaryframework/foundation/early/simple and also access one other source about learning to read.

- Can you remember learning any of these strategies and do you use any now?

Level 2

Find definitions for synthetic and analytic phonics.

- What are the arguments for and against?

Consider your observations of children reading books in school.

- Have you seen any examples of the teaching of phonics or the application of phonics as children read?
- Could you identify them as synthetic or analytic?

Level 3

Find definitions for synthetic and analytic phonics.

- What is the research underpinning the arguments for and against?
- Is it substantial or limited?
- Consider the way phonics is taught in your setting. Is it underpinned by an understanding of the theory behind it?
- Has your reading altered your views about the way phonics is taught in your setting?

Research

Early years literacy – a comparative study

Patricia Beckley, Bishop Grosseteste University College Lincoln

Early years literacy is currently a focus of debate, heightened by the recent publication of the Rose Report (DfES, 2006) encouraging the use of a synthetic phonic approach. Conclusions of the Education Select Committee (*Teaching Children to Read*, DfES, 2005) acknowledged the importance of teaching phonics, but not as an isolated skill for children under 5 years of age. Recommendations included that the DfES should commission further research into early reading.

This empirical study considers comparative approaches to early years literacy between settings in Lincolnshire, England, and Hedmark, Norway. It is drawn from a historical perspective of policies based on early years literacy in the two countries, discussing what factors influenced the evolution of the policies with a comparison of them. From this study findings are made to ascertain the understanding of the policies by the practitioners who are implementing them. Consideration is given as to how the policies work in practice.

Methodology includes interviews and questionnaires with early years policy-makers, practitioners, children, carers and observations of practice. Reflections are made on the Literacy curriculum covered by young children, the perceptions of it by various stakeholders, its implementation and the approaches used in the settings. Positive aspects of the provision will be identified with indications of possible ways forward for the enhancement of early years literacy learning and teaching.

Reflective Tasks

Problem-solving, Reasoning and Numeracy – mathematical development

by Helen Fielding, Bishop Grosseteste University College Lincoln

The Problem-solving, Reasoning and Numeracy development guidance in the Early Years Foundation Stage follows the same categories of mathematics as the National Primary Strategy for Numeracy for Key Stages 1 and 2. The suggested mathematics for this age group is organised into three sections; these are 'Numbers as labels and for counting', 'Calculating' and 'Shape, space and measures'.

Numbers as labels and for counting makes a clear distinction between nominal numbers, which represent objects which not have been allocated in terms of size (for example, house or bus numbers), and counting numbers or cardinal numbers, which are those we count with and are the basis of arithmetic. The recording of 'how many?' or 'how much?' is a vital and basic aspect of our lives from an early age. The consideration of *counting numbers*, e.g. 1, 2, 3, etc. and zero, is an important aspect of early mathematics. Counting, the ordering of whole numbers in a sequence, is a complex process and not as simple as it initially appears.

Gelman and Gallister (1978) identified the principles of counting, all of which are needed in order to do so successfully. These five principles may not all develop at the same rate:

- *One to one correspondence*: each item is to be counted only once, this is often done by touching, pointing, moving or nodding towards each object.
- *Stable order principle*: the understanding that the order of the number names remains in a constant order.
- *Cardinal principle*: (the cardinal number indicates the quantity of a group) this involves knowing that the final number said indicates the number of items in the set.
- *Abstraction principle*: the understanding that any objects can be counted and that they do not need to be exactly the same (3 spaniels and 4 poodles is 7 dogs).
- *Order – irrelevance principle*: objects can be counted beginning with any item whatever its position within the set.

Calculating is very closely linked to 'Numbers as labels and for counting'. Despite its rather theoretical sounding title, the emphasis at this age is very much on the practical and real-life opportunities. The guidance suggests that all the four rules of arithmetic will be encountered in a structured way and possibly in a spontaneous way in response to a child's discoveries or conversation. These should be planned into everyday routines where possible, for example, the sharing of food between a small number of children.

Shape and Space will occur in many activities in an early years setting. Here again, the emphasis is on the practical opportunities, looking at the properties rather than learning names in a rote fashion. Children will inevitably have had a variety of experiences and some may be ready to learn the vocabulary relating to shape and space. Much positional language can be reinforced in an everyday setting in relation to where the children sit and the placing of toys.

Measures at this early stage focuses on the making of comparisons. Much of this occurs using sand or water leading to ideas of full and empty or in the packing away of bricks into the box and seeing how many can be fitted in. There are many occasions in an early years setting to create structured occasions to allow children to discover and compare while reinforcing appropriate vocabulary.

Mathematics is an area of the curriculum which many adults and some practitioners feel less confident in or anxious about. However, it is important to have a confident understanding of the areas of mathematics, the links between them and vocabulary to be taught. When working with young children, we need to take care not to perpetuate a feeling of anxiety, dislike or disinterest in mathematics. It is not always easy to promote a positive approach and attitude towards mathematics when your own early experiences were not encouraging. However, the opportunity to share children's enthusiasm for the discovery of early mathematics can be very refreshing and may shed light on some of the joys of mathematics. 'The teaching of mathematics to young children is a most rewarding adventure, particularly to those [students] who found the subject difficult when they were at school' (Frobisher *et al.*, 1999: iv).

If practitioners can begin to envisage themselves as mathematicians and share a child's natural enthusiasm and interest, this will contribute to the promotion of positive values and effective teaching and learning. (See Picture 9.5.)

Level 1

Use the Foundation Stage Guidance and the 'Supplement of examples: Reception' in the *Framework for teaching mathematics from Reception to Year 6* (DfEE, 1999b), and find statements which exemplify each of Gelman and Gallistel's five counting principles.

Level 2

Reflect on your experiences of counting with young children.

- Which activities have you seen that effectively support one or more of the five counting principles?
- How were these activities planned in order to avoid perpetuating any misconceptions?

Level 3

Consult the guidance for *Mathematics for Foundation Stage: Nursery* and *Reception* (DfES, 2002). These are available on the DCSF website (http://www.standards.dfes.gov.uk/primaryframework/mathematics. Use these resources to help you develop your own subject knowledge. Aim to track the development of counting and consider how it links into early addition.

Picture 9.5 Enjoying maths
Source: John Walmsley/Education Photos

Knowledge and Understanding of the World

Knowledge and Understanding of the World is a very broad area of the Early Years Foundation Stage (DfES, 2007), which encompasses six subjects/areas in the National

Curriculum (DfEE, 1999a); geography, history, design technology, science, information and communication technology (ICT), and citizenship. However, unlike the curriculum at Key Stage 1 (DfEE, 1999a), it does not identify what knowledge should be taught to children, but rather the skills they should be supported in developing, so in many ways Knowledge and Understanding of the World is a misnomer!

The original documentation setting out the foundation stage for learning (SCAA, 1996: 4), identified that children's knowledge and understanding of the world should develop as they, 'explore and recognise features of living things, objects and events in the natural and man made world and look closely at similarities and differences, patterns and change'. This quotation illustrates the skills embodied in the key area of knowledge and understanding of the world: observation, classification and interpretation, developed through exploration. Exploration is a form of play (Johnston, 2005) which supports all aspects of young children's development; is an essential prerequisite in enquiry and embodies many other skills that are essential in young children.

Reflective Tasks

Knowledge and unerstanding of the world

Level 1

Use the EYFS practice guidance document (DfES, 2007) and look at the key area for Knowledge and Understanding of the World. Consider how the following activities fit into the different early learning goals:

- making a musical instrument;
- explore bubbles;
- sorting out family tree pictures;
- observing seeds and leaves using a digital microscope;
- making chapattis.

Level 2

Consider some of the recent experiences you have planned.

- What activities have you used to develop the early learning goals in the key area Knowledge and Understanding of the World (DfES, 2007)?
- How could you change the activities to better meet the early learning goals?

Level 3

- Reflect on the planning in your setting.
- How have you developed each early learning goal in the key area Knowledge and Understanding of the World (DfES, 2007)?
- How could you change the activities to better meet the early learning goals?

Knowledge and Understanding of the World should not be taught as separate strands or even separately from other key areas of development, rather it should be taught in a realistic cross-curricular way. Figure 9.2 shows ideas for cross-curricular development from the starting point of the story book *The Snow Lambs* (Glori, 1995) and using a sheep's fleece (see also de Bóo, 2004, and Picture 9.6).

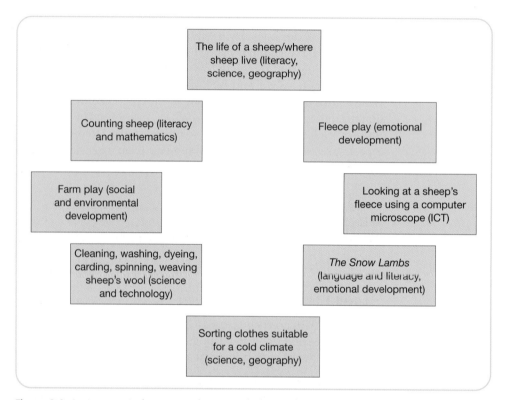

Figure 9.2 A cross-curricular approach to Knowledge and Understanding of the World

Picture 9.6 Sheep play area

Reflective Tasks

Physical Development

Physical development is the way in which children master control of their bodies (Beaver *et al*., 1999; Tassoni, *et al*., 2002). The impact of physical development is clear when we consider the earliest physical reflexes of the newborn and the active 8-year-old with mastery over balance, control and coordination. Physical development not only helps to develop gross and fine motor skills; it has an impact on all other areas of learning. When children can actively explore their environment, using all of their senses, they develop knowledge and understanding of the world in which they live. This then promotes an increasing independence and significantly contributes to a child's social, emotional and intellectual development.

The development of motor skills has three key areas: gross motor skills, locomotor skills and fine motor skills. Gross motor skills enable the child to use large movements and use the large muscles in the body required for movements such as jumping, hopping and climbing. Locomotor skills are closely associated with gross motor skills but are concerned with movement from one place to another (Hughes, 2002), requiring balance and control. Fine motor skills enable children to manipulate objects by using the small muscles in their hands, for example, fastening buttons or threading beads. Bee and Boyd (2007) note that there is a difference between boys and girls in the visible development of bones in the wrist. The full nine bones are visible in girls' wrists (at 51 months) approximately 15 months before they are visible in boys' wrists (at 66 months) (see Chapter 3). This suggests that this physiological difference may well have an impact on the stage of development of fine motor skills, with girls showing earlier mastery of fine manipulative development than boys. In school this may well be significant, particularly in terms of handwriting.

Young children need space to practise their developing physical skills. This space should be planned for, accessible and freely available. The outdoor classroom and the indoor classroom should be treated as equal spaces in which children can experience a wide range of activities, with equal access to both (Lindon, 2005). One of the current issues, often blamed on modern life, is the limited amount of physical exercise and play in the outdoors available to children. There are many reasons for this, such as safety fears, smaller/no gardens, increase in technology and use of the car. There is, however, a concerted effort to reverse this trend, particularly in view of the worrying increase in obesity. Perhaps the sign 'Keep off the grass', seen in many public places, should be altered to read 'Please play on the grass' to indicate the need for more outdoor space and opportunities for children to play.

Level 1

Consider all of the games that you played in the playground as a child.

- What types of motor skills were you developing?
- Do you think children play the same sorts of games today?

Level 2

- How does your setting cater for the three different types of motor development?
- Do you feel that there are areas that could be developed further?
- If so, in what way?

→

Level 3

Consider the provision for physical development in your setting. Draw a plan of your outdoor area. Next to it, draw a plan of your ideal outdoor area to maximise the three types of motor development. How could you go some way towards achieving the ideal in your current space, without need for extra funding? Be creative with your ideas!

Reflective Tasks

Creative development

Ashley Compton, Bishop Grosseteste University College Lincoln

Creativity is a word frequently used in education but it lacks a clear definition. Within Birth to Three Matters (SureStart, 2003) it is associated closely with learning and involves exploration, experimentation, resourcefulness and making connections. However, in the Early Years Foundation Stage (DfES, 2007) it is tied more to the arts since one of the areas of learning is Creative Development, which comprises art, music, dance, role play and imaginative play. When children reach Key Stage 1, creativity has become a key thinking skill in the National Curriculum (DfEE 1999a).

Researchers writing about creativity also lack a common definition, although they often share features. Bruce believes that creativity involves an individual response and 'is about having new ideas and ways of doing things' (Bruce, 2004b: 18). Duffy is reluctant to define creativity because she feels that this could be limiting and restrictive. However, she considers that creativity includes problem-solving and 'connecting the previously unconnected in ways that are new and meaningful to the individual concerned' (Duffy, 1998: 18). Beetlestone (1998) has a construct of creativity that is quite broad. It incorporates the ideas of making new things, making connections and problem-solving, mentioned above, but also includes self-expression, awe and wonder, curiosity and exploration. Craft defines a specific form of creativity, little 'c' creativity (LCC), which is about resourcefulness and the choices you make throughout life. She sees 'possibility thinking as the foundation of creativity' (Craft, 2002: 113) and believes that being imaginative is a vital part of this. Craft makes a distiction between being imaginative and mere imagining. For her, being imaginative involves new ideas or connections, while imagining may be a copy of previous experience. All of these authors are writing about creativity with respect to young children and education and all share the belief that creativity is relevant to children and can be developed. Therefore, whichever definition you choose to adopt, there is a role for educators in developing it.

How can educators help?

- provide opportunities for children to make decisions and encourage such decision-making;
- provide problems for the children to solve and encourage them to find their own solutions when they encounter difficulties;
- provide a range of media, including sound and movement, for children to express their own ideas, not just copy a prescribed model;
- provide role play and small world areas with a range of resources which can be used in many ways;
- be willing to suspend disbelief and enter the play without directing it.

Freya had played 'pass the parcel' at a birthday party. She decided to incorporate this into her play. She had an imaginary parcel and imaginary music but was very clear in passing the parcel and knowing where it stopped. She was also definite about what was in each layer as the parcel was unwrapped. Instead of the usual sweet or pencil there were larger presents such as ladders and live chickens. This spurred the other participants to imagine what could be in their layers. If the adults involved had not allowed the unusual parcels and explained what was realistic, it would have reduced the play to a mere recreation of an event rather than an imaginative exploration of it. In this case no resources were needed but the adults did have to suspend their disbelief and allow the time and space for exploration.

Level 1

Think about what creativity means to you. What are you currently doing to help develop the children's creativity? Read Bruce (2004b). Has this altered your views of creativity? What can you do to the environment you work in to develop children's creativity further?

Level 2

Think about how you identify creativity in children. Read Duffy (1998). How can you create conditions for developing creativity within your setting? How will you assess whether children have developed their creativity?

Level 3

Read Craft (2002). She raises the challenge of balancing a large number of children and a prescribed curriculum with encouraging curiosity and possibility thinking (Craft, 2002: 116). How can you achieve this balance? How can you encourage creative teaching throughout your staff, as well as opportunities for creative learning?

Transition from the Foundation Stage to Key Stage 1

In this chapter we have focused mainly on learning in the Foundation Stage, but at the end of this stage the children will move into Key Stage 1 which is, potentially, a very different, subject-based curriculum. The play-based curriculum of the Foundation Stage is replaced by a different pedagogy with a focus on more formal learning (Dryden *et al.*, 2005). A smooth transition is essential for children to experience continuity and minimal disruption to their learning and security. Sanders *et al.* (2005) conducted a study into the transition from the Foundation Stage to Year 1 and their findings suggested there were some challenges, including moving from a play-based curriculum to a more structured curriculum; difficulties with less mature children; parental concerns. The recommendations include more play-based learning in Year 1; maintenance of friendship groups; good communication between staff and parents; and viewing transition as a process rather than a one-off event, with time to adapt to the new situation.

The Foundation Stage has been welcomed by most practitioners and promotes appropriate early educational experiences for children. The report by Adams *et al.* (2004) into the reception year found that some reception teachers were still feeling pressure from their Key Stage 1 colleagues to prioritise literacy and numeracy, as these are the focus for the SATs at the end of Key Stage 1. Perhaps the changes to the SATs will relieve some of this pressure, but it is down to the Foundation Stage practitioners to have a good knowledge of child development, strong convictions about their practice and to be able to articulate their philosophy confidently to colleagues and parents. This will, perhaps, also impact upon Key Stage 1 practitioners in ensuring the curriculum remains firmly rooted in good early years practice.

Summary

→ Education in the early years did not have equality, consistency or sufficient funding until the changes which began in 1996 with *Desirable Outcomes for Children's Learning* (SCAA, 1996) and government funding for part-time nursery education for 4-year-olds.

→ Changes from 2000 to 2007 have been rapid, culminating in the Early Years Foundation Stage (DfES, 2007), compulsory from September 2008.

→ The Practice Guidance for the Foundation Stage has six areas of learning and development: Personal and Social and Emotional Development; Communication, Language and Literacy; Problem-solving, Reasoning and Numeracy; Knowledge and Understanding of the World; Creative Development; and Physical Development.

→ The Early Years Foundation Stage is from 0 to 5 years and Key Stage 1 from 5 to 7 years.

→ It is important for early years practitioners to provide high-quality experiences based on play and experiential learning initiated by children, rather than a prescribed curriculum.

→ Some schools are using the areas of learning throughout the Foundation Stage and Key Stage 1 to ensure children's experiences do not become too formal and subject-led.

→ In order for practitioners to provide well-planned play experiences they must have a clear understanding of what play is and how to provide for play.

→ A shared understanding and common language about play is vital if practitioners are to justify explicitly what they know instinctively about the importance of play in an educational context.

→ The importance of the role of adults in early years settings should not be underestimated. It is a highly specialised, multifaceted role which perhaps does not get the recognition it deserves.

→ The most effective practitioners ensure there is balance between child-initiated and adult-led activities (Siraj-Blatchford *et al.*, 2002).

→ Communicating with parents/carers is a key role of the early years practitioner and will provide vital insight into each child's experiences before and beyond the classroom.

→ A carefully planned, stimulating environment can help to promote learning and this is particularly relevant in an early years setting. The Reggio Emilia approach to education places an important emphasis on the environment; in fact the environment is seen as an integral part of the education process.

→ The early years curriculum is provided through the careful planning and resourcing of the indoor and outdoor environment. They are of equal importance and should be viewed as one learning environment.

→ The planning and assessment cycle is an important part of any phase of education. A well-planned, appropriate curriculum which builds on the children's previous experiences to develop their learning is at the heart of the process.

→ Planning the curriculum is usually separated into long-, medium- and short-term planning. Fisher (1998) identifies long/medium-term plans as planning for the curriculum and short-term plans as planning for the child.

→ The principles of assessment include using existing skills, knowledge and understanding as a starting point by valuing children's past experiences and existing achievements.

→ Strategies for assessment include observation, talking and listening to children, and assessing products.

→ The Foundation Stage Profile and Key Stage 1 SATs are statutory summative assessments.

→ Although the curriculum should not be compartmentalised in the early years, each area of learning does have distinctive features and specific issues to be considered.

→ A smooth transition from the Foundation Stage to Key Stage 1 is essential for children to experience continuity and minimal disruption to their learning and security.

Key Questions

● What are the key historical developments in policy and practice in early years education?

● What is the value of play in learning?

● What are some of the issues related to the vocabulary of play?

● What different roles can the adult take in supporting children's learning?

● How can the environment promote learning?

● What is meant by the planning and assessment cycle and how are the two dependent upon each other?

● How do each of the six areas of learning and development contribute to a child's knowledge, understanding, skills and attitudes?

References

Adams, S., Alexander, E., Drummond, M. and Moyles, J. (2004) *Inside the foundation Stage – Recreating the Reception Year. Final Report.* London: ATL Publications.

Alliance for Childhood (2004) http://www.allianceforchildhood.org.uk/home/projects_initiatives/campaign_action_from_the_children_are_unbeatable_alliance/

Anning, A. (ed.) (1995) *A National Curriculum for the Early Years.* Buckingham: Open University Press.

Beaver, M., Brewster, J., Jones, P., *et al.* (1999) *Babies and Young Children. Book 1. Early Years Development.* Cheltenham: Stanley Thornes

Bee, H. and Boyd, D. (2007) *The Developing Child.* New York: Pearson Education.

Beetlestone, F. (1998) *Creative Children, Imaginative Teaching.* Buckingham: Open University Press

BERA (British Educational Research Association) Early Years Special Interest Group (2003) *Early Years Research: Pedagogy, Curriculum and Adult Roles, Training and Professionalism.* Southwell: BERA

Bertram, T. and Pascal, C. (2001) *OECD Thematic Review of Education and Care: Background Report for the United Kingdom.* Available from: www.oecd.org.dataoecd/48/16/2479205/pdf

Bilton, H. (1998) *Outdoor Play in the Early Years.* London: David Fulton

Bishop, J. (2001) 'Creating Places for Living and Learning', in Abbott, L. and Nutbrown, C. (eds) *Experiencing Reggio Emilia.* Buckingham: Open University Press

Bowlby, J. (1958) 'The Nature of a Child's Tie to his Mother', *International Journal of Psychoanalysis*, 39: 350–73

Bruce, T. (1987) *Early Childhood Education*. London: Hodder & Stoughton

Bruce, T. (2004a) *Developing Learning in Early Childhood*. London: Paul Chapman

Bruce, T. (2004b) *Cultivating Creativity in Babies, Toddlers and Young Children*. London: Hodder & Stoughton

Bruce, T. (2005) *Early Childhood Education*. London: Hodder Arnold.

Bruner, J., Jolly, A. and Sylva, K. (1976) *Play: Its Role in Development and Learning*. Harmondsworth: Penguin

Consultative Committee (1905) *School Attendance of Children below the Age of Five*. Available from: www.bopins.ac.uk/bopall/ref7535.html

Cooper, P., Arnold, R. and Boyd, E. (2001) 'The Effectiveness of Nurture Groups', *British Journal of Special Education*, 28: 4.

Cox, T. and Sanders, S. (1994) *The Impact of The National Curriculum on the Teaching Of Five Year Olds*. London: Falmer Press

Craft, A. (2002) *Creativity and Early Years Education: A lifewide foundation*. London: Continuum

Daily Telegraph (2007) Letter to the Editor on Play: http://www.telegraph.co.uk/news/main.jhtml?xml=/news/2007/09/10/nplay110.xml

David, T., Goouch, K., Powell, S. and Abbott, L. (2003) *Birth to Three Matters: A Review of the Literature*. Nottingham: DfES.

de Bóo, M. (ed.) (2004) *Early Years Handbook. Support for Practitioners in the Foundation Stage*. Sheffield: The Curriculum Partnership/ Geography Association

DES (1967) *Children and Their Primary Schools – A Report for the Central Advisory Council for Education (Plowden Report)*. London: HMSO

Devereau, J. and Miller, L. (eds) (2003) *Working with Children in the Early Years*. London: David Fulton.

DfEE (1998) *The National Literacy Strategy: Framework for Teaching*. London: DfES

DfEE (1999a) *The National Curriculum: Handbook For Teachers In England*. London: DfEE/QCA

DfEE (1999b) *The National Numeracy Strategy: Framework for Teaching Mathematics from Reception to Year 6*. London: DfEE

DfES (1990) *Starting with Quality:Report of the Committee of Inquiry into the Educational Experiences Offered to 3 and 4 year olds (Rumbold Report)*. London: HMSO

DfES (2002) *Mathematics for Foundation Stage: Nursery* and *Mathematics for Foundation Stage: Reception*. London: DfES

DfES (2004) *Every Child Matters: Change for Children*. London: DfES

DfES (2005) *Teaching Children to Read*. London: DfES

DfES (2006) *Independent Review of the Teaching of Early Reading (The Rose Report)*. Available from www.dfes.gov.uk

DfES (2007) *The Early Years Foundation Stage: Setting the standard for learning, development and care for children from birth to five*. London: DfES

Drake, J. (2001) *Planning Children's Play and Learning in the Foundation Stage*. London: David Fulton.

Dryden, L., Forbes, R., Mukherji, P. and Pound, L. (2005) *Essential Early Years*. London: Hodder Arnold.

Duffy, B. (1998) Supporting Creativity and Imaginaton in the Early Years. Buckingham: University Press

Featherstone, S. and Bayley, R. (2001) *Foundations for Independence*. Lutterworth: Featherstone Education

Fisher, J. (1998) 'The Relationship Between Planning and Assessment', in Siraj-Blatchford, I. (ed.) *A Curriculum Development Handbook for Early Childhood Educators*. Stoke-on-Trent: Trentham Books

Frobisher, L., Monaghan, J., Orton, A., Orton, J., Roper, T. and Threlfall, J. (1999) *Learning to Teach Number*. Cheltenham: Stanley Thornes

Froebel, F. (1826) *On the Education of Man*. Keilhau, Leipzig: Wienbrach

Gelman, R. and Gallister, C.R. (1978) *The Child's Understanding of Number*. Boston: Harvard Press

Glori, D. (1995) *The Snow Lambs*. London: Scholastic

Goleman, D. (1996) *Emotional Intelligence*. New York: Bantam

Hofkins, D. (1996) 'Vouchers do Little for Parental Choice', *The Times Educational Supplement*, 1 November: 6

Hohmann, M. and Weikart, D.P. (2002) *Educating Young Children*. 2nd edn. Ypsilanti, MI: High/Scope Press

Hughes, L. (2002) *Paving Pathways: Child and Adolescent Development*. London: Wadsworth Thomson Learning

Hutt, C., Tyler, S., Hutt, J. and Christopherson, H. (eds) (1988) *Play, Exploration and Learning*. London: Routledge

Isaacs, S. (1954) *The Educational Value of the Nursery School*. London: Headingly Brothers

Johnston, J. (2005) *Early Explorations in Science*, 2nd edn. Buckingham: Open University Press

Lally, M. (1995) Principles and Practice in Early Years Education, in Campbell, R. and Miller, L. *Supporting Children in the Early Years*. Stoke-on-Trent: Trentham Books.

Lindon, J. (2001) *Understanding Children's Play*. Cheltenham: Nelson Thornes

Lindon, J. (2005) *Understanding Child Development: Linking theory and practice*, Abingdon: Hodder Arnold

Macintyre, C. (2001) *Enhancing Learning through Play*. London: David Fulton.

McDonagh, J. and McDonagh, S. (1999) Learning to Talk, Talking to Learn, in Marsh, J. and Hallet, E. (eds) *Desirable Literacies*. London: Paul Chapman

Moyles, J. (1989) *Just Playing? The Role and Status of Play in Early Childhood Education*. Milton Keynes: Open University Press

Moyles, J., Adams, S. and Musgrove, A. (2002) *SPEEL – Study of Pedagogical Effectiveness in Early Learning. Research Report 363*. Nottingham: DfES.

Moyles, J.R. (ed.) (2005) *The Excellence of Play*, 2nd edn. Buckingham: Open University Press

Nahmad-Williams, L. (1998) *The Effect of the National Curriculum and Assessment at Seven on the Education of Four Year Olds in School*. Unpublished MEd Thesis: Bishop Grosseteste College Library

National Commission on Education (1993) *Learning to Succeed. Report of the Paul Hamlyn Foundation*. London: Heinneman.

Norman, K. (1990) *Teaching Talking and Learning in Key Stage 1*. London: National Curriculum Council/National Oracy Project.

Osborne, J., Erduran, S. and Simon, S. (2004) *Ideas, Evidence and Argument in Science (IDEAS) Project*. London: King's College London

Palmer, S. (2006) *Toxic Childhood. How the modern world is damaging our children and what we can do about it*. London: Orion

Pascal, C. (2003) 'Effective Early Learning', *European Early Childhood Education Research Journal*, 11(2): 7–28

Piaget, J. (1950) *The Psychology of Intelligence*. London: Routledge and Keegan Paul

Piaget, J. (1976) 'Mastery Play' and 'Symbolic Play' in Bruner, J., Jolly, A. and Sylva, K. *Play – Its Role in Development and Evolution*. Hammondsworth: Penguin

Pollard, A., Broadfoot, P., Croll, P., Osborn, M., and Abbott, D. (1994) *Changing English Primary Schools*. London: Cassell

PNS (Primary National Strategy) (2007) *Letters and Sounds: Principles and Practice of High Quality Phonics. Six-phase teaching programme*. London: PNS/DfES

QCA (2003) *Foundation Stage Profile Handbook.* London: QCA/DfEE

QCA/DfEE (2000) *Curriculum Guidance for the Foundation Stage.* London: QCA

QCA/DfEE (2001) *Planning for Learning in the Foundation Stage.* London: QCA/DfEE

Sanders, D., White, G., Burge, B., Sharp, C., Eames, A., McEune, R. and Grayson, H. (2005) *A Study of the Transition from the Foundation Stage to Key Stage 1.* Nottingham: DfES/SureStart/NFER

SCAA (School Curriculum and Assessment Authority) (1996) *Desirable Outcomes for Children's Learning on Entering Compulsory Education.* London: DfEE.

Schwienhart, L.J., Weikart, D.P. and Toderan, R. (1993) *High Quality Preschool Programs Found to Improve Adult Status.* Ypsilante, MI: High/Scope Foundation

Siraj-Blatchford, I. (ed.) (1998) *A Curriculum Development Handbook for Early Childhood Educators.* Stoke-on-Trent: Trentham Books

Siraj-Blatchford, I., Sylva, K., Muttock, S., Gilden, R. and Bell, D. (2002) *Researching Effective Pedagogy in the Early Years.* Nottingham: DFES

Steer, A. (2005) *Learning Behaviour – The Report of The Practitioners' Group on School Behaviour and Discipline.* London: DfES

SureStart (2003) *Birth to Three Matters.* London: DfES

Tassoni, P., Beith, K., Eldridge, A. and Gough, A. (2002) *Childcare and Education.* Oxford: Heinemann Child Care

Tizard, B, Mortimore, J. and Burchill, B. (1981) *Involving Parents in Nursery and Infant Schools.* London: Grant McIntyre.

Tough, J (1977) *The Development of Meaning.* London: Allen & Goodwin

Toulmin, S. (1958) *The Uses of Argument.* Cambridge: Cambridge University Press

Vygotsky, L. and Cole, M. (eds) (1978) *Mind in Society, The Development of Higher Psychological Processes.* Cambridge, MA: Harvard University Press

Wells, G. (1986) *The Meaning Makers.* London: Hodder & Stoughton

Chapter 10

Special Needs and Inclusion – Policy and Practice

'When I approach a child, he inspires in me two sentiments; tenderness for what he is, and respect for what he may become'
Louis Pasteur, 1822–1895

Introduction

The first part of this chapter considers the historical perspective on provision for children with special needs and the rationale behind the change in emphasis from special needs provision to the full 'inclusion' of all children in settings providing care and education. It focuses on the legislative framework that supports children across all phases of development, and since 'early years' is defined as applying to children from birth to 8 years, it is essential that practitioners have this overview. The second part of the chapter moves away from mainstream school settings to focus specifically on the provision for children's care and holistic development in early years settings, whether this is in childcare, day nurseries or in nurseries attached to mainstream schools. We will discuss government initiatives specific to this phase, the development of multi-agency working and some of the issues involved, including the considerable emphasis on the rights of parents and children to be included in decision-making about their provision.

An understanding of the models and discourses underpinning the developments for children with special needs is of particular importance as their current influence is as significant as their influence on past provision. Awareness of past legislation in education, as well as of the perspectives on disability and learning difficulties prevalent in society over time, also helps to develop an understanding of current provision. Developments in provision, in England and Wales, for children with disabilities or learning difficulties have been considerable during the past 30 years and, at times, controversial. Recent legislation has strengthened the rights of children, even the very young, and their parents or carers to be involved in decision-making about their provision, and the implementation of the Every Child Matters agenda aims to promote the well-being, achievement and inclusion of all children by ensuring that health care, social services and education practitioners work together to support children and their families.

Aims

→ To provide an overview of the key historical legislation relating to the development of provision for special needs

→ To provide an understanding of the two main models of disability: 'medical' and 'social'

→ To explore the meaning of inclusion and the implications for practitioners

→ To outline the main aspects of the Code of Practice

→ To provide an overview of recent legislation in early years settings

→ To consider the implications for children and their families as part of the multi-agency process

A historical framework

Before the passing of the Education Act 1870, elementary education was provided by the churches and other religious groups. Attendance at school was not compulsory and provision for children with learning difficulties or disabilities was minimal. Private schools for the deaf or blind did exist for those whose parents could afford the fees and there was some provision by charitable institutions. However, the needs of children with disabilities or learning difficulties were largely overlooked. As a result of the 1870 Act, School Boards were established in order to ensure sufficient elementary school places for all children, although attendance did not become compulsory until 1880.

During the nineteenth century the provision of schooling for young people with physical or sensory disabilities developed gradually, and may have been influenced by the system of 'payment by results' also introduced by the 1870 Act. This was a system which used the testing of children in reading, writing and arithmetic to determine teachers' pay. Naturally, it was a disincentive to having children with disabilities in school if their presence was likely to have an adverse impact on test results and, consequently, on teachers' pay. Thus, a need for provision for these children outside the 'normal' school setting was created, and these needs were met through the establishment of 'special schools'. While children who were considered to be 'feeble-minded' received a basic education in a special school, those who were labelled as 'idiots' or 'imbeciles' were not thought to have the ability to benefit from any form of schooling and were either admitted to asylums or cared for by family. From the early twentieth century, local education authorities (LEAs) had a duty to provide an education for 'defective' children, yet it was the middle of the century before responsibility for all such children was transferred from medical care into education. And, not until 1970 were children who had previously been considered 'uneducable' given the right to an education.

Theorists

Maria Montessori

Maria Montessori (see Chapter 1) developed her method of education (Montessori, 1912) to support children with special needs, who were deemed to be uneducable. The structure and repetitiveness of the activities in the Montessori Method (Montessori,1912) support the early development of skills and understandings, particularly for children with special needs. In recent years, the Montessori Method has been adapted for use in mainstream early childhood care, but the extent of adaptation can be quite different, so that some settings can stick fairly rigidly to the Montessori Method, whilst others can be very loosely aligned to Montessori principles.

Nurseries and schools for children with special needs have used the routine and structure of activities to help children to develop for many years.

The Warnock Report (1978) was the outcome of an investigation into the education of children in special schools, which actually listened to the views of the children themselves. It highlighted the dissatisfaction of individuals who were, by this time, referred to as 'handicapped', 'maladjusted' or 'educationally subnormal'. From an early age, they attended day or residential special schools rather than their local, neighbourhood school, with the result that many expressed negative feelings about being isolated from their local community by segregated schooling. This finding is evidence of children's voices being heard and of their opinions being valued, for the first time, at an institutional or governmental level, and is a reflection of a human rights perspective. However, not until some considerable time later were the views of children routinely sought regarding their provision at an individual level. A recommendation resulting from this consultation was that, wherever possible, children with special needs should be educated in their local mainstream schools. Other recommendations in that report (Armstrong, 1998: 39) were:

- the abolition of previously used categories in favour of children's special educational needs (SEN) being described using educational rather than medical criteria;
- the recognition that up to 18 per cent of children in mainstream schools experience difficulties in learning because of SEN;
- more emphasis should be placed on multi-professional assessment and on parents' involvement in decision-making about their children;
- assessment and provision should be extended to include pre-school children.

The report also suggested that all children with special needs would benefit from beginning their education early and advocates that 'early education is the key to their development' (Robson, 1989: 16–17).

The recommendations of the 1981 Education Act reflected the contents of the Warnock Report in that it stated that children with special needs and disabilities should attend local mainstream schools if that is what the parents wished, if the schools had the resources to support them and if it was not detrimental to the learning of the other children. However, the legislation was introduced at a time of economic recession and cuts in government spending; therefore implementation was difficult and the extent to which children with special needs were integrated into their local schools varied considerably between LEAs. The Act also acknowledged the importance of parents as partners with health, social service and education professionals in decision-making about their children, but children were still considered simply as the property of their parents (Freeman, 1987; Armstrong, 1995) and were not viewed as being capable of expressing worthwhile opinions on their needs.

Although the Warnock Report recommended that most children should move from segregated to mainstream settings, the intention was that they should be 'integrated' into these settings rather than 'included'. The difference in terminology is one of degree. Children could be integrated into mainstream classes, or into special classes or units within a mainstream school (where they would have the opportunity to mix with the other children at certain times, such as at breaks or lunch). However, with this approach, the emphasis is on the child with special needs being prepared to cope in a mainstream setting. On the other hand, 'inclusion' places the responsibility on the setting to adapt the curriculum, teaching styles and environment to meet the needs of the individual, and more recent legislation promotes inclusion rather than integration.

The introduction of the National Curriculum in 1988 and the **Special Needs Code of Practice** (DfEE, 1994) are milestones in the move from integration to inclusion. Mittler (2000) described the Special Needs Code of Practice as a 'landmark document'. But, although it did have considerable impact by placing a statutory requirement on schools and LEAs to identify and meet the needs of children with SEN, the first Code (DfEE, 1994) strengthened the rights of parents to be involved in consultation about their children, while only acknowledging the principle of involving the children themselves. It was the revised Code of 2001 that specified that children should be involved in discussion relating to Individual Education Plans (IEPs) and their reviews (DfES, 2001a: 54).

Models of disability

The way we view the issues of including individuals with special needs or disabilities in schools and in society is underpinned by two main models, the 'medical model' and the 'social model', and their associated discourses. The human rights perspective and discourse is also linked inextricably with the social model.

The medical model of disability

During the nineteenth and first part of the twentieth centuries the assessment and diagnosis of children with severe learning disabilities was the responsibility of the medical profession and therefore a medical discourse evolved to discuss anyone who had a physical, sensory or cognitive disability or difficulty. With the medical model of disability the problem was seen to be within the individual. It was thought that certain children would not cope in a mainstream setting because of the disabilities or difficulties with which they were labelled and that they should have the advantage of a special setting, offering them 'the care they need'. Such thoughts and terms locate the difficulty that individuals experience within themselves. So, only if children could overcome their difficulties sufficiently to integrate into the setting would they be allowed to attend. This is a deficit model which relies on the assessments of a range of professionals to determine the child's needs and, as such, does not recognise the child's ability to speak for itself. Closely related to this model are the 'religious' and 'charitable' models, as early provision for disabled children was often provided by the churches or by charitable organisations, and this again is reflected in the associated discourses which imply that the children were tragic individuals, in need of pity and of special care. Although it can be argued that this model still underpins attitudes to individuals with special needs to some extent, there has been a radical move away from it in recent years.

Case Study

Cerebral palsy

Cerebral palsy (CP) is not a disease or an illness, but a physical impairment affecting movement, which varies in severity and includes a variety of conditions.

- Spastic cerebral palsy is characterised by weak and stiff muscles and a lack of control of movement.
- Athetoid cerebral palsy involves loss of control of posture, and unwanted movements.
- Ataxic cerebral palsy involves problems with balance and sometimes shaky hand movements and irregular speech.

Cerebral palsy is commonly caused by failure of part of the brain to develop, either before birth or in early childhood, by injury or oxygen loss during pregnancy or labour or premature birth, or by some childhood illnesses, such as meningitis. Improved maternity and neonatal care has resulted in fewer babies developing cerebral palsy as a result of birth difficulties and a greater rate of survival for severely premature babies. As a result, there has been a slight increase in cerebral palsy in society, with about one in every 400 affected (SCOPE, 2007)

Tom is 7 years old and has cerebral palsy due to complications during birth and a loss of oxygen to his brain. He has problems walking, feeding, talking and using his hands and uses both a walking frame and an electronic wheelchair, and communication aids. He also has some visual impairment. He is of average intelligence and attended a mainstream nursery and school until he was 6 when he and his parents made the decision to send him to a school for severely physically disabled children. This decision was made because Tom was finding it increasingly difficult to develop in a society that assumed he was incapable of communication or any activity. In other words, he found it difficult to fit in. He has settled well in the special school, has made many friends, can access the full curriculum and get health services, such as physiotherapy and speech therapy, as part of his normal day.

Reflective Tasks

How does physical development affect the young child in society?

Level 1

In order to answer this question, you need to research physical development in early childhood. Consider how the developing child is affected by their physical development and how society reacts to physical differences in young children. Consider also Tom's experience outlined in the Case Study above, and try to identify:

- the effect of physical disabilities on cognitive development;
- how the attitudes within society affect children with physical disabilities;
- the effect of society's attitudes towards disability on emotional development.

Level 2

- How could you adapt your daily practice and provision to accommodate a child like Tom?
- How would the other children in your care accommodate a child with physical difficulties?
- How could you support the cognitive, emotional and social development of a child like Tom?

Level 3

- How would a child like Tom cope in your setting?
- Do you consider that a setting like yours is suitable for a child like Tom? Explain your reasons.
- What physical, social and emotional changes would you have to make to ensure that all the children could develop effectively?

(See Picture 10.1.)

Picture 10.1 Communication with a child with special needs
Source: John Walmsley/Education Photos

Human rights and the social model of disability

Human rights movements at a national and international level champion the rights of all children and adults to be fully included in society. Of two key documents promoting the rights of the child to equal opportunities and inclusion in mainstream education, the first is the UN Convention on the Rights of the Child (United Nations, 1989). Article 12 of the Convention emphasises a child's right to be heard in any decisions affecting them, dependent on their age and ability to understand, and this was reflected in the Children Act 1989, which for the first time legislated that children's wishes should be taken into account. However, Article 3, by stating that a child's welfare and the best interests of the child have a higher priority than the individual's wishes, can be problematic at times. Questions arising from this statement revolve around who decides on whether children have the maturity or ability to know what support they need and whether their views should be expressed by the children themselves or by their parents/carers advocating on their behalf. These issues still impact on attitudes to children's involvement in decision-making today.

The second key document on children's rights is the UNESCO Salamanca Statement (1994), which again promotes children's rights to equal opportunities and inclusion in mainstream settings. This statement was signed by the UK and 91 other governments, and reinforces earlier declarations. The importance of these international statements is emphasised by Rustemier (2002: 10) as placing an obligation on governments to ensure inclusive provision:

> One of the main strengths of a human rights approach to education is the recognition that the rights of children and young people to enjoy inclusive education are accompanied by the responsibilities of government to provide it.

As the human rights movement gained strength it also became accepted that the disabling barriers created by society, rather than disability, were the main factors in the marginalisation or exclusion of people with disabilities from full participation in society. This perspective is the 'social model of disability'. It maintains that labels should not be used to draw attention to individuals' disabilities or learning difficulties, as this reflects a deficit model. Its approach has implications for all phases of education, from early years through to post-compulsory education, as it places an obligation on the setting to ensure that buildings and learning experiences are accessible to all, and that discriminatory attitudes of staff or children are challenged. Legislation has promoted equal opportunities in society and in education. Yet it is important to recognise 'the tensions created between a public rhetoric of equal opportunities and activated government policies which in all areas of public life are deepening inequalities rather than reducing them' (Armstrong *et al.*, 2000: 5). While government policy in education promotes the inclusion of children with special needs or disabilities, the pressures from government on schools to achieve good results in tests can lead to some reluctance to accept children with special needs into mainstream settings and to the provision of learning opportunities that may be inappropriate for some children. It is within this framework that inclusive education is currently evolving in our schools.

Tools for Learning

Synthesis

In this chapter we consider the skill of *synthesis* in our Tools for Learning. Synthesis is a very important skill that enables you to take analyses from a wide range of primary and secondary evidence and put them together in order to draw conclusions, make sense of the whole and draw inferences, producing new ideas or models and identifying implications. Howard Gardner (2007) has identified the synthesising mind as essential in modern society (see also Chapter 4), because of the rapidly changing society and the enormous increase in information and sources of information. Synthesis involves having a broad understanding the overall area you are focusing on;

what Gardner likens to a searchlight, having a broad overview, seeing and making use of the links between aspects and being able to monitor changes in the area. It also involves being focused and having in-depth knowledge and understanding; what Gardner describes as a laser beam.

Synthesis should form a major part of the discussion section of any written work. You need to tease out the major issues and engage in a deep and critical discussion of them. This may be structured according to the ideas that have emerged from the analysis of data, or implications of your research on your future practice. Alternatively, it may be structured using the research questions that you have posed and with critical discussion of findings and ideas emerging which help to answer the questions you have posed. This does not mean that you repeat your analysis, but move forward from the analysis.

Practical Tasks

Models of disability

Level 1

Use the internet to search for information on models of disability. Are there differences in opinion? Consider how a setting could ensure that provision would enable a child with special needs to be fully included during day-to-day activities.

Level 2

Use the internet to search for information on models of disability. Note down any differences in opinion and consider why there are differing viewpoints. Through observation of one child with special needs in your setting, identify ways in which barriers have been removed to improve access to the physical setting and to learning.

Level 3

Use the internet to search for information on models of disability. Note down any differences in opinion and consider why there are differing viewpoints.

Drawing on your understanding of models of disability, based on your reading, and your setting's special needs, what policy changes can you suggest that would promote the inclusion of a child with a physical or sensory disability in your setting?

An inclusive approach to education

The National Curriculum, introduced through the Education Reform Act 1988, is frequently cited as the beginning of inclusion for all, as it stated that all children had a right to a broad and balanced curriculum, differentiated to meet their individual needs. This goes beyond a consideration of children with special needs or disabilities to include all children. The revised National Curriculum (DfEE, 1999) took the idea of inclusion further, by setting out three principles as a basis for developing an inclusive teaching and learning environment:

- setting suitable learning challenges;
- responding to children's diverse learning needs;
- overcoming potential barriers to learning and assessment for individuals and groups of children.

However, while schools have a legal obligation to follow the National Curriculum, Knowles suggests that the above are frequently overlooked as working under pressure to plan appropriate learning activities in line with the National Curriculum's programmes of study for any given subject may seem to leave little time to consider the values, aims and purposes that underpin the curriculum (Knowles, 2006: 18).

Government policy promoting moves towards the development of inclusive curricula was accompanied by initiatives to promote the inclusion of children with special needs (see Picture 10.2). An SEN Code of Practice (DfEE, 1994) was introduced to support practitioners in providing for learners with special needs. This Code was criticised because of the bureaucracy involved in its implementation and it was succeeded by a revised Code of Practice (DfES, 2001a), which also supported the implementation of the Special Educational Needs and Disability Act (SENDA) 2001; this is still used to guide special needs provision today. The Code lists areas of need:

- communication and interaction;
- cognition and learning;
- behavioural, emotional and social development;
- sensory and/or physical.

It also sets out a three-stage approach to meeting needs:

1. *School Action/Early Years Action*, where the school provides support with help from the Special Educational Needs Co-ordinator (SENCo), but without the help of outside agencies.

Picture 10.2 Supporting learners with special needs in an inclusive setting
Source: John Walmsley/Education Photos

2. *School Action PlusEarly Years Action Plus*, where outside agencies such as educational psychology services, speech therapy, behaviour support services, health or social services become involved in planning to meet the needs of the child.

3. *Statemented provision*, where a child has a statement from the local authority setting out the additional provision, in terms of extra adult support or special resources, to which he/she is entitled; once a statement has been agreed there is a legal obligation on providers to ensure that the provision is in place.

This Code (DfES, 2001a) gives clearer guidance to practitioners on the writing of **Individual Education Plans** (IEPs) and how frequently they should be reviewed. Labels are still used for administrative purposes in order to get children the support they need. So, while the rights of children are being increasingly acknowledged, a deficit model is still evident. Although Lauchlan and Boyle agree that deficit models have some limited purpose, they propose an end to the overreliance on these as:

> the potential negative impacts are huge: stigmatisation; bullying; reduced opportunities in life; a focus on within-child deficits to the exclusion of other, often more significant, factors; misclassification; and lowered expectations about what a 'labelled' child can achieve.
> (Lauchlan and Boyle, 2007: 41)

The Code also reflects the social model of disability to some extent, locating difficulties encountered by individuals with special needs within society, by stating that 'schools should not assume that children's learning difficulties always result solely, or even mainly, from problems within the child. A school's own practices make a difference – for good or ill' (DfES, 2001a: 47). However, this approach is not without its critics. Lindsay (2003) believes the social model 'actively overlooks' within-child factors in considering the external environment to be the only significant factor that disables an individual.

While the Code of Practice (DfES, 2001a) clearly sets out practitioners' responsibilities, it also states that parents and children have the right to be involved in any decision-making about their education. This includes an involvement in setting targets in IEPs, reviewing whether they have been achieved, and discussing the effectiveness of support. Armstrong acknowledges the difficulty professionals face in gaining children's perspectives, but also that these difficulties are not only with children with special needs: 'gaining access to children's perspectives requires skill in communicating meaning to children and understanding the meanings embedded in children's language and behaviour' (Armstrong, 1995: 67). For very young children, or those with severe learning difficulties or communication problems, the difficulty of expressing their views is complicated further and parents frequently have to voice their child's opinions.

For very young children who find it difficult, or are unable, to express their individual views or concerns, either because they have communication difficulties or because they are still in the Foundation Stage or early Key Stage 1, practitioners must find alternative ways of accessing children's voices. They may be able to express their opinions through writing or drawing. However, all children use body language to make their feelings known. As Mortimer points out, expressions and emotions are closely linked; a full discussion of how very young children can be consulted about their needs can be found in Mortimer (2004).

Shortly after the revised SEN Code of Practice (DfES, 2001a) was introduced, a Disability Code of Practice (Disability Rights Commission, 2002) was issued to support settings in meeting their legal duties set out in SENDA 2001. These duties are that practitioners should not treat children less favourably because of their disability, and they should make reasonable adjustments to include children with disabilities fully in the curriculum. This reflects the social model of disability as it places an obligation on providers to remove the barriers that prevent inclusion. This goes beyond improving physical access for children to include access to all learning opportunities through careful review of the ways in which these opportunities are presented. Although initially educators were concerned that 'reasonable adjustments' could not easily be defined, the Disability Code gives a number of examples in support.

In recent years, much good inclusive practice has evolved as practitioners have become increasingly skilful in providing for children with special needs and disabilities. But inclusion is about much more than this. It is about considering the needs of *all* children. This is clearly stated in the *Curriculum Guidance for the Foundation Stage* (QCA 2000: 17), where the need to provide 'relevant learning and development opportunities and set realistic and challenging expectations that meet the diverse needs of children' is emphasised. It is difficult to name every marginalised group of children for whom inclusive provision should be made. Some that quickly come to mind are children from minority ethnic groups, travellers, those who have English as an additional language, asylum seekers, the gifted and talented, and looked-after children. In order to include and provide equal access to the curriculum for all groups, providers should demonstrate positive values and attitudes. As Mortimer says:

> if you are going to plan a curriculum of activities that is completely unbiased and accessible to all children, then you need to develop positive attitudes about providing equal opportunities and these should pervade all that you think and do at work, at home and in society.
> (Mortimer, 2006: 33)

At a practical level, the Index for Inclusion (CSIE, 2002), and the more recent version for early years and childcare settings, can support the development of inclusive practices in schools and early years settings by encouraging the involvement of all adults within the setting to examine and build on their current practices in terms of inclusive cultures, policies and practices.

Practical Tasks

Inclusive values

The Index for Inclusion suggests indicators for 'establishing inclusive values'. After accessing these indicators in the Index, or online:

Level 1

Can you find examples of how each indicator is practised in any settings you have visited or within your college/learning institution?

Level 2

If a child with English as an additional language (EAL) entered your setting, describe how you would ensure that these indicators were in place for that child.

Level 3

Write how these values would be reflected in your setting, as if you were writing/reviewing your setting's inclusion policy.

Every Child Matters

The introduction of *Every Child Matters: Change for Children* (DfES, 2004a) and *Every Child matters: Change for Children in Schools* (DfES, 2004b) was the government's response to the sad death of Victoria Climbié in 2000, and concern that her death, as a result of horrific abuse, could perhaps have been avoided if there had not been a lack of communication between services such as education, health and social services. Furthermore, there have been many similar cases, both in the past and since Victoria's death, which have not attracted the same media attention. The aim of Every Child Matters is to foster procedures where services can work together and share information, so that children at risk and from the most vulnerable groups in society will be better monitored, and their families better supported in the future.

The five outcomes listed in Every Child Matters, and compiled as a result of discussion with children and young people about their needs, are aimed at achieving well-being for all children, and reflect the positive values of caring about the well-being of others, respecting children's rights to stay safe and to achieve their potential, and the right to be listened to in decisions about themselves and their learning (Smith, 2007). The outcomes are to:

- be healthy;
- stay safe;
- enjoy and achieve;
- make a positive contribution;
- achieve economic well-being.

How these are translated into practice will depend on the setting. Issues related to being healthy and staying safe, for example, will be very different for a child in primary school compared with a teenager at secondary school. Similarly, there will be a different emphasis for a 2-year-old and a young child about to enter Key Stage 2. The early years educator has the responsibility of implementing these outcomes in a way that is appropriate to a child's age and level of maturity.

Removing Barriers to Achievement (DfES, 2004c) focuses on the way in which the education service should respond to the Every Child Matters agenda. Its strategy focuses on four key areas:

- early intervention;
- removing barriers to learning;
- raising expectations and achievement;
- delivering improvements in partnership.

The document focuses strongly on provision for individuals with special needs. However, if its aims are extended to include all marginalised groups, then genuinely inclusive settings will evolve.

Case Study

Suspecting a child is at risk

Cyndy Hawkins, Bishop Grosseteste University College Lincoln

Tannika, aged 3, attends a local nursery class situated in an inner city community college while her guardian, who is also her aunt, attends adult literacy classes.

Her aunt has looked after Tannika since her mother was sent to prison six months ago. The early years practitioners have noticed that since her mother's departure, Tannika's physical appearance has deteriorated through gradual weight loss and an increased lack of personal hygiene.

Tannika is a bright, happy and communicative child, yet of late rarely communicates with the other children or adults. Practitioners have observed Tannika spending much of the time alone and have also observed her at story-time curled up into a ball rocking.

Practitioners think that the separation from her mother has affected Tannika significantly. As a result of their concern, they speak at length with the guardian about their fears. The guardian denies that there is any problem with Tannika's behaviour and insists everything is fine.

Recently practitioners find Tannika foraging in the waste bins for food; when asked the reason for this, she tells a practitioner that she has a tummy ache and is very hungry. At home time the practitioner approaches the guardian about the incident who passes the event off, implying that Tannika is doing things for attention.

The following week Tannika's guardian comes to college alone. She tells the nursery practitioner that Tannika doesn't want to come anymore and that she has arranged for a babysitter to care for her while she attends college. Another mother who lives close by to the family tells practitioners that Tannika is being left alone in the house. The practitioners are extremely alarmed at the news and agree further action is required.

Reflective Tasks

Working in partnership to safeguard children

Cyndy Hawkins, Bishop Grosseteste University College Lincoln
Consider the Case Study above.

Level 1

- Who should practitioners share this information with?
- What agencies might need to be involved in the investigation of the issues?

Level 2

The Children Act 2004 placed a new duty on a wide range of organisations to safeguard and promote the welfare of children by working in partnership and cooperation.

- In the case of 'looked-after children' what local forums are in place to attend to the child's interests?
- How might they respond?

Level 3

Children can only be safeguarded properly if key agencies work effectively together. How far have key agencies progressed towards this model and is 'effective integration of services' a reality or an ideal?

Early years settings and recent legislation

During the past decade there has been increasing focus on inclusion for children and their families within early years education, health and social care provision. Early years setting is a term used to describe the provision of childcare networks, sessional playgroups, children's centres, full day nurseries and pre-schools within local authority maintained and private and voluntary sectors. This provision is constantly adapting and evolving. Free nursery places are now available for all 3- and 4-year-olds and local SureStart programmes created in the 500 most disadvantaged areas are now developing into a network of over 3,000 children's centres. Many sessional and full day-care providers are firming their connections with local schools in order to provide for the requirements of extended provision. Within this complexity of provision the care and learning needs of children from birth to 5 are provided for.

As part of this reconfiguration, education, health and social care are currently adapting to new frameworks that embody a major shift in the thinking that previously categorised care and learning as separate components. A new inspection framework links the standards of care and the quality of provision to the outcomes for children that local authorities must work to. Service providers must consider and be measured against the five outcomes of Every Child Matters (ECM) under the OFSTED regulation and inspection framework. Underpinned by the Children Act 2004, ECM seeks to reduce the gap between those who do well and those who do not and to improve the co-ordination between agencies in order to better respond to the needs of individual children.

The five ECM outcomes are an integral part of the Childcare Act 2006, which is a reinforcement of the Children Act 2004, and is the first ever Act to be exclusively focused on early years and childcare. The Act will provide for consistency across the wide range of provision that caters for early years and is also the first Act to present a legislative framework for children from birth to 5. The new framework is called the Early Years Foundation Stage (EYFS) and is based on the knowledge that high-quality integrated education and childcare provision improves outcomes for all children as identified by Effective Provision of Pre-school Education (EPPE) (DfES, 2004d), a statutory framework from September 2008.

The EYFS (DfES, 2007) supersedes *Curriculum Guidance for the Foundation Stage* (QCA, 2000) and develops and integrates the Birth to Three Matters Framework (SureStart, 2003) and the National Standards for under 8s Daycare and Childminding (DfES, 2003d) to create a single combined care and learning framework for 0–5 yr olds. *Curriculum Guidance for the Foundation Stage* was a leading document in placing emphasis on parent partnership and in stating that no child should be excluded or disadvantaged because of ethnicity, culture, religion, home language, SEN, disability, gender or ability. The EYFS (DfES, 2007) embodies this thinking further by placing a more focused approach on principle into practice for inclusion. The needs of further minority groups such as travellers, refugees and asylum seekers are also included within the framework and partnership working with support agencies is recognised as a key resource for planning to meet the individual needs of children. A core resource of provision is identified as listening to, and respecting the views of, children and their families. The 'Principles into Practice' cards, which are part of the EYFS resources, provide much more evidence and guidance towards inclusion than the previous *Curriculum Guidance for the Foundation Stage* (QCA, 2000). The EYFS should provide an opportunity to embed the most effective approaches and will provide an opportunity to ensure consistency and quality for inclusion across all early years settings.

These legislative developments will have far-reaching effects on universal provision in early years, particularly with regard to inclusion.

Children with additional needs in early years settings

Worldwide there is a changing pattern of need in early childhood. Poverty is an ongoing cause of impoverishment in early childhood, resulting in 'risk' educationally, socially and emotionally. There is a high correlation between poverty and having a child with a disability or special need (Emerson and Hatton, 2005). The increase in survival rates of premature babies and a rise in increasingly complex levels of disability mean that there are more children with complex needs in society. An increase in numbers of children diagnosed with Fragile X and Autism Spectrum Disorders further contributes to a growing population of young children with a diverse range of additional needs, as confirmed by Community Care (2005). Improved diagnosis, better survival rates, and a growing incidence of complex disabilities such as autism have resulted in a 62 per cent increase in the number of disabled children living in the UK. The number of very young children identified with additional needs has increased alongside an increasing responsibility to provide for these children to have access to early years provision for education, health and social care needs. In establishing this background, within which the inclusive agenda for early years must operate, the need for effective intervention at an early stage for all children with additional needs is clearly paramount.

There are many differing descriptors, stages and levels of need within early years settings and there is a gradual tendency within new guidance and documentation to use a more universal descriptor of 'additional needs' as a wider term that also includes 'disabilities' and 'special educational needs'. This can be useful in embracing a practice where the generic principles of inclusion are recognised as effective in supporting not only those children with disabilities and/or SEN but also children who are looked after, ethnic minorities, children with English as an additional language and other marginalised groups.

Research

EPPE Project

Research from the EPPE project (Effective Provision of Pre-school Education, DfES, 2004d) identified that children who do not receive good quality pre-school provision are more at risk of SEN. Likewise children with SEN are likely to benefit most where they attend pre-school settings, especially if they attend a setting which includes children of differing abilities and social backgrounds.

Early years providers registered to receive government funding must have due regard to the Special Educational Needs and Disability Act (SENDA) 2001 in ensuring that young disabled children are not treated less favourably and that reasonable adjustments are made within the setting to avoid disadvantage to the disabled child. The focus on meeting children's special needs within early years settings requires that settings must also have regard to the SEN Code of Practice (DfES, 2001a). This requires that all registered providers must have 'due regard' to the Code in the planning and delivery of services for SEN.

The Code requires that early years settings have a special needs policy which demonstrates a clear commitment to inclusion, a named special needs coordinator and access to appropriate training for all practitioners. Local authorities were required to support private and voluntary settings, who provided for the Early Years Foundation Stage, in this process through a new role identified as Area Special Educational Needs Coordinator (Area SENCo). Local authorities were to establish a minimum ratio of one Area SENCo to

20 non-maintained settings by 2004 in order to oversee policy into practice and to support the government manifesto commitment to identify special needs earlier.

The role of the Area SENCo was initially to empower early years practitioners in effective practice with regard to the Code of Practice. The wider implications of inclusion were recognised in establishing that Area SENCos were also to ensure that practitioners were equipped with the necessary skills, knowledge and understanding to meet the diverse needs of children, including those groups at risk of underachievement. In particular, 'children looked after' were known to be a priority group in terms of risk and many areas have now extended the role of Named Person for Children Looked After in schools to early years settings as part of the Area SENCo role. Local authorities were allowed a great deal of flexibility in the development of this role and this was reflected in the varying responsibilities and structures of provision within different authorities. Most Area SENCOs were individuals within a local authority Early Years Support Service and part of a wider network of Early Year Development Childcare Partnerships. In the longer term local authorities were expected to widen the Area SENCo role to encompass childcare settings providing for under 3s, and consultation was further expected regarding the involvement of Area SENCos within maintained nurseries and reception classes.

Over recent years Area SENCos have seen their role develop and expand to embrace legislative developments. Many local authorities have already changed role titles to reflect these developments; 'Area SENCo' in some local authorities has now become 'Early Years Consultant' or 'Inclusion Consultant' in response to the integrated care/education framework, and it seems that the EYFS (DfES, 2007) has already paved the way for the full 0–5 overview of holistic provision.

Provision for special needs within early years settings follows the graduated three-stage approach as outlined in the Code of Practice (DfES, 2001a). The stages of Early Years Action, Early Years Action Plus and Statemented provision are in alignment with the model provided at statutory school age whereby statutory assessment will only be requested if the special need becomes recognised as a long-term complex need that will require a Statement (approximately 2 per cent of children in England have Statements). For children under 2, Statements are rare; needs are likely to have been identified by parents in conjunction with health and/or social care services. Such cases would most likely reflect a major health difficulty or particular condition but if the parent requests assessment the local authority must carry this out in order to identify appropriate support within an educational setting. The Audit Commission (2002) found that 68 per cent of special needs resources were focused on children with Statements and that statutory assessment was a 'costly and bureaucratic' process allowing for limited flexibility in proactive measures that may in fact reduce the need for Statements. Where authorities have been enabled to delegate resources for children with Statements, thus giving greater flexibility over use of funding, evidence shows that this has in fact reduced further demand for Statements. The DfES encouraged other local authorities to explore this approach (DfES, 2001b).

Flexible funding streams to support preventive measures in early years are a crucial source towards reducing the number of Statements. Funding to support settings developing inclusive early years environments is available within both the Direct Schools Grant and the General SureStart Grant. A specific funding stream that has proved effective is 'Inclusion Funding'. This funding has been targeted particularly towards supporting children who may have long-term complex needs and local authorities have flexibility in its appropriate use, allowing for personalised planning within the child's setting. It is very often a common experience that learning and behaviours in early years are not always clear indicators of where the child's needs may be in, say, 1–2 years time. A child who, for example, has an Autistic Spectrum Disorder (ASD) may display distress at changes in routine in pre-school and may have difficulty playing within close proximity of others.

Increased adult to child ratios within the setting, provided by Inclusion Funding, could enable targeted support using visual timetables and planned times for playing alongside others with adult support, thus reducing social and behavioural difficulties over a period of time, and therefore reducing the need for focused adult support. The diagnosis of ASD may indicate long-term needs for the individual but with early intervention, encouraged by flexible funding streams, this may not become a complex need that requires a Statement. The key, however, lies in the communications between early years and future educational provision.

Case Study

Autism spectrum disorders

Autism spectrum disorders (ASDs) are a group of developmental disorders. The most well known is autism. Children with autism often have impaired social interaction, problems with verbal and non-verbal communication, and unusual, repetitive, or severely limited activities and interests. Between three and six children out of every 1,000 will have autism, with boys being four times more likely than girls. Other ASDs include Asperger syndrome, Rett syndrome, childhood disintegrative disorder, and pervasive developmental disorder – not otherwise specified (PDD-NOS). Children with Asperger syndrome typically have no general delay in language or cognitive development, but atypical use of language and motor clumsiness. Rett syndrome usually affects girls as it is a sex-linked genetic disorder and is characterised by social withdrawal, regressed language skills and hand wringing (NAS, 2007).

Autism is characterised by three distinct problems, which can range from mild to severe:

- difficulties with social interaction;
- problems with verbal and non-verbal communication;
- repetitive behaviours or narrow, obsessive interests.

Autistic children appear to have a higher than normal risk for other conditions, such as Fragile X syndrome (which causes developmental delay and learning disability), tuberous sclerosis (in which tumors grow on the brain), epileptic seizures, Tourette syndrome, learning disabilities, and attention deficit disorder.   About 20–30 per cent of children with autism develop epilepsy by the time they reach adulthood (NAS, 2007).

Jacob's parents first noticed his autistic tendencies as a baby, when he was unresponsive to them. He is now 3 years of age and will spend long periods of time focusing on one toy or rocking and ignore people and other toys. He does not respond to his name and often avoids eye contact. He does not understand social cues, such as tone of voice or facial expressions, and so does not behave as expected or considered appropriate in social contexts. If other children interfere with him, he is likely to bite them or scream. This year, Jacob has undergone a comprehensive evaluation from a multidisciplinary team (psychologist, neurologist, psychiatrist, speech therapist), who will coordinate therapies and interventions. These will include educational or behavioural interventions to help Jacob to develop social and language skills, family counselling for his family and medication in the form of mild antidepressants to reduce his anxiety.

Support for families affected by autism can be found through the National Autistic Society: http://www.autism.org.uk/

Practical Tasks

Autism spectrum disorders

Level 1

- Why do you think visual strategies would support children with ASD in a setting?
- Plan some visual strategies to support Jacob (see Case Study above).
- Can you think of other groups or individuals with other special needs who would benefit from this approach?

Level 2

Sometimes children on the autistic spectrum dread a forthcoming activity, even if it is something they have previously participated in and enjoyed, because they do not remember the emotions they experienced on that occasion.

- What visual strategies could you use to overcome this problem?
- Try out the strategies on any children with ASD in your care and evaluate their success.

Level 3

Social stories are a useful visual tool for supporting children with autism/ASD. As a staff, research this technique and:

- Design a social story to support a child in an area of need in your setting.
- Design a social story to remind a child of the importance of washing hands after going to the toilet.

Historically educational settings have benefited from Statement funding; it is known that even where a child's needs no longer require the level of funding delivered through the Statement it can be perceived as being in the establishment's interest to try to retain the funding since this allows for increased personnel within the staffing structure. Worse than this are the instances where children receive one-to-one provision requiring an adult by their side throughout the day in cases where this is clearly no longer of benefit. The current system of funding is such that the Statement and the accompanying adult can become a fixture that is difficult to remove. Clearly this system has long needed review and early years provision should be the focus for good models of practice and ways forward. In order to effect these changes we need working relationships that share a common language between all our services.

Multi-agency working

Early identification and effective intervention is dependent upon shared understanding and communications between education, health and social care. Multi-agency working in schools was first discussed by the Warnock Report (1978) under the agenda for integration. Within early years provision such developments first became implemented through Early Years Childcare Partnerships in the late 1990s. These early stages of working meant that all agencies working with young children were to plan together in order to oversee provision within the local authority. More recent legislation and guidance is provided in the SEN Code of Practice (DfES, 2001a) which includes a whole chapter related to agency working where the key objective is high-quality integrated support which targets the specific needs of the child. Furthermore registered providers of early years provision in the private and voluntary sector are required to meet the requirements of the National Standards (DfES, 2003b) which identifies that the registered person should be aware of needs and proactive in ensuring that appropriate action is taken. Steps are taken to promote the welfare and development of the child within the setting in partnership with the parents and other relevant parties

Research

Special educational needs

The Audit Commission (2002) undertook an audit of special needs. The main findings are that:

- children with special educational needs (SEN) have remained a low profile group, despite the significant numbers with SEN (1.9 million in England and Wales) or Statements of needs (275,000);
- spending on children with Statements absorbs 69 per cent of SEN budgets, leaving little scope for wider preventive work;
- the arrangements for funding SEN provision in early years settings is incoherent and piecemeal;
- parents of children with SEN often have difficulty with school admissions;
- over two-thirds of children with Statements are educated in mainstream schools but many parents feel that their choice is limited by a lack of suitable provision locally and by unwelcoming attitudes in some schools;
- children with SEN are sometimes excluded from certain lessons, extra-curricular activities and social opportunities – and they are much more likely to be permanently excluded.

The report makes recommendations for the government, local authorities, schools and professionals working with children. The government should establish clear expectations of the advice and support that health and social services should provide and revise national targets and performance tables that fail to reflect the achievements of many children with SEN so that inclusive schools do not appear to perform badly. They should also create a system for recognising and celebrating the good work that does occur in schools and settings. Local authorities should set out a clear timetable for developing both mainstream and special schools. Staff working with young children should have developed skills to enable them to work confidently with children with special needs. They also recommend that schools need to balance pressures, raise standards of attainment and become more inclusive.

There are three important government initiatives which identify the way forward. The Every Child Matters agenda (DfES, 2004a) has measures which include information sharing between agencies, joined-up assessment procedures, multidisciplinary teams, and making one professional a key contact for families. *Together from the Start* (DfES, 2003b) establishes a national set of principles for family-centred working by education, health and social care services and *The National Service Framework* (Department of Health/DfES, 2004) provides a set of standards for health and social care services and their link with education.

Case Study

Special needs awareness

Part of a BA(Hons) in Early Childhood Studies involves understanding child development and factors affecting child development. As part of this students spend two days in a school for physically disabled children in order to develop understanding of the link between physical development, cognition and society.

They spend one day working in class observing young children, helping a range of professionals and undertaking some cognitive activities with children. These may be memory, literacy or mathematical games, sorting activities, jigsaws, exploring sensory playdough, smells or tastes, or water or sand play, focusing on conservation of matter or volume. The purpose here is to ascertain the connection between physical disability and cognition and in most instances the students learn a very valuable lesson about not underestimating children's cognitive abilities.

On the second day, the students take part in a disability awareness workshop (see Picture 10.3) and talk to young people at the school (who are similar in age to most of the students) about what it is to be disabled in society. Many of the disabled young people are able to communicate the frustrations they feel, the prejudices they face and their preference for special schools rather than inclusion, many of them having come from mainstream schools where they failed to achieve or have their special needs met. There is an ongoing debate amongst professionals about whether there should be total inclusion in mainstram schools or if there is the need for specialist schools to cater for specific needs. The children's views in this particular Case Study highlight the importance of appropriate resources, specialist staff and a thorough understanding of a child's needs for total inclusion in mainstream settings to be successful. This is an extremely emotional experience for all our Early Childhood Studies students, but one which challenges their own prejudices and assumptions about society and inclusion in practice.

Picture 10.3 A special needs awareness workshop to promote understanding of special needs

The introduction of early years SENCos within private and voluntary settings and the coordinated support provided by the Area SENCo is an initial outcome of the plan identified in *Removing Barriers to Achievement* (DfES, 2004c), the government's strategy for special needs. Early years settings in receipt of government funding have been enabled to operate according to the Code of Practice, which identifies the need for a multi-agency approach (see also Chapter 13). Early years practitioners have been supported in accessing the same networks of support already in place within maintained educational settings. However, an acknowledgement of private and voluntary early years settings having the same levels of difficulty as maintained settings in accessing this provision needs continued focus; *Removing Barriers to Achievement* (DfES, 2004c) identifies difficulties in accessing support and advice for SEN in private and voluntary settings, where two-thirds of 3-year-olds and a quarter of 4-year-olds are educated. Many authorities have established clear frameworks and time-frames for early years liaison with educational support services such as the Educational Psychology Service and Portage (although that is not to say support is always readily available due to finance and staffing constraints). However, the ongoing difficulties in accessing support from health and social care services remains an issue due to lack of clarity in many authorities about communication frameworks and lack of training and understanding in the Code of Practice. Where support from these services is available and accessed it is often achieved through the perseverance and determination of the early years SENCo in establishing communication.

Thus it can be seen that an individual's strength can be the determining factor towards establishing multi-agency working. Achieving this individual status is dependent upon professional development and networking opportunities in alignment with existing education, health and social care provision. Local authorities have been encouraged to develop joint training for early years practitioners within education, health and social care and this is now to be further enhanced by the shared training to be delivered for EYFS (DfES, 2007).

The need for cohesion and consistency in provision is a recurring theme. Existing frameworks need to move beyond dependency on individuals' perseverance and determination. *Removing Barriers to Achievement* (DfES, 2004c) was a confirmation of strengths and weaknesses within existing practice and a forward move in planning for shared principles and standards, joined-up assessment procedures and key persons to oversee provision throughout the process.

The Early Support Programme (DfES, 2002), launched as a pilot project in 2002, was an early response that anticipated many of the later proposals within ECM (DfES, 2004a). The four-year pilot project was a £13 million programme to improve services for babies and very young children with complex needs through single coordinated assessments, key worker support, clarity about access to local services, and partnership working. Further developments of the programme have been a family toolkit which sets out for families service access and provision, toolkits for professionals offering practical guidance on coordination of services for families, and a national monitoring protocol for deaf children to track their early development.

Through the implementation of Every Child Matters it is envisaged that the Early Support Programme will become integral to practice nationally and will move some way towards addressing the need for shared ways of working between agencies. The main delivery mechanism is expected to be via the 3,500 children's centres to be created by 2010. Early indications of the success of the pilot programme is indicated in a parliamentary report, with particular praise reserved for the government's Early Support Programme, which has done much to coordinate services around the needs of the youngest disabled children. It is interesting to note the government's concept of 'key worker' for the Early Support Programme is described as being 'innovative' when in fact the role of SENCo, which has been in existence for over a decade, exemplifies the same model of provision as that outlined for key persons for the Early Support Programme. Key worker is also the phrase used to describe the coordinator for a model of practice known as Team Around the Child (TAC) (Limbrick, 2004).

Alongside use within children's centres, the Early Support Programme (DfES, 2002) is also to be embedded within the TAC model which has emerged as best practice nationally for a way of working with children who have complex needs. The model has reflected the need for key persons within a multidisciplinary team and the need for children and their families to be a crucial part of the planning and implementation of services. The TAC recognises that each child has a group of professionals specific to their needs and that people within that group may change over time. A key worker is seen as essential for ensuring effective communication and support for the child and their family. The key worker may be an individual already working closely with the family, for example, health visitor or portage worker (see also Chapter 6).

Reflective Tasks

Working with others

Level 1

List all the different professionals and members of staff who work together to support the needs of children in a day nursery.

- Should the diversity of need become more complex, what other professionals might offer support?
- How would the ECM agenda support settings in providing for children with complex needs?

Level 2

From your own experiences and those of colleagues, list the barriers that that can prevent early years practitioners and outside agencies working together in ways that would best support the children in their care. Consider this in the light of the ECM agenda and from your reading about special needs from other literary sources.

- Is what you have read about demonstrated in practice?

Level 3

As a staff, consider ways in which your setting promotes positive links with practitioners, outside agencies and parents/carers.

- Can you suggest strategies for developing this practice further?
- Consider your setting's policy for inclusion and work with other agencies. Does it reflect the ECM agenda?

From your reading on inclusion for different literary sources, consider the different viewpoints and decide which viewpoint your policy most closely resembles.

The Early Support Programme (DfES, 2002; 2004e) and Team around the Child (Limbrick, 2004) are emerging models of support that focus on the early years. Both models are envisaged to fulfil the vision for shared principles and standards, joined-up assessment procedures and key persons identified as ways forward within Every Child Matters (DfES, 2004c). There is lack of clarity about the management of the potential overlap between the two and it would seem important that this is addressed now we are moving beyond the pilot stages. These models of provision are expected gradually to expand into schools and throughout the age range to fall in line with a statutory tool called the Common Assessment Framework (CAF) which may further complicate the issue if finer details are not addressed.

The CAF is the overriding source of support that is likely to establish the lead in providing a cohesive model of provision for the interface between TAC and ESP (DfES, 2004e) in that this is currently being delivered throughout the age range 0–19 and is statutory from March 2008. The CAF provides a standardised approach to conducting a holistic assessment of a child's needs and strengths and enables joint understanding and liaison between child, family and support services. The Framework will help practitioners across universal and specialist services to assess and address children's needs earlier and more effectively.

There is a plethora of information about the CAF and research into the various reports will indicate the lack of clarity regarding its use. It seems that again allowance has been made for local authority agreement. The decision to undertake an assessment is a matter for professional judgement in the light of local practice – the CAF does not lay down a blanket threshold at which a common assessment must always be completed.

Although it could be argued that room is needed for individual adaptations in order to ease the dove-tailing of existing practice, is this not the route by which inconsistency in quality of delivery has existed before? We need standards as promised; standards that are hard and fast, established and agreed.

Further need for consideration is the overlap between CAF and SEN and here it is suggested within guidance that a CAF may be considered if it is believed there are additional needs which go beyond SEN, for example, a domestic situation or a health issue. In such cases the focus of assessment may provide a shift towards the home and therefore require a broader assessment than that indicated by the SEN Code of Practice. This raises the question regarding review meetings which may be better placed as a combined procedure involving CAF and IEP documentation. Again the difficulty regarding 'key'/'lead' persons arises and suggests the SENCo may be a part of this equation to be further discussed.

Early Support Programme (ESP), Team around the Child (TAC) and the Common Assessment Framework are all evolving processes. ESP (DfES, 2004e) and TAC (Limbrick, 2004) are forward-looking in establishing a bottom-up approach using the early years as a baseline from which practices will grow into later years. Multi-agency working in early years, prior to these models, was based on a model already established in educational settings. This required a 'best-fit' approach which made huge demands on services already stretched to meet wider community needs. It is hoped that by establishing new models of practice within early years, early intervention will reduce the need for future individual demands on services as a child moves on and that these examples of good practice and appropriate provision will transfer with the child and their family. Thus the child and their family will become the core agent within a multi-agency delivery. The child and family experience within the early years will strengthen their ability to know and understand service delivery and so empower them to request entitlement on an informed basis throughout 0–19.

Children and their families as part of the multi-agency process

Inter-agency working often fails to recognise the child and their family as priority agents of multi-agency working and it should be argued that any discussion about multi-agency provision must hold the child and family as core communicators and consultants within that process. Government policy focuses on the involvement of young children and their families in the planning, design and governance of services. Education, health and social care partners are expected to seek the views and experiences of young children, including the most vulnerable, and to act upon the information received. Articles 12 and 13 of the United Nations Convention on the Rights of the Child (United Nations, 1989) state that children who are capable of forming views have a right to receive and make known information, to express an opinion, and to have that opinion taken into account in any matters affecting them.

These articles were quoted as part of the framework for the SEN Code of Practice (DfES, 2001a) and the Code became a leading document in placing the emphasis on the child's participation within an inclusive process. However, although the Code refers briefly to 'very young children' and 'early education settings' regarding participation, the detail is mainly concerned with pupil participation in schools and therefore provides minimum support for the early years practitioner. Clarification on the young child's right to be heard was achieved when statutory guidance through the Childcare Act 2006 stated that local authorities must have regard to children's views from birth to 5. Clearly such legislation is far-reaching in the demands it places on the skills of practitioners in fulfilling these requirements. Many early years settings have already embraced this challenge and were proactive in their response to the need to listen to children and their families long before the implementation of the Childcare Act. Active listening has required creativity and imagination on the part of practitioners in adapting to the needs of very young children and those with complex communication difficulties. However, it should be acknowledged that ways of listening to young children are not something new or innovative, they are purely the implementation of interactive processes that have been part of the practice of intuitive practitioners for many years. The skill lies in identifying the ways in which those intuitive practitioners work and embedding those methods of working into all practice.

Successful practice in listening to children is built on a culture of listening to all children. Listening is not an add-on or always an anticipated event; it must lie within the ethos of the setting in order that it is part of an inbuilt approach that becomes a natural way of working. Superficial participation is not enough; listening becomes meaningful when views are acted upon.

The SEN Toolkit (DfES, 2001c: Section 4: Enabling Pupil Participation) which accompanies the SEN Code of Practice (DfES, 2001a), discusses ways forward in seeking young children's views through play observations and non-verbal body language cues, but provides limited advice on putting these ideas into practice and also indicates the risk of misinterpretation on the part of the adult. Effective listening has evolved despite the limitations of this guidance. A publication providing specific information on listening to young children has been produced by Clark and Moss (2001). This outlines a new framework for listening to young children's perspectives on their daily lives. Clark et al. (2003) carried out research commissioned by the SureStart Unit of DfES as a review of the current state with regard to consulting young children. The research has provided a series of partnership leaflets including listening to babies and listening to young disabled children.

Reflective Tasks

Listening to children

Read Clark and Moss (2001) and Clark et al. (2003).

Level 1

- What are the common themes?
- Are there any differences in viewpoint between the two?

Level 2

Consider the ways in which your setting puts any of the suggested strategies into practice. Ask colleagues how they demonstrate that they listen to children. Note where practice concurs with, or differs from, your reading.

Level 3

Find other sources related to 'listening to children'. Ask colleagues how they demonstrate that they listen to children and observe adults interacting with children in your setting.

- Do any of the policies of your setting explicitly mention listening to children or is it implicit within more general statements?

Using all the evidence collected, summarise your viewpoint with justification from the evidence and outline your practice.

Lincolnshire Early Years Support Service has been working on a pilot study in seeking the views of children with SEN regarding their transfer from pre-school into school. The children were encouraged to take photographs of people and places special to them. The photographs were then made into an 'All About Me' book which became used as a source of communication when the children visited their new settings. Similarly these books provided the voice of the child during the SEN review attended jointly by education, health and social care (where appropriate) services to support transition. Practitioners were empowered to use the child's reflections as a source of planning and information for their own setting. For example, one child with cerebral palsy had chosen to use a photo of his rabbit and of a favourite tandem trike he always used in outdoor activities. The school arranged the purchase of an identical trike and also arranged for one of his pre-entry visits to accommodate the rabbit in a 'show and tell' session for existing reception children. Furthermore, having identified through his chosen photos that his Portage worker was special, the school consulted with Portage during the review in order to access on-going intermittent school Portage visits so that his need for a support which normally has a cut-off point at school age was only gradually reduced.

Similar work was carried out as part of Wolfendale's research in 1998. He designed an 'All About Me' profile which was completed jointly by parent and child in order to provide information about young children's feelings and self-perceptions. Local authority developments using the foundation of Wolfendale's model (1998) are more child-focused in that visual rather than written formats enable the young child to use the communicative resources independently in further interactions.

There are also many examples of effective practice in listening to children using puppets and circle time supported by *Social and Emotional Aspects of Learning* (DfES, 2003c). These materials have been incorporated in the Lincolnshire pilot examples. Use of puppets for children exploring individual needs has evolved into a wider development whereby home, support agencies and education are following children's leads in using a generic puppet called Louis as they transfer between home, support agencies and settings. It is now not unusual to have Louis mentioned on an IEP in supporting behavioural, social and emotional targets. Through Louis the children have established a common language for themselves across agencies and settings. Service providers, who historically have had many difficulties in achieving shared understanding and universal languages, have much to learn from children's examples of ways forward. Thus it can be seen that very young children can be enabled to express their views and that adults who are genuinely listening can become active in turning children's opinions about service delivery and individual needs into actions. For more information about use of puppets, see Chapter 6 and Picture 6.3.

Hearing and responding to the views and wishes of children and families is a priority across all aspects of education, health and social care. Encouraging participation in decision-making allows for life choices and fosters a culture of active rather than passive involvement. Children and their families will have expectations raised and will become forthright in achieving their aims.

Case Study

Epilepsy

Epilepsy causes seizures or fits by a sudden burst of excess electrical activity in the brain. The result is a temporary disruption in messages between brain cells and since the brain is responsible for all bodily functions it can be quite disruptive. There are different types of epileptic seizures: partial seizures, which involve part of the brain and generalised seizures which involve the whole brain. In all, there are at least 40 different types of seizure, ranging from brief absent moments, to episodes of losing consciousness, falling to the floor and convulsing (Epilepsy Action, 2007). Many young people with epilepsy do not have special educatonal needs, but it is important that practitioners are trained to understand epilepsy and the implications or education to ensure that the child's needs can be fully addressed.

Sarah's special needs teacher first noticed her epilepsy in one-to-one and small group situations when Sarah appeared to spend large amounts of time daydreaming. Sarah had been recognised as having slight reading delay at 7 years of age and was given additional reading support. When her teacher noticed her daydreaming, she reported it to the school doctor and after tests, including an electroencephalogram (EEG) which records brainwave patterns, it was identified that Sarah suffered from petit mal, a very mild form of epilepsy. This explained her lack of concentration and apparent daydreaming in class and her slow reading development. Once this was recognised medication and a supportive programme could be put in place and Sarah started to make better progress.

Research

Understanding of epilepsy by children with, or without, epilepsy

This was a one-year project conducted between 2006 and 2007. The researchers collected two overlapping sets of primary data: an electronic survey of 44 self-selected children and young people with epilepsy; mainly individual interviews of 22 children/young people in mainstream school with epilepsy and 22 classmates, similar in age, gender and ability.

Children and young people (ages 7–18) with epilepsy were clear about the nature of their condition, including seizures, although some of the younger primary age children were confused about causes and the function of their medication. Epilepsy was regarded as a 'part of them', but the children reported feelings of shame and embarrassment. They wanted professionals to understand their epilepsy better, although they felt that it had a limited impact on school activities.

> Children and young people without epilepsy generally had very little knowledge about epilepsy, although they were positive and understanding towards their class-mates. Where they had specific friends with epilepsy, they were more knowledgeable about the condition. No information about the condition came from the schools.
>
> The research has a number of implications for schools, concerning improved communication, knowledge about the condition and understanding of the challenges faced by individual children with epilepsy.
>
> *Source*: Based on Lewis *et al.*, 2007

Conclusion

Although the importance of early years provision and the early identification of needs had been recognised from the latter half of the twentieth century, provision evolved slowly from that time. However, the twenty-first century has, so far, seen many significant developments which prioritise the well-being, care and learning of the very young. These aim to include all children and ensure that none are disadvantaged because of learning difficulty or disability, social class, 'race', gender or religion. They aim to raise expectations and achievement for *all*, and this is reflected by an increasing emphasis on provision of learning opportunities that enable young children who are gifted or talented to achieve their potential. Some initiatives, such as the ECM agenda (DfES, 2004a), are still at a developmental stage of implementation and there are still difficulties to be overcome. Nevertheless, this is an exciting and challenging time to be involved in the provision of care and of learning experiences for children at this stage of their lives.

Summary

→ During the past 30 years, there have been considerable developments in provision, in England and Wales, for children with disabilities or learning difficulties. Some of these developments have caused controversy.

→ The terms 'integration' and 'inclusion' sound similar but are significantly different in terms of practice. Integration involves a child 'fitting in' to an existing system within a mainstream setting whereas inclusion places the responsibility on the setting to adapt the curriculum, teaching styles and environment to meet the needs of the child. Recent legislation promotes inclusion rather than integration.

→ The Special Needs Code of Practice (2001) has been developed to strengthen the involvement of both the parents/carers and the child in discussions and review of individual support and progress with the setting.

→ The medical model of disability is a deficit model which relies on the assessments of a range of professionals to determine the child's needs and, as such, does not recognise the child's ability to speak for himself or herself.

→ The human rights movement raised the issue that disabling barriers are created by society, rather than disability, excluding people with disabilities from full participation in society. This perspective is the social model of disability and places obligation on the setting to ensure full access to buildings and learning opportunities.

→ The Code of Practice appears to have aspects of both the medical and social model and has come under criticism.

→ Inclusion not only relates to children with disabilities but to many other marginalised groups, such as minority ethnic groups, travellers, those who have English as an additional language, asylum seekers, the gifted and talented, and looked-after children.

→ The EYFS (DfES, 2007) places a focused approach on principle into practice for inclusion.

→ There are many differing descriptors, stages and levels of need within early years settings and there is a gradual tendency within new guidance and documentation to use a more universal descriptor of 'additional needs' as a wider term that also includes 'disabilities' and 'special educational needs'.

→ Early identification and effective intervention is dependent upon shared understanding and communications between education, health and social care services, which is reliant on successful multi-agency working.

→ Provision for special needs within early years settings follows the graduated three-stage approach as outlined in the Code of Practice (DfES, 2001a). The stages are Early Years Action, Early Years Action Plus and Statemented provision in alignment with the model provided at statutory school age.

→ The Special Educational Needs Coordinator (SENCo) oversees the provision for special needs within a setting or, in the case of an Area SENCo, a group of settings.

→ The Common Assessment Framework (CAF) is key to multi-agency working as it provides a standardised approach to conducting a holistic assessment of a child's needs and strengths and enables joint understanding and liaison between child, family and support services.

→ Multi-agency provision must hold the child and family as core communicators and consultants within that process.

Key Questions

- What are some of the key historical legislative documents relating to the development of provision for special needs?
- How have they influenced and changed practice and provision?
- What are the two main models of disability and how might they impact on practice?
- What does inclusion mean and what are the implications for practitioners?
- What are the the main features of the Code of Practice (2001)?
- What are the criticisms of the Code of Practice (2001)?
- What impact has the recent legislation had on early years settings?
- What are the implications for children and their families as part of the multi-agency process?

References

Armstrong, D. (1995) *Power and Planning in Education: Parents, children and special needs.* London: Routledge

Armstrong, D. (1998) Changing Faces, Changing Places: Policy Routes to Inclusion, in Clough, P. (ed.) *Managing Inclusive Education: From Policy to Experience.* London: Paul Chapman

Armstrong, F., Armstrong, D. and Barton, L. (2000) *Inclusive Education: Policy, Contexts and Comparative Perspectives.* London: David Fulton

Audit Commission (2002) *SEN – a mainstream issue.* London: Audit Commission

Clark, A., McQuail, S. and Moss, P. (2003) *Exploring the Field of Listening to and Consulting with Young Children.* Research report 445. London: DfES

Clark, A. and Moss, P. (2001) *Listening to Young Children: The mosaic approach.* London: NCB

Community Care (2005) 'Disability top of the Agenda', *Community Care,* 3 February: 55–6

CSIE (2002) *Index for Inclusion: Developing Learning and Participation in Schools.* Bristol: Centre for Studies in Inclusive Education

Department of Health/DfES (2004) *The National Service Framework.* London: DoH/DfES

DfEE (1994) *Code of Practice on the Identification and Assessment of Special Educational Needs.* London: DfEE

DfEE (1999) *The National Curriculum Handbook for Primary School Teachers.* London: HMSO

DfES (2001a) *Code of Practice on the Identification and Assessment of Children with Special Educational Needs.* London: HMSO

DfES (2001b) *The Distribution of Resources to Support Inclusion.* London: DfES

DfES (2001c) *The SEN Toolkit.* London: DfES

DfES (2002) *Early Support – Helping Every Child Succeed.* London: DfES

DfES (2003a) *Area Special Educational Needs Coordinators (SENCOs) Supporting Early Identification and Intervention for children with SEN.* London: SureStart/DfES

DfES (2003b) *Together from the Start: Practical guidance for professionals working with disabled children (birth to 2) and their families.* London: DfES

DfES (2003c) *Excellence and Enjoyment: Social and Emotional Aspects of Learning.* London: DfES

DfES (2003d) *Full Day Care – National Standards for under 8s daycare and childminding.* London: DfES

DfES (2004a) *Every Child Matters: Change for Children.* London: DfES

DfES (2004b) *Every Child Matters: Change for Children in Schools.* London: DfES

DfES (2004c) *Removing Barriers to Achievement: The Government's Strategy for SEN.* London: DfES

DfES (2004d) Surestart Unit: *The Effective Provision of Pre-school Education (EPPE) Project: Findings from the early primary years.* London: DfES

DfES (2004e) *Early Support Programme: Family pack and professional guidance.* Nottingham: DfES

DfES (2007) *Early Years Foundation Stage: Setting the Standards for Learning Development and Care for children from birth to five.* London: DfES

Disability Rights Commission (2002) *Code of Practice for Schools – Disability Discrimination Act 1995, Part 4.* London: DRC

Emerson, E. and Hatton, C. (2005) *The Socio-economic Circumstances of Families with a Disabled Child.* Lancaster: University of Lancaster.

Epilepsy Action (2007) www.epilepsy.org.uk/info/types.html

Freeman, M. (1987) 'Taking children's rights seriously', *Children and Society,* 1(4): 299–319. Reproduced in Armstrong, D. (1995) *Power and Planning in Education: Parents, children and special educational needs.* London: Routledge.

Gardner, H. (2007) *Five Minds for the Future* Harvard: Harvard Business School Press

Knowles, G. (2006) *Supporting Inclusive Practice.* London: David Fulton

Lauchlan, F. and Boyle, C. (2007) 'Is the use of labels in special education helpful?' *Support for Learning,* 22(1): 36–42

Lewis, A., Parsons, S. and Smith, P. (2007) *Understanding of Epilepsy by Children with, or without, Epilepsy* University of Birmingham: Epilepsy Action

Limbrick, P. (2004) *Early Support for Children with Complex Needs: Team Around the Child and the Multi-agency Keyworker.* Worcester: Interconnections

Lindsay, G. (2003) 'Inclusive education: a critical perspective', *British Journal of Special Education*, 30(1): 3–12

Mittler, P (2000) *Working Towards Inclusive Education: Social Contexts.* London: David Fulton.

Montessori, M. (1912) *The Montessori Method.* London: Heinemann

Mortimer, H. (2004) 'Hearing children's voices in the early years', *Support for Learning* 19(4): 169–74

Mortimer, H. (2006) *Developing an Inclusion Policy in your Early Years Setting.* Stafford: QEd

NAS (National Autistic Society) (2007) www.autism.org.uk/

QCA (2000) *Curriculum Guidance for the Foundation Stage.* London: QCA

Robson, B. (1989) *Pre-school Provision for Children with Special Needs.* London: Cassell Educational

Rustemier, S. (2002) *Social and Educational Justice: The human rights framework for inclusion.* Bristol: CSIE

SCOPE (2007) www.scope.org.uk/information/cp.shtml

Smith, C. (2007) *Demonstrating Positive Values*, in Cole, M. (ed.) *Professional Attributes and Practice for Student Teachers and Teachers Meeting the QTS Standards*, 4th edn. London: Routledge

SureStart (2003) *Birth to Three Matters: A framework to support children in their earliest years.* London: DfES

UNESCO (1994) (Salamanca Statement) World Conference on Special Educational Needs. Paris: UNESCO

United Nations (1989) *Convention on the Rights of the Child.* New York: United Nations.

Warnock, M. (1978) *Special Educational Needs. Report of the Committee of Enquiry into the Education of Handicapped Children and Young People.* London: HMSO

Wolfendale, S. (1998) *All About Me.* Nottingham: NES Arnold

Useful websites

Epilepsy Action: www.epilepsy.org.uk/
SCOPE: www.scope.org.uk/

Part 4

Practitioners in Early Childhood

Chapter 11

The Early Years Professional

"If a child is to keep alive his inborn sense of wonder, he needs the companionship of at least one adult who can share it, rediscovering with him the joy, excitement and mystery of the world we live in"

Rachel Carson (1907–1964)

Introduction

Early childhood is a very large stage in a child's life, especially if we use the international definition of early childhood to mean from birth to 8 years of age. Within this stage are three distinct phases, 0 to 3 years, 3 to 5 years and 5 to 8 years. These phases involve numerous adults and professionals who work together to support children and their families (see Chapter 13). In this chapter we are focusing on those professionals who work with young children on a daily basis and are responsible for their generic care and development, and not those specialists who work together to provide integrated care for children and their families.

Many children are cared for by family members during the first 3 to 5 years of their lives, but others are cared for by nannies in their own homes, childminders in their own homes or the childminders' homes, or they attend playgroups, crèches or nurseries where they will meet and be cared for by play leaders, nursery nurses and managers. Once they start in formal educational settings, such as nurseries and schools, they will be cared for by nursery, Key Stage 1 and Key Stage 2 teachers and teaching assistants. Each of these teaching professionals will have different expertise and experience, with the nursery teacher having knowledge of child development and the education of very young children, and the Key Stage 1 and 2 teachers increasingly focused on cognitive development and the education of children. This diversity of the early years workforce is recognised by the Children's Workforce Development Council (CWDC), who also identify that many settings and professionals now integrate care and education.

Aims

→ To provide an overview of the different types of early years professionals

→ To provide an understanding of the standards for early years professionals and assessment against those standards

→ To consider how different early years professionals ensure they are working to the principles of the Early Years Foundation Stage

→ To explore some of the challenges faced by the diverse range of early years professionals

Different types of early years professionals

Historically, those working with young children come from a variety of different backgrounds, have different expertise and qualifications and different roles and levels of responsibility. These include a variety of professionals with childcare qualifications at the following levels:

- *Level 3*, such as nursery nurses and teaching assistants with BTec, CACHE Diplomas and NVQ3 in early years and childcare;
- *Level 6* (Level 3 Higher Education), such as qualified teachers (Qualified Teacher Status: QTS) and graduate-level managers and leaders (non-QTS), including those with the National Professional Qualification in Integrated Centre Leadership (NPQICL).

There are also unqualified and training professionals who may take on different levels of responsibility for supporting children's development, managing the environment, organising and supervising play activities and supporting and leading colleagues (CWDC, 2007a). However, the situation was confusing, especially for children and their parents, who would not necessarily recognise the differences between the various adults. It was also of concern when in some areas of early childcare just under 50 per cent of professionals in full day-care settings do not have a qualification at supervisory level (Level 3) or above (CWDC, 2007a).

The Childcare Act 2006 removed the distinction between different types of provision in the early years, combining what had been two distinct stages, 0–3 years and 3–5 years, into one coherent stage: the Early Years Foundation Stage (DfES, 2007). The Early Years Foundation Stage (EYFS) does not fully combine what many who work in early childhood consider to be early years, that is, from birth to 8 years of age, but it does go a long way to provide coherence for what was increasingly becoming a fragmented service for children.

Currently the statutory requirements and guidance on the extent to which early years workers need specific qualifications varies between settings. Individuals within the early years workforce have a range of qualifications and undertake various roles with differing levels of responsibility. The Childcare Act 2006 together with the publication of the Ten Year Strategy (DfES, 2004a) set out new duties for local authorities to provide for young children and began the process of changing perceptions of early years professionals. Further publication to support the development of the Every Child Matters agenda (DfES, 2004b) provided a climate for changing the early years workforce, through the setting up of the Children's Workforce Strategy with the aim of improving outcomes for children in five areas,

- health;
- safety;
- enjoyment and achievement;
- positive contribution;
- economic well-being.

The Children's Workforce Strategy identified four challenges in developing and improving the early years workforce (CWDC, 2007b: 4),

- recruiting more people into the children's workforce;
- developing and retaining more people in the workforce;
- strengthening integrated working and developing new workforce roles;
- improving and strengthening leadership, management and supervision.

It is well recognised that quality early years provision has a positive effect on children's future development (Schwienhart *et al.*, 1993; EPPE, 2003) and highly qualified and effective professionals play a major part in supporting development (Moyles *et al.*, 2002; Siraj-Blatchford *et al.*, 2002; BERA, 2003). This has been a persuasive argument in favour of developing the workforce, so that all who work with young children have the necessary skills and understandings, are highly motivated and that quality continuing professional development opportunities are in place (CWDC, 2007a).

Tools for Learning

Writing a literature review

In this chapter we are focusing on how to write a literature review and develop persuasive written arguments. A literature review should be focused on the area you are researching and should use the literature to:

1. set the scene and provide an introduction to the research, through a critical examination of literature in the area;
2. provide a critical analysis to answer the research questions posed.

Selecting literature

Before you start to write a literature review, you need to select the literature. You need to ensure you get a balance between professional and academic; books, journals and websites; seminal and recent texts. It is essential that the balance is correct or your whole work will suffer. You need to ensure that you engage with current work (less than 7 years old), unless it is a seminal text, such as a very important piece of research or an early childhood theorist's original work. You also need to ensure that you read both academic research books and journals, which raise and analyse ideas, and professional books and journals, which apply these ideas in early years settings. There may also be some policy or historical documents that are relevant to your research that should be used.

Using literature

Once you have selected your literature, you need to read it and understand it in order to be able to use it (analyse it) rather than just describe it (see the Tools for Learning in Chapters 8 and 9). Once you have read the literature and have a good idea of your argument, you can use those ideas to support your thinking or argue against and answer your research questions. Make sure you also use secondary data to justify your ideas and answer your research questions. If the literature differs from your view, say why and provide justification for your view from your experience/observation. Be careful not to quote large chunks of the literature as this tends to be more descriptive, and take especial care to ensure that your references are accurate and fully set out in the reference section.

Effective use of reading involves making persuasive arguments (Toulmin, 1958) and using reading to support them, rather than merely citing the reading, as this shows understanding of the issues through analysis of the ideas expressed in the text rather than description. As the skill of using reading develops, then literature needs to be used by the reader to create critical arguments. See Chapter 9 to learn more about creating arguments. In a written literature review, you need to make claims with evidence to support them (data), explaining the relationship between the claim and the evidence/data (warrants) and any specified conditions under which claims hold true (qualifiers), making explicit any underlying assumptions (backings). You also need to make counter-claims and discuss any evidence which contradicts either the data, warrant, backing or qualifier of an argument you are making (counter-claims and rebuttals).

In order to understand how to develop persuasive written arguments and how to use literature, look at how literature is used and referenced in this and other books.

Practical Tasks

Characteristics of early years professionals

Level 1

Look at two of the following pieces of literature and identify what they say about early years professionals:

BERA Early Years Special Interest Group (2003);

CWDC, (2007b);

DfES, (2004a);

DfES, (2004b);

DfES (2007);

EPPE (2003);

Moyles *et al.*, (2002);

Schwienhart *et al.* (1993);

Siraj-Blatchford *et al.* (2002).

> **Level 2**
>
> Use four of the pieces of literature listed under Level 1 to identify characteristics of
> early years professionals
>
> **Level 3**
>
> Use all the pieces of literature listed under Level 1 to identify characteristics of effec-
> tive early years professionals and use this to draw up an action plan to develop your
> own professionalism.

Standards for early years professionals

One aspect of the development of the early years workforce has been the introduction of
standards for leading early years professionals. Local authorities with their partners have
had to translate the principles of *Every Child Matters: Change for Children* (DfES, 2004b) into
local action and this has included plans for a tenfold increase in children's centres in phased
development over 5 years. Each children's centre needs to have lead professionals and these
will be expected to be graduates. This means that the increasing need for early childhood
degree courses is great. Eventually there will be a lead professional supporting groups of
early years professionals, and someone with the early years professional status in all children's centres offering childcare by 2010, and in every full day-care setting by 2015. The aim
is that all professionals working in full day-care settings should be qualified at Level 3 by
2015 and that all supervisors in full day-care settings, sessional care and out-of-school childcare settings should also be qualified at Level 3. All other early years staff should be working
towards relevant qualifications and be supported by the lead professionals.

The CWDC has identified criteria for lead professionals which can be seen in Figure
11.1. Lead early years professionals will need to meet all the standards (CWDC, 2007b)
and also be able to lead and support others in meeting them too, thus ensuring excellent
provision for children in their care.

The standards are divided into six areas:

- knowledge and understanding;
- effective practice;
- relationships with children;
- communicating and working in partnership with families and carers;
- teamwork and collaboration;
- professional development.

They were designed to provide equity between early years professionals and qualified
teachers, that is between the Early Years Professional Status (EYPS) and Qualified Teacher
Status (QTS). However, the standards for EYPS are designed for lead professionals and
those for QTS (TDA, 2006) for beginner teaching professionals. The QTS standards can be
found at www.tda.gov.uk/upload/resources/pdf/s/standards_a4.pdf. They are divided into
three areas:

- attributes;
- knowledge and understanding;
- skills.

Knowledge and understanding: *a secure knowledge and understanding that underpins practice and informs leadership of others*

S1 The principles and content of the Early Years Foundation Stage and how to put them in to practice;

S2 The individual and diverse ways in which children develop and learn from birth to the end of the foundation stage and thereafter;

S3 How children's well-being, development, learning and behaviour can be affected by a range of influences and transitions from inside and outside the setting;

S4 The main provisions of the national and local statutory and non-statutory frameworks within which children's services work and their implications for early years settings;

S5 The current legal requirements, national policies and guidance on health and safety, safeguarding and promoting the well-being of children and their implications for early years settings;

S6 The contribution that other professionals within the setting and beyond can make to children's physical and emotional well-being, development and learning.

Effective practice

S7 Have high expectations of all children and commitment to ensuring that they can achieve their full potential;

S8 Establish and sustain a safe, welcoming, purposeful, stimulating and encouraging environment where children feel confident and secure and are able to develop and learn;

S9 Provide balanced and flexible daily and weekly routines that meet children's needs and enable them to develop and learn;

S10 Use close, informed observation and other strategies to monitor children's activity, development and progress systematically and carefully, and use this information to inform, plan and improve practice and provision;

S11 Plan and provide safe and appropriate child-led and adult-initiated experiences, activities and play opportunities in indoor, outdoor and in out-of-setting contexts, which enable children to develop and learn;

S12 Select, prepare and use a range of resources suitable for children's ages, interests and abilities, taking account of diversity and promoting equality and inclusion;

S13 Make effective personalised provision for the children they work with;

S14 Respond appropriately to children, informed by how children develop and learn and a clear understanding of possible next steps in their development and learning;

S15 Support the development of children's language and communication skills;

S16 Engage in sustained shared thinking with children;

S17 Promote positive behaviour, self-control and independence through using effective behaviour management strategies and developing children's social, emotional and behavioural skills;

S18 Promote children's rights, equality, inclusion and anti-discriminatory practice in all aspects of their practice;

S19 Establish a safe environment and employ practices that promote children's health, safety and physical, mental and emotional well-being;

S20 Recognise when a child is in danger or at risk of harm and know how to act to protect them;

S21 Assess, record and report on progress in children's development and learning and use this as a basis for differentiating provision;

S22 Give constructive and sensitive feedback to help children understand what they have achieved and think about what they need to do next and, when appropriate, encourage children to think about, evaluate and improve on their own performance;

S23 Identify and support children whose progress, development or well-being is affected by changes or difficulties in their personal circumstances and know when to refer them to colleagues for specialist support;

S24 Be accountable for the delivery of high-quality provision.

Relationships with children

S25 Establish fair, respectful, trusting, supportive and constructive relationships with children;

S26 Communicate sensitively and effectively with children from birth to the end of the foundation stage;

S27 Listen to children, pay attention to what they say and value and respect their views;

S28 Demonstrate the positive values, attitudes and behaviour they expect from children.

Figure 11.1 The Standards for Early Years Professional Status (EYPS)
Source: CWDC, 2007b

Communicating and working in partnership with families and carers
S29 Recognise and respect the influential and enduring contribution that families and parents/carers can make to children's development, well-being and learning;
S30 Establish fair, respectful, trusting and constructive relationships with families and parents/carers and communicate sensitively and effectively with them;
S31 Work in partnership with families and parents/carers, at home and in the setting, to nurture children, to help them develop and to improve outcomes for them;
S32 Provide formal and informal opportunities through which information about children's well-being, development and learning can be shared between the setting and families and parents/carers.

Teamwork and collaboration
S33 Establish and sustain a culture of collaborative and cooperative working between colleagues;
S34 Ensure that colleagues working with them understand their role and are involved appropriately in helping children to meet planned objectives;
S35 Influence and shape the policies and practices of the setting and share in collective responsibility for their implementation;
S36 Contribute to the work of a multi-professional team and, where appropriate, coordinate and implement agreed programmes and interventions on a day-to-day basis.

Professional development
S37 Develop and use skills in literacy, numeracy and information and communication technology to support their work with children and wider professional activities;
S38 Reflect on and evaluate the impact of practice, modifying approaches where necessary, and take responsibility for identifying and meeting their professional development needs;
S39 Take a creative and constructively critical approach towards innovation, and adapt practice if benefits and improvements are identified.

Figure 11.1 Continued

Reflective Tasks

Comparing EPYS and QTS standards

Level 1

Look at the sections for knowledge and understanding in the EYPs standards in Figure 11.1 and QTS standards at www.tda.gov.uk/upload/resources/pdf/s/standards _a4.pdf Compare the two sections and identify the similarities and differences between them.

Level 2

Look at the section on professional values and practice in the QTS standards and compare with the EYPS standards in Figure 11.1.

- What sections in the EYPS deal with professional values and practice?
- Are the standards in the EYPS comparable with those in the QTS standards?

Level 3

Look at the section on effective practice in the EYPS standards (Figure 11.1) and compare with the section on teaching in the QTS standards.

- How do the two sections compare?
- How does your setting meet the two different standards?

Both the CWDC and the Training and Development Agency for Schools (TDA), working in partnership with other key providers, plan to develop 'a world-class children's workforce' (CWDC, 2007a) by training and developing the early years workforce. They recognise that their plans are ambitious, but consider that it is essential to be ambitious in order to improve the quality of provision and address the professional needs of both graduate and non-graduate professionals. They also recognise that developing such a diverse group of professionals is a complex and difficult task.

There are four pathways to achieve EYPS (CWDC, 2007b):

1. A three-month part-time validation pathway for professionals who have nearly fulfilled all the standards. This pathway involves the validation of evidence that the professionals meet the standards and have the necessary skills for EYPS, rather than a training programme. A typical professional for whom this is applicable would have a relevant degree (e.g. a BA(Hons) Early Childhood Studies) and have considerable experience of working across the 0–5 age range.

2. A six-month part-time extended professional development pathway (Short EPD). These professionals would have some of the experience necessary for EYPS but would need to undergo extra training. For example, they may be a graduate teacher who has experience of working with 3–5-year-old children. They may need additional experience of working with the under 3s and need some additional child development knowledge and understanding. Another candidate for the short extended development pathway could be an early childhood studies graduate with experience of working with children from birth to 5 years of age, but who needs some additional support within their own setting to lead developments, so they can truly say they are a lead professional.

3. A 15-month part-time extended professional development pathway (Long EPD), for professionals who have some experience or qualifications but need a little more support to fully achieve EYPS. An experienced professional who has a Foundation degree (FdA) in Early Childhood Studies and has considerable experience of working with children from 0 to 5 years of age, would need to undertake the long extended professional development pathway, as they would need to continue their studies to gain a full BA(Hons) in Early Childhood Studies. Another candidate for this pathway could be a graduate in another unrelated subject, but with substantial experience of working across the 0–5 age range. They would need to undertake child development modules of work to expand their understanding of early childhood development. There may also be professionals on this pathway who need to gain experience of working with the 0–5 age group and they would have to undertake over 15 months of placement to gain the necessary professional practice and leadership.

4. A 12-month full training pathway, which accommodates the needs of candidates with graduate level qualifications but very little relevant experience with 0–5-year-olds. A graduate with a degree in psychology or a teacher trained at secondary level would be eligible for this pathway. They would have to undertake at least 18 weeks of placements in early years settings to gain experience in professional practice and leadership, as well as modules that link theory and practice.

Professionals wishing to work in the wider early childhood context, with children from 5 to 8 years of age, would need to undertake a relevant QTS qualification, that is, a QTS degree or a relevant degree and a Postgraduate Certificate in Education (PGCE). In order to achieve QTS they must meet the standards set out by the Training and Development Agency (TDA).

Reflective Tasks

Meeting the Standards

Level 1

Look at the standards for EYPS in Figure 11.1, or QTS www.tda.gov.uk/upload/resources/pdf/s/standards_a4.pdf Your choice of standards depends on which route to early years professional you are following: EYPS for working with children aged 0–5, or QTS for working with children aged 5–8.

- Audit your own skills by identifying which standards you have already achieved and which you need to achieve.
- For each standard you feel you have met, you need to provide evidence as to how and when you met it.
- For the standards you have yet to meet, identify which ones you could achieve in the short, medium and long term and how you can achieve them (that is, produce an action plan to meet the standards).

Level 2

Look at the standards for EYPS in Figure 11.1, or QTS www.tda.gov.uk/upload/resources/pdf/s/standards_a4.pdf. Your choice of standards depends on which route to early years professional you are following: EYPS for working with children aged 0–5, or QTS for working with children aged 5–8.

- Audit your own skills by identifying which standards you have already achieved and which you need to achieve.
- For each standard you feel you have met, you need to provide evidence as to how and when you met it.
- For the standards you have yet to meet, identify which ones you could achieve in the short, medium and long term and how you can achieve them (that is, produce an action plan to meet the standards).
- Look for continuing professional development (CPD) courses which will help you to achieve some of the standards and add to your action plan. Share this plan with your manager, setting leader or headteacher and discuss how they can support you in achieving the standards.

Level 3

Support all your staff in auditing their current expertise, using the tasks set out above. As a staff or within the senior management group, decide how you can support staff in reaching the necessary standards. Are there whole setting courses that would help, or individual training courses? Can you access the support of your local authority?

Assessment against the standards

QTS is acquired through training and education programmes in higher education (HE), national and local consortia and graduate teacher programmes. In order to gain QTS, the standards are assessed during the training programme and during the school placements. In addition, there are online skills tests in numeracy, literacy and information and communication technology (ICT). These are online tests that all trainee teachers need to pass in order to qualify as a teacher. They were introduced in 2001 to ensure that all qualified teachers have the core skills necessary to 'fulfil their wider professional role in schools, rather than the subject knowledge required for teaching' (TDA, 2007). All the test questions are set in the context of the professional role as a teacher and all are written using real professional data and information. In this way the application of skills is tested in real professional contexts. There are about 50 test centres throughout England and the online tests can be retaken a number of times. However, all three tests need to be passed with a mark of at least 60 per cent.

There are a variety of different training providers for EYPS, from higher and further education (FE) institutions, to local authority and independent providers. Some of these (e.g. HE providers) will be able to offer all routes, or ones that involve Level 6 (HE Level 3) training and education, and others will be well placed to offer support for validation and short pathways. All are required to personalise the pathways they offer to meet the individual needs and differing experiences of the professionals. In this way the CWDC (2007b) aim to support the development of a large number of professionals, meet the national targets for EYPS and improve provision for early years children. The process of assessment for EYPS involves a briefing and preparation for assessment, and the final assessment. The assessment begins with a three-day diagnostic process involving an introduction to the standards, an assessment to provide feedback on professionals skills, practical exercises involving relevant professional issues and scenarios, day-to-day work, a group discussion, an interpersonal exercise and a personal interview (CWDC, 2007b). Assessment involves professionals keeping a record of work they do that meets the standards (a portfolio of supporting evidence), so that assessment is evidence-based. The emphasis is on quality rather than quantity of evidence. Assessment also involves a visit from an assessor to the setting, so that the setting, evidence and the professional can be assessed *in situ*. The final assessment aims to be consistent, rigorous, credible and manageable, and recognises that many of the standards are interrelated and can be assessed in a combined way.

The early years professional and the Early Years Foundation Stage (EYFS)

There are a variety of early years professionals (see Pictures 11.1 and 11.2) and they comprise an extremely diverse workforce, which is coordinated by the work of the Children's Workforce Development Council. There are about 500,000 people working in the early years: 80 per cent as employees, 20 per cent self-employed and probably more than 250,000 volunteers (CWDC, 2007c). The CWDC list the different individuals whose work with young children they coordinate (2007c: 1):

- managers, deputies and assistants working in playgroups, children's centres, day nurseries, nursery schools and classes;
- registered childminders working in their own homes, or in a variety of settings such as children's centres, extended schools, etc.;
- nannies;
- portage workers (home visitors providing an educational service for pre-school children and their families who are recognised as needing additional support);
- foster carers;
- children and families' social workers;
- registered managers of children's homes, their deputies and assistants plus all residential child care workers;
- family centre managers, their deputies and assistants plus all family centre workers;

Picture 11.1 A nursery professional
Source: John Harris/Report Digital

- day centre managers, their deputies and assistants plus all day centre workers;
- outreach/family support workers;
- learning mentors, who support individual children in schools and other settings;
- behaviour and education support teams;

Picture 11.2 A pre-school professional
Source: Jacky Chapman/Alamy Images

- education welfare officers;
- educational psychologists;
- other therapists working with children;
- Connexions personal advisers;
- children and family court advisory and support service family court advisers;
- lead inspectors of registered children's services;
- support workers in all the above settings;
- volunteers not otherwise covered above.

To coordinate such a diverse range of individual professionals and volunteers is a mammoth job and one that is fraught with difficulties, as each has different expertise and needs, and faces different challenges. The CWDC have addressed this, in part, by developing a working plan, a single qualifications framework and standards. They also offer training and support for different groups of early years professionals.

Regardless of the diversity among them, there are certain characteristics which the effective early years professionals share. They should be well experienced or have undertaken a period of education (or training). The term education is preferred rather than training, as education implies a proactive approach and an element of understanding of what they should do and why, rather than a mechanistic, reactive approach and knowledge without understanding. Early years professionals also need to know who to go to for advice or leadership (see Chapter 14) and the lines of responsibility. They need to enjoy young children's company and be committed to improving the lives of all children (see Picture 11.3). They need to be reflective (see Chapter 12), reviewing and evaluating their work and striving to improve their practice, and they need to have vision or share and

Picture 11.3 An early years professional
Source: Philip Wolmuth/Alamy Images

understand the vision of those who lead them. In this way an early years professional is more than just someone who works with young children. Below are a number of case studies of different types of early years professionals, with an analysis of some of the challenges they face as they attempt to put into practice the principles of the Early Years Foundation Stage (DfES, 2007).

Research

The lead professional role

The Office for Public Management (OPM) undertook research in 10 localities, on behalf of the Department for Children, Schools and Families (DCSF), to investigate the implementation of the lead professional role. The research looked at the education, health and voluntary sector contexts, as well as younger children and young people with additional and complex needs.

The research identified that policy-makers, commissioners and practitioners support the development of the lead professional role, although there were a number of barriers to effective implementation (OPM, 2006: 5):

- Underdeveloped commissioning and strategic leadership, resulting in lack of clarity about priorities for implementation, innovation and integration locally;

- Confusion about vocabulary and roles, for example the use of the terms 'key worker' and 'case worker' to describe co-ordination and 'first point of contact' roles;

- The challenges of involving all the professional groups and managers from across the sectors, taking account of capacity and other pressures facing different sectors;

- Issues about who could take on the lead professional role (voluntary sector, primary head teachers, teachers, etc.);

- Funding and budgetary constraints – lack of both new funds and resources within mainstream budgets for change agents, and lack of understanding about how to pool resources through integrated commissioning and pooled budgets;

- Lack of wide understanding about the interdependence between the lead professional function, information sharing and CAF. These have recently been linked as part of the same process reform at the DfES. In some areas, developments are still proceeding as two or three separate work streams, and there can be a desire to first embed CAF and other improvements to information sharing before implementing the lead professional function;

- Fears about upsetting arrangements that people think are currently working well for children, young people and families, especially those with additional and complex needs, including sorting out different thresholds;

- The challenges of managing change, notably cultural change.

A qualitative survey by CWDC (2007d) gathered views from attendees at four national CWDC Integrated Working Conferences, five focus groups of health and special needs professionals and 30 telephone interviews. This survey, together with an analysis of the lead professional role, has identified that the lead professional role is welcomed and is felt to be important in the implementation of integrated working. However, without considerable support and raining the role will be less effective. A functional analysis by CWDC (2007d) of the role indicates that there are three emerging models:

- a single role, with one person undertaking the full role;

- a joint role, with more than one person undertaking the role;

- a supported role, with one person undertaking the role, but supported by others.

Most lead professionals were extensions of existing roles, in particular (in rank order), social workers, health visitors and special educational needs coordinators.

Those surveyed felt that certain factors needed to be in place in order for the role of lead professional to be fully effective. These included training programmes to develop skills and support liaison with clients and handling of issues, support from managers and understanding of the role and changes in provision and legislation.

Case Study

A home-based professional

Sally is a 36-year-old mother of three and a registered childminder. She obtained a Level 3 childcare qualification 20 years ago and worked in a local authority day nursery for 10 years, leaving just before the birth of her first child. When her second child started school, she registered as a childminder. She currently has two children in her care and additionally provides pre- and after-school care for two others. She is involved with a local childminding support group and attends regular meetings.

The challenge for Sally is accessing quality advice and support to enable her to develop her provision for children. The local childminding support group is the key to helping Sally meet this challenge as they access support from the National

Childminding Association of England and Wales. The NCMA aims to help every child reach their full potential and to 'ensure that families in every community have access to high quality home-based childcare, play, learning and family support so they can help their children reach their full potential' (NCMA, 2007: 1). The local childminding support group meet in a local children's centre and provide information, discussion and activities to help Sally to understand the following (DfES, 2007):

- each child in her care is a unique individual and competent learner from birth and that children learn and develop in different ways. Sally is able to observe children cared for by different childminders and the different practices that others employ. She is able through this observation, discussion with other childminders and reflection of her own provision to consider alternative ways of supporting individual children in her care and to realise that one approach is not necessarily appropriate for all children;

- positive relationships are an essential element of her work and she needs to develop good, loving and secure relationships with the children in her care. Indeed, there are arguments that early years professionals such as Sally are better placed to develop the secure relationships that very young children need than larger day-care settings which have a large number of staff (Bowlby, 2006; see also Chapter 6);

- the environment in her home can be developed to support and extend children's development. This comes about at the regular meetings of the childminding group through the provision of activities, speakers and role modelling of the types of environment which support child development. During meetings Sally can see how the children in her care interact with the environment and she can discuss with other childminders and experts how she can develop her home environment to impact positively on the children's development.

Case Study

A self-employed manager of a nursery and a Level 3 professional working in the nursery.

Simone is a 39-year-old self-employed manager of a private day nursery for 0–5-year-olds. She has considerable experience as a manager, but no formal childcare qualifications. She has worked extremely hard to set up the nursery and develop quality provision for children. The nursery is OFSTED-registered, as all childminders and day-care providers including playgroups, pre-schools, private nurseries, crèches and out-of-school clubs for under 8s, must be registered by OFSTED in England, or by the Care Standards Inspectorate in Wales. OFSTED registration includes a criminal records check on anyone involved in providing childcare and an inspection of the premises to look at health and safety and educational welfare issues.

Rebecca is a 20-year-old, Level 3 professional, working as an early years practitioner in the nursery.

Simone's challenge is twofold:

1. At present the numbers attending the nursery are low and Simone wants the nursery to achieve a grading of 'outstanding' in a forthcoming inspection, so that parents can see the quality of provision. The development of high-quality childcare is an

essential part of the work of SureStart and the 10-year strategy for childcare (DfES, 2004a). In 2007 the Quality Improvement Project was set up to help childcare providers, local authorities and sector organisations, such as charities, social services, voluntary leisure organisations, etc., work together to promote high-quality childcare and to support continuous improvement in quality, through peer support networks, supporting settings in putting into practice the principles of the Early Years Foundation Stage (DfES, 2007) and developing courses for setting mentors. Simone is accessing this support, which is being provided by the National Children's Bureau, and working towards improving the quality of her nursery's provision 'above and beyond minimum OFSTED standards' (SureStart, 2007a: 1);

2. Simone wishes to develop both her own and Rebecca's expertise and childcare qualifications, as high-quality staff can improve the quality of care, support the achievement of an outstanding OFSTED inspection and empower staff. This can be done through the £250 million the government has invested in improving the qualifications of early years professionals. The money is accessed through the Transformation Fund and will be used to increase the number of leaders in settings taking up the new Early Years Professional Status (CWDC, 2007b). Simone now needs to decide if she will access the funding to help her achieve EYPS and become a lead professional, or support Rebecca in continuing her professional development. If she decides to develop her own expertise, then she runs the risk of sending a message that she does not value Rebecca's contribution, does not care about her personal and professional development and may lose a good professional. If she chooses to invest in Rebecca's personal and professional development, then she will effectively lose control over strategic developments in her nursery and will need to pay Rebecca more money, or risk losing her expertise. Alternatively, she could invest in both her own and Rebecca's development to EYPS, accessing the Transformation Fund for one person and providing the financial assistance for the other from her nursery profits.

Reflective Tasks

Personal and professional development

Read about how to develop quality provision through the personal and professional development of early years professionals. The following texts may help you, but look elsewhere as well and try to find other texts,

CWDC (2007a);

CWDC (2007b);

Dean (2005);

DfES (2007);

Physick (2005);

Whalley (2006).

Level 1

Put yourself in Rebecca's position and write a letter to Simone, providing a persuasive argument as to why you should be supported in your personal and professional development. Use your reading to provide the evidence necessary to make your argument persuasive. Remember the difference between an opinion and an argument: an opinion is an unsubstantiated belief and an argument is an evidence-based belief. Remember too that a persuasive argument is one that convinces the reader of the merit of your view.

Level 2

Consider what the next stage of your own personal and professional development is and use your reading and policy documents (those from government and those from your own setting) to write a persuasive argument that could be presented to your manager or leader.

Level 3

Consider the personal and professional needs of the staff in your setting. Use your reading, policy documents (both the government's and the setting's) and staff appraisal targets to write a persuasive rationale for a plan for developing staff expertise in your setting. This could be a rationale to present to a board of governors, or to the staff as a whole, or to individual staff.

Case Study

A professional working in a children's centre

Susan is a 42-year-old mother of two primary-aged children and has recently completed a work-based Early Years Foundation Degree while employed in a children's centre, offering full day care along with other family support services. Since completing the Foundation degree, she has undertaken a lead role in the setting. Her challenge is to complete the progression route to BA(Hons) and collect evidence to achieve EYPS, but still lead ongoing developments within the setting. The Transformation Fund will support her in this progression route, so the financial implications of her continuing personal and professional development are negligible. However, there are issues to do with work–life balance and longer-term financial reward for work undertaken. In undertaking the Foundation degree and the progression to BA(Hons), Susan has to attend her local university one afternoon and evening a week and complete considerable directed tasks and independent reading and reflection, in addition to her work commitments. This means that she has to study late into the evenings and at weekends in order to achieve the fulfilments of a full-time equivalent, work-based degree, and this is having an effect on the quality of her family life. In addition, the children's centre is making additional demands on her time, as she is becoming more qualified and experienced.

There are two ways in which Susan can meet this challenge. First, she can consider a part-time route for the BA(Hons) Early Childhood Studies. This will take her longer to achieve, but will free up some of her contact commitments (time spent attending the university) and work at home and in the evenings. Secondly, she can discuss with her line manager how the setting can support her in this important year, by decreasing their expectations of her and/or providing her with additional time to support her studies. If the setting is able to provide this support it will be recognising her future potential to develop the setting and enable it to provide quality provision. This may also be the first step towards Susan receiving longer-term financial reward for her endeavours. At the moment, she receives an hourly payment of £6.50 and is aware of the differential between this payment and the initial salary of an early years QTS professional. Because of this, she is considering her longer-term prospects and wondering if she should move towards QTS. This is a dilemma for many early years professionals, who do not receive increases in salary commensurate with their developing expertise and increased qualifications. It is a dilemma that the CWDC will need to address if they are going to retain the quality workforce they are currently investing in.

Marion is 45 years old and also works in the children's centre. She has a BSc in Public Health Nursing and is a Registered Health Visitor. Within the centre, she is part of a multidisciplinary team of professionals and provides health advice for families (sexual health, teenage pregnant mothers, immunisation, etc.), meeting the SureStart agenda of providing 'seamless holistic integrated services and information' SureStart, 2007b) for children up to 5 years of age and their families. Marion would like to develop her qualifications so that she can become a lead professional in the centre. In order to do this she needs to undertake EYPS. Since she already has a degree and considerable experience working with children from 0 to 5 years of age, Marion will need to undertake the extended professional development pathway (Long EPD) to achieve EYPS. Susan likewise will need to take this route to EYPS, but for different reasons, as Marion has an honours degree but not in early childhood and Susan has a Foundation degree in Early Childhood Studies, but not an honours degree. Marion will need to undertake child development modules of work to expand her understanding of early childhood development. Marion will need to ascertain if funding for her to undertake these modules is available via the Transformation Fund and what providers can offer. It may be that part-time child development modules on a Master's degree could help her to gain EYPS and to continue her personal and professional development to Master's level.

Case Study

A reception teacher

Joe is 22 and a recently qualified primary teacher in his first year of teaching, working in a reception class in a large primary school with a 60-place nursery. He achieved a first class honours degree in Education and Early Childhood Studies and obtained his QTS through the PGCE route. The headteacher wants to extend provision within the Early Years Foundation Stage by combining the nursery and reception classes into a Foundation Stage unit where children can develop in a holistic way, and is looking for a lead professional from within the setting who will be part of the senior management team of the school. Joe wants to apply for the post and in order to do this needs to be clear what his particular strengths are and what he sees as his personal and professional challenges.

Reflective Tasks

The lead professional

Level 1

Look at the Job Description in Figure 11.2 and consider how Joe, as a newly qualified practitioner (see Case Study above), can persuade the school that he has the skills and qualities needed to be the lead professional. Use evidence from reading to support your arguments.

Level 2

Look at the Job Description in Figure 11.2 and consider what personal and professional needs Joe will have if he is to achieve in this role. Write a personal and professional development plan for Joe to help him to develop his personal and professional practice and achieve success in this role.

Level 3

Look at Figure 11.2 and consider the appropriateness of the key tasks. Write a person specification for the lead professional for the Early Years Foundation Stage using the headings in Table 11.1. Consider how you could, through personal and professional development, support Joe as the successful applicant.

Main purpose of the job

To lead developments in the Early Years Foundation Stage by forming a Foundation Stage unit and providing quality care and education for children aged between 3 and 5 years of age.

Key tasks

- To assist the headteacher by contributing to the design, development and administration of the Foundation Stage unit.
- To coordinate the planning for the delivery of the Early Years Foundation Stage.
- To be responsible for budget and resource management for the Early Years Foundation Stage unit.
- To contribute to the delivery of the Early Years Foundation Stage.
- To be responsible for tracking, monitoring, assessing and analysing the progress of individuals and groups of children.
- To participate in appropriate training and staff development activities.
- To be responsible for the development of an annual action plan for the Early Years Foundation Stage.
- To undertake any other duties that may reasonably be required.
- To agree objectives and targets with the headteacher in accordance with the school's priorities and to participate in the staff appraisal process.
- To provide written reports on activity to all stakeholders as appropriate and as requested.

Figure 11.2 Job description for a lead professional for the Early Years Foundation Stage

Table 11.1 Person specification for a lead professional for the Early Years Foundation Stage

	Essential	Desirable
Education/qualifications and special training		
Knowledge and skills		
Experience		
Personality requirements		

Case Study

A playgroup leader

Pam is a 29-year-old single mother and a playgroup leader. She has no childcare qualifications, having left school pregnant at 16 without sitting her GCSEs. The playgroup is run on a not-for-profit basis by a parent management committee, charging minimum fees. At the moment the playgroup has morning sessions of three hours a day for children from $2\frac{1}{2}$ years of age and children normally attend a maximum of three sessions a week. The playgroup committee are considering offering extended or full day care to children from the age of 18 months. The playgroup is registered by the government regulatory body and subject to the regulations and inspection regime. These regulations include the need for half the staff to be trained and have staff ratios of 3 to 1 for children under 2 years of age, 4 to 1 for children aged 2 years of age and 8 to 1 for children aged 3–7 years of age.

As a member of the playgroup committee, Pam's dilemma is what effect the provision of extended care will have on both the children and their families. She can seek help from the Pre-school Learning Alliance, a community-run, charitable organisation which provides support for community pre-schools, 'through training courses, quality assurance systems, local visiting by skilled advisers, a range of helpful publications and other merchandise, advice and helplines, advocacy or help with PR and fundraising' (Pre-school Learning Alliance, 2007: 1). They will help Pam to see the advantages and disadvantages of the move to extended day care. The advantages may include:

• increasing day care which will help parents seeking work, helping to raise children out of poverty and support the overall well-being of children in the community (see UNICEF, 2007);
• supporting children's socialisation and language development (EPPE, 2003);
• enabling children to develop friendship groups at an early age which modern lifestyles are making difficult (Children's Society, 2007).

Disadvantages may include:

• the negative effects of extended day care on children's emotional development and stability (Bowlby, 2006);
• the contribution of day care to changes to childhood (Elkind, 2001; Palmer, 2006; and see Chapter 8);
• the effects on the early years workforce within the playgroup and the need to train additional staff.

As an early years professional, Pam also has to consider what her personal and professional development and training needs are and whether the playgroup committee and the Pre-School Alliance could help her to access and finance the training to enable her to become a fully trained early years professional.

Case Study

An educational psychologist

Sita is 31 and an educational psychologist, concerned with helping children or young people who are experiencing problems within an educational setting with the aim of enhancing their learning. She works with individual children who have learning difficulties and social or emotional problems and advises policy-makers, teachers, parents and other professionals who are involved with these children on a range of issues, such as bullying, behaviour, emotional development, etc. Part of her work involves assessing children through observation, interviews and test materials. She also provides training support for teachers and other professionals on behaviour management, stress management and assessment issues.

In order to be an educational psychologist, Sita undertook an honours degree in psychology accredited by the British Psychological Society (BPS), and a PGCE. In 2005, the routes to becoming an educational psychologist changed and, while Sita's route is still applicable, an honours degree that is not in psychology can be converted via a BPS-accredited conversion course (with lists available from the BPS website) and a three-year doctoral training programme. This should be accredited by the BPS and include at least 300 days of professional placement work under supervision. Sita works for a local government employer and they do offer a grant scheme for those who meet the entry criteria and intend to seek employment as an educational psychologist within a local education authority in England or Wales after completion. In order to be accepted onto the postgraduate course relevant experience of working with children in educational, childcare or community settings is required, and Sita obtained this through her PGCE and by working as a teacher for a few years before becoming an educational psychologist. Experience as a teacher is considered very relevant for those wishing to become educational psychologists and teachers may be given exemptions from parts of the doctorate. Apart from academic qualifications, those wishing to become educational psychologists need to be excellent communicators, with sensitivity, tact and diplomacy, coupled with the ability to be assertive, persuasive and effective facilitators, with strong negotiating, administration and time management skills.

Sita is based in the educational offices of the local authority and visits a range of settings, working with children and their families and the professionals who work with them. She attends case conferences involving multidisciplinary teams on how best to meet the social, emotional, behavioural and learning needs of children. Sita's dilemma is how to be more effective in her work, making the best use of her time. She is aware that she is seen as a last resort by many professionals who work daily with children, who see her only on rare occasions and who believe she has little real experience of the daily problems they face in managing challenging behaviour, resolving emotional conflicts and supporting developing children. She wishes to share her expertise and work more effectively in multidisciplinary teams, rather than simply being concerned with one-to-one assessments. To this end, Sita is negotiating with her local authority employers and the local children's centre to be based for three days a week in the community, having a shared office with social and health workers in the children's centre. In this way the centre will provide a fully integrated, multidisciplinary service to the community.

Case Study

An ECS student

Rob is 21 and in the third year of a BA(Hons) degree in Early Childhood Studies. The Early Childhood Studies programme involves the development of understanding of child development (psychology, sociology and physiology) and the nature of childhood, the health of children, and the legislation and provision that underpin early years provision. It also provides understanding and skills in delivering the Early Years Foundation Stage (DfES, 2007) and programmes of study at Key Stages 1 and 2 of the National Curriculum (DfEE, 1999), working with children with diverse needs, observing and assessing children and leading and managing in early childhood settings. Rob is likely to graduate with a good honours degree and wishes to work with children aged between 3 and 5 years of age. His dilemma is whether to do a PGCE or to apply for a position as an early years professional on graduation. A PGCE will extend his student debt and, while it gives him the potential for a higher salary, most early years professionals working in 0–5 settings receive considerably less financial reward. He is more interested in the social and health care of children than their educational development. He is also less keen on working with children aged 0–3 and yet he will need to have this experience in order to achieve EYPS; an essential qualification for those who wish to make their careers with children in the early years. A PGCE may not be the most sensible route for Rob as it is an extremely intensive course and one that will involve him in areas of work and with ages of children that he does not feel comfortable with. He might be better to find a position in an early years setting and work towards EYPS, gaining experience with younger children as he matures and when he feels more comfortable with them. In a few years, he may decide to undertake additional qualifications, such as Master's in the areas of health and social care, thus developing him both personally and professionally.

The challenges facing early years professionals

At a recent Child Development Conference organised by the authors, early years professionals identified a large number of challenges that they face in developing effective childcare provision. These reflected the changes that have occurred in the early years in recent times and the resulting uncertainties.

One of the big questions was whether the Early Years Foundation Stage (DfES, 2007) was really necessary. The EYFS is marketed as a comprehensive framework which sets the standards for learning, development and care of children from birth to 5 (see Chapter 9) and builds on and replaces the existing statutory Curriculum Guidance for the Foundation Stage (DfES, 2007), the non-statutory Birth to Three Matters framework (SureStart, 2003), and the regulatory frameworks in the National Standards for Under 8s Day Care and

Childminding (DfES, 2003). All registered early years providers and schools are required to use the EYFS from September 2008. The purpose and objectives of the EYFS are encompassed within the Every Child Matters agenda (DfES, 2004b) and aim to:

- set the standards for the learning, development and care of children when outside their homes;
- provide for equality of opportunity;
- create the framework for partnerships between early years professionals and parents;
- improve quality and consistency;
- lay a secure foundation for future learning.

These are aims that all involved in childcare and development would share, so why are some early years professionals concerned about the necessity of the EYFS? The professionals felt that while guidance was welcomed, a statutory curriculum for a non-compulsory stage of development was at best rather misguided and at worst insulting to those very experienced professionals who have worked with young children for very many years.

There appear to be three elements to this concern. First, while a common framework is useful and ties up the anomalies in having many different pieces of legislation, the EYFS does cover a huge area of development from 0 to 5 years and enormous differences in development. Professionals working with the youngest children need different types of skills and understandings to those working with older children and this does not appear to be fully recognised in either the Early Years Foundation Stage (DfES, 2007) or the standard for the Early Years Professional Standards (CWDC, 2007b). Secondly, while there was consultation about the EYFS, this was not something to which many professionals appear able to contribute, partly because of the timing of consultation and partly because they do not feel they have a voice. Thirdly, there does appear to be an anomaly between the expectations of skills, knowledge and experience of early years professionals and those of parents, with professionals becoming more and more skilled and confined by legislation and parents becoming deskilled. These three concerns have led some professionals to feel that they have no say in the development of their professionalism, have demands placed on them without consultation and are becoming deskilled. The effects of yet more legislation include increased inspection and a climate of blame, which also has a negative effect on professional morale. Increasing professionalism with better education is having a positive effect on the quality of provision and the quality of the professionals working in the early years. It has also opened the eyes of professionals, who are beginning to question advice and legislation and to engage in the debates called for by many academics and esteemed professionals (Bowlby, 2006; *Daily Telegraph*, 2006). This opening up of professional debate will be supportive of developing effective childcare and should be encouraged. However, it will be necessary to involve the early years professionals in the decisions in a more proactive way, showing that their views and experiences are valued and valuable (see Picture 11.4).

Professionals are very concerned about the part they are playing in changing childhoods and wonder if we are in danger of taking children's childhood away from them. This issue is discussed at length in Chapter 8, but we need to keep this debate alive and move on to practical ways in which we can preserve the good and extend childhood for all children. This is not just in the early years but through to adolescence and adulthood, so that we can show through practice that every child matters (DfES, 2004a) and that every child can:

- be healthy, enjoying physical and mental well-being and living healthily;
- be safe, being safe and protected from any form of harm or neglect;
- enjoy and achieve, having access to and benefiting from opportunities and developing important life skills;

Picture 11.4 Early years professionals debating the nature of childhood

- contribute to community and social life, so that they are able to make a positive contribution to society and take some responsibility for their own actions in society;
- be economically well, being able to achieve their full potential and not be economically disadvantaged later in life because they have not had opportunities to fulfil their potential.

The challenge of empowering parents is considered to be an area in which early years professionals would appreciate help and guidance. Developing positive relationships is a fundamental principle of the EYFS, but there is no common agreement about how to do this. Within this book, Chapter 13 considers this issue, but more practical advice on how to address partnership issues would be welcomed, rather than more legislation or semi-legal contracts such as parenting contracts, which appear to be divisive. Discussion of parental partnership leads to questions about responsibility and whether there has been a cultural shift away from parental responsibility for childcare, emotional development, socialisation, diet, health and indeed all areas of child welfare and development. Over many years more responsibility has fallen on the professionals, with the curriculum, especially at Key Stages 1 and 2, being very structured and focused on cognitive development. In situations where there are no effective partnerships between professionals and parents there may well be some areas of child development and welfare that are not fully addressed, to the detriment of the child. In recent years, the cultural shift for responsibility has moved towards the government, who are expected to comment on and legislate for diverse childhood issues, such as child care, immunization, diet, exercise, education, teaching approaches, social and behavioural issues. But where does this leave parents? Surely we should be supporting parents and empowering them rather than removing their responsibilities?

Professionals would welcome guidance that they can share with parents, providing persuasive evidence on:

- the effects of long days spent in care outside the home (see Bowlby, 2006, and Chapter 6);
- how parents and professionals can work together effectively to settle children into day care (see Chapter 13);
- how professionals can minimise the negative effects of extended day care;
- what playground games and video games are developmentally appropriate;
- what subjects are inappropriate at different ages (e.g. sex and relationships, drugs, moral issues) and how to tackle questions about inappropriate subjects.

An element of professionalism is having a firm philosophy and vision (see Chapter 2). Early years professionals need to work together in an effective team (see Chapters 13 and 14) and develop shared values and teamwork skills. Support and guidance for this is an important prerequisite for all new and changing teams before they embark on supporting children and their families. It is also important for existing teams to reassess their philosophy at reasonably regular intervals to ensure that all professionals working in a team share visions and ways to achieve their collaborative aims as well as the aims of the EYPS (DfES, 2007), or National Curriculum (DfEE, 1999). Professionalism also implies that the practitioner has embarked on a lifelong personal and professional development pathway and this has resource implications for settings and employers, who need to support all appropriate personal and professional development. There is concern at the present time that the support (financial and human/advice) is not always readily accessible to assist their personal and professional development journey and that different types of development are valued more. While some early years professionals have better terms of employment and financial reward than others and while there is no real equivalence between professionals with EYPS and professionals with QTS, there will remain uncertainty and unhappiness in the early years sector. However, the increasing professionalism and empowerment of early years professionals means that they are now much more articulate about injustices and prejudices and so we are in for a real and much needed debate about early years professionalism.

Summary

→ Historically, those working with young children come from a variety of different backgrounds, have different expertise and qualifications and different roles and levels of responsibility.

→ This diversity of the early years workforce is recognised by the Children's Workforce Development Council (CWDC), who also identify that many settings and professionals now integrate care and education.

→ It is well recognised that quality early years provision has a positive effect on children's future development and highly qualified and effective professionals play a major part in supporting development.

→ One aspect of the development of the early years workforce has been the introduction of standards for leading early years professionals.

→ Eventually there will be a lead professional supporting groups of early years professionals, and someone with the early years professional status in all children's centres offering childcare by 2010, and in every full day-care setting by 2015.

→ The CWDC has identified criteria for lead professionals, who will need to meet all the standards and also to demonstrate that they can lead and support others in meeting them too, thus ensuring excellent provision for children in their care.

→ There are four pathways to achieving Early Years Professional Status depending on qualifications and experience.

→ The process of assessment for EYPS involves a briefing and preparation for assessment, and the final assessment.

→ The final assessment aims to be consistent, rigorous, credible and manageable, and recognises that many of the standards are interrelated and can be assessed in a combined way.

→ Regardless of the diversity among early years professionals, there are certain characteristics which effective practitioners need to demonstrate.

→ Case studies of a home-based professional, a self-employed manager of a nursery, a professional working in a children's centre, a reception teacher, a playgroup leader, an educational psychologist and an ECS student demonstrate that there is a diverse range of challenges faced by each.

→ There is debate about some of the changes, including questioning whether or not the Early Years Foundation Stage is necessary and/or appropriate.

→ In recent years, the cultural shift has moved responsibility towards the government, who comment on and legislate for diverse childhood issues which in the past were seen to be the responsibility of the parents.

→ The challenge of empowering parents is considered to be an area in which early years professionals would appreciate help and guidance.

→ A shared philosophy is important to ensure that early years professionals can work effectively as part of a team.

Key Questions

- What are the different types of early years professionals?
- What is your understanding of the standards for early years professionals and how will the assessments take place?
- How do different early years professionals ensure they are working to the principles of the Early Years Foundation Stage?
- What are some of the challenges faced by the diverse range of early years professionals?
- What are the main concerns related to the introduction of the Early Years Foundation Stage and the Early Years Professional Status?

References

BERA Early Years Special Interest Group (2003) *Early Years Research: Pedagogy, Curriculum and Adult Roles, Training and Professionalism.* Southwell: BERA

Bowlby, R. (2006) *The Need for Secondary Attachment Figures in Childcare* www.telegraph.co.uk/opinion/main.jhtml?xml=/opinion/2006/10/21/nosplit/ dt2101.xml#head5Childcare problems

Children's Society (2007) *Good Childhood? A Question for Our Times.* London: The Children's Society

CWDC (2007a) CWDC – *Developing the Early Years Workforce* http://www.cwdcouncil.org.uk/ projects/eypbackground.htm

CWDC (2007b) *Prospectus Early Years Professional Status*. Leeds: CWDC

CWDC (2007c) *About CWDC: What we do* http://www.cwdcouncil.org.uk/aboutcwdc/whatwedo.htm

CWDC (2007d) *Moving Towards Integrated Working. Progress Report 2007*. Leeds: CWDC

Daily Telegraph (2006) Letters to the Editor – Modern Life Leads to More Depression among Children, Tuesday 12 September: 23

Dean, E. (2005) Reform or Rejection? The Impact of Change on the Role of the Pre-school Leader, in Hirst, K. and Nutbrown, C. (2005) *Perspectives on Early Childhood Education: Contemporary research*. Stoke-on-Trent: Trentham Books

DfEE (1999) *The National Curriculum: Handbook For Teachers In England*. London: DfEE/QCA

DfES (2003) *Full Day Care. National Standards for Under 8s Day Care and Childminding*. London: DfES

DfES (2004a) *Choice for Parents, the Best Start for Children: A Ten Year Strategy for Children*. London: DfES

DfES (2004b) *Every Child Matters: Change For Children*. London: DfES

DfES (2007) *Statutory Framework for the Early Years Foundation Stage: Setting the Standards for Learning, Development and Care for children from birth to five. Every Child Matters, Change for Children*. London: DfES

Elkind, D. (2001) *The Hurried Child. Growing Up Too Fast Too Soon*, 3rd edn. Cambridge, MA: Da Capio Press

EPPE (2003) 'Measuring the Impact of Pre-School on Children's Social/Behavioural Development over the Pre-School Period', *The EPPE (Effective Provision of Pre-school Education) Project Technical Paper 8b*. London: Institute of Education

Moyles, J., Adams, S. and Musgrove, A. (2002) *Study of Pedagogical Effectiveness in Early Learning*. London: DfES

NCMA (2007) www.ncma.org.uk

OPM (Office for Public Management) (2006) *Implementation of the Lead Professional Role. A Report for DfES*. London: OPM

Palmer, S. (2006) *Toxic Childhood. How the modern world is damaging our children and what we can do about it*. London: Orion

Physick, R. (2005) Changes and Challenges: Pre-school Practitioners' Responses to Policy Change and Development, in Hirst, K. and Nutbrown, C. *Perspectives on Early Childhood Education: Contemporary research*. Stoke-on-Trent: Trentham Books

Pre-school Learning Alliance (2007) http://www.pre-school.org.uk/

Schwienhart, L.J., Weikart, D.P. and Toderan, R. (1993) *High Quality Preschool Programs Found to Improve Adult Status*. Ypsilante, MI: High/Scope Foundation

Siraj-Blatchford, I., Sylva, K., Muttock, S., Gilden, R. and Bell, D. (2002) *Researching Effective Pedagogy in the Early Years*. London: DfES

SureStart (2003) *Birth to Three Matters. A Framework to Support Children in their Earliest Years*. London: DfES

SureStart (2007a) 'Improving Quality' http://www.surestart.gov.uk/improvingquality/guidance/investorsinchildren/

SureStart (2007b) 'SureStart Services' http://www.surestart.gov.uk/surestartservices/settings/surestartchildrenscentres/

TDA (2006) *Qualifying to Teach. Professional standards for qualified teacher status and requirements for initial teacher training*. London: TDA

TDA (2007) www.TDA.org.uk

Toulmin, S. (1958) *The Uses of Argument*. Cambridge: Cambridge University Press

UNICEF (2007) *An Overview of Child Well-Being in Rich Countries. A comprehensive assessment of the lives and well-being of children and adolescents in the economically advanced nations*. Florence, Italy: UNICEF

Whalley, M. (2006) Working as a Team, in Parker-Rees, R. and Willan, J. (eds) (2006) *Early Years Education. Major Themes in Education*. London: Routledge

Useful reading

Daly, M., Byers, E. and Taylor, W. (2004) *Early Years Management in Practice*. Oxford: Heinemann

Useful websites

British Psychological Society: www.bps.org.uk

The Children's Society Good Childhood Study: www.goodchildhood.org.uk

Children's Workforce Development Council: www.cwdcouncil.org.uk

DCSF: www.dcsf.gov.uk

National Childminding Association: www.ncma.org.uk

Pre-school Learning Alliance: www.pre-school.org.uk

SureStart: www.surestart.gov.uk

Training and Development Agency for Schools (TDA): www.TDA.org.uk

Chapter 12

Reflective Practice

'By three methods we learn wisdom: first, by reflection, which is the noblest; second, by imitation, which is the easiest; and third, by experience, which is the most bitter'

Confucius (551–479 BC)

Introduction

This chapter will consider what is meant by the term 'reflective practitioner' and what this means in practice. We will consider the key elements of reflection and how we can use these to inform our practice and so develop as professionals. There is no blueprint for reflective practice as such, but a number of different models have been suggested to support this process. The value of personal reflection will be considered, alongside working as a reflective practitioner as part of a team and with consideration given to national policy and outcomes.

In a busy setting, it is so easy to be 'doing' all the time that we barely have the chance actually to 'think' about our practice and 'reflect' on it. It could be true to say that more reflection takes place when we are training than when we are qualified, the assumption being that once qualified we know how to do the job and do not have the luxury of college-based sessions when we can talk to student colleagues and tutors about our recent experiences. Moon (1999) discusses the difference between teaching and nursing in terms of reflective practice. She suggests that teacher educators are more interested in reflection than teachers, but that reflective practice is more the realm of the nurse than the nurse educator and is integral to nursing practice. This could be disputed by teachers, particularly in line with performance-related pay, self-evaluation and peer appraisal, and the keenness of many to embark on continuing professional development courses. What is evident, however, is that reflective practice should be integral throughout training and throughout our professional career working with young children. It is important to have a good understanding of what it is and how to do it so that it facilitates our ability not only to *evaluate* our effectiveness, but to move our practice forward so that it impacts positively upon the children and our ability to support their development.

Aims

→ To provide an overview of some of the key theories related to reflective practice

→ To explore some of the characteristics of reflective practice

→ To provide an overview of some of the models of reflective practice

→ To consider how we can develop individual reflective practice

→ To consider how we can work with others to develop reflective practice

→ To provide an understanding of the importance of reflective practice to professional development

Tools for Learning

Writing models for different methodologies

In this chapter we are looking at how you write up research in early childhood. In undertaking any research it is easy to 'fall at the last hurdle', with good research being written up poorly, thus not doing justice to the research itself and to the hard work involved. The first thing to remember when writing up your research is that it takes much longer than you could ever imagine. If you think of the longest amount of time you think writing up will take and then double it and double it again, you might be nearer the time needed. So, when you plan your work you should plan for a considerable amount of time to write it up, leaving time for you to get advice from tutors, colleagues and critical friends and to read and modify it yourself. The second thing to consider, is that different methodologies need to be written up in different ways.

When you decide your methodology, you need to consider what the research will look like in its final written form and this will ensure that you have collected the relevant primary data and recorded them appropriately to help you produce the 'best' piece of work you are able to. For example, a case study will need data to be collected in different fields for each case being studied. It may be that two different family lifestyles are being studied and compared and so the same information will need to be collected from both families in order to make sure an effective comparison can be made. You may be studying the historical development in provision for pre-school children and so you may wish to collect data in a chronological order. You may wish to tell the analytical story of some development in a setting and this would be best written up as a piece of action research, which follows the plan–do–review format common for reflective practice (see Elliott, 1991a). In this case the study should be written up in action steps, with each step being analysed and decisions made which impact on subsequent development. It would be foolish to attempt to undertake some action research and complete the development, collecting data on the way, but not to analyse it until after the development is complete. This is because you need the analysis in order to modify the research and development and to enable you to maximise the impact of the development.

Figure 12.1 provides a guide to the different formats for writing up your research. You need to look at this *before* embarking on the research, that is, at the planning stage.

Survey, Comparative, Historical, Case Study					Narrative, Story		Action Research	
Introduction					Introduction		Introduction	
Review of literature			Methodology and research methods		Methodology and research methods	Review of literature	Review of literature	Methodology and research methods
Methodology and research methods			Review of literature		Review of literature	Methodology and research methods	Methodology and research methods	Review of literature
Analysis and outcomes					Analysis and outcomes		Analysis of action: Step 1	
Method 1	Then	Case study 1	Issue 1	Question 1		Narrative 1	Analysis of action: Step 2	
Method 2	Now	Case study 2	Issue 2	Question 2	Complete story, narrative	Narrative 2	Analysis of action: Step 3	
Method 3 (etc.)		Case study 4 (etc.)	Issue 3 (etc.)	Question 3 (etc.)		Narrative 3	Analysis of action: Step 4 (etc.)	
Discussion of findings Question 1 Question 2 Question 3 (etc.)				Discussion of findings	Discussion of findings Question 1 Question 2 Question 3		Discussion of findings Question 1 Question 2 Question 3	
Conclusion, including evaluation of research and professional development					Conclusion, including evaluation of research and professional development		Conclusion, including evaluation of research and professional development	

Figure 12.1 Writing models for different methodologies

What is reflective practice?

There are a number of definitions of reflective practice, from the very simple: 'to allow the possibility of learning through experience' (Amulya, 2003: 1), to a more complex approach, related to mental processing, which questions the very notion of a single, theoretical definition when there are so many interpretations and variations in practice across professions (Moon, 1999). It is perhaps more important to focus on the characteristics of reflective practice and to ensure that there is consistency and a common understanding within a setting and the wider culture of a particular profession, be it health, social work or education.

Before focusing on these characteristics, it is useful briefly to consider the key theorists who have influenced thinking on reflective practice. Dewey (1859–1952) was an influential figure in education and viewed reflection as a way of purposeful thinking that is systematic and raises questions and answers (see also Chapter 1). In this way, reflective thinking comes about as a response to a problem or dilemma, which should in turn provide a solution (Dewey, 1933). In his pedagogic creed, Dewey (1897: 78), talks about education as a 'continuing re-construction of experience', highlighting the need for a reflective cycle which informs future experience. He was particularly concerned with the process of reflective thought, viewing the final part of the process as a form of testing through action. In this sense, Dewey's approach to reflective thinking is a systematic, scientific process in which a hypothesis can be tested.

Kolb (1984) was influenced by the work of Dewey and is well known for his experiential learning cycle (see Figure 12.2) in which he describes 'reflective observation' as a way of linking 'concrete experience' to 'abstract conceptualisation' and 'active experimentation'. To put it more simply: we experience something (concrete action); we then look back, remember and reflect on that experience (reflective observation); we then think critically about how we might change things for the better (abstract conceptualisation); and then we act on it, implementing the changes to see if they work (active experimentation). Kolb summarised it as: *'the process whereby knowledge is created through transformation of experience'* (Kolb, 1984: 41). The High/Scope approach (Schwienhart *et al.*, 1993) uses a similar cycle, but with only three stages, with its 'plan–do–review' approach. With slight alteration to 'do–review–plan–do', it would virtually mirror Kolb's cycle. Although Kolb's model is useful to see where reflection fits into the learning cycle, it does not provide detail about what reflection is and the processes by which it is achieved.

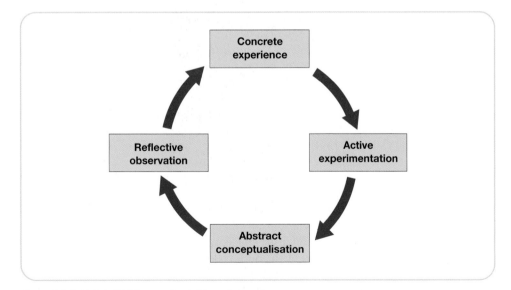

Figure 12.2 Kolb's (1984) experiential learning cycle
Source: Kolb, David, A., *Experiential Learning: Experience as the source of Learning and Development.* © 1984. Electronically reproduced by permission of Pearson Education, Inc., Upper Saddle River, New Jersey.

Reflective Tasks

Kolb's experiential cycle

Level 1

Think about something that you have done recently that you were not happy with. This might be a piece of work, a specific incident during a practical placement, or a personal experience. If you were to repeat the experience, how would you alter things for the better? Consider this in the light of Kolb's experiential cycle.

Level 2

Think about a specific incident in your work with children that did not go as well as you had hoped. This might be the way you handled the behaviour of a child, an organisational or time issue or the way you communicated with a parent. Now consider Kolb's experiential cycle. The concrete experience is already achieved. Go through the other three elements by reflecting on what happened, considering ways in which you could have improved the situation and trying it out. Was it wholly successful or would you need to go through the cycle again to refine it?

Level 3

Think about a situation at work where you needed to solve a problem as a staff. Write the process down under the headings in Kolb's experiential cycle. Are you able to identify each stage clearly? How did you define the difference between 'reflective observation' and 'abstract conceptualisation'?

Consider how you would write up this piece of reflection, using Figure 12.1.

Perhaps one of the most influential writers on reflective practice is Donald Schön (1983). He introduced the phrases 'reflection-in-action' (while doing something) and 'reflection-on-action' (after you have done it). He was critical of training for teachers which focused on the acquisition of knowledge, rather than skills for responding and adapting to different situations as they occur. He felt that there was a gap between the theory that is supposed to underpin professional work and the actual practice, particularly in professions such as teaching and social work, where the reality is often unpredictable and does not fit neatly into a theoretical 'box'. Schön (1987) used the term 'the swamp' to refer to the complexity of the real-life situation and the need for 'swamp knowledge', the tacit knowledge that comes only with experience. Reflection, the construction and reconstruction of real-life experiences, would then develop the 'swamp knowledge' that would link the theory with practice in a more meaningful way.

If we consider the concept of theoretical and experiential knowledge we could formulate a model of different types of knowledge, suggesting that these could be in direct opposition to one another.

The left-hand column in Figure 12.3 is related to 'measurable' knowledge, useful in society's preoccupation with accountability and assessment. The right-hand column is less easily measured, but in that sense perhaps provides the basis and reason for reflection, similar to Schön's 'swamp knowledge'. This model could easily be criticised, as it

Technical Knowledge	*vs.*	**Practical** Knowledge
Knowing **that**	*vs.*	Knowing **how**
Propositional knowledge	*vs.*	**Procedural** knowledge
Conscious knowledge	*vs.*	**Tacit** knowledge
Comprehension (knowledge **about**)	*vs.*	Apprehension (knowledge by **direct acquaintance**)

Figure 12.3 A model of different types of knowledge

suggests one knowledge type versus another and does not advocate a combination of both. Atherton (2003) questions whether reflection can really bring together the practical and theoretical, criticising Schön's work which presupposes a level of articulation in order to do this. It could be argued that professionals should have a sufficient level of articulation to enable constructive reflection and, in fact, that it is vital that they do. The two columns, particularly the right-hand column, have perhaps unconsciously provided guidelines for this.

Atherton (2003) is not alone in the criticism of Schön's work. Moon (1999) presents a whole chapter on Schön and much of this includes criticism of his work from a number of sources. His work is questioned due to lack of precision in his terminology and contradictory statements. The idea of reflection-in-action is hotly debated and Moon comes to the conclusion that it is more to do with a decision-making process, based on *previous* reflection. In contrast, Amulya (2003:2) recognises that reflection during experience differs from that after experience, stating: 'Reflection can also vary in depth, from simply noticing present experience to deep examination of past events.' What Schön did do, however, was to provide a more concrete approach to reflective practice, using more easily accessible terms, which professionals could apply to their practice.

Reflection-in-action is particularly thought-provoking, because when we talk about reflection, we often apply this to looking back at something we have already done, rather than as we are doing it. It could be argued that there is no time for reflection during an event because reflection, by its very nature, requires space for thought and contemplation. In a busy setting with young children, time for contemplation is highly unlikely! The human brain, however, is miraculous in the speed at which it works. I remember driving in fog and realising that I was careering towards a brick wall (I had not taken the bend in the road). The thoughts that went through my head in that split second were remarkable, from chastising myself for not driving more carefully, worrying that I had not taken the advice of my husband to drive slowly, thinking I had not expected to die so young and finally knowing I had a good excuse for being late for work. It will certainly take you far longer to read this or for me to say or type this than it took me to think it. Perhaps this suggests that there are two different types of reflection: high-speed, immediate reflection that directly impacts upon current action, and more in-depth, contemplative reflection that is a slower process and is more wide-ranging with a greater impact upon future practice. It is the latter that we will focus on, although reflection-in-action may well provide the catalyst for reflection-on-action.

Research

Learning How to Learn

Learning How to Learn, a four-year ESRC funded research project as part of the Teaching and Learning Research Programme (James *et al.*, 2007), has identified that teachers are often battling between the demands of league tables and performance targets and their educational principles. They want to allow children to set their own targets or to explore and investigate their own ideas, but they feel constrained by assessment and results. The research indicates that the more reflective teachers become, the easier it is for them to teach with integrity. Schools which actively employ reflective techniques to consider and resolve teaching issues were found to be more successful. The programme (James *et al.*, 2007) has introduced new innovations, such as:

- developing classroom talk and questioning, so that teachers can plan effective questioning techniques and support children in asking questions and reflecting on answers;

- giving appropriate feedback to children, as this is more effective than marks, or marks with comments;

- sharing criteria with learners, as well as learning objectives, goals and targets;

- peer and self-assessment. The research shows that children engaged in peer and self-assessment make the best progress, as they begin the understand their learning needs;

- thoughtful and active learners are those that understand the desired outcomes and how they learn (metacognition).

Characteristics of reflective practice

As there is no specific definition of reflective practice, it is helpful to consider the characteristics of a reflective practitioner. Again, these may vary depending on the discipline in which you are working but there are some commonalities. Moon (1999: 64) outlines some of these:

- It involves reflecting on the subject matter of the individual's practice and the setting in which he or she works.
- It may relate to everyday issues or to more specific, policy-based issues.
- It may result from external influences or from personal interest.
- There may be a final result in which practice is changed but not necessarily, although, if not, understanding should have been enhanced.
- Although reflection is essentially a thinking process, it will probably have been enhanced by oral or written supporting strategies.
- It cannot be separated from emotion and intuition, although these may not be acknowledged.
- It is essentially a critical exercise.
- Sharing reflective practice with others usually serves to enhance the experience and provide more successful outcomes.

- The immediate aim is self and/or professional development which in turn will empower the individual, leading to improvements within the broader context.

Roth (1989) includes:

- Awareness of what, why, and how we do things.
- Questioning what, why and how we do things.
- Asking what, why and how other people do things.

Essentially, reflective practice is an active process which involves enquiry and a motivation to learn from our personal experience.

Reflective Tasks

Characteristics of reflective practice

Level 1

Consider the characteristic adapted from Moon (1999: 64): 'Although reflection is essentially a thinking process, it will probably have been enhanced by oral or written support strategies.' Provide an example where you have talked about or written down your reflections and note how this impacted on your learning. What did you gain from reporting or recording your thinking?

Level 2

Look at the fourth characteristic adapted from Moon (1999: 64) related to the final result in which practice may have changed. Consider a time when you have altered your practice after reflection and review. What prompted the reflection?

- What led to the decision to alter practice?
- How did this change impact upon the experience of the children?

Level 3

Look at the final characteristic in the list adapted from Moon (1999: 64). Provide an example of how you or a colleague has fulfilled a personal/professional aim which has impacted on the setting and led to improvements in the broader context of the setting and perhaps beyond.

- What led to this individual aim being identified and achieved in the first place?
- Why has it had a broader impact?
- How could this inform your policy for staff development?
- If you can't think of an example, what does this suggest about reflective practice in your setting and what are the next steps?

Perhaps one way of summarising these characteristics is by referring to the 'thinking' professional. The more we know, the more realise how little we know. Working in schools with trainee teachers and their teacher mentors, I often hear the same refrain from teachers as they give advice to their trainees: 'We never stop learning; we never know it all. The day you think you do is the day to give up teaching.' This, of course, does not just apply to teaching but to any profession, and this is why the thinking professional is at the core of reflective practice. Sometimes the external pressures can result in professionals being so concerned with the broader issues, related to things such as inspection, that they forget to focus on their own day-to-day practice and the impact this has. It is often the small things that can have a direct and sometimes profound impact on a child's life: a smile and individual greeting every morning; bringing stories to life because of animated and skilful reading; responding to a child's individual idea and acting on it. The ability to home in on relevant detail is a useful skill to aid reflection and development.

Another characteristic that affects reflective practice is attitude. The attitude of individuals within a team can have a profound effect on the morale and effectiveness of that team (Middlewood and Cardno, 2001). Enthusiasm is a good thing, but it sometimes means that new ideas are introduced too quickly, without due thought and consideration about their potential impact. Cynicism can creep into a team, particularly if an experienced professional witnesses a roller coaster of changes, only to find that they are being asked to accept a new initiative which is the same one they were using 30 years ago! Cynicism can, of course, be extremely negative and create tensions within a team. Idealism can raise standards but can also impose unnecessary and stressful pressures on individuals and the team. Nonchalance can result in 'going with the flow' without question, but it is also with minimal commitment and limited understanding. A reflective practitioner needs to have an open, positive but cautious attitude to change, with careful consideration about its potential impact and the pace at which it is introduced. A healthy attitude impacts positively, not only on the team, but also on the children within the setting (Weare, 2004). A positive and open attitude to constructive criticism is also vital and is an essential characteristic for the thinking professional.

While it is useful to consider the characteristics of a reflective practitioner, it is also necessary to consider the processes involved in reflection and how these can support practice. We have discussed the theoretical view of reflective practice and have noted some of the criticisms. To focus on only one theoretical perspective narrows our understanding and limits the potential for reflective processes (York-Barr *et al.*, 2006), so it is important to look at a range of perspectives in order to inform practice. In addition to theoretical frameworks, there are some practical models to support practice. These usually take the form of questions to help to channel our thinking and so support a reflective approach. We will now examine some of these models so that we can see how reflective practice can be developed.

Models to guide reflective practice

Peters (1991) refers to a process called DATA (Describe, Analyse, Theorise and Act) which has similarities to Kolb's experiential learning cycle (Kolb, 1984). Peters refers to DATA as a model or protocol to inform reflective practice:

1. *Describe* – a picture of the experience, identifying key features for the next stage of the model.
2. *Analyse* – identify why and how things happened and what might have influenced these.
3. *Theorise* – think about alternatives, considering the advantages and disadvantages.
4. *Act* – try out the new approach and evaluate its effectiveness.

Smyth (1991: 113) suggests using four questions which include description as the first element as above, but combine Peters's 'analyse' section into two sub-sections which perhaps clarifies how to approach it: 'inform' and 'confront' as outlined below.

1. *Describe*: what do I do?
2. *Inform*: what does this description mean?
3. *Confront*: how did I come to be like this?
4. *Reconstruct:* how might I do things differently?

Gibbs (1988) has a similar set of questions, but includes a question related to how the individual feels about the experience. Moon (1999) notes how literature on learning makes very limited reference to emotion (apart from the inhibiting aspects) despite its inextricable links to the reflection process which in turn promotes learning. Gibbs's cycle (1988) has the following staged questions:

1. *Description*: What happened?
2. *Feelings*: What were you thinking and feeling?
3. *Evaluation*: What was good and bad about the experience?
4. *Analysis*: What sense can you make of the situation?
5. *Conclusion*: What else could you have done?
6. *Action plan*: If it arose again, what would you do?

Having a set of questions can help to focus our thoughts and move from the 'what' to the 'why', 'how' and 'what if'.

Reflective Tasks

Models to guide reflective practice

Level 1

Consider the words: describe, evaluate and analyse. Provide a definition for each.

- Why do we need all three to be a reflective practitioner?
- If you were studying the development of your own professional and reflective practice, what methodology would be appropriate?
- Is there more than one appropriate methodology?

Level 2

Do the Level 1 task.

- Which one of the three words is the most difficult to do in practice?
- Why do you think this is?
- Which of the questions in the previous models would help you to develop reflective practice and why?
- How would you write up the study of your own reflective practice (look at the models in Figure 12.1)?

Level 3

Consider the different models that have been presented.

- If you were to develop reflective practice in your setting, which of these would be the most helpful to share with the staff?

- Add to them to make them more specific to your setting.
- If you were studying the reflective practice of your staff, what methodology would you use and how would you write it up (see Figure 12.1)?

Lindon (2005: 3) presents a cyclical model for developing reflective practice which, unlike the previous generic models, is specific to early years settings. The following are not in any numerical order, but are a part of the cycle of reflection:

- *Doing*: putting ideas into practice and being actively involved or observing children.
- *Thinking*: Being open-minded and tuning in to children.
- *Feeling*: Recognising your emotions and acknowledging the feelings of other adults in the setting as well as the children.
- *Reviewing*: Look, listen and learn by considering what and how.
- *Planning ahead*: What will you try? Provision of resources, experiences and opportunities.

It could be argued that 'thinking' is central to all aspects and should not stand alone as a separate part of the process. As previously stated in relation to High/Scope (Schwienhart *et al.*, 1993), planning, doing and reviewing is a familiar cycle in early years settings and is relatively straightforward. It is the quality of the reviewing element that demonstrates the success of the reflective process.

The Reggio Emilia early childhood programme is a model of good reflective practice in the early years, where the adults working in the settings view themselves as co-learners. Their pedagogy is based on listening, researching and learning (Rinaldi, 2006). Dialogue is at the centre of this approach, with teamwork integral to its success. Callaghan (2002) was impressed when she heard two educators from Reggio Emilia talking about their work together for the past 10 years. They discussed how they used to challenge one another, leading to meaningful discussion, but as they did not appear to do this any more had decided to split up because they were no longer learning from one another. This is a very different culture from that which exists in many settings in England, where conflict is deemed to be a negative characteristic, rather than an impetus for exploring ideas and reflecting on practice. York-Barr *et al.* (2006: 10), refer to an 'open heart', which applies to both openness in thought and openness in relationships. An open attitude and mutual respect is essential, so that challenge is seen to be a positive part of teamwork and moves practice forward.

Working as part of a team is a key feature of practice in early years settings and this includes the reflective process. We will be examining this in more detail later in the chapter, but first we will consider the ways in which individuals can develop personal reflection in order to understand and improve their own performance.

Developing individual reflective practice

There are a number of ways of reflecting, which are all valuable but which may be used for different purposes and in different situations. We might reflect on a whole experience, as an *overview*. If we use a holiday as an example, when we return we are asked 'Did you have a nice holiday?' to which the first, unreflective answer is probably, 'Yes, it was wonderful'. When we actually begin to reflect we start to consider which bits were really wonderful, which bits were okay and which bits we would rather not experience again. We might reflect on a *critical incident*, something significant that happened that prompts us to think further about it. We might have been late getting to the airport and missed our plane. This forces us to reflect and ask questions: What did we do to rectify the situation? How successful was it? Why did it happen? What must we do in the future so that it does not happen again? We might focus on *one particular aspect* of the holiday, such as the location, and consider the positive and negative aspects to help inform our next choice of holiday. We might also focus on a *specific experience* while on holiday, such as the half-day cruise, and ask ourselves similar questions. Moving on from the holiday analogy to our practice in the early years, we could reflect on an overview of our practice over a particular time period (a day, a week or a half-term); we could be motivated to reflect on an aspect of our practice due to a critical incident, positive or negative, that happened in the setting (a confrontation with a parent or informally observing a colleague's good practice); we could select a specific area on which to focus our reflection (organisation of resources); or we could select a specific experience (teaching a PE lesson).

An overview of experience

Looking back at a total experience is particularly useful when that experience is new. When new initiatives are introduced there is often a pilot study which is carried out first and evaluated to inform the initiative before it is introduced more widely. The National Literacy Strategy Framework (DfES, 1998) was introduced into a few pilot areas as the National Literacy Project the year before its introduction as the Strategy Framework, for the purpose of reflection and review. When students go into placements, they are often asked to reflect on the experience as a whole, considering both the positive and negative aspects. Reflection is not only related to teaching (or nursing as described earlier). Grimes (2006) describes how students in law are asked to evaluate a 5–6 week clinical experience. After participating in the clinic, students are required to complete an evaluation form, asking them to think about what they achieved in the centre, what they could have done better and what they might have done differently. They also attend a group evaluation meeting with other participants to discuss in general terms their involvement in the centre's work. Grimes (2006) stresses the importance of learning from the experience of others to facilitate personal reflection. Reflecting on the overview of an experience, however, can become unfocused and can result in a list of moans and complaints. There are two key ways of focusing the reflective process. One is to do as Grimes (2006) suggests, discuss the reflections with others, led by a supervisor to channel the process so that it does not lose the focus. The second is to provide a framework, such as the cycle of experiential learning: reporting the experience, reflecting, accounting the subjective inner experience and then generalising (Moon, 1999).

A critical incident

Critical incidents are often the catalyst for the reflective evaluation process. A critical incident sounds like an emergency, but in fact is not an extreme case at all and can be either positive or negative. It is any professional experience which offers significant meaning for practitioners which prompts them to think further about their practice. An example could be a conversation with a child, in which the child demonstrates a far greater level of understanding than anticipated and so prompts a rethink of future planning. A parent might totally misinterpret a letter that has been sent from the setting, leading to an evaluation not only of the wording of that particular letter, but the way in which the setting communicates with parents in more general terms. Miller *et al.* (2005) cite an example where a parent of a new child, who had recently moved from Sweden, questioned why the children only went outside for short periods in the day. She went on to explain that in Sweden the children were often outside for prolonged periods, wearing appropriate clothing.

This led the practitioner to question the setting's policy for outdoor play and the lack of a clear rationale, leading to a change which involved a more flexible approach.

The reason a critical incident carries significant meaning is that the one incident raises questions about the context more generally and so informs future practice. It does, however, also relate to reflection-in-action (Schön, 1983) when we may need to 'think on our feet' to respond immediately to the situation and then use this situation to prompt more in-depth evaluation in reflection-on-action. Buod (2001: 12) also refers to the importance of 'noticing', which although might appear obvious, is actually a vital component of the critical incident and reflective practice. If a practitioner fails to notice the incident, it will clearly have no impact on practice. The skill of 'noticing' often develops with experience, but needs to be recognised as a significant part of reflection.

Reflective Tasks

A critical incident

Level 1

Think of a specific incident that has had an impact on your life, even though the incident itself might have seemed fairly insignificant to other people. It might be the reason why you chose this course of study or why you wanted to work with children. What was it about the situation that made it significant? Were there any other factors involved (e.g. your frame of mind, the time in your life)?

Level 2

Think of a critical incident that has taken place in your setting that has prompted you to reflect on your future practice. Was it a positive or negative incident? Consider how you dealt with the situation at the time and how the reflective process has moved your practice forward.

Level 3

Think of a critical incident that has taken place in your setting that has prompted a review of policy or a change in practice by the whole staff. Consider whether the critical incident just accelerated a process that would have happened anyway or whether it prompted a new way of thinking or a new approach. Consider what the practice would be like in your setting now if you had not responded to the incident. Reflect on the processes you went through to achieve the changes.

Reflecting on a specific aspect

It is often useful to select a particular aspect of practice as the focus for reflection. A critical incident cannot be planned for and an overview is too general, particularly for a more experienced practitioner. Trainees may need to focus on one particular aspect so that they can concentrate their observations and not be distracted by the many other aspects of the experience going on at the same time. The specific aspect can be chosen for a number of reasons. It may be an area which a practitioner feels needs to be improved or which has been identified on the development plan for the setting; it could be part of a cycle of different foci within the setting; or it could be a particular area of interest for the practitioner. If it is for this final reason, it may well develop into action research and as McNiff and Whitehead (2002: 15) state, when referring to action research; 'the idea of self-reflection is central'.

Once an aspect for focus has been selected, it can be useful to have headings or questions to channel the observations and reflections. Suggestions for specific aspects for reflection could include: use of resources; time management; communication with parents; behaviour management; questioning; record keeping; pupil profiles; health and safety issues; provision for special needs; and any other issue pertinent to the practitioner. If 'use of resources' was chosen, for example, the headings could be:

1. Area of provision.
2. List of resources currently available in that area.
3. How are these resources stored?
4. How are these resources presented to the children?
5. How are these resources used by the children?
6. How frequently are they used?

The next stage would be to reflect on the answers to these questions and consider what will be done next as a result of the evaluation. This is fairly simplistic, but it gives a starting point and can be developed according to the setting and the time available for observation. Another way to begin to think about an aspect is to make a checklist based on good practice and then to check the setting's provision against the criteria in the checklist. The list below is the start of a checklist for storage of resources.

- The resources are low enough to be accessed by all children.
- All boxes are labelled in a way children will understand.
- The boxes are in good condition and fit neatly onto the shelving.
- All boxes can be easily removed and put back.

A list such as this can be a starting point for discussion about good practice and the ways in which the setting needs to move forward. The example given is very practical, but it can also involve analysing the skills and knowledge required to perform a particular job effectively (for example, what is involved in organising your time more efficiently) and identifying where you stand at the moment in relation to these skills There is no suggestion that any one list could encompass all aspects of good practice, nor should it. It is merely a way of focusing on elements of perceived good practice and may well vary from individual to individual or from setting to setting.

Practical Tasks

Reflecting on a specific aspect

Level 1

Choose an aspect of your college experience on which you would like to reflect and improve. It could be writing essays, time-keeping or revising for exams. Write a checklist of good practice and then see how many you can tick. Reflect on what you can do to enable you to tick them all.

Level 2

Choose an aspect of your work with young children on which you would like to reflect and improve. Write a checklist of good practice and share it with a colleague or colleagues to see if they agree with you. Add any of their suggestions and then see how many you can tick. Reflect on what you can do to enable you to tick them all.

Level 3

Choose an aspect in your setting on which you would like to reflect and improve. With colleagues, draw up a checklist of good practice within that area. Use literary sources and evidence from other settings to build up this list. Write an action plan to show how you will meet the aspects that you have been unable to tick.

Reflecting on a specific experience

Trainee professionals are expected to reflect and evaluate their practice and children's development. Trainee teachers evaluate lessons on a regular basis and this is an example of reflecting on a specific experience. Evaluations will take different forms, from short, bullet points at the bottom of a lesson plan to a more narrative approach completed at the end of the day. Teachers by no means evaluate everything they do, but they may choose to evaluate a specific activity, such as a visit or a problematic lesson. Their accountability to external bodies, such as OFSTED, may focus evaluations on areas in which they feel less confident in order to promote their development and expertise in readiness for when the inspector calls! Trainees, on the other hand, could accuse their training institutions of 'death by evaluations', as they are, indeed, asked to evaluate on a very regular basis. Of course it is not only trainee teachers and early childhood professionals who are expected to evaluate, but also students from other disciplines, such as health, social sciences and law. Research into student experiences of reflective practice suggests that many students find written evaluations quite onerous to complete, with considerations such as grammar and punctuation becoming more of the focus than the reflections and the written evaluations not representing students' thoughts (Moore and Ash, 2002; Jindal-Snape and Holmes, 2006). Boud (2001) noted that one of the main inhibiters to reflective writing is the prospect of others reading the evaluations. The perceived expectations of the external reader can profoundly shape the writing, particularly if it is to be assessed. Abbott and Pugh (1998) highlight the fact that reflective practice is a key part of training and therefore forms part of the trainee's assessment. It must therefore be the ability to *reflect* that should be the focus of the assessment, difficult though this may be (Moon, 1999), rather than competency in the classroom, which is a different element within the assessment programme for each student. It is therefore important for any assessor to be able to recognise the key features of reflection. This should be made clear to the student to help develop, rather than inhibit, the reflective process. We will consider writing as one of the techniques for reflection later in the chapter.

What many students initially find difficult is to move from description to evaluation and reflection. The element of description is important in the early stages because it helps to provide a snapshot of the experience; the models discussed earlier all had description as part of the reflective process. What is more challenging is identifying the difference between description and reflection. The following task is based on two narrative accounts, which could have been verbal, designed to highlight the difference between reflection and description. Gura (1996) refers to the important relationship between narrative and reflection. The excerpts are not examples of written evaluations, but aim to illuminate the reflective process.

Reflective Tasks

Reflecting on a specific incident

Extract A

I was in a hurry yesterday morning because I was late. Jane was already in the nursery when I arrived because her mum had to go into work early and Julie asked me to keep an eye on her whilst I was putting out the activities. She seemed fine looking at the books in the book corner and was quiet, which was a relief because I hadn't got time to talk to her and get everything ready for the start of the session. She looked quite tired and curled up on the cushion. I dropped the box of musical instruments on the floor making an almighty clash and expected to have disturbed Jane but she just lay there quietly which was a relief. It didn't take as long as I'd thought to set up so I actually had time for a coffee before the start of the session. I had a quick look but Jane was asleep so I didn't disturb her.

When the other children started to arrive, Jane didn't move. Julie went to wake her but she didn't wake up. It was all action stations then. I called the ambulance and Julie stayed with Jane. She's in hospital now with a suspected fractured skull. She's conscious but they're not sure yet how serious it is. She had looked fine to me. Apparently she'd fallen out of bed at home and felt dizzy but her mum had thought that she was okay. I feel a bit guilty really because I'd been asked to look after her, but if her mum hadn't noticed then I shouldn't be expected to. I keep thinking back to see if I should have noticed, but she just seemed tired.

Extract B

This happened yesterday and I can't get it out of my mind. I was late and feeling flustered and was so focused on getting everything ready for the day that I hadn't noticed that Jane, who had arrived early, was unwell. She did seem unusually quiet and that should have alerted me because she is always so chatty and lively. She's in hospital now with a fractured skull from a fall at home and perhaps if I had noticed her drowsiness earlier, she could have got to hospital earlier and that could make a difference to her recovery. I should have gone over to talk to her first – why didn't I? Why was getting everything ready for the day more important? The one time I should have been alerted is when I dropped the musical instruments; the noise would have woken a sleeping child. I know that, so why did I just carry on? I think I was probably slightly annoyed that Jane was at the nursery before me. It highlighted the fact that I was late. We should be here before the children even if Jane was particularly early.

My first thoughts were that going to talk to her would have delayed me, but now I am beginning to think that I wanted to deny her existence in a way because by acknowledging her I was acknowledging the fact that I should have been here earlier, which is admitting my bad timekeeping and a lack of professionalism. It also shows my lack of flexibility; the first part of my day is getting ready for the children not being with the children. Jane's presence was changing my routine and I couldn't adapt to it. Maybe getting her to hospital a little earlier wouldn't have made any difference, but that doesn't alter anything. I must ensure that I get to work in plenty of time and ultimately, it is the children who matter, not my agenda – they must come first whatever the circumstances.

Both of these extracts are informal narrative accounts relating to a specific incident, but the second one is more reflective than the first, as though the writer is standing back from her actions in order to evaluate them critically.

Level 1

Highlight all the unnecessary factual/descriptive information in extracts A and B. How much is left in extract A in comparison with extract B? Highlight the evidence of reflection in extract B. Use Smyth's model to identify each aspect of the reflective process evident in the extract. Look at the writing models in Figure 12.1 and consider how the narrative in extract B would best be written up.

Level 2

Highlight the evidence of reflection in extract B. Use Smyth's model to identify each aspect of the reflective process evident in the extract. List the emotions likely to have been felt during the experience and during the reflective process. How might these have impacted on the conclusions? Using the writing models in Figure 12.1, map out a structure for the write-up of extract B.

Level 3

Using Gibbs's headings as subtitles, rewrite extract B, using one of the models in Figure 12.1. Do any of the sections need more information? Would you add any more sections for elements that do not fit into Gibbs's model? The experience has clearly had an emotional impact on the writer. Consider whether the emotional response has helped or hindered the reflective process and provide evidence to support your views.

Reflective practice and professional standards

Although the value of reflective practice should be intrinsically beneficial, as already mentioned, external agencies demand evidence of reflective practice in order to meet their standards. The new standards for the early years professional (CWDC, 2006: 11) state that practitioners need to: 'Reflect on and evaluate the impact of practice, modifying approaches where necessary, and take responsibility for identifying and meeting their professional development needs'. This would involve providing evidence of this to meet that particular standard. The Training and Development Agency for schools have standards for qualified teacher status, which include practitioners demonstrating they are able to 'reflect and improve their practice and take responsibility for identifying and meeting their developing professional needs' (TDA, 2007: 8). It is not only those in a position of responsibility that need to show evidence of reflection, all professional qualifications for working with children have reflective practice as part of the National Occupational Standards and the Children's Workforce Strategy (CWDC, 2006). Moore and Ash (2002) refer to reflection which is performed only to meet the requirements of assessment as 'ritualistic reflection' and of little value other than providing spurious evidence. In contrast, the more meaningful 'authentic reflection' seeks to promote development and change and has more intrinsic value. It is important that reflection is valued by the trainees and is not just viewed as another hoop to jump through to gain the qualification.

To enable those starting out in training to develop reflective practice, the role of mentors and supervisors is fundamental. Through their support, trainees should begin to view reflection as integral to practice and become more adept at using the reflective process to become a better practitioner. The value of talking to others has been referred to in previous sections of the chapter and will now be explored in more detail. We will also consider how working with others supports reflective practice and the use of reflection within a team approach.

Working with others to develop reflective practice

'We cannot solve the problems we have created with the same thinking that created them.'
Einstein (1879–1955)

Sometimes we can become so entrenched in our own ways of doing things that we cannot see any other way of doing them. By working with others, we can be offered an alternative perspective that allows us to develop new ways of thinking, opening up different possibilities that would not have been explored without their contributions. One aspect of reflective practice is the ability of practitioners to stand back and view themselves as others might view them. This is not always easy, but by working with others through the reflective process this skill should be developed.

The role of the professional demands the ability to enter into professional dialogue with others and to acknowledge the potential for new ideas and approaches. In a time of constant change of policy and practice, the role of the professional is also under considerable change. Elliot (1991b: 20) discusses the difference between the 'infallible expert model' professional who is reactive, responding to policy change by updating knowledge and skills, and the 'reflective practitioner model' professional who participates in the process of change by 'collaborative problem-solving' which is part of the 'dimension of practice', rather than a 'segregated off-the-job activity'. In other words, accepting change, being a part of change and sometimes being the instrument of change is the role of the professional, rather than continuing the same practice until change is forced by an external influence.

The term **mentoring** is used describe one supportive relationship between colleagues working in a setting (see Picture 12.1). Although the mentor is deemed the more experienced and the mentee a learner, the mentoring relationship has changed considerably

Picture 12.1 Mentoring
Source: Paul Box/Report Digital

from the expert/apprentice model that used to be perceived (Stammers, 1992). Mentoring is used in a variety of circumstances: by trainees, by newly qualified professionals in their first year and by experienced practitioners who are seeking professional development. There are four main types of mentoring relationships:

- Mentoring a trainee who may be undertaking a placement in a setting. The mentor is usually a member of the permanent staff who offers advice, monitors progress and keeps a check on the trainee's welfare. This also involves partnership with the training institution.

- Mentoring a professional newly-appointed into a setting, designed to help a colleague settle in, gain knowledge of procedures in the setting, and ask questions without feeling judged. This can be mentoring a newly-qualified professional or an experienced professional.

- Mentoring an established member of staff who is embarking on a course of study, for example, a nursery nurse doing a Foundation Degree being mentored by the nursery teacher to support work-based tasks and study skills.

- Group mentoring, which involves a small group of professionals at the same level who opt into membership of a group to discuss pertinent, professional issues without feeling inhibited by the presence of a line manager.

The relationship between the mentor and mentee is a crucial part of the mentoring experience. Although the mentee is seen as the learner in the initial stages, the mentoring process also teaches the mentor. Teachers have said to me that having a student has allowed them to reflect on their own practice in addition to supporting their student. York-Barr *et al.* (2006) believe that there are certain characteristics that are essential for a successful mentoring partnership. They suggest specific consideration should be given to clarity of purpose; good listening skills by both partners; the expansion of thinking and enquiry; and a coaching element.

In educational contexts, coaching is a term often used to describe the significant role of another person in reflective practice. Coaching relationships are generally designed to teach a specific set of skills, and once the skills are taught the relationship is no longer needed. Co-coaching relationships, however, are more equal, where colleagues of equal status work together to move practice forward. These may be between two or more colleagues.

One form of coaching, peer observation, is common practice in schools and is designed to support staff development. The environment must be emotionally supportive (Moon, 1999) for this to work and there must be mutual respect between the two colleagues. In Reading, a case study was conducted related to quality assurance through reflective practice. Early years settings were selected for the pilot project to reflect on their provision through peer observations. The DfES stated that 'reflective practice is fundamental to quality assurance' (DfES, 2006: 2). They also related the ability to reflect to the success of self-evaluations for the purpose of OFSTED inspections. The pilot indicated that staff in the early years settings found the experience to be beneficial, with comments including: 'It has helped me analyse things more' and 'I am more aware of my practice and what I'm doing and why' (DfES, 2006: 6). The purpose of the pilot is to encourage settings to gain the quality assurance award through the Investors in Children accredited Reading quality assurance scheme. One caveat might be that the extrinsic award and not the intrinsic value of the reflective process is the motivating factor, potentially resulting in 'ritualistic' reflection rather not the more desired 'authentic' reflection (Moore and Ash, 2002).

It is useful for practitioners to have their practice observed to help them learn and develop, but it is also useful for excellent practitioners to act as role models. Observing good practice can help practitioners to reflect on what they have seen and apply it to their own practice. This is one way of helping less experienced or less accomplished practitioners to develop their skills. Trainees observe practitioners during placements to develop their knowledge and skills from seeing a role model. In schools, advanced skills teachers are selected on the basis of their good practice to 'teach' others and aid professional development. A significant part of the experience is the discussion preceding and following the observation. Without this, the observer is left to make sense of the experience without insights into the thinking that shaped the practice observed. Discussion is therefore a key element of any peer observation.

Peer discussion should expand the thinking capacity of individuals to enable them to address issues, think back on their practice to enable them to think forward about future ideas, promote problem-solving and nurture reflective practice (York-Barr *et al.*, 2006). Jindal-Snape and Holmes (2006) researched the reflective process with educational psychology students. Their findings indicated that discussion with a more experienced practitioner was the most useful for developing professional practice. Although peer support was deemed to have advantages, particularly emotional support, the discussions often lost focus and were dominated by the more vocal members of a group. Students valued the 'reflective skills of the supervisor' as a role model, and speaking to someone who is 'more knowledgeable, better-skilled' (Jindal-Snape and Holmes, 2006: 4). Clearly the verbalisation of thoughts can help the practitioner to think things through and clarify understanding. Amulya (2003) discusses how reflective practice is developed through dialogue and questions and feels that collective reflection and individual reflection are often combined. The discussion is often used to explore a colleague's needs which then supports that individual's reflection and practice, but also contributes to collective learning, and explores the connections through the multiple perspectives.

Reflective Tasks

Mentoring and coaching

Level 1

- As a learner in a placement, how have you felt in the role of mentee?
- How did you view the relationship between you and your mentor?
- Did you feel the environment was emotionally supportive?
- Provide examples as evidence.

Level 2

Select an occasion when you have been a mentee, mentor or coach.

- How did you seek to build a positive relationship?
- Was it successful?
- What did you learn from the experience in terms of your professional development?

Level 3

- Which mentoring/coaching model(s) are used in your setting?
- How did you set up/develop these relationships?
- How do you monitor the success of mentoring and coaching?
- How do you develop peer observation skills with your colleagues?

The whole ethos within a setting can be reflective or, in contrast, can fail to be reflective by the inability of the staff to learn from their own information and experience (Senge *et al.*, 2000). A reflective setting encourages dialogue between staff, creates time for staff to work together and welcomes, rather than resists, challenges to promote new thinking and approaches, leading to growth and improvement.

One of the challenges facing staff working with young children is the potential for conflict between personal and professional philosophies and the ever-changing policies from central government. These come about not only when there is a change in government, but also changes in parliamentary responsibility or values within the same government. Each new education secretary or health minister wants to stamp their authority on their new role and this usually results in policy changes, which in turn has a direct impact on schools, hospitals and related services. A reflective setting should critically evaluate policy change and the potential effects on policy and practice within the setting alongside the overriding philosophy underpinning the values in the setting. If there are conflicts, time will be made for dialogue and questioning to enable a clear articulation of direction with a justifiable approach. A non-reflective setting will either take on any change without question and time to reflect or may resist change totally, treating it with suspicion and disdain, until an outside agency insists on it. With the many changes in policy, it is perhaps understandable that the integrity of some of the changes are questioned, but reflective practitioners, the 'thinking professionals', should view the challenge as a positive forum to re-evaluate practice.

A useful model for responding to change, which could be applied to policy change from central government, would be as follows (adapted from York-Barr *et al.*, 2006):

1. *Ask questions and listen* – by asking questions, practitioners will gain a better understanding of the key principles underpinning the change and once one question has been asked, it may give rise to other questions to widen the debate. Slow down and listen; don't presume.

2. *Acknowledge despair and fear; don't run from it* – it is natural to feel anxious and suspicious of change and practitioners should recognise that some colleagues may feel more threatened than others. Acknowledge that this is a natural phase of the process.

3. *Adopt an 'abundance' mindset* – look for the positive rather than the negative. An abundance mindset acknowledges what we have rather than what we have not. It is an optimist view: 'the glass is half-full, not half-empty'. This helps practitioners to look for the positives within the change and not focus on the negatives.

4. *Remember the past* – this is to encourage practitioners to look back at who or what inspired them; to remember why they have chosen this career and why they want to continue with it. In addition to this, practitioners need to reflect on past practice to analyse how they have got to this point and how their practice has developed. From this, they can then look forward.

5. *Listen and learn from the children* – practitioners need to put the child back at the centre of any policy. What do the children need? Sometimes with all the changes it is easy to forget the very reason we are in our profession. Keep the children in mind at all times.

6. *Express your vision and values* – idealism is not always realism, but without it what are we striving for? Although inflexible idealism can lead to pressure, which must of course be avoided, it is important for practitioners to hold onto their values and integrity and embrace the changes with these firmly in place.

One of the recent policy changes is the introduction of Every Child Matters (DfES, 2003) and the multi-agency approach. To achieve the five outcomes of Every Child Matters (be safe; keep healthy; enjoy and achieve; make a positive contribution; and achieve economic well-being), it is essential that the different children's services work together and share information. One of the potential difficulties is that different agencies have different priorities and different ways of working. Practitioners can learn from one another by acknowledging these different viewpoints. Reflective practice now involves not only reflecting on practice within the discipline, but reflecting on working with other agencies and reflecting on the different perspectives this brings. This provides the opportunity for practitioners to reflect on their own practice in relation to other disciplines and their effectiveness in working as part of an interdisciplinary team.

Reflective Tasks

Working with other agencies

This is a list of some of the people you may work with within your professional career:

- health visitors
- social workers
- parents
- therapists
- education advisers
- psychologists
- SEN service
- OFSTED
- teachers
- volunteer workers.

Level 1

Provide a brief description of the role of each of the people in the above list. Map their responsibilities to the ECM outcomes (DfES, 2003) to show how their role impacts upon these.

Level 2

Map the responsibilities of the people in the list above to the ECM outcomes (DfES, 2003) to show how their role impacts upon these. Consider which of the above you have come into contact with as part of your professional work. Reflect on your communication with them, the time you spent with them, any element of teamwork and the impact of this working relationship. Could it have been improved? If so, how?

Level 3

Consider which of the above you have come into contact with as part of your professional work. Reflect on your communication with them, the time you spent with them, any element of teamwork and the impact of this working relationship. Would you consider that you were working as part of a multi-agency team? Justify your answer. How would working as part of a multi-agency team in your setting help to meet the ECM (DfES, 2003) outcomes?

Responding to policy change and meeting external objectives can be difficult initially, but it is an integral part of working in public services. The services are part of the local and wider community and as such have to respond to the needs of society in the broader context. For practitioners to view their own setting as an island, impervious to outside influences, is a negation of duty to the community in which, and whom, it serves. The integrity of the people working within the setting is crucial for external influences to have a positive, rather than a negative, effect. However, it is also essential for the policy-makers to value this integrity and respond accordingly.

Research

Time to Talk

In 2006, the Department for Children, Schools and Families (DCSF) launched its Time to Talk consultation, inviting views from children and young people, parents, carers and professionals and asking:

- What can be done to make children safer?
- What can be done to make children healthier?
- What can improve support for vulnerable children and young people?
- What would help keep children and young people out of trouble?

The research was conducted by the former Office of the Children's Commissioner, now called 11 Million, and is published in a report entitled *Time to Talk* (11 Million, 2007). This example of reflective practice will inform a 10-year plan, setting out how the DCSF will improve the lives of children and young people. The research does not claim that these views are fully representative and there are no firm policy conclusions made. Some of the key findings are as follows.

Safety

Children tend to see safety as 'the absence of physical harm' (11 Million, 2007: 6), although early years children associate safety with emotional security. As a result, home and family are key places of safety. The research attempted to understand pre-school children's conception of play and risks in public space and discovered that children see risk very differently from adults, so that safety threats to adults are viewed as objects of exploration for children.

Health and happiness

Young children link the ideas of health and happiness so that one is not possible without the other.

Support for vulnerable children

Transition is felt to be especially stressful for vulnerable children. It was suggested that support, discussion, information and training provided by outside services, including regular, consistent support from a social worker to coordinate services to meet children's particular needs would be helpful. Children thought that it was important to break down barriers between children in special schools and the general community.

Keeping children out of trouble

Children and young people are thought to get into trouble for a variety of reasons. Their own bad behaviour is felt to be central and more discipline and emphasis on respect at schools are thought to be solutions.

Supporting and evidencing reflective practice

In the final part of the chapter, we will consider different techniques, or the ways and means, of learning through reflective practice and providing evidence of reflective practice.

Personal reflective journals

There are many different words used to describe journals, such as log books, diaries, workbooks or progress files (Moon, 1999). Journals can be written for many different reasons depending on the purpose. They can record an experience, a specific event, our feelings and our 'story', but ultimately they help us to make sense of something and so enhance our learning (Boud, 2001). A **reflective journal** is contributed to regularly over a period of time and may be totally personal or may be a component of an assessed course. Clearly if it is a piece of assessed work, that fact may well impact on the content and style, as discussed previously, and it will need to be formally written up in a narrative or action research style (see Figure 12.1).

Journal writing can take a number of forms. Personal journals may incorporate creative interpretations, such as poems, pictures and the use of colour and form to express feelings and thoughts. They often incorporate free writing, not based on any structure or pre-set question. These tend to be known as unstructured journals (Moon, 1999), and allow the practitioner to reflect through the process of representation of experiences and thoughts on paper. Some people have a notebook with them all the time to enable them to record thoughts as they occur. They may also have a notebook by their bed so that when that perfect idea pops into their head at 3 o'clock in the morning it can be recorded straight-away and not forgotten by the time the alarm clock goes off, just as they've managed to get to sleep! The act of writing helps the interpretation and clarification of thoughts and ideas, just as verbalising them can do the same.

Structured journals have a more specific outline and purpose. These are primarily used for assessment to ensure criteria have been met, but this is not their only value. Some people prefer to work to a structure, and it certainly helps learners starting reflective writing who need more guidance to arrange their thoughts. The structure could involve the completion of specific tasks or questions. These could be quite vague, such as, 'list three things that you have learnt today', or more specific, such as 'How does your experience in school this week link to your understanding of Bloom's taxonomy?' The journal could be structured through headings pertinent to the practitioner's needs, such as: 'My time management'; 'My impact on the environment'; 'My communication with parents'. The journal could be written from different points of view: 'My perspective'; 'The children's perspective'; 'The parents' perspective', with the practitioner trying to see things from different angles. Lists can also provide a structure, such as 'things I would like to change' or 'things that would help me'. The layout of the journal could be separated into two parallel sections: the left-hand page records the factual experience and the adjacent right-hand page records the reflections on that experience. These are a few examples, but the key point is that the structure must support the reflective process and not be so prescriptive that it inhibits it.

Dialogue journals

These are essentially the same as reflective journals, but involve more than one person. It could be between supervisor and student or between teacher and pupil, but it can also be between peers. The use of technology has enhanced this style of reflection, particularly email and discussion forums. Tutors could pose a question or statement for students to discuss via the forum and the students can then respond to one another, using their personal experience to reflect on the ideas being presented. This is peer discussion in written form, allowing time for reflection not always possible with the immediacy of a verbal discussion. One potential problem is the misunderstandings that could occur through the writing medium. Without the addition of facial expressions and tone of voice that is so central to verbal communication, written communications might be unclear and ambiguous.

Formal written evaluations

The formal evaluation is a specific type of reflection and needs to be relatively succinct if it is to be completed on a daily basis. It provides a summary of a response to an experience. Anyone who has been on a course will probably have been asked to fill in an evaluation form at the end to record their views about the course. This can be quite onerous and I often feel I am doing the trainers' jobs for them because they should be capable of reflecting on their *own* practice and evaluating the way the participants responded to questions and tasks. It is harder, but far more valuable, to evaluate our own practice rather than that of others. To do this effectively, a structure is helpful because it avoids a descriptive account. Consider these two examples:

> I went to bed late because I was trying to get the essay finished and forgot to set the alarm because I was tired, which meant I got up late. I couldn't print it all out because I ran out of ink, so I went to the library to do it, although I felt I deserved a drink first after all the hassle. Finally got it printed out and got to the assignment office two minutes after 4 pm, so it was two minutes after the deadline. The 'rottweiler' admin assistant wouldn't take it, said 'rules were rules' and I should have got there earlier! I'll get a '0' now and I needed to pass!

> I was late handing in my essay and now it will not be marked, resulting in a '0' on my mark profile.
>
> *I learnt that*:
> - I need to give course work priority
> - I need to improve my timekeeping
> - I need to be aware of college protocol and that it is not flexible
>
> *Targets*:
> - Have all essays written and printed out at least one day before they are due in
> - Set my own deadline of 12 noon for handing in assignments to ensure they are not late
> - Check I have spare printing ink cartridges so that I am never left without one

The first is a descriptive narrative; the second is succinct and has a focus. Simple headings such as: 'Positive points'; 'Points for improvement'; and 'Targets', with a limit on the number of each, can provide a useful framework and be less time-consuming than writing in narrative prose. Written evaluations are common practice during placements and therefore it is important for students to develop these skills.

Audio recording and video recording

It can be useful to see or hear yourself as others see or hear you, through the use of video or audio recordings. Students are often asked to watch videos of practitioners to examine the practice that they see, but it is also useful (if somewhat excruciating) to see themselves in action. With the use of small hand-held video cameras this is easier and deleting the video recording after viewing in the setting reduces the problems associated with videos in settings with children. Parents would need to give their permission, but if the purpose was made clear this should not be a significant problem. I often suggest audio recording to my students as a way of examining an aspect of their practice, such as questioning or their general use of voice. York-Barr *et al.* (2006) note how teachers viewing videos of themselves were made aware of habits and mannerisms that they wanted to change, and provide this as an example of how reflection-on-action can impact on reflection-in-action.

Whatever systems we put in place, embedding reflective practice into our professional lives will enhance our practice and make a positive impact on the adults and children with whom we work. It is not always easy and it may be time-consuming, but without it we cannot grow and develop as a professional. It allows us to understand and come to terms with our own feelings; make sense of what is already known and what is new; and gives us ownership of our learning and our practice. This should result in confident, empowered professionals who realise the value of pausing and reflecting to think critically about the impact of their practice. The chapter will end on this final thought:

> People travel to wonder at the height of the mountains, at the huge waves of the sea, at the long courses of rivers, at the vast compass of the ocean … and they pass by themselves without wondering.
> St Augustine (AD 354–430)

Summary

→ Dewey, Kolb and Schön are three of the most well-known writers and theorists on reflective practice.

→ Schön used the terms 'reflection-in-action' (while doing something) and 'reflection-on-action' (after you have done it).

→ Although much of Schön's work has been very influential, it is not without its critics.

→ There are common characteristics of reflective practice, although, essentially, reflective practice is an active process which involves enquiry and a motivation to learn from our personal experience.

→ The thinking professional is at the core of reflective practice.

→ In addition to theoretical frameworks, there are some practical models to support practice. These usually take the form of questions to help channel our thinking and so support a reflective approach.

→ Individuals can develop personal reflection in order to understand and improve their own performance. This can be done in a variety of ways depending on the circumstances and purpose.

→ What many students initially find difficult when reflecting on their own practice is the move from description to evaluation and reflection.

→ To enable those starting out in training to develop reflective practice, the role of mentors and supervisors is fundamental.

→ Reflective practice can also be developed through working with others.

→ The role of the professional demands the ability to enter into professional dialogue with others and to acknowledge the potential for new ideas and approaches.

→ The term mentoring is used describe one supportive relationship between colleagues working in a setting. Mentoring is used in a variety of circumstances: by trainees, by newly-qualified professionals in their first year and by experienced practitioners who are seeking professional development.

→ Coaching relationships are generally designed to teach a specific set of skills, and once the skills are taught the relationship is no longer needed. Co-coaching relationships, however, are more equal, where colleagues of equal status work together to move practice forward.

→ The whole ethos within a setting can be reflective or, in contrast, can fail to be reflective by the inability of the staff to learn from their own information and experience.

→ A reflective setting should critically evaluate policy change and the potential effects on policy and practice within the setting alongside the overriding philosophy underpinning the values in the setting.

→ There are different techniques, or ways and means, of learning through reflective practice and providing evidence of reflective practice, including journals and video recordings.

Key Questions

- What are some of the key theories related to reflective practice and why are some criticised?
- What are some of the characteristics of reflective practice?
- What are some of the models of reflective practice and how to they differ from one another?
- In what ways can we develop individual reflective practice?
- What are some of the issues when working with others to develop reflective practice?
- Why is reflective practice important for professional development?
- What are some of the ways we can record evidence of reflective practice?

References

11 Million (2007) *Time to Talk. DCSF Consultation*. London: 11 Million

Abbott, L. and Pugh, G. (1998) *Training to Work in the Early Years*. Buckingham: Open University Press

Amulya, J. (2003) *What is Reflective Practice?* Cambridge, MA: Massachusetts Institute of Technology, Center for Community Practice

Atherton, J. (2003) *Doceo: Forms of Knowledge*. Available from: http://www.doceo.co.uk/tools/forms.htm (accessed: 5 January 2007)

Boud, D. (2001). Using Journal Writing to Enhance Reflective Practice, in English, L.M. and Gillen, M.A. (eds) *Promoting Journal Writing in Adult Education.* New Directions in Adult and Continuing Education, 90: 9–18. San Francisco: Jossey-Bass

Callaghan, K. (2002) 'Nurturing the Enthusiasm and Ideals of New Teachers through Reflective Practice', *Canadian Children, The Journal of the Canadian Association for Young Children,* 27, 1: 38–41

CWDC (2006) *Early Years Professional National Standards.* Leeds: CWDC

Dewey, J. (1897) 'My pedagogic creed', *The School Journal,* LIV, 3: 77–80. Also available in the *Informal Education Archives,* http://www.infed.org/archives/e-texts/e-dew-pc.htm

Dewey, J. (1933) *How we Think.* Boston: D.C. Heath.

DfES (1998) *The National Literacy Strategy: Framework for Teaching.* London: DfES

DfES (2003) *Every Child Matters – Change for Children.* London: DfES

DfES (2006) *Primary National Strategy – Reading: Developing Reflective Practice Through the Reading Quality Assurance Scheme.* London: DfES

Elliott, J. (1991a) *Action Research for Educational Change.* Buckingham: Open University Press

Elliot, J. (1991b) Two models of Professionalism, in Pollard, A. (ed.) *Readings for Reflective Teaching in the Primary School.* London: Cassell

Gibbs, G. (1988) *Learning by Doing: A Guide to Teaching and Learning Methods.* Birmingham: SCED

Grimes, R. (2006) *Reflection in Legal Clinic.* Available from: www.ukcle.ac.uk/resources/reflection/examples.html

Gura, P. (1996) An Entitlement Curriculum for Early Childhood, in Robson, S. and Smedley, S. *Education in Early Childhood.* London: David Fulton.

James, M., McCormick, R., Black, P., Carmichael, P., Drummond, M., Fox, A., MacBeath, J., Marshall, B., Pedder, D., Procter, R., Swaffield, S., Swann, J. and Wiliam, D. (2007) *Improving Learning How to Learn: Classrooms, Schools and Networks.* London: Routledge

Jindal-Snape, D. and Holmes, E. (2006) *Investigating Methods for Enhancing Reflective Practice used by Educational Psychology Students and Practitioners.* School of Education, Social Work and Community Education, University of Dundee

Kolb, A. (1984) *Experiential Learning: Experience as the Source of Learning and Development.* Englewood Cliffs, NJ: Prentice-Hall

Lindon, J. (2005) *Understanding Child Development.* London: Hodder Arnold.

McNiff, J. and Whitehead, J. (2002) *Action Research Principles and Practice.* London: Routledge Falmer

Middlewood, D. and Cardno, C. (2001) *Managing Teacher Appraisal and Performance.* London: Routledge Falmer

Miller, L., Cable, C. and Devereux, J. (2005) *Developing Early Years Practice.* London: David Fulton

Moon, J. (1999) *Reflection in Learning and Professional Development.* London: Kogan Page

Moore, A. and Ash, A. (2002) *Reflective Practice in Beginning Teachers: Helps, Hindrances and the Role of the Critical Other.* University of Exeter: Paper presented at the BERA Annual Conference, 2002. Available from Education-Line http://www.leeds.ac.uk/educol/

Peters, J. (1991) 'Strategies for Reflective Practice', *Professional Development for Educators of Adults. New Directions for Adult and Continuing Education,* No. 51. San Francisco: Jossey-Bass

Rinaldi, C. (2006) *In Dialogue with Reggio Emilia.* London: Routledge

Roth, R. (1989) 'Preparing the Reflective Practitioner: Transforming the Apprentice Through the Dialectic', *Journal of Teacher Education.* 40: 31–5

Schön, D. (1983) *The Reflective Practitioner.* San Francisco: Jossey-Bass

Schön, D. (1987) *Educating the Reflective Practitioner.* San Francisco: Jossey-Bass

Schwienhart, L., Weikart, D. and Toderan, R. (1993) *High Quality Preschool Programs Found to Improve Adult Status.* Ypsilante, MI: High/Scope Foundation

Senge, P., with Cambron-McCabe, N., Lucas, T., Smith, B., Dutton, J. and Kleiner, A. (2000) *Schools that Learn.* London: Nicholas Brealey

Smyth, J. (1991) *Teachers as Collaborative Learners.* Buckingham: Open University Press.

Stammers, P. (1992) 'The Greeks Had a Name for It...'. *British Journal of Inservice Education*, 18(2): 76–80

TDA (2007) Professional Standards for Teachers: Qualified Teacher Status. London: TDA

Weare, K. (2004) *Developing the Emotionally Literate School.* London: Paul Chapman

York-Barr, J., Sommers, W., Ghere, G. and Montie, J. (2006) *Reflective Practice to Improve Schools.* Thousand Oaks, CA: Corwin Press

Chapter 13

Working Together

'Coming together is a beginning. Keeping together is progress. Working together is success'

Henry Ford (1863–1947)

Introduction

This chapter will consider the issues related to working as part of a team. In addition to exploring the roles of the different professionals involved in working together, we will also consider the impact on the children with whom they work and the importance of working with parents and carers. It is also essential to include the wider community and to explore how the professional can work with all the different individuals and agencies that have an impact on a child's life. Finally, the chapter will seek to identify those key features of effective partnerships and collaborative working that ensure the highest quality provision for every child.

Aims

→ To provide an overview of the different groups of professionals who work together to support children's development

→ To provide an understanding of the centrality of the child to all who work together

→ To explore ways in which the professionals can work effectively with parents and carers

→ To consider the role of the wider community

→ To provide an understanding of effective professional partnerships

Who should work together?

In the area of early childhood, there are many professionals, groups and individuals who need to work together to support children's development (see Figure 13.1). These are represented in Bronfenbrenner's ecological systems theory (1995; see Chapters 1 and 7, and Figure 7.2), as well as Johnston's learning partnership (2002). They are also seen in the themes underpinning the Early Years Foundation Stage (DfES, 2007: 9),

● *A Unique Child* recognises that every child is a competent learner from birth who can be resilient, capable, confident and self-assured. The commitments are focused around development; inclusion; safety; and health and well-being.

● *Positive Relationships* describes how children learn to be strong and independent from a base of loving and secure relationships with parents and/or a key person. The commitments are focused around respect; partnership with parents; supporting learning; and the role of the key person.

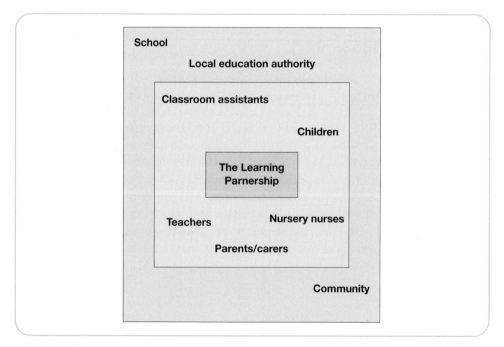

Figure 13.1 The learning partnership
Source: Adapted from Johnston, 2002: 31

- *Enabling Environments* explains that the environment plays a key role in supporting and extending children's development and learning. The commitments are focused around observation, assessment and planning; support for every child; the learning environment; and the wider context – transitions, continuity, and multi-agency working.

- *Learning and Development* recognises that children develop and learn in different ways and at different rates, and that all areas of learning and development are equally important and interconnected.

Case Study

John's first 8 years of life

The complexities of these partnerships are evident if we look at an individual child and all those who have been and are working together to support his early development.

John is 8 years old and is finding school difficult. This is hardly surprising as his life has been traumatic and disrupted. His mother discovered she was pregnant at 14 years of age and kept her pregnancy secret until just before John was born. Her mother and stepfather threw her out of the house and she was taken into care and housed in a teenage mother and baby unit. She was malnourished and when John was born he had a low birth weight (being below the fifth percentile).

When John was 3 years old, his mother was given a council flat and moved in with her boyfriend and John. Two half-siblings arrived within the next two years. His 'stepfather' was a heavy drinker and the police were often called by neighbours during violent attacks on both John, his mother and siblings.

At school, there was concern about John because of his inability to concentrate and he often fell asleep during the school day. He did not have many friends in school and the professionals in the school were concerned about his behaviour as there was evidence that he was bullying other children.

Between the ages of 6 and 7, John, his mother and siblings went into a 'safe house' on three separate occasions, and on one occasion John was put into short-term foster care. Eventually at 8 years old, he moved, with his mother and siblings, into a new flat and school in a new area. As a result of his early circumstances and troubled home life, John had experienced quite a disruptive few years in school, with three different schools in 3 years. He continued to have social and academic problems in school and was supported by a range of professionals to help him overcome them.

Reflective Tasks

The range of professionals

Consider the Case Study above and identify all the professionals who would have worked with John at the different stages of his early life (0–3; 3–5; 5–8).

Level 1

Research the roles of the different professionals who could work with John.

- Do any of the roles overlap?
- How many of the different professionals were you aware of or had had contact with in your own professional life?

Level 2

How many of the different professionals have you worked with in your setting?

- Do you know the different roles and responsibilities of each professional? If not research their roles and responsibilities.
- Are there any children in your care who would benefit from the help of other professionals? If so, how?
- How can you access the help of other professionals?

Level 3

- How many different professionals help your staff in supporting the children in your setting?
- Are there other professional who could help you in your setting?
- Do some of the roles and responsibilities overlap? If so, how?
- How can you and your staff work together with other professionals to support the children in your setting in a coherent and effective way?

All Levels

Now group all the professionals you listed above into those who focus on a child's physical, social, emotional or educational development.

- Is any group under- or over-represented?
- Are there any who span more than one group?

There is a vast array of professionals who need to work together to ensure that a child's holistic development is smooth. Many will focus on the child's physical health and development, such as midwives, health visitors, doctors, paediatricians, physiotherapists and dentists. Others will focus on a child's social development, such as social workers, behaviour and play therapists, probation officers and the police. Psychologists, psychiatrists, counsellors and therapists focus on a child's emotional development. Teachers, teaching assistants, early years professionals, speech therapists and learning support professionals will focus mainly on the educational aspects of a child's development. Many of these professionals are concerned with more than one area of development: play therapists will be concerned with emotional and social aspects; speech therapists are concerned with physical and educational aspects and early years professionals concern themselves with all aspects. Regardless of the individual focus, the most important concern is the child and all professionals should be working together for the holistic development of the child. Each will have different roles and responsibilities, but work together in a partnership with the child in the centre of that partnership. In this way it is essential that we work together effectively, understanding the different roles and responsibilities and how we can facilitate each other as well as support the child. It is when the professionals do not work together effectively or there is a gap in provision and support that children suffer, sometimes disastrously, as in high profile child abuse or death cases.

Tools for Learning

Writing up a thesis

In this chapter we are focusing on writing up a thesis. The decision as to how to structure your work depends initially on the type of research you are undertaking: your research methodology (see Tools for Learning in Chapter 12 and Figure 12.1). Once you have decided the structure, you can then consider what will go into each section. This may include:

- *an introduction*, which describes your research focus, the context and the rationale for the study;
- *research methods*: what you are going to do (research methodology, methods you will use, how you will ensure reliability, validity of data and ethical issues);
- *literature review*: introduction to issues from literature, analysis of secondary data to answer research questions;
- *analysis of primary data*: data should be analysed in as many ways and from as many different perspectives as possible (chronology/history, research questions, patterns emerging, groups of collected data, new ideas and theories, emerging issues, factors affecting data/informants);
- *discussion of findings*: synthesis of ideas, summary of issues/new models/factors, implications (personal and more general), combining primary and secondary data to answer questions, new reading to show understanding and development;
- *evaluation of research*: reflection on the success of your research and the development of your research skills;
- *bibliography*: references and other reading;
- *appendices*.

Working with children

The most important individuals we work with are children. They should be central to all that we do, as it is their development that we are supporting. The importance of child-centred interactions have been recognised by many (see Chapter 1). Look at Table 1.1 and try to identify how many of the theorists mention aspects of child-centred learning. Check your ideas with the text in Chapter 1 and see if you got them all. The first mention of child-centred interaction can be seen in the writings of Rousseau, who identified that we should accommodate children in our work with them and not expect them to accommodate us. Since then the debate has been about how much we should allow children freedom or guidance in their development (Montessori, 1912; Steiner, 1996), or structure their development with artefacts (Froebel, 1826) or skilled interaction (Vygotsky and Cole, 1978).

Recent legislation has also recognised the importance of the individual. The Every Child Matters agenda (DfES, 2003a) is making all who work with children and young people rethink their practice and provision, and the Code of Practice for special needs children (DfES, 2001) emphasises the important of inclusion for all children, regardless of special need. The importance of the individual child taking ownership over their own learning, making their own decisions and reflecting on their achievements are themes in many early years curricula, such as High/Scope (Holt, 2007), Reggio Emilia (Rinaldi,

2006) and Te Whàriki (Nuttall, 2003). This contrasts with provision for older children (8 years of age and above) which has often seen the child as a passive participant (Hendy and Whitebread, 2000; Sanders *et al.*, 2005) in the process of development and learning, with the result that many young adults, who have experienced the full educational process, expect to have little or no responsibility for their own development. Even very young children are well aware of their own abilities and developmental needs and will spend considerable amounts of time perfecting actions. They are quite able to make their own decisions about what they need to learn next and this enables them to differentiate for themselves. Taking ownership over your own learning has a number of important effects. It is motivating and encourages children to keep on developing and learning, as they are more likely to want to find things out and perfect skills if they have decided what to do and how to do it. It also helps to ensure that the learning direction is well matched to the individual child needs and abilities, as children usually start an activity at the stage they are already at and develop from there. If children are actively engaged and motivated, they will have fewer behavioural problems and will take control over their own behaviour as well as learning and development.

The adult's role in this development is to provide the support and space for the children to facilitate their development. The professional early years practitioner will instinctively know when to interact or intervene and when to leave a respectful space to enable the child to complete a task. I once worked with a group of children aged 4 who were playing in a garden centre set up in their class (see de Bóo, 2004). One child wanted to interact and socialise with me, but another wanted to be left alone and spent considerable lengths of time independently observing small details of seeds using a digital microscope attached to a computer (see Picture 13.1). If I attempted to interact with her, she would lower her head and stop what she was doing and I needed to give her the respectful space that she desired.

Picture 13.1 Child independently observing seeds with a computer microscope
Source: Johnston, 2005

In this example the child's 'voice' was non-verbal and I needed to respect her wishes. While working with children we communicate as much to them in non-verbal ways as we do in verbal ways. We model by example behaviours and attitudes that we want them to develop and which will support their future development. We play with them, listen to them and respect ideas. We help them if they are struggling, but only if we are clear they want our help. We leave them alone if they are happy and wish to do something on their own. In this way we model social skills and behaviours, such as cooperation, and also social attitudes, such as respect and tolerance. We also encourage perseverance, self-esteem and creativity, as children come to realise that adults are not infallible founts of knowledge, children themselves can achieve most things if they persevere and that failure is part of learning. This aspect of creativity is not often recognised, but it is important for future development that children are not only able to accept failure, but to build on it to achieve success. Verbal communication supports development through adult questions, challenges, discussions and arguments.

Case Study

Communicating with children as individuals

Megan is rising 5. Her mother and father are both unemployed teenagers and they live in a very damp, cold, high rise flat. Her mother gets very depressed and takes tranquillisers. Her parents row a lot, and after a particularly bad row her father walked out saying he was never coming back. Megan went to school the next day looking pale and was clearly unhappy. The teaching assistant (TA) asked Megan if she would like a drink and, when she said 'yes', took her to the kitchen and gave her a glass of milk and some toast. While she was eating, the TA talked to her about what she wanted to do that day. Megan said that she wanted to paint and so after returning to the classroom Megan went straight to the painting easel and began to paint a picture of her family. When she had finished, she sought out the TA and talked to her about her mum and dad.

Willow is also rising 5 and has muscular dystrophy. She attends the local mainstream primary school, but the access to the school is not good. The place is also dependent on the provision of a full-time classroom assistant to help ensure the safety of Willow, who weighs just 3 stone and is partially sighted. When Willow arrives in school in the morning, her mother has to get her wheelchair up the step into the classroom. Although the main entrance has a wheelchair ramp, the school does not allow children to enter school by the main entrance and Willow wants to be treated like all the other children. During the school day, her classroom assistant is often working with other children in the class and this means that Willow cannot always do the things she wants to do. She rarely goes outside for outside play as she cannot access the step.

Reflective Tasks

Communicating with children as individuals

Consider the Case Study above.

Level 1

- What message were the two teachers communicating about the children as individuals?
- How are the two teachers meeting the Every Child Matters (ECM) agenda (DfES, 2003a) that children should be healthy; stay safe; enjoy and achieve; make a positive contribution; and achieve economic and social well-being?
- What could you do in your next work with children to ensure you are sending positive messages about them as individuals and meeting the ECM agenda?

Level 2

- Do your interactions with children best fit the first or second example?
- How can you ensure that you focus on the individual child's needs and give quality interactions to all children in your care?
- How could you develop your work with children to better meet the ECM agenda?

Level 3

- What messages does your setting send to individuals about their own preferences and needs?
- How can you support your staff to ensure that they address individual needs and provide quality interactions to all children?
- How you support your staff in meeting the ECM agenda?

Article 12 of the UN Convention on the Rights of the Child identifies the right of children to be heard and play a part in decisions that affect them. Cheminais (2006: 22) provides examples of the types of activities that meet the ECM agenda (DfES, 2003a):

- **being healthy** – stress management, relaxation techniques and the provision of a peaceful and multi-sensory room;
- **staying safe** – peer mediation to reduce bullying and discrimination;
- **enjoying and achieving** – personalised learning to meet individual needs, particularly for those with complex learning and physical needs;
- **making a positive contribution** – the inclusion of all children in projects, initiatives and daily routines, and peer mentoring schemes which engage children in helping each other;
- **achieving economic and social well-being** – engaging children in the development of 'life skills', such as financial literacy, problem-solving, team work and the development of self-confidence and self-esteem.

In this way children are placed at the centre of all provision and practice in the early years and inclusion is seen as an important process in achieving this (Jennings, 2005). Practical examples of child-centred inclusion can be found in case studies in a number of publications (Nuttall, 2003; Abbott and Langston, 2005; Jones, 2005), whilst Siraj-

Picture 13.2 Working together to model learning and enjoyment
Source: John Walmsley/Eduction Photos

Blatchford (2005) identifies the principle of inclusive interaction. These include that professionals working with young children should:

- let the child lead;
- listen and respond;
- engage in sustained shared thinking;
- provide time for unhurried interactions;
- interact with all children.

(See Picture 13.2.)

Working with families, parents and carers

Children spend more time with their families than they do in early years settings and schools so it is vitally important that professionals have an effective working relationship with families, parents and carers. This importance has been recognised in many publications (Sage and Wilkie, 2004; Abbott and Langston, 2006; Bastiani and Wolfendale, 1996), and government initiatives (DfES, 2003b; 2007). Vincent (2000) identifies three different roles for parents and carers. First, they can be consumers, receiving a service for their children from the professionals and settings responsible for their children's care. This indicates a passive role for the parent and an unequal working relationship, with the full responsibility for the child's development resting with the professional. Secondly, the parents can be supporters or learners themselves, as defined by parent partnerships in which parents confirm that they will support the setting and professionals in their endeavours. This is less passive than the parent as a consumer, but does not recognise parental individuality, responsibility, expertise and initiative. The third role, as participant, is fully active and recognises the parent as well as the child and professional as full partners with rights and responsibilities.

Working relationships with parents and carers often begin before the children start attending a setting, through home visits where professionals can discuss the nature of the provision they provide for the children and how parents can be involved both in the setting and at home. Professionals need to be well trained to work effectively in the home (Caffrey, 1997) and it should not be seen as simply an extension of the work in the setting. Success in home visits relies on both parent and professional seeing themselves as equal partners. Book and toy loan schemes can help parents to introduce stories and books, play with their children and develop language and imagination. The relationship can continue through visits to the setting and parents can identify vital information about their children, their children's preferences and individual needs, and also parental expertise and experience that the setting can draw upon. In this way the relationship develops into an active partnership with two-way communication. Settings can also communicate with parents through parental information sessions, family learning workshops and newsletters. The most important feature of this working relationship is the two-way communication and consultation, which builds an effective partnership and helps to meet the ECM agenda. The Education Act 2002 identified that professionals should consult with parents and more widely regarding the provision of extended childcare, homework, sport and creative arts clubs. Extended and integrated services enable opportunities for professionals to work together with parents (DfES, 2006), although this involves challenge as to how to work effectively with a range of partners and the whole school community. When children begin to be cared for outside of the family, with childminders, playgroups, nurseries, schools, etc., it is essential that their parents or carers become full partners with the professionals who care for their children. This is important for the following reasons:

- Worried parents can unsettle the children and create difficulties for them as they struggle to gain independence and develop socially, cognitively and emotionally. The evidence discussed in previous chapters (see in particular Chapter 6 and 7) that day care can have negative effects on children's emotional development (Bowlby, 2006) and social development is contrasted by the positive effects on socialisation and independence. If parents are more involved in the care with a positive partnership between the setting and home, then some of the negative effects may be avoided.

- Parents and carers have in-depth knowledge of their children which they can share with professionals to the benefit of children. In an effective partnership both parents and professionals will engage in an honest dialogue about the children's achievements and work together to help them to meet their challenges.

- Parents and carers may have expertise which professionals do not and this expertise can be shared. For example, a parent who is a doctor or nurse or dentist can talk to the children about their job, give them an insight into their responsibilities, allow them to experience some of their equipment (stethoscope, heart monitor, thermometer), play with them in a role play area, etc. Other parents may have access to resources that will support an aspect of the child's development or work of the setting. I was once given a set of wonderful dressing-up clothes from a parent who ran a dance school. These included costumes for rabbits, bees and flowers and a wonderful range of hats. Every parent can contribute in some way to the variety of life within the setting and the challenge for the professional is to find out what they can offer and to capitalise upon it.

- Parents and carers can support the children's development at home in a variety of ways, building on and extending the experiences their children have in the setting. They can read to the child, set up play experiences to extend what they do in the setting, go for walks together, talk to and listen to their child. The setting can provide some simple challenges for parent and child to undertake together, such as practising dressing themselves, or making a joint model or solving a simple problem.

Case Study

Different cultures

Mohammed is 3 years old and lives with his extended family in a white suburban area. He attends a local nursery where he is the only child from an Islamic family. The nursery encourages Mohammed in sharing his cultural experiences with both staff and children. Family members are invited to work in the nursery to extend and develop the children's cultural experiences.

Reflective Tasks

Inclusive partnerships

Consider the Case Study above.

Level 1

- How does the nursery's action benefit both Mohammed and his family?
- How else could they strengthen the working partnership with Mohammed's parents and other parents?

Level 2

- What messages are the professionals in the nursery sending to Mohammed and his family about their culture?
- How else could the professionals develop effective inclusive partnerships with ethnic minority families?

Level 3

- What messages does your setting send to families from ethnic minorities?
- How can you develop effective inclusive partnerships with all families in your setting?

Effective parental inclusion that recognises and celebrates the part that parents play in their child's development and the skills they can bring to a setting is empowering for both the parents and the professionals. It sends powerful messages to parents about their value as parents regardless of family context (Mairs, 1997). This partnership helps children to make sense of the different context that they find themselves in and adapt to the changes in their lives, 'in a dynamic and continuous negotiation process' (Lam and Pollard, 2006: 137) as they enter formal care.

Leaving the care of your primary carer is difficult for both child and parent/carer. There is increasing evidence that early transitions to day care can benefit language development and support socialisation (EPPE, 2003), but adversely affect social (Palmer, 2006) and emotional development (Bowlby, 2006). Transition from home to formal care is best viewed as a process rather than an event (Johnston *et al.*, 2007), and a process that needs an excellent home-school working partnership. Many settings encourage parents to be fully involved with the setting, stay with their children as long as both need to, and help out during the day. Some settings are almost like extensions of home and are designed not only to motivate children but to put them at their ease when they enter the setting. Some settings encourage parents to play with their children at the start and finish of every day and this takes the tension out of partings and reunions and makes the transition between the setting and home smoother. The final report of the EPPE (Effective Provision of Pre-school Education) project has identified the importance of parent interactions in supporting children's development (Sylva *et al.*, 2004). An effective partnership is one where parents work together with professionals to support children by continuing the provision of a high-quality learning environment in the home, by reading to and with their children, singing and teaching them songs and rhymes, and introducing them to number and sounds.

As children move into compulsory care and education the importance of effective working relationships between parents and professionals is recognised in two of the Early Years Foundation Stage themes: positive relationships and enabling environments (DfES, 2007; see beginning of this chapter). Some later transitions between the Foundation Stage and Key Stage 1 and between Key Stage 1 and Key Stage 2 are often characterised by poor parent–professional relationships.

Research

Effective working relationships and transitions

Research (Sanders *et al.*, 2005) has indicated that parents:

- want information about transitions, so they can support their children as to what to expect in the next stage;
- want to meet prospective teachers before they move into new stages;
- want to discuss concerns about the increased demands and workloads placed on children;
- are well placed to make transitions smooth.

Other research (Primary National Strategy, 2006) identifies that parents recognise the importance of good working relationships with professionals. They want their children to be happy, supported by professionals who know them, encourage them, but do not pressurise them. They want to be involved in the life of the setting, and with professionals and other parents. Settings that have effective working relationships with parents, have consulted them, welcomed them, shared with them and involved them fully are more likely to have children who move smoothly through the care and educational system and have fewer developmental problems. Indeed, early transitions are the focus of a great deal of research (e.g. Dunlop and Fabian, 2007) and practical support (e.g. Bayley and Featherstone, 2003). Bia Sena, Foundation Stage Coordinator at the British School, Rio de Janeiro (Johnston *et al.*, 2007) has researched transitions from nursery to reception and identified some barriers to smooth transitions:

- different structures, such as furniture and groupings. The type of furniture differs in the different classes and the children are regrouped on transition, so that six groups become five;
- different pedagogical approaches, with more play-based, child-centred approaches being found in the nursery and more adult-led cognitive activities in reception;

- the role of parents being different in the different classes, but with neither being fully valued.

The results of Bia Sema's research and her action plan can be seen in Figure 14.4. Clearly, effective transition relies on continuity, shared philosophies and approaches. Some of the ideas for developing integrated, collaborative philosophies contained in Chapter 2, will help to ease transitions.

ESRC-funded research (Turner-Cobb, 2006) examined the link between social regulation of stress to learning and health outcomes, in a longitudinal survey of 105 children due to start their first year of formal schooling. Tests were taken on the children six months before starting school and two weeks and six months after transition. Salivary cortisol was measured and parents' reports collected of their children's temperament as well as a health diary, and teacher reports of how they had adapted to the transition. The main findings were:

- cortisol was higher than expected before starting school, increased further at transition, and reduced significantly at follow-up;
- more extroverted children had higher cortisol levels when they started school;
- children who were socially isolated during the first six months of school had significantly higher cortisol levels six months after transition;
- children who were more able to focus their attention and inhibit impulsive behaviour at school had lower morning cortisol levels at transition and follow-up;
- children with higher cortisol levels at transition were less likely to become ill;
- children who tended to be shy at transition were more likely to become ill during the following six months.

Reflective Tasks

Supporting parents

Refer to the Case Study about Megan (see p. 397).

Level 1

- What support is available to help Megan's parents?
- How could you access this support?

Level 2

- What support is available for the parents of children in your care?
- How can you access help for parents of children in your care?

Level 3

- How does your setting access support for parents and children in your care?
- What type of support would help both the parents and children in your setting?

Tools for Learning

Dilemmas in writing up your thesis

Researching can be a long and lonely process. It tends to have certain phases (see Figure 0.1 in the Introduction). Some of these phases can be more comfortable than others and reluctance to move can affect your final outcome, as you will not be giving yourself enough time to write up your work. Below are some of the dilemmas faced by students when writing up their research thesis. If you are facing one of these dilemmas, look at the solutions to help you perfect your work.

1. 'Analysis is scary, so I'll stick to data collection'

You are stuck in the Squirrel Phase, where you know what you are doing and you feel safe and comforted by the amount of information you have collected and reassured by the reading which confirms your initial ideas. This comfort, however, can encourage you to stay in this phase for too long and keep hoarding information which may not see the light of day unless you move on to the Lemming Phase.

Be brave and make the leap. Remember that you are not alone. There are other lemmings out there, who are just as frightened as you and will support you when you make the leap and may even leap with you.

2. 'I have it so I'll use it!'

You have collected a great deal of data and, while much are relevant to the area of research and have informed your conceptual understanding, they are not directly relevant to the study and do not answer your research questions.

Sift through the data and DO NOT use irrelevant material. This material is not wasted as it has informed your ideas. Do not think you can sneak it in the dissertation by adding it in the discussion of findings or putting it in the appendix, as it will just detract from your study. You can always use it in another study or even in a research publication or contribution to a book.

3. 'I am desperately seeking significance'

The data are not as conclusive as you would like, so you try to persuade the reader that they are more significant than is really the case.

The only person you are kidding is yourself, so don't do it. Be honest with yourself and remember that with small-scale qualitative research you are unlikely to find anything of huge significance. Look at the data more deeply and try to understand them. You may find there is more to data if you look carefully. Remember, too, that sometimes things that do not turn out the way you expect prove more interesting than those that do!

4. '20% of children ...'

You have worked with 10 children and so 20 per cent equals two of them.

Don't use statistics unless your sample is big enough to make it sensible. Say 'two of the children' if that is what you mean.

5. 'It is generally believed that ...'

You have a tendency to use 'weasel' words, words which do not really say anything. Other examples include (with thanks to *PsyPAG Quarterly*, June 2005: 48–9):

- '*It has long been known*' or I did not look up the reference;
- '*It is evident ...*' or someone might believe me;
- '*It is believed that ...*', or I think;
- '*Typically ...*' I have not got a clue;
- *Nevertheless ...*', or I am going to keep going.

Use plain English and clarify what you mean. It is not more professional to use 'weasel' words.

6. 'The researcher ...'

You are writing in the third person because you believe it is more professional to do so. Why?
*It is quite acceptable to say '*I ...'

7. 'I'll have time to finish this research after I have ...'

You have lots to do and very little time in which to do it, but you have good intentions and hope to start/continue/finish next week. Every practitioner experiences difficulty in finding the time to complete and write up their research, and it is often easier to look at your research from a distance and hope that the deadline will never arrive.
Prepare a schedule and stick to it as closely as possible. You can adjust your schedule as time goes by but the deadline remains the same, so keep up the momentum. It is sometimes better to dedicate a period of time (a day, two days) to your research, as this will help you to keep up the momentum. Snatched hours are often not enough to really get going and make headway, as it can take you half a day to get back to the position you were in when you last left the work.

8. 'They was the teachers opinons'

Your writing is characterised by bad grammar, spelling and punctuation. You may even have difficulty structuring your work.
Make sure you use your spell check, grammar check and also read through your work. You can even get someone else to check your work (but not before you have had a go yourself). Try reading your work out loud, as this will help you check punctuation and expression.

Working with the wider community

SureStart (2004), a new government initative within the UK to deliver the best start in life for every child, is a good example of early years professionals working effectively with the wider community. SureStart requires effective communication between a range of professionals and the wider community. It does this by consulting with individuals and groups within the community and through community-led provision. In Italy, Reggio Emilia involves partnership with the wider community (Thornton and Brunton, 2005), while in New Zealand, Te Whàriki weaves together the different cultural and pedagogical perspectives for the diverse community (Nuttall, 2003).

Working with the wider community is not easy, as some government initiatives may not be in the best interests of the community members. For example, financial support for partnerships with JobCentre Plus, local training providers and further/higher education institutions to reduce the number of workless households (see, for example,

SureStart, 2004) will only work if the community is one which has jobs available. Support to reduce teenage pregnancies will not work if young girls see pregnancy as a way out of poverty. Extended schools are only useful in communities where parents have jobs and will benefit from the extended care. Financial support is specifically earmarked and cannot be diverted for other more pressing needs if these aims are not met and so the community does not see the benefits as proclaimed by the government.

Children's centres and settings that provide integrated and extended services have a recognised place in the wider community. They impact on the social, moral and educational development of children in the local community and, in turn, the community is enhanced and so has a vested interest in working with settings. Local shops, bus companies, leisure centres and industries are all affected by antisocial behaviour and want to work with children to safeguard their business. In addition, they can impact on the development of the children, the setting and the community through their expertise and by extending learning. Some industries, shops and businesses allow children to visit and experience their work. They may set simple problems for the children to solve and help the children to understand their economic situation, to learn about their business and how it impacts on the local community. When children understand the work of the local services (police, fire and ambulance services), businesses (shops, factories, offices) as well as understand the people and the environment, then they are more likely to respect and care for them. Recycling projects, planting trees, visiting the elderly are all likely to help members of the community understand children and children understand their place in the community, as well as help all to feel a sense of pride and responsibility for the community as a whole.

Research

Partnership within the voluntary and community sector

HM Treasury (2004) conducted a review into four areas of partnerships within the voluntary and community sector:

- improving understanding;
- building local partnerships;
- targeting public services;
- coordinating funding.

A summary of the findings are listed under the different headings below.

Improving understanding (HM Treasury, 2004: 4)

- a lack of coordinated and easily accessible evidence about the 'added value' or impact of the sector beyond qualitative case studies;
- poor levels of understanding of the scale of the government's ambition for the sector's role in public service delivery;
- little in the way of tools for policy-makers to approach the sector with sufficient understanding and confidence;
- difficulty in differentiating between the direct benefits of the sector to public service delivery, and the wider benefits that may accrue to society and the economy.

Building local partnerships (HM Treasury, 2004: 5)

- almost universal recognition of the benefits of working with the sector;

- extreme variety across local areas in the extent to which the sector was involved in public service delivery or community engagement activities;

- while the incidence of local compacts was high, the impact of these compacts was highly variable – from real change at best, to tokenistic or one-sided compacts at worst;

- barriers continue to exist for the sector in the form of lack of capacity and ineffective and short-term funding practices that reduce stability;

- there are sometimes unrealistic expectations and a lack of understanding in the sector about the realities and priorities of working in the public sector;

- all of the above combine to create ongoing difficulties with partnership working between the public and voluntary and community sectors.

Targeting public services (HM Treasury, 2004: 6)

The review asked departments to explore the potential for greater or more effective involvement of the sector in public services by targeting a number of priority areas:

- ethnic minority employment;
- health and social care for older people;
- homeless hostel provision;
- correctional services and the National Offender Management Service;
- children and young people's services.

The review found that there was significant potential for gains to be made by closer working with the sector – ranging from more effective outreach to certain groups in society, joining up provision across service areas, bringing a 'personal touch' to services, creating contestability amongst providers, campaigning for rights, to effective preventive services for vulnerable people in society.

Coordinating funding (HM Treasury, 2004: 7)

The review found that grass-roots activity most at risk included programmes of community involvement and capacity building, early prevention projects, crime reduction and community safety programmes, and initiatives designed to join up local services.

Some communities contain small or larger ethnic groups and these may integrate into the wider community to different degrees. Ethnic tensions have resulted from race riots, as seen in Bradford in 2001, the London bombings in 2005 and the increase in immigration (both legal, due to the opening up of European borders, and illegal, with the high profile deaths of Chinese immigrants in lorries and gangs of cockle-pickers). These tensions do not support cohesion and effective working relationships within a local community which has an ethnic or cultural mix, or within society as a whole. In areas where the community is monocultural, anyone who is obviously different is subject to looks, comments or abuse. A young Hindu man of my acquaintance took up a job in the west of England in a mainly white, working-class community. He began to avoid some public places because of the stares, nudges and whispers. In 2005, he was even asked 'Why did you do it?' referring to the London bombings! Eventually he returned to his family home in multicultural London. Settings can help intra-community understanding by taking children and their families on visits to different places of worship, such as Hindu or Sikh temples, Jewish synagogues, Islamic mosques and Christian churches. They can celebrate the main religions and invite community members to visit the setting and work with the children.

Reflective Tasks

Intra-community understanding

Level 1

- How could a nursery support intra-community understanding within its setting?
- What do you need to do to develop your understanding of different cultural, social, age or racial groups within our society? Write a five-point action plan for your future development.

Level 2

- How does your own community experience differ from the community in which your children live?
- How could you develop your own understanding of different communities? Write a five-point action plan.
- How could you support intra-community understanding with your children?

Level 3

- Is your setting fully integrated within the local community?
- Do all your staff feel comfortable with the community of your setting?
- How could you support intra-community understanding within your setting? With your staff, write a five-point action plan to support intra-community understanding.

Working with other professionals

Within any early years setting, there are a number of different professionals working with children and their families. They all need to work together effectively to support the children in their development and to prevent any children falling through the 'professional net'. Failures in professional cooperation and communication are the cause of high profile cases and have resulted in legislation, such as the Children Act 2004, and initiatives, such as Every Child Matters (DfES, 2003a). Professional standards for higher level teaching assistants (TDA, 2006a), qualified teachers (TDA, 2006b) and early years professionals (CWDC, 2006) all identify the importance of professional communication and integrated practice. At the beginning of this chapter we looked at all the different professionals who could work with an individual child (see the case study about John on p. 393). The working relationships between all these professionals are quite complex, as each one will have different roles and responsibilities, and it must be very easy for individuals to be missed. Effective professionals understand the part played by others in supporting children and their families. They understand the different roles and responsibilities. They trust each other and communicate effectively with each other (see Picture 13.3).

Picture 13.3 Professionals working together

Children and their parents will often not realise that there are different roles and responsibilities. They may not understand the difference between a student, teaching assistant, teacher, manager, physiotherapist, speech therapist and a special needs coordinator. To the child, in particular, all these adults appear to roll into one and they are simply adults who work and play with the child, and who they like and trust to varying degrees (often related to the amount of time spent with them). In reality, the different professionals will work together to their own strengths and expertise. Early years teachers tend to emphasise the cognitive aspects of the curriculum (DfEE, 1999; DfES, 2007), while nursery nurses and teaching assistants are expert in childcare and child development, and therapists and special needs coordinators have expertise for specific programmes of support. When these professionals work together with understanding, trust and good communication skills, they can provide quality and effective support for children's educational, social, emotional and physical development. In educational settings the relationship between teacher and nursery nurse/teaching assistant can be quite delicate if each does not value the expertise of the other. With the introduction of the Early Years Professional Status (EYPS) (CWDC, 2006), the early years workforce is developing expertise and qualifications, so that by 2010 all early childhood settings should have a lead professional with EYPS and graduate qualifications (approximately 25,000 expert professionals nationally). This shift in professional expertise brings with it a shift in the perceived value of early childhood professionals and, it is to be hoped, in remuneration. At present the evidence in educational settings (Cajkler *et al.*, 2006) is that the impact of teaching assistants is dependent on effective professional partnerships and in particular on the support and guidance of teachers and senior managers.

Research

Moving towards integrated working

A qualitative survey by CWDC gathered views from attendees at four national CWDC Integrated Working Conferences, five focus groups of health and special needs professionals and 30 telephone interviews (see also Chapter 11, p. 347). The key messages from the survey include the following (CWDC, 2007a: 6–7):

1. The vast majority of those consulted in the study believed that integrated working, supported by the Common Assessment Framework, the lead professional and information sharing, would ultimately ensure enhanced services for children, young people and their families.

2. There must be recognition that integrated working is a massive cultural change that needs support from every level of the children's workforce, from senior management through to practitioners.

3. Participation – integrated working was more effective when children and young people were present and their voices were heard.

4. Government departments need to provide support infrastructures within which the integrated working agenda can be delivered. Specific messages coming through: Department for Children, Schools and Families (DCSF) – it was reported that it is often difficult to engage all teachers in integrated working, although other education staff were often on board. There was a perception on the ground that there was a tension between the demands of the teaching 'Standards' and the ECM agenda. There were also questions raised about OFSTED inspections and the extent to which ECM and inclusion played a part in them. The Department of Health – the demands on health practitioners to commit to ECM coincides with considerable cuts in children's services. There was a perception that resources allocated for children's services were diverted into adult care. The Youth Justice Board–strategic links between the Youth Inclusion Programme (YIP), the flagship youth crime prevention programme led by third sector organisations, and the ECM agenda were not clear.

5. The private sector needs to be included in partnerships and training locally. Early years staff from the private sector were particularly out of the loop. Nearly all those consulted in this study, while being aware of ECM, had never heard of the Common Assessment Framework or lead professional, despite feeling they were in a strong position to instigate early assessment. Other private sector staff, such as those from residential homes, also reported a lack of engagement.

6. It is important that the third sector is included in integrated working partnerships and training locally. The involvement of the third sector throughout was not consistent. Third sector personnel consulted in the study feel they have a useful role to play, both as a first intervention point and as providers of services. Practitioners commissioning the services of the third sector also reported finding them invaluable to integrated working.

7. Leadership and providing strategic direction was a critical success factor in engaging whole service commitment to integrated working.

8. Once strategic support is in place it is best to 'get on with it' rather than wait for the perfect time. Learning from mistakes is better than doing nothing for fear of making them.

9. There must be continued support after training. Training was not enough on its own. Multi-agency training was considered to be more valuable than training for single agency groups as it helped to break down barriers at an early stage and build professional respect. Co-location of teams had similar benefits and promoted true integrated working. Trainers must come with credibility. About a third of those consulted said the trainers were barely one step ahead of trainees.

10. DCSF guidance was well received, especially the fact sheets. Training materials had a more mixed response. Those which engaged staff in practical activity, particularly introducing case study examples, were deemed most useful. The majority of those consulted were able to adapt materials for local needs.

11. The role of the lead professional was best embraced when it was presented as a change in focus, incorporating the best of current good practice, rather than an add-on which caused additional responsibility.

12. Transition points are times of increased vulnerability when implementing and monitoring integrated working and this needs to be recognised.

13. A mapping exercise linking the CAF to other assessment tools would be helpful.

We have come a long way in recent years in developing effective professional working relationships between teachers and support staff in education settings. However, care needs to be taken to ensure that workforce remodelling and the introduction of 10 per cent PPA (planning, preparation and assessment) time does not misuse the expertise of teaching assistants as underpaid teachers. Teachers need to communicate clearly learning intentions to teaching assistants. Quality time needs to be set aside for both parties to discuss observations of individuals and possible supportive interactions. Any staff development needs should be clearly identified so that both teacher and assistant can see themselves as important in the working relationship and with professional career needs identified and met. In a similar way we have developed effective partnerships with training institutions and settings, so that student professionals can develop experience and expertise in a supportive atmosphere. The most important feature of these working relationships is the mentor. Mentors have a variety of roles from listener and 'critical friend', to supporter and adviser. In training situations, they often also have an assessment role, which can slant the relationship. In work situations they are often peers who can support effective professional communication and solve professional challenges. Within one setting there can be a number of mentor roles. Children may be a mentor to a peer and a mentee when working with a learning mentor. A new teacher, learning mentor or early years professional may have a mentor to help induct them into their new role. Managers and headteachers have school improvement partners (SIPs) and peer mentors who support the setting development. In this way an individual may be a mentor in one situation and a mentee in another (see Robins, 2006).

Whatever the power base within a relationship, it appears that effective professional relationships have certain characteristics (Bolam *et al.*, 2005; CWDC, 2007b), and among the most important are the following:

- values and visions need to be shared;
- roles and responsibilities need to be clearly defined to all within the setting and there should be collective responsibility for the development of children;
- there needs to be mutual trust, respect and support;
- work needs to be regularly evaluated by all involved and the impact on the child considered;

- good practice and success should be shared and celebrated;
- good links need to be developed with parents and outside agencies;
- there needs to be involvement in a wide range of activities inside the setting and within the wider community;
- all work needs to be fully integrated into the work of the setting.

The most important features of effective professional partnerships are the presence of professional dialogue, the use of mentors or 'critical friends', collaborative commitment and motivation, links with other settings, focused CPD coordination, and site facilities that help collaborative work (Bolam *et al.*, 2005). Professionals who resist change, a lack of resources, changes in management, direction and policies are all factors that inhibit good professional working relationships.

Case Study

The role of a learning mentor

Joan works as a learning mentor within a support team in a large children's centre. Her role includes role modelling behaviour, supporting children with behaviour and motivational problems and helping them to achieve their full potential. As part of this role, Joan meets with other professionals, such as teachers, social workers and SENCos, and family members and has to develop positive working relationships with them all as well as the children she is mentoring. She has found that working in a fully integrated setting, where the other professionals are on site and available for informal and formal discussions, is empowering. It has given her skills and expertise that have helped her to fulfil her role effectively and enabled her to understand the roles and responsibilities of other professionals who work with the child and the family.

Reflective Tasks

Professional communication

Level 1

Consider a setting you have experienced as a learner or student.

- How well were the development or learning outcomes communicated to you?
- Were you clear about your role in the setting?
- How could professional communication have been improved?

Level 2

Consider your current role.

- How do you communicate with professionals and adults that you work with?
- How could you improve professional communication?

Discuss with other professionals you work with and find out their feelings about the professional communication issues. Decide as a team how you can work together more effectively to support children in your care. Evaluate any changes you make and discuss your ideas within your team.

Level 3

Consider your setting and all the different people who work within it. Identify how the different professionals in your setting work together.

- Find out from the different professionals how effectively they feel they work together as a team.
- How do you think you can work more effectively as a team?

Discuss this with all the professionals in your setting and decide how to improve working relationships. Try out some of your ideas and evaluate their success.

Effective integrated practice in the early years is a theme of many new initiatives (DfES, 2003a; SureStart, 2004; DfES, 2006), although there is little research into how settings are adjusting to these changes. Integrated front-line service delivery is identified (DfES, 2004a; 2004b; Cheminais, 2006) as the way forward for successful professional services. While I agree that it seems sensible as a principle, I am concerned about what it actually means in practice and about the lack of real support for individual professionals and settings in meeting the Every Child Matters agenda (DfES, 2003a). I am even more concerned about the change of language from a development-driven model to a service-driven model, which takes all the emotion out of the work we do with children and their families and appears cold, hard and efficient, instead of caring, understanding and professional. Whalley identifies how the Pen Green Centre was set up in 1983, in a partnership between social services and education, but with full parental involvement as integral from the outset. All posts at the centre are advertised as 'family workers', 'a generic title that embraces those primarily working with children and those who are chiefly working with adults' (Whalley, 2006: 183), and roles and responsibilities are negotiated depending on expertise and salary. The benefits of integrated professional working are seen clearly in Pen Green. Children and parents are equally important, have equal voices and equally benefit from the professional relationships.

Tools for Learning

Using assessment criteria

When you write up your research thesis, you need to make sure that you are meeting the assessment criteria. Remember that the criteria are what the assessor is looking for and if the evidence of meeting these criteria is weak then your work will be marked as weak. Most criteria will focus on some aspects of the following,

- *Conceptual understanding*: You need to show that through your research your conceptual understanding has become more sophisticated and you have a deep understanding of an issue in early childhood. You should also be able to ask deeper and more sophisticated questions about your research. The difference between your initial thinking about the area and your final conceptual understanding will be evident in your final discussion of your findings and you need to identify clearly what you have learnt through the research. If you undertook an initial concept map to identify your initial understanding, you could now modify, develop or change it or produce a new one. This will show you how your ideas have developed. Now you must persuade the assessor of your work. This persuasion is evident in the strengths of your argument and your use of evidence from secondary and primary data. Evidence that is described or quoted and not used to develop arguments does not show good conceptual understanding. Evidence that is weakly analysed and findings that are not discussed critically and fully do not show developed conceptual understanding.

- *Analytical skills*: Chapters 8 and 9 focus on analysis and how to develop your analytical skills. Assessors will be looking for depth of analysis. A strong thesis will not just present data, it will look at data from different perspectives and in different ways in an attempt to make sense of them and understand them. Look through your work and highlight all pieces which show good analysis. If your data analysis section is more descriptive than analytical, then try to restructure it. At this stage in your studies, you should be able to identify layers of analysis, looking more deeply at issues.

- *Justification*: By now you should be making strong links between ideas, reading, experiences, etc. and creating arguments using these links. This shows greater depth of analysis and understanding and will help you to justify your research decisions, findings and conclusions.

- *Tentativeness*: All work needs to show some tentativeness. Opinions expressed without evidence to support them or assertions made do not show tentativeness. You need to be tentative in your analysis and apply this objectivity in all writing. Be aware of any bias you may have in researching or writing about an issue and any bias the writer of texts may have. Acknowledge this explicitly and use this knowledge to support your argument tentatively. Do not assume that all writers are objective or that you and any informants are objective. Analyse your own and others' objectivity by discussing ideas with others or using more than one source of information (triangulation).

- *Coherence*: There should be explicit links between your research questions (what you were trying to find out), your methods (what you did), your synthesis (what you found out) and the conclusions you came to. Think of your work as a story of your research and the coherence as the storyline or plot. If it has too many threads and complications, then your work is less likely to be coherent. Coherence is also aided by writing seamlessly without too many quotations which break up the text.

- *Referencing*: Make sure that all references are accurately recorded using the method you are advised to use.

Find the criteria that you will be judged by and check your work thoroughly to ensure that you are meeting them fully. It would be a great shame to get to this stage in your research and lose marks because you have not addressed the criteria you are being judged by.

Working with professional associations

Support for professionals has never been so good. There are many government agencies, such as the Children's Workforce Development Council (CWDC), the Training and Development Agency (TDA), the Department for Children, Schools and Families (DCSF). There are numerous websites that give information on child development, planning ideas, key issues in childcare and development, and links to conferences, books and resources. There are numerous professional subject associations: the Early Childhood Forum, the Early Childhood Studies Network and other bodies and associations who provide support for professionals. There are independent and local authority professional development centres, which provide continuing professional development (CPD) or personal and professional development (PPD) and sell resources for settings. There are professional and academic journals and books, with ideas, theories and practical tips. The problem is that the plethora of support can be confusing and contradictory. Professionals need to be willing to challenge ideas and the objectivity and agenda of those who hold them. It is no coincidence that journals have a disclaimer that the ideas expressed are not necessarily those of the journal itself. With an open mind, professionals can navigate their way through the support, taking nothing at face value, applying some useful ideas and evaluating, modifying, changing and implementing them where desirable. In this way effective professionals engage in a professional working relationship with professional associations that supports their development and helps to evaluate new ideas and initiatives. Effective professionals do not take on board new ideas and initiatives just because someone has a 'good idea'. The most successful early years centres (such as Pen Green described above) or local authorities appear to have forceful leaders with vision and drive, who inspire others and instigate new initiatives (see Chapter 14).

Reflective Tasks

Working relationships

Level 1

Identify how you can improve your working relationship with each of the following groups: class teachers, teaching assistants, setting heads and managers, college tutors, learning mentors, parents, children.

- Which of the above groups pose the biggest challenge for you?
- What can you do in the short, medium and long term to develop your professional working relationships, especially with the groups you find the most challenging?
- Keep a record of how successful you are in developing your professional relationships and share you successes and challenges with a peer or tutor, as a critical friend to support you.

Level 2

Reflect on your current working relationships and make a list of all the groups and individuals you work with on a daily, weekly or occasional basis. Put your list in rank order of how effective your professional relationship is.

- How could you develop your professional working relationships with each of the groups and individuals on your list?

Prioritise your list into short, medium and long term and start to develop these relationships. Keep a note of successes and challenges and how you dealt with them. Share this evaluation with others in your setting.

Level 3

Identify how successful your setting is in working effectively and professionally within the setting and the wider community.

- What groups or individuals do you need to work more effectively with?
- How can you and the staff in your setting work together to develop professional working relationships?

Produce a development plan to improve your professional working relationships, identifying the short-, medium- and long-term actions you can make. Keep a record of your plans, achievements and challenges and review the plan after a period of time.

Tools for Learning

Reflecting on your thesis

Work on your own or with a critical friend.

Review your draft dissertation for coherence, continuity and compelling arguments. Be ruthlessly honest about your writing style; you are aiming for a style that is consistent, fluent, and vivid yet not overstated.

You are recommended to read your dissertations using Table 13.1. Make notes at the end of each chapter to suggest how you can improve it further.

Table 13.1 Reflecting on your thesis

Read	Reflect
Discussion	• Are research questions explicitly addressed?
	• Is evidence from personal research used thoroughly?
	• Is new evidence introduced without justification?
	• Is evidence from reading integrated within the argument?
	• Is the argument cogent and compelling or is it overstated, simplistic or over-generalised at times?
Conclusion	• Do you reflect on personal and professional learning through undertaking this research project?
	• Is there an actual conclusion, rather than a summary?
	• Is the conclusion convincing, yet duly tentative?
	• Has the research an apparent or potential impact on the educational setting?
	• Does the dissertation justly claim to enhance our knowledge and understanding in some specific area?
Literature review	
	• Does the argument help to clarify the question(s)?
	• Does the argument show understanding of the conceptual background?
	• Does the review indicate recent relevant research?
	• Is the evidence base of research texts indicated?

Table 13.1 *Continued*

Read	Reflect
	• Are terms used precisely and consistently?
	• Are there parts of the review which now appear irrelevant and could be cut?
	• Are there parts of the review which could now be sharpened or extended to illuminate later discussion?
	• Has the Harvard system been used accurately throughout?
Bibliography	• Are all the works referred to listed in the bibliography?
	• Are the entries consistent and accurate?
	• When secondary sources are used, e.g. 'X cited in Y' , are both X and Y fully detailed in the bibliography?
Methods	• Are the methodology identified and justified?
	• Are the methods explored and explained with reference to the literature on research?
	• Are there an explicit statement of ethical considerations?
	• Are validity and reliability distinguished and addressed?
	• Is the sample and scope of the data collection clear and explicit?
	• Is there an awareness of apparent limitations in the research project?
Analysis	• Are the data clearly presented in text and appendices?
	• Are all tables explicitly titled?
	• Is the analytical method explained and justified?
	• Are data presented in clear, appropriate ways (choice of bar graph or pie chart)?
	• Are there different layers of the analysis (e.g. text level and word level analysis of interview)?
	• Are selection procedures and sorting and classifying methods explained and considered for validity and reliability?
Discussion of findings	• Have you identified the main issues arising from the analysis?
	• Have you identified the implications of the research for your future work?
	• Have you discussed any new ideas?
	• Have you identified new avenues for research and new research questions?
	• Does your synthesis show a more sophisticated conceptual understanding of issues?
	• Have you discussed all the above, introducing new reading to support the arguments you are making?
Appendices	• Is each appendix actually used in the text?
Introduction	• Is there a clear professional purpose to this research?
	• Are the questions as stated actually those that have been addressed?
Abstract	• Does the abstract clearly state the context, the questions, the research project and the conclusions?
Title	• Is the title clear and to the point?

Read	Reflect
Style	● Is there an overuse of colloquial language (e.g. don't, bright)?
	● Is there an overuse of exclamations and rhetorical questions?
	● Is there an overuse of the passive tense?
	● Are gendered pronouns used inappropriately?
	● Are sentences too long and complex?
	● Are paragraphs fragmented and underdeveloped?
	● Is there any confusion when 'its', 'this', etc. are used?
	● Does analysis and synthesis outweigh description?
	● Is there a consistent and attractive personal writing style?
	● Is there a clear flow between chapters?
Presentation	● Are conventions followed consistently?
	● Order of headings
	● Use of capital letters, e.g. key stage or Key Stage?
	● Use of Harvard referencing system (author, date: page)
	● Is punctuation in bibliography and references consistent?
	● Use of particular words, e.g. headteacher or head teacher?
	● Are pages clear and uncluttered?
	● Are all figures and diagrams explicitly titled and listed in the contents?
	● Is anonymity meticulously observed for individuals and institutions?
	● Are commas and apostrophes used accurately?
	● Are there any repetitions that can be cut?

Source: Courtesy of Harriet Marland, Bishop Grosseteste University College Lincoln

Summary

→ In the area of early childhood, there are many professionals, groups and individuals who need to work together to support children's development.

→ Each professional will have a different role and responsibilities, but will need to work together in a partnership, with the child in the centre of that partnership.

→ The adult's role is to provide the support and space for the children to facilitate their development.

→ Children spend more time with their families than they do in early years settings and schools so it is vitally important that professionals have an effective working relationship with families, parents and carers.

→ Professionals need to be well trained to work effectively in the home and it should not be seen as simply an extension of the work in the setting.

→ The most important feature of this working relationship is the two-way communication and consultation, which builds an effective partnership and helps to meet the ECM agenda (DfES, 2003a).

→ Effective parental inclusion that recognises and celebrates the part that parents play in their child's development and the skills they can bring to a setting is empowering for both the parents and professionals.

➜ Working with the wider community is not always easy, as some government initiatives may not be in the best interests of the community members.

➜ SureStart (2004), a government initiative within the UK to deliver the best start in life for every child, is a good example of early years professionals working effectively with the wider community.

➜ Children's centres and settings that provide integrated and extended services have a recognised place in the wider community.

➜ Many different professionals may work together in a setting and their qualifications, experience and roles differ on a number of levels.

➜ One of the most important features of effective professional partnerships is the presence of professional dialogue with collaborative commitment and motivation.

➜ Effective integrated practice in the early years is a theme of many new initiatives, although there is little research into how settings are adjusting to these changes.

➜ Support for professionals has never been so good in terms of the amount of information available. The problem is that the plethora of support can be confusing and contradictory.

Key Questions

- Who are some of the different groups of professionals who work together to support children's development?
- In what ways can early years professionals demonstrate that the centrality of the child is at the heart of their practice?
- How can professionals work effectively with parents and carers?
- How does the wider community impact upon children and their development?
- In what ways can professionals work with the wider community effectively?
- What are the key features of effective professional partnerships?

References

Abbott, L. and Langston, A. (eds) (2005) *Birth to Three Matters. Supporting the Framework of Effective Practice.* Maidenhead: Open University Press

Abbott, L. and Langston, A. (eds) (2006) *Parents Matter. Supporting the Birth to Three Matters Framework.* Maidenhead: Open University Press

Bastiani, J. and Wolfendale, S. (1996) *Home–School Work in Britain: Review, Reflection and Development.* London: David Fulton

Bayley, R. and Featherstone, S. (2003) *Smooth Transitions. Ensuring Continuity from the Foundation Stage.* Husbands Bosworth: Featherstone Education

Bolam, R., McMahon, A., Stoll, L. *et al.* (2005) *Creating and Sustaining Effective Professional Learning Communities* (Research Brief RB637). Nottingham: DfES

Bowlby, R. (2006) *The Need for Secondary Attachment Figures in Childcare* www.telegraph.co.uk/opinion/main.jhtml?xml=/opinion/2006/10/21/nosplit/dt2101.xml#head5Childcare problems

Bronfenbrenner, U. (1995) The Bioecological Model from a Life Course Perspective: Reflections of a participant observer, in Moen P., Elder Jnr, G.H. and Lüscher, L. (eds) *Examining Lives in Context.* Washington, DC: American Psychological Association, pp. 599–618

Caffrey, B. (1997) Working with Parents in the Home, in Whalley, M. (ed.) *Working with Parents*. Abingdon: Hodder & Stoughton

Cajkler, W., Tennant, G., Cooper, P.W., Sage, R., Tansey, R., Taylor, C., Tucker, S.A. and Tiknaz, Y. (2006) 'A systematic literature review on the perceptions of ways in which support staff work to support pupils' social and academic engagement in primary classrooms (1988–2003)', *Research Evidence Education Library*. London: EPPI-Centre, Social Science Research Unit, Institute of Education, University of London

Cheminais, R. (2006) *Every Child Matters. A Practical Guide for Teachers*. London: David Fulton

CWDC (2006) *Early Years Professional Standards*. www.cwdc.org.uk

CWDC (2007a) *Moving Towards Integrated Working. Progress Report 2007*. Leeds: CWDC

CWDC (2007b) *Learning Mentor Practice Guide*. Leeds: CWDC

de Bóo, M. (ed.) (2004) *Early Years Handbook. Support for Practitioners in the Foundation Stage*. Sheffield: Curriculum Partnership/ Geography Association

DfEE (1999) *The National Curriculum. Handbook for primary teachers in England*. London: QCA

DfES (2001) *Special Educational Needs Code of Practice*. London: HMSO

DfES (2003a) *Every Child Matters*. London: DfES

DfES (2003b) *Excellence and Enjoyment. A strategy for primary schools*. London: DfES

DfES (2004a) *Every Child Matters: Change For Children*. London: DfES

DfES (2004b) *Every Child Matters: The Next Steps*. London: DfES

DfES (2006) 'About Integrated Services' www.dfes.gov.uk (accessed February 2006)

DfES (2007) *Statutory Framework for the Early Years Foundation Stage; Setting the Standards for Learning, Development and Care for children from birth to five. Every Child Matters, Change for Children*. London: DfES

Dunlop, A-W. and Fabian, H. (eds) (2007) *Informing Transitions in the Early Years: Research, policy and practice*. Maidenhead: Open University Press

EPPE (2003) 'Measuring the Impact of Pre-School on Children's Social/Behavioural Development over the Pre-School Period', *The EPPE (Effective Provision of Pre-school Education) Project Technical Paper 8b*. London: Institute of Education

Froebel, F. (1826) *On the Education of Man*. Keilhau, Leipzig: Wienbrach

Hendy, L. and Whitebread, D. (2000). 'Interpretations of Independent Learning in the Early Years', *International Journal of Early Years Education*, **8**, 3: 243–52

HM Treasury (2004) *Voluntary and Community Sector Review 2004: Working Together, Better Together*. Available from www.hm-treasury.gov.uk/media/4/3Voluntary_community_sector.pdf

Holt, N. (2007) *Bringing the High/Scope Approach to your Early Years Practice*. London: David Fulton

Jennings, J. (2005) Inclusion Matters, in Abbott, L. and Langton, A. (eds) *Birth to Three Matters. Supporting the Framework of Effective Practice*. Maidenhead: Open University Press

Johnston, J. (2002) Teaching and Learning in the Early Years, in Johnston, J., Chater, M. and Bell, D. (eds) *Teaching the Primary Curriculum*. Buckingham: Open University Press

Johnston, J. (2005) *Early Explorations in Science*. Maidenhead: Open University Press

Johnston, J., Halocha, J. and Chater, M. (2007) *Developing Teaching Skills in the Primary School*. Maidenhead: Open University Press

Jones, P. (2005) *Inclusion in the Early Years: Stories of good practice*. London: David Fulton

Lam, M.S. and Pollard, A. (2006) 'A Conceptual Framework for Understanding Children as Agents in the Transition from Home to Kindergarten', *Early Years*, 26, 2: 123–141

Mairs, K. (1997) Shared Knowledge – Parents and Workers, in Whalley, M. (ed.) *Working with Parents*. Abingdon: Hodder & Stoughton

Montessori, M. (1912) *The Montessori Method*. London: Heinemann

Nuttall, J. (ed.) (2003) *Weaving Te Whàriki* Wellington: New Zealand Council for Educational Research

Palmer, S. (2006) *Toxic Childhood. How the modern world is damaging our children and what we can do about it.* London: Orion

Primary National Strategy (2006) *Seamless Transitions – supporting continuity in young children's learning.* Norwich: SureStart/DfES

Rinaldi, C. (2006) *In Dialogue with Reggio Emilia. Listening, researching and learning.* London: Routledge

Robins, A. (ed.) (2006) *Mentoring in the Early Years.* London: Paul Chapman

Sage, R. and Wilkie, M. (2004) *Supporting Learning in Primary Schools,* 2nd edn. Exeter: Learning Matters

Sanders, D., White, G., Burge, B., Sharp, C., Eames, A., McEune, R. and Grayson, H. NFER (2005) *A Study of the Transition from the Foundation Stage to Key Stage 1.* London: SureStart

Siraj-Blatchford, I. (2005) Interaction Matters, in Abbott, L. and Langston, A. (eds) *Birth to Three Matters. Supporting the Framework of Effective Practice.* Maidenhead: Open University Press

Steiner, R. (1996) *The Education of the Child and Early Lectures on Education.* New York: Anthroposophic Press

SureStart, (2004) *Working Together. A SureStart Guide to the Childcare and Early Education Field.* Annesley: DfES

Sylva, K., Melhuish, E., Sammons, P., Siraj-Blatchford, I. and Taggart, B. (2004) *The Effective Provision of Pre-School Education (EPPE) Project: Final Report. A Longitudinal Study Funded by the DfES* 1997–2004. London: DFES.

TDA (Training and Development Agency) (2006a) *Professional Standards for Higher Level Teaching Assistants.* Available from: www.tda.gov.uk/

TDA (Training and Development Agency) (2006b) *Standards for Classroom Teachers.* Available from: www.tda.gov.uk/

Thornton, L. and Brunton, P. (2005) *Understanding the Reggio Approach.* London: David Fulton

Turner-Cobb, J.M. (2006) *The Social Experience of Transition to School: Learning and Health Outcomes.* Swindon: ESRC

Vincent, C. (2000) *Including Parents? Education, citizenship and parental agency.* Buckingham: Open University Press

Vygotsky, L. and Cole, M. (eds) (1978) *Mind in Society, The Development of Higher Psychological Processes.* Cambridge, MA: Harvard University Press

Whalley, M. (2006) Working as a Team, in Parker-Rees, R. and Willan, J. (eds) *Early Years Education. Major Themes in Education.* London: Routledge

Useful websites

Birth to Three Matters:
   http://www.surestart.gov.uk/resources/childcareworkers/birthtothreematters/

CWDC (Children's Workforce Development Council): www.cwdcouncil.org.uk/

Department for Children, Schools and Families: www.dcsf.gov.uk

Every Child Matters: change for children: www.everychildmatters.gov.uk

Foundation Stage for Learning:
   www.standards.dfes.gov.uk/eyfs/resources/downloads/statutory-framework.pdf

National College for School Leadership: www.ncsl.org.uk

Qualifications and Curriculum Authority: www.qca.org.uk

SureStart: www.surestart.gov.uk

Teachers' TV: www.teachernet.gov.uk/professionaldevelopment/teacherstv/

Training and Development Agency for Schools: www.tda.gov.uk/

Chapter 14

Leadership and Management of Early Years Settings

'If your actions inspire others to dream more, learn more, do more and become more, you are a leader'
John Quincy Adams, 1767–1848

Introduction

This chapter will consider how leadership and management impact upon the effectiveness of early years settings. We will explore the qualities of different types of leadership and identify some of the main issues related to leadership and management within an early years environment. Permeating the chapter is the theme of teamwork and the importance of leading a team, working as part of a team and supporting each individual member of a team to create a dynamic and innovative early years workforce.

Aims

→ To consider the difference between a manager and a leader

→ To provide an overview of the theories of leadership

→ To provide an overview of the different types of leadership and management styles

→ To explore the management of change, organisation and environment

→ To consider the effectiveness of communication within leadership and management

→ To provide an understanding of the main features of effective team leadership

The difference between management and leadership

Early years settings, like all educational settings, need to be managed and led effectively. Leadership and management are 'inherently linked and interwoven' (Rodd, 1998: 5). Management involves a combination of mainly organisational skills which together help to achieve the best results with limited resources. These include the organisation of:

● resources;

● time;

● individuals and teams;

● meetings;

● systems;

● structures;

● money.

In this way, management is more mechanistic and focused on systems and structures, than leadership which is dynamic (van Maurik, 2004), is concerned with people, visions (Dryden *et al.*, 2005), values (Hodgkinson, 1991), innovations, and involves sharing, motivating and challenging. A good leader needs to be a good manager (Rodd, 1998; Sadek and Sadek, 2004) and an administrator (Smith and Langston, 1999), although the skills of leadership and management are not the same. A good leader will set aside time for management and for leadership, so that there is a time for vision and a time for systems. They will maintain and support the team as a whole, developing and supporting individual members of the team, organise the structures and systems necessary for effective functioning and perform the tasks as part of the team (see Figure 14.1). They should also be active, seen to be part of the team, as well as leading it, and approachable to all involved in the setting (staff, parents, children and outside visitors), operating in a transparent way which takes into account Bronfenbrenner's ecological systems (1995; see Chapter 7 and Figure 7.2) and the relationships between different partners and systems.

Theories of leadership

There are a number of different theories of leadership and here we will look at some which are more relevant to early childhood leaders.

Trait theories look for common traits in leaders and assume that leadership is a result of nature and not nurture; leaders are born, not developed. Trait theories are the basis of

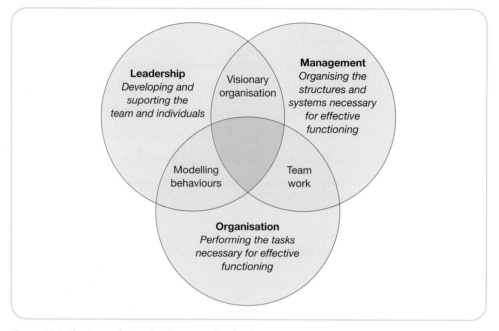

Figure 14.1 The interrelationship between leadership, management and organisation

psychometric tests given at interviews and work developed by the National College for School Leadership (see McClelland, 1987), although they are criticised (van Maurik, 2004; Willan *et al.*, 2004) as being too simplistic and not explaining why some good leaders do not exhibit all requisite traits.

Behavioural theories focus on the behaviours of a good leader and manager, including supporting, interacting and facilitating. Through study of leadership behaviour, Likert (1967) identified four different styles of leadership:

- exploitative/authoritarian;
- benevolent/authoritarian;
- consultative;
- participative.

However, these were not developed with early childhood settings in mind. The changing and dynamic nature of early childhood settings means that styles of leadership are likely to change to meet differing needs of the setting (Rodd, 1998; Willan *et al.*, 2004) and has led to contingency or situational theories. These are based on the premise that different situations need different types of behaviours. This would certainly be the case in a constantly changing early years sector.

Organisational theories relate more to management than leadership and identify the importance of understanding the workings of an organisation (Sadek and Sadek, 2004). Understanding of the past and present functioning of the organisation helps the manager to predict what will happen next and to plan appropriately (Handy, 1992).

Power and influence theories focus on the power that the leader has over the setting and, like transactional theories, are top-down approaches to leadership, with the leader exerting power over or negotiating with those being led. Social exchange theories and transformational theories differ in that they involve the team working together. In social exchange theories, a social contract is developed and the leader provides services in return for compliance within the team. Transformational theories involve a more visionary leadership (Willan *et al.*, 2004) and the team works together to achieve common goals, with the leader empowering the team.

Types of leadership and management

Leadership and management styles can be placed along two continua (see Figure 14.2). The first concerns the relationships between the leader and those involved with the setting. At one end of the continuum, relationships are characterised by support and guidance (coaching), while at the other relationships are more distant and authoritarian. The second continuum is concerned with the way in which tasks are carried out or delegated. At one end the leader directs and controls tasks, while at the other end the tasks are delegated and the leader may not be involved. In the middle, leaders will lead tasks by example, as part of the team, and work with others to support their effective completion.

The most commonly used and traditional styles of leadership and management are set out below. However, it has become clear, in recent times, that leaders and managers may not always adhere to one style and they may adopt different styles depending on the situation.

Autocratic

An autocratic leader in an early years setting may have established the setting for themselves (as in an owner-managed or private organisation) and control all aspects of the structure, organisation, delivery and relationships. Sadek and Sadek (2004) describe this leader as like a spider in the middle of their web. This leader would impose their style and philosophy on those associated with the setting and new staff, parents or children would have to adapt to the imposed style, rather than influencing it by their interactions and inputs. Staff are likely to feel that they are dictated to and their opinions are not valued or even listened to. The advantages of this style are that decisions are easy to make, as they involve one person (Sadek and Sadek, 2004), but undervalued staff are likely to be demotivated and retention of staff may be a problem.

Consultative

The consultative leader is likely to ask questions of the staff and, while expecting a certain answer, will listen to what they have to say. The opinions of staff are likely to be taken

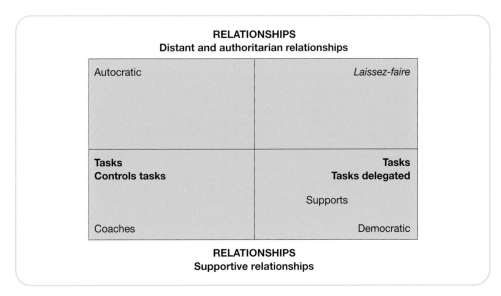

Figure 14.2 Leadership and management styles

into consideration, but ultimately the leader will decide on the direction to take, as they have the vision of where the setting is going and the type of service they provide. If they are an autocratic/consultative leader they may keep this vision a closely guarded secret and this will make the consultation a sham; while goals may be achieved it will be at the expense of staff morale. Staff meetings may be rather one-sided, where the manager issues orders or instructions for the staff to carry out. The autocratic/consultative leader will have few staff meetings, but endless information sheets may be in circulation around the setting or pinned to the noticeboard. They may be a slave to their desk, preferring to manage from the office rather than 'hands-on' and only pass on information to staff when they feel it is necessary. However, this type of leadership and management can appear efficient and the leader seems comfortably 'in charge', especially when talking to parents and others in the community. At the other extreme a democratic/consultative leader may spend endless hours in meetings with staff, discussing issues that none of them have any control over and never reaching a decision. Staff may not be satisfied with the outcomes of decisions as they may involve so many compromises that they cannot see the direction. This can lead to frustration at the seeming inefficiency of the leader, who does not seem to lead or manage effectively; indeed they may appear indecisive and bumbling.

Democratic

The democratic leader discusses options with staff and agrees on the best solution. The democratic leader typically leads by example, welcomes suggestions from staff to improve the setting and allows staff to take the lead in developing their ideas, after initial consultation. Staff meetings may have an agenda and staff would be invited to offer opinions and openly discuss issues as they arise. A democratic style can lead to increased commitment and motivation in staff (Smith and Langston, 1999) and they are likely to feel valued. However, this style can be misinterpreted by staff, as in an effort to engage them the staff may feel that the democratic leader does not have ideas or visions of their own. It may also be that the members of staff are not operating in a unified way (Rodd, 1998) and being democratic does not mean 'letting go', as staff will still need clear leadership. In a democratic setting, information is likely to be well documented and circulated so that everyone has the opportunity to make themselves aware of changes and direction.

Laissez-faire

The *laissez-faire* or laid-back leader will typically leave staff to their own devices, on the understanding that they are sufficiently qualified to know what they are doing. This is similar to the cluster structure of management identified by Sadek and Sadek (2004), which is typical of settings where staff work as individuals, even if apparently as part of a team. This may be characteristic of some integrated provision, where different services are provided in one setting but each service has an individual structure and vision. In this type of situation, the leader is more of a manager and coordinates the different services where necessary, and in this way they are utilising the expertise of team members. The *laissez-faire* leader is likely to leave things to the staff and distance themselves from any responsibility or blame when things go wrong. The *laissez-faire* setting can appear welcoming and friendly to parents and children, but feel chaotic, especially for staff, who may be trying to meet too many different demands. The disadvantages of this style of leadership are that there is no direction or vision and members of staff are likely to feel dissatisfied, which can lead to retention problems.

Situational

A situational leader tends to manage things as they arise, adopting different leadership roles and styles as the situation demands, using their professional judgement to decide how they are going to lead (Willan *et al.*, 2004). They 'play it by ear', waiting to see what the situation demands before they decide what to do. They may decide to be decisive or autocratic leaders, telling staff how to perform a task. They may coach or support individuals to enable them to perform the tasks. They may delegate tasks to staff who have shown competence or empower staff to make their own decisions. A key to this style of leadership is the skill needed to make the decision about direction and style. If the leader is good at making situational decisions and can gauge the expertise and experience of the staff, this will empower staff and lead to a well-run and effective setting. However, if the leader lacks the skills to make these situational decisions, the setting may appear disorganised and be characterised by crisis management, with the leader lurching from one crisis to the next. In such cases, staff who would otherwise be very supportive of the leader and the setting may feel 'put upon'.

Coach

A coaching leader will set roles and tasks for staff, but discuss directions with staff and allow them some freedom in how they achieve the tasks. A coach may offer a form of mentoring to staff (see Robins, 2006), guiding and supporting them in work. Coaching therefore offers high direction and high support for the individual or team and is highly appropriate for students, beginner practitioners or new members of staff.

Supporter

Supporting leaders are similar to the coaching leader, although they give more of the decision-making to their team and facilitate the tasks by supporting the individuals who have been given the control and responsibility. Supporting is appropriate for more experienced staff who are developing their leadership skills and have the expertise to make decisions and do tasks with little direct guidance. Most teams are made up of a variety of staff, with differing experience and expertise and a good leader would coach those with less experience, support those with more and may be more autocratic with any whose work is not effective.

Emotionally intelligent

Emotionally intelligent leaders are empathetic, aware of their own emotions (Willan *et al.*, 2004) and those of others they work with. The ability of practitioners to recognise, understand and manage their own and other people's emotions contributes to the successful execution of professional practice. Emotionally intelligent leaders are able to use this understanding when making decisions and can support their own and others' professional development. Strong emotions play a role in the professional practice of all who work with children (Edginton, 2004, and see Chapter 6).

Research

Sustainable development in schools

Research was undertaken by the National College for School Leadership (NCSL, 2007) to find out about sustainable development in schools. It had five aims:

- To find out why and how some school leaders develop sustainable development within their schools, and how this fits within their wider leadership thinking and approach.

- To provide evidence of the outcomes of these approaches in terms of environmental impact, school ethos and student learning and wider outcomes.

- To provide evidence of the extent to which sustainable development approaches are a feature of schools nationally and the barriers and enablers to more widespread take-up.

- To identify the skills, qualities and development opportunities required by school leaders to make sustainable development a reality.

- To identify the implications of the preceding aims for leadership development and national policy.

The findings indicate that 'leaders who develop sustainability within their school do so with passion and conviction, underpinned by personal values' (NCSL, 2007: 8), influencing all aspects of school life beyond the curriculum, engaging in initiatives such as Healthy Schools, Global Dimension, Eco-schools and Growing Schools, and also extending to external relationships. Often successful schools are ones whose success depends on being inward-looking and the survey indicated that 'most school leaders place the global dimension relatively low on their priorities' (NCSL, 2007: 8). A sustainable leader will support and develop collegiate decision-making and be outward-looking. Distributed leadership appears to be the best sustainable leadership model as sharing responsibility for different tasks reduces the pressure on individual leaders and embeds the principle of sustainability more effectively in the school.

The key qualities of a sustainable school leader are that they are optimistic and outward looking. These leaders are conscious of the place of the school in the local and global community. Many of the case study schools have considerable community and international components to their activities. These leaders have an integrated, systemic understanding of the world and their place in it and can communicate this to others. They understand the interconnectedness of society, the environment and individuals within these contexts.

(NCSL, 2007: 10)

The survey identified a significant mismatch between schools' rhetoric and the reality of practice. Reasons for non-implementation of sustainable schools were identified as lack of time and money.

Tools for Learning

Presenting research

In this chapter we are concerned with presenting research orally and visually. Presenting ideas and findings helps to articulate understandings and ultimately will help with written communication. The findings can be the result of group discussions, individual or group research, which can be small or large-scale.

Oral communication begins in your first year of study, when you communicate ideas in group situations. These can be presentations of the discussions which form the tasks in Chapter 7, leading to more formal presentations of individual research findings. Formally, this develops into group or paired oral presentations of between 5 and 15 minutes. This involves speaking coherently, engaging with the audience and referring to notes rather than reading from them. This develops into longer oral presentations of up to 20 minutes in groups and individually, using notes only as a prompt. The final stage is individual oral presentations of up to 30 minutes, during which you can motivate and engage the audience and have a clear sense of purpose.

Visual presentations can be posters or ICT presentations, which are orally presented and so the same characteristics as described above apply.

Reflective Tasks

Styles of leadership

Level 1

Consider the 'best' leader or manager you have experienced.

- What style of leadership (see above) did they adopt?
- Why was this style effective?
- Are there other styles which would also be effective with you? Explain when they would be effective and why.

Make a poster to articulate your reflections. Share these reflections with a group of your peers.

Level 2

Consider a situation in your own setting when you have had to manage or lead an initiative.

- What style of leadership (see above) did you adopt?
- Was this style effective? Why?
- Are there other styles you could have adopted? Explain when they would be effective and why.

Make a poster to articulate your findings. Present these findings to colleagues.

Level 3

Consider your own recent leadership and management.

- What is the main style of leadership (see above) that you adopt?
- When is this style effective? Why?
- Are there other styles you could adopt? Explain when they would be effective and why.

Make a poster to articulate your findings. Present these findings at a staff meeting and discuss with your staff.

Our own experiences of being led and managed give us valuable information on how best to lead and manage others. If we have good experiences of being managed, we are likely to remember the experiences positively and imitate the style. In this way, how we have felt in situations influences our understanding and shapes our behaviour and interactions with others. Usually we prefer to be consulted about decisions which will affect the way we work. We prefer to know why changes occur, the purpose and direction of change and how this will affect our daily and professional lives. We prefer to make decisions in an emotionally intelligent way that will benefit not only ourselves but other members of staff, and most importantly consider the effect upon the children and their families with whom we work. Realistically though, we are not always objective about the way we feel about decisions and may be influenced by outside factors and past experiences, rather than make rational, objective and emotionally intelligent decisions.

Situational leadership and management

In most cases the style of management adopted will depend on circumstances. This is known as situational leadership and management. There will be times, knowing that staff are qualified and informed, when they are best left to do their work, and others when urgent information will need to be passed on to staff in a direct way, for example, with regard to the safety of the children in their care. There will be times when a democratic approach is wise, especially when planning and organising changes to procedures. For the dissemination of information (for example, considering changes brought about by new government initiatives and legislation), a democratic approach is inclusive of all staff, utilises their training, expertise and knowledge and keeps staff morale high. Therefore the role of the leader and manager should be proactive rather than reactive, taking the lead when necessary, consulting with the staff team and making joint decisions as appropriate and having the vision and confidence to lead the team towards a shared goal: to provide a quality service to the children in their care.

Early childhood leaders have some distinct differences from other leaders (Rodd, 1998), because they are likely to be female and lead teams of other females and work in distinctly different types of settings. They are more likely to empathetic, collaborative leaders. Whether this style of leadership is equally appropriate in all types of early years settings, from groups of childminders to large integrated settings, remains to be seen. The development of the new Early Years Professional Standards (CWDC, 2006) emphasises effective leadership and management in the six strands identified:

- knowledge and understanding;
- effective practice;

- relationships with children;
- communicating and working in partnership with families and carers;
- teamwork and collaboration;
- professional development.

Throughout the document (CWDC, 2006) reference is made to leading teams of professionals and leading initiatives in early childhood and in this way effective leadership is seen as vitally important in driving the changes needed in the early years sector. For example, national initiatives in early childhood, such as Every Child Matters; Change for Children (DfES, 2004), support five outcomes for children up to 19 years of age, that children are healthy, stay safe, enjoy and achieve, make a positive contribution and achieve economic well-being. Embedded in the legislative foundation of the Children Act 2004, this clarifies accountabilities for children's services set out in the national framework for local change programmes by building services around the needs of children and young people. The 10-year strategy for childcare included choice for parents and offered availability, quality and affordability in childcare provision. Local authorities are working with their partners to translate the principles of Every Child Matters; Change for Children into local action. Early childhood leaders are needed to drive these changes, develop children's centres and develop the professionalism of the workforce to support children.

Case Study

What goes on in an early years setting?

Pam Byrd, Curriculum Leader for Early Years, Stamford College of Further Education

There are many different types of early years setting and no single model for managers to follow. Settings may be small, medium or large in their registered capacity, with the number of children varying from about 16 to 100 or more. The setting may include tiny babies from six weeks or the children may start at 2 years of age and stay until school age. The opening hours of a setting may be during term-time only or all year round, and the length of the day can vary with some opening at 7.30 am and others 9.00 am and with closing times varying from 3.00 pm to 7.00 pm. There are even all-night nurseries in some regions. Early years settings may be funded through the local education authority or social services departments. They may operate as school nursery and reception classes, independent businesses, as part of a chain of settings or as organisations with charitable status. The type of building used for early years provision can also differ widely. The buildings range from modified domestic properties or adapted commercial properties, to rooms in a school or purpose-built early years accommodation. This rich tapestry of provision is a testament to the creative thinking of providers, who have identified a need to provide for children's care and early learning and have sought to respond appropriately. Some settings focus primarily on educational aims whereas others offer predominantly childcare for working parents, and yet all tend to be referred to as a 'nursery', even though the term means different things to different people. There are now also multi-purpose children's centres which may be attached to a community school, offering childcare, early education, family support and health advice largely through the government SureStart scheme.

With such diversity there is clearly a need for regulation and inspection to ensure that at least the minimum standards of care are achieved. All settings must be registered to offer childcare (except those on Crown property) and must meet a range of standards, which includes staffing levels, child to adult ratios and premises. Any setting may apply to their local authority to receive nursery grant funding as part of their commitment to offer Foundation Stage experiences. OFSTED undertakes all registrations and inspections following government guidelines to inspect care standards and educational provision. How a setting is managed is a very individual thing, which reflects its underlying aims and ethos.

The aims and ethos expressed in a setting will reflect the staff team views on the nature of childhood itself (see Chapter 2). According to Dahlberg *et al*. (1999), an early years setting has no particular purpose other than that which it is given. This means that early childhood institutions are socially constructed. They have no inherent features, no essential qualities, no necessary purposes. What they are for is not self-evident – they are what we make them. What we think early years institutions are determines what they do and what goes on within them.

Constructions of the early childhood institution

1. a producer of predetermined outcomes;
2. a market-oriented business;
3. as a substitute home;
4. as social intervention and equaliser;
5. a necessary technology for social progress;
6. as a forum in civil society.

These positions follow the various views on the nature of childhood itself.

Read the following views about childhood then consider what your view of childhood is and what you believe an early years setting is for (see also Chapter 2).

The child as knowledge, identity and culture reproducer (*Locke's child*)

The child starts with nothing; is an empty vessel to be filled; is a clean slate. The challenge of early childhood is then to have the child ready for school and for learning. The child needs to be filled with knowledge, skills and the dominant cultural values, which are already predetermined. The child needs to be trained to conform to the fixed demands of compulsory schooling. Early childhood is therefore a foundation for an economically productive adulthood.

The child as an innocent in the golden age of life (*Rousseau's child*)

Childhood is seen as an innocent period in a person's life, a golden age of self-regulation seeking out virtue, truth and beauty before its 'goodness' is corrupted by society. Childhood should therefore be a period of freedom to play, to be expressive and creative. The child needs to be sheltered from the surrounding exploitation and violence of the world by being offered security and continuity.

The young child as nature/the scientific child of biological stages (*Piaget's child*)

The young child is seen as having universal properties and inherent capabilities and therefore development in childhood is viewed as an innate process, that is biologically determined. There is an assessment of what children can or cannot do according to their age and stage, which is seen as a natural and automatic process abstracted from the social context they are in. Development is described in separate, measurable categories rather than complex and interrelated functioning.

The child as labour market supply factor (*Bowlby's child?*)

This view recognises the child as being biologically determined to have a need to be cared for by its mother in its earliest years and that mothers are biologically programmed to provide this care. One-to-one care should be provided in order to avoid undermining this attachment and prevent emotional harm in later life. Provision of quality childcare is therefore seen as a key factor in the employability of parents and the maintaining of a stable, well-prepared workforce. For as long as governments and employers require workers, the provision of substitute parents becomes a national interest.

These constructions have something in common. They produce a 'poor' child, weak and passive, incapable and underdeveloped, dependent and isolated. Contrast these ideas to the 'rich' child:

The child as co-constructor of knowledge, identity and culture (*Postmodern child*)

Children are seen as social actors, participating in constructing and determining their own lives, and also in the lives of those around them and the societies in which they live. They have a voice of their own and should be taken seriously, being involved in democratic dialogue, decision-making and power-sharing. Children are seen as social contributors and not as a cost or burden to society.

What actually goes on in an early years setting will depend on many factors such as management style, operational frameworks, underpinning philosophy, skills and experience of staff, premises and resources available. Quite how the learning and development opportunities are delivered will form the early years 'curriculum' in each setting. The term 'curriculum' can be used and understood in two different ways:

1. A framework for all the learning experienced by a child, whether planned or unplanned.
2. A planned teaching scheme with specified learning objectives that are delivered and assessed.

Since 2000, any setting that is registered to claim nursery education grant funding has needed to demonstrate that it provides a range of opportunities in accordance with the Foundation Stage guidance (QCA, 2000) for the children from ages 3 to 5 years (to the end of the reception year) or in the new Early Years Foundation Stage (DfES, 2006) from birth to 5 years of age. The majority of early years settings are now registered for nursery education grant and are therefore inspected by OFSTED who expect to see the Foundation Stage implemented. Before September 2008, any early years setting that made provision for children under the age of 3 were advised to follow the Birth to Three Matters guidance (SureStart, 2003), which was issued to support practitioners. This was a boxed pack that contained a booklet, DVD, information cards, and a poster with guidance organised into four areas of early experience.

Managing change

Change can be empowering and frightening, exciting and frustrating. Not all teams and individuals who work in teams welcome change, especially when they are comfortable and change threatens this. Change is, however, a normal and essential process in any setting and needs to be managed carefully to alleviate the stress to all concerned in the setting.

Individual members of staff have basic needs, just like those in Maslow's hierarchy (1968; see Figure 1.1). These can also be considered as steps that need to be climbed to achieve effective change and to motivate staff to support and participate in change. This can be seen in Figure 14.3. The first step is comfort, or basic working needs, such as a suitable workspace, pay and access to resources and planning. Staff need to feel comfortable and have their basic needs met before they can move to the next step, which is concerned with security, security that comes with a permanent or fractional contract, being part of an established team and the enjoyment of the work being undertaken. The third step is understanding, which comes when the individual staff member feels they belong in the team of early years professionals. When this happens, they are more likely to understand the needs of the setting and share the vision and strategies of the setting. The final step is fulfilment, which occurs when staff have good self-esteem. In the professional setting, self-esteem comes from empowerment through delegation and when staff are supported through mentoring and appraisal. The fulfilled staff member understands their own abilities and challenges and knows when to take responsibility and when to communicate uncertainties and seek support.

Managing communications

Whatever the preferred style, an effective leader and manager requires a certain kind of interpersonal behaviour and communication skills. Strong leaders are often people who inspire confidence in others and support team members or colleagues to achieve their full

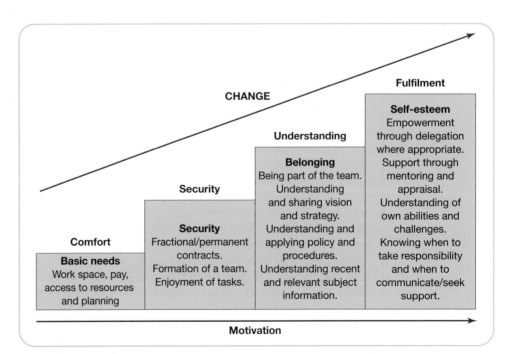

Figure 14.3 Change and emotional support for professional development

potential. Leadership involves getting the very best from people and this seems to be promoted by having common goals, such as meeting the needs of children and awareness of the changing needs of parents and carers. Leaders also deal with these issues in a sensitive manner. Managers should be able to respond to the needs of staff within the setting, ensuring that each one is working to their full potential and using their experiences and qualifications to support the setting. This will ensure that staff feel valued and remain positive about their work, knowing that their contributions are appreciated and their opinions respected. Leaders and managers will ultimately have to be accountable not only to parents/carers, children and the staff team but also under the National Standards for full day care (DfES, 2003a). If the manager is also the 'registered person' (National Standard 1) he/she will be held responsible to show that each of the 14 National Standards are met within the setting. This is the most important role of the manager in funded nurseries as it is against the National Standards that the Office for Standards in Education (OFSTED) will inspect and measure the effectiveness of the setting in meeting the standards of care and protection expected.

Viewpoint

Meetings

Jane Harrison, Proprietor, Red Hen Day Nursery, Legbourne, Lincolnshire

Communication between colleagues is vital for a good working relationship. In our setting the Manager likes to talk to room staff at the beginning of the day to ensure that everyone is feeling well and ready for the children. It is easy for management to become absorbed in the paperwork involved in the day-to-day running of the nursery but in order to understand everyone's well-being we have to be attentive to the needs of the staff, parents and children at all times. We have regular meetings which are important to share meaningful information and also smaller group meetings which lead to a more productive outcome as staff members find it not so daunting to speak out.

It is important for leaders and managers to be aware that not all staff like or enjoy speaking out in front of colleagues whom they might consider to be more experienced or better qualified than them. This is an important point raised in the Viewpoint above. Jane Harrison also identifies other ways, in which a manager can aid communication and understanding between staff.

Managing the organisation

It is the manager's role to organise the setting, ensuring that the nursery is prepared for young children to be welcomed and cared for in a professional and friendly way. Early years managers must also have a vision. Settings require innovative managers who are able to carry forward a set of values and principles, because staff will need guidance on finding the way forward, especially within a dynamic early years sector. As Dean Fink (2005: xix) suggests, 'leadership is not a destination with fixed co-ordinates on a compass, but a journey with plenty of detours and even some dead ends'. Most managers are motivated by a commitment to working with children and families. They may be well organised and proficient managers and be respected for their expertise, for their commitment to work. However, some managers will never be charismatic and so may not be good leaders. Skills of communication and leading are important for managers of early years settings because teams require more than being managed from a 'commercial' viewpoint. Andreski and Nicholas (1996: 10) state that you should not worry that you are not a born leader, these skills can be learned. You should rethink the role and replace the phrase *'leading the team'* with *'managing the work of the team'* to be closer to the truth about running an early years setting.

So what are the key elements of the management leadership role? Andreski and Nicholls (1996: 6) suggest effective leadership is about:

- 'developing a vision and team culture'. This is good for motivation of the staff team and for business;
- setting goals and objectives;
- showing a clear lead and direction for the setting and the staff;
- facilitating the development of others. This would include the children and staff team;
- monitoring and communicating achievements, including effective record keeping, talking to parents, carers and the local community.

Put more simply, four key skills are involved; planning, organising, leading and enthusing, and maintaining authority. How you carry this out depends largely on your personality and behaviour and also depends on the context of what might be happening at any given time.

Managing the environment

The manager has a clear responsibility to the parent/carers, as these are the clients who are purchasing the service, which is the care and education of their child. The rights of the child were identified in the UN Convention on the Rights of the Child. These rights have only been truly recognised under the Children Act 1989, which came into effect in 1991 and emphasises the importance of the welfare of the child (see Curtis and O'Hagan, 2003). The Children Act 1989 also states that parents have a responsibility towards the care of their child. For example, they should not harm, neglect or abandon the child; they should provide physical and moral protection; they should be legally responsible for the child's actions. If parents cannot ensure that a child is cared for as stated above, this responsibility is then assumed by the Director of Social Services. Children therefore have recognisable rights and this is significant for childcare staff who act as legal carers for the child and have the duty to guard the children's rights in the same way as parents. These rights need to be taken into account when organising and managing the environment in which both children and their carers work. We considered the environment of the staff using an adapted hierarchy in Figure 14.3. We can also consider Maslow's hierarchy (1968; see Figure 1.1) when considering the children's environment. Clearly children need to be fed, be safe and emotionally secure in order that they can develop in a holistic way (see Part 2). The importance of a secure, creative and dynamic environment is one that is well recognised (DfES, 2003b; 2006; Johnston, 2005) as essential to enable children to develop and is embedded in the views of many theorists (see Chapter 1). Montessori (1912) identified the need to make the environment child-friendly; Rousseau (1911) identified the need for settings to accommodate individual children; Rousseau (1911), Froebel (1826), Plowden (DES, 1967) and many others identified the need for children to develop and learn through experience, discovery and play (see also Chapter 9).

Managing responsibility, policy and practice and supporting the environment

The outworking of the early years care standards and the rights of the child, referred to above, can be observed within any setting and is often referred to as 'practice'. The practice is generated through the procedures, which are the organisation and execution of daily routines. The routines are laid down for the protection of children and staff within the setting and are directly influenced by the policy of each setting. In any setting there are likely to be policies covering each of the 14 National Standards, and where children under the age of 2 are cared for additional policies will be in operation, covered by Annexe A of the National Standards document (DfES, 2003a). However, the manager is directly responsible for the organisation of the daily routine, which will encompass all aspects of the day for staff dealing with young children. For many this routine will be seen as a very practical list of things to be done at particular times, but the routine is what moulds the environment, creates the feeling of a setting, the culture or philosophy to which staff, parents and children contribute to. In other words, the policies, procedures and routines can help to provide the ethos for the environment and certainly provide the structure that enables the environment and the children within it to flourish.

To ensure that all staff are working in a consistent, efficient and informed way the manager will have to create the correct environment where everyone can work together to get things done. This may be considered as the what, why and when. To ensure that staff are motivated and supportive of the routines, the manager should develop a style of management which empowers and entrusts responsibility to staff with experience and qualifications. As a result of this staff not only feel valued but develop their skills for the job. The manager will also need to consider the involvement and importance of parents in the effective implementation of daily routines by sharing the significance of what occurs in their child's day.

Viewpoint

The view of a day care centre proprietor

Helen Horner, Proprietor, Poppies Day Care Centre, Claypole, Lincolnshire

Creating an environment for learning is a challenge for all policy-makers working towards giving children the best possible start in life. Care needs to be taken to give an equal balance to the child's unique natural ability and their potential ability to achieve in their current environment and culture. As a manager responsible for policy change and development, I feel a weight of burden being lifted from my shoulders as I share my new knowledge with colleagues. Communication between us is improving and a sense of excitement is beginning to form in my heart. My recent learning has already influenced my practice; changes to the staffing structure are starting to take effect with the appointment of higher level supervisors dedicated to specific areas of development. Policy reviews are the next thing for me to address; this will be a time-consuming process and choice of starting point important ...

Reflective Tasks

Routines

Level 1

With a group of peers, consider how different routines could change/influence the ethos of a setting. You may wish to consider how the following influence routines in place:

- free-play activities;
- adult-led activities;
- outdoor play;
- parent helpers/partnerships;
- personal beliefs;
- philosophy;
- the Early Years Foundation Stage (DfES, 2006).

Make a poster of your main issues and present this to others, articulating reasons for your decisions.

Level 2

Consider the routines you have within your setting. How are they influenced by:

- colleagues who work directly with you;
- parents/carers;
- individual children;
- policy and procedures;
- the ethos of the setting;
- your own personal philosophy;
- the philosophy and ethos of the setting.

Make a poster of your reflections and share this with others in your setting to elicit their views and initiate a discussion on the issues raised.

Level 3

In a staff/team meeting, initiate a discussion about how the routines in your setting are influenced from within and outside the setting. You may wish to consider all the bulleted points in the Level 1 and Level 2 tasks above. Produce a poster to summarise the ideas raised by all the staff/groups of staff and use this in a subsequent meeting to encourage/empower staff to decide actions to move the setting forward.

Managing the team

The leader and manager should retain the overall vision of where the setting is going, see the big picture and be able to develop strategies to make it happen. Communication with staff is vital to make this happen. They have a duty to provide high-quality services and should develop their management and organisational skills to manage diverse ranges of services within their settings. They are, however, under enormous pressure to deal with increasing management responsibilities and competing demands from parents, children, the community and the local authority.

The publication of *Every Child Matters* (DfES, 2004) laid out the plan to establish children's centres in each of the 20 most deprived neighbourhoods in the country by 2006. Local authorities now continue to push towards integrated services, which will combine nursery education, family support, employment advice, childcare and health services on one site to provide integrated care and education for young children. The early intervention and effective protection for disadvantaged children, requiring strong leadership with powerful, motivating vision, which has not always been evident, was called for in the report by Lord Laming (2003). Managers should manage more effectively by accepting accountability and being more proactive in developing multidisciplinary training opportunities for all front-line staff. All this requires effective teamwork (Rodd, 2004), which needs skilful leadership and management.

Smith and Langston (1999) identify that the first step in building a team is to become aware of, and understand, individual roles, responsibilities, beliefs and behaviours. This can be done through staff development meetings to share ideas and through team building exercises (see also Chapter 13). All staff need to be involved, the roles and responsibilities of individual team members need to be clearly identified and goals need to be shared and set. To be able to make the setting work in an efficient way and provide a happy, comforting environment for all, the leader/manager needs to motivate staff with the vision for care and education provided in the setting, but also needs to attend to the day-to-day running. This is where policy and procedures come to the fore and policies should be discussed with, written by and disseminated within the team at staff meetings. Sometimes these staff meetings are more difficult than would at first seem, as they usually occur after hours when children have gone home. Of course, not all staff may be working at the end of the day, so there are problems in getting the staff together, but a dedicated time should be agreed at a regular interval, say once a month, when all staff should have the opportunity to attend to discuss overarching policy and procedure, training matters and any other issues of importance. Longer meetings to discuss more important issues should occur on training days, when staff can dedicate themselves to such issues without the care of the children interrupting. This, of course, can also be difficult for settings which are run as businesses and do not close. However, daily concerns and issues needs to be communicated to staff at appropriate times, when they come on duty, change shift or age groups, or need to be kept informed of new developments, such as a new member of staff starting and in need of mentoring and induction. Some settings have a whiteboard, where important daily notices, changes of routine, names of visitors, etc. are displayed. Others have a short meeting at the start of each day or shift when daily issues can be conveyed. These are simply information meetings and do not replace the policy team meetings where staff views can be explored and decisions as to future direction can be discussed in depth.

New and inexperienced members of staff will need some **induction** and training. This may mean separate meetings to support staff development, sending them on courses and opening avenues for the newer members of staff to ask questions. It is not easy for busy managers to find time for this vital induction process and they need to be aware that less experienced staff may be wary about asking questions, which expose their inexperience and lack of knowledge. Induction booklets with information for new staff can help, and having specific times for staff to ask questions or an 'open-door' policy can also help. The most important thing is to develop a supportive atmosphere, in which staff feel able to approach the manager or another senior member of staff.

Viewpoint

The view of a day nursery proprietor

Jane Harrison, Proprietor, Red Hen Day Nursery, Legbourne, Lincolnshire

I find that staff members don't always fully understand what is expected of them and we can improve this by mentoring new staff after their initial induction so that they can get to know how things 'tick'. Looking at the need for staff training and how we implement it and share it will support staff in making use of their knowledge on a practical basis.

A leader or manager must have an up-to-date understanding of what training is available to staff. In the current climate of change there are many demands made of practitioners working in the early years sector. The government policy to provide quality, affordable and accessible childcare to 3- and 4-year-olds has led to a plethora of training opportunities for all levels of staff and the need for practitioners to develop their skills. The Workforce Development Strategy (MLA, 2004) has began to develop a streaming of all training qualifications so that employers can be assured of the skills practitioners will have; more importantly, qualifications providers must also ensure that a variety of different skills are incorporated within the training across the board to assist with service integration and multi-agency working. This is called the Common Core of Skills (HM Government, 2005).

Research

A study about transition from Nursery to Reception

Bia Sena, Foundation Stage Coordinator, British School of Rio de Janeiro, Brazil

I researched transition in order to:

- develop understanding of effective management within the Foundation Stage for Learning;
- develop understanding of how to facilitate effective transition from Nursery to Reception and from Reception to Key Stage 1.

Transitions involve movements from one environment to another and establishing new relationships. It is essential that educators and parents provide a smooth transition. It is also important that transition has continuity and progression, taking place gradually, over time. Some children find it difficult to adjust to new rules and routines, environment, teachers' expectations and styles. The School and I felt that it was important to identify aspects of effective transition practice enabling teachers to find valuable and practical examples of transition practice.

After reading the document *Seamless Transitions* (Primary National Strategy, 2006) we felt some areas should be addressed:

1. **Environment**. The Foundation Stage at the British School of Rio de Janeiro is organised into six nursery classes with 12 children in each class. We also have one teacher and one assistant teacher for each class. It is an independent unit where the children can move around safely and independently. In the Reception year we

have five classes with 20 children, one teacher and one assistant for each class. As a result children need to be regrouped when moving from the Nursery to Reception and are mixed and placed in five new classes. It is a bigger unit placed next to the Key Stage 1 classes. The classrooms are also displayed differently. Nursery has a play/learn-based area. Reception has a more 'teaching approach', with tables and chairs. It is clear that we need to provide a smooth transition to help the Nursery children to feel secure, relaxed and comfortable in their new environment. Teachers should create a more balanced classroom taking into account the children's perspective, interest and needs.

2. **Curriculum**. Another barrier to ensuring smooth transitions was the different pedagogical approaches. The curriculum has two different focuses. The Nursery curriculum is more skill-based, learning through play. The Reception is more based on competence than skills, less playing opportunities. It is important to have a balance of adult-led and a child-led activities. This is crucial for their development and learning process. It is also important to focus on the readiness of the child. What kinds of knowledge, skills and behaviour are expected from the children? The curriculum should have continuity and progression. However, there are some important points that can be considered in relation to pressure for a more formal approach in Reception and at the end of Foundation Stage. As the classrooms are in the same Key Stage 1 unit both year groups' teachers are more in contact and the tendency is to prepare the children for Key Stage 1. Children should not be 'school ready' but teachers need to provide a curriculum that is 'child ready'. Perhaps a change in assessment practices might help to maintain a focus on children's learning throughout this transition period. At the Foundation Stage, learning should be free and playful. Another aspect is that teachers believe that parents value a more formal approach. In this case what is valued as appropriate learning in early childhood is not explained clearly to parents. The school curriculum needs to be a rich daily life which includes learning and development as essential ingredients, along with other children and adults interacting and engaging, and meaningful opportunities.

3. **Communication with parents (partnership)**. Lately relationships between teachers and parents have become more uncertain. Parents have become questioning and more critical about issues of the curriculum, the quality of teaching and practices used to assess and evaluate their children. Again it was felt there was a need to improve communication between staff and parents.

As a middle manager I went to UK for a study visit, so I could coordinate, involve and support staff throughout this process. My research questions were:

- How do managers facilitate effective transition?
- What factors influence effective transition?
- How do teachers record and use assessment materials to inform the next teacher?

After reading and undertaking visits to a variety of early years settings, I decided that the challenges for teachers in my setting were to:

- improve communications with parents and staff;
- provide a classroom that is 'child ready' (that is, more play-based);
- have more outdoor access;
- introduce 'more structured' activities gradually;
- find out what children think.

Action plan

Short term

- Discuss and compare my findings with Nursery and Reception staff
- Find out what is going well and what is not functioning
- Share my UK experience with the Nursery and Reception staff

Medium term

- To create a transition team
- Implement transition ideas

Long term

- Build on findings to improve transitions from Foundation Stage to Key Stage 1

Having concluded her research study (above), Bia produced a Powerpoint presentation to take back to her school and share with both the senior management team, to whom she is accountable, and the Foundation Stage team that she leads. The aim of this Powerpoint was to articulate the findings of her work and to initiate a discussion within the school, so that the subsequent actions would be shared within the team and therefore have a greater chance of success. The main slides from this Powerpoint can be seen in Figure 14.4.

Powerpoint presentations can be a very good way to summarise research findings and present them to others to stimulate discussion and drive any action forward. Keep these short and identify the main aspects:

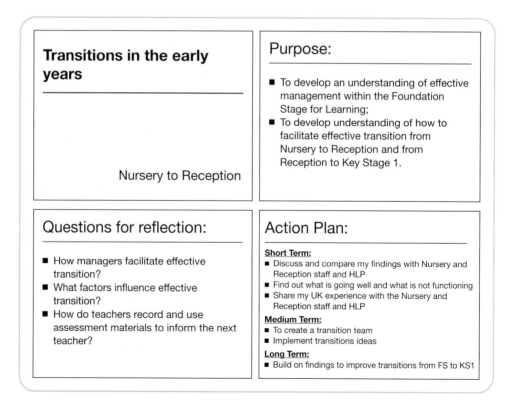

Figure 14.4 Extracts from Bia Sena's Powerpoint presentation

- *What?* what the research is about; the title and research questions;
- *Why?* the rationale behind the research;
- *Who?* who was involved in the research;
- *What?* what you found out;
- *So what?* what the implications of the research are.

Make sure that there are plenty of opportunities to include the team in discussions at every opportunity. Involve them in deciding the research questions and the rationale for the research. Involve them in collecting and analysing data. Work together as a team to decide what the implications are and how the results are going to be used in your setting.

In summary, teamwork is the key behind effective leadership and management of early years settings and the good leader involves the whole team in decisions and tasks.

Summary

→ Leadership and management are linked and interwoven.

→ Management involves a combination of organisational skills which together help to achieve the best results with limited resources.

→ Leadership is dynamic and is concerned with people, visions, values and innovations, and involves sharing, motivating and challenging.

→ A good leader needs to be a good manager.

→ There are a number of different theories of leadership which include trait theories, behavioural theories, organisational theories and power and influence theories.

→ There are commonly used and traditional styles of leadership and management, although leaders and managers may not always adhere to one style and may adopt different styles depending on the situation.

→ These styles include autocratic, consultative, democratic, *laissez-faire*, situational, coach, supporter and emotionally intelligent.

→ Our own experiences of being led and managed give us valuable information on how best to lead and manage others.

→ In most cases the style of management adopted will depend on circumstances. This is known as situational leadership and management.

→ Early childhood leaders have some distinct differences from other leaders because they are likely to be female and lead teams of other females and work in distinctly different types of settings.

→ Effective leadership is seen as vitally important in driving the changes needed in the early years sector.

→ Change is a normal and essential process in any setting but it needs to be managed carefully to alleviate the stress to all concerned in the setting.

→ An effective leader and manager requires a certain kind of interpersonal behaviour and communication skills.

→ Settings require innovative managers who are able to carry forward a set of values and principles, because staff will need guidance on finding the way forward, especially within a dynamic early years sector.

➜ Four key skills are involved: planning; organising; leading and enthusing; maintaining authority.

➜ To ensure that all staff are working in a consistent, efficient and informed way, the leader and manager will have to create the correct environment where everyone can work together to get things done.

➜ The leader and manager will also need to consider the involvement and importance of parents in the effective implementation of daily routines by sharing the significance of what occurs in their child's day.

➜ The leader and manager should retain the overall vision of where the setting is going, see the big picture and be able to develop strategies to make it happen.

➜ The first step in building a team is to become aware of, and understand, individual roles, responsibilities, beliefs and behaviours.

➜ A leader or manager must have an up-to-date understanding of what training is available to staff.

➜ The most important thing is to develop a supportive atmosphere, in which staff feel able to approach the leader and manager with any issue or problem.

Key Questions

- What are the differences between a manager and a leader?
- What are the main theories of leadership and how do they differ from each other?
- Summarise each of the different types of leadership and management styles. Which ones are most likely to be seen in early years settings and why?
- What are the key issues in the management of change, organisation and environment?
- How might a leader and manager ensure effective communication with staff?
- What are the main features of effective team leadership?

References

Andreski, R. and Nicholls, S. (1996) *Managing your Nursery, A Practical Guide for Nursery Professionals.* London: Nursery World Publications

Bronfenbrenner, U. (1995) The Bioecological Model from a Life Course Perspective: Reflections of a participant observer, in Moen, P., Elder, Jnr. G.H. and Lüscher, K. (eds) *Examining Lives in Context.* Washington, DC: American Psychological Association, pp. 599–618

Curtis, A. and O'Hagan, M. (2003) *Care and Education in Early Childhood. A Student's Guide to Theory and Practice.* London: Routledge Falmer

CWDC (Children's Workforce Development Council) (2006) *Early Years Professional National Standards.* London: CWDC

Dahlberg, G., Moss, P. and Pence, A. (1999) *Beyond Quality in Early Childhood Education and Care.* London: Falmer Press

DES (1967) *Children and their Primary School. A report of the Central Advisory Council for Education (England) Vol. 1: Report.* London: HMSO

DfES (2003a) *National Standards for Under 8s day Care and Childminding. Full Day Care.* London: DfES. Available from: www.surestart.gov.uk/_doc/0-ACA52E.PDF

DfES (2003b) *Excellence and Enjoyment. A strategy for primary schools.* London: DfES

DfES (2004) *Every Child Matters: Change For Children.* London: DfES

DfES (2006) *Early Years Foundation Stage.* London: DfES

Dryden, L., Forbes, R., Mukherji, P. and Pound, L. (2005) *Essential Early Years.* London: Hodder Arnold

Edginton, M. (2004) *The Foundation Stage Teacher in Action: Teaching 3, 4 and 5 year olds,* 3rd edn. London: Paul Chapman

Fink, D. (2005) *Leadership for Mortals.* London: PCP

Froebel, F. (1826) *On the Education of Man.* Keilhau, Leipzig: Wienbrach

Handy, C. (1992) *The Gods of Management.* London: Peguin

HM Government (2005) *Common Core of Skills and Knowledge for the Children's Workforce. Every Child Matters, Change for Children.* London: DfES

Hodgkinson, C. (1991) *Educational Leadership: The Moral Art.* Albany: State University of New York

Johnston, J. (2005) *Early Explorations in Science,* 2nd edn. Buckingham: Open University Press

Laming, Lord (2003) *Victoria Climbié Inquiry.* Available from www.victoria-climbie-inquiry.org.uk/finreport/finreport.htm

Likert, R. (1967) *The Human Organization: Its Management and Value.* New York: McGraw-Hill

Maslow, A.H. (1968) *Towards a Psychology of Being.* New York: Van Nostrand

McClelland, D.C. (1987) *Human Motivation.* Cambridge: Cambridge University Press

MLA (Museums, Libraries and Archives Council) (2004) *Learning for Change: Workforce Development Strategy.* London: MLA

Montessori, M. (1912) *The Montessori Method.* London: Heinemann

NCSL (2007) *Leading Sustainable Schools.* Nottingham: NCSL

QCA (2000) *Curriculum Guidance for the Foundation Stage.* London: QCA

Primary National Strategy (2006) *Seamless Transitions – supporting continuity in young children's learning.* Norwich: SureStart/DfES

Robins, A. (ed.) (2006) *Mentoring in the Early Years.* London: Paul Chapman

Rodd, J. (1998) *Leadership in Early Childhood,* 2nd edn. Maidenhead: Open University Press

Rousseau, J.J. (1911) *Emile.* London: J.M. Dent

Sadek, E. and Sadek, J. (2004) *Good Practice in Nursery Management,* 2nd edn. Cheltenham: Nelson Thornes

Smith, A. and Langston, A. (1999) *Managing Staff in Early Years Settings.* London: Routledge

SureStart, (2003) *Birth to Three Matters. A Framework to Support Children in their Earliest Years.* London: DfES

Van Maurik, J. (2004) *Writers on Leadership.* London: Penguin Business

Willan, J., Parker-Rees, R. and Savage, J. (2004) *Early Childhood Studies.* Exeter: Learning Matters

Useful reading

Daly, M., Byers, E. and Taylor, W. (2004) *Early Years Management in Practice.* Oxford: Heinemann.

Handy, C. (1992) *Understanding Organisations.* Harmondsworth: Penguin

Jeffers, S. (1991) *Feel the Fear and Do It Anyway.* London: Random House

O'Sullivan, J. (2003) *Manager's Handbook, Early Years Training and Management.* Leamington Spa: Scholastic

Glossary

Abstraction the ability to form a general concept

Analytic phonics an approach to the teaching of reading in which the phonemes associated with particular graphemes are not pronounced in isolation. Children identify (analyse) the common phoneme in a set of words in which each word contains the phoneme under study

Anthropologist a person who studies human development

Authoritarian strict, controlling, severe, dictatorial

Analysis breaking down ideas, reading or observations to understand them and their constituent parts

Attachment close bond; primary attachments are with main care-giver and secondary attachments with other close indviduals

Attitudes a stance or attribute arising out of a complex interrelationship between the social (behaviour), the affective (feelings/ emotions) and the cognitive (thinking/ ideas)

Behaviourist a person who studies behaviour and considers that behaviour theory explains many/most individual characteristics

Blended family a family consisting of a parent and child(ren) from one broken family combining with another parent and child(ren) from another broken family to make a new family (or step family)

Cephalocaudal development a growth pattern where development begins at the head and works its way downward

Coaching the process of teaching a colleague/peer a specific set of skills

Cognition the construction of idea, knowledge and understanding

Cognitive acceleration the process of supporting the construction of children's ideas

Concept A BIG idea; a picture in the mind

Conditioning the process of training or learning a behaviour, so that it becomes instinctive

Congenital inborn, inherited, hereditary

Consolidator someone who continues to use ideas or theories, which have been introduced by others, in their own practice

Constructivist the development of ideas or behaviours by experience or social interaction

Critical incidents incidents that are critical in determining/developing reflection, ideas and action

Democratic self-governing, autonomous, independent

Early childhood from 0 to 8 years of age

Early years professional generic professionals who work with young children on a daily basis and are responsible for their care and development

Empiricism philosophy characterised by the idea of Locke (1632–1704) that the child is an empty vessel to be filled, or a lump of clay to be moulded

Ethics moral principles/values

Formative assessment informs the planning of the curriculum

Functionalist serving a function

Gender identity the perception that an individual has of themselves in masculine or feminine terms

Genotype our genetic make-up is a result of a mixing of our parents' genes

Implementer someone who introduces the ideas, reforms or theories of another in their practice

Individual Education Plan a plan for a child with special educational needs to help them to achieve

Induction introduction to policy and practice

Innate inborn, instinctive, genetic

Intelligence a measure of thinking ability as measured by intelligence quotients

Interactionism philosophy characterised by Kant (1724–1804) which believes the individual child follows a standard sequence of biological stages that constitute a path to full realisation or a ladder-like progression to maturity

Kinaesthetic concerned with action or movement

Leadership the process of leading a team through example with vision and drive

Linguistics the scientific study of language

Logic the ability to reason

Management the process of organising to achieve the best results

Maturation the rate at which we physically develop motor skills

Mentoring the process of supporting colleagues/peers

Metacognition to be aware of and understand your own thought processes.

Method data collection tool; way of collecting data

Methodology type of research

Moral development the process of developing understanding of society's norms of right or wrong

Morality the doctrine of actions as right or wrong

Morphology the study of word structure

Motor skills skills that involve the use of muscles

Multi-agency working agencies working with young children planning together in order to oversee provision within the local authority

Nativism philosophy characterised by Rousseau (1712–78) that believes the child is vulnerable and generates in adults a desire to shelter them from the corrupt world

Neurophysiologist a person whose focus is on development of the brain and neural pathways

Paralinguistics the way in which we use sound to convey meaning.

Pedagogy the science of teaching

Philosophy the pursuit of wisdom

Phoneme a sound

Phonetics the way we form, transmit and hear sounds

Phonics the teaching and learning of letter/sound correspondence for reading and writing

Phonology the organisation and patterning of sounds in a language

Physiology the study of physical development

Pragmatics the art of conversation

Proximodistal development a growth patters that starts in the centre of the body and works it way outwards.

Psychology the study of the psyche (emotional, cognitive, attitudes, etc.)

Reasoning providing evidence or justification for a belief

Reflection-in-action reflection during the course of an action (while doing something)

Reflection-on-action reflection after an action (after you have done it)

Reflective journal a journal that notes all ideas, reading, observations and analyses and is used to develop reflective practice or research practice

Reflective practice practice that builds on/develops from reflection and analysis

Reflexes reaction, either voluntary (can be controlled) or involuntary (cannot be controlled)

Reinforcement the process of encouraging behaviours

Reformer someone who makes changes or reforms practice and provision, locally, nationally or internationally

Reliability the extent to which something (research) can be repeated with the same/similar results

Self-actualisation reaching full potential; the pinnacle of Maslow's hierarchy of needs

Self-esteem the evaluative aspect of self-concept; what we think of ourselves, or how we judge ourselves

Semantics the study of meaning

Social development the process of learning to live with others in a social learning environment

Social learning the development of behaviours by imitation or interaction with others

Sociology the science of society

Special Needs Code of Practice introduced in 1994, it placed a statutory requirement on schools and LEAs to identify and meet the needs of children with SEN

Summative assessment a summary of a child's attainments

Syntax the study of sentence structure

Synthesis to take analyses from a wide range of primary and secondary evidence and put them back together in order to draw conclusions, make sense of the whole, draw inferences, produce new ideas or models and identify implications.

Synthetic phonics an approach to the teaching of reading in which phonemes (sounds) associated with particular graphemes (letters) are pronounced in isolation and blended together (synthesised)

Theorist someone who develops a theory which has national or international impact on ideas, beliefs, practice and provision

Transition the process of moving from one situation to another

Validity the truth or honesty of data in research

Zone of proximal development the area just beyond current understanding, which sensitive interaction, in ways suited to the child's age, culture and social needs, can help to reach

Index

Note: Page references in *italics* refer to Figure; those in **bold** refer to Table.

abstraction 108
accounts 6
action research 5
Adoption Act 1976 242
adoptive families 242
adults, role of, in early education 276–9
age, cognitive processing and 132–3
Alexander technique 92
analysis **5, 12**
analytic phonics 151, *152*
anthropology 239
antisocial behaviour orders (ASBOs) 62
Area Special Educational Needs
    Coordinator (Area SENCo)
    317–18
Aristotle 50
articulation 148–50, 151
Asperger's syndrome 224
assessment, early education and 282–6
attachment theory (Bowlby) 30,
    176–85, 219, 230
Attention Deficit Hyperactivity Disorder
    (ADHD) 132, 255
attitudes 51, *51*
  development *190*
  influence on social development
    221–5
  reflective practice 370
attributes, parental 245
audio recording 387
auditory methods 40
authoritarian parenting 188, 246
authoritative parenting 188, 246
autism 157, 224
Autism Spectrum Disorders 317,
    318–19
autocratic leadership 425
aversion therapy 225
avoidance attachment 177

babbling 151–3
baby signing 141–2
balance 86
Bandura, Albert 34–5
  social learning theory 194, 213–14
behaviour modification 225
behaviour shaping 225

behavioural disorders 224–5
behavioural tests 223–4
behavioural theories of leadership 424
behaviourism 29, 143, 211–13
bereavement 221
Best Start for Children 70
Birth to Three Matters 42, 70, 89, 141,
    267–8, 316, 355
Birth to Three Study (BTSS) 43
blended families 219, 242, 243
Bobo doll experiment 213–14
bodily-kinaesthetic intelligence 118
body contact 140
body language 139
body orientation 140
BookStart 279
Bowlby, John 29–30
  attachment theory 219, 230
Bowlby, Sir Richard 178–83
brain 108–13, *109*
  development 79–80, 113, 181
  emotion and 175
Brain Gym 41, 126–7
Bronfenbrenner, Urie 33, 231
  ecological systems theory 214, *215*
brook test 223
Bruner, Jerome 33
  cognitive theory 117–18
Bullock report 165
Butler, R.A. 229

calculating 291
carers, working with 399–402
case study research 5
cephalocaudal development 80
cerebral palsy (CP) 307
change management 434
Childcare Act 2006 316, 326, 335, 336
childcare, early, social development and
    221
childhood 253–7
Children Act
  1989 251, 252, 309, 436
  2004 42, 66, 67, 252, 316
children's rights 251–2
Children's Workforce Development
    Council (CWDC) 343–6

Children's Workforce Strategy 336
Choice for Parents 70
Chomsky, Noam
  language acquisition theory 143–4
circle-time 164, *164–5*
classical conditioning 29, 193, 211
coaching 380
coaching leadership 427
cognition 27
cognitive acceleration 41, 125–7
cognitive development
  constructivist theories 123–4
  definition 108
  emotional development and 190
  factor theories of 113–22
cognitive inhibition 132
cognitive theory
  Bruner 117–18
  Piaget 114–16, *114*, **115**, 195, **195**,
    216
  Vygotsky 116
cohabiting–couple families *241*
collaborative play 216
Common Assessment Framework (CAF)
    325
Communication, Language and Literacy
    287–9
communications, management 434–5
community, wider, working with 405–8
concept map *60*
confidence 186–8
confluent processing 121–2
congenital problems 112
consciousness 131–2
constructivism 41
constructivist theories of cognitive
    development 123–4, 216–17
consultative leadership 425–6
control deficiency 132
cooperative/collaborative play 221, 272
coordination 86
correlational research 5
cortisol 181, 182
counting 291
creating mind 120
creative development, early education
    296–7

creativity 37–8, 120
  model of 38–40
  continuum of 39, *39*
  pyramid 39, *40*
critical incident 373–4
cultural differences 249
cultural line 216–17
culture
  cognitive processing and 132–3
  self-esteem and 188
  social development and 226–9
Curriculum Guidance for the
    Foundation Stage 316

dance 92, 97–9
  climax 99
  cool down 99
  planning 98
  skills development 99
  thematic approaches 98
  warm-up 99
DATA 370
death wish 186
declarative memory 129
democratic family 188
democratic leadership 426
dependent children 239, *241*
Desirable Learning Outcomes (DLOs)
    265, 266, 286
development, inter-relationship of *207*
Dewey, John 21, 52
dialogue journals 385–6
Disability Code of Practice 312–13
disability, models of 306–10
  human rights and social model of
      308–9
disciplined mind 120
disorganized, disorientated attachment
    177
divorce 221, 243
domestic violence and abuse 253–4
Down's syndrome 112
Durkheim, Emile 218
dynamic systems theory 214
dyslexia 157
dyspraxia 157

Early Excellence Centres 68
Early Learning Goals (ELGs) 265
Early Support Programme (ESP) 323–5
Early Years Curriculum 280
Early Years Development Childcare
    Partnerships 318
Early Years Foundation Stage (EYFS) 67,
    70, 89, 96, 101, 102, 206, 266,
    268, 316, 335
Early Years Professional Status (EYPS)
    338–41, *339–40*, 343–6, 355,

  409, 430
early years professionals
  challenges facing 355–8
  standards for 338–43
  types 335–6
eating disorders 224
ecological systems theory 214, *215*
ecological transitions 231
ectomorphs 87
Education Act
  1870 304
  1918 263
  ('Butler') 1944 229
  1981 305–6
Education Action Zones 224
Education Reform Act 1988 265, 310
education, early, key developments
    263–70
educational disorders 225
Effective Provision of Pre-school
    Education (EPPE) 43, 316, 317,
    402
effective strategy 132
ego 26, 186
emotional development 174–6, **174–5**
  importance of 189–92
emotionally intelligent leadership 427
emotions 174
empiricism 63
Enabling Environments 393
enactive representation 33, 118
encoding memory 128
endomorphs 87
environment
  influence of, on social development
      231
  learning 280–2
environmental management 436
epilepsy 328–9
episodic memory 129
epistemic play 272
epistemology 216
Erikson, Erik 28–9
  psycho-social stages **191**
ethical mind 121
ethics 3
ethnicity, social development and 220
ethnographic research 6
Every Child Matters 41, 67–8, 70, 88,
    96, 221, 252, 269, 314, 316, 323,
    382, 431
ex post facto research 6
exosystem 33–4, 214
experiential learning cycle 365, *365*
exploratory play 272

facial expression 140
factor theories of cognitive development
    113–22

failure to thrive syndrome, non-organic
    89
families *241*
  social development and 219–25
  structure 239–43
  working with 399–402
Families, Children and Child Care Study
    43
family size
  parenting and 247
  social development and 220
fine motor skills **81–2**, 84, 85
  in indoor nursery environment 92
formal written evaluation 386
formative assessment 283
foster families 242
Foundation Stage 50, 67, 68–70, 267,
    268
Foundation Stage Profile 285
four Ps 251
Fragile X syndrome 112, 317
free play 272–3
Freud, Sigmund 26, 64
  personality development 26, 186
  psychoanalytical theory 186, **186**, 195
  psychosexual development 26
Froebel, Friedrich 20, 20, 64
functionalist view of emotions 189
fuzzy trace 130

games 102–3
Gardner, Howard
  five minds 120–1
  multiple intelligence 41, 118–20
gaze 140
gender identity 187–8
gender typing 187
gender, influence of, on social
    development 219
genotype 86
gesture 139
globalisation 251
grammar 154–7
gross motor skills 80, **81–2**
  in indoor nursery environment 91–2
gymnastic activities 101–2

habit disorders 224
handwriting 84, 289
Healthy Living Blueprint for Schools 88
hereditary factors, physical development
    and 86–7
hierarchical needs, theory of (Maslow)
    31, *31*, 187, 210, 227, 245
High/Scope pre-school programme
    35–6, 43, 365, 395
historical research 6
holistic approach 286

holophrase 153
homes 248–50
household 239
human rights, social model of disability
       and 308–9
Hume, David 50–1

iconic representation 33, 118
id 26, 186
illness, family 221
illuminative research 6
imaginative play 272
implosion therapy 225
imprinting 176, 211
Index for Inclusion 313
Individual Education Plans (IEPs) 306,
       312
inductive reasoning 113
insecure attachment 179, 182
intelligence 108
    general 113
    types 118–19
interactionism 63
intercultural teacher 229
interpersonal intelligence 118
intrapersonal intelligence 118–19

journals
    dialogue 385–6
    personal reflective 385
    structured 385
    unstructured 385

Kane 63
Key Stage 1 84, 97, 101, 102, 269,
       285–6, 289, 297–8
Key Stage 2 269
kinaesthetic methods 40, 41
knowledge 108
    types 366–7, 367
Knowledge and Understanding of the
       World 292–4
Kohlberg, Lawrence 35
    cognitive theory of moral
           development 195–6, **196**
Kolb 365

laissez-faire leadership 426
language 139
    body 139
    cognitive processing and 132–3
    for communication 287
    for thinking 287
    problems 157
    receptive 153–4
    sign 139
Language Acquisition Device (LAD)
       143–4

Language Acquisition Support System
       (LASS) 145
language acquisition theories 142–7
leadership
    vs management 423
    theories of 423–4
    types 425–30
Learning and Development 393
learning environment 280–2
learning partnership 392
learning theories 40–1
libido 186
linguistic intelligence 119
linguistic substitutions **154**
linguistics 139
linking sounds 287
listening 162–7
listening games 166
Literacy Framework 287
Locke, John 50, 63, 211
locomotor skills 81
logic 108
logical mathematical intelligence 119
lone-parent families 241
Lorenz, Konrad 176, 211
ludic play 272

macrosystem 34, 214
Magaluzzi, Loris 34
management
    vs leadership 423
    types 425–7
marginal babbling 151
marriage 218, 239–40
Maslow, Abraham 31–2
    hierarchy of needs 31, 31, 187, 210,
           227, 245
mathematics 290–2
maturation 87
McMillan, Margaret 23, 64, 229
McMillan, Rachel 23, 229
measures 291
medical model of disability 306–7
memory 108, 113, 128–31
mental abilities, primary 113
mental modelling 132
mentoring 379–80, 411, 412
mesomorphs 87
mesosystem 33, 214
metacognition 108, 131–2
methodology 3, **5**, **12**
methods **5**, **12**
microsystem 33, 214
milestones, developmental 27, 81
mind 113
monocultural professional 228–9
Montessori, Maria 21–3, 64
moral development 193
    behaviorist theories of 193–4

cognitive theories 194–6
    supporting 197–9
moral reasoning 35, 186
morality 192–9
morphology 154–7
Motherese 143
motor skills 80–1
multi-family household 239
multicultural teacher 229
multiple intelligence (Gardner) 41,
       118–20
music 191–2
musical intelligence 119

Named Person for Children 318
narratives 6
National Curriculum 70, 251, 265, 267,
       286, 310–11
    physical development and 96–103
    Speaking and Listening 161
National Healthy Schools Standard 88
National Literacy Project 373
National Literacy Strategy 165, 373
National Standards for Under8s Day
       Care and Childminding 70,
       316, 355–6
nativism 63, 143, 144–5
naturalist intelligence 119
Neonatal Behavioral Assessment Scale
       (NBAS) 223
neurophysiology 79–80
non-verbal communication 139–41
noticing 374
nuclear family 240, 241–2
numerical ability 113
nursery rhymes 154
nutrition, physical development and 88

Oberlin, Jean Frederic 19
obesity, physical development and
       88–9
observation 77–8, 82–3
observation schedules 78
operant conditioning 29, 193, 212
oracy 165–7, 289
organisation management 435–6
organisational theories, leadership 424
outdoor classroom 96
outdoor play 273–4, 274

PACE 126
parachute play 192
paralinguistics 147
parallel play 216, 272
parental attributes 245
parenting 245–7
parenting styles 220, 246
parents, working with 399–402

participation rights 251
Pavlov 29, 193, 211
pecking order 212–13
pedagogy 21
peer observation 380
Peers Early Education Partnership
    (PEEP) 43
Pen Green Centre 413
perceptual speed 113
permitting parenting 246
personal identity 50–1
Personal, Social and Emotional
    Development 286
Pestalozzi, Johann Heinrich 17–18
phases of research 5, 12
philosophy 50–4
    continuing development 61–4
    individual, developing 56–7
    integrated 65–7, 66
    personal 54–5
    personal, examination 57–9
    underlying 67–70
philosophy for children (P4C) 162
phoneme 148
phonetics 147
phonics 148, 151, 289
phonology 147–54
physical development 77–8
    delayed 90
    early education 295–6
    factors affecting 86–9
    indoor nursery environment 91–2
    National Curriculum and 96–103
    outdoor play 94–6
Piaget, Jean 27, 27, 63, 64
    cognitive theory 114–16, 114, 115,
        195, 195, 216
    language acquisition theory 145–6
PIES 206
PILES 206
planning and assessment, early
        education and 282–6
Plato 50
play
    development 216
    as education 270–5
    as learning 272
    outdoor 94–6
    as practice 272
    types 271–2
play with rules 272
play therapy 225
Plowden, Bridget 32
Plowden report 69, 265
Positive Relationships 392
posture 140
poverty 221
    physical development and 87–8

special needs and 317
power and influence theories, leadership
    424
pragmatics 52, 161
precise processing 121
prevention rights 251
primary attachment 179
primitive reflexes 79, 209
problem-solving 108
Problem-solving, Reasoning and
        Numeracy 290–2
procedural memory 129
production deficiency 132
professional associations 414–15
professionals, working with 408–13
proprioceptive sense 91, 92
prosody 147
protection rights 251
provision rights 251
proxemics 140
proximodistal development 80
psycho-social stages (Erikson) 191
psychoanalytical therapy 225
psychological disorders 224
psychology 27
psychotic disorders 224
punishment 195
puppets, use of 198, 198
Puritan discourse 251

qualifications, childcare 335, 345
Qualified Teacher Status (QTS) 338,
    346

race, influence of, on social develop-
        ment 226–9
reading 288
reasoning 108
recall 129
receptive language 153–4
reciprocal determinism 34
recognition 129
reconstituted family 219, 242, 243
reconstruction 129
reflection-in-action 366, 367
reflection-on-action 366, 367
reflective journal 385
reflective practice
    characteristics 368–70
    definition 364–8
    individual 372–6
    models 370–2
    professional standards 378–9
    specific aspect 374–5
    specific experience 376
    supporting and evidencing 385–7
    working with others 379–84
reflexes 79, 209

Reggio Emilia early childhood
        programme 34, 372, 396, 405
reinforcement 212
rejecting–neglecting parenting 246
reliability of research 3, 5, 12
remarriage 221
Removing Barrier to Achievement 323
research proposal 6
research questions 5
resistant attachment 177, 180–1
respectful mind 120
responsibility, managing 437
retrieval memory 129
reward 193–4
risk factors, attachment and 181,
        182–3
Romantic discourse 251
Rose Report 151, 276
Rousseau, Jean-Jacques 17, 63, 206, 211
rubella, maternal 112
Rumbold Report 265, 266

sadness 175
scaffolding 145, 147
schema 145
scientific probability 179
secondary attachment 179
secure attachment 177, 179, 182
self-actualisation 31
self-concept 187
self-esteem 89, 186–8
self-regulation 35
semantic memory 130
semantic organisation 130
semantics 159
SEN Toolkit 326
sensori-motor schemes 216
separation anxiety 182
sequential processing 121
sexual disorders 224
shape and space 291
sign language 139
situational leadership 427, 430–1
Skinner, Burrhus F. 29, 64
    behaviourism 193, 211–12
    language acquisition theory 143
SMART 3
smiling 175
social and emotional factors, physical
        development and 89
social constructivism 216–17
social development 206–10
    theories of 211–17
social disorders 224
social exchange theories of leadership
    424
social learning theories 34–5, 193, 194,
        213–14

social mobility 231–2
social policy, influence of, on social
        development 229–30
socialisation 208
society, influence of, on social develop-
        ment 217–18
socio-dramatic play 272
socio-economic factors 221
sociology 205–6
Socrates 50
solitary play 272
sound 147–54, **149–50**
spatial ability 113
spatial intelligence 119
spatial organisation 130
speaking and listening 162–7
Special Educational Needs and
        Disability Act (SENDA) 2001
        311, 312, 317
special needs
    in early years settings 317–20
    historical framework 304–6
    inclusion 310–13
    multi-agency working 320–8
    recent legislation 316
Special Needs (SEN) Code of Practice
        306, 311–12, 317
speech problems 157
stammering 157
Standard Attainment Tests (SATs) 84,
        96, 285–6, 265
Starting with Quality 265
Statementing 319, 320
Steiner, Rudolf 25–6, 25

Sternberg: triarchic theory 118–19
storage memory 128–9
stress in group daycare 178–83
structured play 273
stuttering 157
summative assessment 283
superego 26, 186
supporting leadership 427
SureStart 41, 68, 70, 224, 279, 405
survey 6
sustainable development in schools
        428
sustained shared thinking 162
swamp knowledge 366
symbolic play 272
symbolic representation 33, 118
syntax 154–7
synthesizing mind 120
synthetic phonics 151, *152*
systematic densensitisation 225
systems theories 214

Tabula Rasa 251
tantrums 175
Te Whariki 396, 405
Team Around the Child (TAC) 324, 325
team management 438–43
technical processing 121
temper tantrums 224
thinking 108
tomboyishness 112
tongue twisters 154, *155*
toxic childhood 255–6
transcendental meditation 126

transformational theories of leadership
        424
triarchic theory (Sternberg) 118–19

UN Convention on the Rights of the
        Child 251, 252, 308–9, 326, 398
UN Declaration of Human Rights 251
understanding 108
UNESCO Salamanca statement 309
Unique Child 392
usage-based theory 145
U-shaped curve (Strauss) 123
utilization deficiency 132

validity of research 3, **5**, **12**
verbal reasoning 113
vestibular sense 91, 82
video recording 387
visual methods 40, 41
vocal play 151
Vygotsky, Lev 28, *28*
    cognitive theory 116
    language acquisition theory 145–6
    social constructivism 216–17

Warnock Report (1978) 305–6
Weikart, David 35–6
word fluency 113
words, first 153–4
working parents 221
working together 393–4
writing 84, 289

zone of proximal development
        (Vygotsky) 28, 277

More exciting titles from
Pearson Education

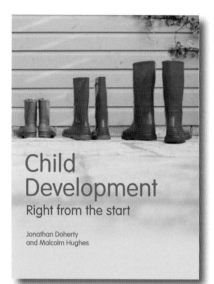
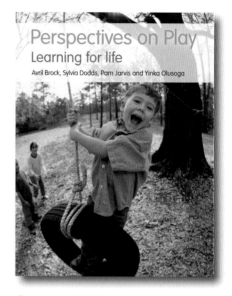
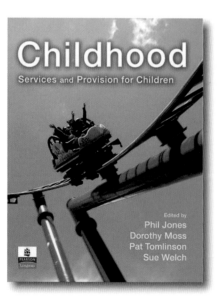